About Language

CONTEXTS FOR COLLEGE WRITING

Second Edition

Selected and Edited by MARDEN J. CLARK

SOREN F. COX

MARSHALL R. CRAIG

Brigham Young University

New York · CHARLES SCRIBNER'S SONS

Acknowledgment is hereby made for "Molly's Soliloquy" from ULYSSES, by James Joyce. Copyright 1914, 1918 and renewed 1942, 1946 by Nora Joseph Joyce. Reprinted by permission of Random House, Inc. This selection is composed of two excerpts (p. 738 and pp. 781–783) from ULYSSES (1961 edition, corrected and reset) and has been titled "Molly's Soliloquy" by the editors.

Library of Congress Cataloging in Publication Data

Clark, Marden J 1916– comp.
About language.

1. English language—Rhetoric. 2. College readers. I. Cox, Soren F., joint comp. II. Craig, Marshall R., joint comp. III. Title.
PE1417.C624 1975 808′.04275 74-13382
ISBN 0-684-14098-5

3 5 7 9 11 13 15 17 19 V/P 20 18 16 14 12 10 8 6 4

Printed in the United States of America

About Language

Second Edition

Introduction

The second edition of this book continues to place the emphasis where we believe the emphasis in freshman composition should have been all along: on language. On language as the appropriate subject for the course, as the medium through which composition takes place, and as the medium for some of the best moments in man's creative life. In other words, the five years since the first edition have not changed but rather have strengthened our commitment to both the basic principles and the approach of the first edition. For this reason, the form and much of the content of the book remain the same, proven in the experience of the teachers and students who have used the book. Especially in the literature, which by its nature defies time, we have found little to change. What has changed in those five years has been the amount and quality of available knowledge and writing about language. The continuing explosion of knowledge about language—often referred to as "the language revolution"—has made available much writing that synthesizes recent developments and much that explores them in detail. We have tried to keep up with that revolution, to make the book as good a reflection, within its scope, of contemporary knowledge about language and rhetoric as we could make it. Beyond this, we have tried to make the book more interesting and useful as a textbook by responding to many practical suggestions from teachers who have used it. The immediate results of such concerns show in the increased number of suggestions for writing and occasionally of questions following the various selections. Some of the introductions to the major parts of the book have been expanded for the same purposes.

We have tried even more in this new edition to avoid the heavy stodginess that seems to afflict most books that discuss language. Yet we believe the book has real substance. As with the previous edition, we wish to provide students, through the use of this book, with an opportunity to learn about language: about the power of language to liberate people from their own ignorance or lethargy, about the impressive and growing body of scientific knowledge that linguists and semanticists have accumulated, about the way in which language functions as a tool for persuasive purposes, about the ability of writers to extend its capacities by experimentation.

Language is a most complex and remarkable and fascinating phenomenon. Even in an age of space exploration and atomic fission, language continues to be the most remarkable of man's inventions—if for no other reason than that space exploration and atomic fission would have been impossible without it. Language is essential to every profession, to every human endeavor. In learning about it and in learning to control it as writers, students improve their capability for coping with an increasingly complex and demanding world. And they learn more about themselves and about their essential humanity.

These considerations have continued to determine the various parts and their arrangement in this book, as well as the choice of materials that make them up.

To help students sense the power of language, Part I features examples of language forcefully at work influencing peoples' lives. One can feel the power in Helen Keller's discovery of words, in Richard Wright's discovery of novels, in Dylan Thomas' and Emily Dickinson's poetry.

The sections that follow present some of the results of the knowledge explosion concerning language. Linguists have recently come to know far more about the nature of language—about its history, grammars, dialects, and usage—than ever before. Part II provides information about the nature of language from such diverse sources as linguist Albert Cook, children's author Lewis Carroll, neurosurgeon Wilder Penfield, and novelist Joseph Conrad. Part III, "The History of Language," includes selections by linguists that indicate why our language is what it is today and selections that clearly show the language in the process of change. Part IV contains selections that present grammatical descriptions of a language and selections by writers whose individual mannerisms in using language virtually constitute a grammar in themselves. Part V provides students with new knowledge and new theories about dialects and usage, selections that may challenge much of what students have been led to believe about language in the past.

Part VI, "Semantics," presents new and significant information about words and how they are used to communicate meaning. Parts VII, "Logic and Persuasion," and VIII, and "Diction, Style, and Tone," bring together elements of writing presented in other sections to demonstrate how practical problems in writing are solved. Part IX, "Experiments with Language," comprises selections by extraordinarily sensitive and creative writers that dramatize the promise and the fulfillment of language.

To keep a focus throughout on the practical problems of writing, we have included as the first selection in the book Wayne Booth's "The Rhetorical Stance," and we repeatedly refer to some of his concepts. We believe, however, that the practical problems of writing have far less to do with such standard concerns as placement of commas or modifiers than with the writer's attitude toward himself and what he is doing. If writing of any kind grows only out of the need to fill a teacher's assignment, there is little chance indeed that it will be effective, vigorous, and convincing. The student may be fully aware of such common qualities of good writing as organization, coherence, effective syntax and diction, but they will remain mere abstractions until he cares enough about his writing to want to make it represent him as effectively as possible. What is at stake, of course, is a meaningful commitment to himself and to his writing. If a writer cares enough about his feelings, responses, and ideas to want to communicate them to others effectively, then such qualities as we usually define by words like *honesty, sincerity,* or *integrity* will almost surely be part of his writing. Even more important, such a commitment will, we are convinced, place in a different and far more meaningful perspective the apparently more practical problems of writing. The student will come to see matters of organization, coherence, sentence structure, word choice, even punctuation, not as pitfalls to be avoided or as sources of mistakes in his papers, but as means of projecting himself and his ideas more vigorously and convincingly. We know of no way to avoid a certain amount of artificiality in classroom writing. But no matter how artificial the situation, the writer should be able to make the experience meaningful. In fact, he should discover fairly early that the writing process itself is one of the best of ways to find ideas, to discover what he really believes, to define himself and his responses.

Once the student realizes that such things are important, then the practical advice Booth gives in "The Rhetorical Stance" should be especially meaningful. To support these concepts and to assist in putting them to practical use, we have included with each of the first six sections a succinct discussion of one of the most common rhetorical methods of developing and supporting an idea. Again we trust that such methods will not remain merely abstractions but will become practical means of giving student writing vitality and conviction. We have also included, following each part of the book, detailed suggestions for writing; shorter writing suggestions follow many of the individual selections.

We believe that the study of language and literature can lead to improved student writing. Literature enables students to see how words function when they are being used most effectively. It exploits all the resources of language to gain effective expression, and an awareness of how this is accomplished should improve students' abilities to control their own language. We have, accordingly, integrated the literary works in this book into all the sections as demonstrations of the relevance of literature to all problems of language. We trust that energy, especially in the form of light, will move both ways between the materials about language and these particularly fine examples of language in action.

Contents

Part V · DIALECTS AND USAGE

Part VI · SEMANTICS

Part VII · LOGIC AND PERSUASION

Part VIII · STYLE AND TONE

Part I

The Power of Language

This first section is frankly proselytizing. It tries to convert you not so much to a religion as to an attitude toward language. It invites you to experience something of the power and fascination of language by sharing what language has meant to others, in both fact and fiction. Our language is so much a part of us, we are ordinarily so unconscious in our use of it, that even when we are thinking *with* it we seldom think *about* it. We may scold it occasionally when it will not behave the way we want it to. We may feel irritation that we have to write papers or make speeches with it. We may even feel resentment when our friends catch us being tripped up in some way by it or when they trip us up with it themselves with an elephant or a "knock-knock" joke. We may dislike the problems language poses for us. But very seldom do we have occasion to marvel at one of the most remarkable facts of our human experience: not only that we can think and speak and hear and read and write well but that we can think and speak and hear and read and write at all. Almost the only time we really pause to look at our language is when someone calls our attention to it or when we suddenly see it from a new perspective. That is the function of this section: first to call your attention to the magic of language and then to let you experience it from a variety of new perspectives.

Most of the selections are concerned, one way or another, with a moment of awakening or with an increasing awareness of language. Not many of us can duplicate Noah Jonathan Jacobs' remarkable imaginative recreation of those first hours in Eden. But we *can* participate in the fun with language and with ideas about language and perhaps even stretch our own imaginations as we do so. Nearly all of us were too young to remember now our first discovery of words, but the excitement of a Helen Keller discovering them in her dark and soundless world should help us know both the excitement of discovery and the implicit value of words. Few of us in these days when books surround us should have to go through Richard Wright's wonderful, agonizing hunger for books, but your editors and your teachers would hope that all of you would share something of his appetite for good ones. You may never become as enamored of words as was Dylan Thomas. Such love almost inevitably leads where it led him, to a career as poet or dramatist or writer of fiction. Some of you may have—or may develop—that kind of love. Instructors will rejoice over those who do. But most of them will be satisfied if you begin to wonder strongly enough to want to find out what it is about words that could elicit such love. With so many Blacks singing wonderful poetry these days, you may need to make a conscious projection of your imagination backwards in time, but you should be able to experience the awe that Countee Cullen feels "at this curious thing: / To make a poet black, and bid him sing."

Such words, and those in the brief poems by Emily Dickinson and others, try to define not so much a moment of awakening as a response, an attitude, toward language. Most of our poets would probably agree with I. A. Richards that "poetry is the supreme use of language, man's chief coordinating instrument, in the service of the most integral purposes of life"; but you need not. Nor need you completely agree with Richards when he argues that the

> . . . study of the modes of language becomes, as it attempts to be thorough, the most fundamental and extensive of all inquiries. It is no preliminary or preparation for our profounder studies. . . . The very formation of the objects which these studies propose to examine takes place through the processes (of which imagination and fancy are modes) by which the words they use acquire their meanings.[1]

These are the words of an enthusiast, though a very important one. When you read Conrad's "Amy Foster" in the next section, you will find complementing evidence of the frighteningly destructive power of language when it fails to communicate. But if when you have finished this section you can wonder, as Amarantha Doggett did in asking, "Is it only crazy folks ever say such things?" then the section will have served its purpose.

[1] I. A. Richards, *Coleridge on Imagination* (London, 1955), pp. 230–31. Reprinted with the permission of Routledge & Kegan Paul Ltd. and W. W. Norton & Company, Inc.

Illustration

Traditionally composition has been divided into four categories—exposition, argument and persuasion, description, and narration. Such a division is made primarily for convenience in discussing composition; in writing, these elements are seldom carefully divided. However most college classes, other than creative writing classes, demand writing which is mainly exposition. Some classes may call upon the student to argue and to persuade other students or the instructor that his idea is *the* correct idea. More commonly the student must present a defensible conclusion or opinion supported by evidence.

If, however, the student wishes a reader to consider the ideas in his writing worthy of serious attention, he will blend argument and persuasion into his exposition to give his paper a rhetorical or persuasive tone. He will suggest that his conclusion, if not *the* correct conclusion, is as good as any other and is perhaps better than most. Similarly, if the student employs description and narration, these elements should serve to support or develop his opinion; they should become a part of his evidence for the exposition.

Exposition is merely that type of composition through which we set forth (or expose) our views about people, places, things, historical events—the list is endless. If you have an opinion, you can present it to an audience. But the audience's reception of your opinion is directly related to the clarity and effectiveness with which you set it forth and the support you can give for holding it. (Of course some part of the audience will accept only those ideas already firmly held, just as a part of the audience will argue with you no matter how excellent your evidence is. Our concern is with audiences in general rather than these fringes.) If you are to please this largest portion of your audience, you must write with your ear cocked for your imaginary reader's questions: over and over he asks "What evidence do you have for that?" "Can you make that any clearer?" "Why do you think that is important?" The careful reader is constantly asking questions.

Perhaps the reader most often asks for clarification. Often you can answer his question best by drawing a mental picture or by giving him an illustration. In addition to clarifying the matter for the reader, an illustration can give support for your opinion at the same time. Illustration is, therefore, one of the most common means of developing exposition. Note, as you read the selections that follow in Part I, how frequently the authors use illustrations and examples to both clarify and support their opinions. One author may use a short illustration to support a point, while another may give a series of illustrations so that we are overwhelmed with the amount or variety of the evidence he is showing us.

Sometimes a single long illustration, presented principally through narration and description, is the sole support for the major point in an expository paper. A student, after explaining his lack of confidence in his scholastic ability and his indecision about going to college, introduced such an example thus: "Then one day something happened, in itself a little thing. But it was significant to me, and it showed me how minor forces influence major decisions." He followed this statement with a single detailed two-page illustration. (The student was consciously imitating the pattern in an essay which the class had just finished reading.)

Usually, however, we find in exposition a number of shorter illustrations. In one paragraph of *The Scientific Outlook* Bertrand Russell refers to Galileo's observations of falling bodies, Kepler's laws of the motion of planets, Newton's laws of gravitation, Einstein's theory of relativity, Pythagoras's theorem, and the Russian mathematician Lobachevsky's non-Euclidean geometry. Obviously Russell could not elaborate the details of each illustration as the student could with his single illustration.

As you use illustrations in your writing, determine for each paper whether you can support and clarify your point best with a single, detailed illustration, with several shorter ones which include some details, or with a series of quick references devoid of any elaboration. Then, having determined the kind of illustration you will use, select those illustrations which have a direct and obvious bearing on your subject and which you can bring to life by the use of specific details. Name names, indicate places and times, give concrete details. Don't say "a scientist once concluded"; it makes a difference whether it was Newton or Einstein and whether the scientist arrived at his conclusion in the fifth century B.C. or in our own century. Be specific.

The Rhetorical Stance

Wayne C. Booth

Professor Booth has become a major spokesman for a new emphasis on rhetoric. His book The Rhetoric of Fiction *(The University of Chicago Press, 1961) has already become something of a classic in the study of rhetoric and in the analysis of fiction. It reminds us once again that writers of fiction do use persuasive techniques, sometimes wondrously complex and powerful. This essay is addressed to teachers of composition, not to freshman students. But it defines with such precision the fundamental problem of making the written word vigorous and powerful that we offer it here as our beginning selection to help you define your own rhetorical stance. We consider the problem of your own stance so basic that we will return to Booth's concepts again and again during the course of this book. Besides, the essay is remarkable for the range of its own illustrative materials—all the way from Booth's experiences as an undergraduate at Brigham Young University to his experiences as a teacher of graduate students at the University of Chicago and other places—allusions that range from classical rhetoric to* Reader's Digest. *You will find it worthwhile to analyze carefully both the ideas and the illustrations of this essay.*

Last fall I had an advanced graduate student, bright, energetic, well-informed, whose papers were almost unreadable. He managed to be pretentious, dull, and disorganized in his paper on *Emma,* and pretentious, dull, and disorganized on *Madame Bovary*. On *The Golden Bowl* he was all these and obscure as well. Then one day, toward the end of term, he cornered me after class and said, "You know, I think you were all wrong about Robbe-Grillet's *Jealousy* today." We didn't have time to discuss it, so I suggested that he write me a note about it. Five hours later I found in my faculty box a four-page polemic, unpretentious, stimulating, organized, convincing. Here was a man who had taught freshman composition for several years and who was incapable of committing any of the more ob-

Wayne C. Booth, "The Rhetorical Stance," *College Composition and Communication,* XIV, No. 3 (October, 1963). Reprinted with the permission of the National Council of Teachers of English and Wayne C. Booth.

vious errors that we think of as characteristic of bad writing. Yet he could not write a decent sentence, paragraph, or paper until his rhetorical problem was solved—until, that is, he had found a definition of his audience, his argument, and his own proper tone of voice.

The word "rhetoric" is one of those catch-all terms that can easily raise trouble when our backs are turned. As it regains a popularity that it once seemed permanently to have lost, its meanings seem to range all the way from something like "the whole art of writing on any subject," as in Kenneth Burke's *The Rhetoric of Religion,* through "the special arts of persuasion," on down to fairly narrow notions about rhetorical figures and devices. And of course we still have with us the meaning of "empty bombast," as in the phrase "merely rhetorical."

I suppose that the question of the role of rhetoric in the English course is meaningless if we think of rhetoric in either its broadest or its narrowest meanings. No English course could avoid dealing with rhetoric in Burke's sense, under whatever name, and on the other hand nobody would ever advocate anything so questionable as teaching "mere rhetoric." But if we settle on the following, traditional, definition, some real questions are raised: "Rhetoric is the art of finding and employing the most effective means of persuasion on any subject, considered independently of intellectual mastery of that subject." As the students say, "Prof. X knows his stuff but he doesn't know how to put it across." If rhetoric is thought of as the art of "putting it across," considered as quite distinct from mastering an "it" in the first place, we are immediately landed in a bramble bush of controversy. Is there such an art? If so, what does it consist of? Does it have a content of its own? Can it be taught? Should it be taught? If it should, how do we go about it, head on or obliquely?

Obviously it would be foolish to try to deal with many of these issues in twenty minutes. But I wish that there were more signs of our taking all of them seriously. I wish that along with our new passion for structural linguistics, for example, we could point to the development of a rhetorical theory that would show just how knowledge of structural linguistics can be useful to anyone interested in the art of persuasion. I wish there were more freshman texts that related every principle and every rule to functional principles of rhetoric, or, where this proves impossible, I wish one found more systematic discussion of why it is impossible. But for today, I must content myself with a brief look at the charge that there is nothing distinctive and teachable about the art of rhetoric.

The case against the isolability and teachability of rhetoric may look at first like a good one. Nobody writes rhetoric, just as nobody ever writes writing. What we write and speak is always *this* discussion of the decline of railroading and *that* discussion of Pope's couplets and the other argument for abolishing the poll-tax or for getting rhetoric back into English studies.

We can also admit that like all the arts, the art of rhetoric is at best very chancy, only partly amenable to systematic teaching; as we are all painfully aware when our 1:00 section goes miserably and our 2:00 section of the same course is a delight, our own rhetoric is not entirely under control. Successful rhetoricians are to some extent like poets, born, not made. They are also dependent on years of practice and experience. And we can finally admit that even the firmest of principles about writing cannot be taught in the same sense that elementary logic or arithmetic or French can be taught. In my first year of teaching, I had a student who started his first two essays with a swear word. When I suggested that perhaps the third paper ought to start with something else, he protested that his high school teacher had taught him always to catch the reader's attention. Now the teacher was right, but the application of even such a firm principle requires reserves of tact that were somewhat beyond my freshman.

But with all of the reservations made, surely the charge that the art of persuasion cannot in any sense be taught is baseless. I cannot think that anyone who has ever read Aristotle's *Rhetoric* or, say, Whateley's *Elements of Rhetoric* could seriously make the charge. There is more than enough in these and the other traditional rhetorics to provide structure and content for a year-long course. I believe that such a course, when planned and carried through with intelligence and flexibility, can be one of the most important of all educational experiences. But it seems obvious that the arts of persuasion cannot be learned in one year, that a good teacher will continue to teach them regardless of his subject matter, and that we as English teachers have a special responsibility at all levels to get certain basic rhetorical principles into all of our writing assignments. When I think back over the experiences which have had any actual effect on my writing, I find the great good fortune of a splendid freshman course, taught by a man who believed in what he was doing, but I also find a collection of other experiences quite unconnected with a specific writing course. I remember the instructor in psychology who pencilled one word after a peculiarly pretentious paper of mine: *bull.* I remember the day when P. A. Christensen talked with me about my Chaucer paper, and made me understand that my failure to use effective transitions was not simply a technical fault but a fundamental block in my effort to get him to see my meaning. His off-the-cuff pronouncement that I should never let myself write a sentence that was not in some way explicitly attached to preceding and following sentences meant far more to me at that moment, when I had something I wanted to say, than it could have meant as part of a pattern of such rules offered in a writing course. Similarly, I can remember the devastating lessons about my bad writing that Ronald Crane could teach with a simple question mark on a graduate seminar paper, or a pencilled "Evidence for this?" or "Why this section here?" or "Everybody says so. Is it true?"

Such experiences are not, I like to think, simply the result of my being a late bloomer. At least I find my colleagues saying such things as "I didn't learn to write until I became a newspaper reporter," or "The most important training in writing I had was doing a dissertation under old *Blank*." Sometimes they go on to say that the freshman course was useless; sometimes they say that it was an indispensable preparation for the later experience. The diversity of such replies is so great as to suggest that before we try to reorganize the freshman course, with or without explicit confrontations with rhetorical categories, we ought to look for whatever there is in common among our experiences, both of good writing and of good writing instruction. Whatever we discover in such an enterprise ought to be useful to us at any level of our teaching. It will not, presumably, decide once and for all what should be the content of the freshman course, if there should be such a course. But it might serve as a guideline for the development of widely different programs in the widely differing institutional circumstances in which we must work.

The common ingredient that I find in all of the writing I admire—excluding for now novels, plays and poems—is something that I shall reluctantly call the rhetorical stance, a stance which depends on discovering and maintaining in any writing situation a proper balance among the three elements that are at work in any communicative effort: the available arguments about the subject itself, the interests and peculiarities of the audience, and the voice, the implied character, of the speaker. I should like to suggest that it is this balance, this rhetorical stance, difficult as it is to describe, that is our main goal as teachers of rhetoric. Our ideal graduate will strike this balance automatically in any writing that he considers finished. Though he may never come to the point of finding the balance easily, he will know that it is what makes the difference between effective communication and mere wasted effort.

What I mean by the true rhetorician's stance can perhaps best be seen by contrasting it with two or three corruptions, unbalanced stances often assumed by people who think they are practicing the arts of persuasion.

The first I'll call the pedant's stance; it consists of ignoring or underplaying the personal relationship of speaker and audience and depending entirely on statements about a subject—that is, the notion of a job to be done for a particular audience is left out. It is a virtue, of course, to respect the bare truth of one's subject, and there may even be some subjects which in their very nature define an audience and a rhetorical purpose so that adequacy to the subject can be the whole art of presentation. For example, an article on "The relation of the ontological and teleological proofs," in a recent *Journal of Religion,* requires a minimum of adaptation of argument to audience. But most subjects do not in themselves imply in any necessary way a purpose and an audience and hence a speaker's tone. The writer who assumes that it is enough merely to write an exposition of what he happens to know on the subject will produce the kind of essay that soils our scholarly journals, written not for readers but for bibliographies.

In my first year of teaching I taught a whole unit on "exposition" without ever suggesting, so far as I can remember, that the students ask themselves what their expositions were *for.* So they wrote expositions like this one—I've saved it, to teach me toleration of my colleagues: the title is "Family relations in More's *Utopia.*" "In this theme I would like to discuss some of the relationships with the family which Thomas More elaborates and sets forth in his book, *Utopia.* The first thing that I would like to discuss about family relations is that overpopulation, according to More, is a just cause of war." And so on. Can you hear that student sneering at me, in this opening? What he is saying is something like "you ask for a meaningless paper, I give you a meaningless paper." He knows that he has no audience except me. He knows that I don't want to read his summary of family relations in *Utopia,* and he knows that I know that he therefore has no rhetorical purpose. Because he has not been led to see a question which he considers worth answering, or an audience that could possibly care one way or the other, the paper is worse than no paper at all, even though it has no grammatical or spelling errors and is organized right down the line, one, two, three.

An extreme case, you may say. Most of us would never allow ourselves that kind of empty fencing? Perhaps. But if some carefree foundation is willing to finance a statistical study, I'm willing to wager a month's salary that we'd find at least half of the suggested topics in our freshman texts as pointless as mine was. And we'd find a good deal more than half of the discussions of grammar, punctuation, spelling, and style totally divorced from any notion that rhetorical purpose to some degree controls all such matters. We can offer objective descriptions of levels of usage from now until graduation, but unless the student discovers a desire to say something to somebody and learns to control his diction for a purpose, we've gained very little. I once gave an assignment asking students to describe the same classroom in three different statements, one for each level of usage. They were obedient, but the only ones who got anything from the assignment were those who intuitively imported the rhetorical instructions I had overlooked—such purposes as "Make fun of your scholarly surroundings by describing this classroom in extremely elevated style," or

"Imagine a kid from the slums accidentally trapped in these surroundings and forced to write a description of this room." A little thought might have shown me how to give the whole assignment some human point, and therefore some educative value.

Just how confused we can allow ourselves to be about such matters is shown in a recent publication of the Educational Testing Service, called "Factors in Judgments of Writing Ability." In order to isolate those factors which affect differences in grading standards, ETS set six groups of readers—business men, writers and editors, lawyers, and teachers of English, social science and natural science—to reading the same batch of papers. Then ETS did a hundred-page "factor analysis" of the amount of agreement and disagreement, and of the elements which different kinds of graders emphasized. The authors of the report express a certain amount of shock at the discovery that the median correlation was only .31 and that 94% of the papers received either 7, 8, or 9 of the 9 possible grades.

But what *could* they have expected? In the first place, the students were given no purpose and no audience when the essays were assigned. And then all these editors and business men and academics were asked to judge the papers in a complete vacuum, using only whatever intuitive standards they cared to use. I'm surprised that there was any correlation at all. Lacking instructions, some of the students undoubtedly wrote polemical essays, suitable for the popular press; others no doubt imagined an audience, say, of *Reader's Digest* readers, and others wrote with the English teachers as implied audience; an occasional student with real philosophical bent would no doubt do a careful analysis of the pros and cons of the case. This would be graded low, of course, by the magazine editors, even though they would have graded it high if asked to judge it as a speculative contribution to the analysis of the problem. Similarly, a creative student who has been getting A's for his personal essays will write an amusing colorful piece, failed by all the social scientists present, though they would have graded it high if asked to judge it for what it was. I find it shocking that tens of thousands of dollars and endless hours should have been spent by students, graders, and professional testers analyzing essays and grading results totally abstracted from any notion of purposeful human communication. Did nobody protest? One might as well assemble a group of citizens to judge students' capacity to throw balls, say, without telling the students or the graders whether altitude, speed, accuracy or form was to be judged. The judges would be drawn from football coaches, hai-lai experts, lawyers, and English teachers, and asked to apply whatever standards they intuitively apply to ball throwing. Then we could express astonishment that the judgments did not correlate very well, and we could do a factor analysis to discover, lo and behold, that some readers concentrated on altitude, some on speed, some on accuracy, some on form—and the English teachers were simply confused.

One effective way to combat the pedantic stance is to arrange for weekly confrontations of groups of students over their own papers. We have done far too little experimenting with arrangements for providing a genuine audience in this way. Short of such developments, it remains true that a good teacher can convince his students that he is a true audience, if his comments on the papers show that some sort of dialogue is taking place. As Jacques Barzun says in *Teacher in America,* students should be made to feel that unless they have said something to someone, they have failed; to bore the teacher is a worse form of failure than to anger him. From this point of view we can see that the charts of grading symbols that mar even the best freshman texts are not the innocent time savers that we pretend. Plausible as it may seem to arrange for more corrections with less time, they inevitably reduce the student's sense of purpose in writing. When he sees innumerable W13's and P19's in the margin, he cannot possibly feel that the art of persuasion is as important to his instructor as when he reads personal comments, however few.

This first perversion, then, springs from ignoring the audience or overreliance on the pure subject. The second, which might be called the advertiser's stance, comes from *under*valuing the subject and overvaluing pure effect: how to win friends and influence people.

Some of our best freshman texts—Sheridan Baker's *The Practical Stylist,* for example—allow themselves on occasion to suggest that to be controversial or argumentative, to stir up an audience is an end in itself. Sharpen the controversial edge, one of them says, and the clear implication is that one should do so even if the truth of the subject is honed off in the process. This perversion is probably in the long run a more serious threat in our society than the danger of ignoring the audience. In the time of audience-reaction meters and pre-tested plays and novels, it is not easy to convince students of the old Platonic truth that good persuasion is honest persuasion, or even of the old Aristotelian truth that the good rhetorician must be master of his subject, no matter how dishonest he may decide ultimately to be. Having told them that good writers always to some degree accommodate their arguments to the audience, it is hard to explain the difference between justified accommodation—say changing *point one* to the final position—and the kind of accommodation that fills our popular magazines, in which the very substance of what is said is accommodated to some preconception of what will sell. "The publication of *Eros* [magazine] represents a major breakthrough in the battle for the liberation of the human spirit."

At a dinner about a month ago I sat between the wife of a famous civil rights lawyer and an advertising consultant. "I saw the article on your book yesterday in the Daily News," she said, "but I didn't even finish it. The title of your book scared me off. Why did you ever choose such a terrible title? Nobody would buy a book with a title like that." The man on my right, whom I'll call Mr. Kinches, overhearing my feeble reply, plunged into a conversation with her, over my torn and bleeding corpse. "Now with my *last* book," he said, "I listed 20 possible titles and then tested them out on 400 businessmen. The one I chose was voted for by 90 percent of the businessmen." "That's what I was just saying to Mr. Booth," she said. "A book title ought to grab you, and *rhetoric* is not going to grab anybody." "Right," he said. "My *last* book sold 50,000 copies already; I don't know how this one will do, but I polled 200 businessmen on the table of contents, and . . ."

At one point I did manage to ask him whether the title he chose really fit the book. "Not quite as well as one or two of the others," he admitted, "but that doesn't matter, you know. If the book is designed right, so that the first chapter pulls them in, and you *keep* 'em in, who's going to gripe about a little inaccuracy in the title?"

Well, rhetoric is the art of persuading, not the art seeming to persuade by giving everything away at the start. It presupposes that one has a purpose concerning a subject which itself cannot be fundamentally modified by the desire to persuade. If Edmund Burke had decided that he could win more votes in Parliament by choosing the other side—as he most certainly could have done—we would hardly hail this party-switch as a master stroke of rhetoric. If Churchill had offered the British "peace in our time," with some laughs thrown in, because opinion polls had shown that more Britishers were "grabbed" by these than by blood, sweat, and tears, we could hardly call his decision a sign of rhetorical skill.

One could easily discover other perversions of the rhetorician's balance—most obviously what might be called the entertainer's stance the willingness to sacrifice substance to personality and charm. I admire Walker Gibson's efforts to startle us out of dry pedantry, but I know from experience that his exhortations to find and develop the speaker's voice can lead to empty colorfulness. A student once said to me, complaining about a colleague, "I soon learned that all I had to do to get an A was imitate Thurber."

But perhaps this is more than enough about the perversions of the rhetorical stance. Balance itself is always harder to describe than the clumsy poses that result when it is destroyed. But we all experience the balance whenever we find an author who succeeds in changing our minds. He can do so only if he knows more about the subject than we do, and if he then engages us in the process of thinking—and feeling—it through. What makes the rhetoric of Milton and Burke and Churchill great is that each presents us with the spectacle of a man passionately involved in thinking an important question through, in the company of an audience. Though each of them did everything in his power to make his point persuasive, including a pervasive use of the many emotional appeals that have been falsely scorned by many a freshman composition text, none would have allowed himself the advertiser's stance; none would have polled the audience in advance to discover which position would get the votes. Nor is the highly individual personality that springs out at us from their speeches and essays present for the sake of selling itself. The rhetorical balance among speakers, audience, and argument is with all three men habitual, as we see if we look at their non-political writings. Burke's work on the Sublime and Beautiful is a relatively unimpassioned philosophical treatise, but one finds there again a delicate balance: though the implied author of this work is a far different person, far less obtrusive, far more objective, than the man who later cried *sursum corda* to the British Parliament, he permeates with his philosophical personality his philosophical work. And though the signs of his awareness of his audience are far more subdued, they are still here: every effort is made to involve the *proper* audience, the audience of philosophical minds, in a fundamentally interesting inquiry, and to lead them through to the end. In short, because he was a man engaged with men in the effort to solve a human problem, one could never call what he wrote dull, however difficult or abstruse.

Now obviously the habit of seeking this balance is not the only thing we have to teach under the heading of rhetoric. But I think that everything worth teaching under that heading finds its justification finally in that balance. Much of what is now considered irrelevant or dull can, in fact, be brought to life when teachers and students know what they are seeking. Churchill reports that the most valuable training he ever received in rhetoric was in the diagramming of sentences. Think of it! Yet the diagramming of a sentence, regardless of the grammatical system, can be a live subject as soon as one asks not simply "How is this sentence put together," but rather "Why is it put together in this way?" or "Could the rhetorical balance and hence the desired persuasion be better achieved by writing it differently?"

As a nation we are reputed to write very badly. As a nation, I would say, we are more inclined to the perversions of rhetoric than to the rhetorical balance. Regardless of what we do about this or that course in the curriculum, our mandate would seem to be, then, to lead more of our students than we now do to care about and practice the true arts of persuasion.

Questions

1. The first paragraph of "The Rhetorical Stance" is illustration-in-advance. Does this beginning seem more apt than some you would find in *Reader's Digest?* Can you understand the full force of the illustration without knowing the meaning of *polemic?*
2. Can you determine how Booth gets from his discussion of whether rhetoric can be taught to his definition of the rhetorical stance? The steps should be easy enough to follow if the lesson he refers to really made an impression: "I should never let myself write a sentence that was not in some way explicitly attached to preceding and following sentences."
3. If you think of the three elements involved in the rhetorical stance as forming the three sides of a triangle, then your problem in any given writing situation is to place yourself somewhere within that triangle so that you are aware not only of all three sides but of something of the relative importance of each side in this particular situation:

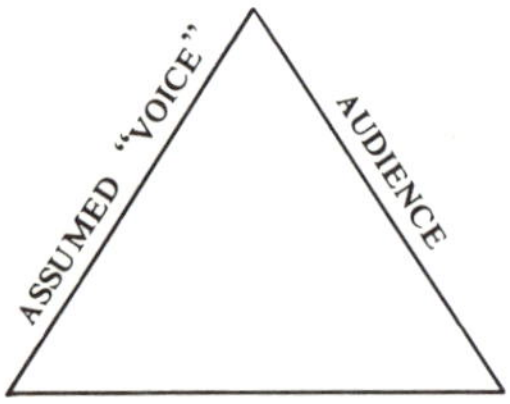

   Since your problem involves "discovering and maintaining in any writing situation a proper balance among the three elements," failure to consider any one of them will cause trouble. You will probably be aware of at least some of the arguments available to you on any subject you are writing about, but many students are aware only vaguely, if at all, of either an audience or an assumed voice for themselves. How does Booth try to convince you that all three are important?
4. Do you recognize in Booth's description of problems in finding the true rhetorical stance any of your own problems in writing? Do the contrasting "corruptions" or "perversions" effectively clarify the true stance? Can you define with any precision Booth's own "voice, the implied character"?
5. Read the essay again, examining it for the range and effectiveness of its illustrations. Are they appropriate to the audience (a large one of fellow teachers of English)? Note how many of the illustrations come from his own experience and fit the personal "voice" he has adopted for the essay: not that of a Mark Twain devastating his audience with irony and satire, nor of a prophet foretelling their doom, but of an urbane and concerned teacher of rhetoric speaking to other concerned teachers. Your own background can hardly be as broad as Booth's, at least not yet. But it is surely broad enough that if you watch for them you can find experiences from your life or from your reading—another part of your life—that can help clarify and sup-

port the position you take. Booth may be talking to teachers of English, but the principles he discusses and the kinds of illustrations he uses can go a long way toward helping you make your own writing more effective.

Suggestions for Writing

1. Remember, if you can—or invent, if you cannot remember—some writing assignment that seemed to you especially meaningless. Try to write a beginning for it as you would if you had seen it before reading this essay. (You needn't try to out-do Booth's student on More's *Utopia.*) Then, after defining as precisely as you can for yourself a true rhetorical stance, write a detailed paper in which you give the subject point and force.
2. You are now a year—or a few years—beyond the sophistication you felt as a high school senior. Write to a group of eager but unconvinced high school sophomores about the importance of taking seriously their English classes, or their math, or biology. Write as effectively and convincingly as you can. You will notice that this assignment determines for you two of the three elements in the writing situation that Booth argues we must keep in balance. Whatever knowledge you now have, reinforced by whatever reading you may do, determines the third. But the balance he insists on is still a problem for you to solve.

Man's Finest Hour

Noah Jonathan Jacobs

This selection is the first chapter of a fascinating book, not widely known, called Naming-Day in Eden: The Creation and Recreation of Language. *The word-play in the sub-title suggests something of the attitude with which the book was written. A major problem in your reading of the selection will be trying to define that attitude. You can help yourself by keeping one simple question before you as you read: How seriously does Jacobs seem to be expecting you to take him? But if the question is simple enough, answering it may be more difficult than it would seem. A final answer may have to wait for more evidence; it will depend on your confidence in his linguistic knowledge, somewhat on your awareness of linguistic problems yet to be raised in this textbook, especially on your sensitivity to what we call* tone *in writing. All this involves your defining Jacobs' rhetorical stance: with what personal voice is he speaking, to what kind of audience, and with what attitude toward his subject? Can you find places where the specific evidence, such as his accounts of word origins, his knowledge of animals, or his own use of words, makes you distrust his linguistic knowledge? As you read, you may want to look at the questions following the selection for other specific hints about the tone.*

Adam was barely one hour old on that fateful fall morning in the springtime of the world (October 4, 4004 B.C., as computed by that exact theologian Bishop Butler) when the Lord assembled the inhabitants of the newly formed earth and paraded them before Adam to see what he would call them. Adam grasped the situation at a glance. He surveyed the line-up before him and, his moist eye, unencumbered by glass or monocle and in a fine frenzy rolling, gave to each of the marchers, whom he now beheld for the first time, a local habitation and a name. In the very infancy of the world man was able to create a symbolic net to capture the fleeting objects before him and make them the object of his intellectual knowledge. With his invisible breath he devised unheard-of names, substantial enough to be freighted with deep thoughts and mobile enough to waft their precious cargo down the ages. God had created the earth, and Adam festooned it with a web of words. With this second creation man gave the world its first constitution. In language he found a foothold and a lever to move the solid world. The verbal execution of this conception deserves the highest praise because it was the greatest single achievement of the human mind and bears the indispensable marks of genius. What man since the Fall, what Solomon among the ancients or Leibniz among the moderns, nay, what logical positivist could undertake such a prodigious task? The prediluvian exploit of the patriarch Noah who, with the help of his wife and wicked sons, rounded up the animals and persuaded them to enter the Ark was a menial chore compared to primal man's linguistic feat. Adam himself stood aghast at the phantom world he had unchained. He could not believe his own ears. *Homo nascitur poeta,* Adam was born a poet. No other animal could have created such an elaborate linguistic edifice, because no animal has the necessary intellectual vigor to represent the world in symbolic forms, unless it were, as the Scotch philosopher Monboddo suggested, that patient architect the beaver.

Armed with this verbal mechanism, man was able to break through every barrier which imprisoned his spirit to assume a commanding position of supremacy. On a bridge of words formed by his lips he crossed the narrow isthmus which separated him from the animals. Halfway across the *pons asinorum,* with one foot in eternity, he looked before him into History (not without misgivings) and behind him on the natural life of Instinct (not without envy, for how could he forget his past?) and, drawing a deep breath, named the cowering beasts as they marked time before him. With these names man drew a line (later ignored by the behaviorists) between the lower animals and himself and thus established his sovereignty over an alien world. This was man's finest hour. He had dissolved the bonds of his origin and had leaped headlong to his new position of freedom, while the incorrigible beasts, loath to break their chains with the past, crept back to their lairs on all fours. They were too absorbed in the satisfaction of their feverish appetites to risk a rupture with their instincts, too steeped in primitive felicity to follow the beckoning ideal. Had they evinced the slightest inclination for that celestial metamorphosis, God would have lent them a Hand. But they stood aside and cried "Nay." They deserved to be left behind.

Numerous instances of animal sagacity have been recorded by psychologists who have made extensive phonetic researches into the sounds with which the animal world regales us. With their customary effrontery these investigators have looked down the throats of animals in an effort to decipher their dark sayings (in the case of the lion from outside the cage) and have made careful notes on the timbre, tempo and motifs of their vocalizations. Extraordinary mental feasts have been revealed by these field auditions. On one occasion a horse was observed working out square roots and a dog was overheard dictating his last will and testament to his spouse as he wiped a tear from his eye. A religious instinct has been detected in the praying mantis (Gr. *mántis,* prophet), a grasshopper that folds its forelegs in an attitude of prayer, and in the elephant, who turns to the east at sundown as it lifts its trunk in worship. It is reported that monkeys, when not involved in arboreal distractions, can speak our language but refrain from doing so lest they be mistaken for men. The experts have also compiled librettos of the woodland concerts of the modulated rhythms of the warbler, the syncopations of the cuckoo and the starling's plagiarisms. The most impressive examples, however, are the recorded bits of human speech of the gifted ibis (venerated by the Egyptians as the inventor of the clyster) and the small talk of the pewit, which is known as the exegete among the birds, for it feeds on delicacies hidden under rocks and excels in interpreting danger signals to its companions.

These vernal researches, though elaborately conducted, are not well authenticated. They exaggerate the mental processes of animals and attribute to them powers they do not possess. The rhinoceros, for example, is extremely dull and short-tempered. Silly hens have been persuaded to sit on addled eggs for days on end. The magpies, lapwings and jackdaws (known in German as *Litauer,* Lithuanians, because of their raucous *k*'s and *r*'s) say harsh things to one another in torrents of excessively bad language. Some birds, as the stork and the woodpecker, are incapable of producing vocal sounds, and some animals, notably the white cat (if it has blue eyes), are stone deaf. It is true that few animals are wholly silent. From the very outset, even before man appeared, each had its own mode of expression when in a talking mood—the asses brayed, the moles rumbled, the doves moaned, the plovers whistled, the gnats hummed, the turtles wept, the monogamous rhinoceros yawned and the lovely elephant blew his trumpet. The fishes too uttered amorous phrases, too delicate for our coarse ears to perceive. But it was an absurd concert wasted on the desert air, for no one really listened. However extraordinary the vocal efforts of animals, they are debarred from human articulation. Speech does not depend on physical endowment but on the wit to connect sound with purpose. The animals are not phonetically defective but semantically blocked. Their speech is hence an unchanging dialect, incapable of variation or improvement, consisting of a limited repertory of vague interjections which are not intended to convey knowledge but merely to voice subjective fears. The duck's dialect, for example, is confined to a monosyllabic, exiguous quack, devoid of variety, wit or compass. The frog's inflections are as infantile and spasmodic today as in the days of Aristophanes. The parrots are generally regarded as having mastered our speech technique, but their speech is unoriginal and profane, and their diction is obscured by an excessive nasality which they have in common with the Puritans, originating in both species from a sanctimonious drawl intoned through cavernous hooked noses. It is true that the serpent's conversation with Eve was marked by careful diction and close reasoning and that Baalam's ass on one occasion indulged in repartee. But the serpent was soon deprived of his gift of speech for abusing his prerogative, and the ass never repeated his initial inspired performance. Man alone is articulate. When an ass speaks, it is a miracle.

It cannot be denied that Adam enjoyed unparalleled advantages in Eden. The Himalayan air of the Garden was favorable to his brooding genius and conducive to "learned leisure." In its solitude, undisturbed by visitors, servants or the clamorous exigencies of domestic life, he found ample material for the application of original principles. Yet Adam labored under incomparable difficulties. He was young in years, anonymous, unchastened by the miscellaneous lessons of experience and hence prone to errors of judgment. His life had struck root in a congenial soil, in the very umbilicus of the world, but his view was confined to the landscape of Eden. Although he was not compelled to submit his random cogitations to a human tribunal for approval, he had no traditional models to emulate, no reference works or maps to consult. There is no more impressive example in history of such an unnatural divorce between inborn talent and acquired experience. His untutored mind was an empty sheet, as Locke assures us, blank on both sides. His chief drawback, however, was neither immature judgment nor inherited weaknesses, but the absence of those powerful incentives to progress: money, alcohol and the fury of fashion.

Nevertheless, our indomitable First Ancestor pressed on with self-assurance. Here was a rank outsider, an orphan and a bachelor to boot, who stepped forward to the dizzy edge and took possession of the world. He accepted his uniqueness. Why could not his horizontal companions rise above themselves to an upright position and escort man to freedom? They could not take off on the wings of abstraction because they failed to understand the nature of language. Hence, they were left to sniff their way along a cul-de-sac while man set out on a limitless road to make his mark in the world.

Questions

1. Jacobs calls language man's greatest invention. In light of the scientific advances of the last century, do you agree or disagree with Jacobs? Why?
2. In this article, Jacobs uses a number of unusual terms and makes frequent

reference to famous men and to widely known ideas. Can you define the following: *prediluvian, incorrigible, arboreal, exegete, exiguous, repartee, umbilicus?* Can you identify such men as Solomon, Leibniz, or Locke? You will be able to respond to Jacobs' essay much more effectively if you know these words and references.

3. Jacobs frequently conveys a great deal of meaning in a single phrase or sentence. What does he mean by the sentence "The animals are not phonetically defective but semantically blocked"? Relate this to the rest of the essay. Later we are going to find some recent evidence that he may be wrong. How might this fact change your response to the selection?
4. In the last sentence Jacobs states somewhat obliquely his central idea, a summary of what he has to say. In your own words explain this idea.
5. If you know the Shakespearian source of "in a fine frenzy rolling" and "a local habitation and a name," you will have a richer response to Jacobs' sentence, but even if you don't you should be able to respond to the effect of these and other poetic expressions: "fateful fall morning in the springtime of the world," "mobile enough to waft their precious cargo down the ages," "festooned it with a web of words," and so forth. Try to define as precisely as you can the effect of these and other forms of somewhat inflated language. Does this quality have anything to do with the statement that "Adam was born a poet"? Relate this quality to Jacobs' rhetorical stance.
6. Examine the third paragraph and try to define Jacobs' attitude toward what he is saying. What effect does he achieve with the parenthetical expression "in the case of the lion from outside the cage"? Relate this expression to such phrases as "customary effrontery," "Decipher their dark sayings," "these field auditions." Find other expressions that point up his attitude or tone.
7. The basic form of this selection seems to be narrative—the story of the naming. But both paragraphs three and four are developed by a series of brief illustrations. Note how illustration combines with and supports the narration and the central idea.

Suggestions for Writing

1. As Jacobs suggests, "Adam enjoyed unparalleled advantages in Eden." One of those advantages was freshness of vision. Everywhere he looked he saw something new. He could not think in cliches as most of us tend to do. Imagine you are Adam confronted with the need to write the world's first report on some such experience as your first bewildering day, your apprehension at the first sunset or night, your first drink of water, your discovery of shade on a sunny day, or your reaction to your shadow. Since reports always go to higher-ups, you have your audience defined for you. Try to catch the freshness of vision Adam would have had.

How I Discovered Words

Helen Keller

By now the story of Helen Keller's battle with blindness and deafness has taken on some of the dimensions of a myth in American thinking, especially in educational circles. This selection from that story fascinates because it records the discovery of language from a process and point of view altogether different from what we usually experience. As you read, try to define as precisely as you can the differences. The selections from Anne Sullivan's letters describe the same experiences from the point of view of her teacher. Both student and teacher reveal their excitement over Miss Keller's discovery of words. Can you see contrasts in their responses?

The most important day I remember in all my life is the one on which my teacher, Anne Mansfield Sullivan, came to me. I am filled with wonder when I consider the immeasurable contrast between the two lives which it connects. It was the third of March, 1887, three months before I was seven years old.

On the afternoon of that eventful day, I stood on the porch, dumb, expectant. I guessed vaguely from my mother's signs and from the hurrying to and fro in the house that something unusual was about to happen, so I went to the door and waited on the steps. The afternoon sun penetrated the mass of honeysuckle that covered the porch, and fell on my upturned face. My fingers lingered almost unconsciously on the familiar leaves and blossoms which had just come forth to greet the sweet southern spring. I did not know what the future held of marvel or surprise for me. Anger and bitterness had preyed upon me continually for weeks and a deep languor had succeeded this passionate struggle.

Have you ever been at sea in a dense fog, when it seemed as if a tangible white darkness shut you in, and the great ship, tense and anxious, groped her way toward the shore with plummet and sounding-line, and you waited with beating heart for something to happen? I was like that ship before my education began, only I was without compass or sounding-line, and had no way of knowing how near the harbour was. "Light! give me

Helen Keller, from *The Story of My Life* (New York, 1903).

light!" was the wordless cry of my soul, and the light of love shone on me in that very hour.

I felt approaching footsteps. I stretched out my hand as I supposed to my mother. Some one took it, and I was caught up and held close in the arms of her who had come to reveal all things to me, and, more than all things else, to love me.

The morning after my teacher came she led me into her room and gave me a doll. The little blind children at the Perkins Institution had sent it and Laura Bridgman had dressed it; but I did not know this until afterward. When I had played with it a little while, Miss Sullivan slowly spelled into my hand the word "d-o-l-l." I was at once interested in this finger play and tried to imitate it. When I finally succeeded in making the letters correctly I was flushed with childish pleasure and pride. Running downstairs to my mother I held up my hand and made the letters for doll. I did not know that I was spelling a word or even that words existed; I was simply making my fingers go in monkey-like imitation. In the days that followed I learned to spell in this uncomprehending way a great many words, among them *pin, hat, cup* and a few verbs like *sit, stand* and *walk.* But my teacher had been with me several weeks before I understood that everything has a name.

One day, while I was playing with my new doll, Miss Sullivan put my big rag doll into my lap also, spelled "d-o-l-l" and tried to make me understand that "d-o-l-l" applied to both. Earlier in the day we had had a tussle over the words "m-u-g" and "w-a-t-e-r." Miss Sullivan had tried to impress it upon me that "m-u-g" is *mug* and that "w-a-t-e-r" is *water,* but I persisted in confounding the two. In despair she had dropped the subject for the time, only to renew it at the first opportunity. I became impatient at her repeated attempts and, seizing the new doll, I dashed it upon the floor. I was keenly delighted when I felt the fragments of the broken doll at my feet. Neither sorrow nor regret followed my passionate outburst. I had not loved the doll. In the still, dark world in which I lived there was no strong sentiment or tenderness. I felt my teacher sweep the fragments to one side of the hearth, and I had a sense of satisfaction that the cause of my discomfort was removed. She brought me my hat, and I knew I was going out into the warm sunshine. This thought, if a wordless sensation may be called a thought, made me hop and skip with pleasure.

We walked down the path to the well-house, attracted by the fragrance of the honeysuckle with which it was covered. Some one was drawing water and my teacher placed my hand under the spout. As the cool stream gushed over one hand she spelled into the other the word *water,* first slowly, then rapidly. I stood still, my whole attention fixed upon the motions of her fingers. Suddenly I felt a misty consciousness as of something forgotten—a thrill of returning thought; and somehow the mystery of language was revealed to me. I knew then that "w-a-t-e-r" meant the wonderful cool something that was flowing over my hand. That living word awakened my soul, gave it light, hope, joy, set it free! There were barriers still, it is true, but barriers that could in time be swept away.

I left the well-house eager to learn. Everything had a name, and each name gave birth to a new thought. As we returned to the house every object which I touched seemed to quiver with life. That was because I saw everything with the strange, new sight that had come to me. On entering the door I remembered the doll I had broken. I felt my way to the hearth and picked up the pieces. I tried vainly to put them together. Then my eyes filled with tears; for I realized what I had done, and for the first time I felt repentance and sorrow.

I learned a great many new words that day. I do not remember what they all were; but I do know that *mother, father, sister, teacher* were among them—words that were to make the world blossom for me, "like Aaron's rod, with flowers." It would have been difficult to find a happier child than I was as I lay in my crib at the close of that eventful day and lived over the joys it had brought me, and for the first time longed for a new day to come.

Anne Sullivan

From Anne Sullivan's Letters

April 3, 1887

The hour from twelve to one is devoted to the learning of new words. *But you mustn't think this is the only time I spell to Helen; for I spell in her hand everything we do all day long, although she has no idea as yet what the spelling means.*

On March 31st I found that Helen knew eighteen nouns and three verbs. Here is a list of the words. Those with a cross after them are words she asked for herself: *Doll, mug, pin, key, dog, hat, cup, box, water, milk, candy, eye* (x), *finger* (x), *toe* (x), *head* (x), *cake, baby, mother, sit, stand, walk.* On April 1st she learned the nouns *knife, fork, spoon, saucer, tea, papa, bed,* and the verb *run.*

April 5, 1887.

I must write you a line this morning because something very important has happened. Helen has taken the second great step in her education. She has learned that *everything has a name and that the manual alphabet is the key to everything she wants to know.*

In a previous letter I think I wrote you that "mug" and "milk" had given Helen more trouble than all the rest. She confused the nouns with the verb "drink." She didn't know the word for "drink," but went through the pantomime of drinking whenever she spelled "mug" or "milk." This morning, while she was washing, she wanted to know the name for "water." When she wants to know the name of anything, she points to it and pats my hand. I spelled "w-a-t-e-r" and thought no more about it until after breakfast. Then it occurred to me that with the help of this new word I might succeed in straightening out the "mug-milk" difficulty. We went out to the pump-house, and I made Helen hold her mug under the spout while I pumped. As the cold water gushed forth, filling the mug, I spelled "w-a-t-e-r" in Helen's free hand. The word coming so close upon the sensation of cold water rushing over her hand seemed to startle her. She dropped the mug and stood as one transfixed. A new light came into her face. She spelled "water" several times. Then she dropped on the ground and asked for its name and pointed to the pump and the trellis, and suddenly turning round she asked for my name. I spelled "Teacher." Just then the nurse brought Helen's little sister into the pump-house, and Helen spelled "baby" and pointed to the nurse. All the way back to the house she was highly excited, and learned the name of every object she touched, so that in a few hours she had added thirty new words to her vocabulary. Here are some of them: *Door, open, shut, give, go, come,* and a great many more.

P. S.—I didn't finish my letter in time to get it posted last night; so I shall add a line. Helen got up this morning like a radiant fairy. She has flitted from object to object, asking the name of everything and kissing me for very gladness. Last night when I got in bed, she stole into my arms of her own accord and kissed me for the first time, and I thought my heart would burst, so full was it of joy.

April 10, 1887.

I see an improvement in Helen from day to day, almost from hour to hour. Everything must have a name now. Wherever we go, she asks eagerly for the names of things she has not learned at home. She is anxious for her friends to spell, and eager to teach the letters to every one she meets. She drops the signs and pantomime she used before, as soon as she has words to supply their place, and the acquirement of a new word affords her the liveliest pleasure. And we notice that her face grows more expressive each day.

Questions

1. Do the early details of biography contribute to the fascination of Miss Keller's selection? If so, how?
2. Why should a blind person have trouble associating the word *"doll"* with each of two different dolls? *Mug* with *water?*
3. How fundamental a fact of language is "everything has a name"?
4. Since this is narrative, the entire selection may be considered an example. That is, the story exemplifies the process by which some blind-deaf people become aware of language. Could its function as an example account for some of the emotion with which we read of Miss Keller's coming to know that everything has a name?
5. Miss Sullivan's letters are written to a specific rather than a general audience. What evidence can you find that this fact shifts her rhetorical stance?

How Beautiful with Shoes

Wilbur Daniel Steele *Unlike Helen Keller, the character in this story named Amarantha has used language for years. Yet the story is very basically concerned with her discovery of certain qualities of language. As you read, try to determine what these qualities are, and why she has not discovered them before.*

By the time the milking was finished, the sow, which had farrowed the past week, was making such a row that the girl spilled a pint of the warm milk down the trough-lead to quiet the animal before taking the pail to the well-house. Then in the quiet she heard a sound of hoofs on the bridge, where the road crossed the creek a hundred yards below the house, and she set the pail down on the ground beside her bare, barn-soiled feet. She picked it up again. She set it down. It was as if she calculated its weight.

That was what she was doing, as a matter of fact, setting off against its pull toward the well-house the pull of that wagon team in the road, with little more of personal will or wish in the matter than has a wooden weather-vane between two currents in the wind. And as with the vane, so with the wooden girl—the added behest of a whip-lash cracking in the distance was enough; leaving the pail at the barn door, she set off in a deliberate, docile beeline through the cow-yard, over the fence, and down in a diagonal across the farm's one tilled field toward the willow brake that walled the road at the dip. And once under way, though her mother came to the kitchen door and called in her high flat voice, 'Amarantha, where you goin', Amarantha?' the girl went on apparently unmoved, as though she had been as deaf as the woman in the doorway; indeed, if there was emotion in her it was the purely sensuous one of feeling the clods of the furrows breaking softly between her toes. It was springtime in the mountains.

'Amarantha, why don't you answer me, Amarantha?'

For moments after the girl had disappeared beyond the willows the widow continued to call, unaware through long habit of how absurd it sounded, the name which that strange man her husband had put upon their daughter in one of his moods. Mrs. Doggett had been deaf so long she did not realize that nobody else ever thought of it for the broad-fleshed, slow-minded girl, but called her Mary or, even more simply, Mare.

Ruby Herter had stopped his team this side of the bridge, the mules' heads turned into the lane to his father's farm beyond the road. A big-barreled, heavy-limbed fellow with a square, sallow, not unhandsome face, he took out youth in ponderous gestures of masterfulness; it was like him to have cracked his whip above his animals' ears the moment before he pulled them to a halt. When he saw the girl getting over the fence under the willows he tongued the wad of tobacco out of his mouth into his palm, threw it away beyond the road, and drew a sleeve of his jumper across his lips.

'Don't run yourself out o' breath, Mare; I got all night.'

'I was comin'.' It sounded sullen only because it was matter of fact.

'Well, keep a-comin' and give us a smack.' Hunched on the wagon seat, he remained motionless for some time after she had arrived at the hub, and when he stirred it was but to cut a fresh bit of tobacco, as if already he had forgotten why he threw the old one away. Having satisfied his humor, he unbent, climbed down, kissed her passive mouth, and hugged her up to him, roughly and loosely, his hands careless of contours. It was not out of the way; they were used to handling animals both of them; and it was spring. A slow warmth pervaded the girl, formless, nameless, almost impersonal.

Her betrothed pulled her head back by the braid of her yellow hair. He studied her face, his brows gathered and his chin out.

'Listen, Mare, you wouldn't leave nobody else hug and kiss you, dang you!'

She shook her head, without vehemence or anxiety.

'Who's that?' She hearkened up the road. 'Pull your team out,' she added, as a Ford came in sight around the bend above the house, driven at speed. 'Geddap!' she said to the mules herself.

But the car came to a halt near them, and one of the five men crowded in it called, 'Come on, Ruby, climb in. They's a loony loose out o' Dayville Asylum, and they got him trailed over somewheres on Split Ridge, and Judge North phoned up to Slosson's store for ever'body come help circle him—come on, hop the runnin'-board!'

Ruby hesitated, an eye on his team.

'Scared, Ruby?' The driver raced his engine. 'They say this boy's a killer.'

'Mare, take the team in and tell pa.' The car was already moving when Ruby jumped it. A moment after it had sounded on the bridge it was out of sight.

'Amarantha, Amarantha, why don't you come, Amarantha?'

Returning from her errand, fifteen minutes later, Mare heard the plaint lifted in the twilight. The sun had dipped behind the back ridge, and though the sky was still bright with day, the dusk began to smoke up out of the plowed field like a ground-fog. The girl had returned through it, got the milk, and started toward the well-house before the widow saw her.

'Daughter, seems to me you might!' she expostulated without change of key. 'Here's some young man friend o' yourn stopped to say howdy, and I been rackin' my lungs out after you. . . . Put that milk in the cool and come!'

Some young man friend? But there was no good to be got from puzzling. Mare poured the milk in the pan in the dark of the low house over the well, and as she came out, stooping, she saw a figure waiting for her, black in silhouette against the yellowing sky.

'Who are you?' she asked, a native timidity making her sound sulky.

' "Amarantha!" ' the fellow mused. 'That's poetry.' And she knew then that she did not know him.

She walked past, her arms straight down and her eyes front. Strangers always affected her with a kind of muscular terror simply by being strangers. So she gained the kitchen steps, aware by his tread that he followed. There, taking courage at sight of her mother in the doorway, she turned on him, her eyes down at the level of his knees.

'Who are you and what d' y' want?'

He still mused. 'Amarantha! Amarantha in Carolina! That makes me happy!'

Mare hazarded one upward look. She saw that he had red hair, brown eyes, and hollows under his cheek-bones, and though the green sweater he wore on top of a gray overall was plainly not meant for him, sizes too large as far as girth went, yet he was built so long of limb that his wrists came inches out of the sleeves and made his big hands look even bigger.

Mrs. Doggett complained. 'Why don't you introduce us, daughter?'

The girl opened her mouth and closed it again. Her mother, unaware that no sound had come out of it, smiled and nodded, evidently taking to the tall, homely fellow and tickled by the way he could not seem to get his eyes off her daughter. But the daughter saw none of it, all her attention centered upon the stranger's hands.

Restless, hard-fleshed, and chap-bitten, they were like a countryman's hands; but the fingers were longer than the ordinary, and slightly spatulate at their ends, and these ends were slowly and continuously at play among themselves.

The girl could not have explained how it came to her to be frightened and at the same time to be calm, for she was inept with words. It was simply that in an animal way she knew animals, knew them in health and ailing, and when they were ailing she knew by instinct, as her father had known, how to move so as not to fret them.

Her mother had gone in to light up; from beside the lamp-shelf she called back, 'If he's aimin' to stay to supper you should've told me, Amarantha, though I guess there's plenty of the side-meat to go 'round, if you'll bring me in a few more turnips and potatoes, though it is late.'

At the words the man's cheeks moved in and out. 'I'm very hungry,' he said.

Mare nodded deliberately. Deliberately, as if her mother could hear her, she said over her shoulder, 'I'll go get the potatoes and turnips, ma.' While she spoke she was moving, slowly, softly, at first, toward the right of the yard, where the fence gave over into the field. Unluckily her mother spied her through the window.

'Amarantha, where *are* you goin'?'

'I'm goin' to get the potatoes and turnips.' She neither raised her voice nor glanced back, but lengthened her stride. 'He won't hurt her,' she said to herself. 'He won't hurt her; it's me, not her,' she kept repeating, while she got over the fence and down into the shadow that lay more than ever like a fog on the field.

The desire to believe that it actually did hide her, the temptation to break from her rapid but orderly walk grew till she could no longer fight it. She saw the road willows only a dash ahead of her. She ran, her feet floundering among the furrows.

She neither heard nor saw him, but when she realized he was with her she knew he had been with her all the while. She stopped, and he stopped, and so they stood, with the dark open of the field all around. Glancing sidewise presently, she saw he was no longer looking at her with those strangely importunate brown eyes of his, but had raised them to the crest of the wooded ridge behind her.

By and by, 'What does it make you think of?' he asked. And when she made no move to see, 'Turn around and look!' he said, and though it was low and almost tender in its tone, she knew enough to turn.

A ray of the sunset hidden in the west struck through the tops of the topmost trees, far and small up there, a thin, bright hem.

'What does it make you think of, Amarantha? . . . Answer!'

'Fire,' she made herself say.

'Or blood.'

'Or blood, yeh. That's right, or blood.' She had heard a Ford going up the road beyond the willows, and her attention was not on what she said.

The man soliloquized. 'Fire and blood, both; spare one or the other, and where is beauty, the way the world is? It's an awful thing to have to carry, but Christ had it. Christ came with a sword. I love beauty, Amarantha. . . . I say, I love beauty!'

'Yeh, that's right, I hear.' What she heard was the car stopping at the house.

'Not prettiness. Prettiness'll have to go with ugliness, because it's only ugliness trigged up. But beauty!' Now again he was looking at her. 'Do you know how beautiful you are, Amarantha, "Amarantha sweet and fair"?' Of a sudden, reaching behind her, he began to unravel the meshes of her hair-braid, the long, flat-tipped fingers at once impatient and infinitely gentle. ' "Braid no more that shining hair!" '

Flat-faced Mare Doggett tried to see around those glowing eyes so near to hers, but wise in her instinct, did not try too hard. 'Yeh,' she temporized. 'I mean, no, I mean.'

'Amarantha, I've come a long, long way for you. Will you come away with me now?'

'Yeh—that is—in a minute I will, mister—yeh . . .'

'Because you want to, Amarantha? Because you love me as I love you? Answer!'

'Yeh—sure—uh . . . *Ruby!*'

The man tried to run, but there were six against him, coming up out of the dark that lay in the plowed ground. Mare stood where she was while they knocked him down and got a rope around him; after that she walked back toward the house with Ruby and Older Haskins, her father's cousin.

Ruby wiped his brow and felt of his muscles. 'Gees, you're lucky we come, Mare. We're no more'n past the town, when they come hollerin' he'd broke over this way.'

When they came to the fence the girl sat on the rail for a moment and rebraided her hair before she went into the house, where they were making her mother smell ammonia.

Lots of cars were coming. Judge North was coming, somebody said. When Mare heard this she went into her bedroom off the kitchen and got her shoes and put them on. They were brand new two-dollar shoes with cloth tops, and she had only begun to break them in last Sunday; she wished afterwards she had put her stockings on too, for they would have eased the seams. Or else that she had put on the old button pair, even though the soles were worn through.

Judge North arrived. He thought first of taking the loony straight through to Dayville that night, but then decided to keep him in the lock-up at the courthouse till morning and make the drive by day. Older Haskins stayed in, gentling Mrs. Doggett, while Ruby went out to help get the man into the Judge's sedan. Now that she had them on, Mare didn't like to take the shoes off till Older went; it might make him feel small, she thought.

Older Haskins had a lot of facts about the loony.

'His name's Humble Jewett,' he told them. 'They belong back in Breed County, all them Jewetts, and I don't reckon there's none on 'em that's not a mite unbalanced. He went to college though, worked his way, and he taught somethin' 'rother in some academy-school a spell, till he went off his head all of a sudden and took after folks with an axe. I remember it in the paper at the time. They give out one while how the Principal wasn't goin' to live, and there was others—there was a girl he tried to strangle. That was four-five year back.'

Ruby came in guffawing. 'Know the only thing they can get 'im to say, Mare? Only God thing he'll say is, "Amarantha, she's goin' with me." . . . Mare!'

'Yeh, I know.'

The cover of the kettle the girl was handling slid off the stove with a clatter. A sudden sick wave passed over her. She went out to the back, out into the air. It was not till now she knew how frightened she had been.

Ruby went home, but Older Haskins stayed to supper with them, and helped Mare do the dishes afterward; it was nearly nine when he left. The mother was already in bed, and Mare was about to sit down to get those shoes off her wretched feet at last, when she heard the cow carrying on up at the barn, lowing and kicking, and next minute the sow was in it with a horning note. It might be a fox passing by to get at the henhouse, or a weasel. Mare forgot her feet, took a broom-handle they used in boiling clothes, opened the back door, and stepped out. Blinking the lamplight from her eyes, she peered up toward the outbuildings, and saw the gable end of the barn standing like a red arrow in the dark, and the top of a butternut tree beyond it drawn in skeleton traceries, and just then a cock crowed.

She went to the right corner of the house and saw where the light came from, ruddy above the woods down the valley. Returning into the house, she bent close to her mother's ear and shouted, 'Somethin's a-fire down to the town, looks like,' then went out again and up to the barn. 'Soh! Soh!' she called in to the animals. She climbed up and stood on the top rail of the cow-pen fence, only to find she could not locate the flame even there.

Ten rods behind the buildings a mass of rock mounted higher than their ridgepoles, a chopped-off buttress of the back ridge, covered with oak scrub and wild grapes and blackberries, whose thorny ropes the girl beat away from her skirt with the broom-handle as she scrambled up in the wine-colored dark. Once at the top, and the brush held aside, she could see the tongue-tip of the conflagration half a mile away at the town. And she knew by the bearing of the two church steeples that it was the building where the lock-up was that was burning.

There is a horror in knowing animals trapped in a fire, no matter what the animals.

'Oh, my God!' Mare said.

A car went down the road. Then there was a horse galloping. That would be Older Haskins probably. People were out at Ruby's father's farm; she could hear their voices raised. There must have been another car up from the other way, for lights wheeled and shouts were exchanged in the neighborhood of the bridge. Next thing she knew, Ruby was at the house below, looking for her probably.

He was telling her mother. Mrs. Doggett was not used to him, so he had to shout even louder than Mare had to.

'What y' reckon he done, the hellion! he broke the door and killed Lew Fyke and set the courthouse afire! . . . Where's Mare?'

Her mother would not know. Mare called. 'Here, up the rock here.'

She had better go down. Ruby would likely break his bones if he tried to climb the rock in the dark, not knowing the way. But the sight of the fire fascinated her simple spirit, the fearful element, more fearful than ever now, with the news. 'Yes, I'm comin',' she called sulkily, hearing feet in the brush. 'You wait; I'm comin'.'

When she turned and saw it was Humble Jewett, right behind her among the branches, she opened her mouth to screech. She was not quick enough. Before a sound came out he got one hand over her face and the other arm around her body.

Mare had always thought she was strong, and the loony looked gangling, yet she was so easy for him that he need not hurt her. He made no haste and little noise as he carried her deeper into the undergrowth. Where the hill began to mount it was harder though. Presently he set her on her feet. He let the hand that had been over her mouth slip down to her throat, where the broad-tipped fingers wound, tender as yearning, weightless as caress.

'I was afraid you'd scream before you knew who 'twas, Amarantha. But I didn't want to hurt your lips, dear heart, your lovely, quiet lips.'

It was so dark under the trees she could hardly see him, but she felt his breath on her mouth, near to. But then, instead of kissing her, he said, 'No! No!' took from her throat for an instant the hand that had held her mouth, kissed its palm, and put it back softly against her skin.

'Now, my love, let's go before they come.'

She stood stock still. Her mother's voice was to be heard in the distance, strident and meaningless. More cars were on the road. Nearer, around the rock, there were sounds of tramping and thrashing. Ruby fussed and cursed. He shouted, 'Mare, dang you, where are you, Mare?' his voice harsh with uneasy anger. Now, if she aimed to do anything, was the time to do it. But there was neither breath nor power in her windpipe. It was as if those yearning fingers had paralyzed the muscles.

'Come!' The arm he put around her shivered against her shoulder blades. It was anger. 'I hate killing. It's a dirty, ugly thing. It makes me sick.' He gagged, judging by the sound. But then he ground his teeth. 'Come away, my love!'

She found herself moving. Once when she broke a branch underfoot with an instinctive awkwardness he chided her. 'Quiet, my heart, else they'll hear!' She made herself heavy. He thought she grew tired and bore more of her weight till he was breathing hard.

Men came up the hill. There must have been a dozen spread out, by the angle of their voices as they kept touch. Always Humble Jewett kept caressing Mare's throat with one hand; all she could do was hang back.

'You're tired and you're frightened,' he said at last. 'Get down here.'

There were twigs in the dark, the overhang of a thicket of some sort. He thrust her in under this, and lay beside her on the bed of groundpine. The hand that was not in love with her throat reached across her; she felt the weight of its forearm on her shoulder and its fingers among the strands of her hair, eagerly, but tenderly, busy. Not once did he stop speaking, no louder than breathing, his lips to her ear.

' "*Amarantha sweet and fair—Ah, braid no more that shining hair . . .*" '

Mare had never heard of Lovelace, the poet; she thought the loony was just going on, hardly listened, got little sense. But the cadence of it added to the lethargy of all her flesh.

' "*Like a clew of golden thread—Most excellently ravellèd . . .*" '

Voices loudened; feet came tramping; a pair went past not two rods away.

' "*. . . Do not then wind up the light—In ribbands, and o'ercloud in night . . .*" '

The search went on up the woods, men shouting to one another and beating the brush.

' "*. . . But shake your head and scatter day!*" I've never loved, Amarantha. They've tried me with prettiness, but prettiness is too cheap, yes, it's too cheap.'

Mare was cold, and the coldness made her lazy. All she knew was that he talked on.

'But dogwood blowing in the spring isn't cheap. The earth of a field isn't cheap. Lots of times I've lain down and kissed the earth of a field, Amarantha. That's beauty, and a kiss for beauty.' His breath moved up her cheek. He trembled violently. 'No, no, not yet!' He got to his knees and pulled her by an arm. 'We can go now.'

They went back down the slope, but at an angle, so that when they came to the level they passed two hundred yards to the north of the house, and crossed the road there. More and more her walking was like sleep-walking, the feet numb in their shoes. Even when he had to let go of her, crossing the creek on stones, she stepped where he stepped with an obtuse docility. The voices of the searchers on the back ridge were small in distance when they began to climb the face of Coward Hill, on the opposite side of the valley.

There is an old farm on top of Coward Hill, big hayfields as flat as tables. It had been half-past nine when Mare stood on the rock above the barn; it was toward midnight when Humble Jewett put aside the last branches of the woods and let her out on the height, and half a moon had risen. And a wind blew there, tossing the withered tops of last year's grasses, and mists ran with the wind, and ragged shadows with the mists, and mares'-tails of clear moonlight among the shadows, so that now the boles of birches on the forest's edge beyond the fences were but opal blurs and now cut alabaster. It struck so cold against the girl's cold flesh, this wind, that another wind of shivers blew through her, and she put her hands over her face and eyes. But the madman stood with his eyes wide open and his mouth open, drinking the moonlight and the wet wind.

His voice, when he spoke at last, was thick in his throat.

'Get down on your knees.' He got down on his and pulled her after. 'And pray!'

Once in England a poet sang four lines. Four hundred years have forgotten his name, but they have remembered his lines. The daft man knelt upright, his face raised to the wild scud, his long wrists hanging to the dead grass. He began simply:

> *' "O western wind, when wilt thou blow*
> *"That the small rain down can rain?" '*

The Adam's-apple was big in his bent throat. As simply he finished.

> *' "Christ, that my love were in my arms*
> *"And I in my bed again!" '*

Mare got up and ran. She ran without aim or feeling in the power of the wind. She told herself again that the mists would hide her from him, as she had done at dusk. And again, seeing that he ran at her shoulder, she knew he had been there all the while, making a race of it, flailing the air with his long arms for joy of play in the cloud of spring, throwing his knees high, leaping the moon-blue waves of the brown grass, shaking his bright hair; and her own hair was a weight behind her, lying level on the wind. Once a shape went bounding ahead of them for instants; she did not realize it was a fox till it was gone.

She never thought of stopping; she never thought anything, except once, 'Oh, my God, I wish I had my shoes off!' And what would have been the good in stopping or in turning another way, when it was only play? The man's ecstasy magnified his strength. When a snake-fence came at them he took the top rail in flight, like a college hurdler and, seeing the girl hesitate and half turn as if to flee, he would have releaped it without touching a hand. But then she got a loom of buildings, climbed over quickly, before he should jump, and ran along the lane that ran with the fence.

Mare had never been up there, but she knew that the farm and the house belonged to a man named Wyker, a kind of cousin of Ruby Herter's, a violent, bearded old fellow who lived by himself. She could not believe her luck. When she had run half the distance and Jewett had not grabbed her, doubt grabbed her instead. 'Oh, my God, go careful!' she told herself. 'Go slow!' she implored herself, and stopped running, to walk.

Here was a misgiving the deeper in that it touched her special knowledge. She had never known an animal so far gone that its instincts failed it; a starving rat will scent the trap sooner than a fed one. Yet, after one glance at the house they approached, Jewett paid it no further attention, but walked with his eyes to the right, where the cloud had blown away, and wooded ridges, like black waves rimmed with silver, ran down away toward the Valley of Virginia.

'I've never lived!' In his single cry there were two things, beatitude and pain.

Between the bigness of the falling world and his eyes the flag of her hair blew. He reached out and let it whip between his fingers. Mare was afraid it would break the spell then, and he would stop looking away and look at the house again. So she did something almost incredible; she spoke.

'It's a pretty—I mean—a beautiful view down that-a-way.'

'God Almighty beautiful, to take your breath away. I knew I'd never loved, Belovéd—' He caught a foot under the long end of one of the boards that covered the well and went down heavily on his hands and knees. It seemed to make no difference. 'But I never knew I'd never lived,' he finished in the same tone of strong rapture, quadruped in the grass, while Mare ran for the door and grabbed the latch.

When the latch would not give, she lost what little sense she had. She pounded with her fists. She cried with all her might: 'Oh—hey—in there—hey—in there!' Then Jewett came and took her gently between his hands and drew her away, and then, though she was free, she stood in something like an awful embarrassment while he tried shouting.

'Hey! Friend! whoever you are, wake up and let my love and me come in!'

'No!' wailed the girl.

He grew peremptory. 'Hey, wake up!' He tried the latch. He passed to full fury in a wink's time; he cursed, he kicked, he beat the door till Mare thought he would break his hands. Withdrawing, he ran at it with his shoulder; it burst at the latch, went slamming in, and left a black emptiness. His anger dissolved in a big laugh. Turning in time to catch her by a wrist, he cried joyously, 'Come, my Sweet One!'

'No! No! Please—aw—listen. There ain't nobody there. He ain't to home. It wouldn't be right to go in anybody's house if they wasn't to home, you know that.'

His laugh was blither than ever. He caught her high in his arms.

'I'd do the same by his love and him if 'twas my house, I would.' At the threshold he paused and thought, 'That is, if she was the true love of his heart forever.'

The room was the parlor. Moonlight slanted in at the door, and another shaft came through a window and fell across a sofa, its covering dilapidated, showing its wadding in places. The air was sour, but both of them were farm-bred.

'Don't, Amarantha!' His words were pleading in her ear. 'Don't be so frightened.'

He set her down on the sofa. As his hands let go of her they were shaking.

'But look, I'm frightened too.' He knelt on the floor before her, reached out his hands, withdrew them. 'See, I'm afraid to touch you.' He mused, his eyes rounded. 'Of all the ugly things there are, fear is the ugliest. And yet, see, it can be the very beautifulest. That's a strange queer thing.'

The wind blew in and out of the room, bringing the thin, little bitter sweetness of new April at night. The moonlight that came across Mare's shoulders fell full upon his face, but hers it left dark, ringed by the aureole of her disordered hair.

'Why do you wear a halo, Love?' He thought about it. 'Because you're an angel, is that why?' The swift, untempered logic of the mad led him to dismay. His hands came flying to hers, to make sure they were of earth; and he touched her breast, her shoulders, and her hair. Peace returned to his eyes as his fingers twined among the strands.

' "Thy hair is as a flock of goats that appear from Gilead . . ." ' He spoke like a man dreaming. ' "Thy temples are like a piece of pomegranate within thy locks." '

Mare never knew that he could not see her for the moonlight.

'Do you remember, Love?'

She dared not shake her head under his hand. 'Yeh, I reckon,' she temporized.

'You remember how I sat at your feet, long ago, like this, and made up a song? And all the poets in all the world have never made one to touch it, have they, Love?'

'Ugh-ugh—never.'

' "How beautiful are thy feet with shoes . . ." Remember?'

'Oh, my God, what's he sayin' now?' she wailed to herself.

' "How beautiful are thy feet with shoes, O prince's daughter! the joints of thy thighs are like jewels, the work of the hands of a cunning workman.
"Thy navel is like a round goblet, which wanteth not liquor; thy belly is like an heap of wheat set about with lilies.
"Thy two breasts are like two young roes that are twins!" '

Mare had not been to church since she was a little girl, when her mother's black dress wore out. 'No, no!' she wailed under her breath. 'You're awful to say such awful things.' She might have shouted it; nothing could have shaken the man now, rapt in the immortal, passionate periods of Solomon's Song.

' ". . . now also thy breasts shall be as clusters of the vine, and the smell of thy nose like apples." '

Hotness touched Mare's face for the first time. 'Aw, no, don't talk so!'

' "And the roof of thy mouth like the best wine for my belovéd . . . causing the lips of them they are asleep to speak." '

He had ended. His expression changed. Ecstasy gave place to anger, love to hate. And Mare felt the change in the weight of the fingers in her hair.

'What do you mean, I mustn't say it like that?' But it was not to her his fury spoke, for he answered himself straightway. 'Like poetry, Mr. Jewett; I won't have blasphemy around my school.'

'Poetry! My God! if that isn't poetry—if that isn't music—' . . . 'It's Bible, Jewett. What you're paid to teach here is *literature*.'

'Doctor Ryeworth, you're the blasphemer and you're an ignorant man.' . . . 'And your Principal. And I won't have you going around reading sacred allegory like earthly love.'

'Ryeworth, you're an old man, a dull man, a dirty man, and you'd be better dead.'

Jewett's hands had slid down from Mare's head. 'Then I went to put my fingers around his throat, so. But my stomach turned, and I didn't do it. I went to my room. I laughed all the way to my room. I sat in my room at my table and I laughed. I laughed all afternoon and long after dark came. And then, about ten, somebody came and stood beside me in my room.'

' "Wherefore dost thou laugh, son?"

'Then I knew who He was, He was Christ.

' "I was laughing about that dirty, ignorant, crazy old fool, Lord."

' "Wherefore dost thou laugh?"

'I didn't laugh any more. He didn't say any more. I kneeled down, bowed my head.

' "Thy will be done! Where is he, Lord?"

' "Over at the girls' dormitory, waiting for Blossom Sinckley."

'Brassy Blossom, dirty Blossom . . .'

It had come so suddenly it was nearly too late. Mare tore at his hands with hers, tried with all her strength to pull her neck away.

'Filthy Blossom! and him an old filthy man, Blossom! and you'll find him in Hell when you reach there, Blossom . . .'

It was more the nearness of his face than the hurt of his hands that gave her power of fright to choke out three words.

'I—ain't—Blossom!'

Light ran in crooked veins. Through the veins she saw his face bewildered. His hands loosened. One fell down and hung; the other he lifted and put over his eyes, took it away again and looked at her.

'Amarantha!' His remorse was fearful to see. 'What have I done!' His hands returned to hover over the hurts, ravening with pity, grief and tenderness. Tears fell down his cheeks. And with that, dammed desire broke its dam.

'Amarantha, my love, my dove, my beautiful love—'

'And I ain't Amarantha neither, I'm Mary! Mary, that's my name!'

She had no notion what she had done. He was like a crystal crucible that a chemist watches, changing hue in a wink with one adeptly added drop; but hers was not the chemist's eye. All she knew was that she felt light and free of him; all she could see of his face as he stood away above the moonlight were the whites of his eyes.

'Mary!' he muttered. A slight paroxysm shook his frame. So in the transparent crucible desire changed its hue. He retreated farther, stood in the dark by some tall piece of furniture. And still she could see the whites of his eyes.

'Mary! Mary Adorable!' A wonder was in him. 'Mother of God!'

Mare held her breath. She eyed the door, but it was too far. And already he came back to go on his knees before her, his shoulders so bowed and his face so lifted that it must have cracked his neck, she thought; all she could see on the face was pain.

'Mary Mother, I'm sick to my death. I'm so tired.'

She had seen a dog like that, one she had loosed from a trap after it had been there three days, its caught leg half gnawed free. Something about the eyes.

'Mary Mother, take me in your arms . . .'

Once again her muscles tightened. But he made no move.

'. . . and give me sleep.'

No, they were worse than the dog's eyes.

'Sleep, sleep! why won't they let me sleep? Haven't I done it all yet, Mother? Haven't I washed them yet of all their sins? I've drunk the cup that was given me; is there another? They've mocked me and reviled me, broken my brow with thorns and my hands with nails, and I've forgiven them, for they knew not what they did. Can't I go to sleep now, Mother?'

Mare could not have said why, but now she was more frightened than she had ever been. Her hands lay heavy on her knees, side by side, and she could not take them away when he bowed his head and rested his face upon them. .

After a moment he said one thing more. 'Take me down gently when you take me from the Tree.'

Gradually the weight of his body came against her shins, and he slept.

The moon streak that entered by the eastern window crept north across the floor, thinner and thinner; the one that fell through the southern doorway traveled east and grew fat. For a while Mare's feet pained her terribly and her legs too. She dared not move them, though, and by and by they did not hurt so much.

A dozen times, moving her head slowly on her neck, she canvassed the shadows of the room for a weapon. Each time her eyes came back to a heavy earthenware pitcher on a stand some feet to the left of the sofa. It would have had flowers in it when Wyker's wife was alive; probably it had not been moved from its dust-ring since she died. It would be a long grab, perhaps too long; still, it might be done if she had her hands.

To get her hands from under the sleeper's head was the task she set herself. She pulled first one, then the other, infinitesimally. She waited. Again she tugged a very, very little. The order of his breathing was not disturbed. But at the third trial he stirred.

'Gently! gently!' His own muttering waked him more. With some drowsy instinct of possession he threw one hand across her wrists, pinning them together between thumb and fingers. She kept dead quiet, shut her eyes, lengthened her breathing, as if she too slept.

There came a time when what was pretense grew a peril; strange as it was, she had to fight to keep her eyes open. She never knew whether or not she really napped. But something changed in the air, and she was wide awake again. The moonlight was fading on the doorsill, and the light that runs before dawn waxed in the window behind her head.

And then she heard a voice in the distance, lifted in maundering song.

It was old man Wyker coming home after a night, and it was plain he had had some whiskey.

Now a new terror laid hold of Mare.

'Shut up, you fool you!' she wanted to shout. 'Come quiet, quiet!' She might have chanced it now to throw the sleeper away from her and scramble and run, had his powers of strength and quickness not taken her simple imagination utterly in thrall.

Happily the singing stopped. What had occurred was that the farmer had espied the open door and, even befuddled as he was, wanted to know more about it quietly. He was so quiet that Mare began to fear he had gone away. He had the squirrel-hunter's foot, and the first she knew of him was when she looked and saw his head in the doorway, his hard, soiled, whiskery face half up-side-down with craning.

He had been to the town. Between drinks he had wandered in and out of the night's excitement; had even gone a short distance with one search party himself. Now he took in the situation in the room. He used his forefinger. First he held it to his lips. Next he pointed it with a jabbing motion at the sleeper. Then he tapped his own forehead and described wheels. Lastly, with his whole hand, he made pushing gestures, for Mare to wait. Then he vanished as silently as he had appeared.

The minutes dragged. The light in the east strengthened and turned rosy. Once she thought she heard a board creaking in another part of the house, and looked down sharply to see if the loony stirred. All she could see of his face was a temple with freckles on it and the sharp ridge of a cheekbone, but even from so little she knew how deeply and peacefully he slept. The door darkened. Wyker was there again. In one hand he carried something heavy; with the other he beckoned.

'Come jumpin'!' he said out loud.

Mare went jumping, but her cramped legs threw her down half way to the sill; the rest of the distance she rolled and crawled. Just as she tumbled through the door it seemed as if the world had come to an end above her; two barrels of a shotgun discharged into a room make a noise. Afterwards all she could hear in there was something twisting and bumping on the floor-boards. She got up and ran.

Mare's mother had gone to pieces; neighbor women put her to bed when Mare came home. They wanted to put Mare to bed, but she would not let them. She sat on the edge of her bed in her lean-to bedroom off the kitchen, just as she was, her hair down all over her shoulders and her shoes on, and stared away from them, at a place in the wallpaper.

'Yeh, I'll go myself. Lea' me be!'

The women exchanged quick glances, thinned their lips, and left her be. 'God knows,' was all they would answer to the questionings of those that had not gone in, 'but she's gettin' herself to bed.'

When the doctor came though he found her sitting just as she had been, still dressed, her hair down on her shoulders and her shoes on.

'What d' y' want?' she muttered and stared at the place in the wallpaper.

How could Doc Paradise say, when he did not know himself?

'I didn't know if you might be—might be feeling very smart, Mary.'

'I'm all right. Lea' me be.'

It was a heavy responsibility. Doc shouldered it. 'No, it's all right,' he said to the men in the road. Ruby Herter stood a little apart, chewing sullenly and looking another way. Doc raised his voice to make certain it carried. 'Nope, nothing.'

Ruby's ears got red, and he clamped his jaws. He knew he ought to go in and see Mare, but he was not going to do it while everybody hung around waiting to see if he would. A mule tied near him reached out and mouthed his sleeve in idle innocence; he wheeled and banged a fist against the side of the animal's head.

'Well, what d' y' aim to do 'bout it?' he challenged its owner.

He looked at the sun then. It was ten in the morning. 'Hell, I got work!' he flared, and set off down the road for home. Doc looked at Judge North, and the Judge started after Ruby. But Ruby shook his head angrily. 'Lea' me be!' He went on, and the Judge came back.

It got to be eleven and then noon. People began to say, 'Like enough she'd be as thankful if the whole neighborhood wasn't camped here.' But none went away.

As a matter of fact they were no bother to the girl. She never saw them. The only move she made was to bend her ankles over and rest her feet on edge; her shoes hurt terribly and her feet knew it, though she did not. She sat all the while staring at that one figure in the wallpaper, and she never saw the figure.

Strange as the night had been, this day was stranger. Fright and physical pain are perishable things once they are gone. But while pain merely dulls and telescopes in memory and remains diluted pain, terror looked back upon has nothing of terror left. A gambling chance taken, at no matter what odds, and won was a sure thing since the world's beginning; perils come through safely were never perilous. But what fright does do in retrospect is this—it heightens each sensuous recollection, like a hard, clear lacquer laid on wood, bringing out the color and grain of it vividly.

Last night Mare had lain stupid with fear on groundpine beneath a bush, loud foot-falls and light whispers confused in her ear. Only now, in her room, did she smell the groundpine.

Only now did the conscious part of her brain begin to make words of the whispering.

'Amarantha,' she remembered, *'Amarantha sweet and fair.'* That was as far as she could go for the moment, except that the rhyme with 'fair' was 'hair.' But then a puzzle, held in abeyance, brought other words. She wondered what 'ravel Ed' could mean. *'Most excellently ravelléd.'* It was left to her mother to bring the end.

They gave up trying to keep her mother out at last. The poor woman's prostration took the form of fussiness.

'Good gracious, daughter, you look a sight. Them new shoes, half ruined; ain't your feet *dead?* And look at your hair, all tangled like a wild one!'

She got a comb.

'Be quiet, daughter; what's ailin' you. Don't shake your head!'

' "But shake your head and scatter day." '

'What you say, Amarantha?' Mrs. Doggett held an ear down.

'Go 'way! Lea' me be!'

Her mother was hurt and left. And Mare ran, as she stared at the wallpaper.

'Christ, that my love were in my arms . . .'

Mare ran. She ran through a wind white with moonlight and wet with 'the small rain.' And the wind she ran through, it ran through her, and made her shiver as she ran. And the man beside her leaped high over the waves of the dead grasses and gathered the wind in his arms, and her hair was heavy and his was tossing, and a little fox ran before them across the top of the world. And the world spread down around in waves of black and silver, more immense than she had ever known the world could be, and more beautiful.

'God Almighty beautiful, to take your breath away!'

Mare wondered, and she was not used to wondering. 'Is it only crazy folks ever run like that and talk that way?'

She no longer ran; she walked; for her breath was gone. And there was some other reason, some other reason. Oh, yes, it was because her feet were hurting her. So, at last, and roundabout, her shoes had made contact with her brain.

Bending over the side of the bed, she loosened one of them mechanically. She pulled it half off. But then she looked down at it sharply, and she pulled it on again.

'How beautiful . . .'

Color overspread her face in a slow wave.

'How beautiful are thy feet with shoes . . .'

'Is it only crazy folks ever say such things?'

'O prince's daughter!'

'Or call you that?'

By and by there was a knock at the door. It opened, and Ruby Herter came in.

'Hello, Mare, old girl!' His face was red. He scowled and kicked at the floor. 'I'd 'a' been over sooner, except we got a mule down sick.' He looked at his dumb betrothed. 'Come on, cheer up, forget it! He won't scare you no more, not that boy, not what's left o' him. What you lookin' at, sourface? Ain't you glad to see me?'

Mare quit looking at the wallpaper and looked at the floor.

'Yeh,' she said.

'That's more like it, babe.' He came and sat beside her; reached down behind her and gave her a spank. 'Come on, give us a kiss, babe!' He wiped his mouth on his jumper sleeve, a good farmer's sleeve, spotted with milking. He put his hands on her; he was used to handling animals. 'Hey, you, warm up a little; reckon I'm goin' to do all the lovin'?'

'Ruby, lea' me be!'

'What!'

She was up, twisting. He was up, purple.

'What's ailin' of you, Mare? What you bawlin' about?'

'Nothin'—only go 'way!'

She pushed him to the door and through it with all her strength, and closed it in his face, and stood with her weight against it, crying, 'Go 'way! Go 'way! Lea' me be!'

Questions

1. To what extent is the rather simple, somewhat melodramatic plot of this story responsible for or detrimental to its success as a piece of writing?
2. Considering the ending, why should Steele go to such pains to establish Mare as a "broad-fleshed, slow-minded," almost unwilled girl? Find other words and phrases that contribute to this picture of her.
3. We don't hear very much of Mare's language juxtaposed with Jewett's. But analyze the effect of juxtaposing Ruby Herter's language with Jewett's when Jewett is first caught. Find other places where Jewett's language, either his own or his language as recited, is juxtaposed to Ruby's or someone else's. What is the effect?
4. We will concentrate on style later in the book. But you ought to be aware of some of the magic in Steele's own language. Note, for example, such expressions as "where the broad-tipped fingers wound, tender as yearning, weightless as caress" or "the hand that was not in love with her throat." Note how these contribute to the terror of the moment. Turn back to the passages (pp. 36–37) in which Steele describes Jewett's reaction to Coward Hill and to Mare's race with him. Try reading aloud these passages

and Mare's recreation of the running (p. 44), feeling or hearing the wonderful prose rhythms as you read.

5. As you think back on the story, who seems to be the "hero"? Does it have a "villain"? In answering these questions try to decide whom you admire most and why.
6. Will Amarantha marry Ruby Herter now? In a way, the question is outside the story. But in another way, the question is crucial to your understanding of it. Think back to the language used to describe Mare and especially their loving. Ruby still calls her Mare at the end. Does she think of herself as Mare? How significant is the play on names? What has happened to Mare to bring about her reaction at the end? The change is of course internal. Define it as precisely as you can. What would their life together be like if they did marry?
7. Notice the effect of Jewett's language on Mare. Steele keeps our attention on it. Is she responding to something new to her during the experience itself rather than to something after it is over? What about the experience has left the strongest impression on Mare?
8. Learning language opened up a new world to Hellen Keller. Does the language used by Humble Jewett contribute to opening a new world to Mare? If so, try to define the new world. What role does language play in whatever you see happening to her?
9. Considered as an illustration or example, what does this story seem to illustrate? How persuasive is it as an illustration?

Suggestions for Writing

1. It may be hard to imagine Ruby Herter writing *anything*. But try to place yourself in his situation, except that you are more perceptive than he is: you recognize something of what has happened to Mare and you want to let her know you do, to show some genuine sympathy and concern, and to get her interested in you again. Since she won't speak to you or see you now, write to her, analyzing what she has been through (for purpose of the paper, you may assume that Ruby knows much of what Mare has heard as well as what she has experienced), what you have learned, and what you will now do that is different. You should be able to use illustration and example to support your plea.

I Hungered for Books

Richard Wright

Richard Wright is one of the most sensitive interpreters of what it means to be a Negro in twentieth-century White America. His novel Native Son *is still having its impact on both black and white. The following selection is the next-to-last chapter of* Black Boy, *in which he records growing up in the South. Wright's excitement over his discovery of Mencken and of the novelists discussed by Mencken is so immediate and so genuine that few could resist its infectiousness. Not many of us have had to scheme and calculate as Wright did to get books to read. But is it this that gives Wright's account its appeal? Have you responded the same way to any other reading? In the earlier parts of* Black Boy *Richard has been pushed from job to job because he was not servile enough. Hence his caginess now.*

One morning I arrived early at work and went into the bank lobby where the Negro porter was mopping. I stood at a counter and picked up the Memphis *Commercial Appeal* and began my free reading of the press. I came finally to the editorial page and saw an article dealing with one H. L. Mencken. I knew by hearsay that he was the editor of the *American Mercury,* but aside from that I knew nothing about him. The article was a furious denunciation of Mencken, concluding with one, hot, short sentence: Mencken is a fool.

I wondered what on earth this Mencken had done to call down upon him the scorn of the South. The only people I had ever heard denounced in the South were Negroes, and this man was not a Negro. Then what ideas did Mencken hold that made a newspaper like the *Commercial Appeal* castigate him publicly? Undoubtedly he must be advocating ideas that the South did not like. Were there, then, people other than Negroes who criticized the South? I knew that during the Civil War the South had hated northern whites, but I had not encountered such hate during my life. Knowing no more of Mencken than I did at that moment, I felt a vague sympathy for him. Had not the South, which had assigned me the role of a non-man, cast at him its hardest words?

Now, how could I find out about this Mencken? There was a huge library near the riverfront, but I knew that Negroes were not allowed to patronize its shelves any more than they were the parks and playgrounds of the city. I had gone into the library several times to get books for the white men on the job. Which of them would now help me to get books? And how could I read them without causing concern to the white men with whom I worked? I had so far been successful in hiding my thoughts and feelings from them, but I knew that I would create hostility if I went about this business of reading in a clumsy way.

I weighed the personalities of the men on the job. There was Don, a Jew; but I distrusted him. His position was not much better than mine and I knew that he was uneasy and insecure; he had always treated me in an offhand, bantering way that barely concealed his contempt. I was afraid to ask him to help me to get books; his frantic desire to demonstrate a racial solidarity with the whites against Negroes might make him betray me.

Then how about the boss? No, he was a Baptist and I had the suspicion that he would not be quite able to comprehend why a black boy would want to read Mencken. There were other white men on the job whose attitudes showed clearly that they were Kluxers or sympathizers, and they were out of the question.

There remained only one man whose attitude did not fit into an anti-Negro category, for I had heard the white men refer to him as a "Pope lover." He was an Irish Catholic and was hated by the white Southerners. I knew that he read books, because I had got him volumes from the library several times. Since he, too, was an object of hatred, I felt that he might refuse me but would hardly betray me. I hesitated, weighing and balancing the imponderable realities.

One morning I paused before the Catholic fellow's desk.

"I want to ask you a favor," I whispered to him.

"What is it?"

"I want to read. I can't get books from the library. I wonder if you'd let me use your card?"

He looked at me suspiciously.

"My card is full most of the time," he said.

"I see," I said and waited, posing my question silently.

"You're not trying to get me into trouble, are you, boy?" he asked, staring at me.

"Oh, no, sir."

"What book do you want?"

"A book by H. L. Mencken."

"Which one?"

"I don't know. Has he written more than one?"

"He has written several."

"I didn't know that."

"What makes you want to read Mencken?"

"Oh, I just saw his name in the newspaper," I said.

"It's good of you to want to read," he said. "But you ought to read the right things."

I said nothing. Would he want to supervise my reading?

"Let me think," he said. "I'll figure out something."

I turned from him and he called me back. He stared at me quizzically.

"Richard, don't mention this to the other white men," he said.

"I understand," I said. "I won't say a word."

A few days later he called me to him.

"I've got a card in my wife's name," he said. "Here's mine."

"Thank you, sir."

"Do you think you can manage it?"

"I'll manage fine," I said.

"If they suspect you, you'll get in trouble," he said.

"I'll write the same kind of notes to the library that you wrote when you sent me for books," I told him. "I'll sign your name."

He laughed.

"Go ahead. Let me see what you get," he said.

That afternoon I addressed myself to forging a note. Now, what were the names of books written by H. L. Mencken? I did not know any of them. I finally wrote what I thought would be a foolproof note: *Dear Madam: Will you please let this nigger boy*—I used the word "nigger" to make the librarian feel that I could not possibly be the author of the note—*have some books by H. L. Mencken?* I forged the white man's name.

I entered the library as I had always done when on errands for whites, but I felt that I would somehow slip up and betray myself. I doffed my hat, stood a respectful distance from the desk, looked as unbookish as possible, and waited for the white patrons to be taken care of. When the desk was clear of people, I still waited. The white librarian looked at me.

"What do you want, boy?"

As though I did not possess the power of speech, I stepped forward and simply handed her the forged note, not parting my lips.

"What books by Mencken does he want?" she asked.

"I don't know, ma'am," I said, avoiding her eyes.

"Who gave you this card?"

"Mr. Falk," I said.

"Where is he?"

"He's at work, at the M—— Optical Company," I said. "I've been in here for him before."

"I remember," the woman said. "But he never wrote notes like this."

Oh, God, she's suspicious. Perhaps she would not let me have the books? If she had turned her back at that moment, I would have ducked out the door and never gone back. Then I thought of a bold idea.

"You can call him up, ma'am," I said, my heart pounding.

"You're not using these books, are you?" she asked pointedly.

"Oh, no, ma'am. I can't read."

"I don't know what he wants by Mencken," she said under her breath.

I knew now that I had won; she was thinking of other things and the race question had gone out of her mind. She went to the shelves. Once or twice she looked over her shoulder at me, as though she was still doubtful. Finally she came forward with two books in her hand.

"I'm sending him two books," she said. "But tell Mr. Falk to come in next time, or send me the names of the books he wants. I don't know what he wants to read."

I said nothing. She stamped the card and handed me the books. Not daring to glance at them, I went out of the library, fearing that the woman would call me back for further questioning. A block away from the library I opened one of the books and read a title: *A Book of Prefaces*. I was nearing my nineteenth birthday and I did not know how to pronounce the word "preface." I thumbed the pages and saw strange words and strange names. I shook my head, disappointed. I looked at the other book; it was called *Prejudices*. I knew what that word meant; I had heard it all my life. And right off I was on guard against Mencken's books. Why would a man want to call a book *Prejudices?* The word was so stained with all my memories of racial hate that I could not conceive of anybody using it for a title. Perhaps I had made a mistake about Mencken? A man who had prejudices must be wrong.

When I showed the books to Mr. Falk, he looked at me and frowned.

"That librarian might telephone you," I warned him.

"That's all right," he said. "But when you're through reading those books, I want you to tell me what you get out of them."

That night in my rented room, while letting the hot water run over my can of pork and beans in the sink, I opened *A Book of Prefaces* and began to read. I was jarred and shocked by the style, the clear, clean, sweeping sentences. Why did he write like that? And how did one write like that? I pictured the man as a raging demon, slashing with his pen, consumed with hate, denouncing everything American, extolling everything European or German, laughing at the weaknesses of people, mocking God, authority.

What was this? I stood up, trying to realize what reality lay behind the meaning of the words . . . Yes, this man was fighting, fighting with words. He was using words as a weapon, using them as one would use a club. Could words be weapons? Well, yes, for here they were. Then, maybe, perhaps, I could use them as a weapon? No. It frightened me. I read on and what amazed me was not what he said, but how on earth anybody had the courage to say it.

Occasionally I glanced up to reassure myself that I was alone in the room. Who were these men about whom Mencken was talking so passionately? Who was Anatole France? Joseph Conrad? Sinclair Lewis, Sherwood Anderson, Dostoevski, George Moore, Gustave Flaubert, Maupassant, Tolstoy, Frank Harris, Mark Twain, Thomas Hardy, Arnold Bennett, Stephen Crane, Zola, Norris, Gorky, Bergson, Ibsen, Balzac, Bernard Shaw, Dumas, Poe, Thomas Mann, O. Henry, Dreiser, H. G. Wells, Gogol, T. S. Eliot, Gide, Baudelaire, Edgar Lee Masters, Stendhal, Turgenev, Huneker, Nietzsche, and scores of others? Were these men real? Did they exist or had they existed? And how did one pronounce their names?

I ran across many words whose meanings I did not know, and I either looked them up in a dictionary or, before I had a chance to do that, encountered the word in a context that made its meaning clear. But what strange world was this? I concluded the book with the conviction that I had somehow overlooked something terribly important in life. I had once tried to write, had once reveled in feeling, had let my crude imagination roam, but the impulse to dream had been slowly beaten out of me by experience. Now it surged up again and I hungered for books, new ways of looking and seeing. It was not a matter of believing or disbelieving what I read, but of feeling something new, of being affected by something that made the look of the world different.

As dawn broke I ate my pork and beans, feeling dopey, sleepy. I went to work, but the mood of the book would not die; it lingered, coloring everything I saw, heard, did. I now felt that I knew what the white men were feeling. Merely because I had read a book that had spoken of how they lived and thought, I identified myself with that book. I felt vaguely guilty. Would I, filled with bookish notions, act in a manner that would make the whites dislike me?

I forged more notes and my trips to the library became frequent. Reading grew into a passion. My first serious novel was Sinclair Lewis's *Main Street*. It made me see my boss, Mr. Gerald, and identify him as an American type. I would smile when I saw him lugging his golf bags into the office. I had always felt a vast distance separating me from the boss, and now I felt closer to him, though still distant. I felt now that I knew him, that I could feel the very limits of his narrow life. And this had happened because I had read a novel about a mythical man called George F. Babbitt.

The plots and stories in the novels did not interest me so much as the point of view revealed. I gave myself over to each novel without reserve, without trying to criticize it; it was enough for me to see and feel something different. And for me, everything was something different. Reading was like a drug, a dope. The novels created moods in which I lived for days. But I could not conquer my sense of guilt, my feeling that the white men around me knew that I was changing, that I had begun to regard them differently.

Whenever I brought a book to the job, I wrapped it in newspaper—a habit that was to persist for years in other cities and under other circumstances. But some of the white men pried into my packages when I was absent and they questioned me.

"Boy, what are you reading those books for?"

"Oh, I don't know, sir."

"That's deep stuff you're reading, boy."

"I'm just killing time, sir."

"You'll addle your brains if you don't watch out."

I read Dreiser's *Jennie Gerhardt* and *Sister Carrie* and they revived in me a vivid sense of my mother's suffering; I was overwhelmed. I grew silent, wondering about the life around me. It would have been impossible for me to have told anyone what I derived from these novels, for it was nothing less than a sense of life itself. All my life had shaped me for the realism, the naturalism of the modern novel, and I could not read enough of them.

Steeped in new moods and ideas, I bought a ream of paper and tried to write; but nothing would come, or what did come was flat beyond telling. I discovered that more than desire and feeling were necessary to write and I dropped the idea. Yet I still wondered how it was possible to know people sufficiently to write about them? Could I ever learn about life and people? To me, with my vast ignorance, my Jim Crow station in life, it seemed a task impossible of achievement. I now knew what being a Negro meant. I could endure the hunger. I had learned to live with hate. But to feel that there were feelings denied me, that the very breath of life itself was beyond my reach, that more than anything else hurt, wounded me. I had a new hunger.

In buoying me up, reading also cast me down, made me see what was possible, what I had missed. My tension returned, new, terrible, bitter, surging, almost too great to be contained. I no longer *felt* that the world about me was hostile, killing; I *knew* it. A million times I asked myself what I could do to save myself, and there were no answers. I seemed forever condemned, ringed by walls.

I did not discuss my reading with Mr. Falk, who had lent me his library card; it would have meant talking about myself and that would have been too painful. I smiled each day, fighting desperately to maintain my old behavior, to keep my disposition seemingly sunny. But some of the white men discerned that I had begun to brood.

"Wake up there, boy!" Mr. Olin said one day.

"Sir!" I answered for the lack of a better word.

"You act like you've stolen something," he said.

I laughed in the way I knew he expected me to laugh, but I resolved to be more conscious of myself, to watch my every act, to guard and hide the new knowledge that was dawning within me.

If I went north, would it be possible for me to build a new life then? But how could a man build a life upon vague, unformed yearnings? I wanted to write and I did not even know the English language. I bought English grammars and found them dull. I felt that I was getting a better sense of the language from novels than from grammars. I read hard, discarding a writer as soon as I felt that I had grasped his point of view. At night the printed page stood before my eyes in sleep.

Mrs. Moss, my landlady, asked me one Sunday morning:

"Son, what is this you keep on reading?"

"Oh, nothing. Just novels."

"What you get out of 'em?"

"I'm just killing time," I said.

"I hope you know your own mind," she said in a tone which implied that she doubted if I had a mind.

I knew of no Negroes who read the books I liked and I wondered if any Negroes ever thought of them. I knew that there were Negro doctors, lawyers, newspapermen, but I never saw any of them. When I read a Negro newspaper I never caught the faintest echo of my preoccupation in its pages. I felt trapped and occasionally, for a few days, I would stop reading. But a vague hunger would come over me for books, books that opened up new avenues of feeling and seeing, and again I would forge another note to the white librarian. Again I would read and wonder as only the naïve and unlettered can read and wonder, feeling that I carried a secret, criminal burden about with me each day.

That winter my mother and brother came and we set up housekeeping, buying furniture on the installment plan, being cheated and yet knowing no way to avoid it. I began to eat warm food and to my surprise found that regular meals enabled me to read faster. I may have lived through many illnesses and survived them, never suspecting that I was ill. My brother obtained a job and we began to save toward the trip north, plotting our time, setting tentative dates for departure. I told none of the white men on the job that I was planning to go north; I knew that the moment they felt I was thinking of the North they would change toward me. It would have made them feel that I did not like the life I was living, and because my life was completely conditioned by what they said or did, it would have been tantamount to challenging them.

I could calculate my chances for life in the South as a Negro fairly clearly now.

I could fight the southern whites by organizing with other Negroes, as my grandfather had done. But I knew that I could never win that way; there were many whites and there were but few blacks. They were strong and we were weak. Outright black rebellion could never win. If I fought openly I would die and I did not want to die. News of lynchings were frequent.

I could submit and live the life of a genial slave, but that was impossible. All of my life had shaped me to live by my own feelings and thoughts. I could make up to Bess and marry her and inherit the house. But that, too, would be the life of a slave; if I did that, I would crush to death something within me, and I would hate myself as much as I knew the whites already hated those who had submitted. Neither could I ever willingly present myself to be kicked, as Shorty had done. I would rather have died than do that.

I could drain off my restlessness by fighting with Shorty and Harrison. I had seen many Negroes solve the problem of being black by transferring their hatred of themselves to others with a black skin and fighting them. I would have to be cold to do that, and I was not cold and I could never be.

I could, of course, forget what I had read, thrust the whites out of my mind, forget them; and find release from anxiety and longing in sex and alcohol. But the memory of how my father had conducted himself made that course repugnant. If I did not want others to violate my life, how could I voluntarily violate it myself?

I had no hope whatever of being a professional man. Not only had I been so conditioned that I did not desire it, but the fulfillment of such an ambition was beyond my capabilities. Well-to-do Negroes lived in a world that was almost as alien to me as the world inhabited by whites.

What, then, was there? I held my life in my mind, in my consciousness each day, feeling at times that I would stumble and drop it, spill it forever. My reading had created a vast sense of distance between me and the world in which I lived and tried to make a living, and that sense of distance was increasing each day. My days and nights were one long, quiet, continuously contained dream of terror, tension, and anxiety. I wondered how long I could bear it.

Questions

1. If you have read any of Mencken's enthusiastic discussions of language, you know how vigorous and biting his prose can be. Why is Wright so affected by the discovery that Mencken is "fighting with words"?
2. When Wright says he "hungered for books, new ways of looking and seeing," can you tell with any precision what he means? Relate it to this sentence which appears three paragraphs later: "The plots and stories in the novels did not interest me so much as the point of view revealed." Would you consider this a mature approach to reading novels?
3. Why, steeped in all this reading, should Wright have had trouble writing? What did he lack that was "more than desire and feeling"?
4. Reading should broaden anyone's perspective and horizons. Why, for Wright, should it have "created a vast sense of distance between me and the world in which I lived and tried to make a living"?

Suggestions for Writing

1. Wright comes out of his experience with the novels a different person, just as Amarantha Doggett does from her experience with the looney and as Helen Keller does from her discovery of words. You must have had similar, if less dramatic, experiences from which you have emerged a different person. Use some experience of awakening as the core of a paper. But use it to illustrate an idea such as "Small experiences can sometimes make a crucial difference in one's life" or "in one's personality" or "in one's character." Other ideas such as "Growing up can be painful" or "exciting" or "awesome" can also be developed. Such personal situations should enable you to give real vitality to the illustration.

Notes on the Art of Poetry

Dylan Thomas *A remarkable Welsh poet, Dylan Thomas in this selection displays an exuberance for words that parallels his enthusiasm for nearly everything else, including life and drinking. You cannot fail to catch his excitement as you read, but the exuberance should show itself not merely in his talking of it but in his own use of words. What evidence of this can you find in his choice of words? Can you find specific words which, in their context, seem especially striking? Try to define for yourself what makes them so. Note especially his comparison of his experiences with words to those of "someone, deaf from birth, who has miraculously found his hearing." The comparison again invites you back to Helen Keller, though she never found her hearing. Could her discovery of language have been analagous to his fascination with sounds? The poem that follows, "Fern Hill," is one of his most delightful. Again as you read, watch for the evidences of his enthusiasm for words.*

You want to know why and how I first began to write poetry, and which poets or kinds of poetry I was first moved and influenced by.

To answer the first part of this question, I should say I wanted to write poetry in the beginning because I had fallen in love with words. The first poems I knew were nursery rhymes, and before I could read them for myself I had come to love just the words of them, the words alone. What the words stood for, symbolised, or meant, was of very secondary importance; what mattered was the *sound* of them as I heard them for the first time on the lips of the remote and incomprehensible grown-ups who seemed, for some reason, to be living in my world. And these words were, to me, as the notes of bells, the sounds of musical instruments, the noises of wind, sea, and rain, the rattle of milkcarts, the clopping of hooves on cobbles, the fingering of branches on a window pane, might be to someone, deaf from birth, who has miraculously found his hearing. I did not care what the words said, overmuch, nor what happened to Jack & Jill & the Mother Goose rest of them; I cared for the shapes of sound that their names, and

Dylan Thomas, "Notes on the Art of Poetry," *Texas Quarterly* (Winter, 1961).

the words describing their actions, made in my ears; I cared for the colours the words cast on my eyes. I realise that I may be, as I think back all that way, romanticising my reactions to the simple and beautiful words of those pure poems; but that is all I can honestly remember, however much time might have falsified my memory. I fell in love—that is the only expression I can think of—at once, and am still at the mercy of words, though sometimes now, knowing a little of their behaviour very well, I think I can influence them slightly and have even learned to beat them now and then, which they appear to enjoy. I tumbled for words at once. And, when I began to read the nursery rhymes for myself, and, later, to read other verses and ballads, I knew that I had discovered the most important things, to me, that could be ever. There they were, seemingly lifeless, made only of black and white, but out of them, out of their own being, came love and terror and pity and pain and wonder and all the other vague abstractions that make our ephemeral lives dangerous, great, and bearable. Out of them came the gusts and grunts and hiccups and hee-haws of the common fun of the earth; and though what the words meant was, in its own way, often deliciously funny enough, so much funnier seemed to me, at that almost forgotten time, the shape and shade and size and noise of the words as they hummed, strummed, jigged and galloped along. That was the time of innocence; words burst upon me, unencumbered by trivial or portentous association; words were their spring-like selves, fresh with Eden's dew, as they flew out of the air. They made their own original associations as they sprang and shone. The words "Ride a cock-horse to Banbury Cross" were as haunting to me, who did not know then what a cock-horse was nor cared a damn where Banbury Cross might be, as, much later, were such lines as John Donne's "Go and catch a falling star, Get with child a mandrake root," which also I could not understand when I first read them. And as I read more and more, and it was not all verse, by any means, my love for the real life of words increased until I knew that I must live *with* them and *in* them, always. I knew, in fact, that I must be a writer of words, and nothing else. The first thing was to feel and know their sound and substance; what I was going to do with those words, what use I was going to make of them, what I was going to *say* through them, would come later. I knew I had to know them most intimately in all their forms and moods, their ups and downs, their chops and changes, their needs and demands. (Here, I am afraid, I am beginning to talk too vaguely. I do not like writing *about* words, because then I often use bad and wrong and stale and wooly words. What I like to do is to treat words as a craftsman does his wood or stone or what-have-you, to hew, carve, mould, coil, polish and plane them into patterns, sequences, sculptures, fugues of sound expressing some lyrical impulse, some spiritual doubt or conviction, some dimly-realised truth I must try to reach and realise.) It was when I was very young, and just at school, that, in my father's study, before homework that was never done, I began to know one kind of writing from another, one kind of goodness, one kind of badness. My first, and greatest, liberty was that of being able to read everything and anything I cared to. I read indiscriminately, and with my eyes hanging out. I could never have dreamt that there were such goings-on in the world between the covers of books, such sand-storms and ice-blasts of words, such slashing of humbug, and humbug too, such staggering peace, such enormous laughter, such and so many blinding bright lights breaking across the just-awaking wits and splashing all over the pages in a million bits and pieces all of which were words, words, words, and each of which was alive forever in its own delight and glory and oddity and light. (I must try not to make these supposedly helpful notes as confusing as my poems themselves.) I wrote endless imitations, though I never thought them to be imitations but, rather, wonderfully original things, like eggs laid by tigers. They were imitations of anything I happened to be reading at the time: Sir Thomas Browne, de Quincey, Henry Newbolt, the Ballads, Blake, Baroness Orczy, Marlowe, Chums, the Imagists, the Bible, Poe, Keats, Lawrence, Anon., and Shakespeare. A mixed lot, as you see, and randomly remembered. I tried my callow hand at almost every poetical form. How could I learn the tricks of a trade unless I tried to do them myself? I learned that the bad tricks come easily; and the good ones, which help you to say what you think you wish to say in the most meaningful, moving way, I am still learning. (But in earnest company you must call these tricks by other names, such as technical devices, prosodic experiments, etc.)

The writers, then, who influenced my earliest poems and stories were, quite simply and truthfully, all the writers I was reading at the time, and, as you see from a specimen list higher up the page, they ranged from writers of school-boy adventure yarns to incomparable and inimitable masters like Blake. That is, when I began, bad writing had as much influence on my stuff as good. The bad influences I tried to remove and renounce bit by bit, shadow by shadow, echo by echo, through trial and error, through delight and disgust and misgiving, as I came to love words more and to hate the heavy hands that knocked them about, the thick tongues that had no feel for their multitudinous tastes, the dull and botching hacks who flattened them out into a colourless and insipid paste, the pedants who made them moribund and pompous as themselves. Let me say that the things that first made me love language and want to work *in* it and *for* it were nursery rhymes and folk tales, the Scottish Ballads, a few lines of hymns, the most famous Bible stories and the rhythms of the Bible, Blake's Songs of Innocence, and the quite incomprehensible magical majesty and nonsense of Shakespeare heard, read, and near-murdered in the first forms of my school.

You ask me, next, if it is true that three of the dominant influences on my published prose and poetry are Joyce, the Bible, and Freud. (I purposely say my "published" prose and poetry, as in the preceding pages I have been talking about the primary influences upon my very first and forever unpublishable juvenilia.) I cannot say that I have been "influenced" by Joyce, whom I enormously admire and whose *Ulysses,* and earlier stories, I have read a great deal. I think this Joyce question arose because somebody once, in print, remarked on the closeness of the title of my book of short stories, "Portrait of the Artist as a Young Dog," to Joyce's title, "Portrait of the Artist as a Young Man." As you know, the name given to innumerable portrait paintings by their artists is, "Portrait of the Artist as a Young Man"—a perfectly straightforward title. Joyce used the painting title for the first time as the title of a literary work. I myself made a bit of doggish fun of the painting-title and, of course, intended no possible reference to Joyce. I do not think that Joyce has had any hand at all in my writing; certainly his *Ulysses* has not. On the other hand, I cannot deny that the shaping of some of my "Portrait" stories might owe something to Joyce's stories in the volume, "Dubliners." But then "Dubliners" was a pioneering work in the world of the short story, and no good storywriter since can have failed, in some way, however little, to have benefited by it.

The Bible, I have referred to in attempting to answer your first question. Its great stories of Noah, Jonah, Lot, Moses, Jacob, David, Solomon and a thousand more, I had, of course, known from very early youth; the great rhythms had rolled over me from the Welsh pulpits; and I read, for myself, from Job and Ecclesiastes; and the story of the New Testament is part of my life. But I have never sat down and studied the Bible, never consciously echoed its language, and am, in reality, as ignorant of it as most brought-up Christians. All of the Bible that I use in my work is remembered from childhood, and is the common property of all who were brought up in English-speaking communities. Nowhere, indeed, in all my writing, do I use any knowledge which is not commonplace to any literate person. I *have* used a few difficult words in early poems, but they are easily looked-up and were, in any case, thrown into the poems in a kind of adolescent showing-off which I hope I have now discarded.

And that leads me to the third "dominant influence": Sigmund Freud. My only acquaintance with the theories and discoveries of Dr. Freud has been through the work of novelists who have been excited by his casebook histories, of popular newspaper scientific-potboilers who have, I imagine, vulgarised his work beyond recognition, and of a few modern poets, including Auden, who have attempted to use psychoanalytical phraseology and theory in some of their poems. I have read only one book of Freud's, "The Interpretation of Dreams," and do not recall having been influenced by it in any way. Again, no honest writer today can possibly avoid being influenced by Freud through his pioneering work into the Unconscious and by the influence of those discoveries on the scientific, philosophic, and artistic work of his contemporaries: but not, by any means, necessarily through Freud's own writing.

To your third question—Do I deliberately utilise devices of rhyme, rhythm, and word-formation in my writing—I must, of course, answer with an immediate, Yes. I am a painstaking, conscientious, involved and devious craftsman in words, however unsuccessful the result so often appears, and to whatever wrong uses I may apply my technical paraphernalia. I use everything and anything to make my poems work and move in the directions I want them to: old tricks, new tricks, puns, portmanteau-words, paradox, allusion, paranomasia, paragram, catachresis, slang, assonantal rhymes, vowel rhymes, sprung rhythm. Every device there is in language is there to be used if you will. Poets have got to enjoy themselves sometimes, and the twistings and convolutions of words, the inventions and contrivances, are all part of the joy that is part of the painful, voluntary work.

Your next question asks whether my use of combinations of words to create something new, "in the Surrealist way," is according to a set formula or is spontaneous.

There is a confusion here, for the Surrealists' set formula was to juxtapose the unpremeditated.

Let me make it clearer if I can. The Surrealists—(that is, super-realists, or those who work *above* realism)—were a coterie of painters and writers in Paris, in the nineteen twenties, who did not believe in the conscious selection of images. To put it in another way: they were artists who were dissatisfied with both the realists—(roughly speaking, those who tried to put down in paint and words an actual representation of what they imagined to be the real world in which they lived)—and the impressionists who, roughly speaking again, were those who tried to give an impression of what they imagined to be the real world. The Surrealists wanted to dive into the subconscious mind, the mind below the conscious surface, and dig up their images from there without the aid of logic or reason, and put them down, illogically and unreasonably, in paint and words. The Surrealists affirmed that, as three quarters of the mind was submerged, it was the function of the artist to gather his material from the greatest submerged mass of the mind rather than from that quarter of the mind which, like the tip of an iceberg, protruded from the subconscious sea. One method the Surrealists used in their poetry was to juxtapose words and images that had no rational relationship; and out of this they hoped to achieve a kind of subconscious, or dream, poetry that would be truer to the real, imaginative world of the mind, mostly submerged, than is the poetry of the conscious mind that relies upon the rational and logical relationship of ideas, objects, and images.

This is, very crudely, the credo of the Surrealists, and one with which I profoundly disagree. I do not mind from where the images of a poem are dragged up: drag them up, if you like, from the nethermost sea of the hidden self; but before they reach paper, they must go through all the rational processes of the intellect. The Surrealists, on the other hand, put their words down together on paper exactly as they emerge from chaos; they do not shape these words or put them in order; to them, chaos is the shape and order. This seems to me to be exceedingly presumptuous; the Surrealists imagine that whatever they dredge from their subconscious selves and put down in paint or in words must, essentially, be of some interest or value. I deny this. One of the arts of the poet is to make comprehensible and articulate what might emerge from subconscious sources; one of the great main uses of the intellect is to *select,* from the amorphous mass of subconscious images, those that will best further his imaginative purpose, which is to write the best poem he can.

And question five is, God help us, what is my definition of Poetry?

I, myself, do not read poetry for anything but pleasure. I read only the poems I like. This means, of course, that I have to read a lot of poems I don't like before I find the ones I do, but, when I *do* find the ones I do, then all I can say is, "Here they are," and read them to myself for pleasure.

Read the poems you like reading. Don't bother whether they're "important," or if they'll live. What does it matter what poetry *is,* after all? If you want a definition of poetry, say: "Poetry is what makes me laugh or cry or yawn, what makes my toenails twinkle, what makes me want to do this or that or nothing," and let it go at that. All that matters about poetry is the enjoyment of it, however tragic it may be. All that matters is the eternal movement behind it, the vast undercurrent of human grief, folly, pretension, exaltation, or ignorance, however unlofty the intention of the poem.

You can tear a poem apart to see what makes it technically tick, and say to yourself, when the works are laid out before you, the vowels, the consonants, the rhymes or rhythms, "Yes, this is *it.* This is why the poem moves me so. It is because of the craftsmanship." But you're back again where you began.

You're back with the mystery of having been moved by words. The best craftsmanship always leaves holes and gaps in the works of the poem so that something that is *not* in the poem can creep, crawl, flash, or thunder in.

The joy and function of poetry is, and was, the celebration of man, which is also the celebration of God.

Fern Hill

Now as I was young and easy under the apple boughs
About the lilting house and happy as the grass was green,
The night above the dingle starry,
Time let me hail and climb
Golden in the heydays of his eyes,
And honoured among wagons I was prince of the apple towns
And once below a time I lordly had the trees and leaves
Trail with daisies and barley
Down the rivers of the windfall light.

And as I was green and carefree, famous among the barns
About the happy yard and singing as the farm was home,
In the sun that is young once only,
Time let me play and be
Golden in the mercy of his means,
And green and golden I was huntsman and herdsman, the
calves
Sang to my horn, the foxes on the hills barked clear and cold,
And the sabbath rang slowly
In the pebbles of the holy streams

All the sun long it was running, it was lovely, the hay
Fields high as the house, the tunes from the chimneys, it
was air
And playing, lovely and watery
And fire green as grass.
And nightly under the simple stars
As I rode to sleep the owls were bearing the farm away,

All the moon long I heard, blessed among stables, the nightjars
Flying with the ricks, and the horses
Flashing into the dark.

And then to awake, and the farm, like a wanderer white
With the dew, come back, the cock on his shoulder: it was all
Shining, it was Adam and maiden,
The sky gathered again
And the sun grew round that very day.
So it must have been after the birth of the simple light
In the first, spinning place, the spellbound horses walking
warm
Out of the whinnying green stable
On to the fields of praise.

And honoured among foxes and pheasants by the gay house
Under the new made clouds and happy as the heart was long,
In the sun born over and over,
I ran my heedless ways,
My wishes raced through the house high hay
And nothing I cared, at my sky blue trades, that time allows
In all his tuneful turning so few and such morning songs
Before the children green and golden
Follow him out of grace,

Nothing I cared, in the lamb white days, that time would
take me
Up to the swallow thronged loft by the shadow of my hand,
In the moon that is always rising,
Nor that riding to sleep
I should hear him fly with the high fields
And wake to the farm forever fled from the childless land.
Oh as I was young and easy in the mercy of his means,
Time held me green and dying
Though I sang in my chains like the sea.

Questions

1. In his "Notes on the Art of Poetry" Thomas tells us that he "had fallen in love with words." This may not have much meaning for you at first. What does Thomas do to make it concrete? In one way or another every writer must have fallen in love with words. It may involve some complex kind of hate-love relationship (see Jeffers' poem "Love the Wild Swan," p. 67), but only some form of love would explain the struggle people go through

to produce significant literature. Thomas's love affair seems almost to lift him above the struggle. Try to find evidence that even for him writing is a struggle.

2. The last four questions Thomas answers may seem of interest only to specialists. But Thomas manages to keep them all tied to the love of words. How? Do his last two paragraphs grow out of the rest of the essay and wrap it up?
3. To really get the feel of the words you must at least read the poem aloud. Better still, if you have access to a record library get the record [1] of Thomas himself reading this and other poems. You would especially enjoy hearing him recite "And Death Shall Have No Dominion." Would the sonorous, heavily rhythmic chant with which he reads that poem suit "Fern Hill"?
4. "As green as grass" is one of our most worn clichés. Would Thomas have been thinking of it when he wrote "as happy as the grass was green"? What does this figure say about Thomas' feeling for words?
5. What effect does Thomas get from such words as "the *lilting* house," "the *heydays* of his eyes," "the *windfall* light," "once *below* a time," "*green* and carefree." Note other striking words and expressions and try to define their effect.
6. Can you define a cumulative effect of the words in the poem? In what ways does it seem to you the work of an enthusiast for words?

Suggestions for Writing

1. Your reaction to Thomas's article may be either positive, negative, or neutral. If it is positive and if you have written poetry or would like to try some, you might enjoy trying a poem that attempts to catch your attitude toward language or words or books or poets. Or you may try to catch your attitude in prose, using Thomas's selection as inspiration or model. If your reaction is negative, you may wish to satirize Thomas's selection or explain your negative reactions to it. And if your reaction is neutral, analyze in detail why the selection "leaves you cold."

[1] Dylan Thomas, *Complete Recorded Poetry,* 1964, Caedmon 2014.

Poems

These poems record with such enthusiasm and such apparent simplicity Miss Dickinson's feeling for words and her art that you could easily miss their actual literary sophistication. You will enjoy looking them over carefully for evidence of that sophistication. But here we want primarily to share the poems—and the enthusiasm—with you. As you read them, and the others that follow, remember that the most characteristic quality of poetry is that it takes advantage of all *resources of language to create tightly compressed and highly effective versions of or responses to experiences, emotions, ideas, problems. Artists often respond in art to their own artistry. How meaningful does this seem as subject matter?*

You will want to contrast the response to words in Bynner's and Jeffers' poem. Are Jeffers' words really the words of a man who hates his verses? If so, why does he write them?

Emily Dickinson

He Ate and Drank the Precious Words

He ate and drank the precious Words—
His Spirit grew robust—
He knew no more that he was poor,
Nor that his frame was Dust—

He danced along the dingy Days
And this Bequest of Wings
Was but a Book—What Liberty
A loosened spirit brings—

I Found the Words to Every Thought

I found the words to every thought
I ever had—but One—

And that—defies me—
As a Hand did try to chalk the Sun

To Races—nurtured in the Dark—
How would your own—begin?
Can Blaze be shown in Cochineal—
Or Noon—in Mazarin?

There Is No Frigate Like a Book

There is no Frigate like a Book
To take us Lands away
Nor any Coursers like a Page
Of prancing Poetry—

This Traverse may the poorest take
Without oppress of Toll—
How frugal is the Chariot
That bears the Human soul.

Witter Bynner

Correspondent

Words, words and words! What else, when men are dead,
Their small lives ended and their sayings said,
Is left of them? Their children go to dust,
As also all their children's children must,
And their belongings are of paltry worth
Against the insatiable consuming earth . . .
I knew a man and almost had forgot
The wisdom of the letters that he wrote,
But words, if words are wise, go on and on
To make a longer note of unison
With man and man than living persons make
With one another for whatever sake.
Therefore I wept tonight when quick words rose
Out of a dead man's grave, whom no one knows.

Robinson Jeffers

Love the Wild Swan

"I hate my verses, every line, every word.
Oh pale and brittle pencils ever to try
One grass-blade's curve, or the throat of one bird
That clings to twig, ruffled against white sky.
Oh cracked and twilight mirrors ever to catch
One color, one glinting flash, of the splendor of things.
Unlucky hunter, Oh bullets of wax,
The lion beauty, the wild-swan wings, the storm of the wings."
—This wild swan of a world is no hunter's game.
Better bullets than yours would miss the white breast,
Better mirrors than yours would crack in the flame.
Does it matter whether you hate your . . . self? At least
Love your eyes that can see, your mind that can
Hear the music, the thunder of the wings. Love the wild swan.

Countee Cullen

Yet Do I Marvel

I doubt not God is good, well-meaning, kind,
And did He stoop to quibble could tell why
The little buried mole continues blind,
Why flesh that mirrors Him must some day die,
Make plain the reason tortured Tantalus
Is baited by the fickle fruit, declare
If merely brute caprice dooms Sisyphus
To struggle up a never-ending stair.
Inscrutable His ways are, and immune
To catechism by a mind too strewn

With petty cares to slightly understand
What awful brain compels His awful hand.
Yet do I marvel at this curious thing:
To make a poet black, and bid him sing!

Writing Projects

We have suggested specific writing assignments following several of the selections, but this section as a whole suggests a rather insistent broader one: your reaction to the section and the relating of the ideas advanced here to your own experiences. In your reading of the varied and contrasting expressions of the power of words, you must have compared some of your own experiences with language to those of the authors you were reading. The possible approaches to writing out of personal experience will vary according to each individual's background and his reaction to the selections read.

Part of the solution to problems in writing is to become as conscious as you can of your own experiences and their implications. Henry James's advice to prospective writers has its immediacy for even writers of freshman papers: "Be one of the people on whom nothing is lost." Conscious attention to your own experiences now with language will help. So will conscious remembering. Your experiences are you. Make them work for you in your writing.

We suggest four categories into which your reactions might fall:

You respond enthusiastically to the selections read.
You feel that the claims for language have been exaggerated.
You are indignant at someone's misuse of the power of language.
You respond mildly to the section.

Below are four writing projects related to these categories. Choose the one that most closely fits your response to the selections. Derive as much vital material as you can from your own experience to illustrate your points. That is, support this essay largely by illustration.

Be especially conscious of the balance Booth defines as the true rhetorical stance. Try carefully to avoid the perversions of it that he calls the pedant's stance, the advertiser's stance, and the entertainer's stance. Your fellow students will be more responsive to the balanced stance, especially since they too have just read the article.

1. Write an essay in which you express your enthusiasm for language. Assume an audience of fellow freshmen interested in language but somewhat resisting your editors' and your own fascination with it. You want to convince them that people other than language-struck lunatics and English teachers with too much vested interest in language can respond to the fascination of words. This may be supported by an experience in which your own enthusiasm was awakened or by several shorter experiences. You might reread Dylan Thomas' and Richard Wright's responses to language for examples.

2. As a student in freshman composition you have been pondering the materials of this section of our text, and especially the high claims for language. You feel that they have been exaggerated, that only for a few special souls like Dylan Thomas can language ever have the significance here ascribed to it.

Write a warning to your fellow students not to be taken in. Find specific illustrative material from the selections themselves and from your own experience to support your thesis. If, for example, you can yourself think without language—in images or mathematical formulae or chemistry equations—you would have a good argument against the several assertions we have seen that one cannot really think without language, or that capacity to think is directly proportional to capacity with language.

3. Suppose you have just discovered how badly some professional users of language—a politician (you name him) or an advertiser or someone else in public life—have misused language to get you to buy them or their products or their ideas. In your indignation you decide to write an essay *exposing* how they misuse language and how dangerous such misuse is. Aim it at the same audience your opponent aimed at. Let the indignation show, but do not merely rant. This will demand an especially careful control of the balance that results in the rhetorical stance. Get as many detailed examples as you can to support your position. Perhaps the most effective kind of example would be that of someone you know who has been misled or damaged somehow by the dishonest use of language.

Those of us who lived through World War II remember the horror of Adolph Hitler mesmerizing a whole nation with his high-pitched, frantic voice. Here, as an example of indignation at the misuse of language, is a brief part of a response to that experience from a German poet who was not mesmerized and who became part of the underground resistance. He is speaking to the youth of Germany after the war:

> And not until now are we ready for the new beginning. Not for the aged but for you and the children. Perhaps you realize that the beginning of all of us was wrong. For we lived according to the word of the Gospel of St. John: "In the beginning was the word." But in the place of God's word we put man's word, and man's word was the curse of the whole age. Consider that well and do not forget it! If you do not want to believe me, only look at the newspapers of these twelve years, nothing else. The leprosy of a nation is rank in them like an evil-smelling ulcer, and on the ulcer the word luxuriates rankly. What is sacred in every language was given into the hands of scroundrels, of paid, cowardly, miserable slaves, and in their hands disfigured into the permanent shame of an entire nation.
>
> If the word had been sacred to the nation, and if its youth had been reared to regard it as sacred, laughter unparalleled would have driven the "superman" back into the cave of his origin. Take two of his words, take the words "fatherland" and "honor," and consider over what an abyss of crime they were stretched like a glittering bridge. Take the word "state," and the word "freedom," and the word "justice"—the great deceivers of mankind when a false hand changes them from an end into a means.[1]

Most of you will not have so emotional or intense a response to the misuse of language, but this example should suggest how such an essay might be written effectively.

4. If none of these assumed situations quite fits your vital experiences with language, set up one of your own. Be careful, however, to avoid the merely

[1] Ernst Wiechert, "Address to the Youth of Germany," *The Poet and His Time* (New York, 1948), pp. 43–44.

general. Be sure your essay has a point that is meaningful to you and that you feel is worth communicating vigorously to your assumed audience. You will need to be even more careful, with this generalized approach, to work consciously for a balance between material, audience, and your "speaker's voice." Make effective use of illustrative materials as you write. Surely you can remember something of your first taste—or distaste—for certain words, your first savoring or flavoring them, your problems in learning certain principles of language, your major successes or failures at communicating some rich new feeling or some frighteningly empty one.

Part II

The Nature of Language

Language has been called man's greatest invention. Normally, when we think of inventions we think of the wheel, telephone, television, machines, and other technological and scientific advances—we do not think of language. But none of these scientific advances compares with language in its influence on the life of man. Man is man because he has language. Yet language seems so intrinsic a part of us that we view it as a part of our being and seldom consider it apart from our humanness or consider its importance to us or what life would be without it. In this section we ask you consciously to consider the nature of language, its importance, its complexity, and its role in making us human.

Because their native language is so much a part of their being, many people are totally unaware of the complexity of the language they use in every aspect of their daily lives. A young child masters this magnificent instrument of communication (indeed he can master several languages early in life) without apparent effort. Consider for a moment what a child has accomplished by the age of five or six. He has mastered a complex system of sounds (phonology), a system that varies from language to language. The English child has learned that certain sound combinations, for example, *sk-, -dst, bl-,* are acceptable in English, but that certain other combinations, such as *ts-, pf-, ng-,* are not a part of normal English. And at this early age (unless he has some problem physically with the organs used to produce speech) the child pronounces English words acceptably in his dialect. Not only does he learn the sounds but he also learns the intonation patterns of English; his voice goes up or down in the right places. Adult speakers of English become aware of the difficulty of this achievement when they struggle and struggle to learn the sounds of a foreign language, never completely mastering them.

The system of sounds is just one of the systems of language that a child masters at an early age. He also masters the grammatical system. He learns how to make nouns mean more than one, how to put the proper endings on verbs to indicate past time, how to compare adjectives and adverbs. It is true that he may have some difficulty with exceptions to the normal rule, but even his handling of exceptions frequently reveals an amazing ability to deal with the system. When the child mistakenly says, "I goed to town today daddy," he reveals a knowledge of the system of English grammar that is truly remarkable. The child has noted that *go* is a verb and he has learned that verbs indicate past time by adding a dental suffix; therefore, he places such a suffix on the word *go*. Because *go* is often used in English, he will soon note that it is an exception to the rule he has formulated and will correctly replace *goed* with *went*. He can make this adjustment in his language use without correction or teaching from his parents.

Not only does he learn how the parts of words go together in English (morphology), he also learns how words pattern in English sentences. He places modifiers before the words they modify; he places subjects before and objects after verbs; he learns that American speakers say "*a* cold" but "*the* flu" and all the other complexities of the article that come so easily to a native speaker of English but that bedevil the speaker of an oriental language who learns English as a second language. In short, he masters the grammar and syntax of English.

Scholars have long been interested in learning more about the nature of language and about what it is in man that enables him to learn language, learn it at an early age, and learn it without apparent conscious effort. Various animals and insects can communicate rather complex messages to each other. Consider, for example, the dance of the bee to tell another bee where to find the nectar or the warning of a mother bear to her cub that danger is near. Extensive studies have been conducted, both with chimpanzees and with dolphins, to discover how they communicate. Parrots, mynah birds, and other birds can actually imitate the words and sentences of language. Are such systems of communication language? Cook, in the first article in this section, offers a careful definition of language which will distinguish language from animal communication. The Premacks, however, report an interesting attempt to teach chimpanzees to deal with a nonvocal system of symbols. Elgin, in her article on psycholinguistics, further explores the nature of language and especially what it may be in man that makes him capable of dealing with his greatest invention, language.

The selections from Plato, Carroll, and Jacobs are commentaries on Cook's definition. Plato raises a question which was a source of controversy for centuries: Are words a matter of "convention and agreement" or are they "natural"? Carroll and Jacobs, exploiting some of the humorous resources of language, also comment on the convention-nature controversy.

Conrad's story illustrates the power of language (or the ignorance of the nature of language) in our lives. Penfield discusses not the nature of language but the nature of the human brain and how that mechanism functions to enable man to learn language. All the articles in this section deal in one way or another with the questions "What is language?" "What is the nature of man that enables him to deal at an early age and to deal so very effectively with the magnificent symbolic system which we call language?" The questions are intriguing; the answers are as yet very tentative.

Definition

When the writer listens for the questions of his imaginary reader, as we suggested the student writer must do in our discussion of "Illustration," he often hears a request for clarification directed at one word or one term. When the student interrupts his professor to ask "What do you mean by a *nuance of color* in music?" he is asking for a definition of terms. Readers are prone to ask the same type of question, and the writer must anticipate these questions before they are asked and define his terms.

A formal definition is the process by which a writer gives both the *genus* (the general class to which the item being defined belongs) and its *differentiae* (those qualities which distinguish the particular item from others in the same class). If the word is completely unknown, the reader needs both its *genus* and *differentiae.* For instance, if we say that a *bark* is a sailing vessel, and thereby give its *genus,* we help the reader somewhat who has no idea what a *bark* is. We do nothing, however, to distinguish the *bark* from the *brig,* the *galleon* and the *sloop*—all of which are also sailing vessels. We need the *differentiae* to accomplish such a distinction. Two ways commonly used to distinguish the various sailing vessels are the number of masts and the manner in which the sails are rigged: square-rigged (athwart the masts on yard arms) or fore-and-aft-rigged (parallel to a line running from the stem to the stern). Using these characteristics, we can give a formal definition of a *bark* as a sailing vessel with three or more masts, the forward masts square-rigged and the rear mast fore-and-aft-rigged. Now even the landlubbers among us could identify the *bark* in a picture of various types of sailing vessels.

Occasionally in his writing the student will want to use a less elaborate definition than the formal one just given. A single word or simple phrase in parentheses after the word or term needing clarification will suffice. Any technical term that is introduced into the composition can thus be defined and then used freely throughout the remainder of the composition. For example, the words *genus* and *differentiae* were defined this way in the illustration given above as were the terms *square-rigged* and *fore-and-aft-rigged.*

A variation of this method occurs when the author defines the word by restating his idea in simpler terms in a following sentence. "During the early days of the campaign, Napoleon's plans remained ephemeral. His communications to his generals indicate that one day's carefully formulated plans were discarded on the following day to be replaced by new plans, which were themselves replaced in turn on the next day." *Ephemeral* here is clearly defined for the reader as "lasting only one day," one definition of the word.

On other occasions, the student will need to provide more than is given in a simple formal definition such as the one we gave for *bark*. He will need an extended definition. Even the entire composition may become a definition of some abstract term—democracy, beauty, bravery, and so on. Frequently the title of an article will suggest that it is such a definition: "What is Democracy?" "The True Meaning of Beauty," or "The Scientific Method." The author of such a selection is careful to point out where the term may overlap another term, where it differs subtly, and precisely how it differs, and he will probably add illustrations to make the definition clearer.

There is a major danger to avoid in using definition—dullness. If you use definitions merely to explain meaning to your readers, the process almost invariably becomes dull. Imagine, for instance, a paper filled with definitions similar to that for *bark,* or an extended definition with no more feeling expressed than in that definition. On the other hand, in the context above, *ephemeral* takes on a negative connotation, from the words the author uses to define it, which it does not necessarily have. When "carefully formulated plans" are "discarded" only one day after being formulated, the reader cannot fail to sense the waste the author felt. Particularly must the writer of an extended definition take care to show his attitude. The titles "What is Democracy?" and "True Bravery" would frighten most teachers of composition. Both such titles suggest dullness. But if you have something pertinent to say about democracy or bravery, or any such abstract term, your definition can be vigorous, exciting, can carry real persuasive energy. Do not write such a theme unless you have something you feel is important to say and then do let your rhetorical stance and energy show in your definition.

Illustration is closely linked with definition as a means of developing exposition. A definition by itself may remain vague; an illustration can provide the additional clarification. Remember how often your dictionary gives a picture of the unusual animal in addition to the definition. That illustration is at least as meaningful as the definition for the imaginary *griffin,* the extinct *dodo* and *glyptodont,* and the unfamiliar *anteater*. Think for a moment how unhelpful a definition of *pun* would be without the illustration. If someone did not know that a pun was a special play on words (the *genus*) involving different meanings for words which are sounded the same (the *differentiae*), he still might not be precisely sure what one was after you had given him the definition, unless you gave him an illustration, an example. And you can influence your reader by the type of illustration you choose. The reader's reactions would be entirely different for each of the following examples from Shakespeare. The witty Mercutio, in *Romeo and Juliet,* expires from Tybalt's sword thrust, punning "Ask for me tomorrow, and you will find me a grave man." In one of Shakespeare's later plays, *Cymbeline,* the young princes intone over a supposed dead page (the heroine in disguise) the poetic pun

> *Golden lads and girls all must,*
> *As chimney-sweepers, come to dust.*

Note that in the Dickinson and Whitman poems at the end of this section a completely different form of definition is used. This form uses the poem as metaphorical definition, a definition which uses words to define other words but which is not restricted by any set pattern.

Looking at Language

Albert B. Cook III

Since we all use language every day, it would seem that devoting an entire essay to defining language would not be necessary. However, as the author of the following essay points out, there are many misconceptions about the terms language, linguist, *and* grammar. *In this essay, which is the first chapter in a grammar text, Professor Cook very carefully defines the key terms that are used again and again by those who write about language. A careful reading of his essay will be rewarding and will establish a firm base for reading and understanding many of the subsequent essays in this book.*

Note how carefully the author works through his definitions, especially his definition of language. *Step by step he leads the reader to an understanding of all the important terms in his definition. Note also the techniques he uses in defining: selecting examples that clarify, making comparisons with familiar terms, pointing out what the term being defined is* not, *making careful definitions of key terms used in defining* language, *comparing his definition with definitions others have written. In his definition he places special emphasis on the terms* system, vocal, arbitrary, *and* symbol. *Do you feel that his emphasis is justified? How does careful definition of terms facilitate communication from writer to reader?*

LINGUISTICS

Language and the Discipline of English

The teacher of English, on whatever level, is involved in a discipline which includes language, composition, and literature, three areas which are seldom interrelated. In fact, the normal arrangement of the subject matter automatically makes these areas discrete and unrelated, despite recent concerted efforts to treat them as interconnected parts of a unified discipline.

This division is evident even in the choice of a vocation. Ordinarily, English teachers become English teachers because they enjoy reading or have some facility in writing, usually creative writing. They virtually never are attracted to the profession because of their public school exposure to language—usually subsumed under the term *grammar*. Many students tend to equate "English" with grammar, a subject usually so grimly presented that they come to loathe it, even though they love to read and often are led to try their hand at writing as a result of their reading.

Several factors contribute to this antipathy toward language studies, one of the biggest being a widespread misunderstanding on the part of public school teachers and administrators of the work being done in the field today. Although this situation is certain to change in the near future, it is probably true that most college students interested in English teaching as a possible vocation had never heard of the work of linguists or of the general discoveries in the field of linguistics, or linguistic science, when they declared a major. The major purpose of this book is to introduce students to the field of linguistics and to show how its findings, as applied to English, can be of more than peripheral importance to them as they continue to specialize in English or in the collateral fields of speech, foreign languages, and dramatics.

The Linguist

To many people, a linguist is the same as a polyglot, one who can speak several languages fluently. For this reason, specialists in the field of linguistics have intermittently been looking for a better occupational word, though without success.[1] In professional usage, the linguist is a scholar who studies language objectively, observing it scientifically, recording the facts of language, and generalizing from them. The use of the term *scientific* should perhaps be soft-pedaled, because language is a human phenomenon which cannot be subclassified so neatly as the natural phenomena of the scientist; but so far as one is able to be scientific *vis-à-vis* human conduct, the linguist certainly adheres to the scientific method. The facts of language which he may observe include its sounds, forms, and syntactic arrangement, and from these he formulates general rules which describe how a specific language is actually used. In addition, the linguist can ob-

[1] The term *linguistician* has been suggested, but it is usually shouted down by those who feel that it is too fancy, or too much like "mortician." Occasionally the expression *linguistic scientist* is used interchangeably with *linguist*, but to the layman it is too close to the laboratory and the test tube.

serve the facts of a language for the purpose of describing its historical development (historical linguistics), its regional and social differences (linguistic geography, or dialectology), its relationship to other languages (comparative linguistics), or its application to other fields, particularly education (applied linguistics). Because the field is so broad and touches so many facets of human conduct, it is a shame that so little real awareness or understanding of it has managed to percolate down to the schools.

The Linguist and His Co-workers

The linguist, primarily concerned with describing the language as it is, should be differentiated from certain other scholars who are also involved, at least peripherally, in language, and usually in the field of English. These include the rhetorician, who is primarily interested in effective written or spoken communication, and the literary critic, who makes value judgments about the worth and effectiveness, the literary merit, of the works of a writer's creative imagination. It sometimes happens that an English teacher can wear all three of these hats. Your instructor in this course, insofar as he assists you in objectively viewing your language, is a linguist. But if he teaches freshman composition, too, he is a rhetorician, using in part the findings of the linguist about social reactions to language to demonstrate to his writers how best to order their prose. Finally, if he also teaches a sophomore literary survey course, he is a critic, using as the basis of his subjective judgments on literature some of the opinions of the rhetorician on what constitutes good writing. Unfortunately, the relationships aren't always this simple, for even in the most enlightened English departments, when specialization is the natural order of things the communication between the linguist and his colleagues sometimes breaks down because of misunderstanding.

Part of the misunderstanding comes from the failure of the linguist (and his lay supporters) to make completely clear his attitude toward language. Too often, he is viewed as one who believes that "everything goes" in language, that "one expression is as good as another," especially in relation to such shibboleths as *ain't*. Actually, he tries to show that in certain communities, under specified conditions, *ain't* (originally a contraction of *am not,* and thus as respectable in its parentage as *isn't* or *aren't*) is in perfectly good spoken usage by all the leading citizens. Some people, unfortunately, see red where *ain't* is concerned, and they won't wait to hear the full explanation: the linguist isn't sanctioning the use of this heinous four-letter word in communities where the leading citizens abjure it; he is simply describing the facts. Other colleagues, depressed by the linguist's descriptions of the grammatical facts of a language, feel that he is complicating things unnecessarily, particularly when they feel they themselves have a sufficient grasp of the "grammar" they learned in school. Besides, they add, with his objective views on usage and his formulaic statements of grammar, the linguist is doing great violence to the language handed down to us from Shakespeare, Milton, and Wordsworth. Finally, there are those colleagues, more amused than alarmed, who profess themselves nonplussed by the preoccupation of some linguists (particularly those who are affiliated with the anthropology departments of major universities) with the "savage tongues" of the American Indians, or of Africa and the Far East. How, they ask, can one take techniques devised to analyze "inarticulate babblings of savages" and use them in the same way on the civilized languages of the West?

This situation is not as pervasive as it was even ten years ago, but there is still a great need for all educators, and laymen as well, to understand more thoroughly the work of the linguist, even if they cannot bring themselves to approve of it. Currently, this need is greatest amongst the English teachers in the public schools, who need to be shown how new language discoveries can benefit them. One place to start is with the future teachers, and the best possible footing comes from knowing what the linguist means when he uses such terms as *language, dialect,* and *grammar,* terms which have suffered from multiplicity of meaning, thereby causing more confusion among the already confused laity.

Definitions

For a start, consider the term *language*. Even though this might seem silly, try to give your definition of it. Here is a word that all of us have used without a second thought, a term which is so obvious that we feel we "know" its "meaning" without inquiring further. Consequently, by now you have probably come up with an answer very much like:

(1) Language is a means of communication.

If we consider this definition for a moment, we must agree that it is just a little bit circular. Furthermore, what is the medium of this "means of communication"? We could name a variety of ways by which communication is carried on: noises in the throat, scribbles on paper, scratches on stone, semaphore, wigwagging flags, smoke signals, Morse code, hand-and-arm signals, deaf-and-dumb signs, and anything else which might "communicate something."

It is a mistake to say that everything on this list is a summation of the instances of language. Consider, first of all, something of the matter of precedence. Some means of communication are less important than others, or are based directly upon them. After pondering this list for a moment, you have probably concluded that all of the various code and signaling devices are secondary to writing—and you are right. The Morse code, for instance, is a system of dots and dashes which is based directly upon the alphabet, and thus could not be devised without the clear and familiar presence of an alphabet system. It is true that before the era of the automatic writing machines, experienced telegraphers had devised a rather large inventory of abbreviations and short-cuts for the commonly used words and expressions in their work, but most of us have never gotten beyond a rather rudimentary knowledge of the Morse system, acquired in our Boy Scout days. At any rate, we can agree that these systems are dependent upon writing, and only a rather obvious sort of hand-and-arm signal could be used with any ease by anyone who was illiterate.

Consequently, we are left with only two means of communication which might be judged primary: noises we make with our throats (speaking) and scribbles we make on a surface (writing). Which is primary? The answer, you would say, is very simple. Remembering that the great tradition of Chaucer, Shakespeare, Milton, the Bible, the whole of literature, is handed down to us in writing; remembering that your basic medium of learning is the written textbook; remembering all of the agony you and your composition teacher put into your written work; perhaps remembering the old injunction to "put it into writing" so that you (or someone else) will remember it—you will immediately leap to the conclusion that:

(2) Language is a *written* means of communication.

Let's look at that a little more closely. Already we can probably frame some rather vague objections to this conclusion. For instance, there are hundreds of different groups of people who have no writting system whatsoever. It is very easy to dismiss them as ignorant, primitive, savage groups, of little account in the modern world, but is it fair to say that they have no language? On the contrary, they probably communicate with one another quite as easily as we do.

Just to make the situation a little plainer, consider the following pieces of information.

1. Mankind was speaking long before the dawn of recorded history. Writing, as we shall see in Chapter 6, is a relatively recent discovery. It is unfortunately true that we know very little about the peoples who leave behind only bits of tools or shards of pottery for archaeologists to uncover, and that "finds" like the Dead Sea Scrolls are far more spectacular, but this does not alter the historical precedence of speech over writing.

2. It is easy to be misled by the emotional appeal of great literature. Yet we must consider that such masterpieces as *Beowulf,* the Norse sagas, the Homeric epics, the "fairy tales" collected by Grimm, even a goodly part of the Bible, were all handed down intact in an oral tradition before someone decided to set them down in writing. Great literature was conceived and passed on without the benefit of writing, and it should also be remembered that the rime and rhythm techniques of poetry (and also of Elizabethan drama) were devised originally as aids to memory.

In connection with this, have you ever had the experience of reading to a young child one of his favorite stories? If, in the course of your reading, you skipped a passage or simply substituted a word, the chances are that you were promptly corrected. The truth of the matter is that all preliterate societies and peoples have remarkable memories and are quite able, even willing, to correct the storyteller who alters the story. Storytellers themselves were not selected for their memories—everyone had a good memory—but rather for their storytelling ability. Today, the sad truth probably is that because of our reliance upon writing, we have allowed a good portion of our faculties for memorization to atrophy.

3. But, you will argue, speech is lost the instant it is uttered by the speaker, whereas there is something permanent and lasting about writing. *Littera scripta manet,* as the old expression goes: "The written word remains." There is no denying this; but unfortunately there is a lot of writing left in the world which is scarcely more than scribbling or ornate carving, simply because there is no one around to decipher it for us. In the last chapter of his book *Lost Languages,* P. E. Cleator describes several of these written remains which give every indication of remaining unknown to us: the Cretan Linear A script, the so-called Eteocyprian script of Cyprus, the Etruscan inscriptions, the Mayan glyphs in the Yucatan, and the *rongo rongo* script of Easter Island, to name a few.[2] Those who could speak the languages inscribed have long since departed, taking with them their knowledge of the correspondence between sound and marking. Indeed, only the written word remains.

4. Finally, those of us who are poor spellers are ruefully aware of the imperfect correspondencies between our alphabet and our language. We have heard of writing systems commonly called "phonetic" in which there is a close correspondency between the letter and the sound. The systems of Spanish and Finnish come most readily to mind. But even here, the relationship is imperfect. And of course in English, there is a good deal of

[2] (New York, 1959), pp. 161–77.

meaningless variation, exemplified by the diverse spelling of the *sh* sound as in *mission,* not to mention the pedantic superfluities in such spellings as *debt, psychology, knight,* and *phthisic.*

By now, I trust that you are convinced of the actual primacy of speaking over writing, and are willing to alter our definition to:

(3) Language is a *vocal* means of communication.

Thus we show that writing is a secondary language form based upon speech, and that Morse code, semaphores, Navy signal flags, deaf-and-dumb signals are all of them tertiary, based upon writing.

But still the definition is incomplete. What, for instance, is it that we are vocalizing? We don't just make a lot of noises; everything we utter is set forth in a meaningful order which we have somehow learned, and from which we depart only within narrow limits, lest we fail to communicate. In order to have communication, we must have system; otherwise we are simply making noises to no purpose. Thus we amend our definition:

(4) Language is a vocal *system* of communication.

The noises in our throats must adhere to some preconceived order and arrangement. All languages have system; the reason why languages other than our own sound like gibberish is because we have not mastered the complexity of their systems. In addition, this system has a framework of ideas built up within it, so that every utterance we make communicates these ideas to the auditor, who in turn responds by framing the same ideas, assuming we have communicated properly. Some of these ideas are lexical, conveying "dictionary" meaning, while others are grammatical, serving only the purpose of maintaining the system. We will call the former symbols, and the latter grammatical signals, both of which we must first learn in order to react to them or utter them. Thus we can further revise the definition to read:

(5) Language is a system of vocal *symbols and grammatical signals* used for communication.

Now let's further consider the nature of the "vocal symbols" in our definition. Take for example the semantic unit *dog.* We are all agreed that this word represents for us the general idea of *Canis domesticus,* with some emotional overtones, depending upon whether we remember a faithful pet, or were bitten once by one of those snarling creatures. Now, to make the problem more complex, consider as well the semantic units *chien, Hund, perro,* which represent respectively the French, German, and Spanish equivalents of our word *dog.* Some might notice that French *chien* seems to be derived from Latin *canis* and will likewise agree that German *Hund* is cognate with the English *hound;* but beyond that no one really can see how any one of these four words innately represents an idea of "dogginess," except that the speakers of the respective languages have all agreed arbitrarily upon the relationship of utterance and concept. In fact, one might almost argue that on the face of it, the infant's spoken *bow-wow* is ideationally more meaningful than *dog.*[3] Be it as it may, *dog* is in English the adult term, and in recognition of the fact that it is only our tacit agreement of utterance and idea at work here, and not any innate relationship bound up in the utterance, we can further alter our definition:

> (6) Language is a system of *arbitrary* vocal symbols and grammatical signals used for communication.

We have now built up the first part of our definition sufficiently well to make that last part seem weak. What is it that this system of arbitrary vocal symbols and grammatical signals can do? We have already listed communication, which suggests the imparting of ideas. But we don't simply listen passively to ideas all the time. Rather, we often find ourselves called upon to lend a helping hand, to assist in an enterprise, to rouse ourselves to action. Thus language is called upon not only for communication, but also for interaction.

But this isn't all. So far we have only implied that this is a human action. What of the so-called language of monkeys, for instance, or dolphins? Apparently they are able to communicate ideas, admittedly rather simple, and interact by means of an arbitrary vocal system. We are told that monkey colonies have signals which seem to mean danger, or food, or a predator. How does human language differ from these rude animal noises? The difference lies in the fact that whereas the monkeys can signal to one another the general concept of *food,* they are unable to communicate information and ideas which they might have acquired about the particular food in question. On the other hand, humans are able to say, "Don't eat that, it's poisonous!" (based upon the recollection of someone's sad experience, or what one has been told about someone who allegedly ate the food); or, "Don't eat that, it's not good for you" (in the situation of parent to child with a hunk of candy only a few minutes before dinner); or, "Eat that, it's good for you" (any parent speaking to any child about

[3] It is instructive to note that even these onomatopoetic representations differ from language to language. See Noel Perrin, "Old Macberlitz Had a Farm," *New Yorker* (January 27, 1962), 28–29; with additions in the February 24, 1962, issue, p. 125.

spinach, about which we have acquired a dubious, but time-honored notion of nutritious goodness); all the way through a scale of associations. We thus have passed on a whole complex of ideas, some of which are the result of personal experience, others of hearsay, and still others of cultural transference, even taboo. This is what makes language a purely human phenomenon, and thus we are ready to add to our definition:

> (7) Language is a system of arbitrary vocal symbols and grammatical signals used for communication, *interaction,* and *cultural transmission.*

This seems pretty good, but it is still a little bit impersonal. Who, we might ask, uses this instrument for communication, interaction, and cultural transmission? Obviously, the speakers of the language, but to refer to them in this way will force us to use in our definition the very word we want to define. Perhaps we should take our hint from Leonard Bloomfield: "Within certain communities successive utterances are alike or partly alike. . . . Any such community is a *speech community.*" [4] Thus we can complete our definition both by making it less impersonal and by specifying the users:

> (8) A language is a system of arbitrary vocal symbols and grammatical signals by means of which *the members of a speech community* communicate, interact, and transmit their culture.

Our definition follows that of Edgar L. Sturtevant,[5] with the addition of the phrase *transmit their culture,* which, as we showed, makes explicit the human quality of language; and the phrase *grammatical signals,* which clarifies the difference between the lexical inventory of the language and the nonlexical portion which orders and regulates the system of the language. We can quote several other definitions as well for the sake of comparison:

> Language is a purely human and non-instinctive method of communicating ideas, emotions, and desires by means of a system of voluntarily produced symbols. These symbols are, in the first instance, auditory and they are produced by the so-called "organs of speech."
>
> EDWARD SAPIR, *Language* (1921)

[4] "A Set of Postulates for the Science of Language," *Language,* II (1926); reprinted in Martin Joos (ed.), *Readings in Linguistics* (3d ed.; New York, 1963), p. 26.

[5] *An Introduction to Linguistic Science* (New Haven, 1947), pp. 2–3.

A language is an arbitrary system of articulated sounds made use of by a group of humans as a means of carrying on the affairs of their society.

W. NELSON FRANCIS, *The Structure of American English* (1958)

[Language is] a system of arbitrary vocal symbols by which thought is conveyed from one human being to another.

JOHN P. HUGHES, *The Science of Language* (1962)

Whatever the definition, it must include directly, or by close implication, all of the following attributes of language:

1. Language has system.
2. Language is vocal.
3. Language is arbitrary.
4. Language is a human activity.
5. Language is noninstinctive.
6. Language is a social activity.
7. Language is related to culture.

Dialect and Language Change

There is still one attribute of language which falls outside of our definition:

8. Language changes.

About language change as a historical phenomenon we will have much to say later, especially as it involves English; but there is another aspect of language change, often misunderstood, which we should clarify now. This is the aspect of change over geographical territory, or between social groups, at a single period of time, generally referred to as dialect.

We should note that language, even as we have defined it, is a relatively abstract concept. Where, for example, should we go to find the English language? England? Scotland? Ireland? Canada? Australia? Perhaps America—but if so, where in America? New England? New York? Texas? California? It is obvious that nowhere in the world is spoken anything which all speakers of English can agree upon as *the* English language. Wherever one goes, one finds a dialect of English, but not "English" itself. The English language, insofar as it has any real existence at all, consists of an abstract system of correspondencies which all the so-called speakers of English adhere to more or less faithfully, and it is the relatively frequent occurrence of these correspondencies which permits, for example, an

American President and a British Prime Minister to communicate one to another on perplexing international problems without the aid of interpreters. Whenever the members of a speech community depart significantly from these language correspondencies, they no longer speak a dialect of language X, but what instead becomes the nucleus of a new language, Y.

This is difficult for many people to understand. Somehow the idea of dialect connotes to them the idea of substandard, or at least different, speech. It's hard for them to realize that they, too, speak a dialect, differing from other regional and social dialects in its sound inventory, its grammatical forms, and its lexicon. They resemble the lady from Fort Worth who was heard to comment, during the 1964 Presidential campaign, "It's nice to have someone in the White House who doesn't speak with an accent." This is an old story; everyone speaks a dialect except me.

Dialect, then, is the concrete manifestation of the abstraction *language*. In fact, it is entirely possible to argue that dialect is only somewhat less abstract than language, that someone with sharp enough ears could note minute differences in the speech of individuals within the same community. This is certainly true, and the term for the dialect of each individual speaker is *idiolect*. It could even be said that each speaker's idiolect is the only concrete manifestation of human speech. However, this complicates matters unnecessarily, and for our purposes, we will consider *dialect* to be the concrete manifestation of the abstraction *language*. What is important here is the realization that *dialect* means simply the regional and social variation of language, and that every utterance represents a concrete instance of that language.[6]

Some might object that the language exists in concrete form in writing, where dialect differences scarcely show up at all, unless the author is consciously trying to re-create them in dialogue. This objection fails to take

[6] Some will perhaps note here a variation of the system devised by the Swiss linguist Ferdinand de Saussure in a sequence of lectures at the University of Geneva in the first decade of this century and published after his death as *Cours de Linguistique Générale*. Saussure posited the division of *le langage* (human speech) into two mutually sustaining parts, *langue* (language) and *parole* (speaking). *Langue* is the essential institution of speech, the social, established system; whereas *parole* is the individual act, accidental, dependent upon the immediate situation. *Langue* can exist without *parole*, as in such "dead" languages as Latin, but the reverse cannot be true. Thus the individual speaker relies upon his intuitive understanding of the system (*langue*) in making his individual utterances (*parole*); but if a significant number of speakers depart in any particular way from the system, the system must be tacitly altered to conform to the alteration, lest a new system be adopted in its place. The presentation which we have made here differs in that by working vertically from the abstraction *language* to the concrete *dialect* (or to *idiolect*, if you prefer) we have considered a situation more in keeping with the reader's experience.

into account the nature of writing as a conventional system, rather than as a faithful reproduction of speech. In particular, the spelling is here confused with the sounds of the language system. Besides, we have already noted that writing is a secondary form, based upon speech. We will discuss later how writing developed and how we have crystallized it into a system which now tends to follow the spoken system at a respectful distance.

GRAMMAR

The Four Meanings

Before we go on to examine English at close hand, we need to consider one more term which we will be using throughout this book. This term, every bit as ambiguous in its unspecified state as the others we have examined, is *grammar.*

To practically everyone, the word *grammar* recalls language workbooks, sentence diagramming, and worry about *will* vs. *shall* and the preposition at the end of the sentence. All of these impressions presuppose the notion of an absolute correctness in language, of "right" and "wrong," "good" and "bad." Insofar as we learned anything at all from these exercises, we learned what was considered the proper use of language. Thus we come to the first consideration of grammar: grammar as linguistic propriety, as in the commonly heard expression, "He doesn't use good grammar." This concept of grammar is usually represented by handbooks of proper usage, such as those often used in the schools or nationally advertised as aids in overcoming one's sense of linguistic inferiority. Thus the first level of the term *grammar* is based upon the concept of language etiquette.

But there are English grammars which are not primarily concerned about the goodness and badness of certain expressions. Such works as those by Henry Sweet and Otto Jespersen make few value judgments, but consist of a detailed description of the language under consideration. In this light, then, we can define the next level of the word *grammar:* a formal description, relatively complete and exhaustive, of a language.

Formal descriptions of languages, however, do not arise out of nothing, *sui generis.* They are developed out of a consistent theory which outlines the descriptive method. Thus, the third level of the term: a theory on which formal descriptions of languages are based. From this level of grammar come such expressions as *descriptive grammar, functional grammar,* and *transformational grammar.*

But description would be impossible if there was no inherent system to be described. Thus we come to the fourth and most abstract level of all: grammar as the system inherent in any language. It is this system which all speakers of a language learn at an early age while scarcely realizing that they are, whether or not a formal description of that language exists. When we speak of the grammar of language X, we are using this particular meaning of the word.

Questions

1. Check the definitions of *language* in a few dictionaries. How many of the definitions include the same limitations as Cook's? Do you agree with Cook that all these limitations are necessary for a precise definition of *language?*
2. Do you understand what Cook means by *system,* by *arbitrary,* by *symbol* and how each of these applies to language? Try to explain each term in your own words.
3. Are you persuaded by Cook's argument that writing is not language? Summarize his arguments for the primacy of speech.
4. Do you agree with Cook's reservation that "the term *scientific* should perhaps be soft-pedaled" in describing the work of a linguist? Why or why not?
5. Are any of the elements in Cook's definitions of grammar new to you? Can you detect any signs of his attitude toward grammar as "the language of etiquette"?
6. What has been your definition of *dialect?* In your experience has the term had negative connotation? Should it have?
7. Does your experience with language seem to justify the implication that a living language constantly changes? What changes have you seen in your own language or in the language of groups with whom you associate?

Suggestions for Writing

1. Choose some technical term with which you are well acquainted. It may be from some subject you have studied, a hobby you have pursued, a job you have done. Write an expanded definition of the term. Use some of the techniques Cook has used—definitions of key words in the term, illustrations to clarify, comparisons, and so forth. You might begin with a formal sentence definition and amplify it so that the term will be meaningful to the reader. Assume that the audience has little or no previous knowledge of the term.
2. On page 89 Cook lists seven attributes of language. Choose one of the seven and write a paper in which you develop the term fully. Think carefully about the implications of the statement you choose and draw from your own experience illustrations to develop and to clarify the points you use in supporting your thesis.

Cratylus

Plato

Plato, Greek philosopher who lived from 428 B.C. to about 348 B.C., here argues through Socrates that language is natural and logical. Hermogenes, on the other hand, holds the position that language is a matter of agreement and convention, the position accepted by contemporary linguists. The early Greek philosophers did not concern themselves with languages other than Greek. Therefore, they did not ask why a word might be dog *in one language and* perro, hund, *and* chien *in others. This dialogue is one of the earliest written examples of concern with language in the western world. Contrast Socrates' argument with Cook's insistence that language is arbitrary. Have you at times unconsciously assumed that the name was the thing or that a word* had *to have a particular meaning? Would Socrates' argument support the position of those people who, during World War I, advocated changing the names of* frankfurter *and* hamburger?

PERSONS OF THE DIALOGUE.

Socrates *Hermogenes* *Cratylus*

Her. I must inform you, Socrates, that Cratylus has been arguing about names; he says that they are natural and not conventional, not sounds which men, giving articulation to a portion of their voice, agree to utter; but that there is a truth or correctness in them, which is the same for Hellenes as for barbarians. Whereupon I ask him, whether his own name of Cratylus is a true name or not, and he answers "Yes." And Socrates? "Yes." Then every man's name, as I tell him, is that which he is called. To this he replies,—"If all the world were to call you Hermogenes, that would not be your name." And when I am anxious to have a further explanation he is ironical and mysterious, and seems to imply that he has a notion in his own mind, if he would only tell, and could entirely convince me, if he chose to be intelligible. Tell me, Socrates, what this oracle means; or rather tell me, if you will be so good, what is your own view of the truth or correctness of names, which I would far sooner hear.

Socrates. Son of Hipponicus, there is an ancient saying, that "hard is the knowledge of the good." And the knowledge of names is a great part of knowledge. If I had not been poor, I might have heard the fifty drachma reading of the great Prodicus, which is a complete education in grammar and language—these are his own words—and then I should have been at once able to answer your question about the correctness of names. But, indeed, I have only heard the single drachma course, and, therefore, I do not know the truth about such matters; I will, however, gladly assist you and Cratylus in the investigation of them. When he declares that your name is not really Hermogenes, I suspect that he is only making fun of you; he means to say that you are no true son of Hermes, because you are always looking after a fortune and never in luck. But as I was saying, there is a great deal of difficulty in this sort of knowledge, and therefore we had better have a council and hear both sides.

Her. I have often talked over this matter, both with Cratylus and others, and cannot convince myself that there is any principle of correctness in names other than convention and agreement; any name which you give, in my judgment, is the right one, and if you change that and give another, the new name is as correct as the old: we frequently change the names of our slaves, and the newly-imposed name is as good as the old: for there is no name given to anything by nature; all is convention and habit of the users; that is my view. But if I am mistaken I shall be happy to hear and learn of Cratylus, or of any one.

Soc. I dare say that you may be right, Hermogenes; let us see: Your meaning is, that the name of each thing is only that name which is given to each thing?

Her. That is my view.

Soc. Whether the giver of the name be an individual or a city?

Her. Yes.

. . . .

[Socrates discusses the nature of names and leads Hermogenes to admit that the law (the legislator) is the originator of names.]

Soc. And is every man a legislator, or the skilled only?

Her. The skilled only.

Soc. Then, Hermogenes, not every man is able to give a name, but only a maker of names; and this is the legislator, who of all skilled artisans in the world is the rarest.

Her. That is true.

Soc. And how does the legislator make names? and to what does he look? Consider this in the light of the previous instances: to what does the carpenter look in making the shuttle? Does he not look to some sort of natural or ideal shuttle?

Her. Certainly.

Soc. And suppose the shuttle to be broken in making, will he make another, looking to the broken one? or will he look to the form which he had in his mind when he made the other?

Her. To the latter, I should imagine.

Soc. Might not that be justly called the true or ideal shuttle?

Her. I should say "Yes" to that.

Soc. And whatever shuttles are wanted, for the manufacture of garments, thin or thick, of woolen, flaxen, or other material, the ideal ought to contain them all; and whatever is the nature best adapted to each kind of work, ought to be the nature which the maker introduces into each sample of his own work.

Her. Yes.

Soc. And the same holds of other instruments: when a man has discovered the instrument which is naturally adapted to each work, he must take care to introduce that into the material of which he makes his work, and in the natural form, not in some other which he fancies; for example, he ought to know how to put into iron the forms of awls, which are adapted by nature to their several works.

Her. Certainly.

Soc. And how to put into wood the proper or natural form of a shuttle?

Her. True.

Soc. For the several forms of shuttles naturally answer to the several kinds of webs; and this is true of instruments in general.

Her. Yes.

Soc. Then, as to names: ought not our legislator also to know how to put the true natural name into sounds and syllables, and to make and give all names with a view to the ideal name, if he is to be a namer in any true sense? And if different legislators do not use the same syllables, that is quite intelligible. For neither does every smith, although he may be making the same instrument for the same purpose, make them all of the same iron. The form must be the same, but the material may vary, and still the instrument may be equally good of whatever iron made, whether in Hellas or in a foreign country; that makes no difference.

Her. Very true.

Soc. And the legislator, whether he be Hellene or barbarian, is not to be deemed by you a worse legislator for that, provided he gives the true and proper form of the name in whatever syllables; this place or any other makes no matter.

Her. Quite true.

Soc. But who then is to determine whether the proper form of the shuttle is given in any sort of wood? the carpenter who makes, or the weaver who is to use them?

Her. I should say, that he who is to use them ought to know, Socrates.

Soc. And who uses the work of the lyre-maker? Will not he be the man who knows how to direct what is being done, and who will know also whether the work is being well done or not?

Her. Certainly.

Soc. And who is he?

Her. The player of the lyre.

Soc. And who will direct the shipwright?

Her. The pilot.

Soc. And who will be best able to direct the legislator in his work, and will know whether the work is well done, in this or any other country? Will not the user be the man?

Her. Yes.

Soc. And this is he who knows how to ask questions?

Her. Yes.

Soc. And how to answer them?

Her. Yes.

Soc. And him who knows how to ask and answer you would call a dialectician?

Her. Yes; that would be the name of him.

Soc. Then the work of the carpenter is to make a rudder, and the pilot has to direct him, if the rudder is to be well made?

Her. True.

Soc. And the work of the legislator is to give names, and the dialectician must be his director if the names are to be rightly given?

Her. That is true.

Soc. Then, Hermogenes, I should say that this giving of names can be no such light matter as you fancy, or the work of light or chance persons; and Cratylus is right in saying that things have names by nature, and that not every man is an artificer of names; but he only who looks to the name which each thing by nature has, and is, will be able to express the ideal forms of things in letters and syllables.

Her. I cannot answer you, Socrates; but I find a difficulty in changing my opinion all in a moment; and I think that I should be more readily persuaded, if you would show me what this is which you term the natural fitness of names.

Soc. My good Hermogenes, I have none to show. Was I not telling you just now (but you have forgotten), that I knew nothing, and proposing to share the inquiry with you? But now that you and I have talked over the matter, a step has been gained; for we have discovered that the name has by nature a truth, and that not every man knows how to give a thing a name.

Questions

1. Plato argues that language is not arbitrary, that it is natural. Review both Plato's and Cook's arguments. Do you see any flaws in either one?
2. Can you think of any words that might be natural rather than arbitrary?
3. Check a dictionary for definitions of the word *barbarian*. Which meaning of the word applies to the word as it is used by Plato?
4. Plato argues that the dialectician should direct the legislator in the task of giving names. Who should give names to new objects, concepts, and ideas? Why?
5. Socrates carefully leads Hermogenes to the answers he wants him to give for certain questions. (This is now called the Socratic method.) Follow the questioning carefully. Would you always give the answers Hermogenes does? Do you always agree with the conclusion Socrates draws?

Adam Names the Animals

Noah Jonathan Jacobs *You were introduced to Jacobs, the author of the delightful essay which follows, in the preceding section. Perhaps you should reread the introduction to "Man's Finest Hour." You will need to consider again Jacobs' attitude toward his subject. As you read, keep in mind Cook's definition of language, particularly his use of the word* arbitrary, *also the nature-convention controversy raised by Plato. Jacobs, of course, is dealing humorously with the issues raised by that controversy and with language origin theories, and is enjoying the delight that can come from using words. Note how he frequently provides clues for the definition of difficult words by the context in which he places them.*

*H*ow did it dawn on first man to use his invisible breath to express the ideas stirring within him? Spirit alone is formless and empty; language alone seduces us from the truth with its syntax and euphony. Which of the two mandates did Adam follow? The problem was how to introduce opaque language into spirit without obscuring it. How did the sounds Adam uttered capture the essence of the animals that passed before him in review? Was the conjunction of the airy concept and the palpable intuition fortuitous? Were the animal names invented for the occasion or were they stored up in some divine greenhouse waiting to be selected by Adam's brooding mind? Did the bewildered beasts fall noiselessly into place when their master's voice fell upon them and slip into their names as if into preexisting garments? And if Adam created these garments a priori, on what principles were the patterns cut? Would another man differently disposed have created other designs? Did man aim his arrowy words at the target's center or was his bow struck at a venture? And if shot from his primal brain in happy ignorance, how did those random verbal darts find their fleshy marks to brand them forever? But our Great Progenitor proceeded confidently and with an air of strong assurance. He himself seems to have set high store on his performance. After he had reviewed the Parade, we see him pacing to and fro, soliloquizing on the import of his linguistic feat, which he straightway made the subject of a panegyric:

> I named them as they passed, and understood
> Their nature; with such knowledge God endued
> My sudden apprehension. . . .
>
> *Paradise Lost,*
> BOOK VIII, ll. 352–354

What *was* the nature of that "sudden apprehension"? Of the infinity of natural sounds ringing in his ears, which did Adam choose to render the essence of the tabanid horsefly, the piebald magpie, the aciculated hedgehog, the wanton lapwing, and all the animals which in that brief review frolicked before him on the green? Was the name he gave the elephant, for example, a faithful reproduction of its roaring (the bow-wow theory) or of some mystic harmony between it and the sound that its vast trunk emitted when struck (the ding-dong theory)? Was the name a rhythmic chant designed to raise its flagging spirit as man goaded it on to do his work (the yo-heave-ho theory) or a vocal reflex signifying his displeasure (the pooh-pooh theory)? It may be that Adam's tongue unwittingly reproduced some typical elephantine gesture, an oral replica of the beast's lithe proboscis, the texture of its wrinkled bulk or the swish of its flapping tail (the ta-ta or the wig-wag theory). Or, to take a more modest example, how did Adam name the bat? Which characteristic impressed him at the moment of naming? Did its blindness move him to call it *murciélago* (Sp.), its baldness *chauve-souris* (Fr.), its shyness *pipistrello* (It.), its leathery skin *Læderlapp* (Dan.) or *böregér* (Hung. from *bör,* leather; *egér,* mouse), its preference for the night *nukteris* (Gr.), its resemblance to the mouse *Fledermaus* (Ger.) or *letutsaya mysh* (Rus.), the sound of its flapping wings *watwat* (Arab.), its winglike hands *chiroptera* (Lat. from Gr. *chir,* hand, plus *pteron,* wing), its resemblance to a lily (!) *liliac* (Rum.), its reputed love of bacon *bat* (OE *backe,* bacon)? The Chinese have conferred a number of laudatory names on this mouselike mammal, such as *embracing wings, heavenly rat, fairy rat, night swallow,* and use it as a symbol of happiness and long life because its name *fu* in Chinese happens to be a homonym which means both *bat* and *prosperity.*

The truth of the matter seems to be that in the short time at his disposal, roughly about thirty minutes, Adam was obliged to employ a number of linguistic devices. The beasts had first to be divided into hoofed and clawed, and the former subdivided into cloven and noncloven hoofed. The question of gender then obtruded itself, and this Adam solved by composition (*she-elephant, nanny goat*), by addition of a suffix (*lioness, tigress*), by inverse deduction, deriving the male from the female (*goose-gander, duck-*

drake, cat-tomcat); and by suppletion, that is, by supplying new forms (*ram-ewe, boar-sow, dog-bitch*). Where the mode of propagation escaped detection because of its rapidity or obscurity, making a responsible decision impossible (as in the case of the rabbit, the turtle and the elephant), Adam disregarded the distinction of sex. The other criteria at his disposal were:

a) place of origin: the *great Dane,* the *Pekingese, Scotty, spaniel* (Spain) and the *tarantula* (Lat. Tarentum, now Taranto in Sicily);

b) size: the *horsefly,* the *bumblebee,* the *bug* (akin to *big?*), and the *chameleon* (Gr. *khamaí,* dwarf, plus *léon,* lion);

c) means of sustenance: the *linnet* which feeds on the seeds of flax and hemp (Lat. *linum,* flax), the *anteater* and the *fish crow;*

d) characteristic sounds emitted: the *bullfrog,* whose croak resembles a bull's roar; the *catbird,* whose call is like the mewing of a cat; and the *partridge* (Gr. *pérdix,* applied to one who expels wind), from the sound it makes when rising;

e) shape: the *ringworm,* the *spoonbill duck,* the *crossbill* and the *fiddler crab,* which holds its large claw as a fiddler his bow;

f) method of locomotion: the *grasshopper, adelopodes* (animals whose feet are hidden), *reptiles* (Lat. *repere,* to creep), *dromedary* (Gr. *dromas,* running—about nine miles an hour), *bustard* (OF *bistarde,* from Lat. *avis tarda,* slow-walking bird), *duck* (from *ducking*) and *dove* (from *diving*);

g) color: the *redbreast,* the *hare* (related to *hazy, gray*), the *oppossum* (Algon. *apasum,* white beast), the *penguin* (Welsh *pen,* head, plus *gwyn,* white), the *pygarg,* a kind of antelope with white hindquarters (Gr. *pugé,* rump, plus *argós,* white), *albatross* (corruption from Lat. *albus,* white, plus Port. *alcatras,* cormorant) and *beaver* (OE *beofor,* brown);

h) odor exuded: the *muskrat* (from its musky smell), the *pismire,* from the urinous smell of an anthill (ME *pissemyre,* from *piss,* plus *mire,* ant), and the Ger. *Stinktier,* skunk;

i) facial expression: the *dodo* (Port. *doudo,* stupid);

j) mode of scratching: *racoon* (Algon. *arathcone,* he scratches with his hands);

k) mode of excretion: the *butterfly,* whose excrement resembles butter, and the *shitepoke heron,* because of the way it empties its bowels when frightened by a shot.

When confronted with two or more criteria, demanding a split decision, Adam adopted more than one name: *turkey* (Turkey) and Fr. *coq d'Inde* (India); *pewit,* from its cry, or *lapwing,* from its motion (OE *hleápan,* to leap, plus *winc,* to totter); the name of the *owl,* which he at first mistook for a feathered cat, he derived from its doleful hooting (Eng. owl, (h)owl; Lat. *ulula,* Swah. *babewatoto*) and also from its glaring eyes (Gr. *glauks* from *glaúkos,* blue, gray, hence glaring); Finn. *pöllö,* owl = staring eyes, *pöllöpää,* to gape; the *lynx* received its name from its light color or from its sharp eyes. An additional factor which complicated Adam's task was the relative distance between the animals and himself. This determined the length of the vowels in the name because the tongue, in accordance with a theory now associated with the name of Piaget but which goes back to Aulus Gellius and Nigidius Figulus, instinctively imitates the space relation of the namer's body to the object, so that the vowels made with the shortened tongue are attached to the animals close by, as the *hen,* the *lamb* or the *squirrel,* and those made with the protruding tongue are extended to those farther removed, as the *mole,* the *cow* and the *owl.*

Adam did not permit himself to be diverted by deceptive sounds or arbitrary combinations at the expense of good sense as did poets of a later age. He did not exploit "apt alliteration's artful aid" to suggest the clatter of hoofbeats (Virgil), hissing serpents (Racine) or the progress of rats (Browning's "The Pied Piper"). Sound alone, which beguiles the ear without engaging the mind, is an unreliable vehicle for thought. The commonplace must not be made alluring by tawdry adornment; the mule's head need not be hung with tinkling bells. Adam called the horse a horse and not Pegasus, the lion a lion and not the father of roaring, the camel a camel and not the ship of the desert. His aim was not to copy reality in every detail in the manner of the "material imitation" of the pre-Platonic philosophers who regarded language as a passive stamp of reality, every sound having an innate quality which makes it suitable to represent certain ideas; he followed Plato's theory of "ideal imitation" where a word expresses the inner essence of a thing, the meaning behind the ever changing object. This view is rejected by those who hold to the "convention theory" according to which words acquire meaning not from their sounds but by common agreement. A word merely provides an appropriate mode of conveying our thoughts, and its meaning is defined by custom and mutual agreement. The sound of a word tells us as little about its meaning as a key about the contents of a room or a seashell about the marine life that haunts the deep. Adam could have given different names to the same creature (Eng. *ewe,* Arab. *najat*) or the same name (Eng. *ewe,* Hung. *juh*); or two different animals could have received the same name (Eng. *dog,* Heb. *dag,* fish). This is the ever recurrent argument advanced against the theory of "ideal imitation" since the days of the Sophists when Democritus refuted Heraclitus: there is no natural connection between a word and the thing it designates. But Adam's names could not have been submitted to anyone for agreement by the very nature of the case. They rang true of their own accord because his speech was a reflection of his reason, his *oratio* flowed from his *ratio*. That is, his basic agreement did not come from the arbitrary corroboration of mortal men but from God who inspired him with the breath of life and who vouched for his speech. . . .

Questions

1. Carefully read the first five sentences in this selection. What does Jacobs mean? Does Jacobs answer the series of questions he asks?
2. From Jacobs' humorous treatment of language emerges a serious point. What is it? Does the point in this essay differ from the one he made in "Man's Finest Hour"?
3. As he discusses the possible ways of naming the bat, he notes that various languages have emphasized particular characteristics of the bat in choosing a name. Is there a single essence of an animal? Does Jacobs himself seem to assume such an essence?
4. What effect does Jacobs achieve by beginning the essay with the assumption that no language exists and then later by having Adam consider the choices from a multitude of languages?
5. In the concluding paragraph Jacobs summarizes the arguments for and against Plato's "natural" theory of language. Are his arguments the same as those presented in "Cratylus"? Do they relate in any way to Cook's definition of language?

Suggestions for Writing

1. Place yourself in Adam's position. Suppose you were surveying a parade which included such animals as a kangaroo, a polar bear, a rabbit. What would you consider the essence of these or other animals that would have to be accounted for in their names? Write a paragraph in which you discuss the possibilities for naming a particular animal.

Humpty Dumpty

Lewis Carroll

In Alice in Wonderland *and* Through the Looking Glass, *Lewis Carroll places Alice in a series of adventures in which she talks to a number of animals. These fantasies have held the interest of children for generations, but the light and humorous tone and Carroll's fascination with language have made the books great favorites with adults also. In this chapter from* Through the Looking Glass *Alice meets and has a conversation with Humpty Dumpty. As you read it, note both Humpty's and Alice's attitudes toward language. Does Humpty's insistence that some words must mean certain things have any relevance to Cook's use of the word* arbitrary *in his definition of language? Although Carroll is humorous in the comments on language, does he make some significant observations about the nature of language? Throughout the essay notice Carroll's interest in language and the attitude he has toward it.*

However, the egg only got larger and larger, and more and more human: when she had come within a few yards of it, she saw that it had eyes and a nose and mouth; and, when she had come close to it, she saw clearly that it was HUMPTY DUMPTY himself. "It ca'n't be anybody else!" she said to herself. "I'm as certain of it, as if his name were written all over his face!"

It might have been written a hundred times, easily, on that enormous face. Humpty Dumpty was sitting, with his legs crossed like a Turk, on the top of a high wall—such a narrow one that Alice quite wondered how he could keep his balance—and, as his eyes were steadily fixed in the opposite direction, and he didn't take the least notice of her, she thought he must be a stuffed figure, after all.

"And how exactly like an egg he is!" she said aloud, standing with her hands ready to catch him, for she was every moment expecting him to fall.

"It's *very* provoking," Humpty Dumpty said after a long silence, looking away from Alice as he spoke, "to be called an egg—*very!*"

"I said you *looked* like an egg, Sir," Alice gently explained. "And some eggs are very pretty, you know," she added, hoping to turn her remark into a sort of compliment.

"Some people," said Humpty Dumpty, looking away from her as usual, "have no more sense than a baby!"

Alice didn't know what to say to this: it wasn't at all like conversation, she thought, as he never said anything to *her:* in fact, his last remark was evidently addressed to a tree—so she stood and softly repeated to herself:—

> *"Humpty Dumpty sat on a wall:*
> *Humpty Dumpty had a great fall.*
> *All the King's horses and all the King's men*
> *Couldn't put Humpty Dumpty in his place again.*

"That last line is much too long for the poetry," she added, almost out loud, forgetting that Humpty Dumpty would hear her.

"Don't stand chattering to yourself like that," Humpty Dumpty said, looking at her for the first time, "but tell me your name and your business."

"My *name* is Alice, but——"

"It's a stupid name enough!" Humpty Dumpty interrupted impatiently. "What does it mean?"

"Must a name mean something?" Alice asked doubtfully.

"Of course it must," Humpty Dumpty said with a short laugh: *"my* name means the shape I am—and a good handsome shape it is, too. With a name like yours, you might be any shape, almost."

"Why do you sit out here all alone?" said Alice, not wishing to begin an argument.

"Why, because there's nobody with me!" cried Humpty Dumpty. "Did you think I didn't know the answer to *that?* Ask another."

"Don't you think you'd be safer down on the ground?" Alice went on, not with any idea of making another riddle, but simply in her good-natured anxiety for the queer creature. "That wall is so *very* narrow!"

"What tremendously easy riddles you ask!" Humpty Dumpty growled out. "Of course I don't think so! Why, if ever I *did* fall off—which there's no chance of—but *if* I did——" Here he pursed up his lips, and looked so solemn and grand that Alice could hardly help laughing. *"If* I *did* fall," he went on, *"the King has promised me*—ah, you may turn pale, if you like! You didn't think I was going to say that, did you? *The King has promised me—with his very own mouth*—to—to——"

"To send all his horses and all his men," Alice interrupted, rather unwisely.

"Now I declare that's too bad!" Humpty Dumpty cried, breaking into a sudden passion. "You've been listening at doors—and behind trees—and down chimneys—or you couldn't have known it!"

"I haven't indeed!" Alice said very gently. "It's in a book."

"Ah, well! They may write such things in a *book,"* Humpty Dumpty said in a calmer tone. "That's what you call a History of England, that is. Now, take a good look at me! I'm one that has spoken to a King, *I* am: mayhap you'll never see such another: and, to show you I'm not proud, you may shake hands with me!" And he grinned almost from ear to ear, as he leant forwards (and as nearly as possible fell off the wall in doing so) and offered Alice his hand. She watched him a little anxiously as she took it. "If he smiled much more the ends of his mouth might meet behind," she thought: "And then I don't know *what* would happen to his head! I'm afraid it would come off!"

"Yes, all his horses and all his men," Humpty Dumpty went on. "They'd pick me up again in a minute, *they* would! However, this conversation is going on a little too fast: let's go back to the last remark but one."

"I'm afraid I ca'n't quite remember it," Alice said, very politely.

"In that case we start afresh," said Humpty Dumpty, "and it's my turn to choose a subject——" ("He talks about it just as if it was a game!" thought Alice.) "So here's a question for you. How old did you say you were?"

Alice made a short calculation, and said "Seven years and six months."

"Wrong!" Humpty Dumpty exclaimed triumphantly. "You never said a word like it!"

"I thought you meant 'How old *are* you?' " Alice explained.

"If I'd meant that, I'd have said it," said Humpty Dumpty.

Alice didn't want to begin another argument, so she said nothing.

"Seven years and six months!" Humpty Dumpty repeated thoughtfully. "An uncomfortable sort of age. Now if you'd asked *my* advice, I'd have said 'Leave off at seven'——but it's too late now."

"I never ask advice about growing," Alice said indignantly.

"Too proud?" the other enquired.

Alice felt even more indignant at this suggestion. "I mean," she said, "that one ca'n't help growing older."

"One ca'n't, perhaps," said Humpty Dumpty; "but *two* can. With proper assistance, you might have left off at seven."

"What a beautiful belt you've got on!" Alice suddenly remarked. (They had had quite enough of the subject of age, she thought: and, if they really were to take turns in choosing subjects, it was *her* turn now.) "At least," she corrected herself on second thoughts, "a beautiful cravat, I should have said—no, a belt, I mean—I beg your pardon!" she added in dismay, for Humpty Dumpty looked thoroughly offended, and she began to wish she hadn't chosen that subject. "If only I knew," she thought to herself, "which was neck and which was waist!"

Evidently Humpty Dumpty was very angry, though he said nothing for a minute or two. When he *did* speak again, it was in a deep growl.

"It is a—*most—provoking*—thing," he said at last, "when a person doesn't know a cravat from a belt!"

"I know it's very ignorant of me," Alice said, in so humble a tone that Humpty Dumpty relented.

"It's a cravat, child, and a beautiful one, as you say. It's a present from the White King and Queen. There now!"

"Is it really?" said Alice, quite pleased to find that she *had* chosen a good subject after all.

"They gave it me," Humpty Dumpty continued thoughtfully as he crossed one knee over the other and clasped his hands round it, "they gave it me—for an un-birthday present."

"I beg your pardon?" Alice said with a puzzled air.

"I'm not offended," said Humpty Dumpty.

"I mean, what *is* an un-birthday present?"

"A present given when it isn't your birthday, of course."

Alice considered a little. "I like birthday presents best," she said at last.

"You don't know what you're talking about!" cried Humpty Dumpty. "How many days are there in a year?"

"Three hundred and sixty-five," said Alice.

"And how many birthdays have you?"

"One."

"And if you take one from three hundred and sixty-five what remains?"

"Three hundred and sixty-four, of course."

Humpty Dumpty looked doubtful. "I'd rather see that done on paper," he said.

Alice couldn't help smiling as she took out her memorandum-book, and worked the sum for him:

$$\begin{array}{r} 365 \\ 1 \\ \hline 364 \end{array}$$

Humpty Dumpty took the book and looked at it carefully. "That seems to be done right——" he began.

"You're holding it upside down!" Alice interrupted.

"To be sure I was!" Humpty Dumpty said gaily as she turned it round for him. "I thought it looked a little queer. As I was saying, that *seems* to be done right—though I haven't time to look it over thoroughly just now—and that shows that there are three hundred and sixty-four days when you might get un-birthday presents——"

"Certainly," said Alice.

"And only *one* for birthday presents, you know. There's glory for you!"

"I don't know what you mean by 'glory,' " Alice said.

Humpty Dumpty smiled contemptuously. "Of course you don't—till I tell you. I meant 'there's a nice knock-down argument for you!' "

"But 'glory' doesn't mean 'a nice knock-down argument,' " Alice objected.

"When *I* use a word," Humpty Dumpty said, in rather a scornful tone, "it means just what I choose it to mean—neither more nor less."

"The question is," said Alice, "whether you *can* make words mean so many different things."

"The question is," said Humpty Dumpty, "which is to be master ——that's all."

Alice was too much puzzled to say anything; so after a minute Humpty Dumpty began again. "They've a temper, some of them—particularly verbs: they're the proudest—adjectives you can do anything with, but not verbs—however, *I* can manage the whole lot of them! Impenetrability! That's what *I* say!"

"Would you tell me please," said Alice, "what that means?"

"Now you talk like a reasonable child," said Humpty Dumpty, looking very much pleased. "I meant by 'impenetrability' that we've had enough of that subject, and it would be just as well if you'd mention what you mean to do next, as I suppose you don't mean to stop here all the rest of your life."

"That's a great deal to make one word mean," Alice said in a thoughtful tone.

"When I make a word do a lot of work like that," said Humpty Dumpty, "I always pay it extra."

"Oh!" said Alice. She was too much puzzled to make any other remark.

"Ah, you should see 'em come round me of a Saturday night," Humpty Dumpty went on, wagging his head gravely from side to side, "for to get their wages, you know."

(Alice didn't venture to ask what he paid them with; and so you see I ca'n't tell *you*.)

"You seem very clever at explaining words, Sir," said Alice. "Would you kindly tell me the meaning of the poem called 'Jabberwocky'?"

"Let's hear it," said Humpty Dumpty. "I can explain all the poems that ever were invented—and a good many that haven't been invented just yet."

This sounded very hopeful, so Alice repeated the first verse:—

" 'Twas brillig, and the slithy toves
Did gyre and gimble in the wabe:
All mimsy were the borogoves,
And the mome raths outgrabe."

"That's enough to begin with," Humpty Dumpty interrupted: "there are plenty of hard words there. '*Brillig*' means four o'clock in the afternoon—the time when you begin *broiling* things for dinner."

"That'll do very well," said Alice: "and '*slithy*'?"

"Well, '*slithy*' means 'lithe and slimy.' 'Lithe' is the same as 'active.' You see it's like a portmanteau—there are two meanings packed up into one word."

"I see it now," Alice remarked thoughtfully: "and what are '*toves*'?"

"Well, '*toves*' are something like badgers—they're something like lizards—and they're something like corkscrews."

"They must be very curious-looking creatures."

"They are that," said Humpty Dumpty: "also they make their nests under sun-dials—also they live on cheese."

"And what's to '*gyre*' and to '*gimble*'?"

"To '*gyre*' is to go round and round like a gyroscope. To '*gimble*' is to make holes like a gimlet."

"And '*the wabe*' is the grass-plot round a sundial, I suppose?" said Alice, surprised at her own ingenuity.

"Of course it is. It's called '*wabe*' you know, because it goes a long way before it, and a long way behind it——"

"And a long way beyond it on each side," Alice added.

"Exactly so. Well then, '*mimsy*' is 'flimsy and miserable' (there's another portmanteau for you). And a '*borogove*' is a thin shabby-looking bird with its feathers sticking out all round—something like a live mop."

"And then '*mome raths*'?" said Alice. "I'm afraid I'm giving you a great deal of trouble."

"Well, a '*rath*' is a sort of green pig: but '*mome*' I'm not certain about. I think it's short for 'from home'—meaning that they'd lost their way, you know."

"And what does '*outgrabe*' mean?"

"Well, '*outgribing*' is something between bellowing and whistling, with a kind of sneeze in the middle: however, you'll hear it done, maybe—

down in the wood yonder—and, when you've once heard it, you'll be *quite* content. Who's been repeating all that hard stuff to you?"

"I read it in a book," said Alice. "But I *had* some poetry repeated to me much easier than that, by—Tweedledee, I think it was."

"As to poetry, you know," said Humpty Dumpty, stretching out one of his great hands, "*I* can repeat poetry as well as other folk, if it comes to that——"

"Oh, it needn't come to that!" Alice hastily said, hoping to keep him from beginning.

"The piece I'm going to repeat," he went on without noticing her remark, "was written entirely for your amusement."

Alice felt that in that case she really *ought* to listen to it; so she sat down, and said "Thank you" rather sadly.

"In winter, when the fields are white,
I sing this song for your delight——

only I don't sing it," he added, as an explanation.

"I see you don't," said Alice.

"If you can *see* whether I'm singing or not, you've sharper eyes than most," Humpty Dumpty remarked severely. Alice was silent.

"In spring, when woods are getting green,
I'll try and tell you what I mean:"

"Thank you very much," said Alice.

"In summer, when the days are long,
Perhaps you'll understand the song:

In autumn, when the leaves are brown,
Take pen and ink, and write it down."

"I will, if I can remember it so long," said Alice.

"You needn't go on making remarks like that," Humpty Dumpty said: "they're not sensible, and they put me out."

"I sent a message to the fish:
I told them 'This is what I wish.'

The little fishes of the sea
They sent an answer back to me.

The little fishes' answer was
'We cannot do it, Sir, because——' "

"I'm afraid I don't quite understand," said Alice.

"It gets easier further on," Humpty Dumpty replied.

"I sent to them again to say
'It will be better to obey.'

The fishes answered, with a grin,
'Why, what a temper you are in!'

I told them once, I told them twice:
They would not listen to advice.

I took a kettle large and new,
Fit for the deed I had to do.

My heart went hop, my heart went thump:
I filled the kettle at the pump.

Then some one came to me and said
'The little fishes are in bed.'

I said to him, I said it plain,
'Then you must wake them up again.'

I said it very loud and clear:
I went and shouted in his ear."

Humpty Dumpty raised his voice almost to a scream as he repeated this verse, and Alice thought, with a shudder, "I wouldn't have been the messenger for *anything!*"

"But he was very stiff and proud:
He said, 'You needn't shout so loud!'

And he was very proud and stiff:
He said, 'I'd go and wake them, if——'

I took a corkscrew from the shelf:
I went to wake them up myself.

And when I found the door was locked,
I pulled and pushed and kicked and knocked.

And when I found the door was shut,
I tried to turn the handle, but——"

There was a long pause.

"Is that all?" Alice timidly asked.

"That's all," said Humpty Dumpty. "Good-bye."

This was rather sudden, Alice thought: but, after such a *very* strong hint that she ought to be going, she felt that it would hardly be civil to stay. So she got up, and held out her hand. "Good-bye, till we met again!" she said as cheerfully as she could.

"I shouldn't know you again if we *did* meet," Humpty Dumpty replied in a discontented tone, giving her one of his fingers to shake: "you're so exactly like other people."

"The face is what one goes by, generally," Alice remarked in a thoughtful tone.

"That's just what I complain of," said Humpty Dumpty. "Your face is the same as everybody has—the two eyes, so——" (marking their places in the air with his thumb) "nose in the middle, mouth under. It's always the same. Now if you had the two eyes on the same side of the nose, for instance—or the mouth at the top—that would be *some* help."

"It wouldn't look nice," Alice objected. But Humpty Dumpty only shut his eyes, and said "Wait till you've tried."

Alice waited a minute to see if he would speak again, but, as he never opened his eyes or took any further notice of her, she said "Good-bye!" once more, and, getting no answer to this, she quietly walked away: but she couldn't help saying to herself, as she went, "of all the unsatisfactory ——" (she repeated this aloud, as it was a great comfort to have such a long word to say) "of all the unsatisfactory people I *ever* met——" She never finished the sentence, for at this moment a heavy crash shook the forest from end to end.

Questions

1. "*Must* a name mean something?" Alice asks. Do you agree with Humpty that it must? Is Humpty being arbitrary, as Cook thinks of it?
2. Closely related, of course, is Humpty's insistence that *glory* means "a nice knockdown argument," that a word means just what he chooses it to mean. With Cook's definition in mind, can you find anything wrong with Humpty's argument? Can you find anything wrong with Alice's attitude toward words? Which seems closer to Cook's attitude?
3. This essay has a light and humorous tone, but what significant observations on language are implicit in the comments by Humpty Dumpty? How do they relate to Cook's discussion?
4. Is Humpty's song merely nonsense as a whole, even though individual parts seem to make sense?
5. Humpty Dumpty calls *slithy* and *mimsy* portmanteau words. What does *portmanteau* mean? Does the context give you any clues to its meaning? Give examples of portmanteau words which have been accepted into the language today. *Smog* is one example.

The Word Was My Agony

Alfred Kazin

This brief selection from Kazin's autobiography, apart from its inherent interest, reveals another quality of language that most of us are ordinarily unaware of: the profound complexity of the language-forming mechanisms. Kazin says nothing about such things. But our awareness of what it takes to form words at all must surely be heightened by hearing a stutterer struggle with a process that comes so naturally to us. Since Kazin is a highly gifted user of words in writing, he makes us feel deeply his "agony" and makes us wonder even more why he would have had such a problem. If you do not have such a problem, you should find in this selection greater awareness and appreciation of the miracle of language. If you have ever had the problem, you should find a kindred and powerful recording of it.

I was awed by this system, I believed in it, I respected its force. The alternative was "going bad." The school was notoriously the toughest in our tough neighborhood, and the dangers of "going bad" were constantly impressed upon me at home and in school in dark whispers of the "reform school" and in examples of boys who had been picked up for petty thievery, rape, or flinging a heavy inkwell straight into a teacher's face. Behind any failure in school yawned the great abyss of a criminal career. Every refractory attitude doomed you with the sound "Sing Sing." Anything less than absolute perfection in school always suggested to my mind that I might fall out of the daily race, be kept back in the working class forever, or—dared I think of it?—fall into the criminal class itself.

I worked on a hairline between triumph and catastrophe. Why the odds should always have felt so narrow I understood only when I realized how little my parents thought of their own lives. It was not for myself alone that I was expected to shine, but for them—to redeem the constant anxiety of their existence. I was the first American child, their offering to the strange new God; I was to be the monument of their liberation from the shame of being—what they were. And that there was shame in this was a fact that everyone seemed to believe as a matter of course. It was in the gleeful discounting of themselves—what do we know?—with which our parents greeted every fresh victory in our savage competition for "high averages," for prizes, for a few condescending words of official praise from the principal at assembly. It was in the sickening invocation of "Americanism"—the word itself accusing us of everything we apparently were not. Our families and teachers seemed tacitly agreed that we were somehow to be a little ashamed of what we were. Yet it was always hard to say why this should be so. It was certainly not—in Brownsville!—because we were Jews, or simply because we spoke another language at home, or were absent on our holy days. It was rather that a "refined," "correct," "nice" English was required of us at school that we did not naturally speak, and that our teachers could never be quite sure we would keep. This English was peculiarly the ladder of advancement. Every future young lawyer was known by it. Even the Communists and Socialists on Pitkin Avenue spoke it. It was bright and clean and polished. We were expected to show it off like a new pair of shoes. When the teacher sharply called a question out, then your name, you were expected to leap up, face the class, and eject those new words fluently off the tongue.

There was my secret ordeal: I could never say anything except in the most roundabout way; I was a stammerer. Although I knew all those new words from my private reading—I read walking in the street, to and from the Children's Library on Stone Avenue; on the fire escape and the roof; at every meal when they would let me; read even when I dressed in the morning, propping my book up against the drawers of the bureau as I pulled on my long black stockings—I could never seem to get the easiest words out with the right dispatch, and would often miserably signal from my desk that I did not know the answer rather than get up to stumble and fall and crash on every word. If, angry at always being put down as lazy or stupid, I did get up to speak, the black wooden floor would roll away under my feet, the teacher would frown at me in amazement, and in unbearable loneliness I would hear behind me the groans and laughter: *tuh-tuh-tuh-tuh.*

The word was my agony. The word that for others was so effortless and so neutral, so unburdened, so simple, so exact, I had first to mediate in advance, to see if I could make it, like a plumber fitting together odd lengths and shapes of pipe. I was always preparing words I could speak, storing them away, choosing between them. And often, when the word did come from my mouth in its great and terrible birth, quailing and bleeding as if forced through a thornbush, I would not be able to look the others in the face, and would walk out in the silence, the infinitely echoing silence behind my back, to say it all cleanly back to myself as I walked in the streets. Only when I was alone in the open air, pacing the roof with pebbles in my mouth, as I had read Demosthenes had done to cure himself of stammering; or in the street, where all words seemed to flow from the length of my stride and the color of the houses as I remembered the perfect tranquillity of a phrase in Beethoven's *Romance in F* I could sing back to myself as I walked—only then was it possible for me to speak without the infinite premeditations and strangled silences I toiled through whenever I got up at school to respond with the expected, the exact answer.

It troubled me that I could speak in the fullness of my own voice only when I was alone on the streets, walking about. There was something unnatural about it; unbearably isolated. I was not like the others! I was not like the others! At midday, every freshly shocking Monday noon, they sent me away to a speech clinic in a school in East New York, where I sat in a circle of lispers and cleft palates and foreign accents holding a mirror before my lips and rolling difficult sounds over and over. To be sent there in the full light of the opening week, when everyone else was at school or going about his business, made me feel as if I had been expelled from the great normal body of humanity. I would gobble down my lunch on my way to the speech clinic and rush back to the school in time to make up for the classes I had lost. One day, one unforgettable dread day, I stopped to catch my breath on a corner of Sutter Avenue, near the wholesale fruit markets, where an old drugstore rose up over a great flight of steps. In the window were dusty urns of colored water floating off iron chains; cardboard placards advertising hairnets, Ex-Lax; a great illustrated medical chart headed THE HUMAN FACTORY, which showed the exact course a mouthful of food follows as it falls from chamber to chamber of the body. I hadn't meant to stop there at all, only to catch my breath; but I so hated the speech clinic that I thought I would delay my arrival for a few minutes by eating my lunch on the steps. When I took the sandwich out of my bag, two bitterly hard pieces of hard salami slipped out of my hand and fell through a grate onto a hill of dust below the steps. I remember how sickeningly vivid an odd thread of hair looked on the salami, as if my lunch were turning stiff with death. The factory whistles called their short, sharp blasts stark through the middle of noon, beating at me where I sat outside the city's magnetic circle. I had never known, I knew instantly I would never in my heart again submit to, such wild passive despair as I felt at that moment, sitting on the steps before THE HUMAN FACTORY, where little robots gathered and shoveled the food from chamber to chamber of the body. They had put me out into the streets, I thought to myself; with their mirrors and their everlasting pulling at me to imitate their effortless bright speech and their stupefaction that a boy could stammer and stumble on every other English word he carried in his head, they had put me out into the streets, had left me high and dry on the steps of that drugstore staring at the remains of my lunch turning black and grimy in the dust.

Questions

1. Kazin tells us that he is a Jew, that he is a "first American child" (hence one of whom much was expected), and that his family spoke another language in the home. How might these facts have affected his problem as a stutterer? Remember as you consider this that most remedial work with stuttering is now approached from a psychological standpoint. Why could Kazin "speak in the fullness of my own voice only when I was alone in the street"?
2. Notice the adjectives that describe the "English that was expected of us at school." Would you use "refined," "correct," and "nice" to describe the language you were and are now expected to use in school? Why or why not? How important would you now consider these qualities in effective writing and speaking?
3. In what ways might Kazin's problems with stuttering support or oppose the idea that language is basically a spoken phenomenon, a system of sounds?
4. Analyze Kazin's use of THE HUMAN FACTORY. Who are "they" at the beginning of the final sentence? The imps? His teachers and fellow students? Both? Students of literature would call this purposeful ambiguity. Is its purpose to suggest that his teachers and students are imps? Robots? Why?

Suggestions for Writing

1. In a crucial moment in Herman Melville's novel *Billy Budd,* Billy faces his accuser Claggart and is asked by Captain Vere to defend himself. Claggart has falsely accused Billy of plotting a rebellion. Billy, a stutterer like Kazin, tries to respond but cannot. In a desperate substitute for speech, he swings an innocent but solid fist at Claggart. Claggart, a petty officer on the ship, dies from the blow, and Captain Vere has to preside over the trial and execution of Billy, who is morally innocent but technically guilty. Most of our failures of communication do not have such drastic consequences, nor do we usually experience them so profoundly as Kazin did. But we all have them. Analyze one such experience you have had and explore its implications. Make your own assumptions about your audience, but at least assume that they are interested in both you and the problem. Perhaps you could do all this as a definition of *communication.*

Amy Foster

Joseph Conrad

This story comes from one of England's most thoughtful, powerful, intense writers of fiction. Everything about his work commands our attention and respect: the seriousness of tone, the sensitivity to ideas and people, the brooding intensity with which he communicates his insights into the human condition, the remarkable control of language. Such control is even the more remarkable when we consider that Conrad was born and raised in Poland (as Jozef Teodor Konrad Korzeniowski) and hence that his great fiction was written in a language not native to him. Our interest in "Amy Foster" here is complex because its implications radiate so far and in so many directions from the basic problem of language that it involves. We hope you will read with an appreciation of Conrad's own fascinating control of English. The story is hardly autobiography, but surely much of its force comes from Conrad's own experiences in coming to a new country and having to live with and master a new language.

Kennedy is a country doctor, and lives in Colebrook, on the shores of Eastbay. The high ground rising abruptly behind the red roofs of the little town crowds the quaint High Street against the wall which defends it from the sea. Beyond the sea-wall there curves for miles in a vast and regular sweep the barren beach of shingle, with the village of Brenzett standing out darkly across the water, a spire in a clump of trees; and still further out the perpendicular column of a lighthouse, looking in the distance no bigger than a lead-pencil, marks the vanishing-point of the land. The country at the back of Brenzett is low and flat; but the bay is fairly well sheltered from the seas, and occasionally a big ship, windbound or through stress of weather, makes use of the anchoring ground a mile and a half due north from you as you stand at the back door of the "Ship Inn" in Brenzett. A dilapidated windmill near by, lifting its shattered arms from a mound no loftier than a rubbish-heap, and a Martello tower squatting at the water's edge half a mile to the south of the Coastguard cottages, are fa-

Joseph Conrad, "Amy Foster," from *Typhoon and Other Stories*. Reprinted with the permission of J. M. Dent and Sons, Ltd., and the Trustees of the Joseph Conrad estate.

miliar to the skippers of small craft. These are the official seamarks for the patch of trustworthy bottom represented on the Admiralty charts by an irregular oval of dots enclosing several figures six, with a tiny anchor engraved among them, and the legend "mud and shells" over all.

The brow of the upland overtops the square tower of the Colebrook Church. The slope is green and looped by a white road. Ascending along this road, you open a valley broad and shallow, a wide green trough of pastures and hedges merging inland into a vista of purple tints and flowing lines closing the view.

In this valley down to Brenzett and Colebrook and up to Darnford, the market town fourteen miles away, lies the practice of my friend Kennedy. He had begun life as surgeon in the Navy, and afterwards had been the companion of a famous traveller, in the days when there were continents with unexplored interiors. His papers on the fauna and flora made him known to scientific societies. And now he had come to a country practice —from choice. The penetrating power of his mind, acting like a corrosive fluid, had destroyed his ambition, I fancy. His intelligence is of a scientific order, of an investigating habit, and of that unappeasable curiosity which believes that there is a particle of a general truth in every mystery.

A good many years ago now, on my return from abroad, he invited me to stay with him. I came readily enough, and as he could not neglect his patients to keep me company, he took me on his rounds—thirty miles or so of an afternoon, sometimes. I waited for him on the roads; the horse reached after the leafy twigs, and, sitting high in the dogcart, I could hear Kennedy's laugh through the half-open door of some cottage. He had a big, hearty laugh that would have fitted a man twice his size, a brisk manner, a bronzed face, and a pair of gray, profoundly attentive eyes. He had the talent of making people talk to him freely, and an inexhaustible patience in listening to their tales.

One day, as we trotted out of a large village into a shady bit of road, I saw on our left hand a low, black cottage, with diamond panes in the windows, a creeper on the end wall, a roof of shingle, and some roses climbing on the rickety trellis-work of the tiny porch. Kennedy pulled up to a walk. A woman, in full sunlight, was throwing a dripping blanket over a line stretched between two old apple-trees. And as the bobtailed, long-necked chestnut, trying to get his head, jerked the left hand, covered by a thick dogskin glove, the doctor raised his voice over the hedge: "How's your child, Amy?"

I had the time to see her dull face, red, not with a mantling blush, but as if her flat cheeks had been vigorously slapped, and to take in the squat figure, the scanty, dusty brown hair drawn into a tight knot at the back of the head. She looked quite young. With a distinct catch in her breath, her voice sounded low and timid.

"He's well, thank you."

We trotted again. "A young patient of yours," I said; and the doctor, flicking the chestnut absently, muttered, "Her husband used to be."

"She seems a dull creature," I remarked, listlessly.

"Precisely," said Kennedy. "She is very passive. It's enough to look at the red hands hanging at the end of those short arms, at those slow, prominent brown eyes, to know the inertness of her mind—an inertness that one would think made it everlastingly safe from all the surprises of imagination. And yet which of us is safe? At any rate, such as you see her, she had enough imagination to fall in love. She's the daughter of one Isaac Foster, who from a small farmer has sunk into a shepherd; the beginning of his misfortunes dating from his runaway marriage with the cook of his widowed father—a well-to-do, apoplectic grazier, who passionately struck his name off his will, and had been heard to utter threats against his life. But this old affair, scandalous enough to serve as a motive for a Greek tragedy, arose from the similarity of their characters. There are other tragedies, less scandalous and of a subtler poignancy, arising from irreconcilable differences and from that fear of the Incomprehensible that hangs over all our heads—over all our heads. . . ."

The tired chestnut dropped into a walk; and the rim of the sun, all red in a speckless sky, touched familiarly the smooth top of a ploughed rise near the road as I had seen it times innumerable touch the distant horizon of the sea. The uniform brownness of the harrowed field glowed with a rose tinge, as though the powdered clods had sweated out in minute pearls of blood the toil of uncounted ploughmen. From the edge of a copse a waggon with two horses was rolling gently along the ridge. Raised above our heads upon the sky-line, it loomed up against the red sun, triumphantly big, enormous, like a chariot of giants drawn by two slow-stepping steeds of legendary proportions. And the clumsy figure of the man plodding at the head of the leading horse projected itself on the background of the Infinite with a heroic uncouthness. The end of his carter's whip quivered high up in the blue. Kennedy discoursed.

"She's the eldest of a large family. At the age of fifteen they put her out to service at the New Barns Farm. I attended Mrs. Smith, the tenant's wife, and saw that girl there for the first time. Mrs. Smith, a genteel person with a sharp nose, made her put on a black dress every afternoon. I don't know what induced me to notice her at all. There are faces that call your attention by a curious want of definiteness in their whole aspect, as, walking in a mist, you peer attentively at a vague shape which, after all, may be nothing more curious or strange than a signpost. The only peculiarity I perceived in her was a slight hesitation in her utterance, a sort of preliminary stammer which passes away with the first word. When sharply spoken to, she was apt to lose her head at once; but her heart was of the kindest.

She had never been heard to express a dislike for a single human being, and she was tender to every living creature. She was devoted to Mrs. Smith, to Mr. Smith, to their dogs, cats, canaries; and as to Mrs. Smith's gray parrot, its peculiarities exercised upon her a positive fascination. Nevertheless, when that outlandish bird, attacked by the cat, shrieked for help in human accents, she ran out into the yard stopping her ears, and did not prevent the crime. For Mrs. Smith this was another evidence of her stupidity; on the other hand, her want of charm, in view of Smith's well-known frivolousness, was a great recommendation. Her short-sighted eyes would swim with pity for a poor mouse in a trap, and she had been seen once by some boys on her knees in the wet grass helping a toad in difficulties. If it's true, as some German fellow has said, that without phosphorus there is no thought, it is still more true that there is no kindness of heart without a certain amount of imagination. She had some. She had even more than is necessary to understand suffering and to be moved by pity. She fell in love under circumstances that leave no room for doubt in the matter; for you need imagination to form a notion of beauty at all, and still more to discover your ideal in an unfamiliar shape.

"How this aptitude came to her, what it did feed upon, is an inscrutable mystery. She was born in the village, and had never been further away from it than Colebrook or perhaps Darnford. She lived for four years with the Smiths. New Barns is an isolated farmhouse a mile away from the road, and she was content to look day after day at the same fields, hollows, rises; at the trees and the hedgerows; at the faces of the four men about the farm, always the same—day after day, month after month, year after year. She never showed a desire for conversation, and, as it seemed to me, she did not know how to smile. Sometimes of a fine Sunday afternoon she would put on her best dress, a pair of stout boots, a large gray hat trimmed with a black feather (I've seen her in that finery), seize an absurdly slender parasol, climb over two stiles, tramp over three fields and along two hundred yards of road—never further. There stood Foster's cottage. She would help her mother to give their tea to the younger children, wash up the crockery, kiss the little ones, and go back to the farm. That was all. All the rest, all the change, all the relaxation. She never seemed to wish for anything more. And then she fell in love. She fell in love silently, obstinately—perhaps helplessly. It came slowly, but when it came it worked like a powerful spell; it was love as the Ancients understood it: an irresistible and fateful impulse—a possession! Yes, it was in her to become haunted and possessed by a face, by a presence, fatally, as though she had been a pagan worshipper of form under a joyous sky—and to be awakened at last from that mysterious forgetfulness of self, from that enchantment, from that transport, by a fear resembling the unaccountable terror of a brute. . . ."

With the sun hanging low on its western limit, the expanse of the grass-lands framed in the counter-scarps of the rising ground took on a gorgeous and sombre aspect. A sense of penetrating sadness, like that inspired by a grave strain of music, disengaged itself from the silence of the fields. The men we met walked past, slow, unsmiling, with downcast eyes, as if the melancholy of an over-burdened earth had weighted their feet, bowed their shoulders, borne down their glances.

"Yes," said the doctor to my remark, "one would think the earth is under a curse, since of all her children these that cling to her the closest are uncouth in body and as leaden of gait as if their very hearts were loaded with chains. But here on this same road you might have seen amongst these heavy men a being lithe, supple and long-limbed, straight like a pine, with something striving upwards in his appearance as though the heart within him had been buoyant. Perhaps it was only the force of the contrast, but when he was passing one of these villagers here, the soles of his feet did not seem to me to touch the dust of the road. He vaulted over the stiles, paced these slopes with a long elastic stride that made him noticeable at a great distance, and had lustrous black eyes. He was so different from the mankind around that, with his freedom of movement, his soft—a little startled, glance, his olive complexion and graceful bearing, his humanity suggested to me the nature of a woodland creature. He came from there."

The doctor pointed with his whip, and from the summit of the descent seen over the rolling tops of the trees in a park by the side of the road, appeared the level sea far below us, like the floor of an immense edifice inlaid with bands of dark ripple, with still trails of glitter, ending in a belt of glassy water at the foot of the sky. The light blurr of smoke, from an invisible steamer, faded on the great clearness of the horizon like the mist of a breath on a mirror; and, inshore, the white sails of a coaster, with the appearance of disentangling themselves slowly from under the branches, floated clear of the foliage of the trees.

"Shipwrecked in the bay?" I said.

"Yes; he was a castaway. A poor emigrant from Central Europe bound to America and washed ashore here in a storm. And for him, who knew nothing of the earth, England was an undiscovered country. It was some time before he learned its name; and for all I know he might have expected to find wild beasts or wild men here, when, crawling in the dark over the sea-wall, he rolled down the other side into a dyke, where it was another miracle he didn't get drowned. But he struggled instinctively like an animal under a net, and this blind struggle threw him out into a field. He must have been, indeed, of a tougher fibre than he looked to withstand without expiring such buffetings, the violence of his exertions, and so much fear. Later on, in his broken English that resembled curiously the speech of a young child, he told me himself that he put his trust in God, believing he was no longer in this world. And truly—he would add—how was he to know? He fought his way against the rain and the gale on all fours, and crawled at last among some sheep huddled close under the lee of a hedge. They ran off in all directions, bleating in the darkness, and he welcomed the first familiar sound he heard on these shores. It must have been two in the morning then. And this is all we know of the manner of his landing, though he did not arrive unattended by any means. Only his grisly company did not begin to come ashore till much later in the day. . . ."

The doctor gathered the reins, clicked his tongue; we trotted down the hill. Then turning, almost directly, a sharp corner into High Street, we rattled over the stones and were home.

Late in the evening Kennedy, breaking a spell of moodiness that had come over him, returned to the story. Smoking his pipe, he paced the long room from end to end. A reading-lamp concentrated all its light upon the papers on his desk; and, sitting by the open window, I saw, after the windless, scorching day, the frigid splendour of a hazy sea lying motionless under the moon. Not a whisper, not a splash, not a stir of the shingle, not a footstep, not a sigh came up from the earth below—never a sign of life but the scent of climbing jasmine: and Kennedy's voice, speaking behind me, passed through the wide casement, to vanish outside in a chill and sumptuous stillness.

". . . . The relations of shipwrecks in the olden time tell us of much suffering. Often the castaways were only saved from drowning to die miserably from starvation on a barren coast; others suffered violent death or else slavery, passing through years of precarious existence with people to whom their strangeness was an object of suspicion, dislike or fear. We read about these things, and they are very pitiful. It is indeed hard upon a man to find himself a lost stranger, helpless, incomprehensible, and of a mysterious origin, in some obscure corner of the earth. Yet amongst all the adventurers shipwrecked in all the wild parts of the world, there is not one, it seems to me, that ever had to suffer a fate so simply tragic as the man I am speaking of, the most innocent of adventurers cast out by the sea in the bight of this bay, almost within sight from this very window.

"He did not know the name of his ship. Indeed, in the course of time we discovered he did not even know that ships had names—'like Christian people'; and when, one day, from the top of Talfourd Hill, he beheld the sea lying open to his view, his eyes roamed afar, lost in an air of wild surprise, as though he had never seen such a sight before. And probably he had not. As far as I could make out, he had been hustled together with many others on board an emigrant ship at the mouth of the Elbe, too bewildered to take note of his surroundings, too weary to see anything, too anxious to care. They were driven below into the 'tween-deck and battened down from the very start. It was a low timber dwelling—he would say—with wooden beams overhead, like the houses in his country, but you went into it down a ladder. It was very large, very cold, damp and sombre, with places in the manner of wooden boxes where people had to sleep one above another, and it kept on rocking all ways at once all the time. He crept into one of these boxes and lay down there in the clothes in which he had left his home many days before, keeping his bundle and his stick by his side. People groaned, children cried, water dripped, the lights went out, the walls of the place creaked, and everything was being shaken so that in one's little box one dared not lift one's head. He had lost touch with his only companion (a young man from the same valley, he said), and all the time a great noise of wind went on outside and heavy blows fell—boom! boom! An awful sickness overcame him, even to the point of making him neglect his prayers. Besides, one could not tell whether it was morning or evening. It seemed always to be night in that place.

"Before that he had been travelling a long, long time on the iron track. He looked out of the window, which had a wonderfully clear glass in it, and the trees, the houses, the fields, and the long roads seemed to fly round and round about him till his head swam. He gave me to understand that he had on his passage beheld uncounted multitudes of people—whole nations—all dressed in such clothes as the rich wear. Once he was made to get out of the carriage, and slept through a night on a bench in a house of bricks with his bundle under his head; and once for many hours he had to sit on a floor of flat stones, dozing, with his knees up and with his bundle between his feet. There was a roof over him, which seemed made of glass, and was so high that the tallest mountain-pine he had ever seen would have had room to grow under it. Steam-machines rolled in at one end and out at the other. People swarmed more than you can see on a feast-day round the miraculous Holy Image in the yard of the Carmelite Convent down in the plains where, before he left his home, he drove his mother in a wooden cart:—a pious old woman who wanted to offer prayers and make a vow for his safety. He could not give me an idea of how large and lofty and full of noise and smoke and gloom, and clang of iron, the place was, but someone had told him it was called Berlin. Then they rang a bell, and another steam-machine came in, and again he was taken on and on through a land that wearied his eyes by its flatness without a single bit of a hill to be seen anywhere. One more night he spent shut up in a building like a good stable with a litter of straw on the floor, guarding his bundle amongst a lot of men, of whom not one could understand a single word he said. In the morning they were all led down to the stony shores of an extremely broad muddy river, flowing not between hills but between houses that seemed immense. There was a steam-machine that went on the water, and they all stood upon it packed tight, only now there were with them many women and children who made much noise. A cold rain fell, the wind blew in his face; he was wet through, and his teeth chattered. He and the young man from the same valley took each other by the hand.

"They thought they were being taken to America straight away, but suddenly the steam-machine bumped against the side of a thing like a great house on the water. The walls were smooth and black, and there uprose, growing from the roof as it were, bare trees in the shape of crosses, extremely high. That's how it appeared to him then, for he had never seen a ship before. This was the ship that was going to swim all the way to America. Voices shouted, everything swayed; there was a ladder dipping up and down. He went up on his hands and knees in mortal fear of falling into the water below, which made a great splashing. He got separated from his companion, and when he descended into the bottom of that ship his heart seemed to melt suddenly within him.

"It was then also, as he told me, that he lost contact for good and all with one of those three men who the summer before had been going about through all the little towns in the foothills of his country. They would arrive on market-days driving in a peasant's cart, and would set up an office in an inn or some other Jew's house. There were three of them, of whom one with a long beard looked venerable; and they had red cloth collars round their necks and gold lace on their sleeves like Government officials. They sat proudly behind a long table; and in the next room, so that the common people shouldn't hear, they kept a cunning telegraph machine, through which they could talk to the Emperor of America. The fathers hung about the door, but the young men of the mountains would crowd up to the table asking many questions, for there was work to be got all the year round at three dollars a day in America, and no military service to do.

"But the American Kaiser would not take everybody. Oh, no! He himself had a great difficulty in getting accepted, and the venerable man in uniform had to go out of the room several times to work the telegraph on his behalf. The American Kaiser engaged him at last at three dollars, he being young and strong. However, many able young men backed out, afraid of the great distance; besides, those only who had some money could be taken. There were some who sold their huts and their land because it cost a lot of money to get to America; but then, once there, you had three dollars a day, and if you were clever you could find places where true gold could be picked up on the ground. His father's house was getting over full.

Two of his brothers were married and had children. He promised to send money home from America by post twice a year. His father sold an old cow, a pair of piebald mountain ponies of his own raising, and a cleared plot of fair pasture land on the sunny slope of a pineclad pass to a Jew inn-keeper, in order to pay the people of the ship that took men to America to get rich in a short time.

"He must have been a real adventurer at heart, for how many of the greatest enterprises in the conquest of the earth had for their beginning just such a bargaining away of the paternal cow for the mirage or true gold far away! I have been telling you more or less in my own words what I learned fragmentarily in the course of two or three years, during which I seldom missed an opportunity of a friendly chat with him. He told me this story of his adventure with many flashes of white teeth and lively glances of black eyes, at first in a sort of anxious baby-talk, then, as he acquired the language, with great fluency, but always with that singing, soft, and at the same time vibrating intonation that instilled a strangely penetrating power into the sound of the most familiar English words, as if they had been the words of an unearthly language. And he always would come to an end, with many emphatic shakes of his head, upon that awful sensation of his heart melting within him directly he set foot on board that ship. Afterwards there seemed to come for him a period of blank ignorance, at any rate as to facts. No doubt he must have been abominably seasick and abominably unhappy—this soft and passionate adventurer, taken thus out of his knowledge, and feeling bitterly as he lay in his emigrant bunk his utter loneliness; for his was a highly sensitive nature. The next thing we know of him for certain is that he had been hiding in Hammond's pig-pound by the side of the road to Norton, six miles, as the crow flies, from the sea. Of these experiences he was unwilling to speak: they seemed to have seared into his soul a sombre sort of wonder and indignation. Through the rumours of the country-side, which lasted for a good many days after his arrival, we know that the fishermen of West Colebrook had been disturbed and startled by heavy knocks against the walls of weather-board cottages, and by a voice crying piercingly strange words in the night. Several of them turned out even, but, no doubt, he had fled in sudden alarm at their rough angry tones hailing each other in the darkness. A sort of frenzy must have helped him up the steep Norton hill. It was he, no doubt, who early the following morning had been seen lying (in a swoon, I should say) on the roadside grass by the Brenzett carrier, who actually got down to have a nearer look, but drew back, intimidated by the perfect immobility, and by something queer in the aspect of that tramp, sleeping so still under the showers. As the day advanced, some children came dashing into school at Norton in such a fright that the schoolmistress went out and spoke indignantly to a 'horrid-looking man' on the road. He edged away, hanging his head, for a few steps, and then suddenly ran off with extraordinary fleetness. The driver of Mr. Bradley's milk-cart made no secret of it that he had lashed with his whip at a hairy sort of gipsy fellow who, jumping up at a turn of the road by the Vents, made a snatch at the pony's bridle. And he caught him a good one, too, right over the face, he said, that made him drop down in the mud a jolly sight quicker than he had jumped up; but it was a good half a mile before he could stop the pony. Maybe that in his desperate endeavours to get help, and in his need to get in touch with someone, the poor devil had tried to stop the cart. Also three boys confessed afterwards to throwing stones at a funny tramp, knocking about all wet and muddy, and, it seemed, very drunk, in the narrow deep lane by the limekilns. All this was the talk of three villages for days; but we have Mrs. Finn's (the wife of Smith's waggoner) unimpeachable testimony that she saw him get over the low wall of Hammond's pig-pound and lurch straight at her, babbling aloud in a voice that was enough to make one die of fright. Having the baby with her in a perambulator, Mrs. Finn called out to him to go away, and as he persisted in coming nearer, she hit him courageously with her umbrella over the head, and, without once looking back, ran like the wind with the perambulator as far as the first house in the village. She stopped then, out of breath, and spoke to old Lewis, hammering there at a heap of stones; and the old chap, taking off his immense black wire goggles, got up on his shaky legs to look where she pointed. Together they followed with their eyes the figure of the man running over a field; they saw him fall down, pick himself up, and run on again, staggering and waving his long arms above his head, in the direction of the New Barns Farm. From that moment he is plainly in the toils of his obscure and touching destiny. There is no doubt after this of what happened to him. All is certain now: Mrs. Smith's intense terror; Amy Foster's stolid conviction held against the other's nervous attack, that the man 'meant no harm'; Smith's exasperation (on his return from Darnford Market) at finding the dog barking himself into a fit, the back-door locked, his wife in hysterics; and all for an unfortunate dirty tramp, supposed to be even then lurking in his stackyard, Was he? He would teach him to frighten women.

"Smith is notoriously hot-tempered, but the sight of some nondescript and miry creature sitting cross-legged amongst a lot of loose straw, and swinging itself to and fro like a bear in a cage, made him pause. Then this tramp stood up silently before him, one mass of mud and filth from head to foot. Smith, alone amongst his stacks with this apparition, in the stormy twilight ringing with the infuriated barking of the dog, felt the dread of an inexplicable strangeness. But when that being, parting with his black hands the long matted locks that hung before his face, as you part the two halves of a curtain, looked out at him with glistening, wild, black-and-white eyes, the weirdness of this silent encounter fairly staggered him. He has admitted since (for the story has been a legitimate subject of conversation about here for years) that he made more than one step backwards. Then a sudden burst of rapid, senseless speech persuaded him at once that he had to do with an escaped lunatic. In fact, that impression never wore off completely. Smith has not in his heart given up his secret conviction of the man's essential insanity to this very day.

"As the creature approached him, jabbering in a most discomposing manner, Smith (unaware that he was being addressed as 'gracious lord,' and adjured in God's name to afford food and shelter) kept on speaking firmly but gently to it, and retreating all the time into the other yard. At last, watching his chance, by a sudden charge he bundled him headlong into the wood-lodge, and instantly shot the bolt. Thereupon he wiped his brow, though the day was cold. He had done his duty to the community by shutting up a wandering and probably dangerous maniac. Smith isn't a hard man at all, but he had room in his brain only for that one idea of lunacy. He was not imaginative enough to ask himself whether the man might not be perishing with cold and hunger. Meantime, at first, the maniac made a great deal of noise in the lodge. Mrs. Smith was screaming upstairs, where she had locked herself in her bedroom; but Amy Foster sobbed piteously at the kitchen-door, wringing her hands and muttering, 'Don't! don't!' I daresay Smith had a rough time of it that evening with one noise and another, and this insane, disturbing voice crying obstinately through the door only added to his irritation. He couldn't possibly have connected this troublesome lunatic with the sinking of a ship in Eastbay, of which there had been a rumour in the Darnford market place. And I daresay the man inside had been very near to insanity on that night. Before his excitement collapsed and he became unconscious he was throwing himself violently about in the dark, rolling on some dirty sacks, and biting his fists with rage, cold, hunger, amazement, and despair.

"He was a mountaineer of the eastern range of the Carpathians, and the vessel sunk the night before in Eastbay was the Hamburg emigrant-ship *Herzogin Sophia-Dorothea,* of appalling memory.

"A few months later we could read in the papers the accounts of the bogus 'Emigration Agencies' among the Sclavonian peasantry in the more remote provinces of Austria. The object of these scoundrels was to get hold of the poor ignorant people's homesteads, and they were in league with the local usurers. They exported their victims through Hamburg mostly. As to the ship, I had watched her out of this very window, reaching close-hauled under short canvas into the bay on a dark, threatening afternoon. She came to an anchor, correctly by the chart, off the Brenzett

Coastguard station. I remember before the night fell looking out again at the outlines of her spars and rigging that stood out dark and pointed on a background of ragged, slaty clouds like another and a slighter spire to the left of the Brenzett church-tower. In the evening the wind rose. At midnight I could hear in my bed the terrific gusts and the sounds of a driving deluge.

"About that time the Coastguardmen thought they saw the lights of a steamer over the anchoring-ground. In a moment they vanished; but it is clear that another vessel of some sort had tried for shelter in the bay on that awful, blind night, had rammed the German ship amidships (a breach—as one of the divers told me afterwards—'that you could sail a Thames barge through'), and then had gone out either scathless or damaged, who shall say; but had gone out, unknown, unseen, and fatal, to perish mysteriously at sea. Of her nothing ever came to light, and yet the hue and cry that was raised all over the world would have found her out if she had been in existence anywhere on the face of the waters.

"A completeness without a clue, and a stealthy silence as of a neatly executed crime, characterize this murderous disaster, which, as you may remember, had its gruesome celebrity. The wind would have prevented the loudest outcries from reaching the shore; there had been evidently no time for signals of distress. It was death without any sort of fuss. The Hamburg ship, filling all at once, capsized as she sank, and at daylight there was not even the end of a spar to be seen above water. She was missed, of course, and at first the Coastguardmen surmised that she had either dragged her anchor or parted her cable some time during the night, and had been blown out to sea. Then, after the tide turned, the wreck must have shifted a little and released some of the bodies, because a child—a little fair-haired child in a red frock—came ashore abreast of the Martello tower. By the afternoon you could see along three miles of beach dark figures with bare legs dashing in and out of the tumbling foam, and rough-looking men, women with hard faces, children, mostly fair-haired, were being carried, stiff and dripping, on stretchers, on wattles, on ladders, in a long procession past the door of the "Ship Inn," to be laid out in a row under the north wall of the Brenzett Church.

"Officially, the body of the little girl in the red frock is the first thing that came ashore from that ship. But I have patients amongst the seafaring population of West Colebrook, and, unofficially, I am informed that very early that morning two brothers, who went down to look after their cobble hauled up on the beach, found a good way from Brenzett, an ordinary ship's hencoop, lying high and dry on the shore, with eleven drowned ducks inside. Their families ate the birds, and the hencoop was split into firewood with a hatchet. It is possible that a man (supposing he happened to be on deck at the time of the accident) might have floated ashore on that hencoop. He might. I admit it is improbable, but there was the man—and for days, nay, for weeks—it didn't enter our heads that we had amongst us the only living soul that had escaped from that disaster. The man himself, even when he learned to speak intelligibly, could tell us very little. He remembered he had felt better (after the ship had anchored, I suppose), and that the darkness, the wind, and the rain took his breath away. This looks as if he had been on deck some time during that night. But we mustn't forget he had been taken out of his knowledge, that he had been sea-sick and battened down below for four days, that he had no general notion of a ship or of the sea, and therefore could have no definite idea of what was happening to him. The rain, the wind, the darkness he knew; he understood the bleating of the sheep, and he remembered the pain of his wretchedness and misery, his heartbroken astonishment that it was neither seen nor understood, his dismay at finding all the men angry and all the women fierce. He had approached them as a beggar, it is true, he said; but in his country, even if they gave nothing, they spoke gently to beggars. The children in his country were not taught to throw stones at those who asked for compassion. Smith's strategy overcame him completely. The wood-lodge presented the horrible aspect of a dungeon. What would be done to him next? . . . No wonder that Amy Foster appeared to his eyes with the aureole of an angel of light. The girl had not been able to sleep for thinking of the poor man, and in the morning, before the Smiths were up, she slipped out across the back yard. Holding the door of the wood-lodge ajar, she looked in and extended to him half a loaf of white bread—'such bread as the rich eat in my country,' he used to say.

"At this he got up slowly from amongst all sorts of rubbish, stiff, hungry, trembling, miserable, and doubtful. 'Can you eat this?' she asked in her soft and timid voice. He must have taken her for a 'gracious lady.' He devoured ferociously, and tears were falling on the crust. Suddenly he dropped the bread, seized her wrist, and imprinted a kiss on her hand. She was not frightened. Through his forlorn conditions she had observed that he was good-looking. She shut the door and walked back slowly to the kitchen. Much later on, she told Mrs. Smith, who shuddered at the bare idea of being touched by that creature.

"Through this act of impulsive pity he was brought back again within the pale of human relations with his new surroundings. He never forgot it—never.

"That very same morning old Mr. Swaffer (Smith's nearest neighbour) came over to give his advice, and ended by carrying him off. He stood, unsteady on his legs, meek, and caked over in half-dried mud, while the two men talked around him in an incomprehensible tongue. Mrs. Smith had refused to come downstairs till the madman was off the premises; Amy Foster, far from within the dark kitchen, watched through the open back-door; and he obeyed the signs that were made to him to the best of his ability. But Smith was full of mistrust. 'Mind, sir! It may be all his cunning,' he cried repeatedly in a tone of warning. When Mr. Swaffer started the mare, the deplorable being sitting humbly by his side, through weakness, nearly fell out over the back of the high two-wheeled cart. Swaffer took him straight home. And it is then that I come upon the scene.

"I was called in by the simple process of the old man beckoning to me with his forefinger over the gate of his house as I happened to be driving past. I got down, of course.

" 'I've got something here,' he mumbled, leading the way to an out-house at a little distance from his other farm-buildings.

"It was there that I saw him first, in a long, low room taken upon the space of that sort of coach-house. It was bare and whitewashed, with a small square aperture glazed with one cracked, dusty pane at its further end. He was lying on his back upon a straw pallet; they had given him a couple of horse-blankets, and he seemed to have spent the remainder of his strength in the exertion of cleaning himself. He was almost speechless; his quick breathing under the blankets pulled up to his chin, his glittering, restless black eyes reminded me of a wild bird caught in a snare. While I was examining him, old Swaffer stood silently by the door, passing the tips of his fingers along his shaven upper lip. I gave some directions, promised to send a bottle of medicine, and naturally made some enquiries.

" 'Smith caught him in the stackyard at New Barns,' said the old chap in his deliberate, unmoved manner, and as if the other had been indeed a sort of wild animal. 'That's how I came by him. Quite a curiosity, isn't he? Now tell me, doctor—you've been all over the world—don't you think that's a bit of a Hindoo we've got hold of here?"

"I was greatly surprised. His long black hair scattered over the straw bolster contrasted with the olive pallor of his face. It occurred to me he might be a Basque. It didn't necessarily follow that he should understand Spanish; but I tried him with the few words I know, and also with some French. The whispered sounds I caught by bending my ear to his lips puzzled me utterly. That afternoon the young ladies from the Rectory (one of them read Goethe with a dictionary, and the other had struggled with Dante for years), coming to see Miss Swaffer, tried their German and Italian on him from the doorway. They retreated, just the least bit scared by the flood of passionate speech which, turning on his pallet, he let out at them. They admitted that the sound was pleasant, soft, musical—but, in conjunction with his looks perhaps, it was startling—so excitable, so utterly unlike anything one had ever heard. The village boys climbed up the bank to have a peep through the little square aperture. Everybody was wondering what Mr. Swaffer would do with him.

"He simply kept him.

"Swaffer would be called eccentric were he not so much respected. They will tell you that Mr. Swaffer sits up as late as ten o'clock at night to read books, and they will tell you also that he can write a cheque for two hundred pounds without thinking twice about it. He himself would tell you that the Swaffers had owned land between this and Darnford for these three hundred years. He must be eighty-five to-day, but he does not look a bit older than when I first came here. He is a great breeder of sheep, and deals extensively in cattle. He attends market days for miles around in every sort of weather, and drives sitting bowed low over the reins, his lank gray hair curling over the collar of his warm coat, and with a green plaid rug round his legs. The calmness of advanced age gives a solemnity to his manner. He is clean-shaved; his lips are thin and sensitive; something rigid and monachal in the set of his features lends a certain elevation to the character of his face. He has been known to drive miles in the rain to see a new kind of rose in somebody's garden, or a monstrous cabbage grown by a cottager. He loves to hear tell of or to be shown something what he calls 'outlandish.' Perhaps it was just that outlandishness of the man which influenced old Swaffer. Perhaps it was only an inexplicable caprice. All I know is that at the end of three weeks I caught sight of Smith's lunatic digging in Swaffer's kitchen garden. They had found out he could use a spade. He dug barefooted.

"His black hair flowed over his shoulders. I suppose it was Swaffer who had given him the striped old cotton shirt; but he wore still the national brown cloth trousers (in which he had been washed ashore) fitting to the leg almost like tights; was belted with a broad leathern belt studded with little brass discs; and had never yet ventured into the village. The land he looked upon seemed to him kept neatly, like the grounds round a landowner's house; the size of the cart-horses struck him with astonishment; the roads resembled garden walks, and the aspect of the people, especially on Sundays, spoke of opulence. He wondered what made them so hardhearted and their children so bold. He got his food at the back-door, carried it in both hands, carefully, to his outhouse, and, sitting alone on his pallet, would make the sign of the cross before he began. Beside the same pallet, kneeling in the early darkness of the short days, he recited aloud the Lord's Prayer before he slept. Whenever he saw old Swaffer he would bow with veneration from the waist, and stand erect while the old man, with his fingers over his upper lip, surveyed him silently. He bowed also to Miss Swaffer, who kept house frugally for her father—a broad-shouldered, big-boned woman of forty-five, with the pocket of her dress full of keys, and a gray, steady eye. She was Church—as people said (while her father was one of the trustees of the Baptist Chapel)—and wore a little steel cross at her waist. She dressed severely in black, in memory of one of the innumerable Bradleys of the neighbourhood, to whom she had been engaged some twenty-five years ago—a young farmer who broke his neck out hunting on the eve of the wedding-day. She had the unmoved countenance of the deaf, spoke very seldom, and her lips, thin like her father's, astonished one sometimes by a mysteriously ironic curl.

"These were the people to whom he owed allegiance, and an overwhelming loneliness seemed to fall from the leaden sky of that winter without sunshine. All the faces were sad. He could talk to no one, and had no hope of ever understanding anybody. It was as if these had been the faces of people from the other world—dead people—he used to tell me years afterwards. Upon my word, I wonder he did not go mad. He didn't know where he was. Somewhere very far from his mountains—somewhere over the water. Was this America, he wondered?

"If it hadn't been for the steel cross at Miss Swaffer's belt he would not, he confessed, have known whether he was in a Christian country at all. He used to cast stealthy glances at it, and feel comforted. There was nothing here the same as in his country! The earth and the water were different; there were no images of the Redeemer by the roadside. The very grass was different, and the trees. All the trees but the three old Norway pines on the bit of lawn before Swaffer's house, and these reminded him of his country. He had been detected once, after dusk, with his forehead against the trunk of one of them, sobbing, and talking to himself. They had been like brothers to him at that time, he affirmed. Everything else was strange. Conceive you the kind of an existence over-shadowed, oppressed, by the everyday material appearances, as if by the visions of a nightmare. At night, when he could not sleep, he kept on thinking of the girl who gave him the first piece of bread he had eaten in this foreign land. She had been neither fierce nor angry, nor frightened. Her face he remembered as the only comprehensible face amongst all these faces that were as closed, as mysterious, and as mute as the faces of the dead who are possessed of a knowledge beyond the comprehension of the living. I wonder whether the memory of her compassion prevented him from cutting his throat. But there! I suppose I am an old sentimentalist, and forget the instinctive love of life which it takes all the strength of an uncommon despair to overcome.

"He did the work which was given him with an intelligence which surprised old Swaffer. By-and-by it was discovered that he could help at the ploughing, could milk the cows, feed the bullocks in the cattle-yard, and was of some use with the sheep. He began to pick up words, too, very fast;

and suddenly, one fine morning in spring, he rescued from an untimely death a grand-child of old Swaffer.

"Swaffer's younger daughter is married to Willcox, a solicitor and the Town Clerk of Colebrook. Regularly twice a year they come to stay with the old man for a few days. Their only child, a little girl not three years old at the time, ran out of the house alone in her little white pinafore, and, toddling across the grass of a terraced garden, pitched herself over a low wall head first into the horsepond in the yard below.

"Our man was out with the waggoner and the plough in the field nearest to the house, and as he was leading the team round to begin a fresh furrow, he saw, through the gap of a gate, what for anybody else would have been a mere flutter of something white. But he had straight-glancing, quick, far-reaching eyes, that only seemed to flinch and lose their amazing power before the immensity of the sea. He was barefooted, and looking as outlandish as the heart of Swaffer could desire. Leaving the horses on the turn, to the inexpressible disgust of the waggoner he bounded off, going over the ploughed ground in long leaps, and suddenly appeared before the mother, thrust the child into her arms, and strode away.

"The pond was not very deep; but still, if he had not had such good eyes, the child would have perished—miserably suffocated in the foot or so of sticky mud at the bottom. Old Swaffer walked out slowly into the field, waited till the plough came over to his side, had a good look at him, and without saying a word went back to the house. But from that time they laid out his meals on the kitchen table; and at first, Miss Swaffer, all in black and with an inscrutable face, would come and stand in the doorway of the living-room to see him make a big sign of the cross before he fell to. I believe that from that day, too, Swaffer began to pay him regular wages.

"I can't follow step by step his development. He cut his hair short, was seen in the village and along the road going to and fro to his work like any other man. Children ceased to shout after him. He became aware of social differences, but remained for a long time surprised at the bare poverty of the churches among so much wealth. He couldn't understand either why they were kept shut up on week-days. There was nothing to steal in them. Was it to keep people from praying too often? The rectory took much notice of him about that time, and I believe the young ladies attempted to prepare the ground for his conversion. They could not, however, break him of his habit of crossing himself, but he went so far as to take off the string with a couple of brass medals the size of a sixpence, a tiny metal cross, and a square sort of scapulary which he wore round his neck. He hung them on the wall by the side of his bed, and he was still to be heard every evening reciting the Lord's Prayer, in incomprehensible words and in a slow, fervent tone, as he had heard his old father do at the head of all the kneeling family, big and little, on every evening of his life. And though he wore corduroys at work, and a slop-made pepper-and-salt suit on Sundays, strangers would turn round to look after him on the road. His foreignness had a peculiar and indelible stamp. At last people became used to see him. But they never became used to him. His rapid, skimming walk; his swarthy complexion; his hat cocked on the left ear; his habit, on warm evenings, of wearing his coat over one shoulder, like a hussar's dolman; his manner of leaping over the stiles, not as a feat of agility, but in the ordinary course of progression—all these peculiarities were, as one may say, so many causes of scorn and offence to the inhabitants of the village. *They* wouldn't in their dinner hour lie flat on their backs on the grass to stare at the sky. Neither did they go about the fields screaming dismal tunes. Many times have I heard his high-pitched voice from behind the ridge of some sloping sheep-walk, a voice light and soaring, like a lark's, but with a melancholy human note, over our fields that hear only the song of birds. And I would be startled myself. Ah! He was different; innocent of heart, and full of good will, which nobody wanted, this castaway, that, like a man transplanted into another planet, was separated by an immense space from his past and by an immense ignorance from his future. His quick, fervent utterance positively shocked everybody. 'An excitable devil,' they called him. One evening, in the tap-room of the Coach and Horses, (having drunk some whisky), he upset them all by singing a love-song of his country. They hooted him down, and he was pained; but Preble, the lame wheelwright, and Vincent, the fat blacksmith, and the other notables, too, wanted to drink their evening beer in peace. On another occasion he tried to show them how to dance. The dust rose in clouds from the sanded floor; he leaped straight up amongst the deal tables, struck his heels together, squatted on one heel in front of old Preble, shooting out the other leg, uttered wild and exulting cries, jumped up to whirl on one foot, snapping his fingers above his head—and a strange carter who was having a drink in there began to swear, and cleared out with his half-pint in his hand into the bar. But when suddenly he sprang upon a table and continued to dance among the glasses, the landlord interfered. He didn't want any 'acrobat tricks in the tap-room.' They laid their hands on him. Having had a glass or two, Mr. Swaffer's foreigner tried to expostulate: was ejected forcibly: got a black eye.

"I believe he felt the hostility of his human surroundings. But he was tough—tough in spirit, too, as well as in body. Only the memory of the sea frightened him, with that vague terror that is left by a bad dream. His home was far away; and he did not want now to go to America. I had often explained to him that there is no place on earth where true gold can be found lying ready and to be got for the trouble of the picking up. How, then, he asked, could he ever return home with empty hands when there had been sold a cow, two ponies, and a bit of land to pay for his going? His eyes would fill with tears, and, averting them from the immense shimmer of the sea, he would throw himself face down on the grass. But sometimes, cocking his hat with a little conquering air, he would defy my wisdom. He had found his bit of true gold. That was Amy Foster's heart; which was 'a golden heart, and soft to people's misery,' he would say in the accents of overwhelming conviction.

"He was called Yanko. He had explained that this meant Little John; but as he would also repeat very often that he was a mountaineer (some word sounding in the dialect of his country like Goorall) he got it for his surname. And this is the only trace of him that the succeeding ages may find in the marriage register of the parish. There it stands—Yanko Goorall—in the rector's handwriting. The crooked cross made by the castaway, a cross whose tracing no doubt seemed to him the most solemn part of the whole ceremony, is all that remains now to perpetuate the memory of his name.

"His courtship had lasted some time—ever since he got his precarious footing in the community. It began by his buying for Amy Foster a green satin ribbon in Darnford. This was what you did in his country. You bought a ribbon at a Jew's stall on a fair-day. I don't suppose the girl knew what to do with it, but he seemed to think that his honourable intentions could not be mistaken.

"It was only when he declared his purpose to get married that I fully understood how, for a hundred futile and inappreciable reasons, how—shall I say odious?—he was to all the countryside. Every old woman in the village was up in arms. Smith, coming upon him near the farm, promised to break his head for him if he found him about again. But he twisted his little black moustache with such a bellicose air and rolled such big, black fierce eyes at Smith that this promise came to nothing. Smith, however, told the girl that she must be mad to take up with a man who was surely wrong in his head. All the same, when she heard him in the gloaming whistle from beyond the orchard a couple of bars of a weird and mournful tune, she would drop whatever she had in her hand—she would leave Mrs. Smith in the middle of a sentence—and she would run out to his call. Mrs. Smith called her a shameless hussy. She answered nothing. She said nothing at all to anybody, and went on her way as if she had been deaf. She and I alone in all the land, I fancy, could see his very real beauty. He was very good-looking, and most graceful in his bearing, with that something wild as of a woodland creature in his aspect. Her mother moaned over her dismally whenever the girl came to see her on her day out. The father was surly, but pretended not to know; and Mrs. Finn once told her plainly that 'this man, my dear, will do you some harm some day yet.' And so it went on. They could be seen on the roads, she tramping stolidly in her finery—gray dress, black feather, stout boots, prominent white cotton gloves that caught your eye a hundred yards away; and he, his coat slung picturesquely over one shoulder, pacing by her side, gallant of bearing and casting tender glances upon the girl with the golden heart. I wonder whether he saw how plain she was. Perhaps among types so different from what he had ever seen, he had not the power to judge; or perhaps he was seduced by the divine quality of her pity.

"Yanko was in great trouble meantime. In his country you get an old man for an ambassador in marriage affairs. He did not know how to proceed. However, one day in the midst of sheep in a field (he was now Swaffer's under-shepherd with Foster) he took off his hat to the father and declared himself humbly. 'I daresay she's fool enough to marry you,' was all Foster said. 'And then,' he used to relate, 'he puts his hat on his head, looks black at me as if he wanted to cut my throat, whistles the dog, and off he goes, leaving me to do the work.' The Fosters, of course, didn't like to lose the wages the girl earned: Amy used to give all her money to her mother. But there was in Foster a very genuine aversion to that match. He contended that the fellow was very good with sheep, but was not fit for any girl to marry. For one thing, he used to go along the hedges muttering to himself like a dam' fool; and then, these foreigners behave very queerly to women sometimes. And perhaps he would want to carry her off somewhere—or run off himself. It was not safe. He preached it to his daughter that the fellow might ill-use her in some way. She made no answer. It was, they said in the village, as if the man had done something to her. People discussed the matter. It was quite an excitement, and the two went on 'walking out' together in the face of opposition. Then something unexpected happened.

"I don't know whether old Swaffer ever understood how much he was regarded in the light of a father by his foreign retainer. Anyway the relation was curiously feudal. So when Yanko asked formally for an interview—'and the Miss, too' (he called the severe, deaf Miss Swaffer simply *Miss*)—it was to obtain their permission to marry. Swaffer heard him unmoved, dismissed him by a nod, and then shouted the intelligence into Miss Swaffer's best ear. She showed no surprise, and only remarked grimly, in a veiled blank voice, 'He certainly won't get any other girl to marry him.'

"It is Miss Swaffer who has all the credit of the munificence: but in a very few days it came out that Mr. Swaffer had presented Yanko with a cottage (the cottage you've seen this morning) and something like an acre of ground—had made it over to him in absolute property. Willcox expedited the deed, and I remember him telling me he had a great pleasure in making it ready. It recited: 'In consideration of saving the life of my beloved grandchild, Bertha Willcox.'

"Of course, after that no power on earth could prevent them from getting married.

"Her infatuation endured. People saw her going out to meet him in the evening. She stared with unblinking, fascinated eyes up the road where he was expected to appear, walking freely, with a swing from the hip, and humming one of the love-tunes of his country. When the boy was born, he got elevated at the 'Coach and Horses,' essayed again a song and a dance, and was again ejected. People expressed their commiseration for a woman married to that Jack-in-the-box. He didn't care. There was a man now (he told me boastfully) to whom he could sing and talk in the language of his country, and show how to dance by-and-by.

"But I don't know. To me he appeared to have grown less springy of step, heavier in body, less keen of eye. Imagination, no doubt; but it seems to me now as if the net of fate had been drawn closer round him already.

"One day I met him on the footpath over the Talfourd Hill. He told me that 'women were funny.' I had heard already of domestic differences. People were saying that Amy Foster was beginning to find out what sort of man she had married. He looked upon the sea with indifferent, unseeing eyes. His wife had snatched the child out of his arms one day as he sat on the doorstep crooning to it a song such as the mothers sing to babies in his mountains. She seemed to think he was doing it some harm. Women are funny. And she had objected to him praying aloud in the evening. Why? He expected the boy to repeat the prayer aloud after him by-and-by, as he used to do after his old father when he was a child—in his own country. And I discovered he longed for their boy to grow up so that he could have a man to talk with in that language that to our ears sounded so disturbing, so passionate, and so bizarre. Why his wife should dislike the idea he couldn't tell. But that would pass, he said. And tilting his head knowingly, he tapped his breastbone to indicate that she had a good heart: not hard, not fierce, open to compassion, charitable to the poor!

"I walked away thoughtfully; I wondered whether his difference, his strangeness, were not penetrating with repulsion that dull nature they had begun by irresistibly attracting. I wondered. . . ."

The Doctor came to the window and looked out at the frigid splendour of the sea, immense in the haze, as if enclosing all the earth with all the hearts lost among the passions of love and fear.

"Physiologically, now," he said, turning away abruptly, "it was possible. It was possible."

He remained silent. Then went on—

"At all events, the next time I saw him he was ill—lung trouble. He was tough, but I daresay he was not acclimatized as well as I had supposed. It was a bad winter; and, of course, these mountaineers do get fits of home sickness; and a state of depression would make him vulnerable. He was lying half dressed on a couch downstairs.

"A table covered with a dark oilcloth took up all the middle of the little room. There was a wicker cradle on the floor, a kettle spouting steam on the hob, and some child's linen lay drying on the fender. The room was warm, but the door opens right into the garden, as you noticed perhaps.

"He was very feverish, and kept on muttering to himself. She sat on a chair and looked at him fixedly across the table with her brown, blurred eyes. 'Why don't you have him upstairs?' I asked. With a start and a confused stammer she said, 'Oh! ah! I couldn't sit with him upstairs, sir.'

"I gave her certain directions; and going outside, I said again that he ought to be in bed upstairs. She wrung her hands. 'I couldn't. I couldn't. He keeps on saying something—I don't know what.' With the memory of all the talk against the man that had been dinned into her ears, I looked at her narrowly. I looked into her short-sighted eyes, at her dumb eyes that once in her life had seen an enticing shape, but seemed, staring at me, to see nothing at all now. But I saw she was uneasy.

" 'What's the matter with him?' she asked in a sort of vacant trepidation. 'He doesn't look very ill. I never did see anybody look like this before. . . .'

" 'Do you think,' I asked indignantly, 'he is shamming?'

" 'I can't help it, sir,' she said, stolidly. And suddenly she clapped her hands and looked right and left. 'And there's the baby. I am so frightened. He wanted me just now to give him the baby. I can't understand what he says to it.'

" 'Can't you ask a neighbour to come in to-night?' I asked.

" 'Please, sir, nobody seems to care to come,' she muttered, dully resigned all at once.

"I impressed upon her the necessity of the greatest care, and then had to go. There was a good deal of sickness that winter. 'Oh, I hope he won't talk!' she exclaimed softly just as I was going away.

"I don't know how it is I did not see—but I didn't. And yet, turning in my trap, I saw her lingering before the door, very still, and as if meditating a flight up the miry road.

"Towards the night his fever increased.

"He tossed, moaned, and now and then muttered a complaint. And she sat with the table between her and the couch, watching every movement and every sound, with the terror, the unreasonable terror, of that man she could not understand creeping over her. She had drawn the wicker cradle close to her feet. There was nothing in her now but the maternal instinct and that unaccountable fear.

"Suddenly coming to himself, parched, he demanded a drink of water. She did not move. She had not understood, though he may have thought he was speaking in English. He waited, looking at her, burning with fever, amazed at her silence and immobility, and then he shouted impatiently, 'Water! Give me water!'

"She jumped to her feet, snatched up the child, and stood still. He spoke to her, and his passionate remonstrances only increased her fear of that strange man. I believe he spoke to her for a long time, entreating, wondering, pleading, ordering, I suppose. She says she bore it as long as she could. And then a gust of rage came over him.

"He sat up and called out terribly one word—some word. Then he got up as though he hadn't been ill at all, she says. And as in fevered dismay, indignation, and wonder he tried to get to her round the table, she simply opened the door and ran out with the child in her arms. She heard him call twice after her down the road in a terrible voice—and fled. . . . Ah! but you should have seen stirring behind the dull, blurred glance of those eyes the spectre of the fear which had hunted her on that night three miles and a half to the door of Foster's cottage! I did the next day.

"And it was I who found him lying face down and his body in a puddle, just outside the little wicker-gate.

"I had been called out that night to an urgent case in the village, and on my way home at daybreak passed by the cottage. The door stood open. My man helped me to carry him in. We laid him on the couch. The lamp smoked, the fire was out, the chill of the stormy night oozed from the cheerless yellow paper on the wall. 'Amy!' I called aloud, and my voice seemed to lose itself in the emptiness of this tiny house as if I had cried in a desert. He opened his eyes. 'Gone!' he said, distinctly. 'I had only asked for water—only for a little water. . . .'

"He was muddy. I covered him up and stood waiting in silence, catching a painfully gasped word now and then. They were no longer in his own language. The fever had left him, taking with it the heat of life. And with his panting breast and lustrous eyes he reminded me again of a wild creature under the net; of a bird caught in a snare. She had left him. She had left him—sick—helpless—thirsty. The spear of the hunter had entered his very soul. 'Why?' he cried, in the penetrating and indignant voice of a man calling to a responsible Maker. A gust of wind and a swish of rain answered.

"And as I turned away to shut the door he pronounced the word 'Merciful!' and expired.

"Eventually I certified heart-failure as the immediate cause of death. His heart must have indeed failed him, or else he might have stood this night of storm and exposure, too. I closed his eyes and drove away. Not very far from the cottage I met Foster walking sturdily between the dripping hedges with his collie at his heels.

" 'Do you know where your daughter is?' I asked.

" 'Don't I!' he cried. 'I am going to talk to him a bit. Frightening a poor woman like this.'

" 'He won't frighten her any more,' I said. 'He is dead.'

"He struck with his stick at the mud.

" 'And there's the child.'

"Then, after thinking deeply for a while—

" 'I don't know that it isn't for the best.'

"That's what he said. And she says nothing at all now. Not a word of him. Never. Is his image as utterly gone from her mind as his lithe and striding figure, his carolling voice are gone from our fields? He is no longer before her eyes to excite her imagination into a passion of love or fear; and his memory seems to have vanished from her dull brain as a shadow passes away upon a white screen. She lives in the cottage and works for Miss Swaffer. She is Amy Foster for everybody, and the child is 'Amy Foster's boy.' She calls him Johnny—which means Little John.

"It is impossible to say whether this name recalls anything to her. Does she ever think of the past? I have seen her hanging over the boy's cot in a very passion of maternal tenderness. The little fellow was lying on his back, a little frightened at me, but very still, with his big black eyes, with his fluttered air of a bird in a snare. And looking at him I seemed to see again the other one—the father, cast out mysteriously by the sea to perish in the supreme disaster of loneliness and despair."

Questions

1. Like Amarantha Doggett in "How Beautiful with Shoes," Amy Foster is depicted as a rather slow-minded, dull girl. Examine some of the language the doctor uses to describe her. Pick out key words. Can you define any basic contrasts between the two girls?
2. To what extent does Yanko's limited experience account for the language throughout Kennedy's narration? Why does Conrad develop the particular quality of Yanko's language in such detail and to such length? Is it related to what happens in the end? In what ways?
3. The key point of the story is, of course, the rejection of Yanko by the whole village but especially by Amy Foster. What are the reasons for that rejection? Is his "lingo" the sole cause? Try especially to account for "the unreasoning terror" Amy develops.
4. Describe and try to account for the effect on you of Yanko's disclosure that "I had only asked for water—only for a little water. . . ."
5. Amy "says nothing at all now. Not a word of him." Why?

6. Does the story seem to overstate the importance of language in human affairs?
7. Conrad, as a Pole in England, must have passed through a similar experience in an alien land with an alien language. To what extent might this fact account for the haunting and terrible power of the story? Cook, in the first article in this section, cites Conrad as an example of a person who gained full mastery over a language other than his native language. Can you find evidences in the language of "Amy Foster" that English is a second language for Conrad?

Suggestions for Writing

1. Write a paper contrasting the responses of Amy and Amarantha Doggett to a "new" language. Since horror plays a central part in the response of each, how can you account for the contrasts? Is the real explanation to be found in the fact that Amy's response is to a completely foreign language while Mare's is to an unusual form or usage in her own language?
2. Few of us experience personally the unreasoning terror that Amy does at the sound of Yanko's lingo. But you must surely have responded at one time or another to people speaking with a strange accent or in a totally strange language. Most of us tend to feel uneasy and superior at the same time. Write a paper in which you analyze in detail one or more such experiences; try to account for your reaction, and decide what it tells you about language.

Psycholinguistics

Suzette Haden Elgin *Two important questions in the study of language in recent years have been: "What is the true nature of language?" and "What is it in man that enables him to learn language?" From an exploration of language and of the nature of man has developed the new field of psycholinguistics. In the following article Elgin discusses four of the questions that have been of major concern in this new discipline. Transformational grammarians, favoring cognitive psychology (the earlier structural grammarians had been primarily influenced by behavioral psychology), have theorized that man has an innate capacity to learn language, that the ability to learn language is "species specific" to humans. These grammarians also argue that learning a language is not a process of forming a habit but is primarily rule-governed behavior. By this they mean that a child does not learn a language merely by imitating what he hears but that he has the inborn capacity to formulate the rules that govern language. With the ability to use these rules, he can create and understand sentences he has never before heard.*

One way of learning about language and about the language acquisition ability of humans is to study the language of people who have various kinds of language disorders. A way of knowing more about what language is or is not is to compare it to communication systems of animals. In the following article Elgin attempts to throw light on the two questions asked above. As the author treats the four questions she raises, she introduces some new terms or uses some familiar terms with a specialized meaning. Does she always clearly define new terms? Note how she uses illustrations to develop and clarify her points.

The basic study of psycholinguistics is the relationship between human language and the human brain. This is an enormous problem to work with, and it covers many kinds and ranges of questions. It would not be possible to cover all of them, even briefly, in one chapter. What *is* possible, however, is to list a number of the questions that are most important to current psycholinguistic work, and then to discuss a few of these in some detail.

Among the questions the psycholinguist wants to answer are the following:

1. Is there any evidence for the reality of the grammatical theory proposed by transformationalists?
2. Is language innate in the human being, is it something inborn, or is it a learned activity?
3. What has happened in those cases where the language mechanism of speakers goes wrong due to injury or disease or some other factor? Can anything be done for such people?
4. Is the assumption that language is uniquely restricted to human beings correct, and if so, why?

Let's examine some of the work being done in the effort to answer these questions.

The Reality of Transformational Grammar

In previous chapters we have often used phrases such as "the operation of rules," "the production of language," "the output of the grammar," and so on. Nonlinguists reading such phrases have in the past mistakenly assumed that their use indicated a mechanistic view of human speech on the part of the linguists. There have been many complaints to the effect that the human being is not a machine, does not operate like a computer, and so on.

In response to these objections, it has become something of a tradition in linguistic texts to include a disclaimer to point out that just because the vocabulary of transformational grammar and the vocabulary of General Motors overlap a bit does not mean that the linguist cannot tell the difference between a human being and a production line.

This disclaimer is certainly a truthful one. Nobody, linguist or not, has very much knowledge about the linguistic structure of the human brain. No linguist for a moment wishes to claim that the brain contains some physiological representation of tree structures and Phrase Structure rules. It goes without saying that linguists do not believe that the human being who says "Jump!" begins by checking a set of rules, noting that the deep structure of the sentence contains a "you," subjecting that output to an examination which indicates that it meets the specifications for *Imperative Deletion,* and so on. Linguists make no claim that the steps outlined in transformational derivations are followed scrupulously by the native speaker like recipes for a casserole. However, even these nonclaims constitute a hypothesis of sorts. They amount to simply taking for granted that we cannot have any real knowledge about such matters.

Recently some psycholinguists have decided that it was time to test these assumptions. Granted that sentences are not put together like casseroles, still we should be able to determine whether the principles outlined by transformational grammar have any *psychological* reality.

In one experiment, linguists (Fodor and Bever, 1965) prepared a set of tape-recorded sentences. Over these sentences they superimposd a number of clicks. The subjects of the experiment listened to the taped sentences and were then asked to judge where the clicks had occurred. A subject would listen to a sentence and then write it down from memory, indicating by a slash his recollection of the position of the click.

The results of this study showed that no matter where the clicks were really located, the subjects' tendency was to hear them as if they were at a major constituent break in the sentence.

After the results of this experiment had been made public, there was some discussion as to whether the displacement of clicks might have been due not to constituent structures but rather to pauses in the sentences. In order to be certain about this, a new experiment was done (Garrett, Bever, and Fodor, 1966) using sentences which had identical sequences but different surface structures. For example, the following pair would show this difference:

(1) a. *In her hope of leaving, Mary showed a lack of common sense.*
b. *Her hope of leaving Mary showed a lack of common sense.*

This experiment maintained the results of the previous one.

These experiments show that there may be some evidence for the psychological reality of constituent structure *at the surface structure level.* This distinction is very important, since often the deep structure of a sentence is quite different from its surface structure. Consider the following sentence:

(2) *It seems that Harry is stubborn.*

The deep structure proposed for this sentence is something like the following:

(3)

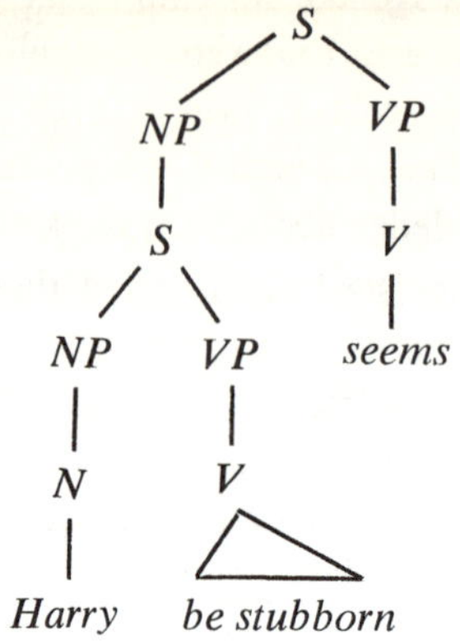

An experiment that shows subjects displacing clicks to a point immediately after surface structure constituent breaks tells us little or nothing about the possible psychological reality of a proposed deep structure like that shown in (3). Psycholinguists are now working with experiments that test for psychological reality of deep structures, and the results of these experiments will be of great interest.

The Innateness of Human Language

If you were asked how children acquire their language, what would you say? It is likely that you might say something like "he learns it from his parents" or "by imitating other people."

This view of language acquisition was once predominant in linguistics. In its most extreme form this theory claimed that the mind of the child is linguistically a blank slate, that the child imitates the speech of other people, and that he is reinforced in his imitations by his success in communicating. The idea that language is learned as a result of stimulus and reinforcement (the behaviorist approach) does have a limited amount of plausibility. It certainly is true that the child who asks for candy and gets it will have a strong tendency to remember the word "candy" correctly thereafter.

However, the evidence is overwhelmingly against anything more than this limited application. It is beyond the scope of this book to go into the technical discussion of the evidence, but it is easily found in the literature.

There is another theory about language acquisition called the *innateness* theory. This is the idea that a human being's language equipment is inborn rather than learned. One of the staunchest advocates of this theory is Eric Lenneberg. Lenneberg claims that man's language ability has been formed by evolution, and that there are crucial times for language development. He contends that the beginning of language in the child depends upon various maturational indices of the brain, and that once the physical maturation of the brain is complete—a condition he places at around puberty—the acquisition of language becomes much more difficult. Lenneberg states that ". . . the child abstracts regularities or relations from the language he hears, which he then applies to building up language for himself as an apparatus of principles" (Lenneberg, 1969). He contends that sometime in their early teens, children in effect outgrow their ability to do this.

This theory is strongly borne out by the facts. The amazing ease with which tiny children learn not only one, but even two or three languages, simply by virtue of being exposed to them, is well known. It does not seem to make a great deal of difference whether the child has the language presented to him in any systematic way; certainly no child is actively "taught" his native language by his parents in the form of lessons and exercises. The amount of talking the child hears, and the type of speech and speech situation vary radically from one child to another; nonetheless, all children learn their native tongue.

Further evidence for Lenneberg's theory is seen in the difficulty the adult has in learning a foreign language. He no longer has the ability to abstract a grammar from the raw data presented to him. Very few adults ever learn to speak a foreign language without an accent, but small children do so with ease.

There is a hypothesis in psycholinguistics, first proposed by Chomsky (1965), that every infant human being is born with something that has been called a *language acquisition device* (LAD for short). This does not mean that he is born with the grammar of his language already in his head—if that were so, the Russian child placed in a French home at birth and hearing only French thereafter would speak Russian, which of course is not the case. Instead, the LAD represents a set of strategies and principles that allow the child to figure out from the language data around him what the rules of his grammar are. This is not a random trial-and-error procedure, but a highly systematic one.

Consider a child who is brought up with English-speaking parents. He hears again and again sentences like "John ate the apple," "Mary saw the baby," "Daddy fixed the car," and so on. From this data he extracts the basic principle that the usual order of English syntactic elements is subject-verb-object. (This is very different from the idea that he simply copies such sentences until he eventually learns to produce others like them.)

A second child, who grows up hearing Diegueño (an American Indian language), will hear sentences whose form is like "Daddy the car fixed," "John the apple ate," and so on. From this data he will extract and internalize the rule that his language has the syntactic order of subject-object-verb.

A child exposed to both languages is able not only to extract both rules but to keep straight which rule applies to which language.

Such facts indicate that a child does not speak some distorted approximation of adult speech, but rather bases his language acts upon a grammar of his own that he has constructed, from data presented to him, and by using the strategies that he was born with. Many interesting studies have been done by psycholinguists in this area, and there are particular differences between adult speech and child speech that can be shown to be completely systematic. For example, studies of the way children form English questions show the following pattern:

(4) a. *Why he is leaving?*
 b. *Who he is kissing?*
 c. *What he is doing?*
 d. *Where the truck is going?*

Such questions are not random "errors." What the child seems to be doing is moving the question word (*why, who,* etc.) to the front of the sentence, just as the adult does, but without following this step with the adult grammar rule that then inverts the subject and the verb. Later, as the child has more data made available to him, he will add the additional rule.

It is easy to see that children attempt to follow definite rules, by observing your own children or the children of your friends. Every adult has heard children say things like "I goed," "Mary singed," and so on. Some children even extend this to the point of saying, "I wented." They do this long before anyone has ever formally said to them anything like, "the sign of the English simple past tense is the suffix *-ed*." They have observed the facts about *-ed* for themselves, and as a productive strategy they apply it to all verbs. One of the most interesting things about this is that often a child who has at an earlier stage used the irregular past forms of verbs correctly will, upon having internalized the rule about *-ed*, suddenly switch to the incorrect forms.

Facts about child language acquisition constitute some of the strongest evidence for the universal grammar hypothesis. For example, we know that in every human society the child begins to talk by about eighteen months, and by the age of five he is able to converse in much the same way that adults do. The child's vocabulary is obviously more limited than the adult's, but it is clear that by roughly the age of five he has mastered the basic grammar of his native language. This is true no matter what the native language may be.

If some languages were "easier" than others, as has been traditionally assumed by students, we would expect to find the children who speak them beginning to speak at a significantly earlier age than the children who speak the "hard" languages. There is no evidence that this is true of any human language whatsoever. Even in the case where a child is exposed from birth to two or more languages and learns them all, there is no really significant difference in the timetable of language acquisition.

Disorders of the Language Mechanism

In this section we will discuss some of the knowledge available about human language when it is not functioning as it should. We are not concerned here with such problems as stuttering or the disorders commonly known as speech impediments, but rather with the large group of language disorders known by the cover term *aphasia.*

In aphasia there is an actual loss of language function. The causes of aphasia are many, the most common being severe organic disease of the brain, or traumatic injuries such as those caused by gunshot wounds and automobile accidents. The types of aphasia are also various, ranging from an impairment so minor as to be hardly noticeable to complete loss of all language ability, including speaking, reading, writing, and understanding. Many combinations are possible in aphasia; a patient may be able to read but not to write, or he may be able to understand speech but not to produce it, and so on. Given the central and urgent necessity for communication in all human beings, it is easy to see that aphasia is one of the most tragic illnesses, particularly since the patient is often in otherwise perfect health and in full possession of his intelligence, and is therefore agonizingly aware of his problems.

At one time it was thought that the brain could be divided up into specific areas, and that these could be specifically diagrammed the way countries are plotted on a map, with Area X responsible for loss of vocal speech, Area Y for loss of reading ability, and so on. There was a great deal of persuasive evidence for this type of classification, particularly from the effects of various kinds of brain surgery upon patients, and from the locations of brain lesions in particular types of disorders. This system is now being seriously questioned, however, in the light of much new evidence; and it appears that we cannot set up any correspondence between brain area and deficiency except in the most general way.

In his book *Psycholinguistics* (1970, pp. 119–20), James Deese states:

> Speech and language seem to be localized in the left cerebral hemisphere, the motor portion of which controls the right side of the body, for most people. . . . The linguistic dominance of the left hemisphere is not complete. Damage in the right cerebral hemisphere (which controls the muscles of the left side of the body) does produce some residual linguistic impairment, but the extent of the impairment is much less than for comparable left cortical damage.

Deese points out that in some left-handed people this situation may be reversed. Lenneberg feels that the localization of language functions in the left hemisphere of the brain is a postpuberty trait and that in the beginning both hemispheres are involved.

The facts about aphasia offer strong evidence for Lenneberg's claim. It is in fact true that although children may become aphasic just as do adults, they almost always recover completely from aphasic disorders and show no aphasic symptoms thereafter. This would seem to indicate that before some critical age it is possible for other areas of the brain to take over language functions formerly maintained by an area damaged by disease or injury. Or, on the other hand, it might indicate that the language function before puberty is distributed throughout the entire brain, and that specialization even to one hemisphere occurs much later. Aphasic recovery in adults shows a very wide range, instead of being a virtual certainty as it is for children.

Psycholinguists are extremely interested in the order in which children acquire various features of their speech. This is of great importance in aphasia, since it has been shown that aphasics lose phonological distinctions between sounds in exactly the reverse order that they are acquired by children learning to speak.

In the treatment of aphasia, since every facet of speech production and comprehension can be involved, it is easy to see that almost every bit of linguistic knowledge is of practical use and potentially of great value. The more we know about the language function in the normal human being, the more chance there is that we will be able to do something significant about cases of language impairment.

Animal Communication

The subject of animal "languages" has always been the source of intense controversy. A glance at any of the large indexes to periodical literature will show that there is a constant flood of articles on the subject, and that this flood is not confined to scholarly journals.

Some of this is no doubt simply due to human ego involvement. As human beings we are already aware that we share many, many characteristics with the other animals, particularly the mammals, and most particularly the primates. Books like Desmond Morris's *The Naked Ape* have brought forcibly to our attention the thinness of the line that separates *homo sapiens* from the gorilla, the chimpanzee, and the rest of the monkey tribes. We can go to any circus and watch these animals, dressed in human clothing, go through one routine after another that mocks our own behavior so closely as to be almost embarrassing. The larger primates are stronger than we are, quicker, and in many ways better equipped for survival. Faced with all this, it is not surprising that we want to cling to what appears to be the one sure evidence of our true superiority—our ability to use language.

At the other end of the scale we have the folklore of animal communication, the stories of talking crows and talking dogs, of horses that can count and spell, and the worrisome theory that the dolphin really has a language but is trapped in the isolation of its dependence upon the sea and its lack of hands and so cannot demonstrate its ability.

We can begin at the very bottom of the scale of animal communication, where it is certain that no actual language is being used. The skunk has a very clear and effective message to deliver—one that endures over an impressive period of time. The tenrec of Madagascar is a mammal, but it produces high-frequency sounds by rubbing together a group of small quills on its back, in what appears to be the mammalian equivalent of cricket noise. The squid in the depths of the ocean emits clouds of color to make it obvious that, like Garbo, it "wants to be alone." The beaver slaps its tail on the ground to warn its fellows of danger. All of these things are sounds, and sounds with meaning. But these meanings are like the meaning of a red traffic light—they are simply signals.

The famous "language of the bees" is confined entirely to the two subjects of food-hunting and house-hunting. There does not seem to be any mechanism for expansion of the set of signals involved. We cannot imagine bees carrying on any sort of conversation. They are simply transmitting facts about two specific situations, and this is not language.

The sounds made by birds are higher on the scale. Linguists have discovered that birds actually have dialects. The calls that American crows make to cause other crows to gather, or to scatter in times of danger, have been tape-recorded; when these recorded calls are played in American woods they have the same effect as live calls. But when they are played for French crows they are not understood, or are ignored entirely (Sebeok, in Fishman, 1968).

Obviously birds do communicate with each other, in the sense of transmitting various informative signals. Their vocal equipment is superb, and we know that many birds are capable of producing all the sounds of human speech. However, the very sophisticated mimicry done by birds like the mynah and the parrot is not true language because it can never be used creatively. No bird that has learned to utter the two sequences "I see the girl" and "the boy is here" will ever spontaneously produce the sequences "I see the boy" and "the girl is here." No bird is able to negate a sentence or to ask a question that he has not been taught. We can be quite certain that the reason birds do not use language other than as signal and mimicry is that they simply cannot do so.

It is with the primates and the whales that we find ourselves with a genuine problem. How do we know, for example, that if we took a baby chimpanzee into a home and raised it like a human child, it would not learn to use human speech? This question becomes doubly crucial when we recall the claim that there is a critical point after which human children cannot learn to speak normally.

The obvious way to answer this question is to try it, and scientists have done just that. The first attempts were very disappointing. In one early experiment a chimpanzee spent six years being cared for just like a human baby, eating in a highchair, being dressed and fed and talked to, yet managed to acquire only four words in all that time.

However, linguists who had studied the construction of the human vocal tract and the mechanics of its use in speech pointed out that this was not a fair test. It happens that the vocal equipment of the chimpanzee is totally unsuited for human speech. On physiological grounds alone, the chimp can never learn human speech—it is *physically* impossible.

Then two scientists, R. Allen Gardner and Beatrice T. Gardner, decided to try a different approach. Again a baby chimpanzee (a female named Washoe) was raised in a home like a human child. But in this case the Gardeners tried to teach the animals to use sign language, thus bypassing her physical limitations. Given the manual dexterity of chimpanzees and their known intelligence, it was felt that this experiment would give the chimp a chance to show its real capability.

The Gardner experiment is still in progress, and the results so far have been interesting. At age five, Washoe had acquired the use of over eighty words, as compared with the four words that the chimpanzee described above learned to say in a similar amount of time. Of particular interest is a remark by the Gardners that "in discussing Washoe's early performance with deaf parents, we have been told that many of her variants of standard signs are similar to the baby-talk variants commonly observed when human children sign." (Gardner and Gardner, 1969). The Gardners also feel that Washoe understands many more signs than she actually produces.

Linguists cannot yet be certain about the speech abilities of the chimpanzee. Perhaps the work being done with Washoe will in time show us that the chimp *can* use human language but simply develops it at a slower rate than human children. Recent reports indicate that Washoe has not yet reached the limits of her language-learning ability, whatever those limits may prove to be. We will have to wait and see. But the results of the work with Washoe certainly indicate that we may have done the chimpanzees a severe injustice, much as if they had judged us to be stupid because we were not capable of swinging arm-over-arm through the trees.

The dolphins (really small toothed whales) are going to be more difficult to study in this regard than the primates. Obviously, you cannot take a dolphin into your home and raise it like a child. The dolphin is doubly handicapped physiologically for human speech; not only is its vocal equipment radically different from man's, but it lacks hands and thus cannot use sign language as Washoe has learned to do.

The most intensive work on dolphin communication has been done by John Lilly, author of *The Mind of the Dolphin.* In his Communication Research Institute in the Virgin Islands, he has constructed environments where it is possible for a human being and a dolphin to live together after a fashion. Lilly claims that not only does the dolphin have a language of its own, but it is willing and able to learn to communicate with man. Opinions of psycholinguists on the correctness of his claim range all the way from total rejection to a guarded support, and only time and more research will allow us to be certain. (This research is of course dependent on restraining man's present trend toward total destruction of these animals; if things go on as they have been, we may find all the whales, including the dolphins, extinct before we ever know if we could have talked together.)

Occasionally one hears linguistics—particularly in the areas of phonology, syntax, and semantics—described as an "ivory tower" discipline with no relation to the nonacademic outside world. This is not too surprising, since the practical applications of the theory in these three areas are not always immediately apparent. But this misconception is never directed toward psycholinguistics. It is obvious even to the individual who is totally uninterested in linguistics that the work of the psycholinguist extends into the most essential areas of man's daily life.

Questions

1. Does the author fully answer the four questions she poses at the beginning of the article? Is it possible to answer such questions with brief answers?

2. What point is Elgin trying to make in reporting the results of the experiments with clicks superimposed on sentences? How do the results support the hypothesis that a human being has an innate ability to deal with language?
3. From your own observations of the language of young children, does it appear that you can explain the language they understand and use on the basis of the language they have heard from their parents and others? Or does it appear that more than imitation of what they have heard is involved in their acquisition of language?
4. What is your response to Elgin's point that no language is more difficult than another? In answering consider the following fact: there is no language that a child cannot learn by about the age of five if he has normal exposure to that language.
5. Can you give a definition of the term *aphasia* on the basis of the information given in this article? What does the term mean?
6. Compare Elgin's statements about the brain and language with Penfield's discussion. Do you find points of disagreement? According to Elgin, are some of Penfield's conclusions now being questioned?
7. Compare Elgin's summary of experiments with the Premacks' discussion in "Teaching Language to an Ape." Are the authors optimistic about the possibilities of animals learning language? Do you think that animals can learn language?

Conditioning the Uncommitted Cortex for Language Learning[1]

Wilder Penfield *In previous articles in this section we have looked at language through the eyes of the linguist and scholar, the humorist, and the literary artist. In this article we get a very different view, through the eyes of a noted neurosurgeon and scientist. Contemporary linguists recognize that a full understanding of the magnificent instrument we call language will come only when linguists, psychologists, mathematicians, physiologists, physicians, and others pool their knowledge. What contribution does Penfield make to your understanding of the nature of language? Although his primary purpose is to show the implications of his findings for the teaching of a second language, what do his findings tell us about the way we learn our "first" language? Notice how he clarifies points with illustrations from his own experience. Do such illustrations add to the interest of the essay? He introduces what is probably a new term, the uncommitted cortex. As you read, note the techniques he uses to make the meaning of the term clear.*

*I*n this changing modern world, it is most urgent for a "well-educated" man to master one or more secondary languages. Once it was the dead languages. Now it is the living languages that are important. This calls for a change in the plan of education. The following discussion of the neurophysiology of speech and its relation to language-learning was prepared for this volume of BRAIN, which honours a neurologist, F. M. R. Walshe. But it is not written for neurologists. It is intended for educators and parents, in the hope that it may help them to adjust school curricula and home instruction to the changing physiology of the brain of childhood.

The human brain is not a previously programmed calculator. It is a living, growing, changing organ. It can even carry out its own repairs to some extent. But it is subject to an inexorable evolution of its functional

[1] A part of this communication was published in different form in *The Atlantic Monthly,* Boston, July 1964, vol. 214, p. 77, entitled *The Uncommitted Cortex.*

Wilder Penfield, "Conditioning the Uncommitted Cortex for Language Learning," *Brain,* LXXXVIII, Part 4 November 1965. Reprinted with the permission of *Brain* and the author.

aptitudes. No one can alter the time schedule of the human brain, not even a psychiatrist, or an educator. The built-in biological clock tells the passage of learning aptitudes and the teacher's opportunity.

When I was in India in 1957, visiting some of the universities under the Commonwealth Colombo Plan, I received a startling invitation from the Department of Education—to give a series of two broadcasts over the All-India Radio on the teaching of secondary languages. Some educator, I reflected, must indeed be desperate! It might well have been so, for the Government of India had laid at the door of the Ministry of Education the task of teaching the people Hindustani and English, although the mother-tongue of the majority was something else. The request was startling to me, not because the problem was new but because an educator had turned to a neurosurgeon.

My wife tried to reassure me by pointing out that our own children had gained a satisfactory command of two added languages. We had done no more than to have them hear German and French well-spoken in their early childhood. Was it, after all, as simple as that? I gave the broadcast and the Department of Education had 10,000 copies of it printed and distributed to the teachers of India. This seemed to leave me with no avenue for retreat. But fortunately this has not been necessary.

For my own part, I had heard no foreign tongue before the age of 16. After that, I studied three modern languages for professional purposes but spoke none well. Before beginning the study of medicine, I even spent a whole year teaching German and was paid for it in an otherwise efficient boys' school. It was, I fear, very poor language teaching. I handed on, as best I could, the words and the grammar I had learned at Princeton to boys who were between 15 and 18 years of age.

On the other hand, my own children learned to use German and French without apparent effort, without foreign accent, and without the long hours of toil that I had sacrificed to language study. They did well what I did badly. There must be a physiological explanation for the difference (unless these children were vastly more intelligent than their father!).

Before saying anything more about the children or the broadcast in India, perhaps the reader will follow me in a short detour. I have had a remarkable opportunity to study speech mechanisms, language learning and bilingualism. Most of my clinical career has been passed in Montreal where my patients were, half of them, French-speaking and half English-speaking. I have seen children, below the age of 10 or 12, lose the power of speech when the speech convolutions in the left hemisphere of the brain had been destroyed by a head injury or a brain tumour. I have seen them recover after a year of dumbness and aphasia. In time, they spoke as well as ever because the young child's brain is functionally flexible for the start of a language. They began all over again. Occasionally when such children had become epileptic because of the brain injury, we were able to study what had happened, while we were trying to cure them. In every case, we found they had established a speech centre located on the other side of the brain in what is called the non-dominant hemisphere. (In a right-handed person, the left hemisphere is normally dominant for speech. That is, it contains the whole specialized speech mechanism.)

When the major speech centre is severely injured in adult life, the adult cannot do what he might have done as a child. He may improve but he is apt to be using the remaining uninjured cortex on the side of the injury. He can never establish a completely new centre on the non-dominant side, as far as our experience goes. That is not because he is senile. It is because he has, by that time, taken over the initially uncommitted convolutions on the non-dominant side of his brain for other uses.

Grey matter is made up of many millions of living nerve cells that are capable of receiving and sending electrical impulses. The cerebral cortex, which is the thick layer of grey matter covering the outer surface of the brain, has been called "new" since it is found to be more and more voluminous as one ascends the philogenetic scale from fish to man. It covers the convolutions and dips down into the fissures between them. The underlying white matter is made up of the branching connexions of the nerve cells. They are capable of transmitting electric potentials like insulated wires. Some of the connexions pass inward from cortex into the "old" grey matter of the brain-stem (the old brain); some unite cortex and brain-stem with the eyes and ears; some pass up and down the spinal cord and along the nerves to the muscles and the skin.

Certain parts of the cerebral cortex are functionally committed from the start. The so-called "sensory cortex" and "motor cortex" can only be used for sensory and motor purposes because these parts seem to have fixed functional connexions from birth onward.

But there is a large area of cortex covering a given, large part of each of the two temporal lobes that is uncommitted at birth. This uncommitted cortex will in time be used for language and for perception. For language, it will make possible the remembrance and use of words. For perception, it will play a part in the recall of the past and the interpretation of present experience. As the child begins to perceive and to speak, electrical currents must be passing in corresponding patterns through this cortex and underlying brain. After each time of passage, it is easier for the passage of later currents along the same trail. This tendency to facilitation of electrical passage results in man's amazingly permanent records of the auditory and visual stream of his conscious life.

Now, if the posterior half of the left uncommitted cortex is used by the child for speech, as it usually is, it becomes the major speech area, or speech cortex.[1] Then the remaining three-quarters is used for interpretation of experience (interpretive cortex). Functional connexions are gradually established by the child and by the time he enters the teens the general uses of the uncommitted areas are apparently fixed for life.

Much of this information about mechanisms of speech and perception has come to us from the well-known work of others. Some has come to us unexpectedly during long operations on conscious alert patients who were kept from pain by local novocain injection into the scalp while a trap door opening was made in the skull. In the attempt to relieve each patient of his attacks of focal epilepsy, a preliminary survey of the brain was made after the exposure was completed.

> A gentle electrical stimulus was applied by touching the cortex here and there with an electrode. This served to map the sensory cortex by causing sensation (visual, auditory or bodily, according to which of the different areas was touched) and the motor cortex by producing crude movement of the face or tongue or limb. When an abnormality in a certain area of brain was suspected of being the cause of fits, the electrode might produce by stimulation there the characteristic beginning of the attack from which the patient sought relief. (Surgical excision of areas of bad cortex is a worth-while method of treatment in case conservative medical therapy has failed in the hands of experienced neurologists.)

The most precious and indispensable portion of the adult's cortex is the major speech area. It might be worth while to forfeit other areas and so lose other functions in order to gain a cure of epilepsy, but never the speech area. Thus the need of a method to map out the exact territory devoted to speech was urgent.

> When the electrode was applied to the speech cortex, it did not cause a man to speak. It seemed at first to have no effect. But if the patient tried to speak while the electrode was in place, he discovered to his astonishment (and to ours at first) that he could not find his words. If shown a pencil, he knew what it was and could make appropriate movements with the hand, but he had lost the power of speaking. He was aphasic. The gentle electric current was blocking the action of the speech cortex, with its underlying connexion, without disturbing the function of the adjacent areas. When the patient was shown an object

[1] There are also two secondary speech areas, both of them in the frontal lobe of the dominant hemisphere: Broca's area in the third frontal convolution, and the supplementary speech area in the supplementary motor area. An adult can recover speech after aphasia of varying lengths of time when either one is destroyed. The posterior speech area (Wernicke's), established in the uncommitted temporal cortex is the major one.

and was asked to name it, he perceived its nature, and he must have dispatched electric potentials along the brain's integrating circuits to the speech mechanism. But, to his surprise, he "drew a blank."

Normally, when the appropriately patterned potentials reach the speech mechanism, the word, by instant reflex action, is made available to consciousness—its sound, how to write it, how to speak it and how to recognize the written word. As long as the electrode continued to paralyse the action of the speech unit, none of these was possible. But as the electrode was lifted, the patient, not knowing what had been done, would exclaim, "Now I can speak! That was a pencil."

So we had a much-needed method of mapping out the major speech area exactly (and the minor ones as well). And we could remove less useful cortex right up to the speech frontier without fear of losing speech function. We mapped out the cortical area thus in hundreds of cases and acquired precise knowledge of the demarcation in each case. This took the place of anatomical conjecture. But what about the similar area in the non-dominant hemisphere and the uncommitted temporal cortex farther forward on both sides? So far, neurologists had found no clear indication of function for these areas.

Stimulation in them never produced aphasia. What were they used for? One day I stumbled on a clue. I applied the electrode to the right temporal cortex (non-dominant). The patient, a woman of middle age, exclaimed suddenly, "I seem to be the way I was when I was giving birth to my baby girl." I did not recognize this as a clue. But I could not help feeling that the suddenness of her exclamation was strange and so I made a note of it.

Several years later during a similar operation, the electrode caused a young girl to describe, with considerable emotion, a specific experience she had when running through a meadow. There is no sensation in the cortex and she could not know when I had touched the electrode to her right temporal lobe but, each time I did so, she described the experience again, and stopped when the electrode was removed. Since that day we have been on the alert and have gathered more and more cases which could be studied critically. We have now published all of them in complete summary.[1]

The conclusion is as follows: There is within the adult human brain a remarkable record of the stream of each individual's awareness. It is as though the electrode cuts in, at random, on the record of that stream. The patient sees and hears what he saw and heard in some earlier strip of time and he feels the same accompanying emotions. The stream of

[1] W. Penfield and Ph. Perot—*Brain* (1963), 86, 595–696.

consciousness flows for him again, exactly as before, stopping instantly on removal of the electrode. He is aware of those things to which he paid attention in this earlier period, even twenty years ago. He is not aware of the things that were ignored. The experience evidently moves forward at the original pace. This was demonstrated by the fact that when, for example, the music of an orchestra, or song or piano, is heard and the patient is asked to hum in accompaniment, the tempo of his humming is what one would expect. He is still aware of being in the operating room but he can describe this other run of consciousness at the same time.

The patient recognizes the experience as having been his own, although usually he could not have recalled it if he had tried. The complete record of his auditory and visual experience is not subject to conscious recall, but it is evidently used in the subconscious brain-transaction that results in perception. By means of it, a man in normal life compares each succeeding experience with his own past experience. He knows at once whether it is familiar or not. If it is familiar, he interprets the present stream of consciousness in the light of the past.

Careful comparison of all the brain maps we have made shows no overlap of the boundaries that separate speech cortex (which endows a man with memory of words) and the interpretive cortex which gives him access to the memory of past similar experience and thus enables him to understand the present.

Before the child begins to speak and to perceive, the uncommitted cortex is a blank slate on which nothing has been written. In the ensuing years much is written, and the writing is normally never erased. After the age of 10 or 12, the general functional connexions have been established and fixed for the speech cortex. After that the speech centre cannot be transferred to the cortex of the lesser side and set up all over again. This "non-dominant" area that might have been used for speech is now fully occupied with the business of perception.

The brain of the 12 year old, you may say, is prepared for rapid expansion of the vocabulary of the mother tongue and of the other languages he may have heard in the formative period. If he has heard these other languages, he has developed also a remarkable *switch mechanism* that enables him to turn from one language to another without confusion, without translation, without a mother-tongue accent.

In my broadcast to the teachers of India, I could only reason as follows: Do not turn without question to the West for your model of teaching secondary languages. Consider first the changing functional capacities of the child's brain. Most of our schools in the West begin the teaching of foreign languages by the dead-language technique. It was designed for adults learning Greek and Latin by means of word-lists and grammar. Your hope that the people of India will speak English and Hindustani as living-languages is doomed to failure if you follow this technique. The dead-language technique has its place, no doubt, but it cannot be used in the years when the child is a genius at language initiation.

But there is another method of beginning a language—the direct method that mothers use. It was used to teach foreign languages as well as the mother-tongue, in the families of ancient Ur and during the Roman Empire. It is used by some parents in the West and in the East today. Even a child's nurse or the least experienced tutor can use the mother's method for a second language. The mother does her teaching when the child's brain is ready for it. In three or four years she may only give the child a few hundred words, perhaps. But he gets the set, acquires the units, creates the functional connexions of the speech cortex. In unilingual countries the mother conducts the first stage of language learning by the direct method and the school carries on easily with the second stage—vocabulary expansion. If a nation is to be bilingual or trilingual, or multilingual, the nation's schools should adopt the mother's direct method for the first stage of foreign language teaching.

In retrospect, I am not sure whether, when I presumed to offer a solution to the teachers of India, I was speaking from scientific evidence,[1] or as a man who had tried unsuccessfully to master secondary languages by the classical methods, or as a teacher of German who had employed the classical method, or, finally, as a father whose children had approached two second languages successfully by the mother's method. In any case, I ventured an opinion:

India's problem is not insuperable. Use the mother's method at the very beginning of formal education with teachers who can speak either English or Hindustani well and who understand kindergarten techniques. Following that, I outlined, in a rather confused manner (my thinking was less clear in this regard then than now) what is described below as *parallel bilingualism* (one language in the morning, the other in the afternoon).

But India, with her most important task of language-teaching, is far away. In other nations of the world the problem of second-language teaching is hardly less urgent, although it presents itself in varying patterns. The urgency of the problem will, I hope, excuse a parent and a clinical neuro-

[1] In 1956, the author had delivered the Vanuxem Lectures at Princeton—"The Physical Basis of Speech," published later as "Speech and Brain Mechanisms," W. Penfield and L. Roberts, Princeton University Press, 1959. The last chapter turns to the subject of language learning. Chapters 12 and 13 of a more recent book, "The Second Career," W. Penfield, Little, Brown, Toronto, 1963, also deal with second-language learning.

physiologist if he addresses school teachers and parents nearer home than India.

There is a good deal of evidence to suggest that when a young child is allowed to hear a second language and learns to use only a few hundred words of that language—he becomes a better potential linguist; his uncommitted cortex is conditioned to further second-language learning. It is difficult or impossible to condition it thus later in life because the functional connexions tend to become fixed.

This would explain the reputed genius of the Swiss, the Poles and the Belgians as linguists. Most of them hear a second language in early childhood in the streets and the playgrounds, if not at home. On the contrary, the average so-called Anglo-Saxon, in Great Britain or the United States, hears only English until possibly he is taught a modern language in his teens at school.

J. B. Conant (former President of Harvard), in his recent studies of American high schools, concluded that in the best schools of today the work is satisfactory, except in one department: the teaching of foreign languages. The classical method, with its grammar and word lists designed to teach dead languages, is the indirect method of the high school. A little child cannot use it. He would only laugh at it, and yet the little child is the genius in our society for starting languages. The brain of the 12 year old is already senescent in that regard. He is ready for vocabulary expansion.

Education, to be scientific, must consider the physiology of a child's brain. When the classical method is used to start a unilingual teenage pupil or adult in the learning of second languages, the procedure is unscientific and not in accordance with the dictates of neurophysiology. With hard work, it may serve the purpose as a second-best method.

The teaching of additional living languages, as intelligent parents have managed it, ever since the society of ancient Ur became bilingual, is in accordance with the modern findings of speech physiology.

The mother's method of initiating the learning of the mother tongue is scientifically correct and successful. This is the original direct method. It conditions the child's uncommitted cortex to the set and the style of the language. Second languages can be started by the same direct method without confusion.

There are examples of early language teaching by the direct method in schools in many parts of the world. But these are still sporadic. It may serve my purpose best to describe a school in Montreal in which the mother's direct method is being well used. The school is available to children from French-speaking homes or English-speaking homes and also to children from Polish or Ukrainian-speaking families.

This is a day-school in which the method of *parallel bilingualism* is used by teachers speaking their native tongue (English or French). They are the teaching nuns of Notre Dame de Sion, 4701 Dornal Avenue, Montreal. The procedure is not at all complicated. Their school has two years of kindergarten and one of first grade. In the morning the children, aged 4 to 6, are received by English-speaking teachers and in the afternoon by French-speaking teachers or vice versa. No time is wasted teaching language as such. The children play and sing and study in one language in the morning and the other in the afternoon. They begin to read and write in two languages. If there is any difficulty of spelling, it disappears spontaneously after the manner of vanishing baby-talk. Every evening the children return to their homes to speak the mother tongue and to receive whatever home religious instruction is desired by their parents.

After two years of bilingual kindergarten and one in the first grade, children of this school have started reading and writing. They are ready to carry on in either language smoothly and without accent or confusion in some other elementary school. They could, of course, transfer to a school that used a third language. Vocabulary expansion could be provided for by reading and conversation almost any time in the first and second decades of life. When they enter middle school, high school or university, these children should be able to study the literature of second languages instead of struggling with grammar.

The child is the genius in our society when it comes to acquiring the early set, the units or the patterns of a language. The enlargement of vocabulary is another story. The 10 year old expands vocabulary as he expands his knowledge miraculously in the direction of his interests.

The secret of the child's freedom from confusion lies in the action of a conditioned reflex that works in his brain automatically from the beginning. It is what might be called the *switch mechanism*. When the English child (or adult) hears a French word or meets a French person or enters a French school, he unconsciously switches on his French "network" with its vocabulary, however meagre it may be. What he proceeds to learn is then added to the French network. In the brain, French, English and Chinese, if learned, seem to utilize the same general area of speech cortex without demonstrable separation into different areas. Every adult who speaks secondary languages is aware of this subconscious reflex which brings the word *bleistift* to his mind instead of "pencil" as he turns to a German companion, or *crayon* as he enters the class conducted in French.

It is preferable in my opinion that, in the early stages, a bilingual adult, charged with the care of a young child, should not switch back and forth too often from one language to another in conversation. But it works well to do what a bilingual mother of my acquaintance has done, establish "upstairs" in the home as a French-speaking area and "downstairs" for

English. Her little children accepted it as no problem at all. Language to them is only a way of getting what is wanted or expressing constructive (or destructive!) ideas.

The first stage of language learning is always in the home. During the first two years of life, imitation of words comes only after months of hearing them.[1] Baby talk shows that the set of the brain for language is not established immediately. It takes time, and the baby's accent and the formal phrasing and organization of sentences alters gradually to that of the adult (without the need of lectures on grammar).

In our own home the two younger children heard German in the nursery from a governess who could speak nothing else. When she took them to French nursery school (aged 3 and 4) they switched to French as they entered the door and switched back again when they found her waiting outside the door at the close of the school. Our two older children, aged 8 and 9, first heard German spoken for a few months in Germany. After that they spoke German to their younger brother and sister and, on occasion, to the governess, but they were never taught the language formally. In spite of that, both older children had excellent command of the language, one for a year of university work in Munich, the other for wireless intelligence in the Second World War.

A unilingual adult, who begins the learning of a second language late, speaks it with a mother-tongue accent and tends to learn by translation. However, the adult who has previously learned some other language in childhood is apt to learn a later third and fourth language faster and probably better than a unilingual adult. It may be suggested that this greater facility of the bilingual adult is due, at least in part, to the well developed "switch mechanism" which he acquired in childhood. He is able to switch off the mother tongue more easily and, thus, to learn directly.

It follows, for example, that in a school district where the only foreign native-born teachers available are Swedish or Spanish, it would be the part of wisdom to have beginning years taught in Swedish (or on a bilingual basis—Swedish in the mornings and Spanish in the afternoons). Those children who continue their schooling in English and eventually go on to college and into professional schools will be better prepared to learn the Russian and Chinese which intelligent English-speaking adults of the future will want to understand. The bilingual child, prepared for formal education by the mother and the child's nurse, or mother and a second language kindergarten, has undoubted advantage over other children whatever the second languages may have been and whatever the eventual work of the individual may prove to be.

[1] According to W. E. Leopold's careful study, there is a lag of two to seven months after the child first hears a word in the second year of life before he uses it in a meaningful manner. (Northwestern University Press, 4 vols., 1939–1949.)

The experience of many parents has, of course, been similar to our own, past and present. It is a common experience that when families immigrate, the children learn the new language by the direct method (without confusion) and unilingual parents learn it less well and more slowly by translation and with a mother-tongue accent. This is the supporting evidence of common sense and common experience. And yet there are those who argue that it is better for a child to establish the mother-tongue well before confusing him by exposure to a second language! The child seems to be protected from confusion by rapidly acquired conditioned reflexes and by the action of the switch mechanism which is a conditioned reflex.

There is other good evidence that even a limited familiarity with additional languages in the first decade endows the normal child with a more efficient and useful brain. In a study supported by the Carnegie Foundation and conducted under W. E. Lambert, Professor of Psychology at McGill University, it was concluded recently that bilingual children, at the 10-year level in Montreal, showed greater intelligence than unilingual children of the same age. They were examined by non-verbal as well as verbal tests.[1]

A second study has been carried out in the same department.[2] In this study, an equal number of bilingual university students was compared with a similar selection of unilingual students. The bilingual students scored higher in intelligence tests when those tests were verbal and also when they were non-verbal. In the bilingual society of the Province of Quebec, those who were bilingual before entering university would have heard the second language early.

In conclusion, man (to a far greater extent than other mammals) is endowed with extensive areas of cerebral cortex which, at birth, are not committed to sensory or motor function. Much of the uncommitted areas covering the temporal lobes that are not used as "speech cortex" will, in time, be used as "interpretive cortex" and so play a rôle in the process of perception. While the mother is teaching the child to understand and to use a few hundred words and teaching the child to perceive the meanings of words and experiences, she is "programming" the brain. Part of the uncommitted cortex is being conditioned or "programmed" for speech, the remaining uncommitted cortex is used as a part of the mechanism of perception. In the second decade of life, functional connexions seem to have become fixed. Vocabulary expansion and multiplication of perceptions then proceed rapidly.

The mother's method of direct language teaching can be used for second languages but this should *begin* before the age of 6 or 8 if possible.

[1] Peel, Elizabeth and Lambert, W.: The Relation of Bilingualism to Intelligence Psychological Monographs, General and Applied, vol. 76, 27, Amer. Psychol. Ass'n. Washington, D.C., 1962.

[2] Anisfeld, Elizabeth Peel: The Cognitive Aspects of Bilingualism. McGill University, Ph.D. thesis.

When the uncommitted cortex is thus conditioned early, the individual becomes a better linguist; the child is better prepared for the long educational climb. In the years of life that follow, the man or woman will more easily become the "well-educated" adult for which the future calls so urgently.

Teachers and parents must always share responsibility for the education of each new generation. This includes the conditioning of each child's brain. How and when it is conditioned, prepares the man for great achievement or limits him to mediocrity. A neurophysiologist can only suggest that the human brain is capable of far more than is demanded of it today. Adjust the time and the manner of teaching to the aptitudes of the growing, changing master-organ. Then, double your demands and your reasonable expectations.

Questions

1. Having read the essay, do you fully understand the term "uncommitted cortex"? Has Penfield defined it completely and precisely?
2. This essay approaches a specific question—how best to teach a foreign language—from the standpoint of the physiology of the brain. Hence the suggestion that educators need to be aware of the findings of neurophysiology. Does the approach tell you more, or less, about the nature of language than have previous essays by linguists? Is language primarily a physiological function? Does Penfield say it is?
3. Specifically, what does Penfield mean by "the mother's method of language teaching"? Do you think you could have learned another language through the simple approach described here? Have you had any experiences which would support or would challenge the statements Penfield makes?
4. After recounting the discovery of the speech center and how it develops and operates, Penfield recounts how he discovered the function of the other side of the cortex: to keep a "record of the stream of each individual's awareness, his consciousness." How does this relate to the basic problem of the speech center?
5. Penfield, in addition to being a prominent neurosurgeon, has written many articles, a novel, and a book-length biography. Did you find his style easy to read? Does he seem to have a serious concern with using words clearly and effectively? In what ways might being able to write well make him more effective as a neurosurgeon?

Teaching Language to an Ape

Ann James Premack and David Premack *In the article "Man's Finest Hour" Noah Jonathan Jacobs noted that "the animals are not phonetically defective but semantically blocked." The authors of this article reverse that statement and operate on the assumption that animals are phonetically defective but do have the ability to deal with meaning and with the abstract systems that constitute language. The beginning of this article and the final section of the article "Psycholinguistics" review a number of attempts to teach animals language. Earlier experiments attempted to teach animals to talk; more recent experiments have abandoned that attempt and try to get animals to deal with concrete objects that substitute for words.*

As the authors note in the second paragraph, their primary purpose in teaching Sarah to use language is to learn something about the nature of language. They are concerned both with the "fundamental nature of language" and with the "human information-processing" mechanism. As you read about their work with Sarah, see if you gain new insights into the nature of language and into the process of communicating meaning. The authors accuse humans of being prejudiced against animals, of denying (without carefully exploring the matter) that animals may have certain language-learning capabilities. After you read this selection, be prepared to respond to their charge. On the basis of the evidence offered here and in the Elgin article, do you think it may be possible to teach some animals to use language?

Over the past 40 years several efforts have been made to teach a chimpanzee human language. In the early 1930's Winthrop and Luella Kellogg raised a female chimpanzee named Gua along with their infant son; at the age of 16 months Gua could understand about 100 words, but she never did try to speak them. In the 1940's Keith and Cathy Hayes raised a chimpanzee named Vicki in their home; she learned a large number of words and with some difficulty could mouth the words "mama," "papa" and "cup." More recently Allen and Beatrice Gardner have taught their chim-

Ann James Premack and David Premack, "Teaching Language to an Ape," *Scientific American,* October 1972, pp. 92–99.

panzee Washoe to communicate in the American Sign Language with her fingers and hands. Since 1966 in our laboratory at the University of California at Santa Barbara we have been teaching Sarah to read and write with variously shaped and colored pieces of plastic, each representing a word; Sarah has a vocabulary of about 130 terms that she uses with a reliability of between 75 and 80 percent.

Why try to teach human language to an ape? In our own case the motive was to better define the fundamental nature of language. It is often said that language is unique to the human species. Yet it is now well known that many other animals have elaborate communication systems of their own. It seems clear that language is a general system of which human language is a particular, albeit remarkably refined, form. Indeed, it is possible that certain features of human language that are considered to be uniquely human belong to the more general system, and that these features can be distinguished from those that are unique to the human information-processing regime. If, for example, an ape can be taught the rudiments of human language, it should clarify the dividing line between the general system and the human one.

There was much evidence that the chimpanzee was a good candidate for the acquisition of language before we began our project. In their natural environment chimpanzees have an extensive vocal "call system." In captivity the chimpanzee has been taught to sort pictures into classes: animate and inanimate, old and young, male and female. Moreover, the animal can classify the same item in different ways depending on the alternatives offered. Watermelon is classified as fruit in one set of alternatives, as food in another set and as big in a third set. On the basis of these demonstrated conceptual abilities we made the assumption that the chimpanzee could be taught not only the names of specific members of a class but also the names for the classes themselves.

It is not necessary for the names to be vocal. They can just as well be based on gestures, written letters or colored stones. The important thing is to shape the language to fit the information-processing capacities of the chimpanzee. To a large extent teaching language to an animal is simply mapping out the conceptual structures the animal already possesses. By using a system of naming that suits the chimpanzee we hope to find out more about its conceptual world. Ultimately the benefit of language experiments with animals will be realized in an understanding of intelligence in terms not of scores on tests but of the underlying brain mechanisms. Only then can cognitive mechanisms for classifying stimuli, for storing and retrieving information and for problem-solving be studied in a comparative way.

The first step in teaching language is to exploit knowledge that is already present. In teaching Sarah we first mapped the simple social transaction of giving, which is something the chimpanzee does both in nature and in the laboratory. Considered in terms of cognitive and perceptual elements, the verb "give" involves a relation between two individuals and one object, that is, between the donor, the recipient and the object being transferred. In order to carry out the act of giving an animal must recognize the difference between individuals (between "Mary" and "Randy") and must perceive the difference between donors and recipients (between "Mary gives Randy" and "Randy gives Mary"). In order to be able to map out the entire transaction of giving the animal has to distinguish agents from objects, agents from one another, objects from one another and itself from others.

The trainer began the process of mapping the social transaction by placing a slice of banana between himself and Sarah. The chimpanzee, which was then about five years old, was allowed to eat the tasty morsel while the trainer looked on affectionately. After the transaction had become routine, a language element consisting of a pink plastic square was placed close to Sarah while the slice of banana was moved beyond her reach. To obtain the fruit Sarah now had to put the plastic piece on a "language board" on the side of her cage. (The board was magnetic and the plastic square was backed with a thin piece of steel so that it would stick.) After Sarah had learned this routine the fruit was changed to an apple and she had to place a blue plastic word for apple on the board. Later several other fruits, the verb "give" and the plastic words that named each of them were introduced.

To be certain that Sarah knew the meaning of "give" it was necessary to contrast "give" with other verbs, such as "wash," "cut" and "insert." When Sarah indicated "Give apple," she was given a piece of apple. When she put "Wash apple" on the board, the apple was placed in a bowl of water and washed. In that way Sarah learned what action went with what verb.

In the first stage Sarah was required to put only one word on the board; the name of the fruit was a sufficient indicator of the social transaction. When names for different actions—verbs—were introduced, Sarah had to place two words on the board in vertical sequence. In order to be given an apple she had to write "Give apple." When recipients were named, two-word sentences were not accepted by the trainer; Sarah had to use three words. There were several trainers, and Sarah had to learn the name of each one. To facilitate the teaching of personal names, both the chimpanzees and the trainers wore their plastic-word names on a string necklace. Sarah learned the names of some of the recipients the hard way. Once she wrote "Give apple Gussie," and the trainer promptly gave the apple to another chimpanzee named Gussie. Sarah never repeated the sentence. At every stage she was required to observe the proper word sequence. "Give apple" was accepted but "Apple give" was not. When donors were to be named, Sarah had to identify all the members of the social transaction: "Mary give apple Sarah."

The interrogative was introduced with the help of the concepts "same" and "different." Sarah was given a cup and a spoon. When another cup was added, she was taught to put the two cups together. Other sets of three objects were given to her, and she had to pair the two objects that were alike. Then she was taught to place the plastic word for "same" between any two similar objects and the plastic word for "different" between unlike objects. Next what amounted to a question mark was placed between pairs of objects. This plastic shape (which bore no resemblance to the usual kind of question mark) made the question explicit rather than implicit, as it had been in the simple matching tests. When the interrogative element was placed between a pair of cups, it meant: "What is the relation between cup *A* and cup *B?"* The choices provided Sarah were the plastic words "same" and "different." She learned to remove the interrogative particle and substitute the correct word. Sarah was able to transfer what she had learned and apply the word "same" or "different" to numerous pairs of objects that had not been used in her training.

Any construction is potentially a question. From the viewpoint of structural linguistics any construction where one or more elements are deleted becomes a question. The constructions we used with Sarah were *"A* same *A"* and *"A* different *B."* Elements in these constructions were removed and the deletion was marked with the interrogative symbol; Sarah was then supplied with a choice of missing elements with which she could restore the construction to its familiar form. In principle interrogation can be taught either by removing an element from a familiar situation in the animal's world or by removing the element from a language that maps the animal's world. It is probable that one can induce questions by purposively removing key elements from a familiar situation. Suppose a chimpanzee received its daily ration of food at a specific time and place, and then one day the food was not there. A chimpanzee trained in the interrogative might inquire "Where is my food?" or, in Sarah's case, "My food is?" Sarah was never put in a situation that might induce such interrogation because for our purposes it was easier to teach Sarah to answer questions.

At first Sarah learned all her words in the context of social exchange. Later, when she had learned the concepts "name of" and "not name of," it was possible to introduce new words in a more direct way. To teach her that objects had names, the plastic word for "apple" and a real apple were placed on the table and Sarah was required to put the plastic word for "name of" between them. The same procedure was repeated for banana. After she had responded correctly several times, the symbol for "apple" and a real banana were placed on the table and Sarah had to put "not name of" between them. After she was able to perform both operations correctly new nouns could be taught quickly and explicitly. The plastic words for "raisin" and "name of" could be placed next to a real raisin and Sarah would learn the noun. Evidence of such learning came when Sarah subsequently requested "Mary give raisin Sarah" or set down "Raisin different apple."

An equally interesting linguistic leap occurred when Sarah learned the predicate adjective and could write such sentences as "Red color of apple," "Round shape of apple" and "Large size of apple." When asked for the relation between "Apple is red? Red color of apple" and given "same" and "different" as choices, she judged the sentences to be the same. When given "Apple is red? Apple is round," she judged the sentences to be different. The distinctions between similar and different, first learned with actual objects, was later applied by Sarah in linguistic constructions.

In English the conditional consists of the discontinuous elements "if-then," which are inconvenient and conceptually unnecessary. In symbolic logic the conditional consists of the single sign $\supset$, and we taught Sarah the conditional relation with the use of a single plastic word. Before being given language training in the conditional, she was given contingency training in which she was rewarded for doing one thing but not another. For example, she was given a choice between an apple and a banana, and only when she chose the apple was she given chocolate (which she dearly loved). "If apple, then chocolate, if banana, then no chocolate" were the relations she learned; the same relations were subsequently used in sentences to teach her the name for the conditional relation.

The subject was introduced with the written construction: "Sarah take apple? Mary give chocolate Sarah." Sarah was provided with only one plastic word: the conditional particle. She had to remove the question mark and substitute the conditional in its place to earn the apple and the chocolate. Now she was presented with: "Sarah take banana? Mary no give chocolate Sarah." Again only the conditional symbol was provided. When Sarah replaced the question mark with the conditional symbol, she received a banana but no chocolate. After several such tests she was given a series of trials on each of the following pairs of sentences: "Sarah take apple if-then Mary give chocolate Sarah" coupled with "Sarah take banana if-then Mary no give chocolate Sarah," or "Sarah take apple if-then Mary no give chocolate Sarah" coupled with "Sarah take banana if-then Mary give chocolate Sarah."

At first Sarah made many errors, taking the wrong fruit and failing to get her beloved chocolate. After several of her strategies had failed she paid closer attention to the sentences and began choosing the fruit that gave her the chocolate. Once the conditional relation had been learned she was able to apply it to other types of sentences, for example, "Mary take red if-then Sarah take apple" and "Mary take green if-then Sarah take banana." Here Sarah had to watch Mary's choice closely in order to take the correct action. With the paired sentences "Red is on green if-then Sarah take apple" and "Green is on red if-then Sarah take banana," which involved a change in the position of two colored cards, Sarah was not confused and performed well.

As a preliminary to learning the class concepts of color, shape and size Sarah was taught to identify members of the classes red and yellow, round and square and large and small. Objects that varied in most dimensions but had a particular property in common were used. Thus for teaching the word "red" a set of dissimilar, unnamed objects (a ball, a toy car, a Life Saver and so on) that had no property in common except redness were put before the chimpanzee. The only plastic word available to her was "red." After several trials on identifying red with a set of red objects and yellow with a set of yellow objects, Sarah was shifted to trials where she had to choose between "red" and "yellow" when she was shown a colored object. Finally completely new red and yellow objects were presented to her, including small cards that were identical except for their color. Again she performed at her usual level of accuracy.

Sarah was subsequently taught the names of shapes, "round" and "square," as well as the size names "large" and "small." These words formed the basis for teaching her the names of the class concepts "color of," "shape of" and "size of." Given the interrogative "Red ? apple" or "Yellow ? banana," Sarah was required to substitute the plastic word for "color of" for the question mark. In teaching class names a good many sentences were not written on the board but were presented as hybrids. The hybrid sentences consisted of a combination of plastic words and real objects arranged in the proper sentence sequence on Sarah's worktable. Typical sentences were "Yellow ?" beside a real yellow balloon or "Red ?" beside a red wood block.

The hybrid sentences did not deter Sarah in the least. Her good performance showed that she was able to move with facility from symbols for objects to actual objects. Her behavior with hybrid constructions recalls the activity of young children, who sometimes combine spoken words with real objects they are unable to name by pointing at the objects.

Was Sarah able to think in the plastic-word language? Could she store information using the plastic words or use them to solve certain kinds of problem that she could not solve otherwise? Additional research is needed before we shall have definitive answers, but Sarah's performance suggests that the answers to both questions may be a qualified yes. To think with language requires being able to generate the meaning of words in the absence of their external representation. For Sarah to be able to match "apple" to an actual apple or "Mary" to a picture of Mary indicates that she knows the meaning of these words. It does not prove, however, that when she is given the word "apple" and no apple is present, she can think "apple," that is, mentally represent the meaning of the word to herself. The ability to achieve such mental representation is of major importance because it frees language from simple dependence on the outside world. It involves displacement: the ability to talk about things that are not actually there. That is a critical feature of language.

The hint that Sarah was able to understand words in the absence of their external referents came early in her language training. When she was given a piece of fruit and two plastic words, she was required to put the correct word for the fruit on the board before she was allowed to eat it. Surprisingly often, however, she chose the wrong word. It then dawned on us that her poor performance might be due not to errors but to her trying to express her preferences in fruit. We conducted a series of tests to determine her fruit preferences, using actual fruits in one test and only fruit names in the other. Sarah's choices between the words were much the same as her choices between the actual fruits. This result strongly suggests that she could generate the meaning of the fruit names from the plastic symbols alone.

We obtained clearer evidence at a later stage of Sarah's language training. In the same way that she could use "name of" to learn new nouns, she was able to use "color of" to learn the names of new colors. For instance, the names "brown" and "green" were introduced in the sentences "Brown color of chocolate" and "Green color of grape." The only new words at this point were "brown" and "green." Later Sarah was confronted with four disks, only one of which was brown, and when she was instructed with the plastic symbols "Take brown," she took the brown disk. Since chocolate was not present at any time during the introduction of the color name "brown," the word "chocolate" in the definition must have been sufficient to have Sarah generate or picture the property brown.

What form does Sarah's supposed internal representation take? Some indication is provided by the results of a test of ability to analyze the features of an object. First Sarah was shown an actual apple and was given a series of paired comparisons that described the features of the apple, such as red v. green, round v. square and so on. She had to pick the descriptive feature that belonged to the apple. Her feature analysis of a real apple agreed nicely with our own, which is evidence of the interesting fact that a chimpanzee is capable of decomposing a complex object into features. Next the apple was removed and the blue plastic triangle that was the word for "apple" was placed before her and again she was given a paired-comparison test. She assigned the same features to the word that she had earlier assigned to the object. Her feature analysis revealed that it was not the physical properties of the word (blue and triangle) that she was describing but rather the object that was represented by the word.

To test Sarah's sentence comprehension she was taught to correctly follow these written instructions: "Sarah insert apple pail," "Sarah insert banana pail," "Sarah insert apple dish" and "Sarah insert banana dish." Next instructions were combined in a one-line vertical sequence ("Sarah insert apple pail Sarah insert banana dish"). The chimpanzee responded appropriately. Then the second "Sarah" and the second verb "insert" were deleted to yield the compound sentence: "Sarah insert apple pail banana dish." Sarah followed the complicated instructions at her usual level of accuracy.

The test with the compound sentence is of considerable importance, because it provides the answer to whether or not Sarah could understand the notion of constituent structure: the hierarchical organization of a sentence. The correct interpretation of the compound sentence was "Sarah put the apple in the pail and the banana in the dish." To take the correct actions Sarah must understand that "apple" and "pail" go together but not "pail" and "banana," even though the terms appear side by side. Moreover, she must understand that the verb "insert" is at a higher level of organization and refers to both "apple" and "banana." Finally, Sarah must understand that she, as the head noun, must carry out all the actions. If Sarah were capable only of linking words in a simple chain, she would never be able to interpret the compound sentence with its deletions. The fact is that she interprets them correctly. If a child were to carry out the instructions in the same way, we would not hesitate to say that he recognizes the various levels of sentence organization: that the subject dominates the predicate and the verb in the predicate dominates the objects.

Sarah had managed to learn a code, a simple language that nevertheless included some of the characteristic features of natural language. Each step of the training program was made as simple as possible. The objective was to reduce complex notions to a series of simple and highly learnable steps. The same program that was used to teach Sarah to communicate has been successfully applied with people who have language difficulties caused by brain damage. It may also be of benefit to the autistic child.

In assessing the results of the experiment with Sarah one must be careful not to require of Sarah what one would require of a human adult. Compared with a two-year-old child, however, Sarah holds her own in language ability. In fact, language demands were made of Sarah that would never be made of a child. Man is understandably prejudiced in favor of his own species, and members of other species must perform Herculean feats before they are recognized as having similar abilities, particularly language abilities. Linguists and others who study the development of language tend to exaggerate the child's understanding of language and to be extremely skeptical of the experimentally demonstrated language abilities of the chimpanzee. It is our hope that our findings will dispel such prejudices and lead to new attempts to teach suitable languages to animals other than man.

Questions

1. As they have worked with Sarah, the authors have been concerned with the "cognitive and perceptual elements" of language. What do these terms mean? How successful has Sarah been in mastering these elements?
2. The authors define the term *displacement* as it relates to language. To what extent was Sarah able to use language in the absence of physical stimuli?
3. Is there evidence that Sarah developed the ability to think? Are the plastic "words" acceptable substitutes for the abstractions that humans use as words? What limitations might you suggest?
4. What evidence is offered that Sarah was able, at least in some respects, to deal with the structure of language?
5. If you have an opportunity to observe the language of a small child, compare the language ability of that child with Sarah's language ability. How long has Sarah been learning language? What percentage of the time is Sarah correct? What percentage of the time is a child correct?

Suggestions for Writing

1. Everyone has had the experience of attempting to teach a difficult concept to someone else. Choose some experience you have had or have witnessed in which someone had difficulty teaching. Analyze the experience and write a paper in which you relate the experience and draw some generalizations from it. Did the difficulty lie in the teaching method used, in the complexity of the idea being taught, in the inability of the subject to learn? Your thesis might be a statement of what you learned from the experience.

Naming of Parts

Henry Reed

This poem tells us something about definition. But it also carries fascinating implications about the nature of language. You might even find relationships between it and "Adam Names the Animals." If you assume a tough sergeant with a rifle demonstrating the parts as he names them, you can see how the poem works. Who is speaking, the sergeant or the listening recruit? Something changes during the fourth line of each stanza. Is the same person speaking? If so, is he speaking out loud?

Today we have naming of parts. Yesterday,
We had daily cleaning. And tomorrow morning,
We shall have what to do after firing. But today,
Today we have naming of parts. Japonica
Glistens like coral in all of the neighboring gardens,
    And today we have naming of parts.

This is the lower sling swivel. And this
Is the upper sling swivel, whose use you will see,
When you are given your slings. And this is the piling swivel,
Which in your case you have not got. The branches
Hold in the gardens their silent, eloquent gestures,
    Which in our case we have not got.

This is the safety-catch, which is always released
With an easy flick of the thumb. And please do not let me
See anyone using his finger. You can do it quite easy
If you have any strength in your thumb. The blossoms
Are fragile and motionless, never letting anyone see
    Any of them using their finger.

And this you can see is the bolt. The purpose of this
Is to open the breech, as you see. We can slide it
Rapidly backwards and forwards: we call this

Easing the spring. And rapidly backwards and forwards
The early bees are assaulting and fumbling the flowers:
    They call it easing the Spring.

They call it easing the Spring: it is perfectly easy
If you have any strength in your thumb: like the bolt,
And the breech, and the cocking-piece, and the point of balance,
Which in our case we have not got; and the almond-blossom
Silent in all of the gardens and the bees going backwards and forwards,
    For today we have naming of parts.

Questions

1. Note how the last line of each stanza, except the last, repeats exactly or with minor variations a large part of a preceding line. Can you decide why? Does the repeated expression "mean" the same as the original? If not, what has changed it? What does this tell us about how the context influences meaning? Why does the last line of the poem repeat the first line?
2. Why in the last line of the fourth stanza does the poet capitalize Spring? Note that the same line, with the capital, begins the final stanza. Does this stanza define precisely who is speaking (note the shift from "your" to "our")?
3. Which do we get defined most precisely, "easing the spring" or "easing the Spring"?

Poems

In certain selections in this section we have been concerned with the rhetorical principle of definition. The definitions we have cited to this point have, for the most part, been examples of formal definition: place the word in a class, then distinguish it from other members of the class. Not all definition is of this sort, however. There is what might be called metaphorical definition. This kind of definition, though not technically as acceptable to the serious scholar, is frequently much more vivid and memorable than the formal definition. The following poems are examples of metaphorical definition. Contrast the definitions of pain, exultation, hope, *and* grass *given by the poets with those in the dictionaries. What are the advantages and the disadvantages of each? In what instances would you be likely to use formal definition? Metaphorical definition? Which "stick in your mind" best? Why?*

Emily Dickinson

"Hope" Is the Thing with Feathers

"Hope" is the thing with feathers—
That perches in the soul—
And sings the tune without the words—
And never stops—at all—

And sweetest—in the Gale—is heard—
And sore must be the storm—
That could abash the little Bird
That kept so many warm—

I've heard it in the chillest land—
And on the strangest Sea—
Yet, never, in Extremity,
It asked a crumb—of Me.

Pain Has an Element of Blank

Pain—has an Element of Blank—
It cannot recollect
When it begun—or if there were
A time when it was not—

It has no Future—but itself—
Its Infinite contain
Its Past—enlightened to perceive
New Periods—of Pain.

Exultation Is the Going

Exultation is the going
Of an inland soul to sea,
Past the houses—past the headlands—
Into deep Eternity—

Bred as we, among the mountains,
Can the sailor understand
The divine intoxication
Of the first league out from land?

Walt Whitman

What Is Grass?

A child said, What is the grass? fetching it to me with full hands;
How could I answer the child? . . . I do not know what it is any more than he.

I guess it must be the flag of my disposition, out of hopeful green stuff woven.

Or I guess it is the handkerchief of the Lord,
A scented gift and remembrancer designedly dropped,
Bearing the owner's name someway in the corners, that we may see and remark, and say Whose?

Or I guess the grass is itself a child . . . the produced babe of the vegetation.

Or I guess it is a uniform hieroglyphic,

And it means, Sprouting alike in broad zones and narrow zones,
Growing among black folks as among white,
Kanuck, Tuckahoe, Congressman, Cuff, I give them the same, I receive them the same.

And now it seems to me the beautiful uncut hair of graves.

Writing Projects

Read the following brief, informal essay by Sydney Harris, a popular newspaper columnist, in which he defines *jerk,* a slang term that became popular among American soldiers during World War II. You will find that, according to a dictionary, a jerk is a foolish, dull, stupid, or unconventional person. Note how Harris' definition differs from the dictionary definition. His is an extended definition, in contrast to the formal definition typically found in a dictionary.

A JERK CAN'T SEE HIMSELF AS OTHERS DO

Sidney J. Harris

I don't know whether history repeats itself, but biography certainly does. The other day, Michael came in and asked me what a "jerk" was—the same question Carolyn put to me a dozen years ago.

At that time, I fluffed her off with some inane answer, such as "A jerk isn't a very nice person," but both of us knew it was an unsatisfactory reply. When she went to bed, I began trying to work up a suitable definition.

> It is a marvelously apt word, of course. Until it was coined, not more than 25 years ago, there was really no single word in English to describe the kind of person who is a jerk—"boob" and "simp" were too old hat, and besides they really didn't fit, for they could be lovable, and a jerk never is.

Thinking it over, I decided that a jerk is basically a person without insight. He is not necessarily a fool or a dope, because some extremely clever persons can be jerks. In fact, it has little to do with intelligence as we commonly think of it; it is, rather, a kind of subtle but persuasive aroma emanating from the inner part of the personality.

I know a college president who can be described only as a jerk. He is not an unintelligent man, nor unlearned, nor even unschooled in the social amenities. Yet he is a jerk *cum laude,* because of a fatal flaw in his nature—he is totally incapable of looking into the mirror of his soul and shuddering at what he sees there.

> A jerk, then, is a man (or woman) who is utterly unable to see himself as he appears to others. He has no grace, he is tactless without meaning to be, he is a bore even to his best friends, he is an egotist without charm. All of us are egotists to some extent, but most of us—unlike the jerk—are perfectly and horribly aware of it when we make asses of ourselves. The jerk never knows.

Nor does he feel the common pangs of remorse or humility. He is locked snugly in his tight little shell and looks out at the world with smug, uncomprehending eyes. He has no real sense of humor, because he thinks the only things that are funny are the things he laughs at, and he has no real sense of values, because he thinks the only things that are true are the things he believes in.

The most serious indictment against the jerk is that he is always trying too hard to get people to like or respect him, without trying to like or respect them at all. It can't be done, but it's impossible to explain this to a jerk. That's what makes him one.

Note that Harris has an introduction to his essay that leads into his definition. In the title and first paragraph he also establishes an audience for his essay. Is there, however, a problem in the matter of audience? After reading paragraph one, how old did you envision Michael to be? Are the vocabulary and structure of the essay really directed to a person that young, or does Harris direct his essay to his adult newspaper audience? Harris also takes an attitude toward his subject. He is not merely defining a term; he wants us to believe that his definition is accurate. He is concerned with himself, his audience, and his subject—he has adopted a rhetorical stance. His definition is not merely a definition. He uses the definition to persuade his audience not to act like a jerk.

In paragraph three he tells what a jerk is *not*—a technique you may find useful in defining terms. In paragraph four he states the term and places it in a class. In the last four paragraphs he extends his definition by illustration and explanation. These last two techniques are most frequently used in constructing extended definitions.

You may or may not agree with Harris' definition of a jerk. But do you see clearly what he means by the term *jerk?* Can you analyze the techniques he has used to make his definition clear? For your own theme choose one of the following topics and write an extended definition of the term or phrase you select.

1. Choose a term you use or hear frequently but that might not be fully understood by someone else. You might choose a slang term, a term used in your hobby or on a job you have some experience with, or a term you have learned in your college major. Write an extended definition of the term which will make its meaning clear to your audience. Be aware of *your* rhetorical stance.

For your audience choose (a) your teacher or your parents—someone of an older generation, (If you choose a slang term assume that the audience does not know contemporary slang and may disapprove of slang.) (b) a younger person or group not acquainted with the term, or (c) people your own age. (For a slang term, in the case of *(b)* and *(c)*, assume that the audience uses slang terms such as the one you have chosen, but because they have lived in another section of the country, they are not acquainted with the term you have chosen.) Note how the essay would be shaped differently by each audience.

2. Choose an abstract term such as *love, beauty,* or *honor* and write an extended definition of what the term means to you. Because this kind of definition can be very dull, be especially concerned with the problem of interest and significance. Draw examples from your own experience that will add interest to your theme. Stipulate the audience to whom you are writing the theme, and persuade them that your attitude is important.

3. Choose some terms or phrases that have a special meaning for you, your family, or some other group you associate intimately with. The terms will have a special meaning for you or the group because of the particular experience you have had with them. Relate what the terms mean and how they developed that meaning for you or for the group. This theme will involve not only defining the term but also noting how the meaning of the term changed. Carefully choose a thesis which will give unity to the paper as a whole.

Part III

The History of Language

Our native language is so much a part of us that we are sometimes surprised to learn that it has a history. But language does have history and that history has apparently always intrigued man. Questions such as the following have appeared in our earliest records: What is the origin of language? Which is the oldest language? Why are there so many languages? How does language change? The story of the Tower of Babel, which appears in this section, has often been seen as an attempt to deal with some of those questions 4000 years before Christ. Herodotus, a Greek historian of the fifth century B.C., reports a language experiment conducted by an Egyptian king. It seems the Egyptians had always considered themselves the oldest race on earth. One of their kings determined to test this claim by isolating two infants where they would never hear a human voice. When the children were about two years old, the herdsman who was caring for them reported that they kept repeating the word "bekos." A consultation with his wise men revealed to the king that "bekos" was the Phoenician word for bread. "In consequence the Egyptians, having deliberately weighed the matter, gave place to the Phoenicians, and granted they were more ancient than themselves," records Herodotus.

Men have studied the history of language because they were interested in answers to such questions as those listed above, but there are a number of other reasons why the study of the history of language is important. As we have noted before, language makes us human. A person who does not know something about the history of language lacks knowledge about one of the major aspects of his humanity. Knowledge of the history of language adds significantly to the knowledge of our race. The language we speak is a heritage passed to us from generation to generation by our linguistic ancestors. Knowing something about our language reveals to us a great deal about the experiences those linguistic ancestors had. In English, for example, the pronouns *they, their,* and *them* are words borrowed from the Scandinavian languages and tell us something about the intimate relationships that developed between the English speakers and Scandinavian invaders (who settled permanently in England in the eighth, ninth, and tenth centuries). The vowel sound in the word *boy* is not native to English but borrowed from the French, a result of the great French influence on English from the twelfth to fifteenth centuries. *Typhoon* is the Anglicized form of the Chinese term for a great storm. When English sailors encountered this new phenomonon, they borrowed a word to name it. The borrowing of the word *algebra* from the Arabic indicates our debt to the Arabs for some of our mathematical concepts. Indeed, knowledge of the history of the English language provides a good deal of information about our nation and about the English-speaking people.

Another reason to study the history of language is to gain a greater understanding of documents written in the past. To know that the word *prevent* once meant "to anticipate" or "to go before" makes the following sentence from some old Pennsylvania records meaningful: "I am glad we have prevented their commands in doing it before they came." If we know that *let* once had the meaning "prevent," we can read *Exodus* 5:4 (King James version of the *Bible*) and understand it: "And the king of Egypt said unto them, Wherefore do ye, Moses and Aaron, let the people from their works? get you unto your burdens." A number of words in Shakespeare, in the Declaration of Independence, and in other great documents of the past have changed in meaning since Elizabethan times or since the eighteenth century. To know something of the language of those periods is to understand such great writing better.

A final benefit gained from the study of the language is to be liberated from a narrow view of language. Such study reveals that all languages in active use change and that change is natural and normal. It also reveals that the rules of "correct usage" are not immutable laws of nature but are determined by the way people use the language. For example, in Shakespeare's time speakers of English would have said, "Go you hence?" and "I know not." We say, "Are you going out?" and "I don't know." The modern speaker must use an auxiliary verb to make such sentences negative or interrogatory; Shakespeare used only the main verb. Such change is normal in a living language and is accepted by the users of that language. Language usage also changes: the double negative which is now viewed as a serious mistake was once acceptable in formal written English. "No man had never yet heard of no ship army" of King Alfred's time and Shakespeare's "I will not budge for no man's pleasure" were acceptable English in their day but have been legislated out of correct English. To have a reasonable attitude toward language change, especially in usage, is not to say that "anything goes," but it should develop greater understanding of and appreciation for the variety that exists in so-called correct English.

In this section Jennings and Roberts write about the relationships among the Indo-European languages and about the history of English. Other selections illustrate English at various stages of its development toward contemporary English and discuss how language change occurs. Craig discusses language change as it has affected American English and British English.

Process

In developing a composition by process the primary concern is to tell how something works or worked. If the process regularly takes place in the same way—as in balancing a checkbook or in training a dog, for example—you must reveal the underlying plan step by step to your reader, so that he understands how to arrive at the desired end—the checkbook balanced correctly, the dog trained, the book rebound, or the cream puffs baked. If on the other hand you are writing of a process that occurred in the past—how Napoleon lost the battle of Waterloo or how the English language developed—you must relate the major steps which occurred to bring about the end result. The aim in either type of process is to reveal the steps involved and the order of those steps.

The usual purposes for a composition developed by process are those of giving directions for doing something, and providing information about how some event occurred. If one of these is your purpose, pick a process you understand well and can make interesting to your readers. A different purpose could call forth a different choice of subject. An entertaining theme could be written, for example, on a process that the writer obviously does not understand. Meticulous directions for a simple process, such as ironing a handkerchief, could become a satire on time-and-motion studies.

The purpose should control both your choice of subject and your attitude toward that subject. The latter will be reflected in the tone used in writing of the process—straight-forward and direct, if the purpose is to give information or instructions; or perhaps mocking, if the purpose is to write satire.

Keep in mind throughout your work on a process that you are directing the theme toward a specific audience, and choose a subject with that audience in mind. Fortunately for the writer of a process, most audiences are eager to know how something works. Articles appear in newspapers and magazines detailing processes from both the past and the present: how a frontiersman smoked meat in a hollow tree, how an astronaut trains for space flight, and how a race horse is eased into retirement.

Students do not often know such unusual processes, but they often know more interesting ones than they at first suppose: how to prepare a slide for a microscope, how to teach a beginner to water ski or scuba dive, how to take a picture of the stars, or how to get a young man to ask for a date. One student's careful instructions on baking an apple pie in a paper bag encouraged the teacher to undertake it, and another student's simple directions for growing orchids in the living room sent several students home to follow the steps of this process.

Having selected a subject, decide what the essential steps in the underlying plan are. Breaking the procedure down into steps will aid you in writing and your audience in understanding and remembering the process. Keep the audience in mind during each step. If you wish your readers to duplicate a process you are describing, ask yourself how much that particular audience needs to know about the process and what steps they would have to follow to duplicate it. Divide the process into as few steps as possible. Fifteen steps are much harder to remember than five or six.

Check your steps carefully, to see that they are ordered correctly. For almost all processes time is the key to the proper order. Ask yourself what must come *first* and what must *follow* that, and then what comes *after* that step. Also consider that there may be something the reader should be warned not to do. A well-known article on making camp, for example, concludes each of the early steps of the process with the same warning for the overeager novice: "Do not unpack your tent."

When you have completed checking your steps, you are ready to begin writing. Here too keep your audience in mind. You are the expert guiding the learners. Guide them; strive for clarity; do not confuse them. In particular avoid any technical terms you understand but which some of your readers may not.

The steps given above are simple: decide on the purpose, pick the subject, break the process down into steps, check the order of the steps carefully, and then write the process, keeping the audience in mind throughout.

The View from the Babel Tower

Gary Jennings

The following selection is a chapter from a book entitled Personalities of Language. *The book is an easy to read, frequently amusing account of the many roles of language in human experience. In this chapter the author deals with some of those questions that have intrigued men for thousands of years: How did language originate? Why are there so many languages? What are the relationships among various languages? In explaining how the various branches of the Indo-European language developed and how languages change, the author is describing processes. Note how he uses illustrations to clarify his points and to add interest to his discussion. Particularly note how he frequently uses a summary of points just made to provide a transition to the next point.*

> *Let clerks indite in Latin, and let Frenchmen in their French also indite their quaint terms, for it is kindly to their mouths; and let us show our fantasies in such wordes as we learned of our mother's tongue.*
>
> —THOMAS USK

When Christopher Columbus set sail into the sunset on his first voyage in 1492, one of his ships carried an under-officer specially assigned to the expedition because he spoke fluent Hebrew. Columbus expected to fetch up in Cipangu, Cathay or Ind, and there was no interpreter available to him who knew Japanese, Chinese or any of the Indian tongues. But it was a common belief in Europe at the time that Hebrew, the language of the Scriptures, was the original tongue of all mankind, so Columbus was confident that even among the Far Easterners he would be able to communicate with their scholars.

He must have been dismayed, when he finally landed in what appeared to be a backwater boondocks of the Indies, to find that the natives were as ignorant of Hebrew as they were of the Scriptures, of biblical history and of everything else in Old World experience. At any rate, there is no record of classical interpreters having been supplied for the subsequent voyages to these new Indies.

But the belief persisted until the middle of the nineteenth century that some single original language had been God's gift to man at the time of Creation, and that in happier days "the whole earth was of one language, and of one speech." The theologians took it on faith and the philologists, such as they were, tried piously to confirm it by tortuous rationalizing. In the 1680s Cotton Mather wrote his M.A. thesis at Harvard in a detailed defense of this supposed linguistic revelation. In 1808 the philosopher Friedrich von Schlegel persuaded himself that the ancestor of all modern tongues was the Sanskrit of ancient India. In the 1830s lexicographer Noah Webster gave it as his opinion that the prototype language must have been "Chaldee," that is, Aramaic, the language of the Holy Land in Christ's day. At various times Hungarian, German, Danish, Basque, Dutch, Swedish—all of these and many others—have been proved, at least to their speakers' satisfaction, to have been the language of Eden.

The sorry diversity of human languages in the latter-day world was neatly explained by the eleventh chapter of Genesis, and that explanation still suffices for the religious fundamentalists. When the overweening descendants of Shem, Ham and Japheth dared to begin building a tower that should rival the heights of heaven, the Lord chastised them with a thunderclap confusion of tongues. Unable even to call for the waterboy, the tower builders had to abandon their project. Each man of them wandered off, burdened with his individual and lonely language, to some far country where he could beget a whole new people of his own and have somebody to talk to.

The Bible called the city of the ill-fated ziggurat Babel (probably from the Hebrew *bilbel,* "confusion"). Hence the fundamentalists could demonstrate through a plausible folk-etymology that the Babel story was confirmed by echoes in many modern languages—the English word "babble," the Italian *balbettio,* the Spanish *balbuceo,* the French *babil,* etc.

But as the nineteenth century moved into its second half, a new generation of linguists, perhaps no less devout than their predecessors but more disposed to scientific discipline, began to question the concept of a divine Ur-language. At the same time, along came Charles Darwin to dispute the whole concept of Creation. Some scholars were so excited by his theory of evolution that they strained as hard to apply it to the origins of language as they had previously strained to validate Babel. Friedrich Max Müller earnestly suggested that the grunts and squeals of man's animal ancestors all over the earth had gradually evolved toward speech in the same way their brains had evolved toward intelligence, and that thus the world's languages would already have been infinitely various even before the genus *Homo* had attained full sapience.

That exegesis was a little too pat, and was never seriously credited. But Darwin's new timetable did at least give the scholars about a million years of human evolution to maneuver in, as against the paltry few thousand the Bible had allowed them. (According to the sober calculations of Archbishop James Ussher in the seventeenth century, Creation had taken place on an October morning in the year 4004 B.C. And Gustav Seyffarth, in the 1820s, asserted that "the alphabet of the races of the world" had been invented the day the Deluge ended: September 7, 3446 B.C.)

After Darwin, a host of anthropologists, archaeologists and paleontologists began to turn up evidence that a fair measure of human civilization had been achieved as long ago as 6000 B.C., and that man-creatures must have been living in passably peaceable intercourse—implying some degree of effective mutual communication—a good three quarters of a million years before that.

And yet to this day we are no nearer knowing how language began than are the fundamentalist endorsers of an archetype tongue divine. For all the proof we have to the contrary, we might as well join them in believing that human speech was a direct and recent gift from the Almighty. Linguists now are fairly sure they know the provenances of the major tongues of today, but the primary sources of those languages are shrouded by time past. Too, there are some current languages which refuse to fit comfortably into the linguists' scheme of things, and there must have been untold numbers of other such tongues which flourished and then fell silent over the ages.

There are probably as many different theories about the origin of languages as there are professional linguists, but four of these should suffice to show their general tenor. The linguists, though not normally inclined to persiflage, have described these four hypotheses by rather chucklesome names: the Bow-Wow theory, the Pooh-Pooh theory, the Ding-Dong theory and the Yo-He-Ho theory.

The Bow-Wow theory supposes that man learned to talk by parroting the cries of animals. Considering that man was first a hunter, the notion has a certain plausibility. Once a group of men had agreed, say, that a boar was an "oink" and an aurochs was a "moo," they would eventually have aspired to naming other things.

The Pooh-Poohists believe that man's first meaningful noises were involuntarily jolted out of him by sudden events or situations, somewhat in the manner of a duchess finding a worm in her salad. It's a little hard to believe that a caveman ever uttered anything quite as finical as "pooh-pooh" but, considering his thorny environment, it's not unlikely that he began to talk by saying a frequent "ow!"

The Ding-Dong theory is based on onomatopoeia, like the Bow-Wow, only predicating that man's first words were echoes of natural sounds other than those of animals. For instance, he may have cried "whack!" in merry mimicry of his club bouncing off a rival's skull, or muttered a fearful "bumble-boom" in imitation of the thunder.

The Yo-He-Ho theory maintains that the earliest effective speech was the result of man's beginning to cooperate and coordinate with his fellows. That is, a group of men may have learned to lighten their labors by shouting some sort of cadence count, like sailors' chanteys or soldiers' marching songs, when they were hauling home a sabertooth's carcass or levering boulders down onto an invading war party.

It seems indisputable that sign language by gestures must have long preceded and then accompanied the development of any meaningful grunts and mumbles. We still find gestures handy for beckoning, shooing, threatening, and even as an aid to exposition (ask anybody, "What is a spiral staircase?" and watch). Sir Richard Paget dwelt on this to suggest, in 1930, an offbeat theory of his own as to the beginnings of speech. It was his hypothesis that the first talking man's tongue movements merely imitated his hand gestures, and that his simultaneous expiration of a breath resulted in the articulation of a specific noise to reinforce each gesture.

For example, to indicate "up" a man would point a finger skyward. At the same time he would unconsciously raise the tip of his tongue to touch the roof of his mouth. If at this moment he grunted, the resulting sound would be approximately "ull" or "oll"—or, as it would be written in Latin, *al*.

Sir Richard pointed out that this word element is still widespread in words signifying "up." Latin has *altus* for "high," whence the English "altitude." The Semitic *al* means "to ascend," whence the Israeli airline El Al. The Melanesian *al* means "to climb." The Kwakiutl Indian *allela* means "up." Other grunts with the tongue variously tilted against the palate give the variant sounds of *at, an, ar* and *atl*. Sir Richard thought it significant that many of the world's upthrusting mountains contain these up-tongued noises in their names: the Alps, Atlas, Andes, Himalaya, Allegheny, Ararat, etc.

It's easy enough to find holes in Paget's theory. For one thing, not all speech sounds involve the manipulation of the tongue, and the rest of our vocal machinery is not adapted for imitating gestures. But, because we can never know the real story of language's beginning, his theory is no more flimsy than the four previously mentioned. There have been stranger ones; Edgar Sturtevant once suggested that man developed language when he first found it profitable to deceive.

The reason for the impossibility of ever tracing back to the beginnings of speech is that there is no "primitive" language surviving on earth for the scholars to study. Early explorers thought they had found something of the sort among the American Indians, the Australian aborigines and such backward peoples. But, crude though their languages sounded to the white man's ear, they proved on investigation to be of a development and complexity easily equal to any "civilized" language. And so the oldest and most basic languages available for scholarly inspection are those whose fragments of writing have been exhumed by archaeologists. But plainly, any ancient language that had attained to writing had already progressed eons beyond the primordial kindergarten.

Most linguistic scholars have ceased to fret over the insoluble. They have contented themselves with visualizing modern-day languages as twigs, so to speak, and with inching backward along them to find the common branches from which the twigs sprouted, thence farther backward to the common limbs from which the branches grew. Thus they have been able to group the world's languages into a system of fairly well-defined families. But if there ever was an archetypal, ancestral language which begat them all—a single trunk to this family tree—it is beyond discovery.

Before we look into the personalities which the various languages developed as they grew, let us briefly see how they *became* separate and disparate.

Our English language is a twig of the so-called Teutonic branch of a limb designated Indo-European. The heftiest and most prolific limb of the language tree, Indo-European has sprouted languages which would seem to be as dissimilar as they are far apart—from Irish in the West to the Bengali of India in the East. The belief is that all the Indo-European languages stem from a single prehistoric tongue, and that its speakers must have lived originally in the area which now comprises Austria, Czechoslovakia and Hungary.

How these people came to be there, whether they had evolved there autochthonously from time beyond reckoning, can only be conjectured. But it is possible that they were a Stone Age mixture of even earlier types from both northern and Mediterranean lands, in which case their "original" language must have been an amalgam of still others. To call these people "Indo-Europeans," as most linguists do, is an obvious *ex post facto* misnomer based on the eventual geographic dispersal of their language. But if they had a name for themselves no one knows it, so we will continue to use the term for convenience's sake.

The Indo-Europeans, then, were nomadic. Over the ages various groups of them went a-roving far, far from home, never to return. As they scattered to all the points of the compass, each group's language began to grow apart from the parent stock and from each of the others'. For example, the Indo-Europeans who first trekked westward gradually developed a proto-Celtic variety of their language during the long march. At one time this must have been the language of almost all western Europe, but it survives today only in its later, splinter languages of Scots Gaelic, Irish, Welsh, Breton on the farthest western coast of France, and the almost extinct Manx.

Following the Celtic groups, a subsequent westward migration spread a Teutonic form of Indo-European all across the northern part of the Continent. This gradually resolved itself into a number of intermediate tongues: Gothic, Old Norse, Englisc, Old Saxon, Franconian—and thence eventually into High and Low German, Dutch, Flemish, the Scandinavian tongues and the various early forms of what finally became English.

Another wave of Indo-Europeans headed straight north to become Lithuanians and Letts. Others moved east and southeast, developing the Slavic body of languages which today includes Polish, Czech, Bulgarian, Serbo-Croatian, the several Russian dialects, etc.

Some of the Stone Age wanderers plodded southeastward all the way across Asia Minor. During this time, they developed a tongue which in a later form became Sanskrit, the oldest Indo-European language with which we are familiar. Various groups dropped out of the line of march here and there, to settle in and bequeath new languages to Armenia, Persia, Afghanistan and Baluchistan. But the most persistently footloose pushed on clear to the Indian subcontinent, where they fanned out into a multitude of settlements and dialects which became the numerous Indic tongues of today.

Still other Indo-Europeans moved southward across the Balkans, developing along the way a proto-Hellenic tongue which was eventually to become classical, then modern, Greek. Another group loitered in Albania, to plant the Thraco-Illyrian still in use there.

Other parties crossed the Alps, developing the Italic languages which eventuated in Latin. Much later, via Roman imperialism, Latin displaced the Celtic tongues of southern Europe to give us the whole body of Romance languages: French, Spanish, Italian, Portuguese, Catalan and Romanian.

My mapping of the spread of the Indo-European tongues is admittedly oversimplified and presumptive; neither mass migrations nor changes in language ever proceed so smoothly. We don't know how long these processes did take, except that they must have occupied glacial ages. We don't know in precisely what order the various migrations took place, or how they might have been affected by rebuffs, checks, retreats and roundabout detours. We don't know how many elementary and intermediate changes the languages may have gone through. We can only trace backward from the numerous language twigs that still are green and from a few dead ones we can recognize as having withered from the same familial branches.

For a small illustration of family resemblance, take the English word "three." In almost every Indo-European language the word for "three" begins with a dental consonant (*t, d* or *th*) followed by an *r*. Among the other languages of the Teutonic branch, for example, it is *thrjá* in Icelandic, *tre* in all the continental Scandinavian tongues, *drei* in German, *drie* in Dutch and Flemish. Among the Romance languages, it is *trois* in French, *tres* in Spanish and Portuguese, *tre* in Italian and *trei* in Romanian. Among the Slavic languages, it is *tri* in Russian, *tři* in Czech, and *trzy* in Polish. It is *tri* in the Celtic languages: Irish, Scots, Gaelic, Welsh and Breton; and *tris* in the Baltic languages: Lettish and Lithuanian. It is *tre* in Albanian. It was *tri* in Sanskrit, *treis* in classical Greek, *tres* in Latin and *thri* in Anglo-Saxon.

The prehistoric Indo-European tide submerged what must have been innumerable earlier languages in both Europe and Asia—as in Italy, where we know that it washed away the Etruscan and Messapian. Only one European tongue dating from before the migrations managed to endure to modern times: the Basque of the French-Spanish Pyrenees. But the Indo-European tongues themselves did not everywhere survive. The Macedonian of northern Greece was extinct before history began. The Tocharian evolved by the Indo-Europeans who penetrated farthest eastward, into the Gobi desert of remotest Turkestan, is known only from scraps of written records.

And even though the Indo-European tongues are spoken today by half of the world's people, there are stubborn islands of unrelated languages flourishing right in the middle of Europe. Basque, for instance, is an entity all to itself, unallied to any other language on earth. Turkish is the European representative of a language group which includes Tataric, Kirghizic and numerous other tongues in use across wide belts of central and northern Asia. What really seems odd is that Hungary, part of the long-ago homeland of the aboriginal Indo-European, should now speak the alien Magyar, a member of a totally unrelated language family (the Finno-Ugric branch of the Ural-Altaic limb) which also includes the Finnish and Lappish of the far north.

Most other languages of the world can similarly be lumped into families whose members all have a common origin. For example, while the two major tongues of India, Hindi and Bengali, are chips off the Indo-European block, the nation also has to cope with some two hundred others, most of them of the Dravidian group: Tamil, Telugu, Canarese, etc. (A ten-rupee note has to proclaim itself in nine different languages.)

The Semitic group once supplied the world with its widest-used languages of commerce and diplomacy: Babylonian-Assyrian, Phoenician, Aramaic. Today its chief representatives are the Arabic of the Near East and Mediterranean Africa, the Amharic of Ethiopia, Maltese and Hebrew, the latter a "dead" language for twenty centuries but successfully resuscitated since 1948 as the national tongue of Israel.

A near limb to the Semitic group is the Hamitic, whose greenest and most fruitful twig was the Egyptian of the pharaohs. A direct descendant, Coptic, is the liturgical language of African Christians, while such relations as Berber, Tamashek and Somali are still spoken by various tribes in the region of the Sahara.

The peoples of the rest of Africa speak some five hundred different tongues, classified by linguists in three main groups—the Sudanese-Guinean group of the Gulf of Guinea coast and the central interior of the continent, the Bantu group farther south, and the Hottentot-Bushman languages of the southwest. It seems probable that the fierce nationalism of Africa's new autonomies will result in a gradual interweaving or lopping off of the lesser language twigs in order to surmount the current communications handicaps. But at this writing Africa is still being hampered by its multiplicity of tongues, from the level of continental progress to that of connubial peace, as witness this letter received by an African newspaper's advice-to-the-lovelorn columnist:

"Being of a different tribe from my wife I do not know what to do every afternoon at four when the radio broadcasts in vernacular. She calls for one tongue, I for another. . . ."

The Sinitic languages of Asia, like the Indo-European, seem to have developed during primeval times when an aboriginal race of people gradually overflowed in all directions from an oriental Eden, situated perhaps in the fertile western valleys of the Yangtze River. The family now includes the myriad spoken dialects of China, plus Tibetan, Burmese, Thai and various other languages of Indo-China. The Japanese and Korean languages may or may not be related to one another—linguists differ on this—but neither of them is related to Chinese or any other of the Sinitic tongues.

The map of the pre-Columbian Americas is a jigsaw puzzle of vaguely defined linguistic families, some forty each in North and South America. This is a conservative estimate, and the families have been determined more or less by guesswork, but any more rigid classification is probably impossible. There were more than a thousand different tongues spoken in the Western hemisphere at the time the white man arrived, but most of these were dead or dying by the time comparative philologists began to study them.

It may be that the first migrants to cross from Asia via the Aleutian stepping stones brought with them a proto-language like the original Indo-European master tongue. Or perhaps they made the crossing long before any of mankind had any well-developed language at all, and the numerous later tongues evolved independently. Or the crossing may have been accomplished in any number of successive waves, each new migration contributing a new tongue. Some linguists claim to have found affinities between the Eskimo family of languages and the Finno-Ugric which includes Hungarian and Finnish. Other scholars, even more imaginative, believe that the Algonquian Indian languages of northern and eastern North America contain elements borrowed from the speech of Viking explorers who visited the New World five centuries before Columbus.

Like the Amerindian, the more than two hundred native languages of Australia and New Guinea had begun to dwindle before they could be seriously studied, and their familial groupings likewise must remain conjectural. The Malayo-Polynesian tongues are rather better known. This limb of language is second only to the Indo-European in its geographical spread. Its related tongues are spoken from Madagascar, off the coast of Africa, all the way to Easter Island in the eastern Pacific, more than halfway around the world. Its branches and twigs include the Tagalog of the Philippines, the Maori of New Zealand, the fast-disappearing Hawaiian, and numerous other languages of Oceania: Fijian, Tahitian, etc.

Not even professional linguists know how many different languages are in use in the world today. The French Academy, a stickler for precision, used to maintain that there were exactly 2,796, exclusive of local dialects. Other estimates have ranged as high as five thousand, because few scholars can agree on just what *is* a "dialect" or when it qualifies as a "language." And, although most of the however-many thousands of tongues have been tucked cozily into families, there are a number of orphans which deny any kinfolk at all. As already mentioned, Basque is one of them. There's an old legend to the effect that the Devil has never been able to tempt a Basque because the language is so uniquely difficult that he's never learned to speak it.

Korean and Japanese may be orphans, too, unless further linguistic research somehow links them together. Others include a number of hermit languages in Kamchatka and far northeast Siberia, the tongue of the Andaman Islands in the Bay of Bengal, and that of the hairy Ainus of northern Japan.

Even the nonlinguist reader has probably recognized most of the names, at least, of the languages mentioned so far in this chapter, and there are professional linguists who speak, read and write a formidable number of them (Charles Berlitz of the Berlitz Schools of Languages reputedly speaks thirty languages with varying degrees of fluency). But there are other tongues, currently or formerly in use, whose very names are little known.

Just for a sampling, consider Pis, a language of the Caroline Islands; Kookie, an Indian dialect akin to Bengali; Flup, spoken along Africa's Gambia River; Saliva, an Orinoco Indian dialect; Gah, the tongue of the Malayan Alfurus; Bzub, a dialect of the Caucasus; Zaza, a Kurdish tongue of northwest Persia; Cullilan-Cunny, an Amerindian language; Kuzzilbash, a Turkish dialect; Jalloof, language of a Senegal tribe; Miao, the dialect of China's Hunan province; Yairy-Yairy and Watty-Watty, two Australian dialects of New South Wales.

It is a little bit droll, a little bit pathetic, that certain peoples all speaking the same language have seen fit to invent a name for themselves which implies that they are the only people on earth, or at least the most important. This hub-of-the-universe ethnocentrism is oftenest to be found among peoples who inhabit an isolated area, or who are wary or contemptuous of their neighbors. The Eskimos, for example, call themselves the Innuit, which means "the people." The name of China comes eponymously from the dynasty of Ch'in, in turn derived from the word *chin* meaning "man," thus the Chinese are "the men." So are the Gilyads of Siberia (*nibach* in their tongue). So are the Illeni Indians (*illeni,* "the men," gave us the name of Illinois). The African name Bantu means "the men." What we call the Hottentots call themselves Khoi-Khoin, the "men among men."

But no nationality and no language has been able to remain completely aloof and uncontaminated. The men of the Innuit are now well versed in GI slang, courtesy of American military outposts in the Arctic. The Hottentot men among men can probably discourse in Hollywood jargon, learned from the location crews of many a jungle movie epic.

Though separate tongues were developed by the various groups of Indo-European migrants (and by the similar offshoots of all the other linguistic limbs), these languages did not just achieve variety and then petrify at that stage. They continued to change, and are still continuing to change, with every passing year.

Some of a language's development is internal in nature. Its speakers invent new words to fit new things and concepts, as civilization inevitably grows more complex. They hatch colloquialisms and slang expressions, and a certain percentage of these become fixtures of the language. The natural elisions of everyday speech, vernacular differences or outright mistakes in pronunciation, passing fads in spoken language, all can become accepted and permanent usages. For example, the Middle English word *napron* became, through the slurring of "a napron," the modern English "an apron." In sixteenth-century France it became fashionable, for some queer reason, to pronounce *r* as *z* (Paris: *Pazi*). Though the cuteness eventually became tiresome and petered out, at least one leftover remains in *chaise* for the original *chaire*.

Even arbitrary legislation has occasionally changed the course of a people's language. As recently as 1938 Norway decreed an end to the modified Danish that had been its "literary language" since the Middle Ages, and substituted a standardized version of the everyday vernacular called Landsmaal as its official national tongue. Kemal Ataturk, upon becoming dictator-president of Turkey in 1923, at once set about abolishing the Arabic script that had previously been used for writing Turkish and ordered the use of the Roman alphabet. The result is that Turkish children can begin to read and write now after about six months of schooling, instead of the two or three years it used to take.

And there are external pressures that mold every language: wartime conquests and defeats, intergroup commerce, cultural and technological exchanges, immigration, tourism. Rome's conquest of all western Europe replaced its numerous Celtic tongues with adaptations of Latin. But the long occupation of those territories also affected the speech of the conquerors; the rankers of the legions returned home with their own language considerably mutated, so that eventually the common folk of Rome spoke a plebeian Latin quite different from the patrician language our schools still teach. For instance, *equus* was the highbrow word for "horse," but it survives only in such equally bookish words as "equine" and "equestrian." The legionnaire and the Roman-in-the-street said *caballus,* which is much more widely represented in the Romance languages of today—the French *cheval,* the Italian *cavallo,* the Spanish *caballo*—and in the English "cavalry," "cavalcade," etc.

Switzerland shows one remarkable effect of commerce on language. Traditionally the world's bank, referee and middleman, Switzerland has never aspired to developing a distinctive language of its own, unless one counts the provincial tongue called Romansch spoken by less than 2 per cent of the population. The Swiss have found it more expedient, prudent and profitable to make do with the French, German and Italian of their three abutting neighbors.

The linguistic largesse of immigration is too well known, especially in the United States, to require elaboration here. The linguistic souvenirs brought home by tourists are perhaps best exemplified in the cocktail-party conversation of any debutante just returned from her "finishing" in Europe. As for cultural exchanges of language, the Western world's musical terminology is predominantly Italian (*piano, fortissimo,* etc.), while art critics rely on both French and Italian expressions (*trompe l'oeil, chiaroscuro,* etc.). Because France gave aviation its earliest impetus, the flyer's technology is still full of French terms (*fuselage, aileron,* etc.).

There is no language in the world whose structure or vocabulary does not exhibit the results of one or several internal ferments and external jostlings. And of them all, English is the one which best illustrates the many ways in which language can change, develop and grow.

Whatever tongue the neolithic Britons may have chanted in their dawn-worship ceremonies at Stonehenge, no one knows. We do know that their language gave way to the Celtic brought from the Continent by the so-called Indo-Europeans. And *that* was largely supplanted by the Teutonic dialects of the later invading Angles, Saxons and Jutes. Their Englisc, which became Anglo-Saxon, gave English its basic structure, its grammar and its stock of common words for common things, acts, concepts and emotions. But Anglo-Saxon words, though the oftenest used, are a minority in modern English, because the vocabulary has so often been enriched by other conquerors, skirmishers and settlers—and it is their words we use most in science, art, religion, technology, politics, literature and other supracommon fields.

Latin came with the Roman legions, the later Christian missionaries and the still later cultural cosmopolitanism of the Renaissance. Norse words were contributed by the Viking invaders. The Norman conquerors brought a sort of bastard French, while Parisian French attended the later succession of the Angevin kings.

By the fourteenth century, the blend of court French (with its admixture of Latin) and the London dialect of Anglo-Saxon (with its traces of Norse and Celtic) had been established as *the* English language. But its speakers continued to borrow words from all the Continental tongues and, during Britannia's heyday of ruling the waves, her explorers and colonizers collected still more words from a multitude of exotic sources.

Meantime, English was constantly enjoying or enduring every possible change from within: simplification of its grammar, shifts in pronunciation and spelling, the invention of neologisms, changes in the meaning of many words, the formalization of slang, colloquialisms and idioms. It gradually sloughed off most of the word-endings—indications of gender, number, case, tense and mood—which still complicate the Continental languages. The inflections which do remain in English are few (*-s* for plural, *'s* for possessive, *-ed* for past tense, etc.) and are seldom irregular (as "men" instead of mans, "his" instead of he's, "went" instead of goed, etc.). In the main, English relies on word order and the addition of modifying words to make its sentences clear. In this it is structurally more like Chinese than like any of its Indo-European cousins.

Its insatiable appetite for other people's words and its uninhibited talent for invention have given English, of all languages, probably the widest scope of expression and the richest potential for euphony. It has a store of synonyms to convey just about every conceivable nuance of meaning; it would be possible to write a lengthy monograph on the subject of Love, for instance, without once repeating the word. And in the rare event that a writer cannot find just the precise locution for his purpose, he can ransack the language's vast stockpile of word elements to compound a brand-new coinage of his own.

The one pressure to which English has never bent is that of legislation, although self-appointed improvers have had a go at it from time to time. The Norman kings decreed the use of their brand of French at court, in the courts of law, in trade and in literature. In 1450 Reginald Pecock sought to jettison the Gallicisms and Latinisms that had crept into English, offering pure Anglian alternatives like "ungothroughable" for impenetrable and "nottobethoughtuponable" for imponderable. When the Puritans came into the ascendancy in England they tried to abolish Roman Catholicism from the language by such sleazy stratagems as substituting "Sir" for Saint in church names—Sir Peter's, Sir Mary's (*sic*), etc.—and promoting "Christ-tide" to delete the despised "mass" from Christmas.

Shortly after the American Revolution, several of the United States founding fathers favored setting up an academy like that of France or Sweden, to standardize and sanctify an "official" American language. And there have been meaningless gestures like the 1923 attempt to have Congress establish that "the national and official language of the Government and people of the United States of America . . . is hereby defined as and declared to be the American language, [i.e.] words and phrases generally accepted as being in good use by the people of the United States of America. . . ." But no do-good decree, proposal or ban has ever stopped the English-speaking people from conducting their lives in whatever vernacular they chose.

I should mention here that any praise of the virtues and advantages of English is an automatic appreciation of the many other tongues which have so heavily contributed to it. And also that the foregoing capsule history of English is intended as microcosm; every other language has manifested similar changes, developments and growth. Thus, every language equally testifies to man's adaptability to shifting circumstances and conditions.

But things do not change everywhere in the same direction or degree. One society becomes urbanized, another remains agrarian; a land-cramped people become migrants or marauders, a comfortable people turn to contemplation and aesthetics. This is not to say that every individual person conforms to a societal way of life—but his native language may. Doubtless the Araucanian Indians of the South American pampas have their sages, rascals, idlers, wits and half-wits, but they all speak the same basic tongue. And that language reflects the pitiful rigors of their existence in that it includes a wide vocabulary of words just to express varying intensities of hunger.

The reasonable man is aware that not all Scots are miserly, not all

Frenchmen are excitable, not all Russians are gloomy—and ditto for all the other facile labels fabricated by superstition, false tradition and standing jokes. But, while it is impossible to assign a stereotyped temperament to every individual of a specific race, color or nationality, it *is* often possible to detect differing and distinctive "personalities" among their languages.

To a non-Scot, the word "burr" perfectly describes both the Gaelic pronunciation and the national flower of Scotland: the language and the thistle are equally rough-edged. The liquid vowels of the Polynesian tongues conjure up visions of loveliness and languor, full moon and blue lagoon.

Contrariwise, the gutturals of the German language sound, to a non-German, as harsh and forbidding as winter in the Black Forest. The swoops and swirls of Persian script seem, to a Westerner, as voluptuous and sensual as the quatrains of Omar Khayyám. But Goethe wrote tender and lyrical word-music in German, and Persian is prosaically utilitarian for keeping the accounts of Iranian oil companies. The personality of a language, like that of a man, is the sum of many things not always apparent to the casual eye or ear.

One factor in the makeup of a language is what the Germans call *Sprachgefühl,* or speech-feeling. In *Words and Their Ways in English Speech* philologists J. B. Greenough and G. L. Kittredge define it as "a regular and persistent mode of thought, and consequently of expression, which more or less dominates the form of the language in the mouths of all its speakers. . . . It affects every word that we utter, though we may think that we are speaking as the whim of the moment dictates; and thus it is the strongest and most pervasive of all conservative forces, and has kept [each] language true to itself." They cite as examples Latin's majestic simplicity of style and the epigrammatic scintillation of French, then add, "Men of genius may take great liberties with their mother tongue without offense; but let them once run counter to its characteristic tendencies, let them violate [its] *Sprachgefühl,* and their mannerism becomes, as it were, a foreign language."

While the national language of a people has its own personality, a *Sprachgefühl* distinct from even closely related tongues, it is at the same time a complex of sublanguages—regional dialects, trade jargons and the like—each of which has its own idiosyncrasies. Take a New York stockbroker and an Alabama sharecropper, a Moscow ballerina and a Pskov muzhik—or, for that matter, any teen-ager and his grandfather. Each pair speaks one national language, but with what worlds-apart difference.

It may be hard to imagine a world in which every town or every social group or even every family spoke a separate language—but it could conceivably have happened. Oral language, like gossip, can undergo remarkable changes even across the space of two backyards, let alone across a country or a century. There is every reason to believe that the world's peace and progress have been retarded by its multifarious tongues. But, horrible to contemplate, these thousands of mutually incomprehensible languages might well have wisped and splintered into thousands of thousands—and mankind into even more fragmented, insular and dissident subcultures—except for one thing. Along came writing.

Questions

1. Jennings discusses some common theories of the origin of language that are also briefly mentioned by Jacobs in "Adam Names the Animals." What does the choice of names indicate about scholars' attitudes toward these theories?
2. Using the information provided by Jennings, construct a "family tree" for the Indo-European language family.
3. Jennings notes that linguists sometimes have difficulty distinguishing between a dialect and a language. Can you explain why such a distinction is difficult to make?
4. According to Jennings, living languages change "with every passing year." Why? How effective do you think governmental or other efforts to prevent or delay change can be?
5. "There is every reason to believe that the world's peace and progress have been retarded by its multifarious tongues." Do you agree with this statement by Jennings? In what ways might a common language promote world peace?
6. Can you find clues in this article which help to identify Jennings' voice in his writing and the audience to which he writes? Is he a scholar writing to other scholars? A scholar writing to laymen? An interested, qualified layman writing to others interested in language? Give specific examples to support your position. Does your answer take into consideration such things as word choice and the level on which the technical information is expressed?

Something About English

Paul Roberts *The preceding selection deals primarily with the Indo-European language family. In this selection Professor Roberts focuses on a single language, English. Very briefly he attempts to tell us how English has changed since about 1000 A.D. Note how, as he relates the processes by which Old English became Modern English, he uses illustration to clarify his points and to add interest to the essay. You might, as you read his discussions of Old English, Middle English, Early Modern English, and Modern English, turn to the comparative passages of Genesis 11:1–9 which follow to see examples of the language at those four stages of its development.*

*N*o understanding of the English language can be very satisfactory without a notion of the history of the language. But we shall have to make do with just a notion. The history of English is long and complicated, and we can only hit the high spots.

The history of our language begins a little after A.D. 600. Everything before that is pre-history, which means that we can guess at it but can't prove much. For a thousand years or so before the birth of Christ our linguistic ancestors were savages wandering through the forests of northern Europe. Their language was a part of the Germanic branch of the Indo-European family.

At the time of the Roman Empire—say, from the beginning of the Christian Era to around A.D. 400—the speakers of what was to become English were scattered along the northern coast of Europe. They spoke a dialect of Low German. More exactly, they spoke several different dialects, since they were several different tribes. The names given to the tribes who got to England are *Angles, Saxons,* and *Jutes.* For convenience, we can refer to them all as Anglo-Saxons.

Their first contact with civilization was a rather thin acquaintance with the Roman Empire on whose borders they lived. Probably some of the Anglo-Saxons wandered into the Empire occasionally, and certainly Roman merchants and traders traveled among the tribes. At any rate, this period saw the first of our many borrowings from Latin. Such words as *kettle, wine, cheese, butter, cheap, plum, gem, bishop, church* were borrowed at this time. They show something of the relationship of the Anglo-Saxons with the Romans. The Anglo-Saxons were learning, getting their first taste of civilization.

They still had a long way to go, however, and their first step was to help smash the civilization they were learning from. In the fourth century the Roman power weakened badly. While the Goths were pounding away at the Romans in the Mediterranean countries, their relatives, the Anglo-Saxons, began to attack Britain.

The Romans had been the ruling power in Britain since A.D. 43. They had subjugated the Celts whom they found living there and had succeeded in setting up a Roman administration. The Roman influence did not extend to the outlying parts of the British Isles. In Scotland, Wales, and Ireland the Celts remained free and wild, and they made periodic forays against the Romans in England. Among other defense measures, the Romans built the famous Roman Wall to ward off the tribes in the north.

Even in England the Roman power was thin. Latin did not become the language of the country as it did in Gaul and Spain. The mass of people continued to speak Celtic, with Latin and the Roman civilization it contained in use as a top dressing.

In the fourth century, troubles multiplied for the Romans in Britain. Not only did the untamed tribes of Scotland and Wales grow more and more restive, but the Anglo-Saxons began to make pirate raids on the eastern coast. Furthermore, there was growing difficulty everywhere in the Empire, and the legions in Britain were siphoned off to fight elsewhere. Finally, in A.D. 410, the last Roman ruler in England, bent on becoming emperor, left the islands and took the last of the legions with him. The Celts were left in possession of Britain but almost defenseless against the impending Anglo-Saxon attack.

Not much is surely known about the arrival of the Anglo-Saxons in England. According to the best early source, the eighth-century historian Bede, the Jutes came in 449 in response to a plea from the Celtic king, Vortigern, who wanted their help against the Picts attacking from the north. The Jutes subdued the Picts but then quarreled and fought with Vortigern, and, with reinforcements from the Continent, settled permanently in Kent. Somewhat later the Angles established themselves in eastern England and the Saxons in the south and west. Bede's account is plausible enough, and these were probably the main lines of the invasion.

We do know, however, that the Angles, Saxons, and Jutes were a long time securing themselves in England. Fighting went on for as long as a hundred years before the Celts in England were all killed, driven into

Wales, or reduced to slavery. This is the period of King Arthur, who was not entirely mythological. He was a Romanized Celt, a general, though probably not a king. He had some success against the Anglo-Saxons, but it was only temporary. By 550 or so the Anglo-Saxons were firmly established. English was in England.

All this is pre-history, so far as the language is concerned. We have no record of the English language until after 600, when the Anglo-Saxons were converted to Christianity and learned the Latin alphabet. The conversion began, to be precise, in the year 597 and was accomplished within thirty or forty years. The conversion was a great advance for the Anglo-Saxons, not only because of the spiritual benefits but because it reëstablished contact with what remained of Roman civilization. This civilization didn't amount to much in the year 600, but it was certainly superior to anything in England up to that time.

It is customary to divide the history of the English language into three periods: Old English, Middle English, and Modern English. Old English runs from the earliest records—i.e., seventh century—to about 1100; Middle English from 1100 to 1450 or 1500; Modern English from 1500 to the present day. Sometimes Modern English is further divided into Early Modern, 1500–1700, and Late Modern, 1700 to the present.

When England came into history, it was divided into several more or less autonomous kingdoms, some of which at times exercised a certain amount of control over the others. In the century after the conversion the most advanced kingdom was Northumbria, the area between the Humber River and the Scottish border. By A.D. 700 the Northumbrians had developed a respectable civilization, the finest in Europe. It is sometimes called the Northumbrian Renaissance, and it was the first of the several renaissances through which Europe struggled upward out of the ruins of the Roman Empire. It was in this period that the best of the Old English literature was written, including the epic poem *Beowulf.*

In the eighth century, Northumbrian power declined, and the center of influence moved southward to Mercia, the kingdom of the Midlands. A century later the center shifted again, and Wessex, the country of the West Saxons, became the leading power. The most famous king of the West Saxons was Alfred the Great, who reigned in the second half of the ninth century, dying in 901. He was famous not only as a military man and administrator but also as a champion of learning. He founded and supported schools and translated or caused to be translated many books from Latin into English. At this time also much of the Northumbrian literature of two centuries earlier was copied in West Saxon. Indeed, the great bulk of Old English writing which has come down to us is in the West Saxon dialect of 900 or later.

In the military sphere, Alfred's great accomplishment was his successful opposition to the Viking invasions. In the ninth and tenth centuries, the Norsemen emerged in their ships from their homelands in Denmark and the Scandinavian peninsula. They traveled far and attacked and plundered at will and almost with impunity. They ravaged Italy and Greece, settled in France, Russia, and Ireland, colonized Iceland and Greenland, and discovered America several centuries before Columbus. Nor did they overlook England.

After many years of hit-and-run raids, the Norsemen landed an army on the east coast of England in the year 866. There was nothing much to oppose them except the Wessex power led by Alfred. The long struggle ended in 877 with a treaty by which a line was drawn roughly from the northwest of England to the southeast. On the eastern side of the line Norse rule was to prevail. This was called the Danelaw. The western side was to be governed by Wessex.

The linguistic result of all this was a considerable injection of Norse into the English language. Norse was at this time not so different from English as Norwegian or Danish is now. Probably speakers of English could understand, more or less, the language of the newcomers who had moved into eastern England. At any rate, there was considerable interchange and word borrowing. Examples of Norse words in the English language are *sky, give, law, egg, outlaw, leg, ugly, scant, sly, crawl, scowl, take, thrust.* There are hundreds more. We have even borrowed some pronouns from Norse—*they, their,* and *them.* These words were borrowed first by the eastern and northern dialects and then in the course of hundreds of years made their way into English generally.

It is supposed also—indeed, it must be true—that the Norsemen influenced the sound structure and the grammar of English. But this is hard to demonstrate in detail.

We may now have an example of Old English. The favorite illustration is the Lord's Prayer, since it needs no translation. This has come to us in several different versions. Here is one:

> Fæder ure þu ðe eart on heofonum si þin nama gehalgod. Tobecume þin rice. Gewurðe þin willa on eorðan swa swa on heofonum. Urne gedæghwamlican hlaf syle us to dæg. And forgyf us ure gyltas swa swa we forgyfaþ urum gyltendum. And ne gelæd þu us on costnunge ac alys us of yfele. Soðlice.

Some of the differences between this and Modern English are merely differences in orthography. For instance, the sign *æ* is what Old English writers used for a vowel sound like that in modern *hat* or *and.* The *th* sounds or modern *thin* or *then* are represented in Old English by þ or ð.

But of course there are many differences in sound too. *Ure* is the ancestor of modern *our,* but the first vowel was like that in *too* or *ooze. Hlaf* is modern *loaf;* we have dropped the *h* sound and changed the vowel, which in *hlaf* was pronounced something like the vowel in *father.* Old English had some sounds which we do not have. The sound represented by *y* does not occur in Modern English. If you pronounce the vowel in *bit* with your lips rounded, you may approach it.

In grammar, Old English was much more highly inflected than Modern English is. That is, there were more case endings for nouns, more person and number endings for verbs, a more complicated pronoun system, various endings for adjectives, and so on. Old English nouns had four cases —nominative, genitive, dative, accusative. Adjectives had five—all these and an instrumental case besides. Present-day English has only two cases for nouns—common case and possessive case. Adjectives now have no case system at all. On the other hand, we now use a more rigid word order and more structure words (prepositions, auxiliaries, and the like) to express relationships than Old English did.

Some of this grammar we can see in the Lord's Prayer. *Heofonum,* for instance, is a dative plural; the nominative singular was *heofon. Urne* is an accusative singular; the nominative is *ure.* In *urum gyltendum* both words are dative plural. *Forgyfaþ* is the third person plural form of the verb. Word order is different: "urne gedæghwamlican hlaf syle us" in place of "Give us our daily bread." And so on.

In vocabulary Old English is quite different from Modern English. Most of the Old English words are what we may call native English: that is, words which have not been borrowed from other languages but which have been a part of English ever since English was a part of Indo-European. Old English did certainly contain borrowed words. We have seen that many borrowings were coming in from Norse. Rather large numbers had been borrowed from Latin, too. Some of these were taken while the Anglo-Saxons were still on the Continent (*cheese, butter, bishop, kettle,* etc.); a large number came into English after the Conversion (*angel, candle, priest, martyr, radish, oyster, purple, school, spend,* etc.). But the great majority of Old English words were native English.

Now, on the contrary, the majority of words in English are borrowed, taken mostly from Latin and French. Of the words in *The American College Dictionary* only about 14 percent are native. Most of these, to be sure, are common, high-frequency words—*the, of, I, and, because, man, mother, road,* etc.; of the thousand most common words in English, some 62 percent are native English. Even so, the modern vocabulary is very much Latinized and Frenchified. The Old English vocabulary was not.

Sometimes between the years 1000 and 1200 various important

changes took place in the structure of English, and Old English became Middle English. The political event which facilitated these changes was the Norman Conquest. The Normans, as the name shows, came originally from Scandinavia. In the early tenth century they established themselves in northern France, adopted the French language, and developed a vigorous kingdom and a very passable civilization. In the year 1066, led by Duke William, they crossed the Channel and made themselves masters of England. For the next several hundred years, England was ruled by kings whose first language was French.

One might wonder why, after the Norman Conquest, French did not become the national language, replacing English entirely. The reason is that the Conquest was not a national migration, as the earlier Anglo-Saxon invasion had been. Great numbers of Normans came to England, but they came as rulers and landlords. French became the language of the court, the language of the nobility, the language of polite society, the language of literature. But it did not replace English as the language of the people. There must always have been hundreds of towns and villages in which French was never heard except when visitors of high station passed through.

But English, though it survived as the national language, was profoundly changed after the Norman Conquest. Some of the changes—in sound structure and grammar—would no doubt have taken place whether there had been a Conquest or not. Even before 1066 the case system of English nouns and adjectives was becoming simplified; people came to rely more on word order and prepositions than on inflectional endings to communicate their meanings. The process was speeded up by sound changes which caused many of the endings to sound alike. But no doubt the Conquest facilitated the change. German, which didn't experience a Norman Conquest, is today rather highly inflected compared to its cousin English.

But it is in vocabulary that the effects of the Conquest are most obvious. French ceased, after a hundred years or so, to be the native language of very many people in England, but it continued—and continues still—to be a zealously cultivated second language, the mirror of elegance and civilization. When one spoke English, one introduced not only French ideas and French things but also their French names. This was not only easy but socially useful. To pepper one's conversation with French expressions was to show that one was well-bred, elegant, *au courant*. The last sentence shows that the process is not yet dead. By using *au courant* instead of, say, *abreast of things,* the writer indicates that he is no dull clod who knows only English but an elegant person aware of how things are done in *le haut monde*.

Thus French words came into English, all sorts of them. There were words to do with government: *parliament, majesty, treaty, alliance, tax, government;* church words: *parson, sermon, baptism, incense, crucifix, religion;* words for foods: *veal, beef, mutton, bacon, jelly, peach, lemon, cream, biscuit;* colors: *blue, scarlet, vermilion;* household words: *curtain, chair, lamp, towel, blanket, parlor;* play words: *dance, chess, music, leisure, conversation;* literary words: *story, romance, poet, literary;* learned words: *study, logic, grammar, noun, surgeon, anatomy, stomach;* just ordinary words of all sorts: *nice, second, very, age, bucket, gentle, final, fault, flower, cry, count, sure, move, surprise, plain.*

All these and thousands more poured into the English vocabulary between 1100 and 1500, until at the end of that time many people must have had more French words than English at their command. This is not to say that English became French. English remained English in sound structure and in grammar, though these also felt the ripples of French influence. The very heart of the vocabulary, too, remained English. Most of the high-frequency words—the pronouns, the prepositions, the conjunctions, the auxiliaries, as well as a great many ordinary nouns and verbs and adjectives—were not replaced by borrowings.

Middle English, then, was still a Germanic language, but it differed from Old English in many ways. The sound system and the grammar changed a good deal. Speakers made less use of case systems and other inflectional devices and relied more on word order and structure words to express their meanings. This is often said to be a simplification, but it isn't really. Languages don't become simpler; they merely exchange one kind of complexity for another. Modern English is not a simple language, as any foreign speaker who tries to learn it will hasten to tell you.

For us Middle English is simpler than Old English just because it is closer to Modern English. It takes three or four months at least to learn to read Old English prose and more than that for poetry. But a week of good study should put one in touch with the Middle English poet Chaucer. Indeed, you may be able to make some sense of Chaucer straight off, though you would need instruction in pronunciation to make it sound like poetry. Here is a famous passage from the *General Prologue to the Canterbury Tales,* fourteenth century:

> Ther was also a nonne, a Prioresse,
> That of hir smyling was ful symple and coy,
> Hir gretteste oath was but by Seinte Loy,
> And she was cleped Madame Eglentyne.
> Ful wel she song the service dyvyne,
> Entuned in hir nose ful semely.

And Frenshe she spak ful faire and fetisly,
After the scole of Stratford-atte-Bowe,
For Frenshe of Parys was to hir unknowe.

Sometime between 1400 and 1600 English underwent a couple of sound changes which made the language of Shakespeare quite different from that of Chaucer. Incidentally, these changes contributed much to the chaos in which English spelling now finds itself.

One change was the elimination of a vowel sound in certain unstressed positions at the end of words. For instance, the words *name, stone, wine, dance* were pronounced as two syllables by Chaucer but as just one by Shakespeare. The *e* in these words became, as we say, "silent." But it wasn't silent for Chaucer; it represented a vowel sound. So also the words *laughed, seemed, stored* would have been pronounced by Chaucer as two-syllable words. The change was an important one because it affected thousands of words and gave a different aspect to the whole language.

The other change is what is called the Great Vowel Shift. This was a systematic shifting of half a dozen vowels and diphthongs in stressed syllables. For instance, the word *name* had in Middle English a vowel something like that in the modern word *father; wine* had the vowel of modern *mean; he* was pronounced something like modern *hey; mouse* sounded like *moose; moon* had the vowel of *moan*. Again the shift was thoroughgoing and affected all the words in which these vowel sounds occurred. Since we still keep the Middle English system of spelling these words, the differences between Modern English and Middle English are often more real than apparent.

The vowel shift has meant also that we have come to use an entirely different set of symbols for representing vowel sounds than is used by writers of such languages as French, Italian, or Spanish, in which no such vowel shift occurred. If you come across a strange word—say, *bine*—in an English book, you will pronounce it according to the English system, with the vowel of *wine* or *dine*. But if you read *bine* in a French, Italian, or Spanish book, you will pronounce it with the vowel of *mean* or *seen*.

These two changes, then, produced the basic differences between Middle English and Modern English. But there were several other developments that had an effect upon the language. One was the invention of printing, an invention introduced into England by William Caxton in the year 1475. Where before books had been rare and costly, they suddenly became cheap and common. More and more people learned to read and write. This was the first of many advances in communication which have worked to unify languages and to arrest the development of dialect differences, though of course printing affects writing principally rather than speech. Among other things it hastened the standardization of spelling.

The period of Early Modern English—that is, the sixteenth and seventeenth centuries—was also the period of the English Renaissance, when people developed, on the one hand, a keen interest in the past and, on the other, a more daring and imaginative view of the future. New ideas multiplied, and new ideas meant new language. Englishmen had grown accustomed to borrowing words from French as a result of the Norman Conquest; now they borrowed from Latin and Greek. As we have seen, English had been raiding Latin from Old English times and before, but now the floodgates really opened, and thousands of words from the classical languages poured in. *Pedestrian, bonus, anatomy, contradict, climax, dictionary, benefit, multiply, exist, paragraph, initiate, scene, inspire* are random examples. Probably the average educated American today has more words from French in his vocabulary than from native English sources, and more from Latin than from French.

The greatest writer of the Early Modern English period is of course Shakespeare, and the best-known book is the King James Version of the Bible, published in 1611. The Bible (if not Shakespeare) has made many features of Early Modern English perfectly familiar to many people down to present times, even though we do not use these features in present-day speech and writing. For instance, the old pronouns *thou* and *thee* have dropped out of use now, together with their verb forms, but they are still familiar to us in prayer and in Biblical quotation: "Whither thou goest, I will go." Such forms as *hath* and *doth* have been replaced by *has* and *does;* "Goes he hence tonight?" would now be "Is he going away tonight?"; Shakespeare's "Fie on't, sirrah" would be "Nuts to that, Mac." Still, all these expressions linger with us because of the power of the works in which they occur.

It is not always realized, however, that considerable sound changes have taken place between Early Modern English and the English of the present day. Shakespearian actors putting on a play speak the words, properly enough, in their modern pronunciation. But it is very doubtful that this pronunciation would be understood at all by Shakespeare. In Shakespeare's time, the word *reason* was pronounced like modern *raisin; face* had the sound of modern *glass;* the *l* in *would, should, palm* was pronounced. In these points and a great many others the English language has moved a long way from what it was in 1600.

The history of English since 1700 is filled with many movements and countermovements, of which we can notice only a couple. One of these is the vigorous attempt made in the eighteenth century, and the rather half-hearted attempts made since, to regulate and control the English language. Many people of the eighteenth century, not understanding very well the forces which govern language, proposed to polish and prune and restrict English, which they felt was proliferating too wildly. There was much talk of an academy which would rule on what people could and could not say and write. The academy never came into being, but the eighteenth century did succeed in establishing certain attitudes which, though they haven't had much effect on the development of the language itself, have certainly changed the native speaker's feeling about the language.

In part a product of the wish to fix and establish the language was the development of the dictionary. The first English dictionary was published in 1603; it was a list of 2500 words briefly defined. Many others were published with gradual improvements until Samuel Johnson published his *English Dictionary* in 1755. This, steadily revised, dominated the field in England for nearly a hundred years. Meanwhile in America, Noah Webster published his dictionary in 1828, and before long dictionary publishing was a big business in this country. The last century has seen the publication of one great dictionary: the twelve-volume *Oxford English Dictionary,* compiled in the course of seventy-five years through the labors of many scholars. We have also, of course, numerous commercial dictionaries which are as good as the public wants them to be if not, indeed, rather better.

Another product of the eighteenth century was the invention of "English grammar." As English came to replace Latin as the language of scholarship it was felt that one should also be able to control and dissect it, parse and analyze it, as one could Latin. What happened in practice was that the grammatical description that applied to Latin was removed and superimposed on English. This was silly, because English is an entirely different kind of language, with its own forms and signals and ways of producing meaning. Nevertheless, English grammars on the Latin model were worked out and taught in the schools. In many schools they are still being taught. This activity is not often popular with school children, but it is sometimes an interesting and instructive exercise in logic. The principal harm in it is that it has tended to keep people from being interested in English and has obscured the real features of English structure.

But probably the most important force on the development of English in the modern period has been the tremendous expansion of English-speaking peoples. In 1500 English was a minor language, spoken by a few people on a small island. Now it is perhaps the greatest language of the world, spoken natively by over a quarter of a billion people and as a second language by many millions more. When we speak of English now, we must specify whether we mean American English, British English, Australian English, Indian English, or what, since the differences are considerable. The American cannot go to England or the Englishman to America confident that he will always understand and be understood. The Alabaman in Iowa or the Iowan in Alabama shows himself a foreigner every time he speaks. It is only because communication has become fast and easy that English in this period of its expansion has not broken into a dozen mutually unintelligible languages.

Questions

1. Old English was a language of many inflections—many grammatical meanings were conveyed with word endings. Modern English has few inflections. Can you read the Old English version of the Lord's Prayer in Roberts' article and determine some of the meanings conveyed by inflections? How does Modern English express those meanings? (Compare also the versions of the Tower of Babel story which follows.)
2. The vocabulary of English is largely borrowed. Can you list the languages from which the largest numbers of words have been borrowed? Can you explain why certain kinds of words have been borrowed from Latin? From Norse? From French?
3. What grammatical devices are used in Modern English to convey the meanings which were expressed by the great number of inflections (word endings) in Old English?
4. What does Roberts mean when he says "Languages don't become simpler; they merely exchange one kind of complexity for another"? This implies that no language is more complex than another. Do you agree? Don't confuse the printed word with language. In your answer consider such questions as "Is it more difficult for the Russian or Chinese child to learn his language than for a child to learn English?"
5. Printing, a conservative influence working against language change, came to England when the Great Vowel Shift was underway. Does this fact suggest any explanation for some spelling problems in Modern English?
6. What major developments influencing the language came out of the 18th century? Does Roberts support or condemn the developments? Why?

Suggestions for Writing

1. Choose a number of specialized terms in a subject such as law, cooking, music, or terms in a hobby which you are well acquainted with. Check a dictionary and list the borrowed words and their source. Then write a paper on the foreign influences in that subject or hobby indicated by the borrowed words.
2. James Joyce in *Ulysses* has Stephen Daedalus imagine that a string of umbilical cords is an unbroken telephone line back to Adam through which Daedalus telephones Adam. In a very real sense language forms an unbroken line to our linguistic ancestors. As a writing assignment imagine that

you have one of your linguistic ancestors on the line. Discuss with that ancestor the problems in communication that are caused by language change or by the different "languages" used by successive generations. Your "line" might be back only one or two generations to your father or mother or grandparents, or it might go back several generations to an ancestor who spoke a different language. Be aware of your audience and the time gap as you write.

Genesis 11:1-9

One of the oldest records of man's interest in language is found in the Bible: the Book of Genesis 11:1–9. Here is a brief attempt to explain why there are so many languages in the world. Though the account is no longer accepted by linguists, it nevertheless reveals one of man's concerns about language over 4000 years ago. Four versions of the story are provided: the first in Old English, probably written about 1000 A.D.; the second in Middle English, written about 1350 A.D.; the third from Early Modern English (The King James version), written about 1600 A.D.; and the last from Modern English, written about 1950. You would do well to read them in reverse order, as we have arranged them, noting changes that have occurred in vocabulary and spelling since Old English times. How much of the Old English version can you understand? Choose a few words from the Modern English version and trace them back through the other versions. For example, note the word built *in the Modern English version. It was* builded *in 1600,* bildeden *in 1350, and* getimbrodon *in 1000. Language scholars, by comparing such changes in words, can construct a very reliable history of a language. Compare the Modern English version with the King James version. Can you give reasons why people sensitive to language prefer the earlier?*

Modern English

Now the whole earth had one language and few words. 2 And as men mi-
grated in the east, they found a plain in the land of Shinar and settled
there. 3 And they said to one another, "Come, let us make bricks, and
burn them thoroughly." And they had brick for stone, and bitumen for
mortar. 4 Then they said, "Come, let us build ourselves a city, and a tower
with its top in the heavens, and let us make a name for ourselves, lest we
be scattered abroad upon the face of the whole earth." 5 And the LORD
came down to see the city and the tower, which the sons of men had built.
6 And the LORD said, "Behold, they are one people, and they have all one
language; and this is only the beginning of what they will do; and nothing
that they propose to do will now be impossible for them. 7 Come, let us go

From the Revised Standard Version of the Bible, copyrighted 1946 and 1952.

down, and there confuse their language, that they may not understand one
another's speech." 8 So the Lord scattered them abroad from there over
the face of all the earth, and they left off building the city. 9 Therefore its
name was called Babel, because there the Lord confused the language of
all the earth; and from there the Lord scattered them abroad over the face
of all the earth.

Early Modern English (*King James Version*)

And the whole earth was of one language, and of one speech. 2 And it
came to pass, as they journeyed from the east, that they found a plain in
the land of Shī′när; and they dwelt there. 3 And they said one to another,
Go to, let us make brick, and burn them thoroughly. And they had brick
for stone, and slime had they for mortar. 4 And they said, Go to, let us
build us a city, and a tower, whose top *may reach* unto heaven; and let us
make us a name, lest we be scattered abroad upon the face of the whole
earth. 5 And the Lord came down to see the city and the tower, which the
children of men builded. 6 And the Lord said, Behold, the people *is* one,
and they have all one language; and this they begin to do: and now nothing
will be restrained from them, which they have imagined to do. 7 Go to, let
us go down, and there confound their language, that they may not under-
stand one another's speech. 8 So the Lord scattered them abroad from
thence upon the face of all the earth: and they left off to build the city.
9 Therefore is the name of it called Bā′bĕl; because the Lord did there
confound the language of all the earth: and from thence did the Lord
scatter them abroad upon the face of all the earth.

Middle English

Forsothe the erthe was of oo lip, and of the same wordis. 2And whan
men shulden go fro the est, thei founden a feeld in the lond of Sennaer,
and thei dwelleden in it. 3And the tother seide to his neiȝbore, Cometh,
and make we tile stoons, and sethe we hem with fier; and thei hadden tiles
for stoons, and towȝ cley for syment. 4And thei seiden, Cometh, and make
we to vs a citee and a towr, whos heiȝt fulli ateyne vnto heuene; and halow

we oure name, or we ben dyuydid into alle londis. 5The Lord forsothe
descendide, that he myȝte se the citee and the towre, the which the children
of Adam bildeden; and seide, 6Se! the puple is oon, and oo lippe is to alle,
and this thei han bigunnen to make, ne thei wolen leeue of fro her
thenkyngis, to the tyme that thei han fulfillid hem in dede; 7thanne come
ȝe, descende we, and confounde we there the tung of hem, that noon here
the vois of his neiȝbore. 8And so the Lord deuydide hem fro that place into
alle londis; and thei sesyden to bilde the citee. 9And therfor was callid
the name of it Babel, for there was confoundid the lippe of al the erthe;
and fro thens the Lord disparpoilide hem vpon the face of alle regiouns.

Old English

Soðlice ealle menn spræcon ða ane spræce. 2Ða ða hi ferdon fram
eastdæle, hi fundon ænne feld on Senaarlande, and wunodon ðæron, 3ða
cwædon hi him betwynan: Vton wyrcean us tigelan and ælan hi on fyre.
Witodlice hi hæfdon tigelan for stan and tyrwan for weall-lim. 4And
cwædon: Vton timbrian us ceastre and stypel oð heofon heahne, and uton
wyrðian urne naman, ær ðam ðe we synd todælede geond ealle eorðan.
5Witodlice Drihten astah nyðer to ðam ðæt he gesawe ða burh and ðone
stypel ðe Adames bearn getimbrodon. 6And he cræð: Ðis is an folc, and
ealle hi specað an leden and hi begunnon ðis to wyrcenne; ne geswycað hi
ær ðan ðe hit geara sy. 7Soðlice uton cuman and todælan ðær heora spæce.
8Swa Drihten hi todælde of ðære stowe geond ealle eorðan. 9And for ðam
man nemde ða stowe Babel, for ðam ðar wæron todælede ealle spæce.

Questions

1. In the first three verses of the Old English version all words are native English words. In the Middle English version the word *syment* is a French borrowing (ultimately) from Latin. In the Early Modern English version the words *journeyed, plain, brick,* and *mortar* are from French. In the modern English version *language, brick,* and *mortar* are from French; *migrated* and *bitumen* are from Latin. On the basis of such information, what statements might you make about relationships between the speakers of English and French? About the kinds of words borrowed from Latin?
2. Take the clause found at the beginning of verse three and note how it is worded in each of the versions. The Old English version should be translated as follows:

ða cwædon	hi	him	betwynan
then said	they	themselves	between.

What differences are there between the versions? How important is word order in Modern English?

Wanderer

The Wanderer, composed about the ninth century by an unknown Anglo-Saxon poet, is one of the great poems that has come to us from Old English. Old English poetry gets its rhythms largely from alliteration and a pause (a caesura) in the middle of each line. You will note that Malone, in his transcription, has attempted to make the poem alliterative in Modern English. The first five lines of the poem are reproduced with a word for word transcription to allow a comparison of the two versions.

In this poem the poet, who has lost his lord and the association of his warrior companions, reflects on the vanity of worldly success and the fleetingness of all material things. He feels a kind of alienation from the world that is perhaps akin to the alienation many people seem to feel today. Note the picturesque compound nouns (called kennings by English scholars) such as gold-friend *and* ring-giver *for lord,* hall-gladness *for good times; also compound adjectives such as* winter-sad, hoar-grey, ice-bound. *Such phrases, characteristic of Old English poetry, add color to the poem.*

Literal Transcription

Oft him anhaga are gebideð
Often the lone man for favor prays

Metudes miltse þeah þe he modcearig
of God the mercy though he sad of heart

geond lagulade longe sceolde
across the sea a long time must [go]

hreran mid hondum hrimcealde sae
stir with hands frosty cold sea

wadan wræ clastas wyrd bi ful aræd.
journey paths of exile fate is fully determined.

WANDERER

Oft the lone man learns the favor,
the grace of God, though go he must
his ways on the deep, dreary and long,
arouse with hands the rime-cold sea,
fare far from home; fate is unswerving.

So quoth the wanderer, of woes mindful,
of fell slaughters, fall of dear ones:
"Oft at each daybreak I am doomed alone
to bewail my cares. Not one now is alive
that I to him openly dare
to say my mind. For sooth I know
that is a worthy wont in a kemp * champion
that fast he bind his breast and keep
his thoughts to himself, think as he will.
No weary mood can ward a man,
no hot head can give help against fate;
therefore he that holds high his good name
oft binds in his bosom the bitter thought.
So I must fetter, lock fast my mood,
oft hounded with care, of home bereft,
far from fellows, friends and kinsmen,
since that day gone by when the dark, the earth,
hid my gold-friend, and I got me thence,
outcast, winter-sad, over ice-bound waves,
with heavy mood a hearth to seek
where I far or nigh might find a lord,
a man in mead-hall mindful of me,
one to befriend me, the friendless waif,
treat me kindly. They ken, the wise,
how grim a mate grief is to him
who lives without a loved master.
The wanderer's path, not wound gold holds him,
a breast frozen, not bliss of earth.
He minds the guests in hall, the gift-taking,
how at the board in years of youth his gold-friend
gave him tokens; gone is kindness, all.

"For that he learns who long must fare without
his beloved leader's lore, wise sayings,
when sorrow and sleep at the same time together
press oft and bind the poor lone one:
to him it seems in mood that his sweet master
he clips and kisses, and clasps at knee
with hands and head, as whilom then
when in days of yore he yet held the throne.
The friendless wight awakes at last,
the fallow flood before him sees,
the birds bathing, broadening their feathers,
frost, snow and hail falling mingled.
Then are the heavier the heart's death-wounds,
sore for the loved one; sorrow is renewed.
Then the mood becomes mindful of kinsmen,
greets them with gladness, gazes fondly
at sight of his fellows; they swim oft away;
the life of the fleeting ones brings little there
of the words he kens; care is renewed
for him who must send his soul wandering
over the ice-bound waves, his weary heart.
Therefore I cannot this world besee
without thinking thoughts of darkness,
when I the life wholly behold of kemps,
how the hall they in haste gave up,
the mood-bold thanes. So this middle earth
with every day down sinks and falls.

"Not one can be wise at once, ere he own
winters in the world. The wise man is patient,
not too hot-headed nor too hasty-tongued,
nor too weak a fighter, nor too foolish-minded,
nor too fearful nor too fain nor too fee-greedy,
never too bold at boasting ere he know the better rede.
The spearman, moved to speak a vow,
must wait, bide his time, till well he know
what turn his mood will take at last.
The tried kemp must grasp how ghastly it will be
when the weal of this world stands waste wholly,
as now in many a spot through this middle earth
the wind-blown walls stand waste, befrosted,
the abodes of men lie buried in snow,

the wine-halls are dust in the wind, the rulers
death, stripped of glee; the dright * all fell, company of retainers
by the wall the proud sought shield. War took off some,
brought some away; a bird took one
over the high sea-flood; the hoar-grey wolf
dealt death to one; with dreary cheer
a kemp hid one in a cave of earth.
So the Maker of men made this borough waste
till all stood idle, the old work of giants,
without the din of dwellers in hall."

He then, wise in soul, with weighty thought
thinks deeply upon this darksome life,
this fallen fastness, far and oft minds
much spilling of blood, and speaks these words:
"Where came the horse, where the rider, where the ring-giver?
Where came the house of feasting? Where is hall-gladness?
Alas, the bright mead-cup! Alas, the mailed fighter!
Alas, the prince's power! Past is that time,
grown dark in the night, as if it never were!
Where the tried warriors once trod stands now
a wall wondrous high, with worm-shapes dight.
The might of spears, of maces death-greedy,
and fate, that famed one, they felled the kemps,
and the storm beats down upon these stone shelters,
the falling snow binds fast the ground,
the blaring winter. Then blackness comes,
night-shades darken, the north sends out
fierce falls of hail to the fright of kemps.
Altogether hard is this earthly kingdom,
the word of the fates shifts the world under heaven.
Here kine are fleeting, here kin are fleeting,
here men are fleeting, here mates are fleeting,
all this earthly frame grows idle at last."

So quoth the sage, sat apart in thought.
He is good who holds troth, his grief must he never
from his breast speak too soon, unless boot * first he know remedy
to win boldly. He does well to seek help
of his Father above, where our bliss all stands.

Questions

1. Would such a title as "Mutability" more accurately describe the theme of this poem?
2. What is the relationship between the beginning and the concluding lines of the poem? What do they reveal about the theme of the poem? Do the references to a Christian God seem intrinsic to the whole poem.

The Tale of the Wyf of Bathe

Geoffrey Chaucer

Chaucer (died 1400 A.D.) was one of the greatest English poets and story tellers. The tale which follows is an example of his poetic greatness and remarkable ability as a story teller, and it also illustrates the language of the Middle English period. Note that some words of that period such as shipnes *for stable (line 15),* undermeles *for afternoons (line 19) have been lost from the language. Other words such as* nice *meaning foolish (line 82) and* coast *meaning region or boundary (line 66) remain in use today with meanings different from Chaucer's. Chaucer used the Old English forms* hir *and* hem *for the Scandinavian borrowings* their *and* them *that we use in Modern English.*

The sounds of Chaucer's English would be quite different from those of Modern English. (Note, for example, Roberts' discussion of the Great Vowel Shift.) Nevertheless, we recommend that you read the lines with their Modern English sounds. You will discover that some lines that do not make sense to you as you read silently will become meaningful when you read them aloud. The language will be somewhat difficult to understand in places; but, because a truly great writer has something significant to say to all people at all times, the effort you put forth will be rewarded.

Chaucer here tells the story of a young knight who will be put to death, as punishment for a crime, unless in one year's time he can discover what it is in life that women desire most.

Heere bigynneth the Tale of the Wyf of Bathe.

In th'olde dayes of the Kyng Arthour,
Of which that Britons speken greet honour,
Al was this land fulfild of fayerye.
The elf-queene, with hir joly compaignye,
Daunced ful ofte in many a grene mede.* meadow
This was the olde opinion, as I rede;

From *The Works of Geoffrey Chaucer*, ed. F. N. Robinson, 2nd ed. (Boston: Houghton Mifflin Co., 1957), pp. 84–88. Reprinted by permission of Houghton Mifflin Company. [Marginal annotations supplied by the editors.]

I speke of manye hundred yeres ago.
But now kan no man se none elves mo,
For now the grete charitee and prayeres
Of lymytours * and othere hooly freres,   begging friars
That serchen every lond and every streem,
As thikke as motes in the sonne-beem,
Blessynge halles, chambres, kichenes, boures,
Citees, burghes, castels, hye toures,
Thropes,* bernes, shipnes,* dayeryes—   villages, stables
This maketh that ther ben no fayeryes.
For ther as wont * to walken was an elf,   used to
Ther walketh now the lymytour hymself
In undermeles * and in morwenynges,   afternoons
And seyth his matyns and his hooly thynges
As he gooth in his lymytacioun.*   assigned area
Wommen may go now saufly * up and doun.   safely
In every bussh or under every tree
Ther is noon oother incubus * but he,   impregnating elf
And he ne wol doon hem * but dishonour.   them
And so bifel it that this kyng Arthour
Hadde in his hous a lusty bacheler,
That on a day cam ridynge fro ryver; *   from hawking
And happed that, allone as he was born,
He saugh a mayde walkynge hym biforn,
Of which mayde anon, maugree hir heed,*   despite her resistance
By verray force, he rafte * hire maydenhed;   took from her
For which oppressioun * was swich clamour   offense
And swich pursute unto the kyng Arthour,
That dampned * was this knyght for to be deed,   condemned
By cours of lawe, and sholde han lost his heed—
Paraventure * swich was the statut tho—   Perhaps
But that the queene and othere ladyes mo
So longe preyeden * the kyng of grace,   begged for
Til he his lyf hym graunted in the place,
And yaf hym to the queene, al at hir wille,
To chese wheither she wolde hym save or spille.*   put to death
The queene thanketh the kyng with al hir myght,
And after this thus spak she to the knyght,
Whan that she saugh hir tyme, upon a day:
"Thou standest yet," quod she, "in swich array *   condition
That of thy lyf yet hastow no suretee.
I grante thee lyf, if thou kanst tellen me

What thyng is it that wommen moost desiren.
Be war, and keep thy nekke-boon from iren!
And if thou kanst nat tellen it anon,* — at once
Yet wol I yeve thee leve for to gon
A twelf-month and a day, to seche and leere * — learn
An answere suffisant in this mateere;
And suretee wol I han, er that thou pace,* — pass
Thy body for to yelden in this place."
Wo was this knyght, and sorwefully he siketh; * — sighs
But what! he may nat do al as hym liketh.
And at the laste he chees hym for to wende,
And come agayn, right at the yeres ende,
With swich answere as God wolde hym purveye; * — provide
And taketh his leve, and wendeth forth his weye.
He seketh every hous and every place
Where as he hopeth for to fynde grace,
To lerne what thyng wommen loven moost;
But he ne koude arryven in no coost * — region
Wher as he myghte fynde in this mateere
Two creatures accordynge in-feere.* — in agreement
Somme seyde wommen loven best richesse,
Somme seyde honour, somme seyde jolynesse,
Somme riche array, somme seyden lust * abedde, — pleasure
And oftetyme to be wydwe and wedde.
Somme seyde that oure hertes been moost esed
Whan that we been yflatered and yplesed.
He gooth ful ny the sothe,* I wol nat lye. — truth
A man shal wynne us best with flaterye;
And with attendance, and with bisynesse,* — diligence
Been we ylymed,* bothe moore and lesse. — trapped
And somme seyen that we loven best
For to be free, and do right as us lest,* — pleases
And that no man repreve us of oure vice,
But seye that we be wise, and no thyng nyce.* — foolish
For trewely ther is noon of us alle,
If any wight wol clawe us on the galle,* — sore spot
That we nel kike * for he seith us sooth. — kick
Assay, and he shal fynde it that so dooth;
For, be we never so vicious withinne,
We wol been holden wise and clene of synne.
And somme seyn that greet delit han we
For to been holden stable, and eek secree,* — able to keep secrets

And in o purpos stedefastly to dwelle,
And nat biwreye * thyng that men us telle. betray
But that tale is nat worth a rake-stele.
Pardee, we wommen konne no thyng hele;
Witnesse on Myda,—wol ye heere the tale?
Ovyde,* amonges othere thynges smale, Roman poet of love
Seyde Myda hadde, under his longe heres,
Growynge upon his heed two asses eres,
The whiche vice he hydde, as he best myghte,
Ful subtilly from every mannes sighte,
That, save his wyf, ther wiste * of it namo. knew
He loved hire moost, and trusted hire also;
He preyede hire that to no creature
She sholde tellen of his disfigure.* disfigurement
She swoor him, "Nay," for al this world to wynne,
She nolde do that vileynye or synne,
To make hir housbonde han so foul a name.
She nolde nat telle it for hir owene shame.
But nathelees, hir thoughte that she dyde,* would die
That she so longe sholde a conseil * hyde; secret
Hir thoughte it swal so soore aboute hir herte
That nedely * som word hire moste asterte; * of necessity, escape
And sith she dorste telle it to no man,
Doun to a mareys * faste * by she ran— marsh, close
Til she cam there, hir herte was a-fyre—
And as a bitore * bombleth * in the myre, bittern, booms
She leyde hir mouth unto the water doun:
"Biwreye me nat, thou water, with thy soun,"
Quod she; "to thee I telle it and namo;
Myn housbonde hath longe asses erys two!
Now is myn herte al hool,* now is it oute. whole
I myghte no lenger kepe it, out of doute.
Heere may ye se, thogh we a tyme abyde,
Yet out it moot; * we kan no conseil hyde. must
The remenant of the tale if ye wol heere,
Redeth Ovyde, and ther ye may it leere.
This knyght, of which my tale is specially,
Whan that he saugh he myghte nat come therby,
This is to seye, what wommen love moost,
Withinne his brest ful sorweful was the goost.* spirit
But hoom he gooth, he myghte nat sojourne;
The day was come that homward moste he tourne.

And in his wey it happed hym to ryde,
In al this care, under a forest syde,
Wher as he saugh upon a daunce go
Of ladyes foure and twenty, and yet mo;
Toward the whiche daunce he drow ful yerne,* — eagerly
In hope that som wysdom sholde he lerne.
But certeinly, er he cam fully there,
Vanysshed was this daunce, he nyste * where. — knew not
No creature saugh he that bar lyf,
Save on the grene he saugh sittynge a wyf—
A fouler * wight * ther may no man devyse. — uglier, person
Agayn * the knyght this olde wyf gan ryse, — to meet
And seyde, "Sire knyght, heer forth ne lith no wey.
Tel me what that ye seken, by youre fey! * — faith
Paraventure it may the bettre be;
Thise olde folk kan * muchel thyng," quod she. — know
"My leeve * mooder," quod this knyght, "certeyn — dear
I nam but deed, but if that I kan seyn
What thyng it is that wommen moost desire.
Koude ye me wisse,* I wolde wel quite youre hire." * — tell, repay you
"Plight * me thy trouthe heere in myn hand," quod she, — Pledge
"The nexte thyng that I requere thee,
Thou shalt it do, if it lye in thy myght,
And I wol telle it yow er it be nyght."
"Have heer my trouthe," * quod the knyght, "I grante." — promise
"Thanne," quod she, "I dar me wel avante * — boast
Thy lyf is sauf; for I wol stonde therby,
Upon my lyf, the queene wol seye as I.
Lat se which is the proudeste of hem alle,
That wereth on * a coverchief or a calle,* — has on, headdress
That dar seye nay of that I shal thee teche.
Lat us go forth, withouten lenger speche."
Tho rowned * she a pistel * in his ere, — whispered, message
And bad hym to be glad, and have no fere.
Whan they be comen to the court, this knyght
Seyde he had holde his day, as he hadde hight,* — promised
And redy was his answere, as he sayde.
Ful many a noble wyf, and many a mayde,
And many a wydwe, for that they been wise,
The queene hirself sittynge as a justise,
Assembled been, his answere for to heere;
And afterward this knyght was bode appeere.

To every wight comanded was silence,
And that the knyght sholde telle in audience
What thyng that worldly wommen loven best.
This knyght ne stood nat stille as doth a best,* beast
But to his questioun anon * answerde at once
With manly voys, that al the court it herde:
"My lige lady, generally," quod he,
"Wommen desiren to have sovereynetee
As wel over hir housbond as hir love,
And for to been in maistrie hym above.
This is youre mooste desir, thogh ye me kille.
Dooth as yow list,* I am heer at youre wille." please
In al the court ne was ther wyf, ne mayde,
Ne wydwe, that contraried that he sayde,
But seyden he was worthy han * his lyf. to have
And with that word up stirte the olde wyf,
Which that the knyght saugh sittynge on the grene:
"Mercy," quod she, "my sovereyn lady queene!
Er that youre court departe, do me right.
I taughte this answere unto the knyght;
For which he plighte me his trouthe there,
The firste thyng that I wolde hym requere,
He wolde it do, if it lay in his myghte.
Bifore the court thanne preye I thee, sir knyght,"
Quod she, "that thou me take unto thy wyf;
For wel thou woost * that I have kept * thy lyf. know, saved
If I seye fals, sey nay, upon thy fey!"
This knyght answerde, "Allas! and weylawey!
I woot right wel that swich was my biheste.* promise
For Goddes love, as chees * a newe requeste! choose
Taak al my good, and lat my body go."
"Nay, thanne," quod she, "I shrewe * us bothe two! curse
For thogh that I be foul, and oold, and poore,
I nolde * for al the metal, ne for oore, would not
That under erthe is grave,* or lith above, buried
But if thy wyf I were, and eek thy love."
"My love?" quod he, "nay, my dampnacioun!
Allas! that any of my nacioun
Sholde evere so foule disparaged * be!" disgraced
But al for noght; the ende is this, that he
Constreyned was, he nedes moste hire wedde;
And taketh his olde wyf, and gooth to bedde.

Now wolden som men seye, paraventure,
That for my necligence I do no cure * care
To tellen yow the joye and al th'array
That at the feeste was that ilke day.
To which thyng shortly answeren I shal:
I seye ther nas no joye ne feeste at al;
Ther nas but hevynesse and muche sorwe.
For prively he wedded hire on the morwe,
And al day after hidde hym as an owle,
So wo was hym, his wyf looked so foule.
Greet was the wo the knyght hadde in his thoght,
Whan he was with his wyf abedde ybroght;
He walweth * and he turneth to and fro. twists
His olde wyf lay smylynge everemo,
And seyde, "O deere housbonde, *benedicitee!* * bless me
Fareth every knyght thus with his wyf as ye?
Is this the lawe of kyng Arthures hous?
Is every knyght of his so dangerous? * offish
I am youre owene love and eek youre wyf;
I am she which that saved hath youre lyf,
And, certes, yet ne dide I yow nevere unright;
Why fare ye thus with me this firste nyght?
Ye faren lyk a man had lost his wit.
What is my gilt? For Goddes love, tel me it,
And it shal been amended, if I may."
"Amended?" quod this knyght, "allas! nay, nay!
It wol nat been amended nevere mo.
Thou art so loothly,* and so oold also, loathsome
And therto comen of so lough a kynde, * race
That litel wonder is thogh I walwe and wynde.
So wolde God myn herte wolde breste!" * burst
"Is this," quod she, "the cause of youre unreste?"
"Ye, certeinly," quod he, "no wonder is."
"Now, sire," quod she, "I koude amende al this,
If that me liste,* er it were dayes thre, please
So wel ye myghte bere * yow unto me. behave
But, for ye speken of swich gentillesse * nobility
As is descended out of old richesse,
That therfore sholden ye be gentil men,
Swich arrogance is nat worth an hen.
Looke who that is moost vertuous alway,
Pryvee * and apert,* and moost entendeth ay privately, publicly

To do the gentil dedes that he kan;
Taak hym for the greetest gentil man.
Crist wole we clayme of hym oure gentillesse,
Nat of oure eldres for hire old richesse.
For thogh they yeve us al hir heritage,
For which we clayme to been of heigh parage,* — rank
Yet may they nat biquethe, for no thyng,
To noon of us hir vertuous lyvyng,
That made hem gentil men ycalled be,
And bad us folwen hem in swich degree.
Wel kan the wise poete of Florence,
That highte * Dant, speken in this sentence. — is named
Lo, in swich maner rym is Dantes tale:
'Ful selde * up riseth by his branches smale — seldom
Prowesse of man, for God, of his goodnesse,
Wole that of hym we clayme oure gentillesse';
For of oure eldres may we no thyng clayme
But temporel thyng, that man may hurte and mayme.
Eek every wight woot this as wel as I,
If gentillesse were planted natureelly
Unto a certeyn lynage doun the lyne,
Pryvee and apert, thanne wolde they nevere fyne * — cease
To doon of gentillesse the faire office; * — duties
They myghte do no vileynye or vice.
Taak fyr, and ber it in the derkeste hous
Bitwix this and the mount of Kaukasous,
And lat men shette the dores and go thenne; * — thence
Yet wole the fyr as faire lye and brenne * — burn
As twenty thousand men myghte it biholde;
His * office natureel ay wol it holde, — Its
Up * peril of my lyf, til that it dye. — upon
Heere may ye se wel how that genterye * — nobility
Is nat annexed * to possessioun, — related
Sith folk ne doon hir operacioun
Alwey, as dooth the fyr, lo, in his kynde.* — nature
For, God it woot, men may wel often fynde
A lordes sone do shame and vileynye;
And he that wole han pris of * his gentrye, — reputation for
For he was boren of a gentil hous,
And hadde his eldres noble and vertuous,
And nel hymselven do no gentil dedis,
Ne folwen his gentil auncestre that deed * is, — dead

He nys nat gentil, be he duc or erl;
For vileyns synful dedes make a cherl.
For gentillesse nys but * renomee * — isn't just, fame
Of thyne auncestres, for hire heigh bountee,
Which is a strange thyng to thy persone.
Thy gentillesse cometh fro God allone.
Thanne comth oure verray gentillesse of grace;
It was no thyng biquethe us with oure place.
Thenketh hou noble, as seith Valerius,
Was thilke * Tullius Hostillius, — that
That out of poverte roos to heigh noblesse.
Reedeth Senek,* and redeth eek Boece; * — moralist, philosopher
Ther shul ye seen expres that it no drede * is — doubt
That he is gentil that dooth gentil dedis.
And therfore, leeve * housbonde, I thus conclude: — dear
Al were it that myne auncestres were rude,* — humble
Yet may the hye God, and so hope I,
Grante me grace to lyven vertuously.
Thanne am I gentil, whan that I bigynne
To lyven vertuously and weyve * synne. — avoid
And ther as ye of poverte me repreeve,
The hye God, on whom that we bileeve,
In wilful poverte chees to lyve his lyf.
And certes every man, mayden, or wyf,
May understọnde that Jhesus, hevene kyng,
Ne wolde nat chese a vicious lyvyng.
Glad poverte is an honest thyng, certeyn;
This wole Senec and othere clerkes seyn.
Whoso that halt hym payd of * his poverte, — is satisfied with
I holde hym riche, al hadde he nat a sherte.
He that coveiteth is a povre wight,
For he wolde han that is nat in his myght;
But he that noght hath, ne coveiteth have,
Is riche, although ye holde hym but a knave.* — peasant
Verray poverte, it syngeth proprely;
Juvenal seith of poverte myrily:
'The povre man, whan he goth by the weye,
Bifore the theves he may synge and pleye.'
Poverte is hateful good and, as I gesse,
A ful greet bryngere out of bisynesse;
A greet amendere eek of sapience * — wisdom
To hym that taketh it in pacience.

Poverte is this, although it seme alenge,* miserable
Possessioun that no wight wol chalenge.
Poverte ful ofte, whan a man is lowe,
Maketh * his God and eek hymself to knowe. makes him
Poverte a spectacle * is, as thynketh me, pair of spectacles
Thurgh which he may his verray freendes see.
And therfore, sire, syn that I noght yow greve,
Of my poverte namoore ye me repreve.* reprove
Now, sire, of elde * ye repreve me; old age
And certes, sire, thogh noon auctoritee
Were in no book, ye gentils of honour
Seyn that men shode an oold wight doon favour,
And clepe * hym fader, for youre gentillesse; address him
And auctours * shal I fynden, as I gesse. authorities
Now ther ye seye that I am foul and old,
Than drede you noght to been a cokewold; * cuckold
For filthe and eelde, also moot I thee,* as I hope to prosper
Been grete wardeyns upon chastitee.
But nathelees, syn I knowe youre delit,
I shal fulfille youre worldly appetit.
Chese now," quod she, "oon of thise thynges tweye:
To han me foul and old til that I deye,
And be to yow a trewe, humble wyf,
And nevere yow displese in al my lyf;
Or elles ye wol han me yong and fair,
And take youre aventure * of the repair * chance, company
That shal be to youre hous by cause of me,
Or in som oother place, may wel be.
Now chese yourselven, wheither * that yow liketh." whichever
This knyght avyseth * hym and sore siketh,* considers, sighs
But atte laste he seyde in this manere:
"My lady and my love, and wyf so deere,
I put me in youre wise governance;
Cheseth youreself which may be moost plesance,
And moost honour to yow and me also.
I do no fors * the wheither of the two; don't care
For as yow liketh, it suffiseth me."
"Thanne have I gete of yow maistrie," quod she,
"Syn I may chese and governe as me lest?" * pleases
"Ye, certes, wyf," quod he, "I holde it best."
"Kys me," quod she, "we be no lenger wrothe;
For, by my trouthe, I wol be to yow bothe,

This is to seyn, ye, bothe fair and good.
I prey to God that I moote sterven wood,* — die mad
But I to yow be also good and trewe
As evere was wyf, syn that the world was newe.
And but I be to-morn as fair to seene
As any lady, emperice, or queene,
That is bitwixe the est and eke the west,
Dooth with my lyf and deth right as yow lest.
Cast up the curtyn, looke how that it is."
And whan the knyght saugh verraily al this,
That she so fair was, and so yong therto,
For joye he hente * hire in his armes two, — took
His herte bathed in a bath of blisse.
A thousand tyme a-rewe * he gan hire kisse, — in a row
And she obeyed hym in every thing
That myghte doon hym plesance or likyng.
And thus they lyve unto hir lyves ende
In parfit joye; and Jhesu Crist us sende
Housbondes meeke, yonge, and fressh abedde,
And grace t'overbyde * hem that we wedde; — outlive
And eek I praye Jhesu shorte * hir lyves — shorten
That wol nat be governed by hir wyves;
And olde and angry nygardes of dispence,* — tightwads
God sende hem soone verray pestilence!

Heere endeth the Wyves Tale of Bathe.

Questions

1. What point is the Wife of Bath making? How seriously does Chaucer seem to want us to accept her thesis?
2. What is the Wife's thesis about the nature of "gentillesse"? Do you agree?
3. In the prologue to this tale, the Wife has stated that she will talk "of the tribulacion in marriage, of which I am expert in al myn age." (She has had five husbands.) What does the fact that she chooses to tell a highly romantic tale filled with a good deal of preaching and moralizing tell about her character? From the story can you cite clues to indicate her attitude toward marriage? Do you agree with her views?
4. What three things does the young knight charge the old hag with in his reasons for not wanting to marry her? Which of the three bothers the hag most?
5. The Wife's story of King Midas seems to be a long digression in the tale. Is

it merely a digression? What does it reveal to us about the character of the Wife? About Chaucer's technique?

6. In other versions of this tale, the hag, upon the promise of marriage, immediately gives the knight the answer to the queen's question. Chaucer, however, has the hag withhold the answer until the couple appear in court. What effect does Chaucer achieve by withholding the answer?
7. Aside from differences in pronunciation and changes in vocabulary, what differences can you point out between Chaucer's language and Modern English? Note the examples of the double negative in this tale. Was Chaucer using substandard English?
8. Chaucer was for a long time considered a clumsy poet, one whose meter was uneven. When scholars discovered that the final *e* in many of Chaucer's words was pronounced, his poetic reputation improved. Can you find lines in which the meter would be uneven unless some final *e's* were pronounced?

On the English Language

Benjamin Franklin *The following letter from Benjamin Franklin to Noah Webster illustrates the state of the language in the late eighteenth century and also a prevailing attitude toward language at that time. Can you find words or phrases that are not used in Modern English? Webster later published a dictionary in which he attempted to bring about significant spelling reform and other language changes. He discovered quickly, however, that his proposals were too radical for the public to accept and greatly modified them in subsequent editions. What would Hayakawa (see "How Dictionaries Are Made") say about Franklin's proposals for "preserving the purity of our language"? How many of the changes Franklin objects to are accepted in current English?*

TO NOAH WEBSTER

On the English Language.—Improper Use of certain Words in America.—Universality of the French Language.—Improvements in Printing.

Philadelphia, 26 December, 1789.

Dear Sir,

I received some time since your *Dissertations on the English Language*. The book was not accompanied by any letter or message, informing me to whom I am obliged for it, but I suppose it is to yourself. It is an excellent work, and will be greatly useful in turning the thoughts of our countrymen to correct writing. Please to accept my thanks for the great honor you have done me in its dedication. I ought to have made this acknowledgment sooner, but much indisposition prevented me.

I cannot but applaud your zeal for preserving the purity of our language, both in its expressions and pronunciation, and in correcting the popular errors several of our States are continually falling into with respect to both. Give me leave to mention some of them, though possibly they may have already occurred to you. I wish, however, in some future publication of yours, you would set a discountenancing mark upon them. The first I remember is the word *improved*. When I left New England, in the year 1723, this word had never been used among us, as far as I know, but in the sense of *ameliorated* or made better, except once in a very old book of Dr. Mather's, entitled *Remarkable Providences.* As that eminent man wrote a very obscure hand, I remember that when I read that word in his book, used instead of the word *imployed,* I conjectured it was an error of the printer, who had mistaken a too short *l* in the writing for an *r,* and a *y* with too short a tail for a *v;* whereby *imployed* was converted into *improved.*

But when I returned to Boston, in 1733, I found this change had obtained favor, and was then become common; for I met with it often in perusing the newspapers, where it frequently made an appearance rather ridiculous. Such, for instance, as the advertisement of a country-house to be sold, which had been many years *improved* as a tavern; and, in the character of a deceased country gentleman, that he had been for more than thirty years *improved* as a justice of the peace. This use of the word *improved* is peculiar to New England, and not to be met with among any other speakers of English, either on this or the other side of the water.

During my late absence in France, I find that several other new words have been introduced into our parliamentary language; for example, I find a verb formed from the substantive *notice; I should not have* NOTICED *this, were it not that the gentleman,* &c. Also another verb from the substantive *advocate; The gentleman who* ADVOCATES *or has* ADVOCATED *that motion,* &c. Another from the substantive *progress,* the most awkward and abominable of the three; *The committee, having* PROGRESSED, *resolved to adjourn.* The word *opposed,* though not a new word, I find used in a new manner, as, *The gentlemen who are* OPPOSED *to this measure; to which I have also myself always been* OPPOSED. If you should happen to be of my opinion with respect to these innovations, you will use your authority in reprobating them.

The Latin language, long the vehicle used in distributing knowledge among the different nations of Europe, is daily more and more neglected; and one of the modern tongues, viz. the French, seems in point of universality to have supplied its place. It is spoken in all the courts of Europe; and most of the literati, those even who do not speak it, have acquired knowledge enough of it to enable them easily to read the books that are written in it. This gives a considerable advantage to that nation; it enables its authors to inculcate and spread throughout other nations such sentiments and opinions on important points, as are most conducive to its interests, or which may contribute to its reputation by promoting the common interests of mankind. It is perhaps owing to its being written in French, that Voltaire's treatise on *Toleration* has had so sudden and so great an effect on the bigotry of Europe, as almost entirely to disarm it. The general use of the French language has likewise a very advantageous effect on the profits of the bookselling branch of commerce, it being well known, that the more copies can be sold that are struck off from one composition of types, the profits increase in a much greater proportion than they do in making a great number of pieces in any other kind of manufacture. And at present there is no capital town in Europe without a French bookseller's shop corresponding with Paris.

Our English bids fair to obtain the second place. The great body of excellent printed sermons in our language, and the freedom of our writings on political subjects, have induced a number of divines of different sects and nations, as well as gentlemen concerned in public affairs, to study it; so far at least as to read it. And if we were to endeavour the facilitating its progress, the study of our tongue might become much more general. Those, who have employed some parts of their time in learning a new language, have frequently observed, that, while their acquaintance with it was imperfect, difficulties small in themselves operated as great ones in obstructing their progress. A book, for example, ill printed, or a pronunciation in speaking, not well articulated, would render a sentence unintelligible; which, from a clear print or a distinct speaker, would have been immediately comprehended. If therefore we would have the benefit of seeing our language more generally known among mankind, we should endeavour to remove all the difficulties, however small, that discourage the learning it.

But I am sorry to observe, that, of late years, those difficulties, instead of being diminished, have been augmented. In examining the English books, that were printed between the Restoration and the accession of George the Second, we may observe, that all *substantives* were begun with a capital, in which we imitated our mother tongue, the German. This was more particularly useful to those, who were not well acquainted with the English; there being such a prodigious number of our words, that are both *verbs* and *substantives,* and spelled in the same manner, though often accented differently in the pronunciation.

This method has, by the fancy of printers, of late years been laid aside, from an idea, that suppressing the capitals shows the character to greater advantage; those letters prominent above the line disturbing its even regular appearance. The effect of this change is so considerable, that a learned man of France, who used to read our books, though not perfectly acquainted with our language, in conversation with me on the subject of our authors, attributed the greater obscurity he found in our modern books, compared with those of the period above mentioned, to change of style for the worse in our writers; of which mistake I convinced him, by marking for him each *substantive* with a capital in a paragraph, which he then easily understood, though before he could not comprehend it. This shows the inconvenience of that pretended improvement.

From the same fondness for an even and uniform appearance of characters in the line, the printers have of late banished also the Italic types, in which words of importance to be attended to in the sense of the sentence, and words on which an emphasis should be put in reading, used to be printed. And lately another fancy has induced some printers to use the short round *s*, instead of the long one, which formerly served well to distinguish a word readily by its varied appearance. Certainly the omitting this prominent letter makes the line appear more even; but renders it less immediately legible; as the paring all men's noses might smooth and level their faces, but would render their physiognomies less distinguishable.

Add to all these improvements *backwards*, another modern fancy, that grey printing is more beautiful than black; hence the English new books are printed in so dim a character, as to be read with difficulty by old eyes, unless in a very strong light and with good glasses. Whoever compares a volume of the *Gentleman's Magazine*, printed between the years 1731 and 1740, with one of those printed in the last ten years, will be convinced of the much greater degree of perspicuity given by black ink than by grey. Lord Chesterfield pleasantly remarked this difference to Faulkener, the printer of the Dublin *Journal*, who was vainly making encomiums on his own paper, as the most complete of any in the world; "But, Mr. Faulkener," said my Lord, "don't you think it might be still farther improved by using paper and ink not quite so near of a color?" For all these reasons I cannot but wish, that our American printers would in their editions avoid these fancied improvements, and thereby render their works more agreeable to foreigners in Europe, to the great advantage of our bookselling commerce.

Further, to be more sensible of the advantage of clear and distinct printing, let us consider the assistance it affords in reading well aloud to an auditory. In so doing the eye generally slides forward three or four words before the voice. If the sight clearly distinguishes what the coming words are, it gives time to order the modulation of the voice to express them properly. But, if they are obscurely printed, or disguised by omitting the capitals and long *s's* or otherwise, the reader is apt to modulate wrong; and, finding he has done so, he is obliged to go back and begin the sentence again, which lessens the pleasure of the hearers.

This leads me to mention an old error in our mode of printing. We are sensible, that, when a question is met with in reading, there is a proper variation to be used in the management of the voice. We have therefore a point called an interrogation, affixed to the question in order to distinguish it. But this is absurdly placed at its end; so that the reader does not discover it, till he finds he has wrongly modulated his voice, and is therefore obliged to begin again the sentence. To prevent this, the Spanish printers, more sensibly, place an interrogation at the beginning as well as at the end of a question. We have another error of the same kind in printing plays, where something often occurs that is marked as spoken *aside*. But the word *aside* is placed at the end of the speech, when it ought to precede it, as a direction to the reader, that he may govern his voice accordingly. The practice of our ladies in meeting five or six together to form a little busy party, where each is employed in some useful work while one reads to them, is so commendable in itself, that it deserves the attention of authors and printers to make it as pleasing as possible, both to the reader and hearers.

After these general observations, permit me to make one that I imagine may regard your interest. It is that *your Spelling Book* is miserably printed here, so as in many places to be scarcely legible, and on wretched paper. If this is not attended to, and the new one lately advertised as coming out should be preferable in these respects, it may hurt the future sale of yours.

I congratulate you on your marriage, of which the newspapers inform me. My best wishes attend you, being with sincere esteem, Sir, &c.

B. FRANKLIN.

Questions

1. Franklin cites French as the first language in international affairs of his time. Today English is without question the most widely used language in the world. Has it become so widely used because it is intrinsically superior to other languages? For what reasons does a language become widely used?
2. Do you agree with Franklin that capitalizing the first letters in nouns would make English more easily comprehended? Why or why not?
3. Franklin assumes that Webster, a lexicographer, can wield a significant influence on the changes the language is undergoing. Is this assumption a sound one? Why or why not?

Suggestions for Writing

1. Choose some changes the language is now undergoing. Write a letter either condemning the changes or approving them to a friend who holds an opposite view. You might choose to write about such things as the widespread use of slang, about changes in the use or meaning of words—*uninterested* being used for *disinterested,* for example—sloppy use of language by younger people, or use of obscene language by certain groups.

Speaking American and Hearing English

Marshall R. Craig *You will recognize the author of this essay as one of your editors. The essay results from a year's stay in England by a family unusually interested in language. Craig is responding to contrasts between American and British English that have intrigued observers of language at least since H. L. Mencken wrote a remarkable analysis entitled* The American Language. *Note Craig's fascination with various dialects of English. Would the contrasts between American and British English be greater than the contrasts between Boston American and Southern American or between Cockney English and Eton English?*

Are you from the States or Canada? I suppose strangers asked our family that question more than any other during our year's stay in England. Once in Smiths, a stationary and book shop, when we answered as usual that we were from the "States," the clerk (pronounced *clark,* of course) who was waiting on us made an unforgettable response. "It's hard to tell, isn't it? Both of you speak so nasal, don't you?" He spoke in a flat, matter-of-fact voice that sounded to us (the only word for it) nasal.

To proclaim ourselves foreigners whenever we opened our mouths to utter our native language was humbling, frustrating, and highly educational. In many ways our family—my wife and I and four children ranging from an eleven-year-old to a junior in college—were better prepared for such a language experience than many visitors to England. Both my wife and I are teachers with extensive language backgrounds, and within our family a dialect debate periodically erupts. Our Utah-reared children scorn the pronunciations of their parents, who unfortunately do not always present a united opposition. When we go to announce that something is horrible, my children insist that it is *hoarable,* I claim it is *hahrable,* and my wife miraculously produces a sound midway between these two extremes. My children almost rhyme *law* with *blah;* my wife and I pronounce it with a rounded vowel sound, but again her vowel is slightly different from mine. For years we have discussed such dialect variations.

In addition, our college-aged daughter had done extensive research for one of her language classes on the differences between American and English speech. Her paper on the subject was a frequent topic of discussion in our family, and we all went to England primed with mental lists of the English equivalents for words we habitually use. We quickly discovered that our lists were far from complete.

On the British plane from New York to London, we encountered our first language difficulty. Our two younger daughters were asked by the steward if they would like some "squash" (a word on no list we had seen). "What is it?" one of them hesitantly asked him. "It's lemon," was his still-puzzling reply. He held a pitcher and cups in his hand, so after an exchange of confused looks on both sides, she ventured, "Is it a *soft* drink?" "Oh, yes." And the girls had their first drink of "squash" as well as their first vocabulary lesson.

We discovered, upon landing at Heathrow Airport, that there is not *a* British accent. We were surrounded by British accents. We heard a greater variety of accents there than we had ever heard in any one place in America, and we reveled in their abundance. A short time later when we stopped at a "layby" and an elderly man gave us directions in a cockney accent better than any stage one we had ever heard, we were even more pleased. He peered at our map, saying, "Oie 'ope yew can read it, 'cause Oie yain't got me glahsses," and all of us melted with delight. When we had driven to the second "round about" as he had carefully instructed and had taken the third "turning," we not only knew we were in England but began to suspect how far from complete were those mental lists each of us carried.

We were startled by the many accents we encountered at Heathrow, but of course we could not distinguish one from another with any precision; later, in the circle of friends we made in southern Greater London, we learned to distinguish ten to twelve different accents. The existence of some of the variations was easily understandable. Katie had a Liverpudlian accent with traces of her mother's Irish speech; the Dromeys, originally from Wales, had a distinctive lilt to their speech; and Ruth, born on the Isle of Man, had still a different accent. But we would have needed the skill of Shaw's Professor Higgins to identify and locate the origin of all of the various London accents we heard just among our friends. These ranged from the precise (the well-known "BBC") speech to the "bovver" boys' almost incomprehensible mutterings. Twelve-year-old twins of our acquaintance substituted *f*'s and *v*'s for *th*'s with the result that they said *fings* and *brovver* for *things* and *brother*. Their speech was not far from that of the then reigning delinquents, the "bovver" boys, who wore heavy boots so that they could "bovver" people with them. The rest of my family was quicker to understand this accent than I was; for weeks and weeks I listened to it uncomprehending, completely baffled.

Our youngest daughter was equally baffled, but only for a few moments, when, on her first day at the high school she attended, a girl asked her, complete with glottal stop, "Go'a rubba?" Another student supplied an eraser.

Although we met "true" cockneys, those born within the sound of the great bell of Bow in the East End of London, none of them spoke with the delightful accent that we heard in our first hour or two in England. They were proud of their heritage and bragged of being cockneys, but they all pronounced their *h*'s.

Varied as the accents were among our friends in London, we later heard others that we remember with equal, or greater, pleasure. None of our friends in London, for instance, used a northern accent. (A friend of ours from Tunbridge Wells tells us that people in the north think that her southern speech is "toffee-nosed.") One of my wife's pleasant memories is from a visit to a school for the blind where she heard a group of girls perform the final scenes from Shakespeare's *A Midsummer Night's Dream.* The girl from northern England who recited the Bottom (Pyramus) lines rhymed naturally in her speech the final words of the couplet "Thy mantle good,/What, stained with blood!" And with even more pleasure, my wife recalls the young boy from Yorkshire who recited for her from the Psalms, in an almost archaic accent: "Whaht is mahn, thaht thew art mindful of him, and the Soon of Mahn that thew visiteth him?"

Our pleasure in the multiplicity of their accents was countered by the English's vocal objection to ours. We quickly found that the tolerant scorn of our children for their parents' pronunciations was nothing compared to the almost universal scorn of the Englishman for American speech. "It's our language, and you have ruined it" summed up the most common reaction to our speech. "What do you call the language you study in school?" we were asked soon after we arrived by one young woman. "You certainly can't call what you speak *English.*" We were reminded of that attitude months later when we met a much-traveled family from India. The eight-year-old daughter, who managed half a dozen languages, had said to her mother during a stay in a cosmopolitan area of Stockholm, "Mother, you know what's the easiest language to learn if you know English? It's American."

There was an open directness about the Englishman's attack on our speech that was disquieting and unanswerable. In a Swedish class my wife attended, one young man was surprised to find that she had been in England for only three months. "I would have thought you had been here much longer than that. Wouldn't you have, Bill?" he asked his friend. Then turning back to my wife he explained, "You speak such *good* English." And when Bill learned that she was to be in England for a year, he added, "You should sound really cultured by then." What does one say to a remark such as that?

Although we identified ourselves as foreigners whenever we spoke, most of the English had a strange perception of American speech, apparently drawn from television westerns. At high school, our daughter Alison's friends greeted her in what they considered an authentic American accent, an exaggerated Texas drawl, "Ho-w-dee, Al." And most of our friends, as well as strangers, found it difficult to identify our accents. "You don't sound like Americans," they would say, or we would be asked the perennial question about whether we were from Canada or the "States." I retain enough of my southern-midland speech for a linguist to "put me in my place" within a few minutes of conversation, but I have spent most of my adult life away from the South and my accent has toned down so much that most American laymen can not place it. My wife, the daughter of Swedish immigrants whose English bore no trace of a Swedish accent but was notably free from regionalisms, has speech patterns which puzzle even the experts. No one from the "States," however, would think of our speech as anything but American.

Since our family has returned to the "States," we have tried a number of times to analyze the attitudes of the English toward their own various accents and toward our speech. Attitudes are especially difficult to analyze and are even more difficult when they are attitudes of large groups of people. However, we have concluded that their attitudes toward their own speech is related to their attitude toward ours.

Perhaps we should have been less surprised at some of their notions about American speech if we had been more aware beforehand of notions prevalent in America about English speech. We remember with amused horror (*hoarror? hahror?*) the "English" accents in the local amateur production we saw just a few weeks after our return from England. Throughout the play, nobility conscientiously dropped their *h*'s. This same misconception was noticed by a young woman from England studying at a university here in America. When she arrived people habitually asked her if she were speaking in a cockney accent. Ignorance of dialect and accents played their part in the English reaction to our speech, just as it did in the two instances listed above.

Another factor was the English attitude toward cultured speech. Not only does the northern English speaker think the southern speech "toffee-nosed," the Englishman, even today, looks down on many of his countrymen's accents as lower class. One of our "true" cockney friends was very proud of her son's "cultured" speech (which seemed artificial to us), and an older woman we met who was acting as a guide for tourists assured us that she did not mind having impoverished herself to send two sons to one of the best known "public" (private, to us) schools because one could tell they were "Eton men" even *before* they spoke. The English themselves, however, scoffed at exaggerated theatrical speech, what they called a "posh" accent. A newspaper editor revealed a slightly different attitude but nevertheless made clear that he believed in a hierarchy of accents when he assured us that the "best" English was spoken in Inverness, Scotland. We never understood who decided what was "best."

We have concluded that this latter attitude is related to English attitudes toward our speech. The English consider Americans as a group to be uncultured and our accents are therefore uncultured.

In addition to our revealing accents, words which were not on our mental lists revealed us as foreigners, particularly during the early part of our stay. My wife at one time had difficulty getting lead for a mechanical pencil. The clerk insisted he had no such lead. Finally, a pantomiming of the rotating of a mechanical pencil enlightened him and he exclaimed, "A propelling pencil!" She got the lead immediately. Also we quickly discovered that what we called a *jug* our English friends called a *pitcher*, and the reverse was true—what we called a *pitcher* is their *jug*. The English *milk jug* is a larger version of our *cream pitcher*. Similarly *basin* and *bowl* are reversed in meaning. Our English friends make bread or cake in a *basin* and wash dishes in a *bowl*.

It was unfortunate that our one daughter did not know the British meaning of *bugger* when she called two male students "lucky buggers." She meant only an almost affectionate substitute for *fellows*—the only meaning of the word for her. Unfortunately, the word for them meant *sodomites* or perhaps was merely an extremely crude expression divorced from any definite meaning. The same daughter also shocked her teacher by referring to a "piddling little essay." The English dictionary we borrowed from our neighbors gave the same meaning for *piddling* as our American ones—*trifling* and *petty*—but the colloquial meaning of *urinating* has removed the word from polite conversations.

One of the major difficulties with vocabulary variations is that even when the new word is understood, the speaker automatically uses the familiar one. We kept saying nice things about people's *yards* instead of their *gardens.* For the Englishman we were praising that small area where he keeps such things as his *dustbins,* their designation for garbage cans. And it took an effort not to ask for a *restroom* at the service station, a request that brought us either a blank stare or a question about our wanting to lie down. We should have said *toilet* or *loo,* both of which words seemed cruder to us than to most of our English friends. The English did not know *john* as a crude name for *toilet,* much to the relief of our son John, although some of the young people we met used *bog* as a term we judged to be about equal to *john* in America.

Because we were used to saying *pants* instead of the British *trousers,* we constantly amused our friends by inadvertently referring to men's underpants. I do not believe that it was the reference to underpants that amused them because the young people had no hesitancy about referring to *knickers,* ladies' underpants. The high school students used *knickers* in their expression equivalent to "keep your shirt on": "Don't get your knickers in a twist." We had some understanding of our friends' smiles because we reacted the same way to the use of *jumper,* which meant for them not the female apparel it does for us but a pullover sweater. We knew this meaning, but we got an amusing mental image when a male friend remarked that he had to buy a jumper or complained that his jumper was too small.

We found that many words in our dialect were stressed differently from the English. Often these were newer or scientific words. We said *MARgarine;* they said *margaREEN.* They also said *caPILLary* for our *CAPillary; skeLEEtal* for our *SKELetal; reSPIRATORY* for our *RESpiraTORy;* and *conTROVersy* for our *CONtroVERsy.* Sometimes they retained the foreign sound of an adopted word. They kept, for example, the *k*-sound in *hydrocephalus* and the *sh*-sound in *schedule,* but all the English we heard anglicized Don Juan to *don jooan* and Don Quixote to *don kwikset.* However, Demesne Road, in the town where we lived, retained the French pronunciation *deemain.*

Try as we would, we could not figure out a pattern for the place names which the English often shortened. We knew many names before we went to England—Worcestershire (*WOOstersher*), Leicester (*LESter*), Birmingham (*BURmingum*), but we had difficulty with Caterham and Westerham, two towns near where we lived. They came out *KAtrm* and *WEStrm,* with the *t*'s sharp against the teeth. The name of another town near us the natives pronounced differently from anyone else; Carshalton by the natives was pronounced *CAR SHALton,* as if there were another Shalton just down the road which they did not want confused with their town. There were also Cirencester, pronounced *SISister,* and the London tube stop Cockfoster, which was called *COFFster.*

The rhythm and intonation of English sentences were often markedly different from ours. For example, the English asked us to repeat something by saying, "Pardon?" For most of them the word was strongly accented on the second syllable and uttered with a sharp, rising, questioning inflection. It came out *p'rDUN?* Our daughter who attended University College London was made aware of this difference in sentence patterns during the rehearsal of a play in which she portrayed, surprisingly enough, an American businesswoman. The director worked with her for some time on one particular speech, trying for a specific rhythm pattern. She finally told him she could not use that rhythm and intonation for the character she was playing. He agreed to allow her to use her own patterns, and as a result we heard a compliment to our accents: people around us at the performance exclaimed at how well that young woman "did an American accent." We did not dare open our mouths to agree with them.

Related to that sharp rising inflection of *p'rDUN?* was the question the English often attached at the end of a statement—"is he?" "doesn't he?" "will they?" and so on. These expressed the multipossibilities of the French *n'est-ce pas?* or the German *nicht wahr?* often with a surprising, to us, positive question added to a positive statement: "You go into the library every day, do you?" Most Americans, I think, would ask "don't you?" instead of "do you?" at the end of such a statement.

Often an unexpected variation in word choice, even the slightest variation, startled us. In a few instances we used an article where our English friends did not. They went *on holiday* or were *in hospital* or were *at university*. Sometimes the reverse was true and they made a slight addition, as they did in *earlier on,* much as we both said *later on.* In our area we hear both *different from* and *different than,* but in England we heard *different to.* The variations were sometimes more complex as in, "Immediately they saw him, they left the room."

We became aware of one interesting vocabulary difference after we had been in England for several months. Our first awareness came when we referred to *British* as a collective name for all inhabitants of the British Islands. A friend of ours, an educator and linguist, told us he would not use *British* as we had done because he made a distinction between the Scots, the English, and the Welsh. We could not make such a distinction. In fact, we invited a young American to our home to meet some of our English friends and introduced him to the Dromeys, who found it amusing that we were introducing them as English—they were Welsh. Later Gordon Dromey told us he was always pleased when someone asked him directions in the city of London, where he worked and which he loved, because the person asking directions never guessed he was getting directions from a foreigner. We did not think of Gordon as Welsh. He was tall and fair, almost the opposite of the short, dark Welshman we had always imagined.

It was not until we traveled in Wales and met Gordon's counterpart on almost every corner in Cardiff that we realized how typical he was of the Welsh.

When I tried to tell our educator friend an amusing story about a marriage between a very homely man and equally homely woman, he was as much at a loss as I had been over distinguishing English, Scots, and Welsh. He had a different meaning for *homely* (for him it was more like our *homey*), but he had no word meaning *homely*—someone was either *plain* or *ugly*. I tried to use *ugly* as my adjective, but the wife of our friend asked if the man in the story was *ugly* enough to be distinctive. The story got lost in a discussion of semantics. *Ugly* had obviously more negative connotations for me than for our English friend. We could not help wondering if many times we were communicating less accurately with our British (English?) friends than we had supposed.

We made a few concessions to English speech during our stay. I think we all learned to say "sorry" instead of "excuse me," which the English considered to be crude. Everyone said "sorry" and so did we. We find ourselves still saying it. My wife asked for *toMAHtoes* at the greengrocers. A helpful neighbor had suggested she do so in order not to be overcharged. We saw no effort by the neighborhood shopkeepers to overcharge us, but it was less trouble to use the English pronunciation there. Our children in school picked up a larger English vocabulary than my wife and I did, and in addition they unconsciously picked up the rhythm and intonation of many expressions.

However, when we had been in England for about nine months, we had all added extensively to our English vocabulary. By that time we automatically kept food in our *larder* and clothes in a *cupboard*. We walked on the *pavement,* and we pulled the car off the highway onto the *verge*. We got our milk from the *milk float* each morning. Our children wrote with a *Biro* instead of a ball point pen. They took the *coach* to school and knew who was really ill and who was *skiving off* from classes. They knew when a teasing friend was *taking the mickey,* and the girls knew when a boy was *chatting them up*, and that when a young man was going to *call* he would not *ring up* but would be knocking on the door. Our son accepted his hair color as *ginger* instead of red, and we all enjoyed standing around *nattering* with our friends.

About this time we had a minor but revealing experience. We were watching the *telly* one evening when we saw a documentary made in the "States." A young man, beginning his college career, drove from his home in the Midwest to California. Along his wandering route—and only someone who had traveled the route would know how wandering it was—he chatted with various people about politics, foreign policy, and college liberals. As the program began, our entire family gasped: the young man was driving on the wrong side of the road! Not only did that surprise us. We winced at the attitudes expressed by those people with whom he chatted and hoped that these were not the typical responses but had been carefully culled from a larger number. But we winced even more at the accents we heard. That was our country and our particular region; yet the accents were often unattractive, harsh, and we could not help laughing—the voices—yes, there was no question about it, some of the voices sounded definitely nasal.

Now that we are home the local dialect sounds, if not beautiful, at least normal to us, but for a short time there in England, hearing that dialect under those circumstances, we could sympathize with the clerk in Smith's. We had a glimpse of how we sounded to the English.

Questions

1. From the evidences of style and tone, to what audience is Craig writing?
2. H. L. Mencken argued for an "American language" (opposed to "English language"). On the evidence presented in this article and from your own knowledge of differences between American and British English, defend or attack his view.
3. Would you expect that differences among the numerous dialects in England would be greater than dialect differences in the United States? As you ponder your answer consider Shuy's discussion of dialects, the length of time groups have been speaking the dialects, the impact of mass education and mass media on language, social classes in the two countries, and mobility of population. Why would there be fewer dialects in America than in England?
4. Many language scholars have noted that transplanted languages tend to be more conservative than the "mother" tongue. As a result, American, Australian, and Canadian English retain pronunciations, words, grammatical items that have been changed in British English. For example, modern speakers of British English would say "autumn," "has got," and "secret'ry"; Shakespeare and American speakers would say "fall," "has gotten," and "secretary." In what ways might the attitudes of a transplanted group lead them to be more conservative in language use?
5. Summarize the reasons Craig gives for many British speakers feeling that British English is superior to American English.
6. What point is Craig making in his last two paragraphs?

Suggestions for Writing

1. Everyone has had the experience of associating with people who have a different "accent" or who speak a different dialect. Craig discusses some of the problems people who speak differently have and some of the reactions other people have to them. Observe the responses people have to language differences and write a paper analyzing the communication situation in terms of the speaker and of the audience.

How Meaning Changes

Thomas Pyles *There are a number of ways in which a language may change. Other authors in this section have discussed change in vocabulary, in the structure of the language (grammar), and in pronunciation. In the following article Pyles discusses semantic change in language: how words change their meanings. Knowledge of the older meanings of words helps you to read the great literature of Middle English and Early Modern English—Chaucer, Shakespeare, The King James Bible—with greater understanding and appreciation.*

Note particularly the organization of this brief essay. Can you find a thesis sentence? How many major parts is the essay divided into? Can you find topic sentences for the major paragraphs?

HOW MEANING CHANGES

Change of meaning—a phenomenon common to all languages—while frequently unpredictable, is not wholly chaotic. Rather, it follows certain paths which we might do well to familiarize ourselves with. Much, probably most, of the illustrative matter which is to follow, like that which precedes, has come from many books read over a long period of years. Some of the examples are by now more or less stock ones, but they make their point better than less familiar ones would do, and hence are used without apology, but with gratitude to whoever first dug them out. It is likely that many of them will be found in James Bradstreet Greenough and George Lyman Kittredge's old, but still good, *Words and Their Ways in English Speech* (New York, 1901).

GENERALIZATION AND SPECIALIZATION

An obvious classification of meaning is that based on scope. This is to say, meaning may be generalized (extended, widened) or it may be specialized (restricted, narrowed). When we increase the scope of a word, we reduce the elements of its contents. For instance, *tail* (from OE *tægl*) in earlier times seems to have meant 'hairy caudal appendage, as of a horse.' When we eliminated the hairiness (or the horsiness) from the meaning, we increased its scope, so that in modern English the word means simply 'caudal appendage.' The same thing has happened to Danish *hale,* earlier 'tail of a cow.' In course of time the cow was eliminated, and in present-day Danish the word means simply 'tail,' having undergone a semantic generalization precisely like that of the English word cited; the closely related Icelandic *hali* still keeps the cow in the picture. Similarly, a *mill* was earlier a place for making things by the process of grinding, that is, for making meal. The words *meal* and *mill* are themselves related, as one might guess from their similarity. A mill is now simply a place for making things: the grinding has been eliminated, so that we may speak of a woolen mill, a steel mill, or even a gin mill. The word *corn* earlier meant 'grain' and is in fact related to the word *grain.* It is still used in this general sense in England, as in the "Corn Laws," but specifically it may mean either oats (for animals) or wheat (for human beings). In American usage *corn* denotes maize, which is of course not at all what Keats meant in his "Ode to a Nightingale" when he described Ruth as standing "in tears amid the alien corn." The building in which corn, regardless of its meaning, is stored is called a barn. *Barn* earlier denoted a storehouse for barley; the word is in fact a compound of two Old English words, *bere* 'barley' and *ærn* 'house.' By elimination of a part of its earlier content, the scope of this word has been extended to mean a storehouse for any kind of grain. American English has still further generalized by eliminating the grain, so that *barn* may mean also a place for housing livestock.

The opposite of generalization is specialization, a process in which, by adding to the elements of meaning, the semantic content of a word is reduced. *Deer,* for instance, used to mean simply 'animal' (OE *dēor*) as its German cognate *Tier* still does. Shakespeare writes of "Mice, and Rats, and such small Deare" (*King Lear* III.iv.144). By adding something particular (the family *Cervidae*) to the content, the scope of the word has been reduced, and it has come to mean a specific kind of animal. Similarly *hound* used to mean 'dog,' as does its German cognate *Hund.* To this earlier meaning we have in the course of time added the idea of hunting, and thereby restricted the scope of the word, which to us means a special sort of dog, a hunting dog. To the earlier content of *liquor* 'fluid' (compare *liquid*) we have added 'alcoholic.' But generalization, the opposite tendency, has occurred in the case of the word *rum,* the name of a specific alcoholic drink, which in the usage of those who disapprove of all alcoholic beverages long ago came to mean strong drink in general, even though other liquors are much more copiously imbibed today. The word has even been personified in *Demon Rum.*

Meat once meant simply 'food,' a meaning which it retains in *sweet-*

meat and throughout the King James Bible ("meat for the belly," "meat and drink"), though it acquired the meaning 'flesh' much earlier and had for a while both the general and the specialized meaning. *Starve* (OE *steorfan*) used to mean simply 'to die,' as its German cognate *sterben* still does.[1] Chaucer writes, for instance, "But as hire man I wol ay lyve and sterve" (*Troilus and Criseyde* I.427). A specific way of dying had to be expressed by a following phrase, for example "of hunger, for cold." The *OED* cites "starving with the cold," presumably dialectal, as late as 1867. The word came somehow to be primarily associated with death by hunger, and for a while there existed a compound verb *hunger-starve*. Usually nowadays we put the stress altogether on the added idea of hunger and lose the older meaning altogether. Although the usual meaning of *to starve* now is 'to die of hunger,' we also use the phrase "starve to death," which in earlier times would have been tautological. An additional, toned-down meaning grows out of hyperbole, so that "I'm starving" may mean only 'I'm very hungry.' The word is of course used figuratively, as in "starving for love," which, as we have seen, once meant 'dying for love.' This word furnishes a striking example of specialization and proliferation of meaning.

Questions

1. Pyles defines the terms *generalization* and *specialization* primarily through illustration. Can you define the two terms in your own words?
2. Later in this same chapter Pyles discusses other changes in meaning such as pejoration (degeneration) in which the meaning of the word moves from positive to negative, and amelioration (elevation) in which the meaning of the word moves from negative to positive. Classify the changes in meaning in the following words.
   disinterested—once meant "impartial, unbiased" now for many people means "no interest."
   knave—once meant "boy" now means "bad person."
   fame—once meant "report, rumor" now means "renown."
   Mickey Mouse—once the name of a cartoon character now means "worthless or corny."
   undertaker—once meant "one who could undertake anything" now means "one who manages funerals."
   ordeal—once meant "trial by physical test" now means "difficult experience."
3. Pyles entitles the section "How Meaning Changes." Does he actually discuss the process of *how* meanings change?

[1] An even earlier meaning may have been 'to grow stiff.'

How Dictionaries Are Made

S. I. Hayakawa *Hayakawa first gained fame as a semanticist (one who studies the meanings of words). He later became known as the president who calmed the campus of San Francisco State University during the student demonstrations of the late 1960's. The brief excerpt which follows is taken from his very popular book* Language in Thought and Action. *In this article he gives an excellent example of how writing about a process can be both clear and interesting. How well does his first paragraph fulfill the functions of an introduction: arousing interest and introducing the topic? Note how he relates the steps in the process, giving illustrations to clarify and to add interest. Note also that he has some negative instruction, telling what making a dictionary is not. Has he explained the process clearly enough so that others could do it?*

It is widely believed that every word has a correct meaning, that we learn these meanings principally from teachers and grammarians (except that most of the time we don't bother to, so that we ordinarily speak "sloppy English"), and that dictionaries and grammars are the supreme authority in matters of meaning and usage. Few people ask by what authority the writers of dictionaries and grammars say what they say. The writer once got into a dispute with an Englishwoman over the pronunciation of a word and offered to look it up in the dictionary. The Englishwoman said firmly, "What for? I am English. I was born and brought up in England. The way I speak *is* English." Such self-assurance about one's own language is not uncommon among the English. In the United States, however, anyone who is willing to quarrel with the dictionary is regarded as either eccentric or mad.

Let us see how dictionaries are made and how the editors arrive at definitions. What follows applies, incidentally, only to those dictionary offices where first-hand, original research goes on—not those in which editors simply copy existing dictionaries. The task of writing a dictionary begins with reading vast amounts of the literature of the period or subject that the dictionary is to cover. As the editors read, they copy on cards every interesting or rare word, every unusual or peculiar occurrence of a common word, a large number of common words in their ordinary uses, and also the sentences in which each of these words appears, thus:

> pail
> The dairy *pails* bring home increase of milk
> Keats, *Endymion*–I, 44–45

That is to say, the context of each word is collected, along with the word itself. For a really big job of dictionary writing, such as the *Oxford English Dictionary* (usually bound in about twenty-five volumes), millions of such cards are collected, and the task of editing occupies decades. As the cards are collected, they are alphabetized and sorted. When the sorting is completed, there will be for each word anywhere from two or three to several hundred illustrative quotations, each on its card.

To define a word, then, the dictionary editor places before him the stack of cards illustrating that word; each of the cards represents an actual use of the word by a writer of some literary or historical importance. He reads the cards carefully, discards some, rereads the rest, and divides up the stack according to what he thinks are the several senses of the word. Finally, he writes his definitions, following the hard-and-fast rule that each definition *must* be based on what the quotations in front of him reveal about the meaning of the word. The editor cannot be influenced by what *he* thinks a given word *ought* to mean. He must work according to the cards or not at all.

The writing of a dictionary, therefore, is not a task of setting up authoritative statements about the "true meanings" of words, but a task of *recording,* to the best of one's ability, what various words *have meant* to authors in the distant or immediate past. *The writer of a dictionary is a historian, not a lawgiver.* If, for example, we had been writing a dictionary in 1890, or even as late as 1919, we could have said that the word "broadcast" means "to scatter" (seed and so on) but we could not have decreed that from 1921 on, the commonest meaning of the word should become "to disseminate audible messages, etc., by radio transmission." To regard the dictionary as an "authority," therefore, is to credit the dictionary writer with gifts of prophecy which neither he nor anyone else possesses. In choosing our words when we speak or write, we can be *guided* by the historical record afforded us by the dictionary, but we cannot be *bound* by it, because new situations, new experiences, new inventions, new feelings, are always compelling us to give new uses to old words. Looking under a "hood," we should ordinarily have found, five hundred years ago, a monk; today, we find a motorcar engine.[1]

Questions

1. Which sentence states Hayakawa's thesis? Does the article fulfill the claims stated in the thesis?
2. List the steps involved in writing a definition for a dictionary entry.
3. Explain what Hayakawa means by the statement "The writer of a dictionary is a historian, not a lawgiver." Do you agree? Is the dictionary the final authority on the meaning of words? Is there a difference between the way people accept the authority of the dictionary on questions of spelling, questions of meaning, questions of pronunciation?
4. Can you explain why Americans say *the* dictionary rather than *a* dictionary even though there are a number of reputable dictionaries published? What do you think of the attitude of the Englishwoman Hayakawa mentions in the first paragraph?

[1] *Webster's Third New International Dictionary* lists the word "hood" also as a shortened form of "hoodlum."

The time that elapsed between *Webster's Second Edition* (1934) and the *Third* (1961) indicates the enormous amount of reading and labor entailed in the preparation of a really thorough dictionary of a language as rapidly changing and as rich in vocabulary as English.

Four Sonnets

Over three centuries separate the first from the last of these sonnets. The sonnets reflect both the changes that have occurred in the English language and its comparative stability since the invention of printing. Shakespeare's Sonnet LV is presented in both the original and modern printing to show changes in alphabet and spelling. Note these carefully. Can you point to other changes in language between Shakespeare's time and Milton's? Wordsworth's? Robinson's? Could you mistake any of the other three sonnets for Robinson's? Do the changes in language itself, or lack of them, explain your answer? Why or why not?

William Shakespeare

Sonnet LV

Not marble, nor the guilded monument,
Of Princes ſhall out-liue this powrefull rime,
But you ſhall ſhine more bright in these contents
Then vnſwept ſtone, beſmeer'd with ſluttiſh time,
When waſtefull warre ſhall *Statues* ouer-turne,
And broiles roote out the worke of maſonry,
Nor *Mars* his ſword, nor warres quick fire ſhall burne
The liuing record of your memory.
Gainſt death, and all obliuious emnity
Shall you pace forth, your praiſe ſhall ſtil finde roome,
Euen in the eyes of all poſterity
That weare this world out to the ending doome.
So til the iudgement that your ſelfe ariſe,
You liue in this, and dwell in louers eies.

Not marble nor the gilded monuments
Of princes shall outlive this pow'rful rhyme,
But you shall shine more bright in these contents

Than unswept stone, besmear'd with sluttish time.
When wasteful war shall statues overturn,
And broils root out the work of masonry,
Nor Mars his sword nor war's quick fire shall burn
The living record of your memory.
'Gainst death and all oblivious enmity
Shall you pace forth, your praise shall still find room
Even in the eyes of all posterity
That wear this world out to the ending doom.
So, till the judgment that yourself arise,
You live in this, and dwell in lovers' eyes.

John Milton

On His Blindness

When I consider how my light is spent,
E're half my days, in this dark world and wide,
And that one Talent which is death to hide,
Lodg'd with me useless, though my Soul more bent
To serve therewith my Maker, and present
My true account, least he returning chide,
Doth God exact day-labour, light deny'd,
I fondly ask; But patience to prevent
That murmur, soon replies, God doth not need
Either man's work or his own gifts, who best
Bear his milde yoak, they serve him best, his State
Is Kingly. Thousands at his bidding speed
And post o're Land and Ocean without rest:
They also serve who only stand and waite.

William Wordsworth

The World Is Too Much with Us

The world is too much with us; late and soon,
Getting and spending, we lay waste our powers:
Little we see in Nature that is ours;
We have given our hearts away, a sordid boon!

The sea that bares her bosom to the moon;
The winds that will be howling at all hours,
And are up-gathered now like sleeping flowers;
For this, for everything, we are out of tune;
It moves us not.—Great God! I'd rather be
A Pagan suckled in a creed outworn;
So might I, standing on this pleasant lea,
Have glimpses that would make me less forlorn;
Have sight of Proteus rising from the sea;
Or hear old Triton blow his wreathéd horn.

Edwin Arlington Robinson

Karma

Christmas was in the air and all was well
With him, but for a few confusing flaws
In divers of God's images. Because
A friend of his would neither buy nor sell,
Was he to answer for the axe that fell?
He pondered; and the reason for it was,
Partly, a slowly freezing Santa Claus
Upon the corner, with his beard and bell.

Acknowledging an improvident surprise,
He magnified a fancy that he wished
The friend whom he had wrecked were here again.
Not sure of that, he found a compromise;
And from the fulness of his heart he fished
A dime for Jesus who had died for men.

Questions

1. The subject of both Shakespeare's sonnet and Milton's is partly their art. Contrast the treatment of it. What do Wordsworth's and Robinson's sonnets have in common? Why should a modern poet pick a form primarily associated with love poetry for a subject like that in "Karma"?
2. How many words did you have to look up in each sonnet to be *assured* of the meaning? From the evidence of these sonnets does word meaning seem to be more, or less, stable than spelling or typography?

3. How strange does sentence structure seem to you in each sonnet? To what extent would the strangeness result from actual changes in language? From what is known as poetic license?
4. We use sonnets for several other purposes in this book. What are the characteristics of a sonnet? How many lines? What rhyme schemes? (Scan the rhymes by calling the first rhyming sound *a*, the second *b*, and so forth. The first four lines of Shakespeare's sonnet rhymes *abab*. Finish scanning it. What rhyme scheme do the other three use?) How many syllables make up most of the lines? With what pattern of accent?

Writing Projects

Clarity is the chief aim when you are giving directions or instructions. Any attempt to embellish your language may detract from your purpose; embellishment will certainly not add to it. Your reader wants a clear statement of the steps involved in the process. Do not confuse him with overwrought language. Be precise and exact.

However, if you are describing a process that can also be an exciting event, you should feel free to use more descriptive and even emotional language. The following is a description of one method of killing the buffalo (actually the American bison) used by the Indians and frontiersmen. Francis Parkman uses the same charged language he would have used to describe the killing of one buffalo, although he has generalized the killing of a number of animals, and in effect gives us the process.

> The buffalo have regular paths by which they come down to drink. Seeing at a glance along which of these his intended victim is moving, the hunter crouches under the bank within fifteen or twenty yards, it may be, of the point where the path enters the river. Here he sits down quietly on the sand. Listening intently, he hears the heavy, monotonous tread of the approaching bull. The moment after, he sees a motion among the long weeds and grass just at the spot where the path is channelled through the bank. An enormous black head is thrust out, the horns just visible amid the mass of tangled mane. Half sliding, half plunging, down comes the buffalo upon the river-bed below. He steps out in full sight upon the sands. Just before him a runnel of water is gliding, and he bends his head to drink. You may hear the water as it gurgles down his capacious throat. He raises his head, and the drops trickle from his wet beard. He stands with an air of stupid abstraction, unconscious of the lurking danger. Noiselessly the hunter cocks his rifle. As he sits upon the sand, his knee is raised, and his elbow rests upon it, that he may level his heavy weapon with a steadier aim. The stock is at his shoulder; his eye ranges along the barrel. Still he is in no haste to fire. The bull, with slow deliberation, begins his march over the sands to the other side. He advances his foreleg and exposes to view a small spot, denuded of hair, just behind the point of his shoulder; upon this the hunter brings the sight of his rifle to bear; lightly and delicately his finger presses the hair-trigger. The spiteful crack of the rifle responds to his touch, and instantly in the middle of the bare spot appears a small red dot. The buffalo shivers; death has overtaken him, he cannot tell from whence; still he does not fall, but walks heavily forward, as if nothing had happened. Yet before he has gone far out upon the sand, you see him stop; he totters; his knees bend under him, and his head sinks forward to the ground. Then his whole vast bulk sways to one side; he falls over on the sand, and dies with a scarcely perceptible struggle.

Parkman, in fact, gives us two processes: the process of killing the buffalo utilized by the hunter and the process of dying through which the buffalo unknowingly goes.

Keeping in mind Parkman's and Hayakawa's techniques,

1. Choose a process you know well, such as polishing a rock, making a certain kind of block in football, stalking a deer, playing a big fish, performing a certain process in sewing or cooking. Specify an audience, for example the football block might be explained to a group of girls, the sewing to a group of boys. Write a process theme so clearly that the members of your audience could repeat the process. Be especially aware of the problem of interest.

2. Select some event in the past with which you are well acquainted and which has particularly intrigued you. Write a process theme in which you detail how that event happened. Examples of such processes are how Helen Keller learned words, how a battle was won or lost, how a person succeeded or failed in a particular endeavor, or how a word has developed a special meaning for your family or for some other group.

3. Select some action with which you are familiar—if you have played football, it might be the action that takes place in the backfield on a particular play, or it might be the process of serving the ball in tennis, or it might be a particularly difficult part of preparing a certain dish. Be sure to explain clearly each step in the process. You may wish to illustrate certain steps with diagrams. Write your paper to someone who is unacquainted with the action you describe.

Part IV

Grammars

As there is a history of language, so too is there a history of the study of language. Unfortunately, such study has developed a negative reputation among many students. Most people are not as enthusiastic about the study of language as they are about the study of physics, mathematics, sociology, or other subjects. To most people, the study of language means being drilled on a few rules of linguistic etiquette, not the study of a complex, interesting, and important subject.

For the word *language* in the above paragraph we should, perhaps, have used the word *grammar*. And it is the study of grammar that has been an unpleasant experience for many. It is important to note, however, that in the title of this section and as we shall use the word in this introduction, *grammar* means something quite different from the usual meaning associated with it. For most people the word means some vaguely defined set of rules that prescribe how a person should use language. It appears in such sentences as "That's not good grammar." When used thus the word *grammar* could more accurately be replaced with the word *usage*. *Grammar* as used here will refer to a study of the system of language—a study that is significant, challenging, and interesting!

Perhaps we can best begin by pointing out a number of definitions that might be applied to the word *grammar*. First, Cook in the second section of this book defines grammar as "the system inherent in any language. It is this system which all speakers of a language learn at an early age." A second definition of grammar, and the one used in this section, is a description of the system of a language. The third and most commonly used definition is that grammar is a set of rules for using correct English, a set of rules for linguistic etiquette. It is in the third of these definitions that the word has negative connotations for many students.

In the past few decades new and often competing approaches to the description of a language (grammar) have been developed. In the 1940's and 1950's structural grammar, an objective, systematic attempt to describe language, was the dominant approach. In the 1960's and 1970's transformational grammar, an attempt not only to describe but also to explain language, has been the prevailing approach. In the 1970's competing versions of transformational grammar have developed. The staid, old, ever-unchanging subject of grammar has become highly controversial, and insights gained by linguists have had significant impact in other scholarly disciplines such as psychology and philosophy. Davy's article, which appears in this section, suggests some of the feeling of excitement and uneasiness that has arisen as a consequence of new approaches developed in the study of language.

The controversy and excitement have not been limited to the world of scholars: new textbooks incorporating some of the new approaches have appeared at all levels in the school systems of the United States—from elementary school to the university. Most English textbooks published in the past ten years have been influenced to some degree by the transformational approach to the analysis of language. Roberts' article in this section compares these different approaches to language analysis. Ross and Miksch humorously illustrate the language problems a speaker of English as a second language and a speaker of substandard dialect have with the grammar of English.

Language is important. The study of the systems language employs to convey meaning can also be important. For too long grammar study has been restricted to the study of a few dos and don'ts. We hope that in this section you will gain new insights into the grammar of English and will conclude that the study of grammar can be interesting and stimulating.

Comparison and Contrast

The method of development called comparison and contrast is used to tell how two or more things are alike or how they differ; frequently it is used to tell how things are alike and how they differ in the same composition. This seems simple enough, and the method is used often, even in casual conversation. "We used to play a game that was a lot of fun. We called it 'Sardines.' It was like 'Hide and Seek' except the one who was 'it' got to go hide and all the rest of the players did the looking. Whenever someone found the hiding place, he had to squeeze in with 'it.' Finally everybody was packed in together." The method is not as simple as it would seem from this short illustration, although the illustration should help you to see some of the precautions that must be taken when using comparison and contrast.

First you must be careful that you are making the comparison and contrast for a purpose. The method is not an end in itself. The student writer often feels that he has said something significant just by showing that some things are alike. In trying to clarify a process new to the audience, the speaker in our illustration had a common purpose for his comparison and contrast. The audience knows how to play "Hide and Seek." He need not go into all the details of the new game. It is like the old familiar one in some ways and differs in other ways. He made the new game understandable by using a brief comparison and contrast.

If your purpose is the same as that of the speaker in the example, that is, to explain something your audience has not previously understood, you can often compare or contrast the unknown to something the audience knows. However, keep that audience in mind; be sure that you use as the base of the comparison something your audience does understand. The speaker used "Hide and Seek" because he was quite sure all his listeners understood that game; he would not use "Ring-a-levio," another hiding game he played as a child, unless he were sure all his listeners understood the rules of that game.

This precaution seems obvious enough when it is stated, but the beginning writer often fails to observe it.

It is of course possible to compare and contrast two items which are both unfamiliar to your audience. In a sense you will utilize a combination of two methods like process and comparison. The major advantage to you as a writer and to your reader in this type of comparison is the economy which results. Two methods of making steel, neither of which your audience is familiar with, could be explained more economically if the second were compared and contrasted with the first rather than presented as an isolated process. The same is true of any number of related processes: two methods of hunting deer, of performing a household task, of bidding in a card game, or of teaching children to sing in parts. Francis Parkman, in *The Oregon Trail,* describes two methods of chasing buffalo. He calls these "running" and "approaching," and assumes that his reader understands neither of these. First he describes "running" (what we would probably think of as "chasing" on horseback) and then points out how "approaching" (stalking on foot) differs from it, very much in the way our speaker described the game "Sardines."

Comparison and contrast, unlike process, which is usually arranged chronologically, has no obvious order. Item one may be presented in detail, followed by item two and the comparison; point *a* of item one may be compared with point *a* of item two, followed by points *b, c, d,* and so on; all the comparisons may be grouped together, followed by all the contrasts; or comparisons and contrasts may be mixed together. Consider the order before you write. Ask yourself if you are pointing out mainly the similarities or mainly the differences. Put the major similarity or difference in an emphatic position. If your concern is with item one compared with item two in a general way, you will probably wish to give a complete presentation of item one followed by a complete presentation of item two. This is the easiest order, but do not use it if you need a point-by-point comparison. This latter order is particularly useful for comparisons and contrasts which involve exact differentiation between items, as in two scientific experiments or other precise processes.

Finally, be sure that you are making comparisons which are honest. The reader who disagrees with your conclusions in a comparison and contrast composition will most often contend that you failed to see major points or that you used items which should never have been compared. Be sure, therefore, that you are making reasonable comparisons and that your comparisons are accurate.

A Revolutionary View of Language

John Davy *Grammar, unfortunately, is a word that has negative connotations for many people. When they think of grammar, they remember being chastised for not using "correct" English; they remember dull classes in school dealing with eight parts of speech, with rules for linguistic etiquette, with filling in blanks in workbooks, in short, with a number of topics that did not seem important or relevant. If this has been your view of grammar, you may be surprised at the sense of excitement conveyed by John Davy as he discusses recent developments in the study of grammar. Davy focuses on the contributions of one person, Noam Chomsky, to the study of grammar and language. The author emphasizes the shift from the study of surface grammar to the analysis of deep grammar, the search for language universals. Though he may, in journalistic style, overstress the significance of some of Chomsky's discoveries, he does reveal some of the excitement that has developed in the past fifteen years in the field of linguistics. Note that, as he reports primarily the changes in the study of grammar, his discussion very naturally leads into other disciplines such as psychology, philosophy, and biology. From the work of Chomsky has come the transformational grammar that has been so influential in American textbooks in the past ten years. This article appeared in the* London Observer. *In what ways does the style, the vocabulary, the paragraphing reflect the audience to which it was addressed? Contrast it with some of the articles in the previous section that originally appeared in scholarly journals.*

At the University of Nevada, not far from Las Vegas, a young female chimpanzee is making an important contribution to a revolution now in progress in the study of language—a revolution that involved a change in our whole view of human nature.

Washoe—for that is the chimpanzee's name—is the subject of a

John Davy, "A Revolutionary View of Language," *English Teaching Forum,* January–February 1971, pp. 2–5. Copyright, *The Observer.* Reprinted with the permission of *Los Angeles Times/Washington Post* News Service.

scientific gamble by two American researchers. Dr. and Mrs. R. A. Gardner, with the help of some devoted assistants, spend all their time looking after Washoe. They communicate with Washoe, and with one another when they are in her presence, in a sign language used for deaf-and-dumb humans.

All past efforts to teach animals to speak (as opposed to training them to produce a few primitive utterances) have failed. Chimpanzees have relatively large and complex brains, and they can learn to perform quite tricky tasks (such as working various forms of puzzle boxes to get at a banana). Why, then, can't they learn to speak? The Gardners concluded that the chimpanzee vocal apparatus may not be adequately formed, or may not be linked appropriately to the brain. But, like many other animal species, chimpanzees can respond to gestures and use them for "communication." So perhaps they could learn to converse with humans in sign language.

The Gardners recently reported that after 31 months of training, Washoe had learned at least 60 "words" and was regularly using them in spontaneous combinations—very simple two-word sentences—much as a human baby might do. "Open key," she might say with her hands, asking for a key to open a locked door.

The inquiry into Washoe's linguistic abilities—and limitations—underlines a growing feeling that human language may represent capacities not merely different in degree, but different in kind, from anything in the animal kingdom. Several branches of science in fact are waking up to a realization that in language we are confronting a major mystery. And the current turmoil in linguistics is showing every sign of involving psychology, philosophy, biology, and our own view of ourselves.

Shock Waves

At the center of these events is a slim but formidable intellectual, Noam Chomsky, currently professor of linguistics at the Massachusetts Institute of Technology. Two sober psychologists recently told me, quite independently, that their first encounter with Chomsky's work had had the quality of "a mythical experience"—a sense of sudden revelation and insight.

Chomsky had this bomb-like effect originally within a small circle of specialists over 10 years ago, when he published *Syntactic Structures,* a short, difficult work pregnant with disturbing implications. This book sent shock waves among students of language and psychology, and it has generated a now rapidly rising tide of research and discussion.

The essence of the situation, perhaps, is this: Prompted by Chomsky, many people have suddenly begun to notice that the ability to acquire and use language is a much more extraordinary thing than we had realized.

This ability appears to be unique to man, and in exploring it we are led to postulate some remarkable and still obscure capacities of mind, which may also demand some quite new ideas about the functioning of the brain.

In this connection, Chomsky—now joined by many allies—has launched a tremendous onslaught on behavioristic psychology (which has dominated a great deal of experimental psychology for half a century), and the repercussions are being felt in the citadels of linguistic philosophy.

These schools have been in the habit of characterizing most talk of "mind" and its properties as scientifically inaccurate and not germane, and they have set out energetically to banish "the ghost in the machine." The new linguistics is conjuring up the "ghost" again, and it is beginning to look not at all ghostly, but like a very substantial feature of the psychological and philosophical scene—a force to be reckoned with even if its precise status and origins are still mysterious.

Clichés for Computers

The central problem in describing the Chomsky revolution lies in what he himself has called the difficulty of establishing "psychic distance" from something that is as close to us as language, and hence very familiar. We all use language all the time, and we normally lose all sense of what extraordinary feats we are performing when we do so.

One group of people who have become vividly aware of the magnitude of these feats are those who have been trying to design computers that can "understand" spoken or written language in more than a very crude fashion. A major problem arises right at the beginning. Untutored computers, like human infants, are first faced with sorting and grouping the sounds of human speech.

Spoken English can be resolved into about 45 distinct sounds, or phonemes, which in normal talk impinge on the ear at the rate of 20 per second. Even with careful pauses and heavy emphasis, computers have the greatest difficulty in identifying particular groups of sounds as words, let alone recognizing certain sequences of words as sentences.

Possibly even more obscure is how a person extracts the meaning from a sequence of words. He hears every day thousands of new sentences that he has never heard before, without any difficulty in understanding them. (Indeed, he gets bored and impatient with speech or writing that is full of sentences he has heard before—that is, clichés. Computers, by contrast, can cope only with clichés. The same applies, apparently, to Washoe.) The native speaker of a language easily recognizes the difference between a random jumble and an orderly sequence of words—even if the sequence makes no sense.

The New Linguistics

Chomsky and his fellow linguists have a happy time inventing examples. Consider, he suggests, *colorless green ideas sleep furiously* and *furiously sleep ideas green colorless.* No human being is likely ever to have heard either of these word sequences before Chomsky published them. But, while both are meaningless, native speakers of English have no difficulty in recognizing the first as "grammatical" and the second as a muddle. This capacity shows that they know, without being consciously aware of it, a great deal about what constitutes orderly English—a knowledge that, when formally written down, constitutes the rules of grammar.

However, conventional grammatical parsing is an inadequate representation of this innate knowledge of the grammar of the language. Two Chomsky sentences have now become a kind of slogan of the new linguistics:

1. John is easy to please.
2. John is eager to please.

These two sentences have, on the surface, an identical structure: In this identical "surface structure" of each, *John* is the "subject of the sentence." But one with an innate feeling for the "deep structure" of the language realizes immediately that in the first sentence, *John* is the LOGICAL (deep-structure) object (*It is easy to please John*), while, in the second, *John* is the logical (deep-structure) as well as the grammatical (surface-structure) subject (*John wants to please*).

On the other hand, sentences can have a different surface structure but the same meaning—the same deep structure. Consider, for example, *John ate the orange* and *The orange was eaten by John.* Somehow a native speaker knows that different surface structures can refer to the same deep structure—that is, to a particular relationship between *John* and *the orange.* In other words, a native speaker of the language instinctively knows a grammar that does not appear on the surface. This being so, he must also know "rules" for transforming various kinds of deep structure into surface structure and back again.

Chomsky has swung the whole of linguistics away from a detailed study of the surface structure of language to an exploration of its deep structure. The effect of this is to draw attention not to the overt behavior of language speakers but to the inner mental processes that are implied in their competence to speak and understand language.

Under the Frosting

It is as though students of cookery were to turn their attention away from analyzing various species of cake—or time-and-motion studies of pastry cooks—to discover the principles of cakemaking that lie behind the activities of cake-makers, the rules they are following, and the complex structure of the concept "cake" that guides their operations. This concept can be transformed, by following the rules, into a number of confections, all of which are digestible. Similarly, we must possess, without realizing it, a concept of language that allows us to produce an infinite variety of comprehensible sentences.

Once we recognize this fact, we can see in it some remarkable implications. To begin with, it is obvious that different languages may have quite different surface structures. On the other hand, if there were no common ground between languages, it would be impossible to translate one language into another. A good deal of research into this question is now going on, but it looks as though at some level all languages share a common deep structure which, if formally defined, would represent a "universal grammar." The differences between languages would then be expressed as distinct sets of rules for transforming the common deep structure into a variety of surface structures.

The second question is how language is acquired. The child hears adults making a variety of noises. These noises, which are almost never exactly repeated, offer only a small sample of the infinite variety of meaningful utterances that adults can produce. Yet, within a couple of years, the child has learned to make appropriate noises, organized in an extremely complex way that obeys the basic rules of adult grammar.

Obviously, the child is not consciously applying rules, any more than adults are. As a matter of fact, detailed study of the problem suggests that there is no conceivable way in which a child—or an adult, for that matter—could discover the relevant rules simply from the noises he hears, any more than a person could arrive at the construction of an internal combustion engine (which is primitive by comparison with the structure of language) by watching the dials on the dashboard.

Baby Talk

The startling implication is that children are born already equipped with a "knowledge" of language—that what linguists are gradually discovering as "universal grammar" is really a way of describing a complex inborn capacity, an innate "idea of language." The child then learns the particular language of his environment by relating what he hears to his unconscious knowledge of the structure that underlies all languages. This may help to explain not only the remarkable fact that babies learn to speak at all but how it is that they seem to learn Bantu, Russian, English, or Japanese with equal facility. They can also learn in the teeth of enormous handicaps—deaf-and-dumb parents, impoverished homes, partial deafness.

Studies of children are revealing further striking facts. In many parts of the world, detailed analyses are now under way, using tape recordings of the developing speech of children over months or years. One important outcome is that researchers have begun to see that "childish" language is not an imperfect copy of adult language but a "language" in its own right.

Thus, between the ages of 18 and 24 months, children characteristically pass through, a stage of forming two-word sentences. There is evidence to suggest that they do not form such sentences at random: They seem, rather, to group the words in their vocabularies into two classes, one much smaller than the other. They then form "sentences" by choosing a word from the first class and adding a word from the second. For example, one boy, whose speech was taped, included *all-gone, bye-bye, big, more, pretty, my see, night-night,* and *hi* in one class, with *boy, sock, boat, fan, Mommy,* and *Daddy* in the other. He would say *Bye-bye celery* and *All-gone lettuce* —but never *Lettuce all-gone.*

The consistency of these constructions suggests that young children follow certain grammatical "rules" that govern "baby talk"; they do not simply copy adult grammar. In the first place, several different kinds of words appear in the first class above: adjectives (*big, pretty*); verbs (*see,* and perhaps *bye-bye* and *night-night*); a pronoun (*my*); and a greeting (*hi*). Furthermore, it is not likely that the child picked up the phrase *all-gone lettuce* from an adult. Indeed, it seems to be more common at this stage for mothers to start imitating the grammar of their children than the other way around!

Universal Grammar

These phenomena have led to the suggestion that the speech of young children may actually embody fundamental language relationships—that their speech may be, so to speak, an expression of universal grammar, not yet transformed into the appropriate surface structures of the surrounding language.

This is still an obscure matter. But recent work with Russian and Japanese children suggests that their early speech has a similar structure despite the great differences in the surface structures of the fully developed adult languages.

Other bits and pieces of evidence are beginning to emerge to support the idea that the formal grammar systems being worked out by Chomsky and others have some real relation to what goes on in the human mind. For example, researchers at the Massachusetts Institute of Technology have been getting people to listen through earphones to sentences that have brief, unrelated "clicks" added at one point or another. It turns out that the listener can seldom tell exactly where the click is located in the sentence. But he tends to place it between particular parts of the sentence structure. It looks as though he might be "punctuating" the sentence in a way that corresponds to a Chomsky-type grammar at a deeper level.

Exploring the Mind

In some recent lectures in California, Chomsky emphasized that the picture of language behavior now emerging is not a fundamentally new one: It was developed by Descartes and later followers, and then forgotten. Shifts in philosophy and intellectual fashion led to concentration on the surface structure of language and to a view of language learning as a process of acquiring verbal behavior from the environment.

The present vivid realization that language would never be learned at all without some elaborate inborn competence has opened the way to a study of language as a "mirror of consciousness," as a way of exploring some of the operating principles of the mind. Chomsky believes that we are still a long way from seeing what these principles are, as far as language is concerned. Indeed, he claims that the processes by which the human mind achieved its present stage of complexity and its particular form of innate organization are a total mystery. He even questions whether Darwinian natural-selection processes can possibly account for the emergence of these language faculties in human evolution, and doubts whether phenomena of the mind can be accounted for by any physical processes in the brain that we yet know of. It may become necessary, he says, to conceive of some quite new principles.

A Scientific Revolution

Chomsky grammar has one crucial characteristic: Although it proposes a finite set of rules, these rules allow the speaker to generate an infinite variety of sentences. This implies that individuals are not condemned to utter mere variations on language they have already heard, or to respond automatically to surrounding stimuli. They have, in principle, the capacity to say new things to use language creatively.

Recently, some students of the history of science—notably T. S. Kuhn—have been emphasizing that science does not evolve along a straight line, gradually accumulating facts and theories to match. The major advances have more often come when scientists have taken a deep breath and started to ask different kinds of questions—when they have turned to new fields of investigation. Behind such changes there may often be deep shifts in the basic assumptions and attitudes that stand behind scientific and intellectual activity.

The Chomsky revolution may be part of such a shift, which may well carry anthropology, biology, and philosophy into quite new territories—territories with an entirely different intellectual climate. As Chomsky says, it is not easy to establish enough "psychic distance" from processes in which one is oneself involved to perceive clearly what is happening. But something is.

One Edinburgh psychologist quite seriously compares Chomsky to Newton, as the initiator of a comparable upheaval in our view of things. It is a large claim. But then language is a large part of our lives. And using language is one of the most essential parts of being human.

Questions

1. In what ways would the task of programming computers to "understand" language require a more rigorous and thorough analysis of language than attempts to teach language to other human beings?
2. The term *grammatical* as used by Chomsky means something quite different from the normal use of the term. By a careful reading of the discussion and examples in this article, can you determine the meaning of the term as Chomsky uses it?
3. Distinguish between the terms *surface structure* and *deep structure* as they are used in this article.
4. Explain in your own words the differences between the sentences "John is easy to please" and "John is eager to please."
5. Does the analogy between cookery and language study clarify the point the author is making about the significance of the study of deep structure? Explain the analogy in your own words.
6. What does Chomsky mean when he says it is difficult for a human being to establish "psychic distance" between himself and the language he uses? Why is such distance important?

Suggestions for Writing

1. One of the noticeable qualities of Davy's article is his sense of excitement about the significance (to him) of the new ideas that Chomsky has expressed. All of us have sometime met a new idea that excited us, developed in us a sense of wonder. Recall from your experience an idea that has affected you in such a way. Write a paper in which you discuss the idea and the circumstances under which you learned it. Try, in relating the experience, to give your reader some feeling for the excitement, the sense of wonder that you felt.

Distinguishing Between Grammars

Paul Roberts

Roberts, in the following essay which originally appeared as the foreword to a book of readings about linguistics, focuses primarily on nineteenth and twentieth-century studies of English.

In the first part of the article Roberts discusses the history of grammar study, specifically the background of what we frequently refer to as traditional or schoolroom grammar. He then discusses structural grammar and transformational grammar. Note that there is an implicit comparison of the three approaches in his discussion. However, near the end of the article he turns to an explicit point-by-point comparison of some features of structural and transformational grammar.

The competing approaches to the study of grammar have raised many questions about the nature of language and about the teaching of grammar. The staid, non-controversial subject of grammar has become very exciting and highly controversial. At the present time transformational grammar is advocated by most linguists and has greatly influenced the grammar presented in textbooks not only in colleges and high schools but in elementary schools as well.

Can you detect the introduction to Roberts' essay? The conclusion? What device does he use to tie the introduction and conclusion together? Is the device effective?

It is a rather depressing thing to be a linguist. One goes to a lot of expense and trouble to prepare oneself in the profession only to discover that the whole population has been practicing it all along, practically since birth. It must happen to a physician only occasionally that he meets some layman convinced that he knows more about medicine than any doctor does. To the linguist it is routine to be instructed in language not only by the man in the street but by the man who cleans it. There are few people who do not have strong views on language—what language is composed of, the relation of language and thought, how to learn languages. The intolerable thing, to the professional man, is that many of these views are correct.

The situation is favorable, of course, for the publication of a book like this one. The reader comes to it not in *statu pupillari,* as he might to a tome on mathematics, but as colleague, ready to dissect, approve, or denounce. He will find here material for all three operations.

The linguist Charlton Laird, in a book called *The Miracle of Language,* conceived of a character named Og who was the first being to speak a human language and therefore the first being to be human. Linguists have long since abandoned serious discussion of the origin of language: the topic has even been barred from the programs of some societies of linguists. We may not know much about language, but we know that we don't know how language originated and that we never will know. There isn't any data. Virtually all the languages of the world have become known by now to linguists, and there aren't any primitive languages among them. All human beings—even those who spend their active years doing nothing but stirring in the mud for worms—speak languages that are highly sophisticated and complicated systems. There are no traces of the steps that must have been taken between Og's first meaningful grunt and the actual languages of today.

Still there must have been an Og, or some Ogs. At some point, some of that species that was to become people must have begun to make sounds that were meaningful to their associates. But this wasn't yet human language. Certain animals can do this much. We are told, by those who have been there, that on the Malaysian Peninsula ape calls to ape, employing a repertoire of nine sentences with such meanings as "There is danger here," "You're asking for trouble," "I love you." This isn't yet human language, however. What the apes do not know how to do is manipulate the parts of their sentences so as to produce new, correct sentences that they had never heard before, like "There is trouble here," "You're dangerous," "Am I troubling you?" If they could just learn this trick, they would be as human as you and I, though of course markedly different in appearance and table manners.

Some Og did learn the trick once. Given "Mbu bork" and "Ho gluck," he made the brand new sentence "Mbu gluck," and some female of the species understood him. They moved shortly after that into a cave that Og had had his eye on and began raising children, who, as they grew to adulthood, were making new sentences like billy-o and wondering how they could use this power to do in their neighbors. And no doubt the senior Ogs were deploring the slovenly pronunciation and bad grammar of the children and reflecting on how all would be up with cave-dwelling culture if the degeneration continued.

Og's descendants have been deploring the degeneration of language ever since. Doubtless Socrates, though well aware that Plato was a bright young chap and a real comer, wished he wouldn't be quite so careless in the use of the aorist tense, and Marcus Antonius may have lost the battle of Actium because he disprized Octavius on account of the latter's bad Latin.

We have had examples in more recent times. In 1961, the Merriam-Webster company published a revision of its unabridged dictionary, the *Webster's Third International.* This company had been infiltrated by linguists, who reported the language as it was in 1961, not as they thought it should be. This radical departure evoked editorial wrath across the nation. The dictionary and its makers were pilloried in the Chicago *Daily News* and *The New York Times,* in *Life Magazine* and the *Atlantic* and *The New Yorker,* because they reported that respectable people sometimes say *ain't* and use *like* as a conjunction. To the writers of the editorials and articles, such admissions seemed a severe, perhaps a fatal, blow to western culture. There was a movement to have Merriam-Webster bought out by people more alive to the sacred responsibility of safe-guarding our tongue, and we were urged meanwhile to use the *Second International* (1934) and not risk moral collapse by dipping into the racy and dangerous *Third.*

There are several interesting implications here: (1) that it was possible, without getting locked up, to speak and write in 1961 as people did in 1934; (2) that people learn to speak and write from dictionaries, however unabridged; (3) that the moral fibre of a nation is actually weakened if its citizens are allowed, without lexicographical reproof, to use *like* as a conjunction or to say *irregardless* instead of *regardless.* But this is now a long quiet battlefield, and I have no wish to roam it further. I use it merely as an example of the deep-seated feelings that people have about language.

A professor of English, a friend of mine with whom I had attended graduate school, once remarked to me that he was all for the scientific study of language *so long as the results were never applied to the teaching of English.* That was about twenty years ago, and I have been wondering ever since what he meant. He *could* have meant that the teaching of English was so bad that it couldn't survive objective appraisal; but I'm pretty sure he didn't think that, as I don't either. I think he felt rather that teaching English—the composition and literature part, that is—was a delicate and somewhat mystical enterprise. If one looks too closely at the flower, the petals fade. His attitude toward Leonard Bloomfield's *Language* might perhaps be compared to that of an enlightened minister to Renan's *Life of Jesus:* one might admire it as an interesting historical document, but naturally one wouldn't quote it in church.

Cherished as it is by so many worthy and eminent people, this attitude is hard to condemn, but it is equally hard to understand. Thomas Pyles, in a book called *Words and Ways of American English,* remarks that Americans, however much they pride themselves on being a free and easy folk, unconfined by tradition, are actually tight to the point of neurosis when it comes to language. They have conceived a correct English, spoken by a few members of the British upper classes and, with slight variations in pronunciation, by the better English teachers in America. This dialect is more for ostentation than for use. One doesn't really expect to speak it; it was given only to Galahad to see the Grail. Those of us with hearts less pure can only try to avoid the company of the better English teachers and members of the British upper classes. It's a point of view, of course, but it does seem to take a lot of fun out of life and literature.

It was with this attitude linguistic science collided when that science emerged in the early twentieth century and with which it is still in collision. In the hierarchy of science, linguistics is a branch of anthropology. Anthropology is the study of man, and one of man's most important attributes is the ability to make sentences. Linguistics studies the sentences that he makes, how he learns to make them, and the effect that making them has on his existence. The study may be said to have begun, in a disciplined way, around 1910 and to have been fostered mainly by American anthropologists interested primarily in the culture of American Indians. The best known names among these early anthropological linguists are Franz Boas and Edward Sapir.

Of course there had been linguists much earlier than Sapir and Boas. Perhaps Og was the first, but the first we have reliable information on was Panini, who described Sanskrit, and described it very well indeed, about four centuries before the birth of Christ. Aristotle had notions, some of them sensible, on language as he did on most other subjects, and he did not withhold them from his public. There were Greek grammars by the second century B.C., and these served as models for what came to be the main textbooks of the Middle Ages—the grammars of Latin.

There are several methods of teaching foreign languages in schools, but the one that seems to have met with most general success is Main Strength and Awkwardness. In the middle of the nineteenth century, Lord Macaulay, faced with the practical problem of how to teach English in India, came to the sensible conclusion that the best way was to start the children young and not teach them much of anything else. For about a century, those Indian children who went to school studied not only English but history in English, science in English, all subjects in English, with the result that millions of Indians today speak English—not very well, to be sure, but a great deal better than any significant number of Americans or Englishmen speak French.

Something like the same method was used for Latin in European countries during the Middle Ages. The school that one attended was called a "grammar school," and this meant specifically a school where one studied Latin grammar. That was essentially what one studied. No English Literature. No Driver Education. Just Latin grammar and the things that Latin might convey. As late as the 1880's, Winston Churchill, arriving at the age of seven at his first school, was set down the very first evening to learn the First Declension. If you start at the age of seven with the First Declension and keep plugging away along these lines until you are seventeen, you're bound to learn quite a lot of Latin, enough to read it with ease, correspond in it, write poetry in it—and educated Europeans were indeed able to do these things, for many hundreds of years.

In all these centuries of preoccupation with Latin, the structure of Latin came to be very finely known. This was what linguistics did in the Middle Ages: it described Latin. It had no truck with contemporary European languages and certainly not with non-European ones. Apart from Greek, which began to interest people in the later years of the Middle Ages, the focus was on Latin, and not just any old Latin, but specifically that of the last years of the Roman Republic and the first of the Empire. If one were to pinpoint it further, it was the Latin of Cicero that was deemed most worthy of study and emulation. Many people tried to emulate it in the Middle Ages, and a few succeeded fairly well.

Thus up to the Renaissance, linguistics was essentially descriptive but with a very small area for description to operate in. There were occasional philosophic speculations about the general nature of language, but they were of trifling importance and drew little attention. With the Renaissance, there was an opening up in several directions. For one thing, people became consciously aware of the vernaculars they spoke—of English, French, Italian, Spanish. Castiglione, in *The Courtier,* has a good deal to say about the kind of Italian a proper person ought to speak and why. In sixteenth-century England, there was much earnest discussion about English: how to spell it, for example, and how and whether to enrich its vocabulary by borrowing words from other languages. At the beginning of the seventeenth century, the first English dictionary appeared, the work of a man named Robert Cawdrey. Cawdrey was speedily plagiarized and improved upon. Other dictionaries followed, growing ever larger, and there were soon other works designed to conduce to a proper use of English the increasing number of people whose prosperity outran their breeding. English grammar was being born.

At roughly the same time, philosophers were beginning to pose more interesting problems, such as how people learn their languages in the first place. Descartes in the early seventeenth century and Locke in the later made suggestions which continue to beset and divide people who are interested in the nature of language.

Until the latter part of the eighteenth century, very little was known about languages other than European languages, and not much about the relationships among the latter. Presumably it was obvious that Italian and Spanish were related and both descendent from Latin, and that English was somehow or other connected with German. There was some knowledge of Old English, or Saxon as it was then generally called. Lexicographers displayed some interest and competence in simple etymology. But in general, awareness of language development and language relationships was slight. The Greeks and Romans had no notion that the Persians and Celts with whom they fought spoke languages related to their own. If put to it, they would no doubt have said that the Persians and Celts didn't really speak languages at all but just made barbaric noises like animals calling to other animals. No more did the educated European of 1750 have any notion that the language he spoke was directly related to languages of India, of Persia, of Russia, of Wales.

But toward the end of the eighteenth century, as scholars became conversant with Sanskrit, a religious language of India first written down around 1500 B.C., they noticed recurring correspondences of the consonants of Sanskrit with those of such languages as Greek, Latin, German, English. In the early nineteenth century, these correspondences were set forth by the Danish scholar Rasmus Christian Rask and a little later were formulated by Jakob Grimm in what came to be known as Grimm's Law or, more soberly, the First Consonant Shift. This demonstrated that such apparently dissimilar words as Latin *lupus* and English *wolf,* English *mother* and Sanskrit *mātṛ* were originally the same and had become differentiated by regular and ascertainable developments of the sound structure of the different languages. Such advances as these brought into being the variety of linguistics called *philology,* which concerns itself with tracing out the historical developments of languages and the relationships among them.

Throughout the nineteenth century and into the early twentieth, linguistics was essentially of this sort. It was historical and comparative and primarily concerned with establishing the facts of the language family to which most of the languages of Europe belong—Indo-European. The work done was enormous and the improvements in theory impressive. After Karl Verner showed that certain apparent irregularities in Grimm's Law weren't irregular at all but were the natural consequence of an ancillary law, people came to the view that, instead of there being no law without an exception, there was no exception without a law. Those who espoused this view, in the latter part of the nineteenth century, were called the Neo-Grammarians. They rode fast, and they rode far, and they filled massive volumes with the historical details of the Indo-European family of languages. They pretty well established linguistics, in its philological aspect, as a science.

But in all this time there was very little interest either in non-Indo-European languages or in the Indo-European languages themselves in their modern shape, and little also—among linguists, at any rate—in what languages are and how human beings learn them. A great many English grammars were produced, since by the nineteenth century, English had become a regular school subject, steadily making way at the expense of Latin. But the grammars were mostly amateurish, dashed off by people who did not in fact devote their lives to the nature of language or think very seriously about it. They often gave wholesome advice on how to use *who* and *whom,* but they did very little to illuminate the structure of English. It has often been said that one cannot really understand English without knowing Latin. Probably it is true that one must know Latin to figure out what the school grammars of English published in the nineteenth century are all about. Latin grammar was the only grammar their authors knew, and so English was presented as a kind of translation of Latin, a procedure that yielded results a good deal less than satisfactory.

There was much more sophistication, in the nineteenth century, in the field of lexicography. The principles developed in the eighteenth by such dictionary makers as Kersey, Bailey, and Johnson were extended and refined. The result was the greatest monument of lexicography of all time, the *Oxford English Dictionary,* first proposed in 1857, seriously undertaken in 1878, and completed in 1928. The late nineteenth century saw also much serious work in English phonetics by such scholars as Henry Sweet, said to be the prototype of the Henry Higgins of Shaw's *Pygmalion.* There began about this time as well what might be called scholarly traditional grammar, which flowered in the works of people like Jespersen, Poutsma, Kruisinga, Curme—multivolumed collections of types of English sentences, painstakingly gathered, arranged, and discussed. This sort of work continues, though with much abatement, and thus overlaps the two movements with which the present book is primarily concerned: structural linguistics and transformationalism.

Structural linguistics is a somewhat misleading term, since all linguistics is concerned with structure and since anyone who devotes himself professionally to the study of language is in some sense a linguist; but it is the most common designation for a kind of linguistic focus that started with the anthropologists early in this century, culminated in the nineteen forties, and then began, under the impact of newer ideas, to change its directions and abandon some of its goals.

The interest of anthropologists at the beginning of the twentieth century in the languages of the American Indian was very practically motivated. These languages were fast disappearing, and though it may not bother a scholar to see something disappear, he hates not to get a record of it before it does so. Accordingly, the anthropologists pursued the departing Indian, sat beside his deathbed, and took notes. The study proved fascinating. The anthropologists did not, of course, share the notion of the layman of the period that Indians communicated mostly by saying "Ugh" and "How" and waving their arms; but even the anthropologists were astonished by the intricate language systems that they found. Many Indian languages proved to be more highly inflected than Greek, though in vastly different ways. Some of their grammars compelled and made commonplace modes of thought not easily even graspable by speakers of Indo-European languages. Their sound structures disclosed that the human articulatory apparatus had capabilities not previously suspected. In short, it became apparent that human language was vastly more complex, diversified, and interesting than anyone in the nineteenth century could have supposed.

One immediate result was the realization that traditional procedures for language description would not serve the new purpose. You can describe Italian pretty well on the Latin model, and maybe you can get by describing English that way if you don't mind quite a few grotesqueries, but when you come to Algonquian, Potawatomi, and Kechua, Latin is largely irrelevant. You have to work out the structure without much help from traditional studies. Doing so, the anthropologist-linguist developed whole new techniques of language analysis.

The anthropologist was not the only one engaged in the endeavor. Equally important was the missionary. If one wishes to convert a people to Christianity, it is, if not indispensable, at least highly desirable to acquaint them with the Bible, and this means translating the Bible into their language, and *that* means learning their language. Many missionaries did this, from New Guinea to Tanganyika, and thus contributed to the growing knowledge of the languages of the world as well as to the technique of language description. Other people, primarily interested neither in religion nor culture but simply in language itself, entered the field, and before long something called linguistics or linguistic science or structural linguistics began to be recognized as a special academic discipline. The universities found themselves harboring professors of it.

It is not within the province of this foreword to describe the principles and practices of structural linguistics. . . . Attention may be drawn, however, to two important facets: the concentration on language as speech rather than as writing, and a different attitude toward correctness. The philologist, dealing necessarily with letters on page or stone, was interested, to be sure, in ascertaining the sounds they signified, but the structural linguist, working with notebook or tape recorder in Borneo or Carson City, Nevada, was in their immediacy and came to a much more profound understanding of them and the systems that contained them than had been attained before. It was this activity that led to refinement of the concept of the *phoneme,* which might be grossly defined as a bundle of similar sounds which seem identical to the native speaker of the language but which may sound quite dissimilar to a speaker of a different language. With the phoneme as a central unit, structural linguistics made extensive studies and inventories of the sound systems of a great many languages, went on to describe their morphological systems, and said something, but not so much that was startling and persuasive, about their syntactic systems. Structural linguistics started with phonology and worked up, so to speak, toward syntax, but it didn't always arrive.

Along with this descriptive and theoretical work went ideas about correctness which weren't exactly new but which tended to strike the layman as revolutionary and very likely dangerous. For reasons which a psychologist could most likely explain, people treasure the notion of a pure variety of whatever language they speak. Nobody is ever able to tell just what this purity consists of, what characteristics make it pure, but most people are sure that it exists somewhere. I was once told, by an educated Italian, that the purest Italian is to be found at a point just ten kilometers south of Siena, along the route of the Via Cassia. He was perfectly serious and thought himself communicating a fact analogous to a statement, say, about the boiling point of water. Always anxious to improve my understanding and extend my frame of reference, I stopped once at Kilometer Stone 214 on the Cassia, which is just ten kilometers south of Siena. There is a little settlement there, with a garage, a tobacco shop, a grocery store, and similar establishments. The residents speak a heavy Tuscan dialect barely understandable to the speaker of standard Italian who strains every auricular muscle. It is no doubt a very good and serviceable dialect, and I'm not saying it isn't. I just wonder what my mentor meant.

The structural linguists, dealing not, at first, with the sophisticated and self-conscious speakers of languages like English and Italian, but with languages of stone-age peoples with no literary tradition, were entirely free of this notion of correctness or purity of language. They did not titter when they heard Sitting Penguin say *ngungho* and tell him that he should say *ngunghu* like Laughing Mongoose. They simply noted that some speakers of the language said *ngungho,* whereas others said *ngunghu.* There was no way of determining that one of these was better or purer or more correct than the other. It could perhaps be ascertained which was the more common, but this was a matter of statistics, not of purity.

Had the structural linguists stuck to languages like Chamorro and Arawak, this century would have been much more peaceful, and the lanes of our universities would have run with far less blood. But they didn't. They got onto English and Italian and other languages which already had academic proprietors. With the disciplining experience of the prairie and the jungle under their belts, they looked with a cool and steady eye on the descriptions of the better known languages and found them sadly wanting. Worse, they said so publicly. Worse still, they said so with a good deal of humorous embroidery, pointing out with some insistence the donkey-like qualities of those to whom the instruction of the youth in their native languages had been entrusted. Very much worse still, they proposed to take over this instruction. The professor of English would be permitted to prattle about Shakespeare and Dickens if he wished, but all serious teaching of language should be confided to the structural linguist.

Naturally, the linguist was regularly clubbed and sometimes smeared, but he did gain enough footholds in the universities to keep the contest lively, and he became a formidable influence in such organizations as the National Council of Teachers of English, which the professor of Shakespeare and Dickens had too often considered beneath his notice. The linguist began to have an effect on teacher-training programs, on textbooks, on the curriculum of the lower schools. The effect was rather slight, actually, but it was enough to alarm the establishment, which launched a vigorous counterattack, oddly enough at the point at which the linguist was least culpable—the idea of correctness. Probably no linguist ever said that it doesn't matter how one speaks or writes, it is what one says that counts. The linguist knows better than most people that the how is at least as important as the what. But he knows also that the choice of one form over another is a sociological rather than a linguistic matter. That is, there are no linguistic reasons why, for example, "I brung it" should be eschewed. No arguments of logic or euphony or analogy can be adduced to establish *brought* as a purer form than *brung*. All that can be said is that, in the world of the closely shaved, the consequences of saying "I brung it" are very serious indeed and that the ambitious young man is well advised to avoid the expression.

Nevertheless, structural linguists were more or less successfully portrayed as champions of an anything-goes school of language. No doubt, they to some extent brought it on themselves. Books with titles like *Leave Your Language Alone* gave a somewhat false impression, and linguists, like stags at bay, often made reckless and inflammatory statements. At any rate, the impression was conveyed that linguists were bent on debasing and dismantling the language. It was suggested that this might be simply part of the permissive attitude that one saw everywhere, though some wondered whether international Communism was not involved in it somehow, and most of the guardians of our culture were quite sure that schools of education were part of the conspiracy. Articles began to appear in the national press about these anarchists who were saying dangerous things about *shall* and *will,* and the whole thing spilled over in the attack, mentioned earlier, on *Webster's Third.*

Ironically, by this time the problem had become, so far as linguists were concerned, largely of historical interest, for linguists had a much more important matter to worry about: generative transformational grammar. It has not been given to many people to change virtually single-handedly the whole course of a scientific discipline. One might think of Galileo, Lavoisier, Freud. If one doesn't rank Noam Chomsky with these, it could only be because one doesn't think linguistics as important as physics, chemistry, or psychology. Chomsky studied linguistics at the University of Pennsylvania and took his Ph.D. degree there. He spent the first part of the fifties thinking and studying and in 1957 published a book called *Syntactic Structures.* . . . Linguistics has not been the same since.

What Chomsky did in *Syntactic Structures* was to ask certain very general questions about language and language learning and to give some partial answers. What do we learn when we learn a language. One might be tempted to say words, or, if one were slightly more sophisticated, sentences. Indeed, most books designed for teaching foreign languages essentially produce words and sentences to be learned. Yet it can be shown that, apart from the simplest formulas and greetings, like "Hello" and "Thank you," and trite expressions of various sorts, like "A good time was had by all," the chances that any particular learner will have occasion to use any particular sentence are quite small. This is so even in cases where the needs of the learner are pretty well known in advance—those of tourists, for example. Countless British tourists preparing for continental travel have memorized the French, German, and Spanish equivalents of "I have two pounds of tea and three bars of chocolate for my own personal use," but it is doubtful that any considerable number have stammered out the sentences. What happens is that the customs man who boards the train at Modane, anxious to get back to his card game, says hopefully, *"Rien à déclarer?"* and you say *"Rien à déclarer,"* and return to your study of the phrase book.

The views of people who write phrase books on what phrases might come in handy are sometimes peculiar. A Dutch book on *Useful English Words and Phrases* contains the sentence "Our postillion has been struck by lightning." One is not likely to find use for this, which is a pity, because it is a sentence with a certain euphony and a kind of dignity. But in fact the chances that a Hollander visiting New York will have occasion to say, for example, "Where are my suitcases?" are not much greater than they are for "Our postillion has been struck by lightning." They are a little greater, but not much. He would have to lose his suitcases, first of all, a thing not really easy to do, and then be in a situation in which "Where are my suitcases?" is the proper thing to say. Maybe "A thief just made off with my suitcases" or "Have you happened to see any unclaimed suitcases in the lobby?" would be more to the point. The orders of probability of "Where are my suitcases?" and "Our postillion has been struck by lightning" are quite similar. Both are near zero.

What, then, do we learn when we learn a language, if it is not words and phrases and sentences? Obviously, what we learn is a sentence-making mechanism of some sort. Chomsky pointed out that the number of possible sentences for any language is, if not infinite, at least on the order of magnitude of the particles of the universe. What is not so immediately obvious is that the number of sentence *types* is not appreciably smaller. The structures of syntax can combine and embed and intertwine and extend in such an endless number of ways that it is far beyond the power of any grammar, however multivolumed, to set them forth. One can come pretty close to listing the words of a language, if *word* is defined narrowly enough, but one can't even begin to list the sentences or the sentence types.

What one must therefore conclude is that we Ogs, in contrast to the Malaysian ape, have acquired a power to *generate* sentences—just those which will serve our unpredictable needs. The mechanism that enables us to do this is called grammar. Apparently every human child who is not deaf or functionally malformed builds himself a grammar. From the random sentences that he hears from the people around him, he builds a sentence-making system, going through some sort of process of theory construction. As Chomsky has pointed out, this goes to essential completion at a very early age—say around five or six years. The operation goes on indifferently to the particular language involved; that is, the Chinese child builds his grammar of Chinese with about as much ease or difficulty as the American child builds his of English and in about the same time. Also it goes on, apparently, indifferently to intelligence. You don't have to be bright to learn Chinese or French. All you have to have are Chinese or French parents. Once you have built your grammar, you can choose, among the trillion plus sentences at your disposition, just those which fill the need of the moment. You can locate the bathroom, complain about not being permitted to watch television, inquire about your suitcases, or report to the police a recent unpleasantness suffered by your postillion.

There are still a large number of unanswered questions about this grammar-building ability. One is whether the ability atrophies after a certain age. Little children are notoriously the most able learners of languages. Some tots build not just one grammar but three or four simultaneously and chatter with equal skill in English, French, Turkish, and Egyptian Arabic, according to the company in which they find themselves. Some psychologists feel that doing so is bad for their mental health, but nothing conclusive is known. Anyway, though the reasons are murky, it is certain that the older you get the harder it is to learn a new language. An English-speaking child of eight can learn French only laboriously if at all, but it isn't clear what the impeding factors are. Probably the self-conscious possession of a prior language is an important one. People have often speculated on what would happen if a child were raised for a certain time in the absence of language—say six or seven years—and then confronted with it. Herodotus reports one such experiment, and King James the First is said to have made another, but in modern times it is hard to find a subject. Anyone who comes across a ten-year-old human child who has been raised by wolves should report at once to the nearest linguist.

All of these matters are in the realm of speculation and are unlikely to be understood soon, if ever. But if one can't very hopefully go about understanding the learning process, one can with more confidence try to figure out the thing learned, the grammar. Transformationalists have argued that a grammar consists of three components—the syntactic, the phonological, and the semantic. The syntactic component is in some sense prior to the other two in the setting forth of the grammar. (We may note that the point of entry for transformationalists is the opposite of that for structuralists and more in accord with traditional grammar.) This syntactic component is generated by two sets of rules. One set is called phrase-structure, or kernel, rules, the other transformational rules. The phrase-structure rules generate the elements of sentences in a simple order. The following might be said roughly to be generated by phrase-structure rules: "The suitcases are somewhere," "The children whine," "Lightning has struck the postillion." Transformational rules ring changes on such kernel sentences, reordering their parts, combining them, adding items and deleting others. The following are sentences to which transformational rules have been applied: "Where are my suitcases?" "I took steps to stop the whining of the children," "Our postillion has been struck by lightning."

The structures generated by phrase-structure rules are sometimes called deep structures; those generated by transformational rules are called surface structures. A pair of sentences may be quite similar in surface structure and yet quite different in deep structure. To employ a much used example, "John is eager to please" and "John is easy to please" have about the same surface structure but differ fundamentally in deep structure, since in the first John is the pleaser but in the second he is the pleasee. The other two components of the grammar, the semantic and the phonological, relate respectively to the deep structure and the surface structure. It is the deep structure that provides the basic meaning of sentences. It is the surface structure that has to be pronounced. The grammar might be diagramed as follows:

SYNTACTIC COMPONENT

phrase-structure rules
↓ ——————→ SEMANTIC COMPONENT
deep structures
↓
transformational rules
↓ ——————→ PHONOLOGICAL COMPONENT
surface structures

Thus transformational grammar provides a framework in which answers to the three basic questions one can ask of any sentence may be sought: (1) of what elements is it composed? (syntax), (2) what does it mean? (semantics), (3) how is it pronounced? (phonology).

All this may seem harmless enough, and even obvious, but it rocked the world of linguistics. Structural linguists had confined themselves, at least in theory, to describing the sentences found in corpora. A corpus might be a set of tapes of conversations by speakers of Navajo. Or it might be the complete works of Jonathan Swift. Whatever it was, the structuralist kept within it, describing the sentences as accurately as possible and making inventories of their elements. He never tried to predict what a Navajo or Jonathan Swift would have said if he had said something else. The transformationalist tries to do just that. His intent is to project, from a finite set of known sentences, an illimitable number of others and to show that these will be accepted as grammatical when and if they are ever used.

Along with this went a new view of correctness, or grammaticalness. The structuralist tended to take a whatever-is-is-right view of things. If a Navajo said something, it was accepted as correct Navajo. The transformationalist is more subtle, or more cautious. He would point out that interferences of many kinds might have derailed the Navajo from the track of Navajo grammar. He might have had a lapse of memory; he might have been drunk; one of his kids might have annoyed him just as he was getting into the predicate and made him forget what the subject was. The transformationalist would say, in fact, that speakers of a language are ungrammatical more often than not, hitting near the mark but not often on it. Transformationalists make a distinction between *competence* and *performance*. The competence is the grammar itself which the speaker has internalized as a result of the theory-construction process mentioned earlier. The performance is what he actually does with it, beset by such distractions as screaming children, shyness, hysteria, LSD. Beyond this is the fact that we sometimes sport with the grammar, departing from it deliberately in order to be humorous or poetic. E. E. Cummings' "He danced his did," in which the grammatical "He did his dance" is deliberately inverted, is a frequently cited example. But also

"Are you the waiter?"
"No, I'm not. I'm a waitee."

Here the rule for forming words with the morpheme *ee* is pushed into new territory, and the expression is ungrammatical. Of course, if the usage became common, the grammatical rule would change in this particular to accommodate it. Transformationalists do not say, any more than structuralists did, that grammars are static.

Transformationalists differ from their predecessors also in their attitude toward the notions of rule and exception. Structuralists were pretty chary about rules, looking on them as somehow unscientific, whereas transformationalists take them to their bosoms whenever at all possible. The structuralists seem to have inverted the Neo-Grammarians' "There is no exception without a rule" to "If there is an exception, there can be no rule." For example, in English the ending *-ate* has a fairly regular effect on the placement of the primary stress: it tends to put it on the antepenultimate syllable: *démonstrate, víolate, cálculate*. But there are exceptions. Some people say not *rémonstrate* but *remónstrate*. Such irregularities led many structuralists not only to shrink from stating a rule for the stress effect of *-ate* but to adopt the much more far-reaching conclusion that stress is phonemic in English—that is, that, for any particular sentence you wish to say, you must learn previously which syllables have the various grades of stress. The transformationalist, on the other hand, would say that any rule, no matter how many the exceptions, is better than no rule at all, because if there is no rule, then everything is exception. If, confronted by a thousand items, he can take just ten of them together in a rule, the transformationalist joyfully does so, because that leaves him with only 990 exceptions, not a thousand. So naturally he gives a stress rule for *-ate:* it puts the stress on the antepenultimate syllable, with a few exceptions, like *remónstrate*. This leads him to the vaster conclusion that stress is largely predictable in English and hence, from his point of view, not phonemic.

As this is being written, we await the publication of *The Sound Pattern of English* by Chomsky and Morris Halle. Transformationalists were merely irritating to structuralists when they confined themselves to syntax, because structuralists had not travelled much in that realm anyway. But *The Sound Pattern of English* is, among other things, an attack on the concept of the phoneme, which has been the cornerstone of linguistics since about 1935. It will be interesting to see how the issue is resolved.

One may well ask what good linguistics is—transformationalist, structuralist, or other. How does it help us feed the chickens? There is, as a matter of fact, quite a large application. Linguistics contributes importantly to such sister disciplines as psychology, medicine, communication theory, as well as being the heart and soul of anthropology. But the most obvious application would seem to be to language teaching, whether to the teaching of foreign languages or to the improvement of the native one. The first time that linguistics was applied on a large scale to foreign-language teaching was during World War II. Leonard Bloomfield himself, sometimes called the Father of linguistics, was associated with the effort, and many of the great names of linguistics came to public attention at that time. Readers of newspapers learned of a marvelous new technology for language teaching. Our soldiers and sailors were being taught so efficiently and well that, after a short course of instruction, they could be dropped, say, behind Japanese lines in China and, with a little bit of makeup, pass as Japanese and steal secrets.

Undoubtedly, it was the journalists and not the linguists who were responsible for most of the exaggeration. When the war was over, Professors Frederick B. Agard and Harold B. Dunkel were commissioned to find out what had actually happened, to what extent the methods advocated by linguists had proved superior to traditional methods. Agard and Dunkel were linguists and would have been pleased to report that we had here a real cure for tooth decay, but they were also responsible scholars, and they stated that it was impossible to prove the fact one way or the other. The factors involved in language learning are so extraordinarily complex that it cannot be shown conclusively that particular methodologies contribute to or detract from the desired result.

It was certainly true that some of the language schools during the war achieved spectacular results, but it is impossible to know how much these results owed to techniques derived from linguistics and how much to Main Strength and Awkwardness. If you put a bright young soldier into a room with a native speaker of Japanese and keep them there eight hours a day for eighteen months, the soldier will learn quite a lot of Japanese, even if his text is just a Japanese translation of Cicero and his instructor is a nitwit. Unless, of course, the soldier simply goes mad, which also happened now and then.

Nevertheless, the euphoria felt during the war about new methods of language teaching survived the war and probably rightly so. It is no doubt true that linguistics has contributed importantly to language learning. It is hard to believe that one can teach something as well or better if he doesn't understand it than if he does. It would seem that the more we know about language, the more we are in a position to choose intelligently and effectively among methods of teaching it. This is not the same, however, as saying that we have a technology for foreign-language teaching in the sense that physics provides a technology for bridge-building. Linguistics has produced no simple and certain method for learning languages. It may some day, but it hasn't yet.

The problems of the application of linguistics to the improvement of the pupil in the use of his native language are more subtle and have been longer argued. Specifically, the problem is this: does it pay, if you are a native speaker of English and wish to improve your use of it, to study English grammar? In the twenties and thirties there were several investigations of this problem, and they were impressively unanimous in their conclusion: that it doesn't pay. Pupils who didn't study grammar seemed to improve as much or as little as those who did. It should be noted, however, that the grammar studied in the test cases was of a rudimentary type, unaffected by any doctrines of linguistics, and also that the variables are staggering. It is probably impossible to control an experiment of this type in any really effective way.

The essential question, actually, is this: how do people who write well learn to write well? And nobody really knows the answer. Obviously they must have a great deal of experience in reading and writing, but they must have other capacities as well—power of observation and of applying what is observed, intelligence, memory, willingness to take pains. It is quite possible that our best writers are not significantly assisted by what they learn in schools and that they would be just as good if they didn't go to school at all beyond the first few grades. This doesn't mean, however, that everybody would write just as well with little or no schooling. Indeed, the teaching and learning problem does not affect the Faulkners and E. B. Whites of this world but rather the great mass of citizens who, more and more in this age of paper, find that their careers and earning power and happiness are closely related to their ability to write sentences. The feeling persists in the schools that such people will do better in proportion as they understand the structure of the sentences they write. This may be a fallacy, but it is far from having been proved to be so. If a better method of teaching writing exists, it has yet to be demonstrated.

At any rate, the question is only whether or not the student in school or college should be subjected, or treated, to the study of his language, not what theory of the language should be presented to him. For this latter question eventually solves itself. Different theories contend in the forums of the Linguistic Society of America and the International Congresses of Linguists, in the classrooms of Berkeley, California, and University College, London. It doesn't really matter much, in the long run, how clever in debate the proponents of a particular theory are or how devastatingly they write. It is the theory that counts. If it gets us closer to a satisfactory notion of what language is like, it ultimately prevails; otherwise it doesn't. And when it prevails, those who deal with language in some professional way are stuck with it. The physicist might think that the world would be a happier place if neutrons behaved in some fashion different from the one they do, but he can't do anything about it. Neither can the language teacher—whether of a third grade in Mason City, Iowa, or of a Berlitz school in Vienna—do anything about the facts of language, except perhaps to avoid learning about them. It is hard to become unignorant, but it is nearly impossible, once unignorant, to become ignorant again. Linguistics may teach the teacher of language things that will make his work more simple or more difficult, more pleasant or more painful, more effective or less. However it is, there is nothing he can do about it. He has to accept what he knows, what he believes to be true, and operate from there.

It is to be supposed that most readers of this book are not expecting to become teachers of language and so are in no danger professionally of absorbing prickly and painful knowledge. They can relax and enjoy the ride down the rapids and perhaps even find some amusement in the imprecations that the boatmen scream at one another. Language ranks only slightly behind sex in the universal interest it inspires. If it is true that there is nothing like a dame (and it certainly is), it is equally true that there is nothing like a sentence. We who are descendants of Og cannot avoid speculation over the miracle of language. It is a great thing to have a grammar; it puts us one up on the Malaysian ape. And it's an even greater thing not to have to take the grammar too seriously, to be able to kick it around a little if we like. The only thing we have to fear is that some day linguists will know all there is to know about language, be able to lay it out completely and say it is just such and so, and there are no more questions. But we don't have to fear this very much.

Questions

1. What are the two definitions of *linguist* that Roberts implies at the beginning of this article?
2. Roberts does not discuss fully the method of structural linguistics but he does stress two important principles of structuralists. What are the two principles? How do they differ from the approach of traditional grammarians?
3. Structuralists begin their analysis of language with phonology, move next to morphology, and end with syntax. Can you define the three terms? Why would structuralists consider them in the order listed?
4. What is the difference between a prescriptive approach to grammar and a descriptive approach? In which category would traditional grammar be placed? Structural? Transformational?

5. What does Roberts mean by his statement that when we learn a language "what we learn is a sentence-making mechanism of some sort"?
6. In what sense does a five or six year old native speaker "know" the grammar of his language? In your experience do children of this age have problems with grammar? If so, what kinds of problems?
7. What would be Penfield's explanation (see page 153) of Roberts' statement "that the older you get the harder it is to learn a new language"?
8. Distinguish between deep structure and surface structure. How do they relate to competence and performance in language?
9. Why do the generative-transformational grammarians insist that we must study not only the structure of language but also the nature of the human if we are to produce acceptable grammars?
10. Roberts, who spent his last years writing transformational grammars, is very cautious about the claims he makes for the new approaches to language study. Can you see any reasons why? Is he overly cautious?

Suggestions for Writing

1. Knowing your own language involves more than knowing the vocabulary of the language. Explain, in terms of what Roberts says in this article, and in terms of your own knowledge of the language, what else you must know before you can adequately use a language.
2. Contrast the different views toward grammar and usage held by two of your former English teachers. Select a specific purpose to give your theme unity and significance. Use concrete and specific examples to support your points. You can make a point-by-point contrast or you might choose to describe one teacher fully before you describe the second.

Jabberwocky

Lewis Carroll

In "Jabberwocky" Carroll deals with the structure of the language. He has used nonsense words for most of those words that carry meaning in a sentence, but has retained the structure of English. Humpty Dumpty in Part Two of this book gives his interpretation of the first verse of the poem. You might refer to his analysis and see if you agree. Though referential or vocabulary meanings are largely absent from the poem, structural or grammatical meanings are still discernible. After reading the poem through a couple of times, just for the fun it offers, you might try to determine the parts of speech represented by some words. Can you identify nouns, verbs, adjectives? Can you determine whether nouns are singular or plural, whether verbs are present or past tense? How are you able to determine such matters when you do not know the meanings of the words?

'Twas brillig, and the slithy toves
  Did gyre and gimble in the wabe:
All mimsy were the borogoves,
  And the mome raths outgrabe.

"Beware the Jabberwock, my son!
  The jaws that bite, the claws that catch!
Beware the Jubjub bird, and shun
  The frumious Bandersnatch!"

He took his vorpal sword in hand:
  Long time the manxome foe he sought—
So rested he by the Tumtum tree,
  And stood awhile in thought.

And, as in uffish thought he stood,
  The Jabberwock, with eyes of flame,
Came whiffling through the tulgey wood,
  And burbled as it came!

One, two! One, two! And through and through
  The vorpal blade went snicker-snack!

He left it dead, and with its head
He went galumphing back.

"And hast thou slain the Jabberwock?
Come to my arms, my beamish boy!
O frabjous day! Callooh! Callay!"
He chortled in his joy.

'Twas brillig, and the slithy toves
Did gyre and gimble in the wabe:
All mimsy were the borogoves,
And the mome raths outgrabe.

Questions

1. Carroll contributed some new words to the English language. Two of these were *chortle* and *galumph*. Can you analyze them as blends of two familiar words the way Humpty Dumpty analyzes words earlier in this book? Other examples of words resulting from blending are *smog, brunch, motel*. What effect is achieved by blending? (Some dictionaries cite *galumph* as a combination of *gallop* + *triumph*, others imply it is a combination of *gallop* + *bump* with corresponding differences in meaning. Can you give reasons for the differences in meaning?)
2. If you are able to identify parts of speech and to determine such grammatical meanings as number and tense from the nonsense words, which grammar or grammars discussed by Roberts are you using?

Who Flang That Ball?

W. F. Miksch *Authors in preceding selections have discussed a number of ways in which languages change. In the following selection the author illustrates language change by analogy. Analogy has been a significant factor in the changes from Old English to Modern English. If a regular pattern exists in the system of language, it creates a very strong force to make all other irregular items of the same type in the language conform to that pattern. In Old English there were about 312 strong verbs, verbs with three parts such as* sing, sang, sung. *Only about 65 strong verbs remain in Modern English. Verbs like* strive *are now being regularized by analogy. The old past tense form* strove *is being replaced by the regular form* strived. *Children sometimes make errors in grammar by following the principle of analogy: "It hurted me." Can you think of other examples of analogical change?*

Miksch has Infield reverse the tendency to regularize verbs by having him use strong verbs as the basis for his analogical change. Can you provide the analogical forms of all the verbs he changes? Although he deals with a serious linguistic principle, Miksch's purpose, which is to amuse, dictates a certain approach to his subject. Does Miksch make any assumptions about the background of his audience?

My assignment was to interview Infield Ingersoll, one-time shortstop for the Wescosville Wombats and now a radio sports announcer. Dizzy Dean, Red Barber and other sportscasters had taken back seats since the colorful Ingersoll had gone on the air. The man had practically invented a new language.

"I know just what you're gonna ask," Infield began. "You wanna know how come I use all them ingrammatical expressions like 'He swang at a high one.' You think I'm illitrut."

"No, indeed," I said. Frankly, I *had* intended to ask him what effect he thought his extraordinary use of the King's English might have on future generations of radio listeners.

But a gleam in Infield's eyes when he said "illitrut" changed my mind.

"What I'd really like to get," I said, "is the story of how you left baseball and became a sportscaster."

Infield looked pleased. "Well," he said, "it was the day us Wombats plew the Pink Sox . . ."

"Plew the Pink Sox?" I interrupted. "Don't you mean played?"

Infield's look changed to disappointment. "Slay, slew. Play, plew. What's the matter with that?"

"Slay is an irregular verb," I pointed out.

"So who's to say what's regular or irregular? English teachers! Can an English teacher bat three hundred?"

He paused belligerently, and then went on. "What I'm tryin' to do is easify the languish. I make all regular verbs irregular. Once they're all irregular, then it's just the same like they're all regular. That way I don't gotta stop and think."

He had something there. "Go on with your story," I said.

"Well, it was the top of the fifth, when this Sox batter wang out a high pop fly. I raught for it."

"Raught?"

"Past tense of verb to Reach. Teach, taught. Reach,—"

"Sorry," I said. "Go ahead."

"Anyhow I raught for it, only the sun blound me."

"You mean blinded?"

"Look," Infield said patiently, "you wouldn't say a pitcher winded up, would you? So there I was, blound by the sun, and the ball just nuck the tip of my glove—that's nick, nuck; same congregation as stick, stuck. But luckily I caught it just as it skam the top of my shoe."

"Skam? Could that be the past tense of to skim?"

"Yeah, yeah, same as swim, swam. You want this to be a English lesson or you wanna hear my story?"

"Your story please, Mr. Ingersoll."

"Okay. Well, just then the umpire cell, 'Safe!' Naturally I was surprose. Because I caught that fly, only the ump cell the runner safe."

"Cell is to call as fell is to fall, I suppose?" I inquired.

"Right. Now you're beginning to catch on." Infield regarded me happily as if there was now some hope for me. "So I yold at him, 'Robber! That decision smold!' "

"Yell, yold. Smell, smold," I mumbled. "Same idea as tell, told."

Infield rumbled on, "I never luck that umpire anyway."

"Hold it!" I cried. I finally had tripped this backhand grammarian. "A moment ago, you used nuck as the past for nick, justifying it by the verb to stick. Now you use luck as a verb. Am I to assume by this that luck is the past tense of to lick?"

"Luck is past for like. To like is a regular irregular verb of which there are several such as strike, struck. Any farther questions or should I go on?"

"Excuse me," I said. "You were saying you never luck that umpire."

"And neither did the crowd. Everyone thrould at my courage. I guess I better explain thrould," Infield said thoughtfully. "Thrould comes from thrill just like would comes from will. Got that? Now to get back to my story: 'Get off the field, you bum, and no back talk!' the umpire whoze."

"Whoze?"

"He had asthma," Infield pointed out patiently.

I saw through it instantly. Wheeze, whoze. Freeze, froze.

"And with those words, that ump invote disaster. I swang at him and smeared him with a hard right that lood square on his jaw."

"Lood? Oh, I see—Stand, stood. Land, lood—it lood on his jaw."

"Sure. He just feld up and went down like a light. As he reclone on the field, he pept at me out of his good eye."

"Now wait. What's this pept?" I asked.

"After you sleep, you've did what?" Infield inquired.

"Why, slept—oh, he peeped at you, did he?"

"You bet he pept at me. And in that peep I saw it was curtains for me in the league henceforward. So I beat him to it and just up and quat."

"Sit, sat. Quit—well, that gets you out of baseball," I said. "Only you still haven't told me how you got to be on radio and television."

"I guess that'll have to wait," Infield said, "on account I gotta hurry now to do a broadcast."

As he shade my hand good-by, Infield grun and wank at me.

*Mr. K*A*P*L*A*N, the Comparative, and the Superlative*

Leonard Q. Ross *Many people have become acquainted with Hyman Kaplan, the delightful creation of Leonard Q. Ross. Mr. Kaplan, an immigrant to the United States, is attending night school and attempting to learn English. The experiences Mr. Kaplan and his struggling fellow students have provide many pleasant moments for the reader. But the author, with his insight into the problems of students attempting to learn English as a second language, reveals a good deal about the system of the English language that can be of interest to the native speaker of English.*

Mr. Kaplan and his friends struggle mightily with some of the systems of English—systems that the native speaker uses without conscious awareness that they exist. Read the following selection for the pleasure it gives you, but also be aware of the kinds of problems Mr. Parkhill's students are having. You may envy Mr. Kaplan's originality in spelling, but be especially alert for the problems he has with the very system of English; with the use of the articles a, an, *and* the; *with prepositions; and with word order. What is Mr. Kaplan's problem with the comparative and the superlative? Why does the principle of analogy fail him in his attempts to deal with* good *and* bad?

For two weeks Mr. Parkhill had been delaying the inescapable: Mr. Kaplan, like the other students in the beginners' grade of the American Night Preparatory School for Adults, would have to present a composition for class analysis. All the students had had their turn writing the assignment on the board, a composition of one hundred words, entitled "My Job." Now only Mr. Kaplan's rendition remained.

It would be more accurate to say Mr. K * A * P * L * A * N's rendition the assignment remained, for even in thinking of that distinguished student, Mr. Parkhill saw the image of his unmistakable signature, in all its red-blue-green glory. The multicolored characters were more than a trademark; they were an assertion of individuality, a symbol of singularity, a proud expression of Mr. Kaplan's Inner Self. To Mr. Parkhill, the signature took on added meaning because it was associated with the man who had said his youthful ambition had been to become "a physician and sergeant," the Titan who had declined the verb "to fail": "fail, failed, bankropt."

One night, after the two weeks' procrastination, Mr. Parkhill decided to face the worst. "Mr. Kaplan, I think it's your turn to—er—write your composition on the board."

Mr. Kaplan's great, buoyant smile grew more great and more buoyant. "My!" he exclaimed. He rose, looked around at the class proudly as if surveying the blessed who were to witness a linguistic *tour de force,* stumbled over Mrs. Moskowitz's feet with a polite "Vould you be so kindly?" and took his place at the blackboard. There he rejected several pieces of chalk critically, nodded to Mr. Parkhill—it was a nod of distinct reassurance—and then printed in firm letters:

My Job A Cotter In Dress Faktory
Comp. by
H * Y *

"You need not write your name on the board," interrupted Mr. Parkhill quickly. "Er—to save time . . ."

Mr. Kaplan's face expressed astonishment. "Podden me, Mr. Pockheel. But de name is by me *pot* of mine composition."

"Your name is *part* of the composition?" asked Mr. Parkhill in an anxious tone.

"Yas*sir!*" said Mr. Kaplan with dignity. He printed the rest of H * Y * M * A * N K * A * P * L * A * N for all to see and admire. You could tell it was a disappointment for him not to have colored chalk for this performance. In pale white the elegance of his work was dissipated. The name, indeed, seemed unreal, the letters stark, anemic, almost denuded.

His brow wrinkled and perspiring, Mr. Kaplan wrote the saga of A Cotter In Dress Faktory on the board, with much scratching of the chalk and an undertone of sound. Mr. Kaplan repeated each word to himself softly, as if trying to give to its spelling some of the flavor and originality of his pronunciation. The smile on the face of Mr. Kaplan had taken on something beatific and imperishable: it was his first experience at the blackboard; it was his moment of glory. He seemed to be writing more slowly than necessary as if to prolong the ecstasy of his Hour. When he had finished he said "Hau Kay" with distinct regret in his voice, and sat down. Mr. Parkhill observed the composition in all its strange beauty:

My Job A Cotter In Dress Faktory
Comp. by
H * Y * M * A * N K * A * P * L * A * N

Shakspere is saying what fulls man is and I am feeling just the same way when I am thinking about mine job a cotter in Dress Faktory on 38 st. by 7 av. For why should we slafing in dark place by laktric lights and all kinds hot for $30 or maybe $36 with overtime, for Boss who is fat and driving in fency automobil? I ask! Because we are the deprassed workers of world. And are being exployted. By Bosses. In mine shop is no difference. Oh how bad is laktric light, oh how is all kinds hot. And when I am telling Foreman should be better conditions he hollers, Kaplan you redical!!

At this point a glazed look came into Mr. Parkhill's eyes, but he read on.

So I keep still and work by bad light and always hot. But somday will the workers making Bosses to work! And then Kaplan will give to them bad laktric and positively no windows for the air should come in! So they can know what it means to slafe! Kaplan will make Foreman a cotter like he is. And give the most bad dezigns to cot out. Justice.

Mine job is cotting Dress dezigns.

T-H-E E-N-D

Mr. Parkhill read the amazing document over again. His eyes, glazed but a moment before, were haunted now. It was true: spelling, diction, sentence structure, punctuation, capitalization, the use of the present perfect for the present—all true.

"Is planty mistakes, I s'pose," suggested Mr. Kaplan modestly.

"Y-yes . . . yes, there are many mistakes."

"Dat's because I'm tryink to give *dip ideas,*" said Mr. Kaplan with the sigh of those who storm heaven.

Mr. Parkhill girded his mental loins. "Mr. Kaplan—er—your composition doesn't really meet the assignment. You haven't described your *job,* what you *do,* what your work *is.*"

"Vell, it's not soch a interastink jop," said Mr. Kaplan.

"Your composition is not a simple exposition. It's more of a—well, an *essay* on your *attitude.*"

"Oh, fine!" cried Mr. Kaplan with enthusiasm.

"No, no," said Mr. Parkhill hastily. "The assignment was *meant* to be a composition. You see, we must begin with simple exercises before we try—er—more philosophical essays."

Mr. Kaplan nodded with resignation. "So naxt time should be no ideas, like abot Shaksbeer? Should be only *fects?"*

"Y-yes. No ideas, only—er—facts."

You could see by Mr. Kaplan's martyred smile that his wings, like those of an eagle's, were being clipped.

"And Mr. Kaplan—er—why do you use 'Kaplan' in the body of your composition? Why don't you say *'I* will make the foreman a cutter' instead of *'Kaplan* will make the foreman a cutter?' "

Mr. Kaplan's response was instantaneous. "I'm so glad you eskink me dis! Ha! I'm usink 'Keplen' in de composition for plain and tsimple rizzon: becawss I didn't vant de reader should tink I am *prajudiced* aganst de foreman, so I said it more like abot a strenger: *'Keplen* vill make de foreman a cotter!' "

In the face of this subtle passion for objectivity, Mr. Parkhill was silent. He called for corrections. A forest of hands went up. Miss Mitnick pointed out errors in spelling, the use of capital letters, punctuation; Mr. Norman Bloom corrected several more words, rearranged sentences, and said, "Woikers is exployted with an *'i,'* not 'y' as Kaplan makes"; Miss Caravello changed "fulls" to "fools," and declared herself uncertain as to the validity of the word "Justice" standing by itself in "da smalla da sentence"; Mr. Sam Pinsky said he was sure Mr. Kaplan meant *"oppressed* voikers of de voild, not *deprassed,* aldough dey are deprassed *too,"* to which Mr. Kaplan replied, "So ve bote got right, no? Don' *chenge* 'deprassed,' only *add* 'opprassed.' "

Then Mr. Parkhill went ahead with his own corrections, changing tenses, substituting prepositions, adding the definite article. Through the whole barrage Mr. Kaplan kept shaking his head, murmuring "Mine gootness!" each time a correction was made. But he smiled all the while. He seemed to be proud of the very number of errors he had made; of the labor to which the class was being forced in his service; of the fact that his *ideas,* his creation, could survive so concerted an onslaught. And as the composition took more respectable form, Mr. Kaplan's smile grew more expansive.

"Now, class," said Mr. Parkhill, "I want to spend a few minutes explaining something about adjectives. Mr. Kaplan uses the phrase—er—'most bad.' That's wrong. There is a word for 'most bad.' It is what we call the superlative form of 'bad.' " Mr. Parkhill explained the use of the positive, comparative, and superlative forms of the adjective. " 'Tall, taller, tallest.' 'Rich, richer, richest.' Is that clear? Well then, let us try a few others."

The class took up the game with enthusiasm. Miss Mitnick submitted "dark, darker, darkest"; Mr. Scymzak, "fat, fatter, fattest."

"But there are certain exceptions to this general form," Mr. Parkhill went on. The class, which had long ago learned to respect that gamin, The Exception to the Rule, nodded solemnly. "For instance, we don't say 'good, gooder, goodest,' do we?"

"No, sir!" cried Mr. Kaplan impetuously. " 'Good, gooder, good*est?'* Ha! It's to leff!"

"We say that X, for example, is good. Y, however, is—?" Mr. Parkhill arched an eyebrow interrogatively.

"Batter!" said Mr. Kaplan.

"Right! And Z is—?"

"High-cless!"

Mr. Parkhill's eyebrow dropped. "No," he said sadly.

"Not high-cless?" asked Mr. Kaplan incredulously. For him there was no word more superlative.

"No, Mr. Kaplan, the word is 'best.' And the word 'bad,' of which you tried to use the superlative form . . . It isn't *'bad, badder, baddest.'* It's 'bad' . . . and what's the comparative? Anyone?"

"Worse," volunteered Mr. Bloom.

"Correct! And the superlative? Z is the—?"

" 'Worse' also?" asked Mr. Bloom hesitantly. It was evident he had never distinguished the fine difference in sound between the compartive and superlative forms of "bad."

"No, Mr. Bloom. It's not the *same* word, although it—er—sounds a good deal like it. Anyone? Come, come. It isn't hard. X is *bad,* Y is *worse,* and Z is the—?"

An embarrassed silence fell upon the class, which, apparently, had been using "worse" for both the comparative and superlative all along. Miss Mitnick blushed and played with her pencil. Mr. Bloom shrugged, conscious that he had given his all. Mr. Kaplan stared at the board, his mouth open, a desperate concentration in his eye.

"Bad—worse. What is the word you use when you mean 'most bad'?"

"Aha!" cried Mr. Kaplan suddenly. When Mr. Kaplan cried "Aha!" it signified that a great light had fallen on him. "I know! De exect void! So easy! *Ach!* I should know dat ven I vas wridink! *Bad—voise—"*

"Yes, Mr. Kaplan!" Mr. Parkhill was definitely excited.

"Rotten!"

Mr. Parkhill's eyes glazed once more, unmistakably. He shook his head dolorously, as if he had suffered a personal hurt. And as he wrote "W-O-R-S-T" on the blackboard there ran through his head, like a sad refrain, this latest manifestation of Mr. Kaplan's peculiar genius: "bad—worse—rotten; bad—worse . . ."

Questions

1. You will gain an increased appreciation for the complexity of English grammar if you work with some of the problems that foreign students have as they learn English. Doing one or two of the following exercises should make you aware of some of the systems of English grammar.
   a. Read Mr. Kaplan's theme carefully, changing all the verb forms so that they would be acceptable in standard written English. Which verb forms seem most troublesome to Mr. Kaplan? Are these forms ever difficult for a native speaker?
   b. Check the use of prepositions in the language of the students throughout the article. Can you give any explanation of why prepositions should be so difficult for the foreign student, yet offer the native speaker no problem?
   c. Change the word order of any sentences used by the students that are not acceptable in standard English. What are the students' major problems in word order?
   d. Note the use of articles in the speech and writing of the students. Could you offer clear explanations to the students to help them avoid errors in the use of the articles?
2. In addition to the students' use of grammar, note their pronunciation of English. Does the spelling of the words seem to indicate the pronunciation of the foreign students adequately? Can the letters on the printed page fully convey the rich variety of sound and tone that can be expressed by the voice? What devices are available to a writer as he attempts to represent dialects and other pronunciation variations?

Of This Time, of That Place

Lionel Trilling *Grammar, we have seen, involves more than parts of speech and sentence structure. It describes the broad structure of a language. And in this sense everyone has his own unique language and his own individual grammar. In the following story you will meet two young men, students like yourselves, who have such radically different and opposing ways of writing as to constitute, at least for one of them, a private grammar, as you will see. The two contrast with each other in many ways. (Try to define the contrasts as you read.) You will find other meaningful contrasts in the story if you watch for them. Do Tertan and Blackburn resemble students you know?*

I

It was a fine September day. By noon it would be summer again, but now it was true autumn with a touch of chill in the air. As Joseph Howe stood on the porch of the house in which he lodged, ready to leave for his first class of the year, he thought with pleasure of the long indoor days that were coming. It was a moment when he could feel glad of his profession.

On the lawn the peach tree was still in fruit and young Hilda Aiken was taking a picture of it. She held the camera tight against her chest. She wanted the sun behind her, but she did not want her own long morning shadow in the foreground. She raised the camera, but that did not help, and she lowered it, but that made things worse. She twisted her body to the left, then to the right. In the end she had to step out of the direct line of the sun. At last she snapped the shutter and wound the film with intense care.

Howe, watching her from the porch, waited for her to finish and called good morning. She turned, startled, and almost sullenly lowered her glance. In the year Howe had lived at the Aikens', Hilda had accepted him as one of her family, but since his absence of the summer she had grown shy. Then suddenly she lifted her head and smiled at him, and the humorous smile confirmed his pleasure in the day. She picked up her bookbag and set off for school.

The handsome houses on the streets to the college were not yet fully awake, but they looked very friendly. Howe went by the Bradby house where he would be a guest this evening at the first dinner party of the year. When he had gone the length of the picket fence, the whitest in town, he turned back. Along the path there was a fine row of asters and he went through the gate and picked one for his buttonhole. The Bradbys would be pleased if they happened to see him invading their lawn and the knowledge of this made him even more comfortable.

He reached the campus as the hour was striking. The students were hurrying to their classes. He himself was in no hurry. He stopped at his dim cubicle of an office and lit a cigarette. The prospect of facing his class had suddenly presented itself to him and his hands were cold; the lawful seizure of power he was about to make seemed momentous. Waiting did not help. He put out his cigarette, picked up a pad of theme paper, and went to his classroom.

As he entered, the rattle of voices ceased, and the twenty-odd freshmen settled themselves and looked at him appraisingly. Their faces seemed gross, his heart sank at their massed impassivity, but he spoke briskly.

'My name is Howe,' he said, and turned and wrote it on the blackboard. The carelessness of the scrawl confirmed his authority. He went on, 'My office is 412 Slemp Hall, and my office-hours are Monday, Wednesday and Friday from eleven-thirty to twelve-thirty.'

He wrote, 'M., W., F., 11:30–12:30.' He said, 'I'll be very glad to see any of you at that time. Or if you can't come then, you can arrange with me for some other time.'

He turned again to the blackboard and spoke over his shoulder. 'The text for the course is Jarman's *Modern Plays,* revised edition. The Co-op has it in stock.' He wrote the name, underlined 'revised edition' and waited for it to be taken down in the new notebooks.

When the bent heads were raised again he began his speech of prospectus. 'It is hard to explain—' he said, and paused as they composed themselves. 'It is hard to explain what a course like this is intended to do. We are going to try to learn something about modern literature and something about prose composition.'

As he spoke, his hands warmed and he was able to look directly at the class. Last year on the first day the faces had seemed just as cloddish, but as the term wore on they became gradually alive and quite likable. It did not seem possible that the same thing could happen again.

'I shall not lecture in this course,' he continued. 'Our work will be carried on by discussion and we will try to learn by an exchange of opinion. But you will soon recognize that my opinion is worth more than anyone else's here.'

He remained grave as he said it, but two boys understood and laughed. The rest took permission from them and laughed too. All Howe's private ironies protested the vulgarity of the joke, but the laughter made him feel benign and powerful.

When the little speech was finished, Howe picked up the pad of paper he had brought. He announced that they would write an extemporaneous theme. Its subject was traditional, 'Who I am and why I came to Dwight College.' By now the class was more at ease and it gave a ritualistic groan of protest. Then there was a stir as fountain pens were brought out and the writing arms of the chairs were cleared, and the paper was passed about. At last, all the heads bent to work, and the room became still.

Howe sat idly at his desk. The sun shone through the tall clumsy windows. The cool of the morning was already passing. There was a scent of autumn and of varnish and the stillness of the room was deep and oddly touching. Now and then a student's head was raised and scratched in the old, elaborate, students' pantomime that calls the teacher to witness honest intellectual effort.

Suddenly a tall boy stood within the frame of the open door. 'Is this,' he said, and thrust a large nose into a college catalogue, 'is this the meeting place of English 1A? The section instructed by Dr. Joseph Howe?'

He stood on the very sill of the door, as if refusing to enter until he was perfectly sure of all his rights. The class looked up from work, found him absurd and gave a low mocking cheer.

The teacher and the new student, with equal pointedness, ignored the disturbance. Howe nodded to the boy, who pushed his head forward and then jerked it back in a wide elaborate arc to clear his brow of a heavy lock of hair. He advanced into the room and halted before Howe, almost at attention. In a loud, clear voice he announced, 'I am Tertan, Ferdinand R., reporting at the direction of Head of Department Vincent.'

The heraldic formality of this statement brought forth another cheer. Howe looked at the class with a sternness he could not really feel, for there was indeed something ridiculous about this boy. Under his displeased regard the rows of heads dropped to work again. Then he touched Tertan's elbow, led him up to the desk and stood so as to shield their conversation from the class.

'We are writing an extemporaneous theme,' he said. 'The subject is, "Who I am and why I came to Dwight College." '

He stripped a few sheets from the pad and offered them to the boy. Tertan hesitated and then took the paper, but he held it only tentatively. As if with the effort of making something clear, he gulped, and a slow smile fixed itself on his face. It was at once knowing and shy.

'Professor,' he said, 'to be perfectly fair to my classmates'—he made a large gesture over the room—'and to you'—he inclined his head to Howe—'this would not be for me an extemporaneous subject.'

Howe tried to understand. 'You mean you've already thought about it —you've heard we always give the same subject? That doesn't matter.'

Again the boy ducked his head and gulped. It was the gesture of one who wishes to make a difficult explanation with perfect candor. 'Sir,' he said, and made the distinction with great care, 'the topic I did not expect, but I have given much ratiocination to the subject.'

Howe smiled and said, 'I don't think that's an unfair advantage. Just go ahead and write.'

Tertan narrowed his eyes and glanced sidewise at Howe. His strange mouth smiled. Then in quizzical acceptance, he ducked his head, threw back the heavy, dank lock, dropped into a seat with a great loose noise and began to write rapidly.

The room fell silent again and Howe resumed his idleness. When the bell rang, the students who had groaned when the task had been set now groaned again because they had not finished. Howe took up the papers, and held the class while he made the first assignment. When he dismissed it, Tertan bore down on him, his slack mouth held ready for speech.

'Some professors,' he said, 'are pedants. They are Dryasdusts. However, some professors are free souls and creative spirits. Kant, Hegel and Nietzsche were all professors.' With this pronouncement he paused. 'It is my opinion,' he continued, 'that you occupy the second category.'

Howe looked at the boy in surprise and said with good-natured irony, 'With Kant, Hegel, and Nietzsche?'

Not only Tertan's hand and head but his whole awkward body waved away the stupidity. 'It is the kind and not the quantity of the kind,' he said sternly.

Rebuked, Howe said as simply and seriously as he could, 'It would be nice to think so.' He added, 'Of course I am not a professor.'

This was clearly a disappointment but Tertan met it. 'In the French sense,' he said with composure. 'Generically, a teacher.'

Suddenly he bowed. It was such a bow, Howe fancied, as a stage-director might teach an actor playing a medieval student who takes leave of Abelard—stiff, solemn, with elbows close to the body and feet together. Then, quite as suddenly, he turned and left.

A queer fish, and as soon as Howe reached his office, he sifted through the batch of themes and drew out Tertan's. The boy had filled many sheets with his unformed headlong scrawl. 'Who am I?' he had begun. 'Here, in a mundane, not to say commercialized academe, is asked the question which from time long immemorably out of mind has accreted doubts and thoughts in the psyche of man to pester him as a nuisance. Whether in St.

Augustine (or Austin as sometimes called) or Miss Bashkirtsieff or Frederic Amiel or Empedocles, or in less lights of the intellect than these, this posed question has been ineluctable.'

Howe took out his pencil. He circled 'academe' and wrote 'vocab.' in the margin. He underlined 'time long immemorably out of mind' and wrote 'Diction!' But this seemed inadequate for what was wrong. He put down his pencil and read ahead to discover the principle of error in the theme. 'Today as ever, in spite of gloomy prophets of the dismal science (economics) the question is uninvalidated. Out of the starry depths of heaven hurtles this spear of query demanding to be caught on the shield of the mind ere it pierces the skull and the limbs be unstrung.'

Baffled but quite caught, Howe read on. 'Materialism, by which is meant the philosophic concept and not the moral idea, provides no aegis against the question which lies beyond the tangible (metaphysics). Existence without alloy is the question presented. Environment and heredity relegated aside, the rags and old clothes of practical life discarded, the name and the instrumentality of livelihood do not, as the prophets of the dismal science insist on in this connection, give solution to the interrogation which not from the professor merely but veritably from the cosmos is given. I think, therefore I am (cogito etc.) but who am I? Tertan I am, but what is Tertan? Of this time, of that place, of some parentage, what does it matter?'

Existence without alloy: the phrase established itself. Howe put aside Tertan's paper and at random picked up another. 'I am Arthur J. Casebeer, Jr.,' he read. 'My father is Arthur J. Casebeer and my grandfather was Arthur J. Casebeer before him. My mother is Nina Wimble Casebeer. Both of them are college graduates and my father is in insurance. I was born in St. Louis eighteen years ago and we still make our residence there.'

Arthur J. Casebeer, who knew who he was, was less interesting than Tertan, but more coherent. Howe picked up Tertan's paper again. It was clear that none of the routine marginal comments, no 'sent. str.' or 'punct.' or 'vocab.' could cope with this torrential rhetoric. He read ahead, contenting himself with underscoring the errors against the time when he should have the necessary 'conference' with Tertan.

It was a busy and official day of cards and sheets, arrangements and small decisions, and it gave Howe pleasure. Even when it was time to attend the first of the weekly Convocations he felt the charm of the beginning of things when intention is still innocent and uncorrupted by effort. He sat among the young instructors on the platform, and joined in their humorous complaints at having to assist at the ceremony, but actually he got a clear satisfaction from the ritual of prayer and prosy speech, and even from wearing his academic gown. And when the Convocation was over the pleasure continued as he crossed the campus, exchanging greetings with men he had not seen since the spring. They were people who did not yet, and perhaps never would, mean much to him, but in a year they had grown amiably to be part of his life. They were his fellow-townsmen.

The day had cooled again at sunset, and there was a bright chill in the September twilight. Howe carried his voluminous gown over his arm, he swung his doctoral hood by its purple neckpiece, and on his head he wore his mortarboard with its heavy gold tassel bobbing just over his eye. These were the weighty and absurd symbols of his new profession and they pleased him. At twenty-six Joseph Howe had discovered that he was neither so well off nor so bohemian as he had once thought. A small income, adequate when supplemented by a sizable cash legacy, was genteel poverty when the cash was all spent. And the literary life—the room at the Lafayette, or the small apartment without a lease, the long summers on the Cape, the long afternoons and the social evenings—began to weary him. His writing filled his mornings and should perhaps have filled his life, yet it did not. To the amusement of his friends, and with a certain sense that he was betraying his own freedom, he had used the last of his legacy for a year at Harvard. The small but respectable reputation of his two volumes of verse had proved useful—he continued at Harvard on a fellowship and when he emerged as Doctor Howe he received an excellent appointment, with prospects, at Dwight.

He had his moments of fear when all that had ever been said of the dangers of the academic life had occurred to him. But after a year in which he had tested every possibility of corruption and seduction he was ready to rest easy. His third volume of verse, most of it written in his first years of teaching, was not only ampler but, he thought, better than its predecessors.

There was a clear hour before the Bradby dinner party, and Howe looked forward to it. But he was not to enjoy it, for lying with his mail on the hall table was a copy of this quarter's issue of *Life and Letters,* to which his landlord subscribed. Its severe cover announced that its editor, Frederic Woolley, had this month contributed an essay called 'Two Poets,' and Howe, picking it up, curious to see who the two poets might be, felt his own name start out at him with cabalistic power—Joseph Howe. As he continued to turn the pages his hand trembled.

Standing in the dark hall, holding the neat little magazine, Howe knew that his literary contempt for Frederic Woolley meant nothing, for he suddenly understood how he respected Woolley in the way of the world. He knew this by the trembling of his hand. And of the little world as well as the great, for although the literary groups of New York might dismiss

Woolley, his name carried high authority in the academic world. At Dwight it was even a revered name, for it had been here at the college that Frederic Woolley had made the distinguished scholarly career from which he had gone on to literary journalism. In middle life he had been induced to take the editorship of *Life and Letters,* a literary monthly not widely read but heavily endowed, and in its pages he had carried on the defense of what he sometimes called the older values. He was not without wit, he had great knowledge and considerable taste, and even in the full movement of the 'new' literature he had won a certain respect for his refusal to accept it. In France, even in England, he would have been connected with a more robust tradition of conservatism, but America gave him an audience not much better than genteel. It was known in the college that to the subsidy of *Life and Letters* the Bradbys contributed a great part.

As Howe read, he saw that he was involved in nothing less than an event. When the Fifth Series of *Studies in Order and Value* came to be collected, this latest of Frederic Woolley's essays would not be merely another step in the old direction. Clearly and unmistakably, it was a turning point. All his literary life Woolley had been concerned with the relation of literature to mortality, religion, and the private and delicate pieties, and he had been unalterably opposed to all that he had called 'inhuman humanitarianism.' But here, suddenly, dramatically late, he had made an about-face, turning to the public life and to the humanitarian politics he had so long despised. This was the kind of incident the histories of literature make much of. Frederic Woolley was opening for himself a new career and winning a kind of new youth. He contrasted the two poets, Thomas Wormser, who was admirable, Joseph Howe, who was almost dangerous. He spoke of the 'precious subjectivism' of Howe's verse. 'In times like ours,' he wrote, 'with millions facing penury and want, one feels that the qualities of the *tour d'ivoire* are well-nigh inhuman, nearly insulting. The *tour d'ivoire* becomes the *tour d'ivresse,* and it is not self-intoxicated poets that our people need.' The essay said more: 'The problem is one of meaning. I am not ignorant that the creed of the esoteric poets declares that a poem does not and should not *mean* anything, that it *is* something. But poetry is what the poet makes it, and if he is a true poet he makes what his society needs. And what is needed now is the tradition in which Mr. Wormser writes, the true tradition of poetry. The Howes do no harm, but they do no good when positive good is demanded of all responsible men. Or do the Howes indeed do no harm? Perhaps Plato would have said they do, that in some ways theirs is the Phrygian music that turns men's minds from the struggle. Certainly it is true that Thomas Wormser writes in the lucid Dorian mode which sends men into battle with evil.'

It was easy to understand why Woolley had chosen to praise Thomas

Wormser. The long, lilting lines of *Corn Under Willows* hymned, as Woolley put it, the struggle for wheat in the Iowa fields, and expressed the real lives of real people. But why out of the dozen more notable examples he had chosen Howe's little volume as the example of 'precious subjectivism' was hard to guess. In a way it was funny, this multiplication of himself into 'the Howes.' And yet this becoming the multiform political symbol by whose creation Frederic Woolley gave the sign of a sudden new life, this use of him as a sacrifice whose blood was necessary for the rites of rejuvenation, made him feel oddly unclean.

Nor could Howe get rid of a certain practical resentment. As a poet he had a special and respectable place in the college life. But it might be another thing to be marked as the poet of a wilful and selfish obscurity.

As he walked to the Bradbys', Howe was a little tense and defensive. It seemed to him that all the world knew of the 'attack' and agreed with it. And, indeed, the Bradbys had read the essay but Professor Bradby, a kind and pretentious man, said, 'I see my old friend knocked you about a bit, my boy,' and his wife Eugenia looked at Howe with her childlike blue eyes and said, 'I shall *scold* Frederic for the untrue things he wrote about you. You aren't the least obscure.' They beamed at him. In their genial snobbery they seemed to feel that he had distinguished himself. He was the leader of Howeism. He enjoyed the dinner party as much as he had thought he would.

And in the following days, as he was more preoccupied with his duties, the incident was forgotten. His classes had ceased to be mere groups. Student after student detached himself from the mass and required or claimed a place in Howe's awareness. Of them all it was Tertan who first and most violently signaled his separate existence. A week after classes had begun Howe saw his silhouette on the frosted glass of his office door. It was motionless for a long time, perhaps stopped by the problem of whether or not to knock before entering. Howe called, 'Come in!' and Tertan entered with his shambling stride.

He stood beside the desk, silent and at attention. When Howe asked him to sit down, he responded with a gesture of head and hand, as if to say that such amenities were beside the point. Nevertheless, he did take the chair. He put his ragged, crammed briefcase between his legs. His face, which Howe now observed fully for the first time, was confusing, for it was made up of florid curves, the nose arched in the bone and voluted in the nostril, the mouth loose and soft and rather moist. Yet the face was so thin and narrow as to seem the very type of asceticism. Lashes of unusual length veiled the eyes and, indeed, it seemed as if there were a veil over the whole countenance. Before the words actually came, the face screwed itself into an attitude of preparation for them.

'You can confer with me now?' Tertan said.

'Yes, I'd be glad to. There are several things in your two themes I want to talk to you about.' Howe reached for the packet of themes on his desk and sought for Tertan's. But the boy was waving them away.

'These are done perforce,' he said. 'Under the pressure of your requirement. They are not significant; mere duties.' Again his great hand flapped vaguely to dismiss his themes. He leaned forward and gazed at his teacher.

'You are,' he said, 'a man of letters? You are a poet?' It was more declaration than question.

'I should like to think so,' Howe said.

At first Tertan accepted the answer with a show of appreciation, as though the understatement made a secret between himself and Howe. Then he chose to misunderstand. With his shrewd and disconcerting control of expression, he presented to Howe a puzzled grimace. 'What does that mean?' he said.

Howe retracted the irony. 'Yes. I am a poet.' It sounded strange to say.

'That,' Tertan said, 'is a wonder.' He corrected himself with his ducking head. 'I mean that is wonderful.'

Suddenly, he dived at the miserable briefcase between his legs, put it on his knees, and began to fumble with the catch, all intent on the difficulty it presented. Howe noted that his suit was worn thin, his shirt almost unclean. He became aware, even, of a vague and musty odor of garments worn too long in unaired rooms. Tertan conquered the lock and began to concentrate upon a search into the interior. At last he held in his hand what he was after, a torn and crumpled copy of *Life and Letters*.

'I learned it from here,' he said, holding it out.

Howe looked at him sharply, his hackles a little up. But the boy's face was not only perfectly innocent, it even shone with a conscious admiration. Apparently nothing of the import of the essay had touched him except the wonderful fact that his teacher was a 'man of letters.' Yet this seemed too stupid, and Howe, to test it, said, 'The man who wrote that doesn't think it's wonderful.'

Tertan made a moist hissing sound as he cleared his mouth of saliva. His head, oddly loose on his neck, wove a pattern of contempt in the air. 'A critic,' he said, 'who admits *prima facie* that he does not understand.' Then he said grandly, 'It is the inevitable fate.'

It was absurd, yet Howe was not only aware of the absurdity but of a tension suddenly and wonderfully relaxed. Now that the 'attack' was on the table between himself and this strange boy, and subject to the boy's funny and absolutely certain contempt, the hidden force of his feeling was revealed to him in the very moment that it vanished. All unsuspected, there had been a film over the world, a transparent but discoloring haze of danger. But he had no time to stop over the brightened aspect of things. Tertan was going on. 'I also am a man of letters. Putative.'

'You have written a good deal?' Howe meant to be no more than polite, and he was surprised at the tenderness he heard in his words.

Solemnly the boy nodded, threw back the dank lock, and sucked in a deep, anticipatory breath. 'First, a work of homiletics, which is a defense of the principles of religious optimism against the pessimism of Schopenhauer and the humanism of Nietzsche.'

'Humanism? Why do you call it humanism?'

'It is my nomenclature for making a deity of man,' Tertan replied negligently. 'Then three fictional works, novels. And numerous essays in science, combating materialism. Is it your duty to read these if I bring them to you?'

Howe answered simply, 'No, it isn't exactly my duty, but I shall be happy to read them.'

Tertan stood up and remained silent. He rested his bag on the chair. With a certain compunction—for it did not seem entirely proper that, of two men of letters, one should have the right to blue-pencil the other, to grade him or to question the quality of his 'sentence structure'—Howe reached for Tertan's papers. But before he could take them up, the boy suddenly made his bow-to-Abelard, the stiff inclination of the body with the hands seeming to emerge from the scholar's gown. Then he was gone.

But after his departure something was still left of him. The timbre of his curious sentences, the downright finality of so quaint a phrase as 'It is the inevitable fate' still rang in the air. Howe gave the warmth of his feeling to the new visitor who stood at the door announcing himself with a genteel clearing of the throat.

'Doctor Howe, I believe?' the student said. A large hand advanced into the room and grasped Howe's hand. 'Blackburn, sir, Theodore Blackburn, vice-president of the Student Council. A great pleasure, sir.'

Out of a pair of ruddy cheeks a pair of small eyes twinkled good-naturedly. The large face, the large body were not so much fat as beefy and suggested something 'typical'—monk, politician, or innkeeper.

Blackburn took the seat beside Howe's desk. 'I may have seemed to introduce myself in my public capacity, sir,' he said. 'But it is really as an individual that I came to see you. That is to say, as one of your students to be.'

He spoke with an English intonation and he went on, 'I was once an English major, sir.'

For a moment Howe was startled, for the roast-beef look of the boy and the manner of his speech gave a second's credibility to one sense of his statement. Then the collegiate meaning of the phrase asserted itself, but some perversity made Howe say what was not really in good taste even with so forward a student, 'Indeed? What regiment?'

Blackburn stared and then gave a little pouf-pouf of laughter. He waved the misapprehension away. '*Very* good, sir. It certainly is an ambiguous term.' He chuckled in appreciation of Howe's joke, then cleared his throat to put it aside. 'I look forward to taking your course in the romantic poets, sir,' he said earnestly. 'To me the romantic poets are the very crown of English literature.'

Howe made a dry sound, and the boy, catching some meaning in it, said, 'Little as I know them, of course. But even Shakespeare who is so dear to us of the Anglo-Saxon tradition is in a sense but the preparation for Shelley, Keats and Byron. And Wadsworth.'

Almost sorry for him, Howe dropped his eyes. With some embarrassment, for the boy was not actually his student, he said softly, 'Wordsworth.'

'Sir?'

'Wordsworth, not Wadsworth. You said Wadsworth.'

'Did I, sir?' Gravely he shook his head to rebuke himself for the error. 'Wordsworth, of course—slip of the tongue.' Then quite in command again, he went on. 'I have a favor to ask of you, Doctor Howe. You see, I began my college course as an English major,'—he smiled—'as I said.'

'Yes?'

'But after my first year I shifted. I shifted to the social sciences. Sociology and government—I find them stimulating and very *real*.' He paused, out of respect for reality. 'But now I find that perhaps I have neglected the other side.'

'The other side?' Howe said.

'Imagination, fancy, culture. A well-rounded man.' He trailed off as if there were perfect understanding between them. 'And so, sir, I have decided to end my senior year with your course in the romantic poets.'

His voice was filled with an indulgence which Howe ignored as he said flatly and gravely, 'But that course isn't given until the spring term.'

'Yes, sir, and that is where the favor comes in. Would you let me take your romantic prose course? I can't take it for credit, sir, my program is full, but just for background it seems to me that I ought to take it. I do hope,' he concluded in a manly way, 'that you will consent.'

'Well, it's no great favor, Mr. Blackburn. You can come if you wish, though there's not much point in it if you don't do the reading.'

The bell rang for the hour and Howe got up.

'May I begin with this class, sir?' Blackburn's smile was candid and boyish.

Howe nodded carelessly and together, silently, they walked to the classroom down the hall. When they reached the door Howe stood back to let his student enter, but Blackburn moved adroitly behind him and grasped him by the arm to urge him over the threshold. They entered together with Blackburn's hand firmly on Howe's biceps, the student inducting the teacher into his own room. Howe felt a surge of temper rise in him and almost violently he disengaged his arm and walked to the desk, while Blackburn found a seat in the front row and smiled at him.

II

The question was, At whose door must the tragedy be laid?

All night the snow had fallen heavily and only now was abating in sparse little flurries. The windows were valanced high with white. It was very quiet; something of the quiet of the world had reached the class, and Howe found that everyone was glad to talk or listen. In the room there was a comfortable sense of pleasure in being human.

Casebeer believed that the blame for the tragedy rested with heredity. Picking up the book he read, 'The sins of the fathers are visited on their children.' This opinion was received with general favor. Nevertheless, Johnson ventured to say that the fault was all Pastor Manders' because the Pastor had made Mrs. Alving go back to her husband and was always hiding the truth. To this Hibbard objected with logic enough, 'Well then, it was really all her husband's fault. He *did* all the bad things.' De Witt, his face bright with an impatient idea, said that the fault was all society's. 'By society I don't mean upper-crust society,' he said. He looked around a little defiantly, taking in any members of the class who might be members of upper-crust society. 'Not in that sense. I mean the social unit.'

Howe nodded and said, 'Yes, of course.'

'If the society of the time had progressed far enough in science,' De Witt went on, 'then there would be no problem for Mr. Ibsen to write about. Captain Alving plays around a little, gives way to perfectly natural biological urges, and he gets a social disease, a venereal disease. If the disease is cured, no problem. Invent salvarsan and the disease is cured. The problem of heredity disappears and li'l Oswald just doesn't get paresis. No paresis, no problem—no problem, no play.'

This was carrying the ark into battle, and the class looked at De Witt with respectful curiosity. It was his usual way and on the whole they were sympathetic with his struggle to prove to Howe that science was better than literature. Still, there was something in his reckless manner that alienated them a little.

'Or take birth-control, for instance,' De Witt went on. 'If Mrs. Alving had some knowledge of contraception, she wouldn't have had to have li'l Oswald at all. No li'l Oswald, no play.'

The class was suddenly quieter. In the back row Stettenhover swung his great football shoulders in a righteous sulking gesture, first to the right, then to the left. He puckered his mouth ostentatiously. Intellect was always ending up by talking dirty.

Tertan's hand went up, and Howe said, 'Mr. Tertan.' The boy shambled to his feet and began his long characteristic gulp. Howe made a motion with his fingers, as small as possible, and Tertan ducked his head and smiled in apology. He sat down. The class laughed. With more than half the term gone, Tertan had not been able to remember that one did not rise to speak. He seemed unable to carry on the life of the intellect without this mark of respect for it. To Howe the boy's habit of rising seemed to accord with the formal shabbiness of his dress. He never wore the casual sweaters and jackets of his classmates. Into the free and comfortable air of the college classroom he brought the stuffy sordid strictness of some crowded, metropolitan high school.

'Speaking from one sense,' Tertan began slowly, 'there is no blame ascribable. From the sense of determinism, who can say where the blame lies? The preordained is the preordained and it cannot be said without rebellion against the universe, a palpable absurdity.'

In the back row Stettenhover slumped suddenly in his seat, his heels held out before him, making a loud, dry, disgusted sound. His body sank until his neck rested on the back of his chair. He folded his hands across his belly and looked significantly out of the window, exasperated not only with Tertan, but with Howe, with the class, with the whole system designed to encourage this kind of thing. There was a certain insolence in the movement and Howe flushed. As Tertan continued to speak, Howe stalked casually toward the window and placed himself in the line of Stettenhover's vision. He stared at the great fellow, who pretended not to see him. There was so much power in the big body, so much contempt in the Greek-athlete face under the crisp Greek-athlete curls, that Howe felt almost physical fear. But at last Stettenhover admitted him to focus and under his disapproving gaze sat up with slow indifference. His eyebrows raised high in resignation, he began to examine his hands. Howe relaxed and turned his attention back to Tertan.

'Flux of existence,' Tertan was saying, 'produces all things, so that judgment wavers. Beyond the phenomena, what? But phenomena are adumbrated and to them we are limited.'

Howe saw it for a moment as perhaps it existed in the boy's mind—the world of shadows which are cast by a great light upon a hidden reality as in the old myth of the Cave. But the little brush with Stettenhover had tired him, and he said irritably, 'But come to the point, Mr. Tertan.'

He said it so sharply that some of the class looked at him curiously. For three months he had gently carried Tertan through his verbosities, to the vaguely respectful surprise of the other students, who seemed to conceive that there existed between this strange classmate and their teacher some special understanding from which they were content to be excluded. Tertan looked at him mildly, and at once came brilliantly to the point. 'This is the summation of the play,' he said and took up his book and read, ' "Your poor father never found any outlet for the overmastering joy of life that was in him. And I brought no holiday into his home, either. Everything seemed to turn upon duty and I am afraid I made your poor father's home unbearable to him, Oswald." Spoken by Mrs. Alving.'

Yes, that was surely the 'summation' of the play and Tertan had hit it, as he hit, deviously and eventually, the literary point of almost everything. But now, as always, he was wrapping it away from sight. 'For most mortals,' he said, 'there are only joys of biological urgings, gross and crass, such as the sensuous Captain Alving. For certain few there are the transmutations beyond these to a contemplation of the utter whole.'

Oh, the boy was mad. And suddenly the word, used in hyperbole, intended almost for the expression of exasperated admiration, became literal. Now that the word was used, it became simply apparent to Howe that Tertan was mad.

It was a monstrous word and stood like a bestial thing in the room. Yet it so completely comprehended everything that had puzzled Howe, it so arranged and explained what for three months had been perplexing him that almost at once its horror became domesticated. With this word Howe was able to understand why he had never been able to communicate to Tertan the value of a single criticism or correction of his wild, verbose themes. Their conferences had been frequent and long but had done nothing to reduce to order the splendid confusion of the boy's ideas. Yet, impossible though its expression was, Tertan's incandescent mind could always strike for a moment into some dark corner of thought.

And now it was suddenly apparent that it was not a faulty rhetoric that Howe had to contend with. With his new knowledge he looked at Tertan's face and wondered how he could have so long deceived himself. Tertan was still talking, and the class had lapsed into a kind of patient unconsciousness, a coma of respect for words which, for all that most of them knew, might be profound. Almost with a suffusion of shame, Howe believed that in some dim way the class had long ago had some intimation of Tertan's madness. He reached out as decisively as he could to seize the thread of Tertan's discourse before it should be entangled further.

'Mr. Tertan says that the blame must be put upon whoever kills the joy of living in another. We have been assuming that Captain Alving was a wholly bad man, but what if we assume that he became bad only because Mrs. Alving, when they were first married, acted toward him in the prudish way she says she did?'

It was a ticklish idea to advance to freshmen and perhaps not profitable. Not all of them were following.

'That would put the blame on Mrs. Alving herself, whom most of you admire. And she herself seems to think so.' He glanced at his watch. The hour was nearly over. 'What do you think, Mr. De Witt?'

De Witt rose to the idea; he wanted to know if society couldn't be blamed for educating Mrs. Alving's temperament in the wrong way. Casebeer was puzzled, Stettenhover continued to look at his hands until the bell rang.

Tertan, his brows louring in thought, was making as always for a private word. Howe gathered his books and papers to leave quickly. At this moment of his discovery and with the knowledge still raw, he could not engage himself with Tertan. Tertan sucked in his breath to prepare for speech and Howe made ready for the pain and confusion. But at that moment Casebeer detached himself from the group with which he had been conferring and which he seemed to represent. His constituency remained at a tactful distance. The mission involved the time of an assigned essay. Casebeer's presentation of the plea—it was based on the freshmen's heavy duties at the fraternities during Carnival Week—cut across Tertan's preparations for speech. 'And so some of us fellows thought,' Casebeer concluded with heavy solemnity, 'that we could do a better job, give our minds to it more, if we had more time.'

Tertan regarded Casebeer with mingled curiosity and revulsion. Howe not only said that he would postpone the assignment but went on to talk about the Carnival, and even drew the waiting constituency into the conversation. He was conscious of Tertan's stern and astonished stare, then of his sudden departure.

Now that the fact was clear, Howe knew that he must act on it. His course was simple enough. He must lay the case before the Dean. Yet he hesitated. His feeling for Tertan must now, certainly, be in some way invalidated. Yet could he, because of a word, hurry to assign to official and reasonable solicitude what had been, until this moment, so various and warm? He could at least delay and, by moving slowly, lend a poor grace to the necessary, ugly act of making his report.

It was with some notion of keeping the matter in his own hands that he went to the Dean's office to look up Tertan's records. In the outer office the Dean's secretary greeted him brightly, and at his request brought him the manila folder with the small identifying photograph pasted in the corner. She laughed. 'He was looking for the birdie in the wrong place,' she said.

Howe leaned over her shoulder to look at the picture. It was as bad as all the Dean's-office photographs were, but it differed from all that Howe had ever seen. Tertan, instead of looking into the camera, as no doubt he had been bidden, had, at the moment of exposure, turned his eyes upward. His mouth, as though conscious of the trick played on the photographer, had the sly superior look that Howe knew.

The secretary was fascinated by the picture. 'What a funny boy,' she said. 'He looks like Tartuffe!'

And so he did, with the absurd piety of the eyes and the conscious slyness of the mouth and the whole face bloated by the bad lens.

'Is he *like* that?' the secretary said.

'Like Tartuffe? No.'

From the photograph there was little enough comfort to be had. The records themselves gave no clue to madness, though they suggested sadness enough. Howe read of a father, Stanislaus Tertan, born in Budapest and trained in engineering in Berlin, once employed by the Hercules Chemical Corporation—this was one of the factories that dominated the sound end of the town—but now without employment. He read of a mother Erminie (Youngfellow) Tertan, born in Manchester, educated at a Normal School at Leeds, now housewife by profession. The family lived on Greenbriar Street which Howe knew as a row of once elegant homes near what was now the factory district. The old mansion had long ago been divided into small and primitive apartments. Of Ferdinand himself there was little to learn. He lived with his parents, had attended a Detroit high school and had transferred to the local school in his last year. His rating for intelligence, as expressed in numbers, was high, his scholastic record was remarkable, he held a college scholarship for his tuition.

Howe laid the folder on the secretary's desk. 'Did you find what you wanted to know?' she asked.

The phrases from Tertan's momentous first theme came back to him. 'Tertan I am, but what is Tertan? Of this time, of that place, of some parentage, what does it matter?'

'No, I didn't find it,' he said.

Now that he had consulted the sad, half-meaningless record he knew all the more firmly that he must not give the matter out of his own hands. He must not release Tertan to authority. Not that he anticipated from the Dean anything but the greatest kindness for Tertan. The Dean would have the experience and skill which he himself could not have. One way or another the Dean could answer the question, 'What is Tertan?' Yet this was precisely what he feared. He alone could keep alive—not forever but for a somehow important time—the question, 'What is Tertan?' He alone could keep it still a question. Some sure instinct told him that he must not surrender the question to a clean official desk in a clear official light to be dealt with, settled and closed.

He heard himself saying, 'Is the Dean busy at the moment? I'd like to see him.'

His request came thus unbidden, even forbidden, and it was one of the surprising and startling incidents of his life. Later when he reviewed the events, so disconnected in themselves, or so merely odd, of the story that unfolded for him that year, it was over this moment, on its face the least notable, that he paused longest. It was frequently to be with fear and never without a certainty of its meaning in his own knowledge of himself that he would recall this simple, routine request, and the feeling of shame and freedom it gave him as he sent everything down the official chute. In the end, of course, no matter what he did to 'protect' Tertan, he would have had to make the same request and lay the matter on the Dean's clean desk. But it would always be a landmark of his life that, at the very moment when he was rejecting the official way, he had been, without will or intention, so gladly drawn to it.

After the storm's last delicate flurry, the sun had come out. Reflected by the new snow, it filled the office with a golden light which was almost musical in the way it made all the commonplace objects of efficiency shine with a sudden sad and noble significance. And the light, now that he noticed it, made the utterance of his perverse and unwanted request even more momentous.

The secretary consulted the engagement pad. 'He'll be free any minute. Don't you want to wait in the parlor?'

She threw open the door of the large and pleasant room in which the Dean held his Committee meetings, and in which his visitors waited. It was designed with a homely elegance on the masculine side of the eighteenth-century manner. There was a small coal fire in the grate and the handsome mahogany table was strewn with books and magazines. The large windows gave on the snowy lawn, and there was such a fine width of window that the white casements and walls seemed at this moment but a continuation of the snow, the snow but an extension of casement and walls. The outdoors seemed taken in and made safe, the indoors seemed luxuriously freshened and expanded.

Howe sat down by the fire and lighted a cigarette. The room had its intended effect upon him. He felt comfortable and relaxed, yet nicely organized, some young diplomatic agent of the eighteenth century, the newly fledged Swift carrying out Sir William Temple's business. The rawness of Tertan's case quite vanished. He crossed his legs and reached for a magazine.

It was that famous issue of *Life and Letters* that his idle hand had found and his blood raced as he sifted through it, and the shape of his own name, Joseph Howe, sprang out at him, still cabalistic in its power. He tossed the magazine back on the table as the door of the Dean's office opened and the Dean ushered out Theodore Blackburn.

'Ah, Joseph!' the Dean said.

Blackburn said, 'Good morning, Doctor.' Howe winced at the title and caught the flicker of amusement over the Dean's face. The Dean stood with his hand high on the door-jamb and Blackburn, still in the doorway, remained standing almost under his long arm.

Howe nodded briefly to Blackburn, snubbing his eager deference. 'Can you give me a few minutes?' he said to the Dean.

'All the time you want. Come in.' Before the two men could enter the office, Blackburn claimed their attention with a long full 'Er.' As they turned to him, Blackburn said, 'Can *you* give *me* a few minutes, Doctor Howe?' His eyes sparkled at the little audacity he had committed, the slightly impudent play with hierarchy. Of the three of them Blackburn kept himself the lowest, but he reminded Howe of his subaltern relation to the Dean.

'I mean, of course,' Blackburn went on easily, 'when you've finished with the Dean.'

'I'll be in my office shortly,' Howe said, turned his back on the ready 'Thank you, sir,' and followed the Dean into the inner room.

'Energetic boy,' said the Dean. 'A bit beyond himself but very energetic. Sit down.'

The Dean lighted a cigarette, leaned back in his chair, sat easy and silent for a moment, giving Howe no signal to go ahead with business. He was a young Dean, not much beyond forty, a tall handsome man with sad, ambitious eyes. He had been a Rhodes scholar. His friends looked for great things from him, and it was generally said that he had notions of education which he was not yet ready to try to put into practice.

His relaxed silence was meant as a compliment to Howe. He smiled and said, 'What's the business, Joseph?'

'Do you know Tertan—Ferdinand Tertan, a freshman?'

The Dean's cigarette was in his mouth and his hands were clasped behind his head. He did not seem to search his memory for the name. He said, 'What about him?'

Clearly the Dean knew something, and he was waiting for Howe to tell him more. Howe moved only tentatively. Now that he was doing what he had resolved not to do, he felt more guilty at having been so long deceived by Tertan and more need to be loyal to his error.

'He's a strange fellow,' he ventured. He said stubbornly, 'In a strange way he's very brilliant.' He concluded, 'But very strange.'

The springs of the Dean's swivel chair creaked as he came out of his sprawl and leaned forward to Howe. 'Do you mean he's so strange that it's something you could give a name to?'

Howe looked at him stupidly. 'What do you mean?' he said.

'What's his trouble?' the Dean said more neutrally.

'He's very brilliant, in a way. I looked him up and he has a top intelligence rating. But somehow, and it's hard to explain just how, what he says is always on the edge of sense and doesn't quite make it.'

The Dean looked at him and Howe flushed up. The Dean had surely read Woolley on the subject of 'the Howes' and the *tour d'ivresse*. Was that quick glance ironical?

The Dean picked up some papers from his desk, and Howe could see that they were in Tertan's impatient scrawl. Perhaps the little gleam in the Dean's glance had come only from putting facts together.

'He sent me this yesterday,' the Dean said. 'After an inverview I had with him. I haven't been able to do more than glance at it. When you said what you did, I realized there was something wrong.'

Twisting his mouth, the Dean looked over the letter. 'You seem to be involved,' he said without looking up. 'By the way, what did you give him at mid-term?'

Flushing, setting his shoulders, Howe said firmly, 'I gave him A-minus.'

The Dean chuckled. 'Might be a good idea if some of our nicer boys went crazy—just a little.' He said, 'Well,' to conclude the matter and handed the papers to Howe. 'See if this is the same thing you've been finding. Then we can go into the matter again.'

Before the fire in the parlor, in the chair that Howe had been occupying, sat Blackburn. He sprang to his feet as Howe entered.

'I said my office, Mr. Blackburn.' Howe's voice was sharp. Then he was almost sorry for the rebuke, so clearly and naïvely did Blackburn seem to relish his stay in the parlor, close to authority.

'I'm in a bit of a hurry, sir,' he said, 'and I did want to be sure to speak to you, sir.'

He was really absurd, yet fifteen years from now he would have grown up to himself, to the assurance and mature beefiness. In banks, in consular offices, in brokerage firms, on the bench, more seriously affable, a little sterner, he would make use of his ability to be administered by his job. It was almost reassuring. Now he was exercising his too-great skill on Howe. 'I owe you an apology, sir,' he said.

Howe knew that he did, but he showed surprise.

'I mean, Doctor, after your having been so kind about letting me attend your class, I stopped coming.' He smiled in deprecation. 'Extracurricular activities take up so much of my time. I'm afraid I undertook more than I could perform.'

Howe had noticed the absence and had been a little irritated by it after Blackburn's elaborate plea. It was an absence that might be interpreted as a comment on the teacher. But there was only one way for him to answer. 'You've no need to apologize,' he said. 'It's wholly your affair.'

Blackburn beamed. 'I'm so glad you feel that way about it, sir. I was worried you might think I had stayed away because I was influenced by ——' He stopped and lowered his eyes.

Astonished, Howe said, 'Influenced by what?'

'Well, by——' Blackburn hesitated and for answer pointed to the table on which lay the copy of *Life and Letters*. Without looking at it, he knew where to direct his hand. 'By the unfavorable publicity, sir.' He hurried on. 'And that brings me to another point, sir. I am vice president of Quill and Scroll, sir, the student literary society, and I wonder if you would address us. You could read your own poetry, sir, and defend your own point of view. It would be very interesting.'

It was truly amazing. Howe looked long and cruelly into Blackburn's face, trying to catch the secret of the mind that could have conceived this way of manipulating him, this way so daring and inept—but not entirely inept—with its malice so without malignity. The face did not yield its secret. Howe smiled broadly and said, 'Of course I don't think you were influenced by the unfavorably publicity.'

'I'm still going to take—regularly, for credit—your romantic poets course next term,' Blackburn said.

'Don't worry, my dear fellow, don't worry about it.'

Howe started to leave and Blackburn stopped him with, 'But about Quill, sir?'

'Suppose we wait until next term? I'll be less busy then.'

And Blackburn said, 'Very good, sir, and thank you.'

In his office the little encounter seemed less funny to Howe, was even in some indeterminate way disturbing. He made an effort to put it from his mind by turning to what was sure to disturb him more, the Tertan letter read in the new interpretation. He found what he had always found, the same florid leaps beyond fact and meaning, the same headlong certainty. But as his eye passed over the familiar scrawl it caught his own name, and for the second time that hour he felt the race of his blood.

'The Paraclete,' Tertan had written to the Dean, 'from a Greek word meaning to stand in place of, but going beyond the primitive idea to mean traditionally the helper, the one who comforts and assists, cannot without fundamental loss be jettisoned. Even if taken no longer in the supernatural sense, the concept remains deeply in the human consciousness inevitably.

Humanitarianism is no reply, for not every man stands in the place of every other man for this other comrade's comfort. But certain are chosen out of the human race to be the consoler of some other. Of these, for example, is Joseph Barker Howe, Ph.D. Of intellects not the first yet of true intellect and lambent instructions, given to that which is intuitive and irrational, not to what is logical in the strict word, what is judged by him is of the heart and not the head. Here is one chosen, in that he chooses himself to stand in the place of another for comfort and consolation. To him more than another I give my gratitude, with all respect to our Dean who reads this, a noble man, but merely dedicated, not consecrated. But not in the aspect of the Paraclete only is Dr. Joseph Baker Howe established, for he must be the Paraclete to another aspect of himself, that which is driven and persecuted by the lack of understanding in the world at large, so that he in himself embodies the full history of man's tribulations and, overflowing upon others, notably the present writer, is the ultimate end.'

This was love. There was no escape from it. Try as Howe might to remember that Tertan was mad and all his emotions invalidated, he could not destroy the effect upon him of his student's stern, affectionate regard. He had betrayed not only a power of mind but a power of love. And, however firmly he held before his attention the fact of Tertan's madness, he could do nothing to banish the physical sensation of gratitude he felt. He had never thought of himself as 'driven and persecuted' and he did not now. But still he could not make meaningless his sensation of gratitude. The pitiable Tertan sternly pitied him, and comfort came from Tertan's never-to-be-comforted mind.

III

In an academic community, even an efficient one, official matters move slowly. The term drew to a close with no action in the case of Tertan, and Joseph Howe had to confront a curious problem. How should he grade his strange student, Tertan?

Tertan's final examination had been no different from all his other writing, and what did one 'give' such a student? De Witt must have his A, that was clear. Johnson would get a B. With Casebeer it was a question of a B-minus or a C-plus, and Stettenhover, who had been crammed by the team tutor to fill half a blue-book with his thin feminine scrawl, would have his C-minus which he would accept with mingled indifference and resentment. But with Tertan it was not so easy.

The boy was still in the college process and his name could not be omitted from the grade sheet. Yet what should a mind under suspicion of madness be graded? Until the medical verdict was given, it was for Howe to continue as Tertan's teacher and to keep his judgment pedagogical. Impossible to give him an F: he had not failed. B was for Johnson's stolid mediocrity. He could not be put on the edge of passing with Stettenhover, for he exactly did not pass. In energy and richness of intellect he was perhaps even De Witt's superior and Howe toyed grimly with the notion of giving him an A, but that would lower the value of the A De Witt had won with his beautiful and clear, if still arrogant, mind. There was a notation which the Registrar recognized—Inc. for Incomplete, and in the horrible comedy of the situation, Howe considered that. But really only a mark of M for Mad would serve.

In his perplexity, Howe sought the Dean, but the Dean was out of town. In the end, he decided to maintain the A-minus he had given Tertan at mid-term. After all, there had been no falling away from that quality. He entered it on the grade sheet with something like bravado.

Academic time moves quickly. A college year is not really a year, lacking as it does three months. And it is endlessly divided into units which, at their beginning, appear larger than they are—terms, half-terms, months, weeks. And the ultimate unit, the hour, is not really an hour, lacking as it does ten minutes. And so the new term advanced rapidly, and one day the fields about the town were all brown, cleared of even the few thin patches of snow which had lingered so long.

Howe, as he lectured on the romantic poets, became conscious of Blackburn emanating wrath. Blackburn did it well, did it with enormous dignity. He did not stir in his seat, he kept his eyes fixed on Howe in perfect attention, but he abstained from using his notebook, there was no mistaking what he proposed to himself as an attitude. His elbow on the writing-wing of the chair, his chin on the curled fingers of his hand, he was the embodiment of intellectual indignation. He was thinking his own thoughts, would give no public offense, yet would claim his due, was not to be intimidated. Howe knew that he would present himself at the end of the hour.

Blackburn entered the office without invitation. He did not smile; there was no cajolery about him. Without invitation he sat down beside Howe's desk. He did not speak until he had taken the blue-book from his pocket. He said, 'What does this mean, sir?'

It was a sound and conservative student tactic. Said in the usual way it meant, 'How could you have so misunderstood me?' or 'What does this mean for my future in the course?' But there were none of the humbler tones in Blackburn's way of saying it.

Howe made the established reply, 'I think that's for you to tell me.'

Blackburn continued icy. 'I'm sure I can't, sir.'

There was a silence between them. Both dropped their eyes to the blue-book on the desk. On its cover Howe had penciled: 'F. This is very poor work.'

Howe picked up the blue-book. There was always the possibility of injustice. The teacher may be bored by the mass of papers and not wholly attentive. A phrase, even the student's handwriting, may irritate him unreasonably. 'Well,' said Howe, 'let's go through it.'

He opened the first page. 'Now here: you write, "In *The Ancient Mariner,* Coleridge lives in and transports us to a honey-sweet world where all is rich and strange, a world of charm to which we can escape from the humdrum existence of our daily lives, the world of romance. Here, in this warm and honey-sweet land of charming dreams we can relax and enjoy ourselves." '

Howe lowered the paper and waited with a neutral look for Blackburn to speak. Blackburn returned the look boldly, did not speak, sat stolid and lofty. At last Howe said, speaking gently, 'Did you mean that, or were you just at a loss for something to say?'

'You imply that I was just "bluffing"?' The quotation marks hung palpable in the air about the word.

'I'd like to know. I'd prefer believing that you were bluffing to believing that you really thought this.'

Blackburn's eyebrows went up. From the height of a great and firm-based idea he looked at his teacher. He clasped the crags for a moment and then pounced, craftily, suavely. 'Do you mean, Doctor Howe, that there aren't two opinions possible?'

It was superbly done in its air of putting all of Howe's intellectual life into the balance. Howe remained patient and simple. 'Yes, many opinions are possible, but not this one. Whatever anyone believes of *The Ancient Mariner,* no one can in reason believe that it represents a—a honey-sweet world in which we can relax.'

'But that is what I *feel,* sir.'

This was well-done, too. Howe said, 'Look, Mr. Blackburn. Do you really relax with hunger and thirst, the heat and the sea-serpents, the dead men with staring eyes, Life in Death and the skeletons? Come now, Mr. Blackburn.'

Blackburn made no answer, and Howe pressed forward. 'Now, you say of Wordsworth, "Of peasant stock himself, he turned from the effete life of the salons and found in the peasant the hope of a flaming revolution which would sweep away all the old ideas. This is the subject of his best poems." '

Beaming at his teacher with youthful eagerness, Blackburn said, 'Yes, sir, a rebel, a bringer of light to suffering mankind. I see him as a kind of Prothemeus.'

'A kind of what?'

'Prothemeus, sir.'

'Think, Mr. Blackburn. We were talking about him only today and I mentioned his name a dozen times. You don't mean Prothemeus. You mean——' Howe waited, but there was no response.

'You mean Prometheus.'

Blackburn gave no assent, and Howe took the reins. 'You've done a bad job here, Mr. Blackburn, about as bad as could be done.' He saw Blackburn stiffen and his genial face harden again. 'It shows either a lack of preparation or a complete lack of understanding.' He saw Blackburn's face begin to go to pieces and he stopped.

'Oh, sir,' Blackburn burst out, 'I've never had a mark like this before, never anything below a B, never. A thing like this has never happened to me before.'

It must be true, it was a statement too easily verified. Could it be that other instructors accepted such flaunting nonsense? Howe wanted to end the interview. 'I'll set it down to lack of preparation,' he said. 'I know you're busy. That's not an excuse, but it's an explanation. Now, suppose you really prepare, and then take another quiz in two weeks. We'll forget this one and count the other.'

Blackburn squirmed with pleasure and gratitude. 'Thank you, sir. You're really very kind, very kind.'

Howe rose to conclude the visit. 'All right, then—in two weeks.'

It was that day that the Dean imparted to Howe the conclusion of the case of Tertan. It was simple and a little anticlimactic. A physician had been called in, and had said the word, given the name.

'A classic case, he called it,' the Dean said. 'Not a doubt in the world,' he said. His eyes were full of miserable pity, and he clutched at a word. 'A classic case, a classic case.' To his aid and to Howe's there came the Parthenon and the form of the Greek drama, the Aristotelian logic, Racine and the Well-Tempered Clavichord, the blueness of the Aegean and its clear sky. Classic—that is to say, without a doubt, perfect in its way, a veritable model, and, as the Dean had been told, sure to take a perfectly predictable and inevitable course to a foreknown conclusion.

It was not only pity that stood in the Dean's eyes. For a moment there was fear too. 'Terrible,' he said, 'it is simply terrible.'

Then he went on briskly. 'Naturally, we've told the boy nothing. And, naturally, we won't. His tuition's paid by his scholarship, and we'll continue him on the rolls until the end of the year. That will be kindest. After that the matter will be out of our control. We'll see, of course, that he gets into the proper hands. I'm told there will be no change, he'll go on like this, be as good as this, for four to six months. And so we'll just go along as usual.'

So Tertan continued to sit in Section 5 of English 1A, to his classmates still a figure of curiously dignified fun, symbol to most of them of the respectable but absurd intellectual life. But to his teacher he was now very different. He had not changed—he was still the grayhound casting for the scent of ideas, and Howe could see that he was still the same Tertan, but he could not feel it. What he felt as he looked at the boy sitting in his accustomed place was the hard blank of a fact. The fact itself was formidable and depressing. But what Howe was chiefly aware of was that he had permitted the metamorphosis of Tertan from person to fact.

As much as possible he avoided seeing Tertan's upraised hand and eager eye. But the fact did not know of its mere factuality, it continued its existence as if it were Tertan, hand up and eye questioning, and one day it appeared in Howe's office with a document.

'Even the spirit who lives egregiously, above the herd, must have its relations with the fellowman,' Tertan declared. He laid the document on Howe's desk. It was headed 'Quill and Scroll Society of Dwight College. Application for Membership.'

'In most ways these are crass minds,' Tertan said, touching the paper. 'Yet as a whole, bound together in their common love of letters, they transcend their intellectual lacks since it is not a paradox that the whole is greater than the sum of its parts.'

'When are the elections?' Howe asked.

'They take place tomorrow.'

'I certainly hope you will be successful.'

'Thank you. Would you wish to implement that hope?' A rather dirty finger pointed to the bottom of the sheet. 'A faculty recommender is necessary,' Tertan said stiffly, and waited.

'And you wish me to recommend you?'

'It would be an honor.'

'You may use my name.'

Tertan's finger pointed again. 'It must be a written sponsorship, signed by the sponsor.' There was a large blank space on the form under the heading, 'Opinion of Faculty Sponsor.'

This was almost another thing and Howe hesitated. Yet there was nothing else to do and he took out his fountain pen. He wrote, 'Mr. Ferdinand Tertan is marked by his intense devotion to letters and by his exceptional love of all things of the mind.' To this he signed his name, which looked bold and assertive on the white page. It disturbed him, the strange affirming power of a name. With a businesslike air, Tertan whipped up the paper, folded it with decision and put it into his pocket. He bowed and took his departure, leaving Howe with the sense of having done something oddly momentous.

And so much now seemed odd and momentous to Howe that should not have seemed so. It was odd and momentous, he felt, when he sat with Blackburn's second quiz before him, and wrote in an excessively firm hand the grade of C-minus. The paper was a clear, an indisputable failure. He was carefully and consciously committing a cowardice. Blackburn had told the truth when he had pleaded his past record. Howe had consulted it in the Dean's office. It showed no grade lower than a B-minus. A canvass of some of Blackburn's previous instructors had brought vague attestations to the adequate powers of a student imperfectly remembered, and sometimes surprise that his abilities could be questioned at all.

As he wrote the grade, Howe told himself that his cowardice sprang from an unwillingness to have more dealings with a student he disliked. He knew it was simpler than that. He knew he feared Blackburn: that was the absurd truth. And cowardice did not solve the matter after all. Blackburn, flushed with a first success, attacked at once. The minimal passing grade had not assuaged his feelings and he sat at Howe's desk and again the blue-book lay between them. Blackburn said nothing. With an enormous impudence, he was waiting for Howe to speak and explain himself.

At last Howe said sharply and rudely, 'Well?' His throat was tense and the blood was hammering in his head. His mouth was tight with anger at himself for his disturbance.

Blackburn's glance was almost baleful. 'This is impossible, sir.'

'But there it is,' Howe answered.

'Sir?' Blackburn had not caught the meaning but his tone was still haughty.

Impatiently Howe said, 'There it is, plain as day. Are you here to complain again?'

'Indeed I am, sir.' There was surprise in Blackburn's voice that Howe should ask the question.

'I shouldn't complain if I were you. You did a thoroughly bad job on your first quiz. This one is a little, only a very little, better.' This was not true. If anything, it was worse.

'That might be a matter of opinion, sir.'

'It is a matter of opinion. Of my opinion.'

'Another opinion might be different, sir.'

'You really believe that?' Howe said.

'Yes.' The omission of the 'sir' was monumental.

'Whose, for example?'

'The Dean's, for example.' Then the fleshy jaw came forward a little. 'Or a certain literary critic's, for example.'

It was colossal and almost too much for Blackburn himself to handle. The solidity of his face almost crumpled under it. But he withstood his own audacity and went on. 'And the Dean's opinion might be guided by the knowledge that the person who gave me this mark is the man whom a famous critic, the most eminent judge of literature in this country, called a drunken man. The Dean might think twice about whether such a man is fit to teach Dwight students.'

Howe said in quiet admonition, 'Blackburn, you're mad,' meaning no more than to check the boy's extravagance.

But Blackburn paid no heed. He had another shot in the locker. 'And the Dean might be guided by the information, of which I have evidence, documentary evidence,'—he slapped his breast pocket twice—'that this same person personally recommended to the college literary society, the oldest in the country, that he personally recommended a student who is crazy, who threw the meeting into an uproar—a psychiatric case. The Dean might take that into account.'

Howe was never to learn the details of that 'uproar.' He had always to content himself with the dim but passionate picture which at that moment sprang into his mind, of Tertan standing on some abstract height and madly denouncing the multitude of Quill and Scroll who howled him down.

He sat quiet a moment and looked at Blackburn. The ferocity had entirely gone from the student's face. He sat regarding his teacher almost benevolently. He had played a good card and now, scarcely at all unfriendly, he was waiting to see the effect. Howe took up the blue-book and negligently sifted through it. He read a page, closed the book, struck out the C-minus and wrote an F.

'Now you may take the paper to the Dean,' he said. 'You may tell him that after reconsidering it, I lowered the grade.'

The gasp was audible. 'Oh, sir!' Blackburn cried. 'Please!' His face was agonized. 'It means my graduation, my livelihood, my future. Don't do this to me.'

'It's done already.'

Blackburn stood up. 'I spoke rashly, sir, hastily. I had no intention, no real intention, of seeing the Dean. It rests with you—entirely, entirely. I *hope* you will restore the first mark.'

'Take the matter to the Dean or not, just as you choose. The grade is what you deserve and it stands.'

Blackburn's head dropped. 'And will I be failed at mid-term, sir?'

'Of course.'

From deep out of Blackburn's great chest rose a cry of anguish. 'Oh, sir, if you want me to go down on my knees to you, I will, I will.'

Howe looked at him in amazement.

'I will, I will. On my knees, sir. This mustn't, mustn't happen.'

He spoke so literally, meaning so very truly that his knees and exactly his knees were involved and seeming to think that he was offering something of tangible value to his teacher, that Howe, whose head had become icy clear in the nonsensical drama, thought, 'The boy is mad,' and began to speculate fantastically whether something in himself attracted or developed aberration. He could see himself standing absurdly before the Dean and saying, 'I've found another. This time it's the Vice-president of the Council, the manager of the debating team and secretary of Quill and Scroll.'

One more such discovery, he thought, and he himself would be discovered! And there, suddenly, Blackburn was on his knees with a thump, his huge thighs straining his trousers, his hand outstretched in a great gesture of supplication.

With a cry, Howe shoved back his swivel chair and it rolled away on its casters half across the little room. Blackburn knelt for a moment to nothing at all, then got to his feet.

Howe rose abruptly. He said, 'Blackburn, you will stop acting like an idiot. Dust your knees off, take your paper and get out. You've behaved like a fool and a malicious person. You have half a term to do a decent job. Keep your silly mouth shut and try to do it. Now get out.'

Blackburn's head was low. He raised it and there was a pious light in his eyes. 'Will you shake hands, sir?' he said. He thrust out his hand.

'I will not,' Howe said.

Head and hand sank together. Blackburn picked up his blue-book and walked to the door. He turned and said, 'Thank you, sir.' His back, as he departed, was heavy with tragedy and stateliness.

IV

After years of bad luck with the weather, the College had a perfect day for Commencement. It was wonderfully bright, the air so transparent, the wind so brisk that no one could resist talking about it.

As Howe set out for the campus he heard Hilda calling from the back yard. She called, 'Professor, professor,' and came running to him.

Howe said, 'What's this "professor" business?'

'Mother told me,' Hilda said. 'You've been promoted. And I want to take your picture.'

'Next year,' said Howe. 'I won't be a professor until next year. And you know better than to call anybody "professor." '

'It was just in fun,' Hilda said. She seemed disappointed.

'But you can take my picture if you want. I won't look much different next year.' Still, it was frightening. It might mean that he was to stay in this town all his life.

Hilda brightened. 'Can I take it in this?' she said, and touched the gown he carried over his arm.

Howe laughed. 'Yes, you can take it in this.'

'I'll get my things and meet you in front of Otis,' Hilda said. 'I have the background all picked out.'

On the campus the Commencement crowd was already large. It stood about in eager, nervous little family groups. As he crossed, Howe was greeted by a student, capped and gowned, glad of the chance to make an event for his parents by introducing one of his teachers. It was while Howe stood there chatting that he saw Tertan.

He had never seen anyone quite so alone, as though a circle had been woven about him to separate him from the gay crowd on the campus. Not that Tertan was not gay, he was the gayest of all. Three weeks had passed since Howe had last seen him, the weeks of examination, the lazy week before Commencement, and this was now a different Tertan. On his head he wore a panama hat, broad-brimmed and fine, of the shape associated with South American planters. He wore a suit of raw silk, luxurious, but yellowed with age and much too tight, and he sported a whangee cane. He walked sedately, the hat tilted at a devastating angle, the stick coming up and down in time to his measured tread. He had, Howe guessed, outfitted himself to greet the day in the clothes of that ruined father whose existence was on record in the Dean's office. Gravely and arrogantly he surveyed the scene—in it, his whole bearing seemed to say, but not of it. With his haughty step, with his flashing eye, Tertan was coming nearer. Howe did not wish to be seen. He shifted his position slightly. When he looked again, Tertan was not in sight.

The chapel clock struck the quarter hour. Howe detached himself from his chat and hurried to Otis Hall at the far end of the campus. Hilda had not yet come. He went up into the high portico and, using the glass of the door for a mirror, put on his gown, adjusted the hood on his shoulders and set the mortarboard on his head. When he came down the steps, Hilda had arrived.

Nothing could have told him more forcibly that a year had passed than the development of Hilda's photographic possessions from the box camera of the previous fall. By a strap about her neck was hung a leather case, so thick and strong, so carefully stitched and so molded to its contents that it could only hold a costly camera. The appearance was deceptive, Howe knew, for he had been present at the Aikens' pre-Christmas conference about its purchase. It was only a fairly good domestic camera. Still, it looked very impressive. Hilda carried another leather case from which she drew a collapsible tripod. Decisively she extended each of its gleaming legs and set it up on the path. She removed the camera from its case and fixed it to the tripod. In its compact efficiency the camera almost had a life of its own, but Hilda treated it with easy familiarity, looked into its eye, glanced casually at its guages. Then from a pocket she took still another leather case and drew from it a small instrument through which she looked first at Howe, who began to feel inanimate and lost, and then at the sky. She made some adjustment on the instrument, then some adjustment on the camera. She swept the scene with her eye, found a spot and pointed the camera in its direction. She walked to the spot, stood on it and beckoned to Howe. With each new leather case, with each new instrument, and with each new adjustment she had grown in ease and now she said, 'Joe, will you stand here?'

Obediently Howe stood where he was bidden. She had yet another instrument. She took out a tape-measure on a mechanical spool. Kneeling down before Howe, she put the little metal ring of the tape under the tip of his shoe. At her request, Howe pressed it with his toe. When she had measured her distance, she nodded to Howe who released the tape. At a touch, it sprang back into the spool. 'You have to be careful if you're going to get what you want,' Hilda said. 'I don't believe in all this snap-snap-snapping,' she remarked loftily. Howe nodded in agreement, although he was beginning to think Hilda's care excessive.

Now at last the moment had come. Hilda squinted into the camera, moved the tripod slightly. She stood to the side, holding the plunger of the shutter-cable. 'Ready,' she said. 'Will you relax, Joseph, please?' Howe realized that he was standing frozen. Hilda stood poised and precise as a setter, one hand holding the little cable, the other extended with curled dainty fingers like a dancer's, as if expressing to her subject the precarious delicacy of the moment. She pressed the plunger and there was the click. At once she stirred to action, got behind the camera, turned a new exposure. 'Thank you,' she said. 'Would you stand under that tree and let me do a character study with light and shade?'

The childish absurdity of the remark restored Howe's ease. He went to the little tree. The pattern the leaves made on his gown was what Hilda was after. He had just taken a satisfactory position when he heard in the unmistakable voice, 'Ah, Doctor! Having your picture taken?'

Howe gave up the pose and turned to Blackburn who stood on the walk, his hands behind his back, a little too large for his bachelor's gown. Annoyed that Blackburn should see him posing for a character study in light and shade, Howe said irritably, 'Yes, having my picture taken.'

Blackburn beamed at Hilda. 'And the little photographer?' he said. Hilda fixed her eyes on the ground and stood closer to her brilliant and aggressive camera. Blackburn, teetering on his heels, his hands behind his back, wholly prelatical and benignly patient, was not abashed at the silence. At last Howe said, 'If you'll excuse us, Mr. Blackburn, we'll go on with the picture.'

'Go right ahead, sir. I'm running along.' But he only came closer. 'Doctor Howe,' he said fervently, 'I want to tell you how glad I am that I was able to satisfy your standards at last.'

Howe was surprised at the hard, insulting brightness of his own voice, and even Hilda looked up curiously as he said, 'Nothing you have ever done has satisfied me, and nothing you could ever do would satisfy me, Blackburn.'

With a glance at Hilda, Blackburn made a gesture as if to hush Howe —as though all his former bold malice had taken for granted a kind of understanding between himself and his teacher, a secret which must not be betrayed to a third person. 'I only meant, sir,' he said, 'that I was able to pass your course after all.'

Howe said, 'You didn't pass my course. I passed you out of my course. I passed you without even reading your paper. I wanted to be sure the college would be rid of you. And when all the grades were in and I did read your paper, I saw I was right not to have read it first.'

Blackburn presented a stricken face. 'It was very bad, sir?'

But Howe had turned away. The paper had been fantastic. The paper had been, if he wished to see it so, mad. It was at this moment that the Dean came up behind Howe and caught his arm. 'Hello, Joseph,' he said. 'We'd better be getting along, it's almost late.'

He was not a familiar man, but when he saw Blackburn, who approached to greet him, he took Blackburn's arm, too. 'Hello, Theodore,' he said. Leaning forward on Howe's arm and on Blackburn's he said, 'Hello, Hilda dear.' Hilda replied quietly, 'Hello, Uncle George.'

Still clinging to their arms, still linking Howe and Blackburn, the Dean said, 'Another year gone, Joe, and we've turned out another crop. After you've been here a few years, you'll find it reasonably upsctting—you wonder how there can be so many graduating classes while you stay the same. But of course you don't stay the same.' Then he said, 'Well,' sharply, to dismiss the thought. He pulled Blackburn's arm and swung him around to Howe. 'Have you heard about Teddy Blackburn?' he asked. 'He has a job already, before graduation—the first man of his class to be placed.' Expectant of congratulations, Blackburn beamed at Howe. Howe remained silent.

'Isn't that good?' the Dean said. Still Howe did not answer and the Dean, puzzled and put out, turned to Hilda. 'That's a very fine-looking camera, Hilda.' She touched it with affectionate pride.

'Instruments of precision,' said a voice. 'Instruments of precision.' Of the three with joined arms, Howe was the nearest to Tertan, whose gaze took in all the scene except the smile and the nod which Howe gave him. The boy leaned on his cane. The broad-brimmed hat, canting jauntily over his eye, confused the image of his face that Howe had established, suppressed the rigid lines of the ascetic and brought out the baroque curves. It made an effect of perverse majesty.

'Instruments of precision,' said Tertan for the last time, addressing no one, making a casual comment to the universe. And it occurred to Howe that Tertan might not be referring to Hilda's equipment. The sense of the thrice-woven circle of the boy's loneliness smote him fiercely. Tertan stood in majestic jauntiness, superior to all the scene, but his isolation made Howe ache with a pity of which Tertan was more the cause than the object, so general and indiscriminate was it.

Whether in his sorrow he made some unintended movement toward Tertan which the Dean checked, or whether the suddenly tightened grip on his arm was the Dean's own sorrow and fear, he did not know. Tertan watched them in the incurious way people watch a photograph being taken, and suddenly the thought that, to the boy, it must seem that the three were posing for a picture together made Howe detach himself almost rudely from the Dean's grasp.

'I promised Hilda another picture,' he announced—needlessly, for Tertan was no longer there, he had vanished in the last sudden flux of visitors who, now that the band had struck up, were rushing nervously to find seats.

'You'd better hurry,' the Dean said. 'I'll go along, it's getting late for me.' He departed and Blackburn walked stately by his side.

Howe again took his position under the little tree which cast its shadow over his face and gown. 'Just hurry, Hilda, won't you?' he said. Hilda held the cable at arm's length, her other arm crooked and her fingers crisped. She rose on her toes and said 'Ready,' and pressed the release. 'Thank you,' she said gravely and began to dismantle her camera as he hurried off to join the procession.

Questions

1. From the moment we see Tertan's late arrival (Can you see why Trilling has him arrive late?), Trilling emphasizes his strangeness. Can you define the strangeness? Does he seem just another "square"?
2. From the moment Dr. Howe thinks the word "mad," Tertan gradually recedes from person to fact. Why? Has Dr. Howe committed the semantic error of mistaking the word for the thing it signifies? Note how both he and the Dean cling to the words "a classic case."
3. Did you suspect Tertan of madness before Dr. Howe used the term? How

mad is he? As you approach the end of the story do you *want* it to be madness? Is Tertan's language lacking enough in coherence and direction to indicate madness?

4. Though Dr. Howe does not narrate the story, we see everything from his point of view. How does he feel toward Tertan? Does his attitude affect yours?
5. Blackburn is a senior. He has thrived in the system until he meets Dr. Howe. Why? His writing is a little florid but clear and direct enough. What is the matter with it? What is he trying to do with it? If you know "The Rime of the Ancient Mariner" you know, even before Dr. Howe tells him, how completely Blackburn misses the poem. Similarly with Wordsworth. Has he been merely bluffing?
6. Blackburn's attempts to manipulate Dr. Howe are overt and vicious. But note that in his way Tertan also manipulates him, somewhat more successfully (for example, in getting him to sign as faculty sponsor). Contrast the motives of the two. Dr. Howe uses the word "mad" with Blackburn too. Does it have the same meaning? The same effect on Howe as with Tertan? Is Blackburn mad?
7. Other than giving Blackburn something of a wedge, why should Trilling have Howe stress the article in *Life and Letters?* It contrasts two poets. Does the contrast have anything to do with that between Tertan and Blackburn?
8. Why should Trilling begin and end his story with Hilda taking Dr. Howe's picture? Does Tertan include the people in his comment, "Instruments of precision"? Does he now include Dr. Howe?

Suggestions for Writing

1. Write an essay in which you compare or contrast the two characters and the two kinds of madness. Is the story saying merely that society will accept one kind and not the other? Your own as well as Dr. Howe's responses to the characters will be important. Can we have any final question about the validity of the psychiatrists' judgment of Tertan? Would any psychiatrist find Blackburn mad?
2. Dr. Howe and the Dean may not contrast quite as sharply, but they do make an interesting study in contrasts as academic people. If you try this one, give close attention to the article on Dr. Howe.
3. The story also suggests writing possibilities with many kinds of comparisons or contrasts outside the story itself: two kinds of madness (different from those developed in the story) embodied in people you know or imagine, two contrasting students.

Writing Projects

1. Choose two teachers whose methods of teaching have favorably impressed you. Consider the approaches which made them effective. Then make a point-by-point comparison of their methods. In order to make your theme say something significant, choose a controlling purpose for the comparison. Consider the audience for which you are writing. For what purpose might you make such a comparison for them?

2. Choose two or three hobbies, majors in college, kinds of schools you are acquainted with, sports, or similar subjects. Compare or contrast them. Explain each one fully before moving to the next one. Be especially aware of the need for effective transitions between major points in this theme.

3. Compare and contrast your expectations for a particular event or experience and the reality of that event. You might, for example, contrast what you expected dormitory living, social life, or a particular subject to be like before you came to college with what it actually is. Other possibilities include a camping trip, a big social happening in your life, a big sports event, or your participation in a school play, debate, or contest of some sort. There are good possibilities in a number of these subjects for a humorous theme. Take care, however, to keep your reader in mind and to develop your points with careful attention to order and to detail.

4. Compare or contrast a scene at two different times of day or two different seasons of the year. Assume contrasting attitudes toward the times of day or the seasons and show these attitudes in your writing.

Part V

Dialects and Usage

In a precise sense each individual has his own peculiar rules of usage and his own peculiar dialect (called by the linguist an idiolect). Speech sounds, vocabulary, and usage practices vary within a single family from member to member. However, the majority of the native speakers in any particular area have enough in common in their pronunciation, vocabulary, and grammatical usage that dialectologists can distinguish them from speakers in other areas.

On a map showing dialects of the United States, a few lines, mostly running east and west, divide the map into large geographical regions of speech patterns. Much work has been done on regional dialects, but much more needs to be done before linguists can reproduce a comprehensive regional dialectal map of the country as a whole. When their knowledge is complete, an irregular grid of wavey lines across the map will delineate the approximate boundaries of all regional dialect areas. They know now, for example, that north of a certain line, native speakers use the word *pail* instead of *bucket,* and east of another line native speakers pronounce *Mary, merry,* and *marry* exactly alike. They have not charted such distinctions, however, for the entire country.

But even if the regional dialect areas were carefully charted, the modern dialectologist would know that the charting was far from complete. He is also concerned with charting the "social" dialects: those dialects spoken by different groups living within a single regional dialect area. Often the speakers of one social dialect are convinced that their own dialect is acceptable, is somehow *the* dialect, and another spoken side by side with it is an inferior one. Some southern speakers, acquainted with "hill" speech, avoid the perfectly good Anglo-Saxon word *fetch,* except in "Jack and Jill went up a hill/ To fetch a pail of water," because it is related in their thinking with a "poor" dialect.

Usage variations are closely related to both regional and social dialects. Various regional dialects exhibit differences in grammatical usage. Whether you say *waked* or *woke, dived* or *dove* is probably determined by where you learned to speak English. Similiarly, social dialects existing within a regional dialect area exhibit differences in what is adopted as accepted usage. Compare, for example, "Shall you be there tomorrow evening?" and "Will you go over there tomorrow night?"

Two of the selections in this section deal with the technical distinctions of dialect and usage: Roger W. Shuy's "Dialects: What They Are" and David DeCamp's "Dimensions of English Usage." Shuy discusses both regional and social dialects, including a clear definition of dialect. DeCamp makes a brief statement about usage controversies in this country, identifying three attitudes toward usage. He then discusses the complexities involved in any attempt to deal comprehensively with usage problems. In the article "Ghetto Children Know What They're Talking About," John M. Brewer discusses a distinctive social dialect. As you might expect, this article contains many illustrations. Twain and Thurber, in their unique styles, comment on English usage. The Papashivilys' "For All But the Breaking Heart" illustrates what might be called the dialect of a minority group. This delightful story also illustrates the kinds of usage problems speakers of English as a second language have.

A number of the selections contain examples of dialects. Unfortunately the representation of a dialect in written English presents almost insurmountable difficulties. Our sound system, particularly our vowels, cannot be represented with phonetic accuracy with the alphabet we employ. The sound /e/, our long *a,* is represented at least eight different ways in our English spelling, although some are far from common spellings, and the letter *a* itself represents at least eight different sounds. Joel Chandler Harris' claim in 1880 that his Uncle Remus stories were "phonetically correct" can be true only in part. Linguists are even uncertain as to the exact pronounciation Harris meant to reproduce with his famous *Brer,* Uncle Remus' pronounciation of *brother,* which he prefixed to all the animals in his stories. An elderly Negro woman in a remarkably natural recording of a folk variation of one of the Brer Rabbit tales pronounced the word as if it were the first syllable of *brother* with the *th* completely suppressed and with the faintest suggestion of a final *r*. Her pronunciation, close certainly to what Harris meant to reproduce, is far removed from that of generations of readers of *Uncle Remus.*

James Russell Lowell in his *Biglow Papers,* first published thirty-two years before Harris' *Uncle Remus,* was aware of this difficulty and says that he "endeavored to adapt the spelling as nearly as possible to the ordinary mode of pronunciation" of the Yankee dialect he was representing. Later in a discussion of specific sounds of the dialect, he adds that "To the sound *ou*" the Yankee "prefixes an *e* (hard to exemplify otherwise than orally.)" He gives the example *now,* pronounced "neou."

Lowell is also aware of a second difficulty, the manner in which the sounds are spoken. He concludes his description of the dialect by saying,

"To the dish thus seasoned add a drawl *ad libitum.*" But can you understand what is meant by an eastern drawl, a southern drawl, a western drawl without having heard them? Writing makes no provision for reproducing the rhythms of speech. There is no way to reproduce the cadence of the native speaker of Swedish speaking in English, the lilt of the Yiddish dialect, or the musical Negro speech for the reader who has not already heard them. In fact the most deft representation of dialect often achieves its effect through vocabulary and phrasing, and the slightest variation in spelling that will suggest the sound of the speech.

Much so-called dialect in literature tends to follow set patterns that often smack more of the sentimental than of a true dialect. The farmer resorts to "shucks!" when he wants to be forceful and his wife exclaims "land's sakes" and "shaw" or "I be!" The Negro sounds like a Stephen Foster lyric, and each national group has its obvious characteristics. Mark Twain slyly gibes at this tendency in a *Connecticut Yankee in King Arthur's Court.* The Yankee, as he listens to a story, objects that "Sir Marhaus the king's son of Ireland talks like all the rest," and suggests he be given "a brogue, or at least a characteristic expletive." He claims, "It is a common literary device with great authors. You should make him say, 'In this country, be jabers, came never knight since it was christened, but he found strange adventures, be jabers.' You see how much better that sounds." James Whitcomb Riley and Edgar Guest rely heavily on such sentimental devices. As you read the selections in this section, try to determine whether any of the authors represented slip into set patterns as opposed to accurate reporting of an actual dialect.

Classification and Division

Much of the work of the scientist involves classification and division. The botanist, for example, classifies plants by putting the individual plant in the large group to which it belongs, then deciding which of the subgroups to put it in, and finally locating it in the particular minor grouping which identifies it. He speaks of the order, the family, the genus and the species, but he is merely giving a name to each step of the classification. We are doing the same thing whenever we identify a book as a novel of science fiction dealing with ocean exploration. We have put the book in a large class, the novel; then into a smaller subclass of the novel, science fiction; and finally into a particular grouping of science fiction, those books dealing with ocean exploration.

When the life scientist dissects, he is in a literal sense dividing. But so is the critic who talks of the three qualities needed for a good poem, the director who explains that each action must have motivation and direction, and the coach who insists that a winning team must have "know-how," strength, and determination.

Both of these processes are common in our lives and both are common methods of developing compositions. Classification involves a group of units which are "classed" with other units having similar characteristics. Division involves separating a single unit into parts. However, division is easily confused with classification when the unit being divided is a group. The same rules apply to both processes, and for practical purposes in composition these two processes can be considered as one.

Strictly logical classification and division—that used by the scientist—demands that three conditions be observed. First, each step must be made as the result of one characteristic only. This rule would not allow *college students* to be classed as *freshmen girls, freshmen boys, sophomore girls, sophomore boys,* and so on, in one step. The rule calls for an intermediate step of classing the students as *freshmen, sophomores, juniors,* and *seniors*. Second, the subclasses must contain all the units contained in the class itself. This rule provides for a proper number of subclasses. (If you are sorting a pile of fruit of many varieties and find that you have no basket for one fruit, you get another basket. It is as simple as that.) And third, each unit must fit into one, and only one, subclass. (If one fruit fits into more than one basket, you have labeled your baskets incorrectly.) Similarly, division is made on the basis of one characteristic for each step, the parts must total the whole, and never should one part fit into two or more categories.

In composition these rules are usually not followed as closely as they are in logic or in science, but an awareness of the rules will help you to avoid fuzzy writing. Make clear to the reader the basis for your classification or division; he will then sense the logic behind your work, whether or not he knows the rule that each step is made on the basis of only one characteristic. If you are classifying the sights in your community according to those a visitor should see if he has one day to spend, those to add to the list if he has two days, and those to add if he has even longer, you are classifying on the basis of interest priorities for a visitor. Keep that basis in mind and do not confuse the reader by trying to judge those sights at the same time by their cost and the ease with which a visitor can reach them. Those are legitimate characteristics for a classification, but they demand additional steps or a different classification entirely.

Often in composition you do not have to discuss in detail all the units in your classification or even to include all of the units, but you must indicate that you are not doing so. David DeCamp in "Dimensions of English Usage," which is included in this section, is primarily concerned about the school teacher's shifting attitude toward English usage, but he first makes clear that other attitudes exist. Likewise a writer may say he is considering the "four main dialects" or only the "common beliefs about evolution." Such a statement presupposes an earlier classification into two classes, "main" and "minor" dialects or "common" and "unusual" beliefs.

Because scientists use the methods of classifying and dividing, and because we have been taught to accept the scientist as an objective observer, we tend to think of classification and division as strictly logical, impartial means of development. But a human being is doing the classifying or the dividing and his stance begins to show as soon as he names the classes or divisions. Sometimes the title itself will tell us the author's stance: "The Promises and Perils of the New Genetics," "Knowledge and Opinion," or "Accuracy and Fallacy in Reporting." The attitude of the author is immediately apparent. As a writer, the title you use or the names you apply to your classes are important in revealing your attitudes to your readers.

Dialects: What They Are

Roger W. Shuy *The following article is an attempt to define a very difficult-to-define term. All of us have our own views of what dialects are, and many of us have quite unconsciously developed negative attitudes toward dialect differences in language. After all, dialects are what other people speak. Shuy suggests that* dialect *is a neutral term and that all of us speak a dialect. Are you convinced by his reasoning? He also divides dialects into two types: regional and social. Read carefully to see if you can define what he means by the term "social dialect." Do you feel that people should have neutral attitudes toward social dialects?*

Many Americans are unaware that they and their friends speak a variety of English which can be called a dialect. Many even deny it and say something like this: "No, we don't speak a dialect around here. They speak more harshly and strangely out East and down South, but we just don't have anything like that in *our* speech."

Most Southerners know that people from other parts of the country are either pleased or annoyed by their Southern pronunciations and expressions. Many Easterners are aware of the reactions of people from west of the Alleghenies to typical Eastern speech patterns. On the other hand, many Midwesterners, for some reason, seem oblivious to the fact that Americans from other areas find something strange about the vocabulary, pronunciation, and grammar characteristic of the Midwest.

People tend to describe the differences between their speech and that of others in certain conventional terms. *Harshness* and *nazalized drawl* are often used to describe the speech of any area other than that of the speaker. Another popular term, *guttural,* is also used with little precision. Strangely enough, many people will insist that they hear a *guttural* quality in the speech of another person *even though they cannot define the term.*

Linguists who specialize in the study of dialects describe American speech systematically and with precision. They avoid terms like *harsh* and *dull,* for such words are closer to condemnation than description, and terms like *soft* and *musical,* for they are too general to be useful. Like many common English terms, these words have been used so widely that it is difficult to say exactly what they *do* mean.

How, then, can linguists go about describing dialect differences systematically and precisely? Perhaps we should begin with what we already know. In an age in which people often move from one area of the country to another, it is rather common for us to have neighbors or classmates whose dialect may be somewhat "different." Furthermore, the summer (or winter) vacation has enabled many of us to enter different dialect areas. Television and radio have brought speakers from many social and geographical dialect areas into our homes. We may begin, then, by recognizing that there *are* dialect differences.

Besides the facts, however, we also begin with attitudes. Since language is a form of social behavior, we react to a person's speech patterns as we would react to any of his actions. If his dialect differs from our own, we may consider him quaint, naive, stupid, suave, cultivated, conceited, alien, or any number of other things. Most frequently, however, our attitude toward the outsider tends to be negative, since, after all, he is not one of *our* group. Recently a graduate school professor at a large Midwestern university asked his students to describe various unidentified persons whose voices were recorded on tape. The class described one voice as rustic and uncultivated. The voice was that of their professor!

It is clear, then, that most people recognize dialect differences of some sort and have certain feelings or attitudes toward them. A classic example of this recognition and reaction occurred during a survey of Illinois speech conducted in 1962. Many people from the middle of the state and most from the southern part pronounced *greasy* something like *greezy.* On the other hand, people in the northern counties of the state pronounced the word *greecey.* The northern Illinois informants felt that the southern pronunciation was crude and ugly; it made them think of a very messy, dirty, sticky, smelly frying pan. To the southern and midland speakers, however, the northern pronunciation connoted a messy, dirty, sticky, smelly skillet.

Which of the two pronunciations and reactions are right? The answer is easy: The southern Illinois pronunciation and reaction are appropriate in southern Illinois, and the northern Illinois pronunciation and reaction are proper in northern Illinois. Educated *and* uneducated speakers say *greezy* in southern Illinois. Educated *and* uneducated speakers say *greecey* in northern Illinois. Although we must not be surprised that people tend to believe their own way is the "right way," it should be clear that there are two acceptable pronunciations of this word in Illinois, reflecting different dialects.

The word "dialect" is associated with speech communities, groups of people who are in constant internal communication. Such a group speaks its own dialect; that is, the members of the group have certain language habits in common. For example, a family is a speech community; the members of the family talk together constantly, and certain words have certain special meanings within the family group. The people who belong to your class in school form a speech community, sharing certain special ways of talking together—the latest slang, for instance. The people who work together in a single office are a speech community. Larger speech communities may be the members of a single occupation or profession. Carpenters share certain typical carpentry terms; lawyers use special legal terms.

An even larger speech community is made up of people who live in a particular geographic region. Such regional speech communities are the special concern of this book. The study of these communities is called "dialect geography" or "linguistic geography" or, simply, "dialectology." The scholar who studies varieties of a language is called a "dialect geographer," or a "linguistic geographer," or a "dialectologist."

Dialectology is concerned with the regional and social aspects of language. The intermingling of these regional and social aspects is clearly illustrated in American English. We are all aware of the fact that relatively uneducated people tend to use certain pronunciations, grammar, and vocabulary which easily identify them as uneducated. We know, furthermore, that people from certain areas speak in such a way that we can make a good general guess as to where they are from. The speech of any such person, then, is a mixture of social and geographical features. The educated person will undoubtedly share some of the geographical features found in the speech of his uneducated townsman, but he will probably *not* share the speech features which label the other man uneducated (at least not in his more formal utterances). Here we discover two different aspects of dialectology—*regional dialects* and *social dialects.*

We might say that there are at least three degrees of understanding of what dialects are. First, some people think that a dialect is something spoken by a white-bearded old man in an out-of-the-way area.

Once we became aware of the fact that we *all* speak a dialect of some sort, we recognize dialects in a geographical sense, the second degree of understanding.

The third degree of understanding comes when we realize that social layers exist *within* regional dialect areas. That is, well-educated, partly-educated, and uneducated people may all live within the boundaries of a well-defined dialect area. In one sense, they all speak dialect X. It is also true, however, that they speak different varieties of this dialect. Certain aspects of the dialect are shared by all social levels; others are used by only one or two of the groups.

A case in point is the past tense of the verb *climb*. Well-educated people in all dialect areas favor *climbed* as the past tense form. Some uneducated speakers in certain Northern dialect areas may say *clim.* In some parts of the Midland and Southern dialect areas, many uneducated speakers say *clum;* in Virginia, many uneducated speakers say *clome.* With this verb, then, we find dialect variants only among uneducated speakers. The variants, *clim, clum,* and *clome,* have geographical *and* social patterns. Both must be taken into account.

A dialect, then, is a variety of a language. It differs from other varieties in certain features of pronunciation, vocabulary, and grammar ("grammar" will be used to mean both word construction *and* syntax). It may reveal something about the social or regional background of its speakers, and it will be generally understood by speakers of other dialects of the same language.

Questions

1. Were you aware that the language you speak is a dialect of English? What are some characteristics of the dialect of your region?
2. Distinguish between regional and social dialects.
3. Shuy states that the pronunciations *greezy* and *greecey* are both correct. What reasoning does he use to draw this conclusion? Do you agree with him? What implications does your answer have as you consider other usage differences?

Suggestions for Writing

1. Almost all students have been in situations where some characteristics of their dialects have been challenged—pronunciation of words, expressions, choice of words. Teachers, visitors (who are convinced that only their own dialect is acceptable), and parents (who want to show their offspring in the best light) have all been known to urge a different dialect on young people. Trips away from the home community, sometimes only a few miles away, will call forth comparisons of pronunciation. Write about such an experience, or experiences, stressing how you felt about the challenge.

An Ephraimite Perspective on Bidialectalism

David W. Cole *In the past, educators generally accepted the view that one task of the schools was to eliminate dialect differences among students and to teach all students to use standard (correct) English. In recent years, with increasing attention being given to the needs of minority groups, Black English, Chicano English, and a number of other social dialects have become the dominant language in some areas. The differences between these dialects and standard English are significant enough that some linguists have argued that the dialects really have different grammars—that the differences are more than merely dialectal differences. As the groups who speak these dialects have asserted themselves politically, economically, and socially, they have also demanded acceptance of the language forms characteristic of their group.*

Traditional educators still insist that speakers of these dialects give up their "incorrect" usage and learn standard English. Others have urged the groups to hold to their dialects and to resist efforts by school systems to force them to learn standard English. A third view is that speakers of such dialects should hold on to their dialects where they are appropriate, but also learn to use standard English in appropriate situations. The term bidialectalism *is used to describe this view. Its advocates argue that just as there is no stigma attached to the bilingual person who can shift from one language to another as circumstances require, so should there be no stigma attached to the person who can shift from one social dialect to another. The following article is a discussion between a professor who urges members of a particular language group to defend the equality of their dialect and a young man who sees some practical problems in such a course of action. Many young speakers of a social dialect face the kind of decision discussed here. What would be your advice to them?*

And the Gileadites took the passages of Jordan before the Ephraimites, and it was so, that when those Ephraimites which were escaped said, Let me go over; that the men of Gilead said unto him, Art thou an Ephraimite? If he said, Nay;
Then said they unto him, Say now Shibboleth: and he said Sibboleth: for he could not frame to pronounce it right. Then they took him, and slew him at the passages of Jordan: and there fell at that time of the Ephraimites forty and two thousand.

—JUDGES 12:5–6

A professor of English and Linguistics appeared in great glory among the Ephraimites, saying, Fear not: for lo, I bring you glad tidings. The difference between Shibboleth and Sibboleth is not phonological, but merely phonetic; and the differences between the dialects of the Ephraimites and the Gileadites are relatively superficial; and the two dialects are linguistically equal.

Then a young man of the Ephraimites answered and said, Who art thou that darkenest counsel by words without knowledge? For thou knowest not the need of Ephraim.

The Professor in his glory demanded of him, Is not intelligibility the need of all who speak? And do the men of Ephraim not understand what the Gileadites mean when they say Shibboleth? And do they not understand what ye Ephraimites mean when ye say Sibboleth? How then do I not know the need of Ephraim?

Then the young man of the Ephraimites replied unto him, "Sir, we do understand them, as do they also understand us when we speak: but that is not the need of Ephraim. They slay us at the passages of Jordan. And so we wish to learn to say S-sibboleth, even as the Gileadites do, so that we may pass over Jordan when we will. That is the need of Ephraim.

The Professor of English and Linguistics said, Ye are Ephraimites: and ye cannot frame your tongues to speak as the Gileadites do.

But the young man of the Ephraimites said, Some men speak in more than one tongue. We too will do even so: for that is how we may pass over Jordan.

Then the Professor in his glory said sternly, To learn to say Shibboleth and to speak in the speech of the Gileadites is to lose thine heritage, and to become less than an Ephraimite, and less than a man. This thou must not do, but speak in thine own speech with pride, and proudly say Sibboleth.

But the young man said unto him, To be beheaded at the passage of Jordan is to become less than an Ephraimite, and less than a man.

Then said the Professor in his glory, Pass not over Jordan, but stay among the Ephraimites, thine own people, and speak in thine own speech, and say Sibboleth.

The young man of the Ephraimites replied unto him, Some of us will do even so: but some of us wish to pass over Jordan into the land of Gilead to enjoy the fruits of the land: and some of us wish to pass over Jordan to fight against the Gileadites. And all of us who wish to pass over Jordan wish to learn to say S-sibboleth, even as the Gileadites do, so that they may not slay us at the passages of Jordan.

Then the Professor spake from his glory and said, It is well to pass over Jordan to fight against the Gileadites. It may be well to pass over even to enjoy the fruits of the land of Gilead. But do not allow the Gileadites to require you to say Shibboleth, that ye may pass. Who are they, that they may say unto you, Pass, or, Do not pass?

But the young man of the Ephraimites said, They guard the passages over Jordan with swords, and with spears: and they are many and powerful: and they will let no one pass who cannot frame his tongue to say S-sibboleth, even as they do. Canst thou take from them their swords and spears? Canst thou stop their ears, so that they cannot hear us, when we say Sibboleth? Canst thou change their hearts, so that they will embrace the Ephraimites, instead of slaying us?

And the Professor said unto him, I would take from the Gileadites their swords and spears: and I would change their hearts.

And the Professor bowed his head and said, But I have not yet done these things.

Then the young man of the Ephraimites looked upon him and said, Will these things be done soon?

But the Professor said, No, not soon.

Then said the young man of the Ephraimites unto him, Neither canst thou stop up their ears.

And again the Professor said, No.

The young man of the Ephraimites fixed his eyes upon the Professor, whose glory was departed. Finally he said, Thou art a wise man: and thou understandest the speech of the Gileadites, even as thou understandest the speech of the Ephraimites. Thou understandest the framing of the tongue. Leave those who will dwell in the land of Ephraim to dwell in peace, but teach us who would pass over Jordan, so that we may say S-sibboleth, even as the Gileadites do, and pass by the Gileadites at the passages of Jordan.

Questions

1. The word *shibboleth* originally meant "a stream at flood." Because of the incident related here, the word has lost its original meaning and developed a series of new meanings. Look the word up in a good dictionary and note the new meanings. Can you see the relationship between the various meanings and the incident recorded in *Judges* 12:5–6?
2. In one sense the discussion in this article revolves around the issue of upholding a principle versus being practical. What is the central point of the professor's argument? What does the young man counter this argument with?
3. From your own experience relate incidents in which a person was discriminated against because of the way he pronounced a word, a vocabulary choice he made, or a grammatical structure he used.
4. Do you feel that judgments relating to one's educational status, to one's fitness for employment, to one's acceptance into a particular social group should be made on the basis of the dialect he speaks? Defend your position.
5. What is the tone of this article? How were you able to determine the tone?

Ghetto Children Know What They're Talking About

John M. Brewer *John M. Brewer, an ex-principal of "a large elementary school in the heart of a Negro slum," tells of the private language he encountered there—a colorful, graphic, picturesque social dialect, which thrives on its very secrecy. As you read of the vigorous language of children, ask yourself the question: "Should educators make an attempt to eradicate this dialect?" What does the language provide for the children? Could the language work as a means of communication beyond its immediate environment?*

Broken homes are "trees without roots."

Meat markets are "great flesh parlors."

Outsiders looking for thrills are "toys on a fairy lake."

This is the colorful, private speech of the children of America's ghettos, a "hidden language" of haunted phrases and striking subtlety. It is a language little known in the world outside, but for many it is more meaningful, more facile and more developed than the language of standard English.

During the period I was the principal of a large elementary school in the heart of a Negro slum, I became fascinated by this secret language developed by a rough-and-ready group of ghetto children. I found this idiom to be as dazzling as a diamond, invested with the bitter-sweet soulfulness bred by the struggle against poverty's dehumanizing forces.

I discovered that it was developed by the children even before they came to school, passed on from mother to child, and that a quarter of the students came from homes where it is the usual household speech. It is equipment for survival in the black ghetto. Normally it is used only in easy social settings like the home and after-school gatherings, and not in front of outsiders—which helps to explain why the children are often inarticulate when they try to use conventional English in talking to teachers, doctors, the school staff, etc.

As they advance in their schooling, these children also advance their hidden language vocabulary, become infatuated with this kind of verbal play and help it to flower with additions from the standard English they meet in class. They, and their parents, are fully aware of the aliveness of their words and make a serious effort to master the idiom. But, of course, this development conflicts with the formal school pattern and teachers who demand that only conventional English be used, and it often happens that verbally bright children suddenly clam up or become inarticulate in the classroom.

An illustration of the wonderful possibilities of the language of the ghetto helps one to judge how rich and interesting it is.

About 9:45 A.M. one day, Junebug—a small, wiry, shabbily dressed boy with large brown eyes—came into my office. As I looked up, it was obvious that he was hosed down and deep in the mud [embarrassed and had a problem]. Very quickly I got up and asked, "Why are you stretched so thin by joy? Are you flying backwards?" ["Why are you so sad? Are you in trouble?"]

Junebug took a cool view [looked up], cracked up [smiled] and answered, "My special pinetop [favorite teacher] is smoking [angry] and wants to eyeball [see] you fast." I said to him, "I'm stalled [puzzled]. What is this all about?"

He answered, "I wasted [punched] one of the studs [boys] for capping [insulting] me. Teach blasted [yelled] at me and told me to fade away [go] to the hub [office] and fetch you."

I stood up and told Junebug to cool it. "Don't put your head in the bowl and pull the chain" ["Don't do anything rash"]. Hurriedly he grabbed my arm and said: "I hope I don't get a big slap on the rump."

As I headed up the stairs toward his classroom I was deeply concerned. What did he mean by that "slap-on-the-rump" remark? A paddling never fazed him before. Suddenly the message came through loud and clear: He had played the part of an unlikely wrongdoer to tell me something was wrong in his classroom. He was tough and cruel, cunning and ruthless, a master of all the skills needed to survive in his jungle; he was too shrewd to be trapped this way, with so many witnesses, without a motive. He was very fond of his teacher.

I knew his twisted code of honor, which did not allow him to be an informer. He had got in trouble himself so that I would see and uncover something about his class.

Very reluctantly I eased open the classroom door and entered the room. I could sense that the hum of industry was missing. The children

—chronologically aged 11–13 but actually precocious young adults —were impenetrable, as though encased in glass, sitting stiffly at their desks. The teacher walked over to me and said, "Whatever has come over this class this morning defies interpretation by anyone—most of all myself."

In a booming voice I said to the class, "Operation Jappin' [teacher harassment] has shot its load [is all over]." Operation Jappin' goes like this:

The tomcat [the sly and ruthless student leading the operation] begins with a stinging hit [first attack] and the sandbaggin' starts—things are thrown, strange noises come out of nowhere, children are unresponsive. The tomcat tells all his tadpoles [classmates] that it is now time for the chicken to become an eagle [for more aggressive action] and they had better trilly along [join his group] because the sun has fallen on its belly [it's too late to back out].

The first step is to unzip the teacher [make her back down], so the tomcat takes the long dive [openly defies her], hoping she puts him in cold storage [punishes him] so he can then dress her in red tresses [insult her]. He and his friends get bolder, and outflap [out wit] and scramble [gang up on] her daily. All morning they shoot her down with grease [play dirty tricks on her] until finally she is ready for the big sleep [gives in]. They continue the heart-deep kicks [fun] until they are sure she is frozen on the needle [does not know what to do].

The tomcat then decides to wring [exploit] the scene. Now his glasses are on [he's in control], his ashes have been hauled away [his problems are gone]. He sends hotcakes [notes] to some of the children demanding money; the rabbits [timid children] know they will be erased [beat up] unless they pay him. He tells them he is a liberty looter [good crook] who will protect them because he carries a twig [big club]. Five-finger discount [stealing] pays off. The cockroaches crow [gang members are happy].

Poor Tiny Tim [the teacher], her nerve ends are humming [she is overwhelmed], her fleas [nice children] and bust-heads [smart children] have twisted the knob [lost respect for her]. The tomcat doesn't have to waste any more hip bullets on her [continue the harassment]—after all, a cat can't tell a dog what to do [he is the new leader]. He will keep his shoe laces tied [control everything]. Hail the Stinking King.

Quickly I singled out the group I thought was capable of organizing Operation Jappin', and together we went to my office. I told Junebug to go to the outer office and sit down. In spite of the imperturbable look on his face, I knew he was aware that I had captured the scene [found out what was going on]: these cub scouts [amateurs] were bleedin' [exposed].

The climate was a sticky one. I had to converse with them in their hidden language. But since I was a ghetto linguist, they could not victimize me by their idiomatic ambushes so neatly booby-trapped with sudden jolts and dead-end phrases.

I also had to ready them to pay their dues [accept disciplinary action]. I could not offer them two tricks for one until they were ready to turn a somersault [promise them anything until they confessed]. And I had to burn some time [give them time] to talk it over.

Finally, of course, I had to discipline the ringleaders. Operation Jappin' was sandbagged. In the end, I couldn't help but feel sorry for Junebug, and yet how could I tell his teacher how he had sacrificed himself in her behalf? Conceivably all of this might terrify her.

Yet I had to try to provide a bridge between her world and his. It is imperative that teachers see the ways in which the hidden and formal languages cut across, support or collide with each other. In fact, the term "hidden language" is really a misleading one, because in the out-of-school setting it becomes the primary language while the formal language used in the schools is secondary.

I suspect that many teachers are unaware of this inversion. And they are baffled as well by the odd structure of the primary language of the street-corner society. The logic is nonlogic, for instance: "I am full of the joy of being up front" means I am disgusted with my circumstances. The appeal is illusion and fantasy: "It goes to the back of your head and pulls out beautiful things."

If one looks for substance instead of smut, meaning instead of obfuscation, it is possible to harness some of the positive features that lie behind the crust of degradation and depravation explicit in the hidden language. The schools in our urban ghettos are full of children who communicate this way.

It was to make clear the hidden dynamics of the hidden language—realistic, tough, practical, with a broad sweep of understanding—and to explore the inversion process that I began "Operation Capping."

Operation Capping can best be described as a "tug of war" between formal and restrictive language. The long-range goal was systematically to strip away the students' addiction to a hidden language that thwarted their progress with the language of the school and textbook.

I developed a two-pronged approach. One was not to deny the validity of the child's world, his pragmatism, his unwillingness to be deluded, his suspicious nature and his perceptions, his quickness, toughness, and agile imagination. The other was to manipulate and redirect what was already a favorite pastime of the children, called "Capping," which in my youth was called "Playing the Dozens." In it, children try to outdo each other in trading insults and deprecating each other's family. For example: "Your Mama wasn't born, she was trapped"; "Your sisters are side-show bait"; "You ain't got no pappy, you're a S.O.B."; or "So's your Mama."

I decided to borrow this practice and give it a classy academic personality. The technique was simple, because the kids were already highly motivated to surpass each other in verbal intercourse. So I would meet a group for a "buzz session" [dictionary skills and English grammar] and introduce one of their well-known idioms, such as "pad," "crib" or "bread," and the children had to "cap" each other in formal English by providing a synonym.

As time passed we introduced antonyms and moved from simple sentences to complex ones. The kids were so highly competitive that they took up practices to which they previously were indifferent: They used the dictionary, read books, brought samples of word lists and resorted to all the conventional practices of the classroom. They had to win the capping game at any cost.

The spin-off from Operation Capping touched many sensitive and intriguing areas. The students discovered for themselves the built-in disadvantages of their idiomatic phrases; it didn't take them long to determine that these phrases didn't convey the meanings to others that their hidden language did: For example, they were stumped as they tried to find a standard English idiom for such hidden language phrases as: "rising on the wings of power" [a pocketful of money]; "gold is my color" [pay me in advance]; "trailing dark lines" [a hopeless search for something]; "I'm on ice" [in trouble].

The students openly expressed a real concern about their verbal deficit in formal language. But at the end of Operation Capping, they had become less dependent on their hidden language to express themselves, and began to stockpile new standard words and phrases and to wrestle successfully with grammar for the first time.

They also had a purpose for reading, and their ability improved significantly. Learning became fun and exciting because they no longer labored under unfair handicaps. There was a change in their value system, and they had a new sense of identity.

I believe that the operation helped to provide richer opportunities for these children to experience the forces in the tug of war between their two languages and to come to know the language necessary for effective communication in the mainstream of contemporary American society.

Color It Vivid

Adapting the hidden language to their own experience, slum children turn standard English into phrases like these:

A nice teacher . . . *My golden butterfly, my luscious lollipop, my special pinetop, Little Eva, star apple-smooth.*

A mean teacher . . . *Headshrinker, killer ape, Bloody Mary, Swinging Tillies, The Vulture, The Beast.*

A strict teacher . . . *Clyde Beatty, Smokey the Bear, caged quiet, my ball and chain, rifle-hard, double-edged.*

Patronizing teacher . . . *Untouchable, tack-head, huckster, hard and odd, foggy, my caddy.*

A well-taught lesson . . . *Easy eats, heart-deep kicks.*

Poor lesson . . . *Same tired paths, cracked my skull, tucked me in tight.*

Textbooks . . . *Passport, license, retreads, sheets.*

To cheat in class . . . *Fix the meter, boosted goods.*

A reading class . . . *Living it twice, the line up, here comes the birds.*

An arithmetic lesson . . . *Tops and bottoms, halving, splitting.*

Questions

1. Brewer talks of the sources of the ghetto dialect in a general way ("The logic is nonlogic. . . . The appeal is illusions and fantasy. . . ."), but find specific examples and determine, if you can, the source of the imagery. What seem to be the predominant sources?
2. Some recent studies of dialect insist that the language of the ghetto should not be considered a dialect of English, but rather an independent language itself, with different structure and patterns as well as a different vocabulary. Does Brewer's use of speech in his long illustration indicate primarily a vocabulary difference or do there seem to be broader differences?
3. What is your reaction to the game "capping" which Brewer played with the students? Should he have made this effort to change their language?
4. Brewer says the students were "stumped" when they tried to find standard English idioms for such phrases as "rising on the wings of power," "gold is my color," "trailing dark lines," and "I'm on ice." Can you find standard English phrases which are as meaningful and as expressive?
5. Do you know of any other language which is as vivid and expressive as this? Do you know of any other private language children use among themselves?

Suggestions for Writing

1. Some linguists have suggested that we teach students to be bidialectical (that is, have a dialect for home and friends and a dialect for job or business), but

some teachers have objected to this plan, feeling that the aim should be to bring all the language to an agreed upon level. Looking at dialect in its broadest meaning, we all have more than one dialect that we use. One with family and close friends, another with casual acquaintances, and perhaps others to use on more formal occasions. Think of expressions you would use among friends and family, some that you would use in informal situations, and others you would use only in the most formal of situations. Write an essay in which you discuss your various dialects, pointing out how they differ.

The Braw Wooer

Robert Burns *The following poem, written originally as a song, was one of the many composed during the last few years of Burns's short life. Perhaps we need a Scotsman to give the poem its authentic sound, but even a silent reading of the poem suggests the lively swing of the music and reveals that Burns was using the unique qualities of his dialect as effectively as any other writer of songs uses English. We need not think of dialect literature as in any way inferior to that produced in standard English.*

Last May a braw* wooer cam doun the lang glen, *gallant*
  And sair* wi' his love he did deave* me; *sore, deafen*
I said there was naething I hated like men—
  The deuce gae wi'm, to believe me, believe me;
  The deuce gae wi'm to believe me.

He spake o' the darts in my bonie black een,* *eyes*
  And vow'd for my love he was diein',
I said he might die when he liket—for Jean—
  The Lord forgie me for liein', for liein';
  The Lord forgie me for liein'!

A weel-stocket mailen,* himsel for the laird,* *farm, owner*
  And marriage aff-hand, were his proffers;
I never loot on that I kenn'd* it, or car'd, *knew*
  But thought I might hae waur* offers, waur offers; *worse*
  But thought I might hae waur offers.

But what wad ye think?—in a fortnight or less—
  The deil tak his taste to gae near her!
He up the *Gate-slack* to my black* cousin, Bess— *dark*
  Guess ye how, the jad*! I could bear her, could bear her; *jade* (wench)
  Guess ye how, the jad! I could bear her.

But a' the neist week, as I petted* wi' care, *sulked*
  I gaed to the tryst* o' Dalgarnock; *cattle fair*

And wha but my fine fickle wooer was there,
    I glowr'd as I'd seen a warlock,* a warlock, *wizard*
    I glowr'd as I'd seen a warlock.

But owre my left shouther I gae him a blink,
    Lest neibours might say I was saucy;
My wooer he caper'd as he'd been in drink,
    And vow'd I was his dear lassie, dear lassie
    And vow'd I was his dear lassie.

I spier'd* for my cousin fu' couthy* and sweet, *inquired, kind*
    Gin* she had recover'd her hearin', *if*
And how her new shoon* fit her auld shachl't* feet, *shoes, shapeless*
    But heavens! how he fell a swearin', a swearin',
    But heavens! how he fell a swearin'.

He begged, for gudesake, I wad be his wife,
    Or else I wad kill him wi' sorrow;
So e'en to preserve the poor body in life,
    I think I maun* wed him to-morrow, tomorrow; *must*
    I think I maun wed him to-morrow.

Skipper Ireson's Ride

John Greenleaf Whittier

Unlike Burns, who was writing in his own dialect, Whittier had the help of someone else in working up the dialect in this ballad. Lowell, then the editor of the Atlantic Monthly, *either supplied or embellished the Marblehead dialect. Why do you suppose that the dialect is not used as a refrain for each stanza of the poem? How effective is the dialect? Can you read it, or is the spelling too contorted?*

OF all the rides since the birth of time,
Told in story or sung in rhyme,—
On Apuleius's Golden Ass,
Or one-eyed Calender's horse of brass,
Witch astride of a human back,
Islam's prophet on Al-Borák,—
The strangest ride that ever was sped
Was Ireson's, out from Marblehead!
    Old Floyd Ireson, for his hard heart,
    Tarred and feathered and carried in a cart
        By the women of Marblehead!

Body of turkey, head of owl,
Wings a-droop like a rained-on fowl,
Feathered and ruffled in every part,
Skipper Ireson stood in the cart.
Scores of women, old and young,
Strong of muscle, and glib of tongue,
Pushed and pulled up the rocky lane,
Shouting and singing the shrill refrain:
    "Here's Flud Oirson, fur his horrd horrt,
    Torr'd an' futherr'd an' corr'd in a corrt
        By the women o' Morble'ead!"

Wrinkled scolds with hands on hips,
Girls in bloom of cheek and lips,

Wild-eyed, free-limbed, such as chase
Bacchus round some antique vase,
Brief of skirt, with ankles bare,
Loose of kerchief and loose of hair,
With conch-shells blowing and fish-horns' twang,
Over and over the Mænads sang:
"Here's Flud Oirson, fur his horrd horrt,
Torr'd an' futherr'd an' corr'd in a corrt
By the women o' Morble'ead!"

Small pity for him!—He sailed away
From a leaking ship, in Chaleur Bay,—
Sailed away from a sinking wreck,
With his own town's-people on her deck!
"Lay by! lay by!" they called to him.
Back he answered, "Sink or swim!
Brag of your catch of fish again!"
And off he sailed through the fog and rain!
Old Floyd Ireson, for his hard heart,
Tarred and feathered and carried in a cart
By the women of Marblehead!

Fathoms deep in dark Chaleur
That wreck shall lie forevermore.
Mother and sister, wife and maid,
Looked from the rocks of Marblehead
Over the moaning and rainy sea,—
Looked for the coming that might not be!
What did the winds and the sea-birds say
Of the cruel captain who sailed away?—
Old Floyd Ireson, for his hard heart,
Tarred and feathered and carried in a cart
By the women of Marblehead!

Through the street, on either side,
Up flew windows, doors swung wide;
Sharp-tongued spinsters, old wives gray,
Treble lent the fish-horn's bray.
Sea-worn grandsires, cripple-bound,
Hulks of old sailors run aground,
Shook head, and fist, and hat, and cane,
And cracked with curses the hoarse refrain:
"Here's Flud Oirson, fur his horrd horrt,

Torr'd an' futherr'd an' corr'd in a corrt
By the women o' Morble'ead!"

Sweetly along the Salem road
Bloom of orchard and lilac showed.
Little the wicked skipper knew
Of the fields so green and the sky so blue.
Riding there in his sorry trim,
Like an Indian idol glum and grim,
Scarcely he seemed the sound to hear
Of voices shouting, far and near:
"Here's Flud Oirson, fur his horrd horrt,
Torr'd an' futherr'd an' corr'd in a corrt
By the women o' Morble'ead!"

"Hear me, neighbors!" at last he cried,—
"What to me is this noisy ride?
What is the shame that clothes the skin
To the nameless horror that lives within?
Waking or sleeping, I see a wreck,
And hear a cry from a reeling deck!
Hate me and curse me,—I only dread
The hand of God and the face of the dead!"
Said old Floyd Ireson, for his hard heart,
Tarred and feathered and carried in a cart
By the women of Marblehead!

Then the wife of the skipper lost at sea
Said, "God has touched him! why should we?"
Said an old wife mourning her only son,
"Cut the rogue's tether and let him run!"
So with soft relentings and rude excuse,
Half scorn, half pity, they cut him loose,
And gave him a cloak to hide him in,
And left him alone with his shame and sin.
Poor Floyd Ireson, for his hard heart,
Tarred and feathered and carried in a cart
By the women of Marblehead!

A Winter Courtship

Sarah Orne Jewett

Sarah Orne Jewett (1849–1909) was born and died in South Berwick, a small town in southern Maine. Her stories and novels are about the unhurried life in rural or small-town New England. Little of the harsh struggle against nature shows itself in her work, although the problems of genteel poverty and old age often appear. Her themes frequently skirt the sentimental. Most often she avoids its pitfalls with a humorous revelation of personality. Little happens in the following story. Only two characters appear, but through their conversation much of the life of the nineteenth-century New England village is recreated. Observe how the thoughts and silent plans of both the man and woman help us keep a detached view of the courtship. Note also that on a symbolic level as well as an actual level this is a winter courtship. Miss Jewett has been praised for delicately capturing the New England dialect. Can you see how she does it?

The passenger and mail transportation between the towns of North Kilby and Sanscrit Pond was carried on by Mr. Jefferson Briley, whose two-seated covered wagon was usually much too large for the demands of business. Both the Sanscrit Pond and North Kilby people were stayers-at-home, and Mr. Briley often made his seven-mile journey in entire solitude, except for the limp leather mail-bag, which he held firmly to the floor of the carriage with his heavily shod left foot. The mail-bag had almost a personality to him, born of long association. Mr. Briley was a meek and timid-looking body, but he held a warlike soul, and encouraged his fancies by reading awful tales of bloodshed and lawlessness in the far West. Mindful of stage robberies and train thieves, and of express messengers who died at their posts, he was prepared for anything; and although he had trusted to his own strength and bravery these many years, he carried a heavy pistol under his front-seat cushion for better defense. This awful weapon was familiar to all his regular passengers, and was usually shown to strangers by the time two of the seven miles of Mr. Briley's route had been passed. The pistol was not loaded. Nobody (at least not Mr. Briley himself) doubted that the mere sight of such a weapon would turn the boldest adventurer aside.

Protected by such a man and such a piece of armament, one gray Friday morning in the edge of winter, Mrs. Fanny Tobin was traveling from Sanscrit Pond to North Kilby. She was an elderly and feeble-looking woman, but with a shrewd twinkle in her eyes, and she felt very anxious about her numerous pieces of baggage and her own personal safety. She was enveloped in many shawls and smaller wrappings, but they were not securely fastened, and kept getting undone and flying loose, so that the bitter December cold seemed to be picking a lock now and then, and creeping in to steal away the little warmth she had. Mr. Briley was cold, too, and could only cheer himself by remembering the valor of those pony-express drivers of the pre-railroad days, who had to cross the Rocky Mountains on the great California route. He spoke at length of their perils to the suffering passenger, who felt none the warmer, and at last gave a groan of weariness.

"How fur did you say 't was now?"

"I do' know 's I said, Mis' Tobin," answered the driver, with a frosty laugh. "You see them big pines, and the side of a barn just this way, with them yellow circus bills? That's my three-mile mark."

"Be we got four more to make? Oh, my laws!" mourned Mrs. Tobin. "Urge the beast, can't ye, Jeff'son? I ain't used to bein' out in such bleak weather. Seems if I could n't git my breath. I'm all pinched up and wigglin' with shivers now. 'T ain't no use lettin' the hoss go step-a-ty-step, this fashion."

"Landy me!" exclaimed the affronted driver. "I don't see why folks expects me to race with the cars. Everybody that gits in wants me to run the hoss to death on the road. I make a good everage o' time, and that's all I *can* do. Ef you was to go back an' forth every day but Sabbath fur eighteen years, *you*'d want to ease it all you could, and let those thrash the spokes out o' their wheels that wanted to. North Kilby, Mondays, Wednesdays, and Fridays; Sanscrit Pond, Tuesdays, Thu'sdays, an' Saturdays. Me an' the beast 's done it eighteen years together, and the creatur' warn't, so to say, young when we begun it, nor I neither. I re'lly did n't know 's she'd hold out till this time. There, git up, will ye, old mar'!" as the beast of burden stopped short in the road.

There was a story that Jefferson gave this faithful creature a rest three times a mile, and took four hours for the journey by himself, and longer whenever he had a passenger. But in pleasant weather the road was delightful, and full of people who drove their own conveyances, and liked to stop and talk. There were not many farms, and the third growth of white pines made a pleasant shade, though Jefferson liked to say that when he began to carry the mail his way lay through an open country of stumps and sparse underbrush, where the white pines nowadays completely arched the road.

They had passed the barn with circus posters, and felt colder than ever when they caught sight of the weather-beaten acrobats in their tights.

"My gorry!" exclaimed Widow Tobin, "them pore creatur's looks as cheerless as little birch-trees in snow-time. I hope they dresses 'em warmer this time o' year. Now, there! look at that one jumpin' through the little hoop, will ye?"

"He could n't git himself through there with two pair o' pants on," answered Mr. Briley. "I expect they must have to keep limber as eels. I used to think, when I was a boy, that 't was the only thing I could ever be reconciled to do for a livin'. I set out to run away an' follow a rovin' showman once, but mother needed me to home. There warn't nobody but me an' the little gals."

"You ain't the only one that's be'n disapp'inted o' their heart's desire," said Mrs. Tobin sadly. " 'T warn't so that I could be spared from home to learn the dressmaker's trade."

" 'T would a come handy later on, I declare," answered the sympathetic driver, "bein' 's you went an' had such a passel o' gals to clothe an' feed. There, them that 's livin' is all well off now, but it must ha' been some inconvenient for ye when they was small."

"Yes, Mr. Briley, but then I've had my mercies, too," said the widow somewhat grudgingly. "I take it master hard now, though, havin' to give up my own home and live round from place to place, if they be my own child'en. There was Ad'line and Susan Ellen fussin' an' bickerin' yesterday about who'd got to have me next; and, Lord be thanked, they both wanted me right off but I hated to hear 'em talkin' of it over. I'd rather live to home, and do for myself."

"I've got consider'ble used to boardin'," said Jefferson, "sence ma'am died, but it made me ache 'long at the fust on 't, I tell ye. Bein' on the road 's I be, I could n't do no ways at keepin' house. I should want to keep right there and see to things."

"Course you would," replied Mrs. Tobin, with a sudden inspiration of opportunity which sent a welcome glow all over her. "Course you would, Jeff'son,"—she leaned toward the front seat; "that is to say, onless you had jest the right one to do it for ye."

And Jefferson felt a strange glow also, and a sense of unexpected interest and enjoyment.

"See here, Sister Tobin," he exclaimed with enthusiasm. "Why can't ye take the trouble to shift seats, and come front here long o' me? We could put one buff'lo top o' the other,—they're both wearin' thin,—and set close, and I do' know but we sh'd be more protected ag'inst the weather."

"Well, I could n't be no colder if I was froze to death," answered the widow, with an amiable simper. "Don't ye let me delay you, nor put you out, Mr. Briley. I don't know 's I 'd set forth to-day if I 'd known 't was so cold; but I had all my bundles done up, and I ain't one that puts my hand to the plough an' looks back, 'cordin' to Scriptur'."

"You would n't wanted me to ride all them seven miles alone?" asked the gallant Briley sentimentally, as he lifted her down, and helped her up again to the front seat. She was a few years older than he, but they had been schoolmates, and Mrs. Tobin's youthful freshness was suddenly revived to his mind's eye. She had a little farm; there was nobody left at home now but herself, and so she had broken up housekeeping for the winter. Jefferson himself had savings of no mean amount.

They tucked themselves in, and felt better for the change, but there was a sudden awkwardness between them; they had not had time to prepare for an unexpected crisis.

"They say Elder Bickers, over to East Sanscrit, 's been and got married again to a gal that's four year younger than his oldest daughter," proclaimed Mrs. Tobin presently. "Seems to me 't was fool's business."

"I view it so," said the stage-driver. "There 's goin' to be a mild open winter for that fam'ly."

"What a joker you be for a man that 's had so much responsibility!" smiled Mrs. Tobin, after they had done laughing. "Ain't you never 'fraid, carryin' mail matter and such valuable stuff, that you 'll be set on an' robbed, 'specially by night?"

Jefferson braced his feet against the dasher under the worn buffalo skin. "It is kind o' scary, or would be for some folks, but I 'd like to see anybody get the better o' me. I go armed, and I don't care who knows it. Some o' them drover men that comes from Canady looks as if they did n't care what they did, but I look 'em right in the eye every time."

"Men folks is brave by natur'," said the widow admiringly. "You know how Tobin would let his fist right out at anybody that ondertook to sass him. Town-meetin' days, if he got disappointed about the way things went, he 'd lay 'em out in win'rows; and ef he had n't been a church-member he 'd been a real fightin' character. I was always 'fraid to have him roused, for all he was so willin' and meechin' to home, and set round clever as anybody. My Susan Ellen used to boss him same 's the kitten, when she was four year old."

"I 've got a kind of sideways cant to my nose, that Tobin give me when we was to school. I don't know 's you ever noticed it," said Mr. Briley. "We was scufflin', as lads will. I never bore him no kind of a grudge. I pitied ye, when he was taken away. I re'lly did, now, Fanny. I liked Tobin first-rate, and I liked you. I used to say you was the han'somest girl to school."

"Lemme see your nose. 'T is all straight, for what I know," said the widow gently, as with a trace of coyness she gave a hasty glance. "I don't know but what 't is warped a little, but nothin' to speak of. You 've got real nice features, like your marm's folks."

It was becoming a sentimental occasion, and Jefferson Briley felt that he was in for something more than he had bargained. He hurried the faltering sorrel horse, and began to talk of the weather. It certainly did look like snow, and he was tired of bumping over the frozen road.

"I should n't wonder if I hired a hand here another year, and went off out West myself to see the country."

"Why, how you talk!" answered the widow.

"Yes 'm," pursued Jefferson. " 'T is tamer here than I like, and I was tellin' 'em yesterday I 've got to know this road most too well. I 'd like to go out an' ride in the mountains with some o' them great clipper coaches, where the driver don't know one minute but he 'll be shot dead the next. They carry an awful sight o' gold down from the mines, I expect."

"I should be scairt to death," said Mrs. Tobin. "What creatur's men folks be to like such things! Well, I do declare."

"Yes," explained the mild little man. "There 's sights of desp'radoes makes a han'some livin' out o' followin' them coaches, an' stoppin' an' robbin' 'em clean to the bone. Your money *or* your life!" and he flourished his stub of a whip over the sorrel mare.

"Landy me! you make me run all of a cold creep. Do tell somethin' heartenin', this cold day. I shall dream bad dreams all night."

"They put on black crape over their heads," said the driver mysteriously. "Nobody knows who most on 'em be, and like as not some o' them fellows come o' good families. They 've got so they stop the cars, and go right through 'em bold as brass. I could make your hair stand on end, Mis' Tobin,—I could *so!*"

"I hope none on 'em 'll git round our way, I 'm sure," said Fanny Tobin. "I don't want to see none on 'em in their crape bunnits comin' after me."

"I ain't goin' to let nobody touch a hair o' your head," and Mr. Briley moved a little nearer, and tucked in the buffaloes again.

"I feel considerable warm to what I did," observed the widow by way of reward.

"There, I used to have my fears," Mr. Briley resumed, with an inward feeling that he never would get to North Kilby depot a single man. "But you see I had n't nobody but myself to think of. I 've got cousins, as you know, but nothin' nearer, and what I 've laid up would soon be parted out;

and—well, I suppose some folks would think o' me if anything was to happen."

Mrs. Tobin was holding her cloud over her face,—the wind was sharp on that bit of open road,—but she gave an encouraging sound, between a groan and a chirp.

" 'T would n't be like nothin' to me not to see you drivin' by," she said, after a minute. "I should n't know the days o' the week. I says to Susan Ellen last week I was sure 't was Friday, and she said no, 't was Thursday; but next minute you druv by and headin' toward North Kilby, so we found I was right."

"I 've got to be a featur' of the landscape," said Mr. Briley plaintively. "This kind o' weather the old mare and me, we wish we was done with it, and could settle down kind o' comfortable. I 've been lookin' this good while, as I drove the road, and I 've picked me out a piece o' land two or three times. But I can't abide the thought o' buildin',—'t would plague me to death; and both Sister Peak to North Kilby and Mis' Deacon Ash to the Pond, they vie with one another to do well by me, fear I 'll like the other stoppin'-place best."

"*I* should n't covet livin' long o' neither one o' them women," responded the passenger with some spirit. "I see some o' Mis' Peak's cookin' to a farmers' supper once, when I was visitin' Susan Ellen's folks, an' I says 'Deliver me from sech pale-complected baked beans as them!' and she give a kind of a quack. She was settin' jest at my left hand, and could n't help hearin' of me. I would n't have spoken if I had known, but she need n't have let on they was hers an' make everything unpleasant. 'I guess them beans taste just as well as other folks',' says she, and she would n't never speak to me afterward."

"Do' know 's I blame her," ventured Mr. Briley. "Women folks is dreadful pudjicky about their cookin'. I 've always heard you was one o' the best o' cooks, Mis' Tobin. I know them doughnuts an' things you 've give me in times past, when I was drivin' by. Wish I had some on 'em now. I never let on, but Mis' Ash's cookin' 's the best by a long chalk. Mis' Peak's handy about some things, and looks after mendin' of me up."

"It does seem as if a man o' your years and your quiet make ought to have a home you could call your own," suggested the passenger. "I kind of hate to think o' your bangein' here and boardin' there, and one old woman mendin', and the other settin' ye down to meals that like 's not don't agree with ye."

"Lor', now, Mis' Tobin, le 's not fuss round no longer," said Mr. Briley impatiently. "You know you covet me same 's I do you."

"I don't nuther. Don't you go an' say fo'lish things you can't stand to."

"I 've been tryin' to git a chance to put in a word with you ever sence

— Well, I expected you 'd want to get your feelin's kind o' calloused after losin' Tobin."

"There 's nobody can fill his place," said the widow.

"I do' know but I can fight for ye town-meetin' days, on a pinch," urged Jefferson boldly.

"I never see the beat o' you men fur conceit," and Mrs. Tobin laughed. "I ain't goin' to bother with ye, gone half the time as you be, an' carryin' on with your Mis' Peaks and Mis' Ashes. I dare say you 've promised yourself to both on 'em twenty times."

"I hope to gracious if I ever breathed a word to none on 'em!" protested the lover. " 'T ain't for lack o' opportunities set afore me, nuther;" and then Mr. Briley craftily kept silence, as if he had made a fair proposal, and expected a definite reply.

The lady of his choice was, as she might have expressed it, much beat about. As she soberly thought, she was getting along in years, and must put up with Jefferson all the rest of the time. It was not likely she would ever have the chance of choosing again, though she was one who liked variety.

Jefferson wasn't much to look at, but he was pleasant and appeared boyish and young-feeling. "I do' know 's I should do better," she said unconsciously and half aloud. "Well, yes, Jefferson, seein' it 's you. But we 're both on us kind of old to change our situation." Fanny Tobin gave a gentle sigh.

"Hooray!" said Jefferson. "I was scairt you meant to keep me sufferin' here a half an hour. I declare, I 'm more pleased than I calc'lated on. An' I expected till lately to die a single man!"

" 'T would re'lly have been a shame; 't ain't natur'," said Mrs. Tobin, with confidence. "I don't see how you held out so long with bein' solitary."

"I 'll hire a hand to drive for me, and we 'll have a good comfortable winter, me an' you an' the old sorrel. I 've been promisin' of her a rest this good while."

"Better keep her a steppin'," urged thrifty Mrs. Fanny. "She'll stiffen up master, an' disapp'int ye, come spring."

"You 'll have me, now, won't ye, sartin?" pleaded Jefferson, to make sure. "You ain't one o' them that plays with a man's feelin's. Say right out you 'll have me."

"I s'pose I shall have to," said Mrs. Tobin somewhat mournfully. "I feel for Mis' Peak an' Mis' Ash, pore creatur's. I expect they 'll be hardshipped. They 've always been hard-worked, an' may have kind o' looked forward to a little ease. But one on 'em would be left lamentin', anyhow," and she gave a girlish laugh. An air of victory animated the frame of Mrs. Tobin. She felt but twenty-five years of age. In that moment she made plans for cutting her Briley's hair, and making him look smartened-up and ambitious. Then she wished that she knew for certain how much money he had in the bank; not that it would make any difference now. "He need n't bluster none before me," she thought gayly. "He 's harmless as a fly."

"Who 'd have thought we 'd done such a piece of engineerin', when we started out?" inquired the dear one of Mr. Briley's heart, as he tenderly helped her to alight at Susan Ellen's door.

"Both on us, jest the least grain," answered the lover. "Gimme a good smack, now, you clever creatur';" and so they parted. Mr. Briley had been taken on the road in spite of his pistol.

Questions

1. When do you first realize that Mrs. Tobin has designs on Mr. Briley? Reread the beginning of the story and notice if you can discover anything in Mrs. Tobin's earlier speeches which would indicate her interest?
2. Does the dialect seem to be a real dialect to you or merely a literary one, that is, one that uses certain nonstandard forms and a suggestion or two of pronunciation differences? Does the dialect seem sentimental in any way?
3. Do you discover any differences in the two characters' speech? Do they both speak the same social dialect?

Munn Short's Story

Robert Penn Warren *Robert Penn Warren has had a distinguished career as a man of letters—as teacher, critic, editor, novelist, short story writer, and poet. He received the Pultizer Prize in 1947 for his novel* All the King's Men. *In the novel* World Enough and Time *Munn Short tells the following story to Jeremiah Beaumont, who is waiting in prison to be executed. Like many a sermon, for it is a sermon, Munn's story concentrates more on the sinning than on the reformation. But ask yourself as you read if Munn seems sincere in his conversion and in his desire to allay any fear of death Jeremiah may have? Read for the language also. Warren is giving us both a dialect and a highly individualized character. Finally, of course, read for the story. Warren is an excellent teller of tales.*

Dyin," Munn Short said, and pivoted on his good leg, the dirty platter tilting from his hand. "Yeah, dyin," he said, and let the platter sink back to the table, among the clutter of dishes. "Yeah," he said, "hit ain't lak they say, something of angrish and moan. Hit ain't to be feared of."

"What makes you think I am afraid?" Jeremiah demanded angrily. "And want your comfort?" He shoved his chair back from the table.

Short shook his head, and peered down at Jeremiah. "I knows you ain't a-feared," he said. "Air-man could look at you and know, and I has seen 'em feared and not a-feared, and knowed their faces. Ain't no call to be a-feared. Why, Lawd, the graveyard, hit is the cheapest boardin house. Don't cost nobody nuthin, not the man nor the worm neither. Why, Lawd, ain't but one thing more natchel than breathin and that is not breathin. Hit comes easy, and don't take much sleight nor practice. Come the end, and ever-body learn hit. Ain't no call fer a man to be a-feared, and he knows how to come to hit."

"If you mean salvation," Jeremiah said, "what's that to me? You know I am not a believer."

"A pity you ain't, and I'll say hit," Short said. "Fer believin is a help in the dark when the fear comes. But they ain't no call fer the fear, no way, believin or not. Not of the dyin. The angrish and moan is of the livin time, not of the dyin. I knows. Fer I died once."

Jeremiah leaned a little forward, peering at that innocent, old, hairy face, with snub nose and watery-blue, quizzical slit eyes. "You died?" he asked.

"A long time back," Munn Short said. He sat down, and stretched out the bad leg before him like a stick. "Time I got this here," he said, and tapped the bad knee.

"How?" Jeremiah asked. "How did you die?"

"How old you reckin I am?" Munn Short demanded.

Jeremiah studied him. "Maybe fifty-five, fifty-seven."

"Naw, I am seventy, goin on seventy-one. Been forty years since I died. A long time ago, after I come to this here country. Fer I warn't born here. I was born in Virginie, nigh Ca-lina, in them hills. I knows the year, but I done fergot the day. My mammy tole me, but I done fergot, hit is so long. But I rickerlict she said hit was fodder-pullin time and they taken me outa a punkin. Hit was the way she talked to me and me leetle, not much outa swaddlins and hippins. She talked to me by the fire while I come on. She taught me head-countin and tole me about Jesus when I got big to hear. Hit was all the learnin I got, what you might call a fireside eddication. When I learnt to read, hit was later and me growed, after I had done died and I yearned to read the Holy Word how hit is writ.

"But my mammy died when I warn't naught but a sprig, and left me, and hit is hard to see her face, the time is so long. Then my pappy died. They was good folks, my foreparents, but they never had no money and the world's goods to any extreme. They warn't nuthin fer 'em to leave me, but I made hit and growed. Growed to be big and I fit them British the fust time. Virginie and Ca-lina. I was at the Mountin. King's Mountin, and I seen men die, but nuthin tetched me, lead nor sharp steel, and I says to myseff, like a man will and him young, hit ain't for me, the dyin, fer I ain't gonna die.

"Come over the mountins, into Kaintuck. The war warn't over, but folks was movin and goin a-ready. They hear'd how the land laid sweet over the mountins, and they moved toward hit. Folks moved toward land layin sweet and new, lak water down hill. Hit is nay-tur. And me too, and I lived in the new land.

"Lived lak a man will, and labored fer bread. I seen the belt tight and I seen the gut full to plenish, in the change of time and the seasons, how they come. I taken what come and ne'er give thanks, fer hit was my strenth I laid trust in. And I taken my pleasure. I drunk likker and laid on the ground lak a hog. I fit with folks fer no cause, and cut men to let the blood come out. I stole, and I grieve to say hit. A man layin drunk, and I taken what he had. I laid out with women in the bresh. I done all the meanness of man. But a man comes along and he falls in the world and the mud lak a man will. Ain't nuthin to tell him, if he don't harken soft, fer the world, hit is a quagmire and don't hang out no sign.

"One time I was at a station west of here. Tubb's Station, they named hit. We was forted thar agin the Injuns, nineteen folks, ten of us men and the rest women and some chillen. They was a man named Perk, but his last name I fergit, had a wife not more'n a bitsy gal looked lak, sixteen year, maybe. Her hair was dark to night and plenty, and her eyes was blue and she walked the ground light nigh to dancin. Lottie was her name, but we called her Sis fer her littleness and bein so big-eyed to look at you. Perk was old, gittin on to sixty, maybe. He had taken Sis when her folks got kilt nigh Lexington, and he loved her fer a wife, and she loved him and done her duty.

"We made one crop at Tubb's Station, and laid in fer the weather, close but fer the huntin. They was Injuns that fall. We seen their signs, but ne'er hair ner hide. But we hear'd 'em call in the night. Call lak a owl. We laid close, and Sis moved amongst us. I seen her, and I was nigh thirty but my sap was green and she come on my mind. I done hit. Tuk me nigh all winter but I done hit. Made eyes to her and helt her hand, and she jerked hit away, and then time comes she didn't jerk hit away, and one time I put my hand in to lay holt on her sweet little titties, and she just stood thar in the dark a minute and shaken lak a chill, then she run away. She never tole Perk nuthin, so I knowed hit was a-comin.

"Come sugar time. We was gittin sap outa them sugar trees, and I tolled her off in the bresh and done hit. Warn't no trouble, she ne'er strove none, but she cried, and I ast why, didn't she lak hit? She shaken and said how she cried fer Perk. And I said, Perk be damned, and laughed, and said how I had done Perk a favor.

"We laid up close in the Station and hit was hard to git a gal off. Then full spring and they was no more signs of Injuns and folks moved out to make a crop, and hit was more easy. Then she said how she was gonna have a baby, and hit was mine, but Perk never knowed and he was glad. I said to her how I had done Perk a favor, and she cried agin, lak the fust time.

"The cawn was in and folks worked in the crop. They taken the rifles, and some stayed in the Station to keep watch, but we taken no good keer. One day I said to Sis how I would slip off from the fer field and go down the branch and fer her to come. Hit was berry time and she could go to git berries, but hit would not be berries she would git. Hit will be sweeter'n berries, I says to her, and she looked at me big-eyed and her breath come sharp. So I laughed, and went my way. I knowed she would come.

"She come. I was down by the branch, scrouched down in the green bresh, and seen her comin. I whistled low, and she harkened, but never seen me. She come long the branch, footin slow and light on the ground, and lookin all round her, big-eyed. I never stirred, but just lay fer the joy of watchin her come so, lak a pretty critter, shy-lak and touchous and wild. Then I stood up, and put out my hand.

"We had done hit, and laid in the green shade fer breath. Then I hear'd hit. Hit was a man yellin, fer off. Then a rifle, fer off. I lept up to listen, then I knowed, fer thar was the horn from the Station, blowin the sign. Come on, I said, and started, fer I had left my rifle agin a tree towards the field. Come on, I yelled agin, before I got to my rifle, and looked back.

"She had done riz up in the green and whilst I seen her the arrow come. Hit went in, in the chist under the neck, and she didn't make no sound. She just throwed up her arms lak she was liftin 'em up to somebody to hug 'em maybe. Then she fell down.

"A arrow missed me, and I made hit to my rifle. I grabbed hit and dodged behind the tree, and behind another tree, gittin toward the Station. I knowed that Injun was in the woods a-comin, but I did not see him. I never seen him till I got towards the nigh field to the Station, and I seen him and give hit to him. I started to run agin, totin my rifle and hit not loaded now, when the bullet come. Some them Injuns had rifles. The bullet hit me in the leg and I come down. I was tryin to load my rifle, but did not make hit. A Injun come out the woods and run towards me. He grabbed me by the hair and thowed me back. He lifted up his knife, and I knowed I was dead. Hit seemed lak hit taken ferever, me thowed back to look up towards the sky, and that Injun's face and paint dabbed on hit lak hit was floatin in the sky and that-air knife high in the sky ready to come down on me, but hit looked lak hit would never come.

"Hit come. Hit taken me in the chist, towards the left side. I knowed hit was in me, but I never felt hit, just a lettle push lak.

"That Injun thowed my head back holding my hair, and I felt that-air knife tetch my head, fer he was startin to take my scalp. I knowed I was dead. Hit was the last I knowed, fer I was dead and gone.

"Night and I come to. Knowed I was dead and did not know whar I was. I laid a long time not knowin and my eyes shet. Then I hear'd a stir, but hit was fer off and nuthin, lak hit was a dream. Then somethin tetched my mouth, and hit was water, and I opened my eyes. They was somebody thar, but I was too weak to keer. I taken the water, a sup, and shet my eyes.

"I laid long, hit was days and nights, and knowed leetle or nuthin, just layin, and they taken keer fer me. Then I opened my eyes, and hit was toward evenin, and somebody was settin thar. I looked at him, and seemed lak I could not rickerlict nuthin, who hit was setting thar. Hit looked lak time had done gone and left me. Then I knowed I knowed hit all, how hit had been. Hit was Perk settin thar.

"I studied on him and he was lookin at me. I said to him then, how I had been dead. And he said, you was more nigh dead than you knowed.

"Hit was Perk had shot that Injun fixin to scalp me. Perk had been in them woods and not in the field ner the Station. He shot the Injun and he toted me to the Station, and him a old man, while them Injuns was shootin. They started fer him, but them fellers in the Station hit one and skeered 'em back. He got me in, and hit was him taken keer fer me most. He done fer me when he could and would not let other folks. Hit was lak I was his blood-kin, they said. Fer all his grievin fer Sis he done hit. They tole me how Sis was gone.

"My strenth was comin on, slow but hit was comin. Perk would set with me and he would watch me. Sometimes I would shet my eyes lak I was asleep, but squinch-eyed I would be a-watchin him, and he would still be lookin at me and never stop. I studied on hit.

"One day I ast him why he taken keer fer me. And he said, because you air mine. And he looked at me lak he done.

"I was much obleeged, and thanked him kindly fer savin my life. And he said, I never saved yore life. So I tole him what folks said, how he brung me in.

"He said, I brung you in, but I ne'er saved yore life, hit was that Injun saved yore life. And I said, that Injun, why he nigh kilt me. And he said, that Injun nigh kilt you, but me, I'd a kilt you.

"Then I looked at him stidy, and he looked at me, and I knowed that he knowed. I did not say nuthin, but he looked at me and then he said, yeah, I knows, I knows all hit, and I was in the woods, fer I knowed Sis never went fer no berries and I had found you I'd a-kilt you and ne'er said by yore leave.

"I studied on him a minute and I said, why didn't you let me lay and that Injun had kilt me. And he said, I nigh done hit, but hit come on me sudden, how you was mine, and that Injun had no right on you fer you was mine.

"He looked at me, and a skeer growed in me. Hit was not lak the skeer when the Injun lifted up the knife. Hit was another kind, and more deep. My lips was dry, but then I said, what you goin to do?

"Nuthin, he said. And I said, nuthin?

"God damn you, he said, I caint do nuthin, I caint do nuthin I aimed to do and studied on, fer I done brung you in and laid you down and I done give you water to sup, and I set here and aimed to, when you got yore strenth and could know, fer you was mine, but God damn you, I caint, fer I done give you water and they is just us here and them woods, and we air togither, but God damn you, fer I give you water to sup.

"He got up from his cheer, and laid a curse on me, sayin fer God to damn me to hell, fer hit had not been fer me Sis would ne'er left the Station and gone in the green woods and ne'er been taken by them Injuns.

"And I said, taken by them Injuns, did you say taken? And he said, yeah, they taken her, and men done trailed them Injuns, but they never seen 'em. And I ast him how they knowed she was taken, and he said how they had looked good in all them woods whar she went in, and it was the part them Injuns come through and they must of taken her.

"Then I almost bust out and said how Sis was dead and the arrow in her chist, but I could not say hit fer fear and my tongue stuck in my mouth hit was so dry. So I laid thar, and he went away. I laid thar all night, and sweat fer the fear. But ever time I shet my eyes, I seen Sis layin on the ground in the green bresh, and I could not sleep. Then it come so when I laid with my eyes open, I seen Sis layin on the cold ground and the arrow in her leetle chist.

"Hit was nigh day when I called out loud. I yelled, and they come, and I said to git Perk, which they done. He come and I taken his hand and said, the Injuns ne'er taken her, she is dead, and a arrow in her chist. And I told him the part of the woods and the green bresh.

"He did not say nuthin. He looked at me clost, fer the light was comin on, and he went out the door. After sun he come back. He come in and looked down on me whar I laid. Scalped, he said, and looked down on me. Then he said, varmints, varmints and birds, they been at her. They done et they fill of her, and her layin thar. And I thought he was not goin to stand, fer he called out loud, Oh, God, she laid on the cold ground.

"But he stood and looked down on me. Then he said, you had not tole me and I had come thar, I'd a-kilt you, had I given you sup or not, I'd a-kilt you, fer oh, God, I seen the place in the bresh whar you laid and her layin on the cold ground.

"He beat his hands togither, and said, you done kilt her, but I caint do to you lak I aimed, and go yore way, but never fergit you air mine and my name and my mark, they air on you, fer I saved you and brung you in, and you air mine.

"He run out the room, and I never seen him agin. He left the Station. Back towards Lexington in that country, but whar I ne'er knowed.

"I got my strenth, and went forth. But hit was ne'er the same. I knowed how I had laid dead, and come alive, and walked with folks, but inside me I was dead, fer Perk had put his mark on me. I could not rickerlict how it was to be alive lak a-fore, fer last year's hot spell cools off mighty fast in December. And I cried out why I had not been let lay dead on the ground and fergot. Body-dyin was easy when I laid on the ground, but dyin ever day when you walk in the sun, hit is hard, and I cried out fer the mercy.

"Long time, and hit come. Come in the night when I laid and seen how them varmints had come and Sis on the cold ground, and they et on her while she lay, and I cried out how Perk had laid a curse on me and I was his'n and could not git away. Then hit come, how I did not have to be Perk's and his mark on me. I could be Jesus', and the mark plum washed away, lak I had hear'd tell. And I cried out, Oh, kin hit be! I was layin in the night.

"I found the way and the promise, and Jesus come in my heart. He is hung on my heart lak a cow-bell and a cow-bell caint keep no secret. I move and I got to tell about Jesus, how he come. I know you ain't no believer, but . . ."

Jeremiah shoved his chair back sharply on the bricks, and grasped the edge of the table as though about to rise. "But what?" he demanded.

Munn Short looked at him across the dirty dishes under the candle. "Body-dyin," he said, "hit ain't nuthin. I done hurt worse, stubbin my toe in the dark when I was a sprout and runnin. Fer a fack, fer I been dead. But the dyin what ain't body, hit is different. Hit begins and hit don't stop. Till Jesus come in my heart. Red rose don't brag in the dark, but hit shore smell sweet, and Jesus lays in my heart in the dark and is sweet-smellin. I smells Jesus in the dark. Hit ain't lak hit was when I laid and I smelled all night how them varmints had come and Sis a-layin on the bare ground all that time with the weather and that place a-smellin. I smelled hit in the dark, nigh to puke."

Questions

1. What is the effect of having Munn's story told in dialect? What would be lost if Warren had narrated the story in his own words?
2. Munn says he was "born in Virginie, nigh Ca-line, in them hills," and thus places the area in which he learned to speak. After he was "growed" he "come over the mountins, into Kaintuck." Assume that Munn is an informant for a dialect study. You have recorded the story he tells here. What characteristics do you find in his language patterns which would help you to construct a dialect for his area? What specific words and phrases would you want to check against other informants'? What grammatical usage?
3. What vocabulary of Munn's do you fail to understand, even in context? Can you find expressions which Warren seems to use to reveal Munn's character, rather than show his dialect?
4. Warren often presents a character who, outwardly religious, is revealed as a hypocrite. In the headnote you were asked to determine if Munn seemed sincere. Does he or does he not? How does the language he uses help to reveal his true character?

Dimensions of English Usage

David DeCamp *One result of linguists' investigations of English has been a confusion in the minds of teachers and students concerning usage problems. The Miss Fidditch of an earlier generation knew precisely what was right and what was wrong. Her rule book told her. Students may have continued saying what family and friends said, but she pressed for the "correct" form. When grammarians began to look closely at the history of the language and to survey English usage more closely, many of the so-called laws of language on which those rules were based proved to be not laws but some grammarian's assumptions. Often Latin rules were imposed upon English; often the rules were "logical" assumptions. Without the infallibility of the rule book, today's teacher and student have no single standard by which to determine usage. David DeCamp, a contemporary linguist, discusses the twentieth-century background of usage study and the vexing complexity of the problem. As he discusses the six dimensions of usage, try to draw examples from your own experience to illustrate each. In his own attitude toward usage problems, does DeCamp seem to be closer to Miss Fidditch or to "the simple sliding scale" proponents?*

The Tragerian structural linguist, the Chomskian generative linguist, and Miss Fidditch, our dear old English teacher from P. S. 19, are all plagued with the same problem: that of reconciling two very different views of language. Most of the time the linguist looks on language as an abstract theoretical structure, which exists—if it can be said to exist anywhere—in the mind of its speaker, perhaps in the collective mind of all its speakers. He hopes that the grammar he is writing will be an accurate map of that structure, but the means of verifying his hypotheses are complicated and indirect. He will never with his own eyes actually see such a thing as "the English verb" naked and pure. Similarly when Miss Fidditch teaches her

David DeCamp, "Dimensions of English Usage," from *Reflections on High School English*, ed. Gary Tate. Reprinted by permission of The University of Tulsa Press.

grammar class, she too deals in abstract structures and moves in a world of nouns, verbs, subjunctives, gerunds, and other "unreal" postulated entities. Her theories may differ slightly from the linguist's theories, but they are still theories rather than observed facts.

When the linguist heads for a Navajo village and a summer of field-work, however, or when he dabbles in dialectology or phonetics, he must see language not as an abstraction but as people talking and writing, a complicated profusion of people and circumstances and social mores and sounds and marks on paper. Similarly Miss Fidditch faces three or four classes, consisting of more than a hundred bewilderingly diverse youngsters, all of them constantly engaged in unique and unpredictable acts of language. That odd sentence in Johnny's last composition, the even odder one in the poem assigned for next week—how to reconcile these with the comfortable mathematical security of the grammar class? For there is indeed something comfortable and secure about grammar. It is like geometry with its ideal perfect circles, squares, and triangles, whereas most of English teaching is more like surveying, where none of the measurements ever come out exactly right, where even a straight line is only approximated, and where the surveyor must triangulate on the basis of imperfect triangles.

This double view of language was most articulately expressed at the turn of the century by the Swiss linguist de Saussure, who applied the term *la langue* to the underlying, abstract, constant structure, and applied the term *la parole* to the infinitely variable, empirically observable acts of language. The dictionary translations of these two terms (*language* for *la langue* and *word* or *speech* for *la parole*) fail to convey the same idea, and many linguists continue to use the French words as technical terms. Linguists since de Saussure have developed various approaches to reconciling these two views of language. The Tragerians, for example, have tried to structure both an "overall pattern" to account for the composite of all English language acts and a "common core" restricted to those characteristics which all varieties of the language share in common. The generative linguists are working on sets of supplementary rules which, hopefully, may map out the relationships between the general grammatical principles which you find in your textbooks and the linguistic diversity which you daily face in your classrooms. Much progress has been made; much more such work needs to be done.

In this lecture, however, I wish to discuss not linguistic theory but Miss Fidditch's own approaches to the paradox of *la langue* and *la parole*. The older Miss Fidditch operated on the principle that optional alternatives were intolerable. There was one and only one correct form for everything. Free choice was anarchy. Try to imagine how many arguments were settled, thanks to her influence, and how many bets paid off by looking up a word in the dictionary to see which form came first and which second—all this despite the fervent disclaimer by the editors in the prefaces to most dictionaries, insisting that the second entry is in no way substandard. After all, you can't print two alternatives and have them both come first! The half truth so widely mouthed by the semanticists in the 1930's, that there are no synonyms, only confirmed her conviction that there is no permissible variation in language. The parents of her pupils were bent on middle-class social climbing, a parlor game in which gaucheries like *it don't* automatically disqualify a player, and any teacher foolish enough to deviate from the unrelenting pursuit of the one and only correct form of English would be crucified at the next PTA meeting.

The older Miss Fidditch's intuitions on this matter were not entirely wrong. They seldom were. Like her rules of grammar, they were too vague and too limited and sometimes erred in detail, but they had some basis in fact. No sensible, well-informed person today wants to leave your language alone, not even the author of the book whose first edition bore that unfortunate title. Given enough context, not only the linguistic context of what is said before and after the form in question but also the social and cultural context in which it is used, it is almost always possible to choose and say that this word is better than that one *under these circumstances.* Value judgments can be—in fact, must be—made, but only in reference to larger contexts. We cannot evaluate elements in isolation. Hydrogen supports life when we drink it in water, but few of us choose concentrated hydrochloric acid as our cup of tea. Hydrogen is not in itself either a good element or a bad element. It is indeed better to use the letter *c* than the letter *k* in spelling the word *cat,* but we hardly insist that *c* is a better letter of the alphabet than *k*. Miss Fidditch stopped short of this absurdity of evaluating letters of the alphabet, but she did consider herself capable of isolated and absolute judgments on *shall, irregardless, might could,* and *you all.* For one thing, this simplified her problem of reconciling *la langue* and *la parole.* By outlawing all variation, she thought she could establish a simple one-to-one relationship between her grammatical principles and the written and spoken word. This she called logic. At this point my grammar has only triangular holes; square and oval pegs need not apply!

The 1920's were a decade of usage surveys. J. Leslie Hall's book *English Usage* had appeared in 1917, challenging the single standard. Hall's source was 75,000 pages of English and American literature, and his book bristled with incontrovertable statistics; e.g., found in 65 reputable authors 453 times. Yet teachers did not accept Hall's conclusion that "Custom is the most certain mistress of language." Even Matthew Arnold and Walter Pater may have exercised poetic license, the teachers argued, and little Johnny had darn well better learn correct English first; there will be plenty of time for him to experiment with the language after he has become an established great author. So do as I preach, not as Pater practices.

The presence of variable usage in literary masterpices failed to move Miss Fidditch. In the 1920's, therefore, three major surveys were launched, attempting this time to examine the living usage. In 1927, Sterling Leonard and H. Y. Moffett published their article "Current Definition of Levels in English Usage." [1] Their research was expanded to a survey of the usage attitudes of 229 prominent members of our society, including well-known authors, editors of influential publications, and leading businessmen, and was published in full by Leonard in 1932 in his *Current English Usage.* In 1926, C. C. Fries began his survey of the English usage found in about three thousand letters written to a U. S. government agency. The socio-economic backgrounds of the people who wrote these letters were correlated with the usage in the letters, and Fries' report, *American English Grammar,* not published until 1940, divided English into three types: *standard* English, characteristic of writers with college education and professional standing in the community, *popular* or *common English,* normally used by high school graduates, and *vulgar* English, characteristic of uneducated laborers. Both the Leonard and the Fries surveys were published by the National Council of Teachers of English. In their time they were shockingly controversial, though they seem quite innocuous to us now. Fries was—and still occasionally is—subjected to many vitriolic attacks as the advocate of laissez-faire in linguistics and in morality in general, the arch-conspirator whose treason finally culminated in the great betrayal at Springfield in 1961. The third great survey begun in the 1920's was the Linguistic Atlas of America. Although field work for the atlas did not begin until 1931, the project began with the formal proposal in 1928, and plans involving the social levels to be surveyed were worked out before the end of the decade. Hans Kurath, director of the atlas, adopted Fries' three types, and the tradition became firmly established that American English exists in high, middle, and lowbrow varieties.

Miss Fidditch was not quick to change. Unless she was the type who attended NCTE meetings and regularly read such publications as the *English Journal,* she probably did not even know about these surveys until the 1940's when the publication of Fries created such a stir. R. C. Pooley's *Handbook of Current English Usage* [2] appeared in 1930, but it had little immediate influence; Pooley did not become a common classroom word until 1946, when his *Teaching English Usage* was published. And of course

[1] *English Journal,* XVI (May, 1927), 345–56.

[2] Colorado State Teachers College Bulletin, Series 30, June, 1930, No. 3.

the appearance in 1934 of the second edition of *Webster's New International Dictionary* set off a flurry of controversy as violent as that following the publication of the third edition in 1961. But few changes in the teaching of usage filtered down to the classroom until the postwar years.

The status of linguistics was considerably elevated by the success of the wartime accelerated language courses. Both the colleges and the high schools installed language labs and overhauled their creaky curricula in foreign languages. It is inconceivable that we would ever go back to the slow old translation methods by which languages were taught in the 1930's. The teaching of English as a foreign language became a recognized and respectable professional specialty, a branch of applied linguistics. It was inevitable that linguistics would invade Miss Fidditch's grammar class. Textbooks in the new English grammar began to appear. The NCTE, which always had been sympathetic toward linguistics, was thoroughly infiltrated by linguists and became the subversive organization it is today. A course in English structure became a requirement for the teacher's certificate in most states. The summer institutes pioneered by the College Board's Commission on English and now the entry of the U. S. Office of Education have hastened the capitulation, and Miss Fidditch has been so thoroughly brainwashed that she no longer opposes the linguists' theories of grammar, but too often expects the linguist to bring her the revealed word of truth from on high.

A revised attitude toward usage entered the classroom as a fellow-traveler with the new grammar. Miss Fidditch reluctantly gave up the fight for *I shall* as a lost cause. The three Fries-Kurath types (standard, common, and vulgar) became the new dogma. Miss Fidditch stopped thinking about correct and incorrect English and began to think in terms of good, not so good, and awful. With the dike breached by the acceptance of *I will* and *it's me* even in her textbooks, she believed that the good was no longer attainable, that she had no choice but to support the not-so-good and to shore up fragments against the influx of the awful. Quit trying so hard for perfection, she was told, or just quit trying altogether. Leave your language alone. Be descriptive, not prescriptive—whatever that means.

The results have been dismal. Miss Fidditch now vacillates between her old unenlightened despotism and a new unenlightened anarchy. She is trapped in a pincer maneuver between the NCTE and the PTA. The confusion in today's attitudes toward usage is well illustrated in an Ann Landers column which appeared recently:

> *"Dear Ann Landers:*
>
> "I'm a Chicagoan who is stationed at Fort Hood, Texas. Your answer will settle a small civil war in our barracks. We have guys in our

outfit who hail from all parts of the country. The fellows from New York and Texas pronounce the letters 'u' and 'ew' as if there was a 'Y' in front. It comes out 'You.' For example, they say 'Nyoo York' and 'nyoospaper.' The midwesterners and the west coast guys say 'Noo York' and 'noozpaper.'

"The words 'produce,' 'consume,' and 'student' get the same treatment from the Texans and New Yorkers. They put a little 'y' sound in. We notice that Chet Huntley says, 'N.B.C. Nyoos, Nyoo York' and David Brinkley says, 'N.B.C. Nooz, Washington.'

"Can you tell us which is correct?—FORT HOOD GANG.

"Dear Gang:

"I have checked four dictionaries. No two agree.

"The best answer to your question is in Fowler's Modern English Usage. It says 'We deserve not praise but censure, if we decline to accept the popular pronunciation of popular words.' This means there is no right or wrong, so imitate the natives.

"Good night, David. Good night, Chet. We enjoy your nooz in Chicago."

Of course Ann Landers' answer is half right, but oh that statement that there is no right or wrong in language—and imagine citing Fowler, of all people, to support it!

If Ann Landers is indeed echoing the new popular attitude toward usage, as I fear, then it is later than we think. It means that the authors of all those slick shiny new pretty textbooks and handbooks, each of which competes to be the most modern and up to date, have so distorted the real and eminently sensible conclusions of Fries and Kurath and the other surveyors of usage that it may take us a decade to get back to sanity. For when these textbook writers and a whole gaggle of new self-appointed experts on English language teaching who have never even read those surveys, though they invariably cite the titles in their footnotes and bibliographies—when these camp followers substituted the Fries-Kurath scale for the old invariable absolute, they loaded that scale with all kinds of extraneous junk. The "standard" end of the scale was equated with literary, formal, rhetorically effective, and other irrelevant adjectives. The "vulgar" end was equated with illiterate, slang, colloquial, jargon, and dialect.

Such a composite scale is, of course, illogical and unusuable. Is *ain't* to be considered literary because it appears in *Huckleberry Finn,* or illiterate because it is used by the garbage man? And how about those little dialogues between Mercutio and his friends in *Romeo and Juliet?* Are they literary or vulgar? The Bostonian "Pahk youh cah beside the Hahvahd pahts depahtment" is a local dialect, but hardly restricted to the speech of illiterates. Faced with such an inconsistent scale, on which one end was obviously mother, home, and heaven, the other end the black pit, but along which Miss Fidditch was completely unable to navigate because these inconsistencies kept spinning the compass, she simply gave up and concluded that all virtue is relative and it doesn't really matter very much. Let's be descriptive, not prescriptive, anyway!

Even some of the highly competent and responsible authorities must share some of the blame for this absurd all-purpose usage scale and the consequent lapse into laissez-faire. Porter Perrin's *Writer's Guide and Index of Usage* replaced the conservative *Harbrace Handbook* as the most widely adopted freshman text, largely because of his elaborate scale of usage, ranging from literary at one end (the highest, naturally) to vulgate, slang, and dialect at the other. Pooley's *Teaching English Usage,* the most influential of the how-to-do-it books, used a five-tone scale: Literary, Standard Formal, Standard Informal, Homely, and Illiterate. Pooley was apparently following George Philip Krapp, one of the finest scholars on the English language, whose classification was Literary, Formal Colloquial, General Colloquial, Popular, and Vulgar.

In 1948 John S. Kenyon published a very important paper entitled "Cultural Levels and Functional Varieties of English" [3] in which he attacked the single, multi-purpose scale and insisted that functional varieties (i.e., written vs. spoken) must be considered separately from cultural levels (i.e., upper vs. lower class usage). One dimension is not enough to fix a point of usage. The same warning had appeared in the first chapter of Fries, but no one had paid it much attention. Kenyon's article did indeed have some effect: Subsequent editions of Perrin, for example, adopted a two-dimensional scale of usage. But only a few of the textbook writers heeded the warning.

Even Kenyon combined many incompatibles. His examples of the lower cultural level included "illiterate speech, narrowly local dialect, ungrammatical speech and writing, excessive and unskilful slang, slovenly and careless vocabulary and construction, exceptional pronunciation." Kenyon was committing the very sin against which he preached so eloquently: loading one end of the value scale with a whole wastebasketful of miscellaneous evils. The "Hahvahd Yahd" pronunciation is "narrowly local" and perhaps even "exceptional" but certainly not of low cultural level. The slang of our teenagers may be inappropriate in an essay on *Silas Marner,* but it has little in common with the speech of illiterates. And I have been most offended by "slovenly and careless vocabulary" in graduate

[3] *College English,* X (October, 1948), 31–36.

theses and dissertations written by pompous prudes who would sooner die than to ever split an infinitive.

Today we find three different and incompatible attitudes toward usage simultaneously current: The old invariable absolute of Miss Fidditch, moribund but not yet dead; the single sliding scale of the early Perrin, unfortunately now the most popular in the classroom; and Kenyon's two-dimensional scale distinguishing functional varieties from cultural levels. Now two dimensions are better than one, or none, but I suggest that they are not enough. To push the geometrical metaphor a bit further, two intersecting lines can indeed define a point, but it takes three dimensions to define a solid object, and a fourth to place it in time. For a concept so complex and elusive as usage, we need at least six dimensions.

One of these dimensions, as Kenyon quite rightly insisted, is functional variety or style. This is not a single binary contrast between written and spoken English, however, for there are many occasions on which we talk like a book, and we often write, or try to write, in a friendly conversational style. I am now speaking to you, but from a prepared written text. Does that make this lecture a sample of spoken English or of written English? No, style is a scale with more than two values, perhaps a continuous dimension. The most sensitive and sensible attempt I have yet seen to articulate this scale is Martin Joos's *The Five Clocks*—an absolute essential on your reading lists, for it is written both to and for the new enlightened Miss Fidditch. Joos calibrates this scale with five values, five styles, each of which may be either written or spoken: The *intimate* style, which communicates the person and the situation rather than information (after all, who could paraphrase the content of the "conversation" of nuzzling young lovers?); the *casual* style, that easy discourse which so comfortably keeps you a member of your in-group; the *consultative* style with which we earn and buy our daily bread, informative conversation normally punctuated at six-second intervals with cooperative interruptions from the listener (. . . yes . . . that's right . . . m-hm . . . yeah); the *formal* style, to be interrupted only by someone raising his hand or invoking some similar device of parliamentary procedure; and the *frozen* style, the language of those texts which we value enough to keep intact and periodically repeat verbatim, each time thawing the frozen text enough to savor the taste and aroma. It is no wonder that we prefer reading literature to hearing public lectures: any normal child prefers sucking a popsicle to drinking orange pop.

A second dimension of usage is geographical. Too many English teachers still think of a dialect as "what the other fellow speaks; I myself speak General American." The myth of a "general American" dialect was obsolete even before Kurath published his *World Geography of the Eastern United States* in 1949, yet it lingers on in our classrooms. Yankee Miss

Fidditches still condemn *you-all* as an illogical, illiterate vulgarism, just as they did when I was a child in their classes. And the Yankee is in turn reviled for his use of *dove* as the past tense of *dive*. Indeed some expressions are so narrowly localized, like the Bostonion *tonic,* for example, that they are better avoided when writing for nationwide publication, but they are certainly not substandard. Each of us speaks a dialect, and our regionalisms inevitably creep into our writing. If we try to avoid them, or warn our students to avoid them, it should be because they interfere with communication. If and when there is a case against *you-all,* it must rest on grounds very different from those relevant to *ain't* and *it don't.*

A third dimension is time. Historical change in language is both inevitable and continuous, not just something that happened at the time of the Norman Conquest. Nostalgia for the linguistic past is also nothing new. Remember that Spenser thought of Chaucer as a "well of English undefiled." The smart Miss Fidditch no longer cites Shakespeare to prove a point of usage, for she has learned that the Bard can be a two-edged sword in the hands of a bright and rebellious student. Yet she often uses *Silas Marner* and *A Tale of Two Cities* as prescriptive models for her students' prose. No one really wants or welcomes linguistic change, but the teacher is powerless to stop or even to retard it. She should be moderately conservative linguistically and there is no need for her to champion every emergent neologism just because it has appeared once in *Time* magazine. But continued tilting at the windmill of *disinterested/uninterested* only reduces her to an anachronism without any of the nobility of the gentle knight.

A fourth dimension is age. There is no reason why the child should talk like his grandfather, or vice versa. The language of Holden Caulfield's monologue would be singularly inappropriate for Hemingway's old man talking to his fish, but it is not in and of itself bad English. The speeches of John F. Kennedy were youthful and vigorous; we can only guess how he might have written as an elder statesman. A fifth dimension is sex. Can you imagine one of the football players in your senior English class describing the day of the big game as "utterly lovely"? We recognize that the masculine idiom differs from the feminine when we make critical judgements about Jane Austen, but do we sufficiently recognize the rights and needs of our students to speak and write in a manner appropriate to their sex and age group?

This leaves a sixth dimension, that of cultural level. Does Johnny speak and write in a social dialect which types him as coming from the wrong side of the tracks? If so, it is not because he is stupid or sloppy-thinking or even ignorant of English grammar. Explaining the principles of English verb agreement will not make him stop saying *it don't.* If you try to tell him that *I don't have no money* really means "I do have some money," he merely recognizes you for the fool you are. He knows very well—and so do you—that his sentence means nothing of the sort. He speaks this way because his parents and his friends speak this way. We acquire a social dialect the same way we acquire a geographical dialect, and no study of grammar (traditional, structural, or transformational) is going to change it. Dialects cannot be compared and evaluated in terms of logic, only in terms of appropriateness to the situation. After all, one can make a pretty strong logical case for *ain't: He's a student, isn't he? You're a student, aren't you? I'm a student, . . .?* The research of my students in a seminar on social dialectology has clearly established that this linguistic social stratification in usage is firmly ingrained by kindergarten age. This is the logic in which these children think; to them, the teacher's dialect seems illogical.

If we tell Johnny that the use of *ain't* in certain social circles may prevent him from getting an invitation to join the country club (and from getting a good enough job to pay the club dues), then he starts to listen. But—and here is the controversial point on which so many critics have misinterpreted the linguists—we should not condemn *ain't* as a word, only its use in circumstances where it will evoke social disapproval. We hear a lot about aid to "disadvantaged youth" in these days of the War on Poverty, but no one holds that making a child ashamed of his family and friends is a legitimate goal of such programs. Ideally we should make Johnny bidialectal, able to travel in the country-club set without linguistic handicap, yet able to return to his home and friends without alienating them with pretentious manners and speech. We should help him to social-climb without becoming a snob, minimize rather than contribute to the cultural conflict which results from social mobility. People used to think that they could improve a bilingual child's English by stamping out his foreign language. Therefore Spanish-speaking children in Texas were punished for speaking Spanish, and both Spanish language and Spanish culture (except Castillian, of course) were treated with contempt. We now know that this unfortunate policy only rendered the child incapable of living comfortably in either culture. We found that when we encouraged pride in his bilingualism and in his Spanish heritage, he actually learned English faster, provided, of course, that he could see the important social and economic motives for doing so.

Bidialectism is like bilingualism, better approached positively than negatively. If your school has a dominant clique of students from "culturally advantaged" middle-class homes, your job is easy. You have only to assist Johnny in acquiring the linguistic social tools he needs to break into the circle of friends he admires. Teenagers are great conformists, with a classicist's respect for proper form, and they will learn more about usage on the ballfield and in the schoolyard than you can teach them in the classroom. But if the top dogs in your school are the gang of leather jacket and *it don't* boys, you have a problem, for the child will inevitably adopt whatever English usage gives him the most status among his peers. All you can do is try to supply the motivation which he does not get through natural channels. If your invocations of the country club and good job and your parade of heroes who don't say *it don't* all fail to move him, then you will almost certainly fail. In either case, you will get further with a positive approach. Johnny is a lot more likely to say *isn't* in the English class if you don't try to stop him from saying *ain't* in the schoolyard.

Even if the worst happens: the social organization of your student body does make your task hopeless and you do fail, and Johnny goes right on saying *ain't,* this is not a very important failure, certainly not worth making nagging old curmudgeons out of yourselves and breaking diplomatic relations with your students. There are so many things that you can do to help your students, even if you can't make a dent in their vulgate. You teach them composition, literature, grammar. And there are the other five dimensions of usage, in which you are not bucking the system and so can get through to the student. Johnny may be very interested in learning how language varies geographically, for example, and an understanding of regional variation may awaken an interest in how language can also vary socially, so that you eventually get through to him after all. Perhaps the society on the right side of the tracks is too remote and alien to motivate him at all; then let him wait a few years. When his life later does produce a need to associate with people outside his purloined-hubcap fraternity, he will make his own adjustments in social usage; that is, he will if you have given him some understanding of the usage problem rather than just loading him down with so many negative inhibitions that they only block his later attempts to find himself linguistically. Your proper goal is linguistic awareness, of self and of society.

These six dimensions of usage must be carefully distinguished, both from one another and from a seventh but different scale, what we might call the scale of *responsibility*. On this scale, value judgements are indeed relevant: how responsible has Johnny been in selecting exactly those points on the other six dimensions which will make his language most appropriate for this specific occasion, and how responsibly has he combined these language forms into a logical, coherent, effective discourse? It is this which we should be evaluating when we put a grade on his composition. Another name for this scale is *rhetoric*. It is the legitimate subject matter of the course in composition. The six dimensions of usage must also be taught in the English class, however, for they are the factors which condition the long, almost continuous string of the linguistic decisions which one must make in putting together a responsible composition.

But, Miss Fidditch will protest, how can we teach Johnny to make the hundreds of decisions on English usage which are so necessary in any responsible writing or speaking if every decision is itself such a complicated problem as you say, a function of six variable factors? Wouldn't he be paralyzed by having to stop at each word and work out the mathematics? Indeed he would, *if* the entire process had to operate at the deliberate, fully-conscious level. Fortunately our minds contain a wonderful mechanism which reduces a great deal of this decision-making to subconscious habit. Given enough experience—and good English teaching is mostly a matter of providing and directing that experience—a good writer or speaker learns to continuously evaluate the context and the situation and make the proper choices with little or no conscious awareness of the process.

Permit me another analogy: When you first learned to drive a car, you perhaps despaired of ever mastering the complicated coordination of your hands on the wheel and gearshift lever and your feet on the pedals. The worst part was that the proper thing to do with your hands and feet kept changing from moment to moment, depending on what you saw through the windshield and on the dashboard dials and what you heard and felt the car do. If your approach to this complex problem was to oversimplify it by reducing it to a set of invariable rules ("Always keep your eyes on the road." "Apply the brakes when you see danger ahead."), then you became a bad driver, the kind that slams on the brakes when skidding on an icy road, and who forgets to look in the rear-view mirror before changing lanes. If you are a good driver (as I am sure that all of you are), it is because you developed flexibility rather than rigidity in your reactions to new situations, and because you practiced driving under varying conditions until the appropriate reactions became second nature to you, so that now people compliment you by saying that you "instinctively" do the right thing in an emergency.

When I was a child in seventh grade, the local school system decided that we young barbarians needed social polish and so hired to lecture to us on etiquette an elderly widow, then living in modest circumstances but earlier, so she told us, the flower of Eastern Society. Her lectures were straight out of Emily Post, and the society she described might as well have been on Mars. I remember her telling us that when we went to call on our little friends, their butler would of course greet us at the door. If the young master were not at home, the butler would always present a silver tray, on which we were to lay our visiting cards. But, she warned us, before we placed the card on the tray, we had to bend down the proper corner of the card—I believe it was to be the lower right-hand corner, but I have forgotten that detail. Now in that little piney-woods community, a few of the more affluent families may have owned silver trays, but certainly no butlers. And visiting cards?! No, this instruction was absurd, not because there was anything wrong with butlers and visiting cards, nor because her rule of the proper corner was incorrect, but because she presented these as inflexible absolutes, ideals of social behavior for anyone anywhere. Even if we were too poor to buy visiting cards, she graciously assured us, we could write them out ourselves in a good Palmer hand and carry them along with us when we went to ask Butch or Spike to come out for an afternoon of stealing apples from the orchard behind the insane asylum.

Certainly we show much more sense today, both in driver training and in teaching our kids social manners. What excuse then is there for the English teacher's vacillating between the old invariable absolute and a game of laissez-faire on a sliding scale. I don't propose a compromise, for I believe that both alternatives are equally dead wrong. To insist that square pegs go in square holes, triangular pegs in triangular holes, is not a proposal of a compromise between the idiocy of one fool who insists that square pegs are always nicer than triangular ones, and that of the other fool who claims that the shape of the pegs isn't really very important. What I propose is that we be uncompromisingly demanding of our students that they employ the *correct usage,* the *responsible* usage.

Of course you will be criticized for doing so, but then the good teacher has always found his cup of hemlock to be both inevitable and strangely rewarding. There are conservatives who will accuse you of "giving up all standards of right and wrong." There will be liberals who, with equal injustice, will accuse you of being "prescriptive old grammarians hostile to modern linguistic science." Hardest of all to bear will be those who will accuse you of being compromisers or, even worse, eclectics.

But you can defend yourselves. I was recently interviewed by a news reporter who was preparing a syndicated feature series on the "new grammar" and English teaching. I talked with him for two hours, but I am afraid that he went back to his newspaper not yet thoroughly converted, for a few days later I received the following letter from him:

"*Dear Dr. DeCamp:*

"Many, many thanks for the interesting interview last week. I came away from our talk much better informed than before.

"However (life is a whole series of "howevers"), there is something that bothers me. This is in what my limited knowledge of the modern movement sees as a too indulgent attitude toward the standard or prestige dialect.

"If the standard dialect were divested of its authority, if the level of language represented for example in the writing of Churchill is placed on the same value scale as the cottonfield jargon of Alabama—if we no longer have the goal of "correct" English, then what will we really have?

"As I see it the existence of a prescriptive norm creates an upward thrust to the language. That is, the existence of a The Correct Way tends to urge an upward striving which continuously works for the betterment of communication. Without an authority level would not the upward striving be brunted? Would not the course of the language's evolution become slightly degraded?

"As I see it there must be a prescribed goal to all human endeavor. As I see it a bad king given to arbitrary, inconsistent action is to be preferred, still, to anarchy. A semblance of order is better than confusion, I feel."

This is not a foolish letter. This newsman is not an idiot or a fanatic. He is an intelligent man of affairs, genuinely trying to find out what is going on in English classes today. That even he would write such a letter proves what a great task lies before us to inform the public as well as to teach their children. The newsman deserved an extended reply, and I wrote one. I will conclude today by reading that reply, not that I offer it as a model for replies to letters of this sort which you will certainly receive, but because it sums up most of the ideas of this lecture and arrays them in battle formation. For it is your battle too: a fight for your rights to be prescriptive, but correctly prescriptive, a fight for your freedom to get on with the job of helping Johnny learn, not to use better English, but to use English better. And that is really what usage is all about. Here is what I wrote:

There is no danger of "the course of the language's evolution" becoming "degraded," as you fear. Language is only the medium of communication. Shakespeare was a great dramatist because he knew how to write well, not because Elizabethan English was superior. To assume otherwise is like saying that Rembrandt was a great painter because he had better paints and canvas than modern artists have. The English language is now, always has been, and probably always will be perfectly adequate—*equally* adequate—as a medium of good writing. Unfortunately not all people are equally adept at using that medium. Therefore we need English teachers.

The attitude toward the standard or prestige dialect held by the linguist or the responsible English teacher is no more indulgent than it ever has been in any century. Of course we do not place the writing of Churchill on the same value scale as the cottonfield jargon of Alabama

—your example—because there is no value scale including both these. There are at least three variables involved here. Remember my telling you about the several dimensions in which language may vary? Well, to begin with, Churchill is formal writing; the cottonfield is informal conversation. Second, Churchill was a well-to-do, upper-class English gentleman, whereas the cottonfield worker is economically and culturally lower class. Third, Churchill was a disciplined mind and an experienced and talented writer, whereas very few of the field workers would have the ability to write the history of the second world war even if someone gave them the opportunity. The first of these is a dimension (or scale, if you prefer) of functional varieties of language. After all, Churchill did not always speak as he wrote; he was a delightful informal conversationalist. Of course his informal conversation was not the same as that of the field worker, but we would have to compare the two men either by their formal writing or by their informal speech. Formal written prose is not in and of itself better than conversation. Each has its place; each is out of place in situations demanding the other—could you imagine your wife greeting you in Churchillian periods?—and there are both good and bad examples of each.

The second dimension by which your two examples vary is cultural level. The kid from the slums speaks differently, despite our efforts at democratic education. This is one way we can tell a judge from a janitor even if both are wearing bathing suits at the beach and we only hear them talking about the weather. The two simply speak different dialects, social dialects.

The third dimension relevant here is rhetorical. In this dimension, value judgments are indeed in order. A disciplined, logical mind, a clear sense of organization, a feel for the most effective and persuasive expression. We admire these characteristics in Churchill and deplore their absence in the field laborer, though they occasionally do appear in the speech and writing of an uneducated laborer. No one defends sloppy thinking. Now it is true that the clear-thinking, rhetorically-competent man is often upper class socially, simply because his competence advances him to a higher income bracket. It is also true that he is usually in a position where he will be producing more formal writing than will the laborer. But the three dimensions are not necessarily correlated. Disorganized, illogical trash is written in formal style by persons of upper class using impeccable "grammar"—witness the current government gobbledygook or the correspondence and memos written by most industrial executives. I won't even mention journalese. Churchill's table talk was colloquial yet superb. So was Mark Twain, even when through the mouth of Huck Finn he used *ain't* and all the other shibboleths of lower class usage.

No, we are not "indulgent." We complain that the old-line English teachers were too indulgent. They gave (and some still do give) the student an A on a paper, no matter how inane and disorganized, just as long as the verbs all agreed in number, the commas were in the right places, and the student refrained from using *ain't*. Therefore, as you yourself admitted, their training had little to offer you in your career as a writer.

We believe that the teacher should be far more demanding rhetorically than ever before, that there should be no compromise with sloppiness in composition. On the cultural dimension, we believe that the teacher should deal with all the social variants, giving the student facility in shifting to different varieties, and being honest about the social implications of using each; after all, in some circumstances saying *it don't* is indeed socially equivalent to spitting on the carpet, but *I shall* and *Whom did you meet* are kisses of death to a politician—and possibly to a newspaper writer as well. Finally, on the functional or stylistic dimension, the teacher should give attention to all the stylistic levels which her students are likely to use. Instead of damning informal English or apologizing for it, she should help her students use it well.

In summary, I find it as illogical to attribute Churchill's greatness as a writer to his use of upper-class standard grammar as to attribute it to the fact that he always smoked big cigars.

Questions

1. Explain in your own words the two views of language DeCamp discusses at the beginning of this article.
2. What are the common expressions in colloquial English in your community that would not be acceptable to the teachers who followed Miss Fidditch? How successful has the school been in removing these expressions from everyday speech?
3. At this point in your study of language, how do you feel about change in language? Are all changes bad? Does no change mean that the language is dead? Do you think there should be some change but some restraint also? Or do you feel that the language should be completely unhampered, that the more it changes the better it becomes?
4. Explain DeCamp's statement that students should learn "not to use better English, but to use English better."
5. Distinguish between "cultural levels" and "functional varieties" of language.

6. What does DeCamp mean when he says that the goal of the English teacher in working with students should be helping them to achieve "linguistic awareness, of self and of society"? How does this goal differ from Miss Fidditch's goal of teaching the student correct English?
7. How apt is DeCamp's analogy comparing learning to drive a car well with learning to use language effectively?
8. As DeCamp analyzes it, English usage is a very complex (and vexing) problem. Do you feel that the problem is as complex as he indicates? Do you agree with him that the "invariable absolute" (right and wrong) and "single sliding scale" (formal, informal, substandard) are totally inadequate? Explain.
9. Using DeCamp's terminology, how would you describe such expressions as "I will," "it's me," and "who did you meet"?

Suggestions for Writing

1. To illustrate one of his points, DeCamp relates an experience he had as a seventh grade student. Choose some experience you have had which involves several people and which has some point to it. Retell the experience using specific and concrete detail effectively. You may choose not to state your point (thesis) directly but let it be implicit in the experience you relate.
2. There are three letters expressing concern about English usage in this article. Select some concern you have had with usage or a concern you have heard others express. Now that you are acquainted with DeCamp's views on usage, write a letter to him or to some other interested party discussing how DeCamp's views have influenced your position or how you disagree with his point of view. Be sure to state your points clearly and to develop them with specific and concrete detail.

For All But the Breaking Heart

George and Helen Waite Papashvily *The following is an entertaining story taken from a delightful book entitled* Anything Can Happen. *You will be impressed with the fresh figures of speech in the conversation and you will be delighted with the characters. Our major concern, however, is with the language used in the story. We are all acquainted with the "accents" of foreigners who have learned English as adults. We can identify the speech of people from France, from Germany, from Spanish-speaking countries. Because learning English presents different problems to speakers of other languages, speakers of each foreign language develop their own peculiar dialect of English. In the following story you will see characteristics of the English spoken by speakers from Russia. The authors have indicated these characteristics occasionally by the spelling of a word but more frequently by word choice or use of grammatical structures.*

When we discuss dialect or usage differences, we discuss pronunciation, vocabulary, and grammatical differences. In this story such differences make the speech more vivid and add to the creation of the characters in the story. Note especially the grammatical differences —particularly in the use of verbs and in word order. These differences add to our appreciation of the story and our enjoyment of the characters. Would you advocate that these people eliminate their dialect of English and learn standard English? We think you will agree that the language used adds a great deal to the vividness and the vitality of the story.

One of our boys, Illarion, worked in a big college. He had there duties to watch through a telescope at the stars and see they stayed all in their places and between times he taught the students what tricks he knew like the way to measure the sun and what gonna be the shortest distance to get up on the moon or where the comets hurrying when they go so fast by. He was, how they call in English, an astronomer.

It didn't pay much, his job, considering there was such lot a night shift to it, but Illarion, thank God, hasn't got the kind of heart that's always aching after money. No, his pleasure was study and more study, and now and then for recreation maybe to catch a couple of stars that weren't around before and give them nice names and write them down in book. That, and a glass of wine once a week with his friends, he'd be a perfectly satisfied man, Illarion.

Now it was his usual custom to meet us every Friday night in a restaurant and have a good time together with us. Because even if Illarion was big professor and sat on platforms with a black board to cover his head, and people bowing down, still when he came in a party he had sense enough to leave his education home and sing and dance and drink and tell stories and enjoy himself like a human being.

Well, came this Friday and he didn't show up. Boiled *beche* we ordered, too. That's a piece of veal shoulder boiled with herbs. His favorite.

"I hope nothing be wrong," Vactangi told us, "but Illarion reads too much. Specially out of those thick heavy books. I warned him it gonna give him trouble some day. Not even pictures in them to break up the pages."

"I don't believe it hurts him," Challico said. "Us Khevsouris has eyes like a eagle's. Ever I told you about my uncle? He could shoot——"

Yes, yes, but we not interested to hear all over again how Challico's uncle can hit a wild boar exactly through the center of the heart at half a mile. Makes at least a hundred tellings now and each time Challico's uncle gets farther and farther away from pig.

"Boar again?" Vactangi asked. "Watch out, Challico, pretty soon gonna have to kill him by radio, your uncle."

"Well maybe Illarion's busy," I said, to stop the argument. "Moon eclipsing or something, keeps him on the job."

So we didn't bother too much and it went until the next Friday. Still no Illarion.

"After all," Vactangi said, "now is something wrong. The moon can't be on a rampage every week. Have to go in a college, one of us, and find out what's the trouble."

So we appointed Challico for a committee. "O.K.," he said. "If my countryman is in danger I go after him. If it's my duty to rescue my friend, it don't matter what kind of a place you send me in. I gonna go."

Comes he back the next day with news we didn't like to hear. Illarion was sick, very sick.

"What's the matter with him?" Vactangi wanted to know. "Describe me how he's a sick."

"Well, he's in a place like a hospital that belongs to the college. They say nothing's wrong. They say only he's tired. But I think they're trying to fool us."

"Did you see him?"

"Yes, they took me in a room, Illarion is lying with his face to the wall. 'My God, man,' I told in Georgian, 'what's the matter?!' Nurse makes me, 'Ssssh. Don't excite your friend. He's just a little bit overworked. He finished up important research and now he's resting.' 'Resting!' I said. 'Must be he's sick.' 'No, he's not sick.' She has a smile, that lady, flashes off and on her mouth like a light bulb. Makes me nervous. 'Gotta be sick,' I insist, 'a grown man laying in bed in the middle of the daytime. Illarion! What's the matter?' 'Nothing,' he says. He sounds weaker than an orphan lamb."

"Illarion? In a bed?" I said. "A hundred and ninety pounds? Six foot three-inch man?"

"So I went and asked the doctor, a big, big professor. He tells me Illarion was working too hard, and now they don't want him to get nervous broke down."

"Nervous broke down?" Vactangi asked. "What means that?"

"It's American sickness," I said. "When your brain ain't interested in you any more."

"Must be awful thing that. Except once in while I forget where I put something, otherwise I'm on good terms with my own brains. I can't imagine not getting along together O.K."

"Why can't he have his head cracked in from fight, or a dagger wound?" I said. "A bullet through his leg? Something, at least, that a person can understand. Nervous broke down!"

So we decided the best thing is to go all together in the hospital see what can we do.

He was in a bathrobe this time, sitting in chair, but no life at all to his face. "Illarion," I said, "man, you want to eat?"

"We had a lovely dish of spinach for lunch," starched lady taking care of him said, "and if we good—" She shook her finger at him, "we gonna eat nice cup custard for our supper. Aren't we?"

"Illarion," Vactangi said in Georgian, "want lamb? Stick of *shashlik,* good broiled? Give you blood."

Illarion shaked his head, no.

"A glass of good black wine," Challico proposed. "That brings your strength back."

"Maybe you like us to give you a little song to cheer you up." My suggestion.

"No, gentlemen. Not today." The starched lady was putting us out. "But you can come again tomorrow."

"Look, boys. We gotta do something quick," I said. We was walking home. "Dzea Vanno's coming back from Fresno tomorrow. Dzea's lived through eighty years now. Surely he must know the answer to a thing like this."

So immediately Dzea came home we told him the story. He thought it over while he smoothed a nice point to his beard. "Is he disappointed in love, Illarion?" he asked finally.

"No," Challico said, "can't be that. First time I was there, just to see if I can shake him up, I said, 'Illarion, a young lady stopped me downstairs and asked how is Mr. Illarion, today? As beautiful as running deer she was. Maybe you special friend?' He don't even turn his head."

"Well, only one solution then," Dzea Vanno said. "We'll have to try garlic sauce. I don't like man that boasts but it could make cripples to dance or mutes to sing; it would bring the dead alive, my garlic sauce. Can cure everything in fact but man in love."

"I agree a hundred per cent," I told. "I tasted already. Will open Illarion's appetite and if he eats naturally he has to get better."

"And if it doesn't help?"

"Then nothing be any use," Dzea said. "We might as well make plans where we gonna have his funeral party. He ought to be ashamed of himself, a young fellow, strong body, all his arms and legs on, to get sick. I'm eighty-five years old. You ever see me lay in a bed to worry my friends?"

"There'll be plenty of time later to give him hell," Vactangi said. "Just now, let's we be practical. How we gonna give him this garlic sauce? If we try to take it in the hospital they'll smell us coming from the streetcar stop."

"I gonna phone," Challico said, "ask the doctor can we come and take our friend Illarion for a little ride?"

"Yes?"

"Then we drive some place, make a party, have the sauce."

"After one whiff such delicious aroma," I said, "can't refuse Illarion to take a bite of meat, a swallow of wine, and first thing we know he be all well again, our Illarion."

"But what thinks the hospital when he don't come back right away?"

"After we get him out we phone again and tell he likes to stay for a few hours more with us. We take good care of him."

"Where shall we go? In the park?"

"No. We can't build big enough fire there."

"Beach?"

"Much better. We go far down away from the towns."

"Full with bootleggers all those little beaches," Vactangi said. "They unload their boats there."

"That's just a story," Challico told him. "For my part, I hope we see some. I'm gonna get five, six gallons. Buy wholesale, that's the way to save money."

So we phoned; doctor said O.K. and we called for Illarion in our car.

"We gonna take you on the beach," we told him. "Make a nice party, all be in honor of you."

"I don't care."

"And build a fire. Make *shashlik.*"

"I don't care."

"Ajepsandal Dzea seasoned special your taste?"

"I don't care."

He was like a clock with no tick to it.

We drove along the coast twenty, twenty-five miles to a nice quiet spot. Parked in a field and climbed down the path to the beach. Clean white sand, cliffs on three sides to break the wind. Ideal. We fixed a place for Illarion with blankets against a big log so he could face the ocean.

"Now cheer up," Vactangi told him. "Breathe the sea air. You'll be well in no time. Breathe deep."

Meanwhile Challico and me gathered driftwood for the fire and Dzea Vanno began to make the sauce. In his wooden mortar he put the garlic pearls and salt and pepper and our herb kinsey, and a pinch of dill. Then with his pestle Pound—Pound—Pound—and between each pound, he added little drops of tarragon vinegar, and again Pound—Pound—Pound. When the whole thing turned smooth as cream and the aroma filled the air it was ready to eat.

Illarion, an invalid, couldn't eat *shashlik* off a stick so Vactangi arranged a few of the tenderest pieces of meat on a nice leaf for him, put a drop of sauce beside it, broke him bread.

Then we ate, drank our wine. The sauce made us so hungry we broiled a few more sticks of lamb again; had another little glass of wine. Uncle John told some stories. Vactangi played us tune on his *chongouri.*

And the whole time out of our eye corners we were watching Illarion. He ate, yes, but from his interest he might as well be chewing sawdusts.

"Well, there's no use to expect miracles," Challico said when him and me went down the beach for more driftwood. "Maybe he needs to eat twice even garlic sauce before it cures him. A severe case like this."

When we came back Challico tried to brighten up Illarion by remembering things about home. Both they were Khevsouris, these two, from villages way, way up in our mountains. Kind of odd peoples, these Khevsouris, in their habits. Still to this very day they're wearing the helmets and chain-mail coats left over from the Crusades and jousting with lances and if they don't have any real fights on a hand, for pastime they stage mock ones with each other. Bravest fellows in the world, but not a lot of progress to them.

Usually Illarion liked to talk about this. He was proud he was a Khevsouri and had a right to bring his men through any gate of the Holy City wearing arms and with all their battle flags flying. Only of course I don't think he ever did it so far. And him and Challico always enjoyed to show how they can play with broadswords so big that most men couldn't even lift them.

"Come on, man," Challico encouraged, "this is a lonesome place. It won't bother nobody if we sound some of the battle calls. The one from the siege before Acre? How about that?"

"No." Illarion didn't want.

"How about our rally that saved the day at Doryleum? We don't often get a chance like this. Holler all we want."

"No."

"Allright, then I gonna sing and you keep me chorus. Come on. 'The Frankish men they have a Queen, Eléanor, Eléanor.' "

"No." Nothing suited.

So Vactangi tuned the strings on his *chongouri* again, and we made a nice quartette, me and Uncle John and Challico, and for fourth we had the waves rolling in—Boom—Boom—Boom to carry our bass. Boom. Boom.

And, just in that minute when we were so happy with a glass in hand watching our fire burn gold and green and blue, a bullet spit the sand not ten feet back of us.

"Down," Dzea said and we went flat behind the log. The gun spattered again.

"Only BB's," Vactangi listened to the third burst, "and from one gun, air rifle."

"Still, I don't want in my skin," Challico told. "Why they shooting on us?"

"Why? That's your bootleggers you gonna buy wholesale from. Better forget it. Try instead to remember some undertaker that'll give you a funeral for half price."

The bootleggers were back of us. We could hear them talking.

"Must they come up while we sang," Dzea Vanno said. "Probably they expecting boats tonight. That's why they give us a hint to go away."

"Then why don't they tell us nice way?" Challico said. "How can we go now? Impossible! Means we runned away."

We stayed quiet for a few minutes behind the log. Dzea was on one side of me, Illarion at the end.

"How we gonna manage?" Challico whispered. "Maybe they rush us?"

Something moved on the beach. Was it a man? No. I looked again. Maybe seaweed? Couldn't be sure. I nudged Dzea. He couldn't see nothing. Only a shadow.

"How we manage?" Vactangi was answering, "why we gonna manage usual way. Stick together and fight and when last man is left alone he can do how he pleases."

"Let's wait," Dzea said, "few——"

Then we heard a bellow, a sound that split open the night like a cleaver.

"Son of gun!" Challico said, "it's Illarion."

I felt the place next to me. Empty! It was Illarion all right and he's still yelling. Would turn a person's blood to sherbet that noise he makes.

"I got the one with the gun," he was hollering. "Give me hand, boys, is two others left." He was on the ledge halfway down the path with them. And how he got there? Why naturally it was nothing for him to creep the length of the beach, walk straight up the cliff and then jump down on the bootleggers. Regular mountain goats, anyway, all these Khevsouris.

So we went up, too, and after a little damages all around, finally we got the whole bunch together and tied them up with our belts.

"Now we have an armistice," Dzea, our oldest man, was spokesman— "Why you shoot us?"

"You breaka law," fellows told him. Must be he was Italian. Not speaking so good English.

"I break the law," Challico said. "You're funny, huh? Maybe President don't allow no more picnics on beach? Is that it?"

"Yuh, we know your picnics," biggest Italian said and won't talk more.

"If you was nice fellows we'd let you go." Dzea said. "But how we know what you'll do? You're too wild."

"No." Illarion said. "No, we can't fool around. We have to go to the nearest farm, phone the police."

"Police?" big fellow hollered, "whassa matter you? Crazy? Bootleggers."

"I don't care if you are or not," Illarion said, "but you can't shoot people. Dangerous. It's your own fault we have to call the police."

"You won't call the police," second fellow, red handkerchief on a neck, was speaking. The third bootlegger so far only made mumble, mumble. I don't know what was wrong with him. "You don't fool us. Police look two years for you. They lock you up in two minutes, you bootleggers!"

"We bootleggers?" Vactangi said. "You the bootleggers."

"You! You!" Big Italian was so mad he's jumping. "You! You!"

"Wait," Dzea Vanno said. "Let's get it straight who's who. I'm a man, by trade a cook, living in San Francisco. I comed here on a picnic. These my friends all. So you're the bootleggers, isn't it?"

"Certainly not," big fellow talked. "I'm a farmer. This my two neighbors. Week after week all the gangsters unloading their boats here——"

"Yes," Red Handkerchief put in his word, "and tramp down our artichoke fields carrying stuff to the trucks. Ruin my crops. I told to stay away ten times. No stay. So tonight I and my friends wait for when they get drunk like usual sing, holler, then we fill fulla pepper shot."

"Well," Challico said politely, "mistakes can happen, isn't it true?"

I untied the belts.

"How about damages?" Big Fellow wanted to know. "All our clothes tore. And your friend bent my rifle over his knee."

"Hocked hall my heeth hout," the little fellow, the mumbling one, crept around on the ground lighting matches. "Han't hind. Hup. No, hat's a hock. Houldn't I hollowed, hould I?"

"His teeth are gone," Red Handkerchief told us.

"My God," Illarion said, "I didn't mean to do that."

"False teeth," Red Handkerchief explained. "Could be worse."

"Well, we very, very sorry, anyway," Dzea Vanno said. "Would fifteen dollars make our apology?"

They guessed it would.

"O.K. boys," Dzea told us, "get together money."

"No, I gonna pay," Illarion said. "I feel good. I didn't feel so good in years. Let it be my treat."

So we paid over the money. Shook hands all around. "Now we friends." Dzea Vanno said.

"Pardon me," Little One said, he found his teeth and got them in, "ain't you eating something with garlic in?"

Well next thing they were down on the beach and we broiled more lamb and Big Fellow, Tony was his name, sent Red Handkerchief home across the fields for two jugs. "I gonna give you drink good wine," he promised.

And Illarion, my God, he was eating and singing and doing somersaults backwards, and showing us how they dance in his village and shaking himself all over like happy dog got off a chain.

Finally fire was out; food all gone; songs all sung, our party was over. "Son a gun!" Tony said, after they promised to come the next Sunday and visit us in the city, "I never see fellows fight so good. You must like, huh? Zim-Zam," he smacked his fists in his hand. "Must be a regular hobby for you boys?"

It was after eight o'clock in the morning when we deposited Illarion back in college. "Don't take me to the hospital," he told us. "Leave me off at my room." He felt full of snort and ready to get on his job.

"Well, Dzea," Challico said when we were driving down our street, "just like you promised. That garlic sauce, it cures everything."

"Everything," Dzea said twinkling his eyes. "Everything but a man in love."

"And what cures that, Dzea?" I asked him.

Dzea smoothed the white wings of his mustache. "Only the grave," he said, "or another prettier face."

Questions

1. In Shuy's terms, the language of the characters in this story would be classified as a social dialect. Which of the following views would you favor? (a) These people should leave the dialect they now speak and learn standard English. (b) These people should insist that their dialect is acceptable and use it in place of standard English. (c) They should continue to use this dialect when appropriate but should learn standard English to use in appropriate situations. Why have you adopted the position you have chosen?
2. Give examples of some fresh figures of speech used by the characters. What effect does the word choice have on the reader?
3. How do the authors distinguish between the kind of English used by the characters whose native speech was Russian and those whose native speech was Italian?

Buck Fanshaw's Funeral

Mark Twain

Roughing It, *from which the following selection is taken, must be loosely classed as autobiography. Twain did journey to Nevada in 1861 and did reside in Carson City and Virginia City for several years. But Twain's humorous account, written after he left Nevada, is unencumbered by facts. Chapter after chapter smacks of the tall tale. In "Buck Fanshaw's Funeral" Twain contrasts two social dialects. Through Scotty Briggs's evaluation of Buck Fanshaw, we do glimpse much of the violent masculinity of the frenzied gold mining days, and through Scotty's appeal to the stiff, bookish minister, we can sense the community's striving for respectability. But Twain is interested in the humor inherent in the situation. He would only have chuckled at those critics who find the minister too bookish. Note particularly how the minister "simplifies" his responses when Scotty fails to understand.*

Somebody has said that in order to know a community, one must observe the style of its funerals and know what manner of men they bury with most ceremony. I cannot say which class we buried with most éclat in our "flush times," the distinguished public benefactor or the distinguished rough—possibly the two chief grades or grand divisions of society honored their illustrious dead about equally; and hence, no doubt, the philosopher I have quoted from would have needed to see two representative funerals in Virginia before forming his estimate of the people.

There was a grand time over Buck Fanshaw when he died. He was a representative citizen. He had "killed his man"—not in his own quarrel, it is true, but in defense of a stranger unfairly beset by numbers. He had kept a sumptuous saloon. He had been the proprietor of a dashing helpmeet whom he could have discarded without the formality of a divorce. He had held a high position in the fire department and been a very Warwick in politics. When he died there was great lamentation throughout the town, but especially in the vast bottom-stratum of society.

On the inquest it was shown that Buck Fanshaw, in the delirium of a wasting typhoid fever, had taken arsenic, shot himself through the body, cut his throat, and jumped out of a four-story window and broken his neck—and after due deliberation, the jury, sad and tearful, but with intelligence unblinded by its sorrow, brought in a verdict of death "by the visitation of God." What could the world do without juries?

Prodigious preparations were made for the funeral. All the vehicles in town were hired, all the saloons put in mourning, all the municipal and fire-company flags hung at half-mast, and all the firemen ordered to muster in uniform and bring their machines duly draped in black. Now—let us remark in parenthesis—as all the peoples of the earth had representative adventurers in the Silverland, and as each adventurer had brought the slang of his nation or his locality with him, the combination made the slang of Nevada the richest and the most infinitely varied and copious that had ever existed anywhere in the world, perhaps, except in the mines of California in the "early days." Slang was the language of Nevada. It was hard to preach a sermon without it, and be understood. Such phrases as "You bet!" "Oh, no, I reckon not!" "No Irish need apply," and a hundred others, became so common as to fall from the lips of a speaker unconsciously—and very often when they did not touch the subject under discussion and consequently failed to mean anything.

After Buck Fanshaw's inquest, a meeting of the short-haired brotherhood was held, for nothing can be done on the Pacific coast without a public meeting and an expression of sentiment. Regretful resolutions were passed and various committees appointed; among others, a committee of one was deputed to call on the minister, a fragile, gentle, spiritual new fledgling from an Eastern theological seminary, and as yet unacquainted with the ways of the mines. The committeeman, "Scotty" Briggs, made his visit; and in after days it was worth something to hear the minister tell about it. Scotty was a stalwart rough, whose customary suit, when on weighty official business, like committee work, was a fire helmet, flaming red flannel shirt, patent leather belt with spanner and revolver attached, coat hung over arm, and pants stuffed into boot tops. He formed something of a contrast to the pale theological student. It is fair to say of Scotty, however, in passing, that he had a warm heart, and a strong love for his friends, and never entered into a quarrel when he could reasonably keep out of it. Indeed, it was commonly said that whenever one of Scotty's fights was investigated, it always turned out that it had originally been no affair of his, but that out of native goodheartedness he had dropped in of his own accord to help the man who was getting the worst of it. He and Buck Fanshaw were bosom friends, for years, and had often taken adventurous "potluck" together. On one occasion, they had thrown off their coats and taken the weaker side in a fight among strangers, and after gaining a hard-earned victory, turned and found that the men they were helping had deserted early, and not only that, but had stolen their coats and made off with them! But to return to Scotty's visit to the minister. He was on a sorrowful mission, now, and his face was the picture of woe. Being admitted to the presence he sat down before the clergyman, placed his fire-hat on an unfinished manuscript sermon under the minister's nose, took from it a red silk handkerchief, wiped his brow and heaved a sigh of dismal impressiveness, explanatory of his business. He choked, and even shed tears; but with an effort he mastered his voice and said in lugubrious tones:

"Are you the duck that runs the gospel-mill next door?"

"Am I the—pardon me, I believe I do not understand?"

With another sigh and a half-sob, Scotty rejoined:

"Why you see we are in a bit of trouble, and the boys thought maybe you would give us a lift, if we'd tackle you—that is, if I've got the rights of it and you are the head clerk of the doxology-works next door."

"I am the shepherd in charge of the flock whose fold is next door."

"The which?"

"The spiritual adviser of the little company of believers whose sanctuary adjoins these premises."

Scotty scratched his head, reflected a moment, and then said:

"You ruther hold over me, pard. I reckon I can't call that hand. Ante and pass the buck."

"How? I beg pardon. What did I understand you to say?"

"Well, you've ruther got the bulge on me. Or maybe we've both got the bulge, somehow. You don't smoke me and I don't smoke you. You see, one of the boys has passed in his checks, and we want to give him a good send-off, and so the thing I'm on now is to roust out somebody to jerk a little chin-music for us and waltz him through handsome."

"My friend, I seem to grow more and more bewildered. Your observations are wholly incomprehensible to me. Cannot you simplify them in some way? At first I thought perhaps I understood you, but I grope now. Would it not expedite matters if you restricted yourself to categorical statements of fact unencumbered with obstructing accumulations of metaphor and allegory?"

Another pause, and more reflection. Then, said Scotty:

"I'll have to pass, I judge."

"How?"

"You've raised me out, pard."

"I still fail to catch your meaning."

"Why, that last lead of yourn is too many for me—that's the idea. I can't neither trump nor follow suit."

The clergyman sank back in his chair perplexed. Scotty leaned his head on his hand and gave himself up to thought. Presently his face came up, sorrowful but confident.

"I've got it now, so's you can savvy," he said. "What we want is a gospel-sharp. See?"

"A what?"

"Gospel-sharp. Parson."

"Oh! Why did you not say so before? I am a clergyman—a parson."

"Now you talk! You see my blind and straddle it like a man. Put it there!"—extending a brawny paw, which closed over the minister's small hand and gave it a shake indicative of fraternal sympathy and fervent gratification.

"Now we're all right, pard. Let's start fresh. Don't you mind my snuffling a little—becuz we're in a power of trouble. You see, one of the boys has gone up the flume—"

"Gone where?"

"Up the flume—throwed up the sponge, you understand."

"Thrown up the sponge?"

"Yes—kicked the bucket—"

"Ah—has departed to that mysterious country from whose bourne no traveler returns."

"Return! I reckon not. Why, pard, he's *dead!*"

"Yes, I understand."

"Oh, you do? Well I thought maybe you might be getting tangled some more. Yes, you see he's dead again—"

"Again! Why, has he ever been dead before?"

"Dead before? No! Do you reckon a man has got as many lives as a cat? But you bet you he's awful dead now, poor old boy, and I wish I'd never seen this day. I don't want no better friend than Buck Fanshaw. I knowed him by the back; and when I know a man and like him, I freeze to him—you hear *me*. Take him all round, pard, there never was a bullier man in the mines. No man ever knowed Buck Fanshaw to go back on a friend. But it's all up, you know, it's all up. It ain't no use. They've scooped him."

"Scooped him?"

"Yes—death has. Well, well, well, we've got to give him up. Yes, indeed. It's a kind of a hard world, after all, *ain't* it? But pard, he was a rustler! You ought to seen him get started once. He was a bully boy with a glass eye! Just spit in his face and give him room according to his strength, and it was just beautiful to see him peel and go in. He was the worst son of a thief that ever drawed breath. Pard, he was *on* it! He was on it bigger than an Injun!"

"On it? On what?"

"On the shoot. On the shoulder. On the fight, you understand. *He* didn't give a continental for *any*body. *Beg* your pardon, friend, for coming so near saying a cuss-word—but you see I'm on an awful strain, in this palaver, on account of having to cramp down and draw everything so mild. But we've got to give him up. There ain't any getting around that, I don't reckon. Now if we can get you to help plant him—"

"Preach the funeral discourse? Assist at the obsequies?"

"Obs'quies is good. Yes. That's it—that's our little game. We are going to get the thing up regardless, you know. He was always nifty himself, and so you bet you his funeral ain't going to be no slouch—solid silver door-plate on his coffin, six plumes on the hearse, and a nigger on the box in a biled shirt and a plug hat—how's that for high? And we'll take care of *you,* pard. We'll fix you all right. There'll be a kerridge for you; and whatever you want, you just 'scape out and we'll 'tend to it. We've got a shebang fixed up for you to stand behind, in No. 1's house, and don't you be afraid. Just go in and toot your horn, if you don't sell a clam. Put Buck through as bully as you can, pard, for anybody that knowed him will tell you that he was one of the whitest men that was ever in the mines. You can't draw it too strong. He never could stand it to see things going wrong. He's done more to make this town quiet and peaceable than any man in it. I've seen him lick four Greasers in eleven minutes, myself. If a thing wanted regulating, *he* warn't a man to go browsing around after somebody to do it, but he would prance in and regulate it himself. He warn't a Catholic. Scasely. He was down on 'em. His word was, 'No Irish need apply!' But it didn't make no difference about that when it came down to what a man's rights was—and so, when some roughs jumped the Catholic boneyard and started in to stake out town-lots in it he *went* for 'em! And he *cleaned* 'em, too! I was there, pard, and I seen it myself."

"That was very well indeed—at least the impulse was—whether the act was strictly defensible or not. Had deceased any religious convictions? That is to say, did he feel a dependence upon, or acknowledge allegiance to a higher power?"

More reflection.

"I reckon you've stumped me again, pard. Could you say it over once more, and say it slow?"

"Well, to simplify it somewhat, was he, or rather had he ever been connected with any organization sequestered from secular concerns and devoted to self-sacrifice in the interests of morality?"

"All down but nine—set 'em up on the other alley, pard."

"What did I understand you to say?"

"Why, you're most too many for me, you know. When you get in with your left I hunt grass every time. Every time you draw, you fill; but I don't seem to have any luck. Let's have a new deal."

"How? Begin again?"

"That's it."

"Very well. Was he a good man, and—"

"There—I see that; don't put up another chip till I look at my hand. A good man, says you? Pard, it ain't no name for it. He was the best man that ever—pard, you would have doted on that man. He could lam any galoot of his inches in America. It was him that put down the riot last election before it got a start; and everybody said he was the only man that could have done it. He waltzed in with a spanner in one hand and a trumpet in the other, and sent fourteen men home on a shutter in less than three minutes. He had that riot all broke up and prevented nice before anybody ever got a chance to strike a blow. He was always for peace, and he would *have* peace—he could not stand disturbances. Pard, he was a great loss to this town. It would please the boys if you could chip in something like that and do him justice. Here once when the Micks got to throwing stones through the Methodis' Sunday-school windows, Buck Fanshaw, all of his own notion, shut up his saloon and took a couple of six-shooters and mounted guard over the Sunday-school. Says he, 'No Irish need apply!' And they didn't. He was the bulliest man in the mountains, pard! He could run faster, jump higher, hit harder, and hold more tanglefoot whisky without spilling it than any man in seventeen counties. Put that in, pard—it'll please the boys more than anything you could say. And you can say, pard, that he never shook his mother."

"Never shook his mother?"

"That's it—any of the boys will tell you so."

"Well, but why *should* he shake her?"

"That's what *I* say—but some people does."

"Not people of any repute?"

"Well, some that averages pretty so-so."

"In my opinion the man that would offer personal violence to his own mother, ought to—"

"Cheese it, pard; you've banked your ball clean outside the string. What I was a drivin' at, was, that he never *throwed off* on his mother—don't you see? No indeedy. He give her a house to live in, and town lots, and plenty of money; and he looked after her and took care of her all the time; and when she was down with the smallpox I'm d——d if he didn't set up nights and nuss her himself! *Beg* your pardon for saying it, but it hopped out too quick for yours truly. You've treated me like a gentleman, pard, and I ain't the man to hurt your feelings intentional. I think you're white. I think you're a square man, pard. I like you, and I'll lick any man that don't. I'll lick him till he can't tell himself from a last year's corpse! Put it *there!*" [Another fraternal hand-shake—and exit.]

The obsequies were all that "the boys" could desire. Such a marvel of funeral pomp had never been seen in Virginia. The plumed hearse, the dirge-breathing brass bands, the closed marts of business, the flags drooping at half-mast, the long, plodding procession of uniformed secret societies, military battalions and fire companies, draped engines, carriages of officials, and citizens in vehicles and on foot, attracted multitudes of spectators to the sidewalks, roofs, and windows; and for years afterward, the degree of grandeur attained by any civic display in Virginia was determined by comparison with Buck Fanshaw's funeral.

Scotty Briggs, as a pall-bearer and a mourner, occupied a prominent place at the funeral, and when the sermon was finished and the last sentence of the prayer for the dead man's soul ascended, he responded, in a low voice, but with feeling:

"AMEN. No Irish need apply."

As the bulk of the response was without apparent relevancy, it was probably nothing more than a humble tribute to the memory of the friend that was gone; for, as Scotty had once said, it was "his word."

Scotty Briggs, in after days, achieved the distinction of becoming the only convert to religion that was ever gathered from the Virginia roughs; and it transpired that the man who had it in him to espouse the quarrel of the weak out of inborn nobility of spirit was no mean timber whereof to construct a Christian. The making him one did not warp his generosity or diminish his courage; on the contrary it gave intelligent direction to the one and a broader field to the other. If his Sunday-school class progressed faster than the other classes, was it matter for wonder? I think not. He talked to his pioneer small-fry in a language they understood! It was my large privilege, a month before he died, to hear him tell the beautiful story of Joseph and his brethren to his class "without looking at the book." I leave it to the reader to fancy what it was like, as it fell, riddled with slang, from the lips of that grave, earnest teacher, and was listened to by his little learners with a consuming interest that showed that they were as unconscious as he was that any violence was being done to the sacred proprieties!

Questions

1. Many of Scotty's expressions, the "metaphor and allegory" the minister complains of, derive from poker—"I'll have to pass," "you've raised me out," "I can't call that hand," and others. What other sources can you discover for his expressions? What would be the source of "No Irish need apply"?

2. Do you understand every expression? In other words, has Twain included too many expressions which belonged peculiarly to the Nevada of that time?
3. Is one of the individuals more to blame than the other for the lack of communication in this dialogue? Cite specific evidence to support your idea.
4. In a real-life situation similar to this—the ghetto children with their teachers, for instance—who has the major responsibility for getting to the others' level? Or is the responsibility shared equally? Does one party sometimes insist that the other do all the adjusting?

Suggestions for Writing

1. Reproduce the conversation between two characters in which one speaks in the slang of his group or the jargon of his profession which the other fails to understand. One speaker could be a child talking to an adult, a teenager to a counselor, a water skier to a mountain skier, a sailor to a landlubber, a long-haired rock and roll musician to a long-haired classical musician, or any such combination. Try to have the person using the slang explain something to the other person which that person fails to understand.

Ladies' and Gentlemen's Guide to Modern English Usage

James Thurber *Inspired by Fowler's* Modern English Usage *and Mencken's* The American Language, *James Thurber turned out his own inimitable guide to usage. Although both Fowler and Mencken have been revised, you may be more familiar with recent works by Bergen and Cornelia Evans, Margaret Bryant, or Wilson Follett. (The latter presents a conservative view of usage.) The more rules of usage you know, the more you will enjoy Thurber. Do not fail to note, however, Thurber's use of* whom *in his own sentences after he has decided on the proper usage.*

I. WHO AND WHOM

The number of people who use "whom" and "who" wrongly is appalling. The problem is a difficult one and it is complicated by the importance of tone, or taste. Take the common expression, "Whom are you, anyways?" That is of course, strictly speaking, correct—and yet how formal, how stilted! The usage to be preferred in ordinary speech and writing is "Who are you, anyways?" "Whom" should be used in the nominative case only when a note of dignity or austerity is desired. For example, if a writer is dealing with a meeting of, say, the British Cabinet, it would be better to have the Premier greet a new arrival, such as an under-secretary, with a "Whom are you, anyways?" rather than a "Who are you, anyways?"—always granted that the Premier is sincerely unaware of the man's identity. To address a person one knows by a "Whom are you?" is a mark either of incredible lapse of memory or inexcusable arrogance. "How are you?" is a much kindlier salutation.

The Buried Whom, as it is called, forms a special problem. This is where the word occurs deep in a sentence. For a ready example, take the common expression: "He did not know whether he knew her or not because he had not heard whom the other had said she was until too late to see her." The simplest way out of this is to abandon the "whom" altogether and substitute "where" (a reading of the sentence that way will show how much better it is). Unfortunately, it is only in rare cases that "where" can be used in place of "whom." Nothing could be more flagrantly bad, for instance, than to say "Where are you?" in demanding a person's identity. The only conceivable answer is, "Here I am," which would give no hint at all as to whom the person was. Thus the conversation, or piece of writing, would, from being built upon a false foundation, fall of its own weight.

A common rule for determining whether "who" or "whom" is right is to substitute "she" for "who," and "her" for "whom," and see which sounds the better. Take the sentence, "He met a woman who they said was an actress." Now if "who" is correct then "she" can be used in its place. Let us try it. "He met a woman she they said was an actress." That instantly rings false. It can't be right. Hence the proper usage is "whom."

In certain cases grammatical correctness must often be subordinated to a consideration of taste. For instance, suppose that the same person had met a man whom they said was a street-cleaner. The word "whom" is too austere to use in connection with a lowly worker, like a street-cleaner, and its use in this form is known as False Admiration or Pathetic Fallacy.

You might say: "There is, then, no hard and fast rule?" ("was then" would be better, since "then" refers to what is past). You might better say, then (or have said): "There was then (or is now) no hard and fast rule?" Only this, that it is better to use "whom" when in doubt, and even better to re-word the statement, and leave out all the relative pronouns, except ad, ante, con, in, inter, ob, post, prae, pro, sub, and super.

II. WHICH

The relative pronoun "which" can cause more trouble than any other word, if recklessly used. Foolhardy persons sometimes get lost in which-clauses and are never heard of again. My distinguished contemporary, Fowler, cites several tragic cases, of which the following is one: "It was rumoured that Beaconsfield intended opening the Conference with a speech in French, his pronunciation of which language leaving everything to be desired. . . ." That's as much as Mr. Fowler quotes because, at his age, he was afraid to go any farther. The young man who originally got into that sentence was never found. His fate, however, was not as terrible as that of another adventurer who became involved in a remarkable which-mire. Fowler has followed his devious course as far as he safely could on foot: "Surely what applies to games should also apply to racing, the leaders of which being the very people from whom an example might well be looked for. . . ." Not even Henry James could have successfully emerged from a sentence with "which," "whom," and "being" in it. The safest way to avoid such things is to follow in the path of the American author, Ernest Hemingway. In his youth he was trapped in a which-clause one time and barely escaped with his mind. He was going along on solid ground until he got into this: "It was the one thing of which, being very much afraid—for whom has not been warned to fear such things—he . . ." Being a young and powerfully built man, Hemingway was able to fight his way back to where he had started, and begin again. This time he skirted the treacherous morass in this way: "He was afraid of one thing. This was the one thing. He had been warned to fear such things. Everybody has been warned to fear such things." Today Hemingway is alive and well, and many happy writers are following along the trail he blazed.

What most people don't realize is that one "which" leads to another. Trying to cross a paragraph by leaping from "which" to "which" is like Eliza crossing the ice. The danger is in missing a "which" and falling in. A case in point is this: "He went up to a pew which was in the gallery, which brought him under a colored window which he loved and always quieted his spirit." The writer, worn out, missed the last "which"—the one that should come just before "always" in that sentence. But supposing he had got it in! We would have: "He went up to a pew which was in the gallery, which brought him under a colored window which he loved and which always quieted his spirit." Your inveterate whicher in this way gives the effect of tweeting like a bird or walking with a crutch, and is not welcome in the best company.

It is well to remember that one "which" leads to two and that two "whiches" multiply like rabbits. You should never start out with the idea that you can get by with one "which." Suddenly they are all around you. Take a sentence like this: "It imposes a problem which we either solve, or perish." On a hot night, or after a hard day's work, a man often lets himself get by with a monstrosity like that, but suppose he dictates that sentence bright and early in the morning. It comes to him typed out by his stenographer and he instantly senses that something is the matter with it. He tries to reconstruct the sentence, still clinging to the "which," and gets something like this: "It imposes a problem which we either solve, or which, failing to solve, we must perish on account of." He goes to the water-cooler, gets a drink, sharpens his pencil, and grimly tries again. "It imposes a problem which we either solve or which we don't solve and . . ." He begins once more: "It imposes a problem which we either solve, or which we do not solve, and from which . . ." The more times he does it the more "whiches" he gets. The way out is simple: "We must either solve this problem, or perish." Never monkey with "which." Nothing except getting tangled up in a typewriter ribbon is worse.

Questions

1. Thurber, like Twain, is more interested in the humor inherent in a situation than in making a profound statement, but if we analyze Thurber's stance we can see behind the wit a position Thurber has taken about usage. What does this selection reveal about Thurber's attitude toward books on usage? On the problem of deciding what usage is preferable? How seriously should we take Thurber's advice on the use of *which?* Is there a danger of awkwardness in its overuse?
2. How does Thurber's method of achieving humor differ from Twain's? Cite specific examples to support your opinion.

Suggestions for Writing

1. Write two paragraphs on the same subject—describe a person, a place, a reaction you have had, or narrate a short event. Give the same information in both paragraphs. Write the first ultracorrectly and keep your own personality out of it as much as you can; write the second as you would tell it to a friend. Then write a third paragraph in which you contrast the usage in the two earlier paragraphs. Ask yourself what is different about the sentences, what is different about the words you use, and what is different about the overall effect of the paragraphs.

The Man Who Was Almost a Man

Richard Wright *The first section of this book contains Richard Wright's account of his own insatiable reading when he was a young man in Memphis. In "The Man Who Was Almost a Man" Wright pictures a life he knew earlier in a dialect he spoke himself. Although the place is not designated, Dave's story could have taken place in the Mississippi of Wright's childhood. Dave, seventeen and striving to be a man, hardly seems aware of the suppression of the Negroes as a group. He is aware of his own suppression. His indignation turns almost as much against his own group and family as against his employer. Examine the dialect and the character of Dave. Are they believable?*

Dave struck out across the fields, looking homeward through paling light. Whut's the use talkin wid em niggers in the field? Anyhow, his mother was putting supper on the table. Them niggers can't understan nothing. One of these days he was going to get a gun and practice shooting, then they couldn't talk to him as though he were a little boy. He slowed, looking at the ground. Shucks, Ah ain scareda them even ef they are biggern me! Aw, Ah know whut Ahma do. Ahm going by ol Joe's sto n git that Sears Roebuck catlog n look at them guns. Mebbe Ma will lemme buy one when she gits mah pay from old man Hawkins. Ahma beg her t gimme some money. Ahm ol ernough to hava gun. Ahm seventeen. Almost a man. He strode, feeling his long loose-jointed limbs. Shucks, a man oughta hava little gun aftah he done worked hard all day.

He came in sight of Joe's store. A yellow lantern glowed on the front porch. He mounted steps and went through the screen door, hearing it bang behind him. There was a strong smell of coal oil and mackerel fish. He felt very confident until he saw fat Joe walk in through the rear door, then his courage began to ooze.

"Howdy, Dave! Whutcha want?"

"How yuh, Mistah Joe? Aw, Ah don wanna buy nothing. Ah jus wanted t see ef yuhd lemme look at tha catlog erwhile."

"Sure! You wanna see it here?"

"Nawsuh. Ah wans t take it home wid me. Ah'll bring it back termorrow when Ah come in from the fiels."

"You plannin on buying something?"

"Yessuh."

"Your ma lettin you have your own money now?"

"Shucks. Mistah Joe, Ahm gittin t be a man like anybody else!"

Joe laughed and wiped his greasy white face with a red bandanna.

"Whut you plannin on buyin?"

Dave looked at the floor, scratched his head, scratched his thigh, and smiled. Then he looked up shyly.

"Ah'll tell yuh, Mistah Joe, ef yuh promise yuh won't tell."

"I promise."

"Waal, Ahma buy a gun."

"A gun? Whut you want with a gun?"

"Ah wanna keep it."

"You ain't nothing but a boy. You don't need a gun."

"Aw, lemme have the catlog, Mistah Joe. Ah'll bring it back."

Joe walked through the rear door. Dave was elated. He looked around at barrels of sugar and flour. He heard Joe coming back. He craned his neck to see if he were bringing the book. Yeah, he's got it. Gawddog, he's got it!

"Here, but be sure you bring it back. It's the only one I got."

"Sho, Mistah Joe."

"Say, if you wanna buy a gun, why don't you buy one from me? I gotta gun to sell."

"Will it shoot?"

"Sure it'll shoot."

"Whut kind is it?"

"Oh, it's kinda old . . . a left-hand Wheeler. A pistol. A big one."

"Is it got bullets in it?"

"It's loaded."

"Kin Ah see it?"

"Where's your money?"

"Whut yuh wan fer it?"

"I'll let you have it for two dollars."

"Just two dollahs? Shucks, Ah could buy tha when Ah git mah pay."

"I'll have it here when you want it."

"Awright, suh. Ah be in fer it."

He went through the door, hearing it slam again behind him. Ahma git some money from Ma n buy me a gun! Only two dollahs! He tucked the thick catalogue under his arm and hurried.

"Where yuh been, boy?" His mother held a steaming dish of black-eyed peas.

"Aw, Ma, Ah just stopped down the road t talk wid the boys."

"Yuh know bettah t keep suppah waitin."

He sat down, resting the catalogue on the edge of the table.

"Yuh git up from there and git to the well n wash yosef! Ah ain feedin no hogs in mah house!"

She grabbed his shoulder and pushed him. He stumbled out of the room, then came back to get the catalogue.

"Whut this?"

"Aw, Ma, it's jusa catlog."

"Who yuh git it from?"

"From Joe, down at the sto."

"Waal, thas good. We kin use it in the outhouse."

"Naw, Ma." He grabbed for it. "Gimme ma catlog, Ma."

She held onto it and glared at him.

"Quit hollerin at me! Whut's wrong wid yuh? Yuh crazy?"

"But Ma, please. It ain mine! It's Joe's! He tol me t bring it back t im termorrow."

She gave up the book. He stumbled down the back steps, hugging the thick book under his arm. When he had splashed water on his face and hands, he groped back to the kitchen and fumbled in a corner for the towel. He bumped into a chair; it clattered to the floor. The catalogue sprawled at his feet. When he had dried his eyes he snatched up the book and held it again under his arm. His mother stood watching him.

"Now, ef yuh gonna act a fool over that ol book, Ah'll take it n burn it up."

"Naw, Ma, please."

"Waal, set down n be still!"

He sat down and drew the oil lamp close. He thumbed page after page, unaware of the food his mother set on the table. His father came in. Then his small brother.

"Whutcha got there, Dave?" his father asked.

"Jusa catlog," he answered, not looking up.

"Yeah, here they is!" His eyes glowed at blue-and-black revolvers. He glanced up, feeling sudden guilt. His father was watching him. He eased the book under the table and rested it on his knees. After the blessing was asked, he ate. He scooped up peas and swallowed fat meat without chewing. Buttermilk helped to wash it down. He did not want to mention money before his father. He would do much better by cornering his mother when she was alone. He looked at his father uneasily out of the edge of his eye.

"Boy, how come yuh don quit foolin wid tha book n eat yo suppah?"

"Yessuh."

"How you n ol man Hawkins gitten erlong?"

"Suh?"

"Can't yuh hear? Why don yuh lissen? Ah ast yu how wuz yuh n ol man Hawkins gittin erlong?"

"Oh, swell, Pa. Ah plows mo lan than anybody over there."

"Waal, yuh oughta keep yo mind on whut yuh doin."

"Yessuh."

He poured his plate full of molasses and sopped it up slowly with a chunk of cornbread. When his father and brother had left the kitchen, he still sat and looked again at the guns in the catalogue, longing to muster courage enough to present his case to his mother. Lawd, ef Ah only had tha pretty one! He could almost feel the slickness of the weapon with his fingers. If he had a gun like that he would polish it and keep it shining so it would never rust. N Ah'd keep it loaded, by Gawd!

"Ma?" His voice was hesitant.

"Hunh?"

"Ol man Hawkins give yuh mah money yit?"

"Yeah, but ain no usa yuh thinking bout throwin nona it erway. Ahm keepin tha money sos yuh kin have cloes t go to school this winter."

He rose and went to her side with the open catalogue in his palms. She was washing dishes, her head bent low over a pan. Shyly he raised the book. When he spoke, his voice was husky, faint.

"Ma, Gawd knows Ah wans one of these."

"One of whut?" she asked, not raising her eyes.

"One of these," he said again, not daring even to point. She glanced up at the page, then at him with wide eyes.

"Nigger, is yuh gone plumb crazy?"

"Aw, Ma—"

"Git outta here! Don yuh talk t me bout no gun! Yuh a fool!"

"Ma, Ah kin buy one fer two dollahs."

"Not ef Ah knows it, yuh ain!"

"But yuh promised me one—"

"Ah don care whut Ah promised! Yuh ain nothing but a boy yit!"

"Ma, ef yuh lemme buy one Ah'll *never* ast yuh fer nothing no mo."

"Ah tol yuh t git outta here! Yuh ain gonna toucha penny of tha money fer no gun! Thas how come Ah has Mistah Hawkins t pay yo wages t me, cause Ah knows yuh ain got no sense."

"But, Ma, we needa gun. Pa ain got no gun. We needa gun in the house. Yuh kin never tell whut might happen."

"Now don yuh try to maka fool outta me, boy! Ef we did hava gun, yuh wouldn't have it!"

He laid the catalogue down and slipped his arm around her waist.

"Aw, Ma, Ah done worked hard alla summer n ain ast yuh fer nothing, is Ah, now?"

"Thas whut yuh spose t do!"

"But Ma, Ah wans a gun. Yuh kin lemme have two dollahs outta mah money. Please, Ma. I kin give it to Pa . . . Please, Ma! Ah loves yuh, Ma."

When she spoke her voice came soft and low.

"Whut yu wan wida gun, Dave? Yuh don need no gun. Yuh'll git in trouble. N ef yo pa jus thought Ah let yuh have money t buy a gun he'd hava fit."

"Ah'll hide it, Ma. It ain but two dollahs."

"Lawd, chil, whut's wrong wid yuh?"

"Ain nothin wrong, Ma. Ahm almos a man now. Ah wans a gun."

"Who gonna sell yuh a gun?"

"Ol Joe at the sto."

"N it don cos but two dollahs?"

"Thas all, Ma. Jus two dollahs. Please, Ma."

She was stacking the plates away; her hands moved slowly, reflectively. Dave kept an anxious silence. Finally, she turned to him.

"Ah'll let yuh git tha gun ef yuh promise me one thing."

"Whut's tha, Ma?"

"Yuh bring it straight back t me, yuh hear? It be fer Pa."

"Yessum! Lemme go now, Ma."

She stooped, turned slightly to one side, raised the hem of her dress, rolled down the top of her stocking, and came up with a slender wad of bills.

"Here," she said. "Lawd knows yuh don need no gun. But yer pa does. Yuh bring it right back t me, yuh hear? Ahma put it up. Now ef yuh don, Ahma have yuh pa lick yuh so hard yuh won fergit it."

"Yessum."

He took the money, ran down the steps, and across the yard.

"Dave! Yuuuuuh Daaaaave!"

He heard, but he was not going to stop now. "Naw, Lawd!"

The first movement he made the following morning was to reach under his pillow for the gun. In the gray light of dawn he held it loosely, feeling a sense of power. Could kill a man with a gun like this. Kill anybody, black or white. And if he were holding his gun in his hand, nobody could run over him; they would have to respect him. It was a big gun, with a long barrel and a heavy handle. He raised and lowered it in his hand, marveling at its weight.

He had not come straight home with it as his mother had asked; instead he had stayed out in the fields, holding the weapon in his hand, aiming it now and then at some imaginary foe. But he had not fired it; he had been afraid that his father might hear. Also he was not sure he knew how to fire it.

To avoid surrendering the pistol he had not come into the house until he knew that they were all asleep. When his mother had tiptoed to his bedside late that night and demanded the gun, he had first played possum; then he had told her that the gun was hidden outdoors, that he would bring it to her in the morning. Now he lay turning it slowly in his hands. He broke it, took out the cartridges, felt them, and then put them back.

He slid out of bed, got a long strip of old flannel from a trunk, wrapped the gun in it, and tied it to his naked thigh while it was still loaded. He did not go in to breakfast. Even though it was not yet daylight, he started for Jim Hawkins' plantation. Just as the sun was rising he reached the barns where the mules and plows were kept.

"Hey! That you, Dave?"

He turned. Jim Hawkins stood eying him suspiciously.

"What're yuh going here so early?"

"Ah didn't know Ah wuz gittin up so early, Mistah Hawkins. Ah wuz fixin t hitch up ol Jenny n take her t the fiels."

"Good. Since you're so early, how about plowing that stretch down by the woods?"

"Suits me, Mistah Hawkins."

"O.K. Go to it!"

He hitched Jenny to a plow and started across the fields. Hot dog! This was just what he wanted. If he could get down by the woods, he could shoot his gun and nobody would hear. He walked behind the plow, hearing the traces creaking, feeling the gun tied tight to his thigh.

When he reached the woods, he plowed two whole rows before he decided to take out the gun. Finally, he stopped, looked in all directions, then untied the gun and held it in his hand. He turned to the mule and smiled.

"Know whut this is, Jenny? Naw, yuh wouldn know! Yuhs jusa ol mule! Anyhow, this is a gun, n it kin shoot, by Gawd!"

He held the gun at arm's length. Whut t hell, Ahma shoot this thing! He looked at Jenny again.

"Lissen here, Jenny! When Ah pull this ol trigger, Ah don wan yuh t run n acka fool now!"

Jenny stood with head down, her short ears pricked straight. Dave walked off about twenty feet, held the gun far out from him at arm's length, and turned his head. Hell, he told himself, Ah ain afraid. The gun felt loose in his fingers; he waved it wildly for a moment. Then he shut his eyes and tightened his forefinger. Bloom! A report half deafened him and he thought his right hand was torn from his arm. He heard Jenny whinnying and galloping over the field, and he found himself on his knees, squeezing his fingers hard between his legs. His hand was numb; he jammed it into his mouth, trying to warm it, trying to stop the pain. The gun lay at his feet. He did not quite know what had happened. He stood up and stared at the gun as though it were a living thing. He gritted his teeth and kicked the gun. Yuh almos broke mah arm! He turned to look for Jenny; she was far over the fields, tossing her head and kicking wildly.

"Hol on there, ol mule!"

When he caught up with her she stood trembling, walling her big white eyes at him. The plow was far away; the traces had broken. Then Dave stopped short, looking, not believing. Jenny was bleeding. Her left side was red and wet with blood. He went closer. Lawd, have mercy! Wondah did Ah shoot this mule? He grabbed for Jenny's mane. She flinched, snorted, whirled, tossing her head.

"Hol on now! Hol on."

Then he saw the hole in Jenny's side, right between the ribs. It was round, wet, red. A crimson stream streaked down the front leg, flowing fast. Good Gawd! Ah wuzn't shootin at tha mule. He felt panic. He knew he had to stop that blood, or Jenny would bleed to death. He had never seen so much blood in all his life. He chased the mule for half a mile, trying to catch her. Finally she stopped, breathing hard, stumpy tail half arched. He caught her mane and led her back to where the plow and gun lay. Then he stooped and grabbed handfuls of damp black earth and tried to plug the bullet hole. Jenny shuddered, whinnied, and broke from him.

"Hol on! Hol on now!"

He tried to plug it again, but blood came anyhow. His fingers were hot and sticky. He rubbed dirt into his palms, trying to dry them. Then again he attempted to plug the bullet hole, but Jenny shied away, kicking her heels high. He stood helpless. He had to do something. He ran at Jenny; she dodged him. He watched a red stream of blood flow down Jenny's leg and form a bright pool at her feet.

"Jenny . . . Jenny," he called weakly.

His lips trembled. She's bleeding t death! He looked in the direction of home, wanting to go back, wanting to get help. But he saw the pistol lying in the damp black clay. He had a queer feeling that if he only did something, this would not be; Jenny would not be there bleeding to death.

When he went to her this time, she did not move. She stood with sleepy, dreamy eyes; and when he touched her she gave a low-pitched whinny and knelt to the ground, her front knees slopping in blood.

"Jenny . . . Jenny . . ." he whispered.

For a long time she held her neck erect; then her head sank, slowly. Her ribs swelled with a mighty heave and she went over.

Dave's stomach felt empty, very empty. He picked up the gun and held it gingerly between his thumb and forefinger. He buried it at the foot of a tree. He took a stick and tried to cover the pool of blood with dirt—but what was the use? There was Jenny lying with her mouth open and her eyes walled and glassy. He could not tell Jim Hawkins he had shot his mule. But he had to tell something. Yeah, Ah'll tell em Jenny started gittin wil n fell on the joint of the plow. . . . But that would hardly happen to a mule. He walked across the field slowly, head down.

It was sunset. Two of Jim Hawkins' men were over near the edge of the woods digging a hole in which to bury Jenny. Dave was surrounded by a knot of people, all of whom were looking down at the dead mule.

"I don't see how in the world it happened," said Jim Hawkins for the tenth time.

The crowd parted and Dave's mother, father, and small brother pushed into the center.

"Where Dave?" his mother called.

"There he is," said Jim Hawkins.

His mother grabbed him.

"Whut happened, Dave? Whut yuh done?"

"Nothin."

"C mon, boy, talk," his father said.

Dave took a deep breath and told the story he knew nobody believed.

"Waal," he drawled. "Ah brung ol Jenny down here sos Ah could do mah plowin. Ah plowed bout two rows, just like yuh see." He stopped and pointed at the long rows of upturned earth. "Then somethin musta been wrong wid ol Jenny. She wouldn ack right a-tall. She started snortin n kickin her heels. Ah tried t hol her, but she pulled erway, rearin n goin in. Then when the point of the plow was stickin up in the air, she swung erroun n twisted herself back on it . . . She stuck herself n started t bleed. N fo Ah could do anything, she wuz dead."

"Did you ever hear of anything like that in all your life?" asked Jim Hawkins.

There were white and black standing in the crowd. They murmured. Dave's mother came close to him and looked hard into his face. "Tell the truth, Dave," she said.

"Looks like a bullet hole to me," said one man.

"Dave, whut yuh do wid the gun?" his mother asked.

The crowd surged in, looking at him. He jammed his hands into his pockets, shook his head slowly from left to right, and backed away. His eyes were wide and painful.

"Did he hava gun?" asked Jim Hawkins.

"By Gawd, Ah tol yuh tha wuz a gun wound," said a man, slapping his thigh.

His father caught his shoulders and shook him till his teeth rattled.

"Tell whut happened, yuh rascal! Tell whut . . ."

Dave looked at Jenny's stiff legs and began to cry.

"Whut yuh do wid tha gun?" his mother asked.

"Whut wuz he doin wida gun?" his father asked.

"Come on and tell the truth," said Hawkins. "Ain't nobody going to hurt you . . ."

His mother crowded close to him.

"Did yuh shoot tha mule, Dave?"

Dave cried, seeing blurred white and black faces.

"Ahh ddinn gggo tt sshooot hher . . . Ah ssswear ffo Gawd Ahh ddin. . . . Ah wuz a-tryin t sssee ef the old gggun would sshoot—"

"Where yuh git the gun from?" his father asked.

"Ah got it from Joe, at the sto."

"Where yuh git the money?"

"Ma give it t me."

"He kept worryin me, Bob. Ah had t. Ah tol im t bring the gun right back t me . . . I was fer yuh, the gun."

"But how yuh happen to shoot that mule?" asked Jim Hawkins.

"Ah wuzn shootin at the mule, Mistah Hawkins. The gun jumped when Ah pulled the trigger . . . N fo Ah knowed anythin Jenny was there a-bleedin."

Somebody in the crowd laughed. Jim Hawkins walked close to Dave and looked into his face.

"Well, looks like you have bought you a mule, Dave."

"Ah swear fo Gawd, Ah didn go t kill the mule, Mistah Hawkins!"

"But you killed her!"

All the crowd was laughing now. They stood on tiptoe and poked heads over one another's shoulders.

"Well, boy, looks like yuh done bought a dead mule! Hahaha!"

"Ain tha ershame."

"Hohohohoho."

Dave stood, head down, twisting his feet in the dirt.

"Well, you needn't worry about it, Bob," said Jim Hawkins to Dave's father. "Just let the boy keep on working and pay me two dollars a month."

"Whut yuh wan fer yo mule, Mistah Hawkins?"

Jim Hawkins screwed up his eyes.

"Fifty dollars."

"Whut yuh do wid tha gun?" Dave's father demanded.

Dave said nothing.

"Yuh wan me t take a tree n beat yuh till yuh talk!"

"Nawsuh!"

"Whut yuh do wid it?"

"Ah throwed it erway."

"Where?"

"Ah . . . Ah throwed it in the creek."

"Waal, c mon home. N firs thing in the mawnin git to tha creek n fin tha gun."

"Yessuh."

"Whut yuh pay fer it?"

"Two dollahs."

"Take tha gun n git yo money back n carry it t Mistah Hawkins, yuh hear? N don fergit Ahma lam you black bottom good fer this! Now march yosef on home, suh!"

Dave turned and walked slowly. He heard people laughing. Dave glared, his eyes welling with tears. Hot anger bubbled in him. Then he swallowed and stumbled on.

That night Dave did not sleep. He was glad that he had gotten out of killing the mule so easily, but he was hurt. Something hot seemed to turn over inside him each time he remembered how they had laughed. He tossed on his bed, feeling his hard pillow. N Pa says he's gonna beat me . . . He remembered other beatings, and his back quivered. Naw, naw, Ah sho don wan im t beat me tha way no mo. Dam em all! Nobody ever gave him anything. All he did was work. They treat me like a mule, n then they beat me. He gritted his teeth. N Ma had t tell on me.

Well, if he had to, he would take old man Hawkins that two dollars. But that meant selling the gun. And he wanted to keep that gun. Fifty dollars for a dead mule.

He turned over, thinking how he had fired the gun. He had an itch to fire it again. Ef other men kin shoota gun, by Gawd, Ah kin! He was still, listening. Mebbe they all sleepin now. The house was still. He heard the soft breathing of his brother. Yes, now! He would go down and get that gun and see if he could fire it! He eased out of bed and slipped into overalls.

The moon was bright. He ran almost all the way to the edge of the woods. He stumbled over the ground, looking for the spot where he had buried the gun. Yeah, here it is. Like a hungry dog scratching for a bone, he pawed it up. He puffed his black cheeks and blew dirt from the trigger and barrel. He broke it and found four cartridges unshot. He looked around; the fields were filled with silence and moonlight. He clutched the gun stiff and hard in his fingers. But, as soon as he wanted to pull the trigger, he shut his eyes and turned his head. Naw, Ah can't shoot wid mah eyes closed n mah head turned. With effort he held his eyes open; then he squeezed. *Blooooom!* He was stiff, not breathing. The gun was still in his hands. Dammit, he'd done it! He fired again. *Blooooom!* He smiled. *Bloooom! Blooooom! Click, click.* There! It was empty. If anybody could shoot a gun, he could. He put the gun into his hip pocket and started across the fields.

When he reached the top of a ridge he stood straight and proud in the moonlight, looking at Jim Hawkins' big white house, feeling the gun sagging in his pocket. Lawd, ef Ah had just one mo bullet Ah'd taka shot at tha house. Ah'd like t scare ol man Hawkins jusa little . . . Jusa enough t let im know Dave Saunders is a man.

To his left the road curved, running to the tracks of the Illinois Central. He jerked his head, listening. From far off came a faint *hoooof-hoooof; hoooof-hoooof; hoooof-hoooof*. . . . He stood rigid. Two dollahs a mont. Les see now . . . Tha means it'll take bout two years. Shucks! Ah'll be dam!

He started down the road, toward the tracks. Yeah, here she comes! He stood beside the track and held himself stiffly. Here she comes, erroun the ben . . . C mon, yuh slow poke! C mon! He had his hand on his gun; something quivered in his stomach. Then the train thundered past, the gray and brown box cars rumbling and clinking. He gripped the gun tightly; then he jerked his hand out of his pocket. Ah betcha Bill wouldn't do it! Ah betcha . . . The cars slid past, steel grinding upon steel. Ahm ridin yuh ternight, so hep me Gawd! He was hot all over. He hesitated just a moment; then he grabbed, pulled atop of a car, and lay flat. He felt his pocket; the gun was still there. Ahead the long rails were glinting in the moonlight, stretching away, away to somewhere, somewhere where he could be a man . . .

Questions

1. Do you detect any sentimental elements in Wright's reporting of the dialect of his characters? If so, what expressions seem unrealistic?

2. Are the dialects of the white characters reported differently from that of the Negroes? Differently from each other? How differently would such persons —a farmer and a storekeeper—talk from each other in real life? How differently from the Negroes?
3. Does Dave seem as old as he says he is? Before you answer consider his desire for a gun, his manner of looking at the catalog, the way he talks to his parents, his reactions to both the storekeeper and the farmer, his actions after he has shot the mule, the lie he tells about the mule, and his running away. If you find speeches, actions, or thoughts that suggest he is either presented as being too old or too young, do you find any justification for these in the story itself?
4. What usages do Dave and his parents have that are not heard in your community? Does Wright exaggerate the usage differences?
5. Is the desire for a gun a good way to express Dave's desire for manhood? Why, or why not? Does Wright convince you that Dave would leave home rather than give up the gun?

Writing Projects

1. Write an essay in which you classify speakers not by their purposes or subjects but on the basis of their use of language. You can take any large group—politicians, teachers, visitors, friends—and decide on a specific area of language usage for the basis of your classification—their manner of speaking, their words and phrases, their cliches, their humor. Indicate your attitude in the names and descriptions you give to the classes.

2. Classify any large group of people you know on any basis you desire. Possibilities include the following: classify students by their dress, their study habits, their major interests; professors or teachers by their grading practices, their teaching methods. Other possible groups are parents, salesmen, and high school problem students. Be sure that you make a distinction between the classes and that your reader can see clearly the basis of the classification. As directed in the previous suggestion, indicate your attitude. Make your paper both classify the group and show your response to each class.

3. If you know a dialect other than your own, either regional or social, write a conversation between two individuals, one of whom speaks the dialect. Or have the character tell a story in his own words much as Munn Short does in the Warren selection. Try to use the vocabulary the speaker would use and suggest the sound of his speech through your spelling.

4. Classify attitudes or ideas held by people you know. Choose some basis for the classification such as a particular interest some people have or a prejudice or bias they have. Attitudes towards sports; towards controversial topics such as ecology, censorship, energy problems, abortion; towards particular groups such as teachers or politicians all offer possibilities for a paper. Choose a thesis and rhetorical stance that will give point to your classifying.

5. In our education we are largely learning about divisions that have already been established. As noted earlier, the scientist who dissects is dividing, as is the coach who talks about know-how, strength, and determination. Write a paper in which you explain how something is divided into units. Possibilities are such things as how a course you took was divided into units, how you divide the activities of a typical day, how a job is divided among workers, or how an experience can be divided into parts (for example, a vacation might be divided into preparation, activities, retrospect). Again, give point to such a paper by your stance and thesis.

Part VI

Semantics

The comparatively new science—or is it an art?—of semantics has done much to dispel old myths and misunderstandings about language, and has provided fascinating new insights into the way language takes on and communicates meaning. Our sense, for example, that somehow the word *is* the thing it stands for has become deeply ingrained in our emotional if not our intellectual responses. We may know well enough that to call a thing a spade does not make it a spade, especially if it is a scoopshovel or a pitchfork. But to call a man a communist can have fearsome consequences in our society, whether we give sound evidence that he really is one or give no evidence at all. Or to call a proposal or an idea or even an action (protests against pollution or proceedings to impeach a president) "communist inspired" is to turn off thinking about such things and turn on emotions: simply because we accept the word as the thing. Modern techniques in propaganda, advertising, and politics may not have grown out of semantics, but they certainly make use (often negatively) of insights from semantics. Our responses to these techniques are often laughably—or frighteningly—naive. People must actually buy dog food when they see that little cart pulled into the kitchen—or the manufacturers would have stopped such inanities long ago.

The techniques of modern propaganda, largely developed during World War I and including such devices as name-calling, glittering generalities, card-stacking (presenting only that evidence which supports a position), and bandwagon appeal culminated in Hitler's "Big Lie" of World War II: repeat anything, no matter how absurd, often enough and people will believe it if they want to. The development of such techniques, accompanied by the widespread fear of communism, made possible the "semantic smear," the single most distinguishing technique of those who operated during what we now call "The McCarthy Era," early in the 1950's. Today such appeals surround us, and though we are swayed emotionally our minds have become numbed by them. We pay no attention to either smear or "purr." Or we think ourselves immune to both.

Semanticists provide us with warnings about such things as smear and purr words, with careful analysis of the emotional charge in most words, with an awareness of our individual reactions to words, and with a complex and fascinating approach to logic: semantic logic. But their main concern was defined early by the title of a book, *The Meaning of Meaning,* by C. K. Ogden and I. A. Richards. This enigmatic title suggests, among other things, that *meaning* is the subject matter, that the concept of *meaning* has significance, and, since it is the title of a rather long book, that the concept is rather complex. Later semanticists like Korzybski have shown that Ogden and Richards had only begun to suggest how complex.

This section can include only a sampling of the wide range of achievement and complexity in semantics. The selection from Hayakawa is the only one from a recognized scholar in semantics. It introduces both the problems and the approach. The other selections show implications of semantics in writing and thinking. We can hardly read with awareness Aldous Huxley on "Words and Behavior" without sensing some of the profoundly moral implications of semantic problems. Nor can we explore with Jean-Paul Sartre the semantic base of Anti-Semitism without much the same response. Flannery O'Connor's amazing short story and Robert Frost's poem should help show how intimately involved in our immediate lives are the problems of semantics.

Even this much semantic knowlege should make you both aware and wary: aware of the powers and potentials of semantics, wary of the misuse and manipulation of semantics. You should also become more aware of the power and energy of language in your own writing, and wary of the pitfalls that the semantic complexity of our language keeps setting for readers and writers.

Cause and Effect

Much daily conversation implies that there exists a cause and effect relationship in most activities. "Marian! Why in the world did you cut your hair?" "What made you decide to go into medicine, Dr. Williams?" Think for a moment how often you hear such questions, and how often you ask them. "Why did he do this?" "Why do they do that?" Such questions and their answers make up a large part of the everyday communication between human beings.

Moreover the questions suggest that there are simple answers. Marian usually gives one. "Well, I saw this picture in the magazine. . . ." Or "I decided to do a lot of swimming this summer. . . ." Or "I give all kinds of reasons, but the truth is that I just couldn't face brushing it one more morning." Marian, and Dr. Williams, may give several causes for the one effect. And each may be a partial cause for that effect. The motivation behind any action is usually very complex, a network of multiple causes resulting in a minor effect, which in turn becomes the cause—along with still others perhaps—of another effect. We are all aware that Marian may not know exactly why she cut her hair. And Dr. Williams' uncle, who was a doctor, could have been the major influence on Dr. Williams' decision to go into medicine, but that was probably not the only influence. There may be influences that Dr. Williams does not admit publicly, such as his desire for prestige and a well-paying position.

If the answers we hear, and read, to the large number of *why* questions we ask are oversimplified, why do we use the cause and effect development so often? (Please note that cause and effect question.) One answer is fairly obvious. Even if we do not get the total answer, we are interested in knowing *why* something happened. Why did Henry VIII divorce Catherine of Aragon? Why does *blank* (supply the name of any new movie starlet) love, hate, fear, depend upon, or avoid *blank* (supply the name of any established star or director)? Why is there so much unrest among college students? Or, on a different level, why did Rome fall? (The English historian Gibbon spent the major portion of his life answering that one.)

Cause and effect, then, is a very popular method of development, but it is also frequently oversimplified. Use it, but use it with caution. Show a *major* cause, not the *only* cause. Show three *possible* causes, not *the* three causes. Students hesitate to use such caution, feeling that this somehow weakens their thesis. Surprisingly, it does the opposite. If you are cautious about your findings, your composition manifests a suggestion of scientific objectivity. The scientist who cautiously prefaces his findings with "to the best of our knowledge" or "as nearly as we can tell at this time" impresses us much more than the one who finds the truth, the whole truth, and is ready to quit looking. Develop the cautious approach and give your readers the feeling that an authority is talking.

Use caution also in deciding just what is a cause and what merely is an accompanying event. The mistaken assumption that because one event precedes another it is necessarily the cause of the other is named the *post hoc* fallacy in logic. (The Latin expression *post hoc ergo propter hoc* means "after this, therefore because of it.") It rains. The neighbor to your south says, "Well, I should have known it was going to rain. We planned a picnic." The one to the north says, "Any time I want it to rain, I just have to wash my car." Neither of your neighbors believes what he has said; he is repeating a formula which he has heard over and over. If anyone pressed him he would deny that his action was the cause. But, and this is a much more serious charge, he is very likely to believe that he knows the cause of many major occurrences. The answer is simple. Usually as simple as Marian's or Dr. Williams'. "Will Simm's boy is mixed up with those college radicals," says your neighbor to the south. "I knew that would happen if they let him go to California to work last summer." The neighbor to the north also has an answer just as simple, but quite different. "They let that boy read too much. Some reading is all right, but that kid read all the time. What do they expect?" You smile at the neighbors and say nothing. You know the answer though, the real answer. Be cautious with that answer. Does that cause always result in that effect? Does it always accompany it? Does the effect never happen without it?

All inductive reasoning, the logic behind the scientific method, is based on a belief in cause and effect relationships. The scientist says that under these conditions when these factors are introduced, this is the result. In other words this cause produces that effect in these circumstances. But note that the scientist is cautious. He hesitates to say this will *always* cause that; he is more likely to say that this will *probably* always cause that.

Symbols

S. I. Hayakawa

You were introduced to Hayakawa and his book Language in Thought and Action, *through the selection "How Dictionaries Are Made." He has introduced semantic concepts to a whole generation of college students. He may oversimplify some of the concepts, but he also presents them graphically and with a real sense of their importance, even urgency. You may have trouble with some unfamiliar words, or with familiar words used for unfamiliar concepts. Most such words, like* extensional, *Hayakawa defines in context, sometimes elaborately. Study them in their context before you reach for the dictionary. As you read, be aware of the many different kinds of cause and effect relations Hayakawa establishes. Why do we use symbols? What are some of the results? When he argues that "society itself is often to blame" for our "improper habits of evaluation," he is assigning a cause. How convincingly?*

> This basic need, which certainly is obvious only in man, is the need of symbolization. The symbol-making function is one of man's primary activities, like eating, looking, or moving about. It is the fundamental process of the mind, and goes on all the time.
>
> —SUSANNE K. LANGER

> Man's achievements rest upon the use of symbols.
>
> —ALFRED KORZYBSKI

THE SYMBOLIC PROCESS

Animals struggle with each other for food or for leadership but they do not, like human beings, struggle with each other for things that *stand for* food or leadership: such things as our paper symbols of wealth (money, bonds, titles), badges of rank to wear on our clothes, or low-number license plates, supposed by some people to stand for social precedence. For animals, the relationship in which one thing *stands for* something else does not appear to exist except in very rudimentary form.[1]

The process by means of which human beings can arbitrarily make certain things *stand for* other things may be called the *symbolic process*. Whenever two or more human beings can communicate with each other, they can, by agreement, make anything stand for anything. For example, here are two symbols:

X *Y*

We can agree to let *X* stand for buttons and *Y* stand for bows; then we can freely change our agreement and let *X* stand for the Chicago White Sox and *Y* for the Cincinnati Reds; or let *X* stand for Chaucer and *Y* for Shakespeare, *X* for North Korea, and *Y* for South Korea. *We are, as human beings, uniquely free to manufacture and manipulate and assign values to our symbols as we please.* Indeed, we can go further by making symbols that stand for symbols. If necessary we can, for instance, let the symbol *M* stand for all the *X*'s in the above example (buttons, White Sox, Chaucer, North Korea) and let *N* stand for all the *Y*'s (bows, Cincinnati Reds, Shakespeare, South Korea). Then we can make another symbol, *T,* stand for *M* and *N,* which would be an instance of a symbol of symbols of symbols. This freedom to create symbols of *any* assigned value and to create *symbols that stand for symbols* is essential to what we call the symbolic process.

Everywhere we turn, we see the symbolic process at work. Feathers worn on the head or stripes on the sleeve can be made to stand for military rank; cowrie shells or rings of brass or pieces of paper can stand for wealth; crossed sticks can stand for a set of religious beliefs; buttons, elks' teeth, ribbons, special styles of ornamental haircutting or tattooing, can stand for social affiliations. The symbolic process permeates human life at the most primitive and the most civilized levels alike. Warriors, medicine

[1] One investigator, J. B. Wolfe, trained chimpanzees to put poker chips into an especially constructed vending machine ("chimpomat") which supplied grapes, bananas, and other food. The chimpanzees proved to be able to distinguish chips of different "values" (1 grape, 2 grapes, zero, and so on) and also proved to be willing to work for them if the rewards were fairly immediate. They tended, however, to stop work as they accumulated more chips. Their "money system" was definitely limited to rudimentary and immediate transactions. See Robert M. Yerkes' *Chimpanzees: A Laboratory Colony* (1943).

Other examples of animals successfully learning to react meaningfully to things-that-stand-for-other-things can readily be offered, but as a general rule these animal reactions are extremely simple and limited when contrasted with human possibilities in this direction. For example, it appears likely that a chimpanzee might be taught to drive a simplified car, but there would be one thing wrong with its driving: its reactions are such that if a red light showed when it was halfway across a street, it would stop in the middle of the crossing, while, if a green light showed when another car was stalled in its path, it would go ahead regardless of consequences. In other words, so far as such a chimpanzee would be concerned, the red light could hardly be said to *stand for* stop; it *is* stop.

men, policemen, doormen, nurses, cardinals, and kings wear costumes that symbolize their occupations. American Indians collected scalps, college students collect membership keys in honorary societies, to symbolize victories in their respective fields. There are few things that men do or want to do, possess or want to possess, that have not, in addition to their mechanical or biological value, a symbolic value.

All fashionable clothes, as Thorstein Veblen has pointed out in his *Theory of the Leisure Class* (1899), are highly symbolic: materials, cut, and ornament are dictated only to a slight degree by considerations of warmth, comfort, or practicability. The more we dress up in fine clothes, the more we restrict our freedom of action. But by means of delicate embroideries, easily soiled fabrics, starched shirts, high heels, long and pointed fingernails, and other such sacrifices of comfort, the wealthy classes manage to symbolize, among other things, the fact that they don't have to work for a living. On the other hand, the not-so-wealthy, by imitating these symbols of wealth, symbolize their conviction that, even if they do work for a living, they are just as good as anybody else.

With the changes in American life since Veblen's time, many changes have taken place in our ways of symbolizing social status. Except for evening and party wear, fashionable clothes nowadays are often designed for outdoor life and therefore stress comfort, informality, and above all, freedom from the conventions of business life—hence the gaily colored sports shirts for men and capri pants for women.

In Veblen's time a deeply tanned skin was indicative of a life spent in farming and other outdoor labor, and women in those days went to a great deal of trouble shielding themselves from the sun with parasols, wide hats, and long sleeves. Today, however, a pale skin is indicative of confinement in offices and factories, while a deeply tanned skin suggests a life of leisure—of trips to Florida, Sun Valley, and Hawaii. Hence, a sun-blackened skin, once considered ugly because it symbolized work, is now considered beautiful because it symbolizes leisure. "The idea is," as Stanton Delaplane said in the San Francisco *Chronicle,* "to turn a color which, if you were born with it, would make it extremely difficult to get into major hotels." And pallid people in New York, Chicago, and Toronto who cannot afford midwinter trips to the West Indies find comfort in browning themselves with drugstore tanning solutions.

Food, too, is highly symbolic. Religious dietary regulations, such as those of the Catholics, Jews, and Mohammedans, are observed in order to symbolize adherence to one's religion. Specific foods are used to symbolize specific festivals and observances in almost every country—for example, cherry pie on George Washington's birthday; haggis on Burns' Nicht. And eating together has been a highly symbolic act throughout all of man's known history: "companion" means one with whom you share your bread.

The white Southerner's apparently illogical attitude toward Negroes can also be accounted for on symbolic grounds. People from outside the South often find it difficult to understand how many white Southerners accept close physical contact with Negro servants and yet become extremely upset at the idea of sitting beside Negroes in restaurants or buses. The attitude of the Southerner rests on the fact that the ministrations of a Negro servant—even personal care, such as nursing—have the symbolic implication of social inequality; while admission of Negroes to buses, restaurants, and nonsegregated schools has the symbolic implication of social equality.

We select our furniture to serve as visible symbols of our taste, wealth, and social position. We often choose our residences on the basis of a feeling that it "looks well" to have a "good address." We trade in perfectly good cars for later models, not always to get better transportation, but to give evidence to the community that we can afford it.[2]

Such complicated and apparently unnecessary behavior leads philosophers, both amateur and professional, to ask over and over again, "Why can't human beings live simply and naturally?" Often the complexity of human life makes us look enviously at the relative simplicity of such lives as dogs and cats lead. But the symbolic process, which makes possible the absurdities of human conduct, also makes possible language and therefore all the human achievements dependent upon language. The fact that more things can go wrong with motorcars than with wheelbarrows is no reason for going back to wheelbarrows. Similarly, the fact that the symbolic process makes complicated follies possible is no reason for wanting to return to a cat-and-dog existence. A better solution is to understand the symbolic process so that instead of being its victims we become, to some degree at least, its masters.

LANGUAGE AS SYMBOLISM

Of all forms of symbolism, language is the most highly developed, most subtle, and most complicated. It has been pointed out that human beings, by agreement, can make anything stand for anything. Now, human beings have agreed, in the course of centuries of mutual dependency, to let the

[2] The writer once had an eight-year-old car in good running condition. A friend of his, a repairman who knew the condition of the car, kept urging him to trade it for a new model. "But why?" the writer asked. "The old car's in fine shape still." The repairman answered scornfully, "Yeah, but what the hell. All you've got is transportation."

Recently, the term "transportation car" has begun to appear in advertisements: for example, " '48 Dodge—Runs perfectly good; transportation car. Leaving, must sell. $100." (Classified section of the *Pali Press*, Kailua, Hawaii.) Apparently it means a car that has no symbolic or prestige value and is good only for getting you there and bringing you back—a miserable kind of vehicle indeed!

various noises that they can produce with their lungs, throats, tongues, teeth, and lips systematically stand for specified happenings in their nervous systems. We call that system of agreements *language*. For example, we who speak English have been so trained that, when our nervous systems register the presence of a certain kind of animal, we may make the following noise: "There's a cat." Anyone hearing us expects to find that, by looking in the same direction, he will experience a similar event in his nervous system—one that will lead him to make an almost identical noise. Again, we have been so trained that when we are conscious of wanting food, we make the noise "I'm hungry."

There is, as has been said, *no necessary connection between the symbol and that which is symbolized*. Just as men can wear yachting costumes without ever having been near a yacht, so they can make the noise "I'm hungry" without being hungry. Furthermore, just as social rank can be symbolized by feathers in the hair, by tattooing on the breast, by gold ornaments on the watch chain, or by a thousand different devices according to the culture we live in, so the fact of being hungry can be symbolized by a thousand different noises according to the culture we live in: *"J'ai faim,"* or *"Es hungert mich,"* or *"Ho appetito,"* or *"Hara ga hetta,"* and so on.

However obvious these facts may appear at first glance, they are actually not so obvious as they seem except when we take special pains to think about the subject. Symbols and things symbolized are independent of each other; nevertheless, we all have a way of feeling as if, and sometimes acting as if, there were necessary connections. For example, there is the vague sense we all have that foreign languages are inherently absurd: foreigners have such funny names for things, and why can't they call things by their right names? This feeling exhibits itself most strongly in those tourists who seem to believe that they can make the natives of any country understand English if they shout loud enough. Like the little boy who was reported to have said, "Pigs are called pigs because they are such dirty animals," they feel that the symbol is inherently connected in some way with the thing symbolized. Then there are the people who feel that since snakes are "nasty, slimy creatures" (incidentally, snakes are *not* slimy), the word "snake" is a *nasty, slimy word*.

THE PITFALLS OF DRAMA

Naïveté regarding the symbolic process extends to symbols other than words, of course. In the case of drama (stage, movies, television), there appear to be people in almost every audience who never quite fully realize that a play is a set of fictional, symbolic representations. An actor is one who symbolizes other people, real or imagined. In a movie some years ago, Fredric March enacted with great skill the role of a drunkard. Florence Eldridge (Mrs. March) reports that for a long time thereafter she got letters of advice and sympathy from women who said that they too were married to alcoholics. Also some years ago it was reported that when Edward G. Robinson, who used to play gangster roles with extraordinary vividness, visited Chicago, local hoodlums would telephone him at his hotel to pay their professional respects.

One is reminded of the actor, playing the role of a villain in a traveling theatrical troupe, who, at a particularly tense moment in the play, was shot by an excited cowpuncher in the audience. But this kind of confusion does not seem to be confined to unsophisticated theatergoers. In recent times, Paul Muni, after playing the part of Clarence Darrow in *Inherit the Wind,* was invited to address the American Bar Association; Ralph Bellamy, after playing the role of Franklin D. Roosevelt in *Sunrise at Campobello,* was invited by several colleges to speak on Roosevelt. Also, there are those astonishing patriots who rushed to the recruiting offices to help defend the nation when, on October 30, 1938, the United States was "invaded" by an "army from Mars" in a radio dramatization.[3]

THE WORD IS NOT THE THING

The above, however, are only the more striking examples of confused attitudes toward words and symbols. There would be little point in mentioning them if we were *uniformly and permanently aware* of the independence of symbols from things symbolized, as all human beings, in the writer's opinion, *can be* and *should be*. But we are not. Most of us have, in some area or other of our thinking, improper habits of evaluation. For this, society itself is often to blame: most societies systematically encourage, concerning certain topics, the habitual confusion of symbols with things symbolized. For example, if a Japanese schoolhouse caught on fire, it used to be obligatory in the days of emperor-worship to try to rescue the emperor's *picture* (there was one in every schoolhouse), even at the risk of one's life. (If you got burned to death, you were posthumously ennobled.) In our society, we are encouraged to go into debt in order that we may display, as symbols of prosperity, shiny new automobiles. Strangely enough, the possession of shiny automobiles even under these conditions makes their "owners" *feel* prosperous. In all civilized societies (and probably in many primitive ones as well), the symbols of piety, of civic virtue, or of patriotism are often prized above actual piety, civic virtue, or patriotism. In one way or another, we are all like the brilliant student who cheats on his

[3] See Hadley Cantril's *The Invasion from Mars* (1940); also John Houseman's "The Men from Mars," *Harper's* (December 1948).

exams in order to make Phi Beta Kappa: it is so much more important to have the symbol than the things it stands for.

The habitual confusion of symbols with things symbolized, whether on the part of individuals or societies, is serious enough at all levels of culture to provide a perennial human problem.[4] But with the rise of modern communications systems, the problem of confusing verbal symbols with realities assumes peculiar urgency. We are constantly being talked at, by teachers, preachers, salesmen, public-relations counsels, governmental agencies, and moving-picture sound tracks. The cries of the hawkers of soft drinks, detergents, and laxatives pursue us into our homes, thanks to radio and television—and in some houses the sets are never turned off from morning to night. The mailman brings direct-mail advertising. Billboards confront us on the highway, and we even take portable radios with us to the seashore.

We live in an environment shaped and largely created by hitherto unparalleled semantic influences: mass-circulation newspapers and magazines which are given to reflecting, in a shocking number of cases, the weird prejudices and obsessions of their publishers and owners; radio programs, both local and network, almost completely dominated by commercial motives; public-relations counsels who are simply highly paid craftsmen in the art of manipulating and reshaping our semantic environment in ways favorable to their clients. It is an exciting environment, but fraught with danger: it is only a slight exaggeration to say that Hitler conquered Austria by radio. Today, the full resources of advertising agencies, public-relations counsels, radio, television, and slanted news stories are brought to bear in order to influence our decisions in election campaigns, especially in years of presidential elections.

Citizens of a modern society need, therefore, more than that ordinary "common sense" which was defined by Stuart Chase as that which tells you that the world is flat. They need to be systematically aware of the powers and limitations of symbols, especially words, if they are to guard against being driven into complete bewilderment by the complexity of their semantic environment. The first of the principles governing symbols is this: The symbol is NOT the thing symbolized; the word is NOT the thing; the map is NOT the territory it stands for.

MAPS AND TERRITORIES

There is a sense in which we all live in two worlds. First, we live in the world of happenings which we know at first hand. This is an extremely

[4] The charge against the Pharisees, it will be remembered, was that they were obsessively concerned with the symbols of piety at the expense of an adequate concern with its spirit.

small world, consisting only of that continuum of the things that we have actually seen, felt, or heard—the flow of events constantly passing before our senses. So far as this world of personal experience is concerned, Africa, South America, Asia, Washington, New York, or Los Angeles do not exist if we have never been to these places. Jomo Kenyetta is only a name if we have never seen him. When we ask ourselves how much we know at first hand, we discover that we know very little indeed.

Most of our knowledge, acquired from parents, friends, schools, newspapers, books, conversation, speeches, and television, is received *verbally*. All our knowledge of history, for example, comes to us only in words. The only proof we have that the Battle of Waterloo ever took place is that we have had reports to that effect. These reports are not given us by people who saw it happen, but are based on other reports: reports of reports of reports, which go back ultimately to the first-hand reports given by people who did see it happening. It is through reports, then, and through reports of reports, that we receive most knowledge: about government, about what is happening in Korea, about what picture is showing at the downtown theater—in fact, about anything that we do not know through direct experience.

Let us call this world that comes to us through words the *verbal world,* as opposed to the world we know or are capable of knowing through our own experience, which we shall call the *extensional world*. (The reason for the choice of the word "extensional" will become clear later.) The human being, like any other creature, begins to make his acquaintance with the extensional world from infancy. Unlike other creatures, however, he begins to receive, as soon as he can learn to understand, reports, reports of reports, reports of reports of reports. In addition he receives inferences made from reports, inferences made from other inferences, and so on. By the time a child is a few years old, has gone to school and to Sunday school, and has made a few friends, he has accumulated a considerable amount of second- and third-hand information about morals, geography, history, nature, people, games—all of which information together constitutes his verbal world.

Now, to use the famous metaphor introduced by Alfred Korzybski in his *Science and Sanity* (1933), this verbal world ought to stand in relation to the extensional world as a *map* does to the *territory* it is supposed to represent. If a child grows to adulthood with a verbal world in his head which corresponds fairly closely to the extensional world that he finds around him in his widening experience, he is in relatively small danger of being shocked or hurt by what he finds, because his verbal world has told him what, more or less, to expect. He is prepared for life. If, however, he grows up with a false map in his head—that is, with a head crammed with error and superstition—he will constantly be running into trouble, wasting his efforts, and acting like a fool. He will not be adjusted to the world as it is; he may, if the lack of adjustment is serious, end up in a mental hospital.

Some of the follies we commit because of false maps in our heads are so commonplace that we do not even think of them as remarkable. There are those who protect themselves from accidents by carrying a rabbit's foot. Some refuse to sleep on the thirteenth floor of hotels—a situation so common that most big hotels, even in the capitals of our scientific culture, skip "13" in numbering their floors. Some plan their lives on the basis of astrological predictions. Some play fifty-to-one shots on the basis of dream books. Some hope to make their teeth whiter by changing their brand of tooth paste. All such people are living in verbal worlds that bear little, if any, resemblance to the extensional world.

Now, no matter how beautiful a map may be, it is useless to a traveler unless it accurately shows the relationship of places to each other, the structure of the territory. If we draw, for example, a big dent in the outline of a lake for, let us say, artistic reasons, the map is worthless. But if we are just drawing maps for fun without paying any attention to the structure of the region, there is nothing in the world to prevent us from putting in all the extra curlicues and twists we want in the lakes, rivers, and roads. No harm will be done *unless someone tries to plan a trip by such a map.*

Similarly, by means of imaginary or false reports, or by false inferences from good reports, or by mere rhetorical exercises, we can manufacture at will, with language, "maps" which have no reference to the extensional world. Here again no harm will be done unless someone makes the mistake of regarding such "maps" as representing real territories.

We all inherit a great deal of useless knowledge, and a great deal of misinformation and error (maps that were formerly thought to be accurate), so that there is always a portion of what we have been told that must be discarded. But the cultural heritage of our civilization that is transmitted to us—our socially pooled knowledge, both scientific and humane—has been valued principally because we have believed that it gives us accurate maps of experience. The analogy of verbal worlds to maps is an important one and will be referred to frequently throughout this book. It should be noticed at this point, however, that there are two ways of getting false maps of the world into our heads: first, by having them given to us; second, by creating them ourselves when we misread the true maps given to us.

Questions

1. Considering the whole selection, why does Hayakawa begin with the broad discussion of the symbolic process? Is it necessary for us to understand the broad process in order to understand the specific one in language? Does the broad analysis help convince us of the dangers or of the values he later finds in semantic awareness?
2. Relate the discussion of "transportation" cars (see also the footnote) to a billboard advertising, "We sell only experienced cars." What is the difference between "used" cars, "pre-owned" cars, and "experienced" cars?
3. Hayakawa's discussion of the relation of maps to territories suggests that not only our social but our private mental health may be profoundly influenced by the accuracy with which our verbal map corresponds to reality. Does he exaggerate? To decide, you will have to weigh both his evidence and the evidence of your own experience.
4. Note Hayakawa's analysis of cause and effect in the relations between Southern whites and Negroes. Perhaps the most basic logic underlying the essay is expressed in the paragraph just preceding the section on "Language as Symbolism." Analyze this paragraph carefully, especially its last sentence. Does the rest of the essay convince you that understanding the symbolic process (cause) can help us become its masters rather than its victims?
5. If we really commit follies because of false maps in our heads or because we habitually confuse symbols with things symbolized, point to some commonplace ones other than those Hayakawa lists. Can you point to much more serious and dangerous ones? Could the revolt against the "establishment" have any cause in false maps? Could the establishment's reaction?

Suggestions for Writing

1. One TV commercial shows a husband early in this century punishing his wife when he catches her smoking in the basement, or elsewhere. Then to the catchy tune of "You've come a long way, Baby," a smartly dressed, mini-skirted modern wife struts forward: "You've got your own cigarette now, baby./You've come a long, long way." The commercial is of course a clever one, and loaded with semantic suggestion. Many people object to the continued advertising of tobacco in the face of all the evidence that connects smoking to lung cancer. (That the tobacco industry could insist for so long that no cause and effect relationship had been conclusively proved should emphasize the loopholes in cause and effect reasoning.) Surely you can find just as serious examples of symbols being used to violate or destroy or promote something you feel strongly about. Choose a major example or a related series of lesser examples as the basis for a paper. Develop a cause-effect analysis to express your vigorous distaste or support for this particular use of symbols. As always, work consciously toward solving the problem of rhetorical stance.

An Academic Concern

George Bennion *Semanticists often talk about words that ordinarily would have quite specific meanings but when used in certain contexts, usually social, have almost no meaning except as a kind of generalized response. When someone says, "How are you?" and you respond, "I'm fine," very seldom would either of you be really concerned about the state of your health: the last thing your friend really wants is a detailed report. Both question and response are close to what Hayakawa in another chapter calls "purr" words, just as much of the cursing we hear he calls "snarl" words. We do not really want God to damn someone to Hell, nor do we mean to insult someone's mother: we are simply snarling, or something less. This selection shows what a sensitive observer of language can do with this phenomenon. It would make a good model for you to use in describing some related semantic phenomenon you have observed.*

Some time ago I read an essay about an interesting feature of language called "caressing speech," a sub-language, I suppose, in which tone is crucial but words are nonsignificant. I put the essay aside recalling instances in which men had talked to spooky horses soothingly, softly, using outrageous words, and to dogs lovingly, casting awful aspersions on their ancestors, the horses pacified and the dogs ingratiated. But last summer I witnessed a remarkable example of caressing speech applied to humans.

I had taken a job on a water crew where there was a fairly standard variety of personalities—some friendly, some sullen, all immediately suspicious of an English teacher. One among them, a mechanic in the repair shop, I soon marked as perhaps the crudest, most vile-talking man I had ever met. I had to go a long way back to remember speech like his, all the way back to a time in Luzon, when I waited at a replacement depot with some creatures whose mouths were awash with the slime of all the back doors of the world. The mechanic reminded me of them. About sixty, he was short, fat, unwashed every time I saw him, always with a three-day stubble on his face. That was Willy.

Also employed there was Willy's son—maybe twenty-seven years old—whose name was Richard. Richard, a true son of the vile old man, drove a huge garbage truck that accepted the smaller collections of swill from all over the city. I tell you, never was a man more in his niche than Willy's Richard. His crude language, his disheveled clothing, his sloppy bearing—even his personality it seemed, all fit in marvelously with the heavy effluvium hovering inseparably about the truck. I wondered if Richard didn't awaken nights, aware of an absence, and have to go down to the garbage truck for a moment before he could get back to sleep.

But there was something else about Willy and Richard I failed to notice at first, perhaps because the hand holding my nose obscured my vision.

One Saturday, not a regular working day, I was called to help tap a major water pipe from which we were to take an eight-inch line. Willy was to do the cutting and welding; Richard was there, leech-like I readily perceived, looking for overtime. They came to the job together, and throughout the day, as the work was trying or slack, Richard fussed about his father with a gentle helpfulness and concern that would have annoyed another man. It was the same Richard, all right: his mouth vomited an unending stream of obscenities; but they were not intended as imprecations. They were administered on and around Willy with a tenderness I don't recall seeing before between grown men. It was the "caressing speech" of the essay. Willy, intent on his difficult task, was silent most of the day, but Richard maintained a smooth soft flow of words that I'm certain, however shocking to other ears, eased the father's chores and made pleasant an otherwise beastly day.

Some days later, working at a routine job in town, I discovered we were in front of Willy's house. His wife kept tabs on our progress, frequently inviting the strawboss into the shade and plying him with beer. In every way that woman belonged to Willy. She was a complete fishwife. Her hair stood out in every way, tousled and unbrushed; her toothless mouth, forever open, made loud talk and raucous laughter; her large belly demanded attention in spite of a dress nondescript in color and design, and her short legs, almost always wide apart to accommodate their considerable task, moved her about impressively.

She had the same speech as Willy and Richard—disgusting in its raucous assault on the sensibilities. We hear of men with sepulchral voices or funereal speech; hers was sewer speech. Yet like Richard's, it wasn't only that: where his ribaldry had been gentle and tender, hers was jolly and gay. She maintained a happy cacophony that spoke of enormous enjoyment.

Presently her children appeared—six, eight, maybe twelve years old, all girls, all stocky, all happy, all noisy. And then came Willy, home from the shop. He moved into the assemblage like a well-fed hog—grunting, blaspheming, cursing just as usual, only there really was no sting in it, no meanness. And the little girls were tugging at him and hugging and fondling him, all the while his swear words dropping and splattering about like manure from a cow at the manger.

Finally I climbed out of the shallow hole where I had been at work and sat down at the edge, my feet hanging into it. Willy, with all the thoughtfulness of an accomplished host, waddled over and acknowledged my presence, squatting a moment at the side of the hole. In no time two of the little girls were with him, one on either side, patting, purring, playing, Willy all the while addressing them by filthy names in the gentlest, most affectionate tones his whisky voice could manage.

I ventured an ambiguity: "Willy, you have a remarkable family."

He looked at me a moment, kindly, seriously, like a pastor knowing the importance of choice family relations; and then patting his girls: "These little bastards? Well I guess you're right. That's one thing, George; the Lord has always blessed me with a goddam good family."

Words and Behavior

Aldous L. Huxley *Mr. Huxley is best known as a novelist, especially as the author of* Brave New World, *a frightening projection into the future of tendencies toward state and mechanistic control over human life and thought. George Orwell's* 1984 *and* Brave New World, *along with modern warfare, the experience of the world with communism and naziism, and the possibility of annihilation of the race by the nuclear bomb, have made the world aware of the implications and dangers of science and dictators. The mechanized humans pictured in either book may never come into being, but the capabilities for producing them already exist, both Huxley and Orwell argue, and the dangers of such a development are far greater and more frightening than most of us like to admit.*

Huxley was also a tireless and biting critic of other qualities in modern civilization. This selection does not discuss semantic problems as such. But nearly every idea Huxley explores has semantic implications, some of them almost as disturbing as his picture of the Brave New World. *As you read, keep in mind Hayakawa's distinctions between maps and territories.*

Words form the thread on which we string our experiences. Without them we should live spasmodically and intermittently. Hatred itself is not so strong that animals will not forget it, if distracted, even in the presence of the enemy. Watch a pair of cats, crouching on the brink of a fight. Balefully the eyes glare; from far down in the throat of each come bursts of a strange, strangled noise of defiance; as though animated by a life of their own, the tails twitch and tremble. With aimed intensity of loathing! Another moment and surely there must be an explosion. But no; all of a sudden one of the two creatures turns away, hoists a hind leg in a more than fascist salute and, with the same fixed and focused attention as it had given a moment before to its enemy, begins to make a lingual toilet. Animal love is as much at the mercy of distractions as animal hatred. The dumb creation lives a life made up of discrete and mutually irrelevant episodes.

Such as it is, the consistency of human characters is due to the words upon which all human experiences are strung. We are purposeful because we can describe our feelings in rememberable words, can justify and rationalize our desires in terms of some kind of argument. Faced by an enemy we do not allow an itch to distract us from our emotions; the mere word "enemy" is enough to keep us reminded of our hatred, to convince us that we do well to be angry. Similarly the word "love" bridges for us those chasms of momentary indifference and boredom which gape from time to time between even the most ardent lovers. Feeling and desire provide us with our motive power; words give continuity to what we do and to a considerable extent determine our direction. Inappropriate and badly chosen words vitiate thought and lead to wrong or foolish conduct. Most ignorances are vincible, and in the greater number of cases stupidity is what the Buddha pronounced it to be, a sin. For, consciously, or subconsciously, it is with deliberation that we do not know or fail to understand—because incomprehension allows us, with a good conscience, to evade unpleasant obligations and responsibilities, because ignorance is the best excuse for going on doing what one likes, but ought not, to do. Our egotisms are incessantly fighting to preserve themselves, not only from external enemies, but also from the assaults of the other and better self with which they are so uncomfortably associated. Ignorance is egotism's most effective defense against that Dr. Jekyll in us who desires perfection; stupidity, its subtlest stratagem. If, as so often happens, we choose to give continuity to our experience by means of words which falsify the facts, this is because the falsification is somehow to our advantage as egotists.

Consider, for example, the case of war. War is enormously discreditable to those who order it to be waged and even to those who merely tolerate its existence. Furthermore, to developed sensibilities the facts of war are revolting and horrifying. To falsify these facts, and by so doing to make war seem less evil than it really is, and our own responsibility in tolerating war less heavy, is doubly to our advantage. By suppressing and distorting the truth, we protect our sensibilities and preserve our self-esteem. Now, language is, among other things, a device which men use for suppressing and distorting the truth. Finding the reality of war too unpleasant to contemplate, we create a verbal alternative to that reality, parallel with it, but in quality quite different from it. That which we contemplate thenceforward is not that to which we react emotionally and upon which we pass our moral judgments, is not war as it is in fact, but the fiction of war as it exists in our pleasantly falsifying verbiage. Our stupidity in using inappropriate language turns out, on analysis, to be the most refined cunning.

The most shocking fact about war is that its victims and its instruments are individual human beings, and that these individual human beings are condemned by the monstrous conventions of politics to murder or be murdered in quarrels not their own, to inflict upon the innocent and, innocent themselves of any crime against their enemies, to suffer cruelties of every kind.

The language of strategy and politics is designed, so far as it is possible, to conceal this fact, to make it appear as though wars were not fought by individuals drilled to murder one another in cold blood and without provocation, but either by impersonal and therefore wholly non-moral and impassible forces, or else by personified abstractions.

Here are a few examples of the first kind of falsification. In place of "cavalrymen" or "foot-soldiers" military writers like to speak of "sabres" and "rifles." Here is a sentence from a description of the Battle of Marengo: "According to Victor's report, the French retreat was orderly; it is certain, at any rate, that the regiments held together, for the six thousand Austrian sabres found no opportunity to charge home." The battle is between sabres in line and muskets in échelon—a mere clash of ironmongery.

On other occasions there is no question of anything so vulgarly material as ironmongery. The battles are between Platonic ideas, between the abstractions of physics and mathematics. Forces interact; weights are flung into scales; masses are set in motion. Or else it is all a matter of geometry. Lines swing and sweep; are protracted or curved; pivot on a fixed point.

Alternatively the combatants are personal, in the sense that they are personifications. There is "the enemy," in the singular, making "his" plans, striking "his" blows. The attribution of personal characteristics to collectivities, to geographical expressions, to institutions, is a source, as we shall see, of endless confusions in political thought, of innumerable political mistakes and crimes. Personification in politics is an error which we make because it is to our advantage as egotists to be able to feel violently proud of our country and of ourselves as belonging to it, and to believe that all the misfortunes due to our own mistakes are really the work of the Foreigner. It is easier to feel violently toward a person than toward an abstraction; hence our habit of making political personifications. In some cases military personifications are merely special instances of political personifications. A particular collectivity, the army or the warring nation, is given the name and, along with the name, the attributes of a single person, in order that we may be able to love or hate it more intensely than we could do if we thought of it as what it really is: a number of diverse individuals. In other cases personification is used for the purpose of concealing the fundamental absurdity and monstrosity of war. What is absurd and monstrous about war is that men who have no personal quarrel should be trained to murder one another in cold blood. By personifying opposing armies or countries, we are able to think of war as a conflict between individuals. The same result is obtained by writing of war as though it were carried on exclusively by the generals in command and not by the private soldiers in their armies. ("Rennenkampf had pressed back von Schubert.") The implication in both cases is that war is indistinguishable from a bout of fisticuffs in a bar room. Whereas in reality it is profoundly different. A scrap between two individuals is forgivable; mass murder, deliberately organized, is a monstrous iniquity. We still choose to use war as an instrument of policy; and to comprehend the full wickedness and absurdity of war would therefore be inconvenient. For, once we understood, we should have to make some effort to get rid of the abominable thing. Accordingly, when we talk about war, we use a language which conceals or embellishes its reality. Ignoring the facts, so far as we possibly can, we imply that battles are not fought by soldiers, but by things, principles, allegories, personified collectivities, or (at the most human) by opposing commanders, pitched against one another in single combat. For the same reason, when we have to describe the processes and the results of war, we employ a rich variety of euphemisms. Even the most violently patriotic and militaristic are reluctant to call a spade by its own name. To conceal their intentions even from themselves, they make use of picturesque metaphors. We find them, for example, clamoring for war planes numerous and powerful enough to go and "destroy the hornets in their nests"—in other words, to go and throw thermite, high explosives and vesicants upon the inhabitants of neighboring countries before they have time to come and do the same to us. And how reassuring is the language of historians and strategists! They write admiringly of those military geniuses who know "when to strike at the enemy's line" (a single combatant deranges the geometrical constructions of a personification); when to "turn his flank"; when to "execute an enveloping movement." As though they were engineers discussing the strength of materials and the distribution of stresses, they talk of abstract entities called "man power" and "fire power." They sum up the long-drawn sufferings and atrocities of trench warfare in the phrase, "a war of attrition"; the massacre and mangling of human beings is assimilated to the grinding of a lens.

A dangerously abstract word, which figures in all discussions about war, is "force." Those who believe in organizing collective security by means of military pacts against a possible aggressor are particularly fond of this word. "You cannot," they say, "have international justice unless you are prepared to impose it by force." "Peace-loving countries must unite to use force against aggressive dictatorships." "Democratic institutions must be protected, if need be, by force." And so on.

Now, the word "force," when used in reference to human relations, has no single, definite meaning. There is the "force" used by parents when, without resort to any kind of physical violence, they compel their children to act or refrain from acting in some particular way. There is the "force" used by attendants in an asylum when they try to prevent a maniac from hurting himself or others. There is the "force" used by the police when they control a crowd, and that other "force" which they used in a baton charge. And finally there is the "force" used in war. This, of course, varies with the technological devices at the disposal of the belligerents, with the policies they are pursuing, and with the particular circumstances of the war in question. But in general it may be said that, in war, "force" connotes violence and fraud used to the limit of the combatants' capacity.

Variations in quantity, if sufficiently great, produce variations in quality. The "force" that is war, particularly modern war, is very different from the "force" that is police action, and the use of the same abstract word to describe the two dissimilar processes is profoundly misleading. (Still more misleading, of course, is the explicit assimilation of a war, waged by allied League-of-Nations powers against an aggressor, to police action against a criminal. The first is the use of violence and fraud without limit against innocent and guilty alike; the second is the use of strictly limited violence and a minimum of fraud exclusively against the guilty.)

Reality is a succession of concrete and particular situations. When we think about such situations we should use the particular and concrete words which apply to them. If we use abstract words which apply equally well (and equally badly) to other, quite dissimilar situations, it is certain that we shall think incorrectly.

Let us take the sentences quoted above and translate the abstract word "force" into language that will render (however inadequately) the concrete and particular realities of contemporary warfare.

"You cannot have international justice, unless you are prepared to impose it by force." Translated, this becomes: "You cannot have international justice unless you are prepared, with a view to imposing a just settlement, to drop thermite, high explosives and vesicants upon the inhabitants of foreign cities and to have thermite, high explosives and vesicants dropped in return upon the inhabitants of your cities." At the end of this proceeding, justice is to be imposed by the victorious party—that is, if there is a victorious party. It should be remarked that justice was to have been imposed by the victorious party at the end of the last war. But, unfortunately, after four years of fighting, the temper of the victors was such that they were quite incapable of making a just settlement. The Allies are reaping in Nazi Germany what they sowed at Versailles. The victors of the next war will have undergone intensive bombardments with thermite, high explosives and vesicants. Will their temper be better than that of the Allies in 1918? Will they be in a fitter state to make a just settlement? The answer, quite obviously, is: No. It is psychologically all but impossible that justice should be secured by the methods of contemporary warfare.

The next two sentences may be taken together. "Peace-loving countries must unite to use force against aggressive dictatorships. Democratic institutions must be protected, if need be, by force." Let us translate. "Peace-loving countries must unite to throw thermite, high explosives and vesicants on the inhabitants of countries ruled by aggressive dictators. They must do this, and of course abide the consequences, in order to preserve peace and democratic institutions." Two questions immediately propound themselves. First, is it likely that peace can be secured by a process calculated to reduce the orderly life of our complicated societies to chaos? And, second, is it likely that democratic institutions will flourish in a state of chaos? Again, the answers are pretty clearly in the negative.

By using the abstract word "force," instead of terms which at least attempt to describe the realities of war as it is today, the preachers of collective security through military collaboration disguise from themselves and from others, not only the contemporary facts, but also the probable consequences of their favorite policy. The attempt to secure justice, peace and democracy by "force" seems reasonable enough until we realize, first, that this noncommittal word stands, in the circumstances of our age, for activities which can hardly fail to result in social chaos; and second, that the consequences of social chaos are injustice, chronic warfare and tyranny. The moment we think in concrete and particular terms of the concrete and particular process called "modern war," we see that a policy which worked (or at least didn't result in complete disaster) in the past has no prospect whatever of working in the immediate future. The attempt to secure justice, peace and democracy by means of a "force," which means, at this particular moment of history, thermite, high explosives and vesicants, is about as reasonable as the attempt to put out a fire with a colorless liquid that happens to be, not water, but petrol.

What applies to the "force" that is war applies in large measure to the "force" that is revolution. It seems inherently very unlikely that social justice and social peace can be secured by thermite, high explosives and vesicants. At first, it may be, the parties in a civil war would hesitate to use such instruments on their fellow-countrymen. But there can be little doubt that, if the conflict were prolonged (as it probably would be between the evenly balanced Right and Left of a highly industrialized society), the combatants would end by losing their scruples.

The alternatives confronting us seem to be plain enough. Either we invent and conscientiously employ a new technique for making revolutions and settling international disputes; or else we cling to the old technique and, using "force" (that is to say, thermite, high explosives and vesicants), destroy ourselves. Those who, for whatever motive, disguise the nature of the second alternative under inappropriate language, render the world a grave disservice. They lead us into one of the temptations we find it hardest to resist—the temptation to run away from reality, to pretend that facts are not what they are. Like Shelley (but without Shelley's acute awareness of what he was doing) we are perpetually weaving

> A shroud of talk to hide us from the sun
> Of this familiar life.

We protect our minds by an elaborate system of abstractions, ambiguities, metaphors and similes from the reality we do not wish to know too clearly; we lie to ourselves, in order that we may still have the excuse of ignorance, the alibi of stupidity and incomprehension, possessing which we can continue with a good conscience to commit and tolerate the most monstrous crimes:

> The poor wretch who has learned his only prayers
> From curses, who knows scarcely words enough
> To ask a blessing from his Heavenly Father,
> Becomes a fluent phraseman, absolute
> And technical in victories and defeats,
> And all our dainty terms for fratricide;
> Terms which we trundle smoothly o'er our tongues
> Like mere abstractions, empty sounds to which
> We join no meaning and attach no form!
> As if the soldier died without a wound:
> As if the fibers of this godlike frame
> Were gored without a pang: as if the wretch
> Who fell in battle, doing bloody deeds,
> Passed off to Heaven translated and not killed;
> As though he had no wife to pine for him,
> No God to judge him.

The language we use about war is inappropriate, and its inappropriateness is designed to conceal a reality so odious that we do not wish to know it. The language we use about politics is also inappropriate; but here our mistake has a different purpose. Our principal aim in this case is to arouse and, having aroused, to rationalize and justify such intrinsically agreeable sentiments as pride and hatred, self-esteem and contempt for others. To achieve this end we speak about the facts of politics in words which more or less completely misrepresent them.

The concrete realities of politics are individual human beings, living together in national groups. Politicians—and to some extent we are all politicians—substitute abstractions for these concrete realities, and having done this, proceed to invest each abstraction with an appearance of concreteness by personifying it. For example, the concrete reality of which "Britain" is the abstraction consists of some forty-odd millions of diverse individuals living on an island off the west coast of Europe. The personification of this abstraction appears, in classical fancy-dress and holding a very large toasting fork, on the backside of our copper coinage; appears in verbal form, every time we talk about international politics. "Britain," the abstraction from forty millions of Britons, is endowed with thoughts, sensibilities and emotions, even with a sex—for, in spite of John Bull, the country is always a female.

Now, it is of course possible that "Britain" is more than a mere name—is an entity that possesses some kind of reality distinct from that of the individuals constituting the group to which the name is applied. But this entity, if it exists, is certainly not a young lady with a toasting fork; nor is it possible to believe (though some eminent philosophers have preached the doctrine) that it should possess anything in the nature of a personal will. One must agree with T. H. Green that "there can be nothing in a nation, however exalted its mission, or in a society however perfectly organized, which is not in the persons composing the nation or the society. . . . We cannot suppose a national spirit and will to exist except as the spirit and will of individuals." But the moment we start resolutely thinking about our world in terms of individual persons we find ourselves at the same time thinking in terms of universality. "The great rational religions," writes Professor Whitehead, "are the outcome of the emergence of a religious consciousness that is universal, as distinguished from tribal, or even social. Because it is universal, it introduces the note of solitariness." (And he might have added that, because it is solitary, it introduces the note of universality.) "The reason of this connection between universality and solitude is that universality is a disconnection from immediate surroundings." And conversely the disconnection from immediate surroundings, particularly such social surrounding as the tribe or nation, the insistence on the person as the fundamental reality, leads to the conception of an all-embracing unity.

A nation, then, may be more than a mere abstraction, may possess some kind of real existence apart from its constituent members. But there is no reason to suppose that it is a person; indeed, there is every reason to suppose that it isn't. Those who speak as though it were a person (and some go further than this and speak as though it were a personal god) do so, because it is to their interest as egotists to make precisely this mistake.

In the case of the ruling class these interests are in part material. The personification of the nation as a sacred being, different from and superior to its constituent members, is merely (I quote the words of a great French jurist, Léon Duguit) "a way of imposing authority by making people believe it is an authority *de jure* and not merely *de facto*." By habitually talking of the nation as though it were a person with thoughts, feelings and a will of its own, the rulers of a country legitimate their own powers. Personification leads easily to deification; and where the nation is deified, its government ceases to be a mere convenience, like drains or a telephone system, and, partaking in the sacredness of the entity it represents, claims to give orders by divine right and demands the unquestioning obedience due to a god. Rulers seldom find it hard to recognize their friends. Hegel, the man who elaborated an inappropriate figure of speech into a complete philosophy of politics, was a favorite of the Prussian government. *"Es ist,"* he had written, *"es ist der Gang Gottes in der Welt, das der Staat ist."* The decoration bestowed on him by Frederick William III was richly deserved.

Unlike their rulers, the ruled have no material interest in using inappropriate language about states and nations. For them, the reward of being mistaken is psychological. The personified and deified nation becomes, in the minds of the individuals composing it, a kind of enlargement of themselves. The superhuman qualities which belong to the young lady with the toasting fork, the young lady with plaits and a brass *soutien-gorge,* the young lady in a Phrygian bonnet, are claimed by individual Englishmen, Germans and Frenchmen as being, at least in part, their own. *Dulce et decorum est pro patria mori*. But there would be no need to die, no need of war, if it had not been even sweeter to boast and swagger for one's country, to hate, despise, swindle and bully for it. Loyalty to the personified nation, or to the personified class or party, justifies the loyal in indulging all those passions which good manners and the moral code do not allow them to display in their relations with their neighbors. The personified entity is a being, not only great and noble, but also insanely proud, vain and touchy; fiercely rapacious; a braggart; bound by no considerations of right and wrong. (Hegel condemned as hopelessly shallow all those who dared to apply ethical standards to the activities of nations. To condone and applaud every iniquity committed in the name of the State was to him a sign of philosophical profundity.) Identifying themselves with this god, individuals find relief from the constraints of ordinary social decency, feel themselves justified in giving rein, within duly prescribed limits, to their criminal proclivities. As a loyal nationalist or party-man, one can enjoy the luxury of behaving badly with a good conscience.

The evil passions are further justified by another linguistic error—the error of speaking about certain categories of persons as though they were mere embodied abstractions. Foreigners and those who disagree with us are not thought of as men and women like ourselves and our fellow-countrymen; they are thought of as representatives and, so to say, symbols of a class. In so far as they have any personality at all, it is the personality we mistakenly attribute to their class—a personality that is, by definition, intrinsically evil. We know that the harming or killing of men and women is wrong, and we are reluctant consciously to do what we know to be wrong. But when particular men and women are thought of merely as representatives of a class, which has previously been defined as evil and personified in the shape of a devil, then the reluctance to hurt or murder disappears. Brown, Jones and Robinson are no longer thought of as Brown, Jones and Robinson, but as heretics, gentiles, Yids, niggers, barbarians, Huns, communists, capitalists, fascists, liberals—whichever the case may be. When they have been called such names and assimilated to the accursed class to which the names apply, Brown, Jones and Robinson cease to be conceived as what they really are—human persons—and become for the users of this fatally inappropriate language mere vermin or, worse, demons whom it is right and proper to destroy as thoroughly and as painfully as possible. Wherever persons are present, questions of morality arise. Rulers of nations and leaders of parties find morality embarrassing. That is why they take such pains to depersonalize their opponents. All propaganda directed against an opposing group has but one aim: to substitute diabolical abstractions for concrete persons. The propagandist's purpose is to make one set of people forget that certain other sets of people are human. By robbing them of their personality, he puts them outside the pale of moral obligation. Mere symbols can have no rights—particularly when that of which they are symbolical is, by definition, evil.

Politics can become moral only on one condition: that its problems shall be spoken of and thought about exclusively in terms of concrete reality; that is to say, of persons. To depersonify human beings and to personify abstractions are complementary errors which lead, by an inexorable logic, to war between nations and to idolatrous worship of the State, with consequent governmental oppression. All current political thought is a mixture, in varying proportions, between thought in terms of concrete realities and thought in terms of depersonified symbols and personified abstractions. In the democratic countries the problems of internal politics are thought about mainly in terms of concrete reality; those of external politics, mainly in terms of abstractions and symbols. In dictatorial countries the proportion of concrete to abstract and symbolic thought is lower than in democratic countries. Dictators talk little of persons, much of personified abstractions, such as the Nation, the State, the Party, and much of depersonified symbols, such as Yids, Bolshies, Capitalists. The stupidity of politicians who talk about a world of persons as though it were not a world of persons is due in the main to self-interest. In a fictitious world of symbols and personified abstractions, rulers find that they can rule more effectively, and the ruled, that they can gratify instincts which the conventions of good manners and the imperatives of morality demand that they should repress. To think correctly is the condition of behaving well. It is also in itself a moral act; those who would think correctly must resist considerable temptations.

Questions

1. To what extent is Huxley's metaphor in the first sentence intrinsic to the paragraph it introduces? To the whole essay? Is it effective? How is his description of the cats related to the metaphor? That is, does his analysis really show words to be a thread on which we string our experiences?
2. Though the concepts Huxley explores are perhaps no more difficult or profound than those discussed by Hayakawa, his language is more abstract and difficult. You may need to consult a dictionary for words like *intermittently, discrete, vitiate, incessantly*. Can you decide why Huxley uses so many abstract words? Do they work harmoniously with such expressions as *stupidity, in cold blood, scrap* (for *fight*)?
3. One of the central concerns of semantics is with connotations of words. Huxley generalizes that "in war, 'force' connotes violence and fraud used to the limit of the combatants' capacity." Hasn't Huxley's analysis already shown that the word "connotes" almost anything but violence and fraud? Is he just careless here? Or is there some sense in which he can be right?
4. Huxley maneuvers words semantically himself. What happens to the word *rich* in the expression "a rich variety of euphemism"? What happens to the words in Huxley's "translation" of the sentences used to justify "force" in international relations? What happens to "intrinsically agreeable sentiments" when he applies this to "pride and hatred, self-esteem and contempt for others"?

Suggestions for Writing

1. Huxley's contrast between the abstraction "Britain" and the concrete reality of which "Britain" is the abstraction suggests an intriguing similar analysis of "America." Some of his comparisons would work point for point with America but many qualities of America would be quite different. The problem suggests a development of your paper by comparison and contrast. But in this section we are suggesting that you work with cause and effect. One way to approach this would be to analyze the causes for the abstract "America" as contrasted with the concrete, and then to examine, as Huxley does, one or more effects that follow from the abstraction.

2. Huxley wrote this selection just as the forces were gathering which resulted in the mass extermination of millions of Jews in Nazi Germany and its conquered nations. Any quick review of that period shows the terrifying extent to which these mass murders were carried out in the name of semantic abstractions, like "Pure Aryan Race" and "Jew." You may want to turn back to the brief quotation from the poet Wiechert (see p. 70) to see a reaction to all this. Even superficial examination of our problems with civil rights, ecology and pollution, the energy crisis, population control, and so forth should show distressing similar misuse of both semantic abstraction and semantic personification (note Huxley's analysis of these). Using a cause-effect analysis, write a paper in which you explore one or more of these problems, or some other current problem, in terms of its semantics.
3. Select a political speech or a particular politician or political movement and analyze the semantic abstractions and/or personifications that contribute to success or to broad dangers for you or for society at large.

Dulce Et Decorum Est

Wilfred Owen *This famous poem is part of a small legacy of poetry left us by Wilfred Owen before he was killed near the end of World War I. The evidence of this and other poems indicates that we lost one of the most promising poets of our time to that war. The poem is one of the most effective war poems in our or any language. Careful analysis with Huxley's discussion of the semantics of war in mind should show why.*

Bent double, like old beggars under sacks,
Knock-kneed, coughing like hags, we cursed through sludge,
Till on the haunting flares we turned our backs
And towards our distant rest began to trudge.
Men marched asleep. Many had lost their boots
But limped on, blood-shod. All went lame; all blind;
Drunk with fatigue; deaf even to the hoots
Of tired, outstripped Five-Nines that dropped behind.

Gas! GAS! Quick, boys!—An ecstasy of fumbling,
Fitting the clumsy helmets just in time;
But someone still was yelling out and stumbling
And flound'ring like a man in fire or lime . . .
Dim, through the misty panes and thick green light,
As under a green sea, I saw him drowning.

In all my dreams, before my helpless sight,
He plunges at me, guttering, choking, drowning.

If in some smothering dreams you too could pace
Behind the wagon that we flung him in,
And watch the white eyes writhing in his face,
His hanging face, like a devil's sick of sin;
If you could hear, at every jolt, the blood

Come gargling from the froth-corrupted lungs,
Obscene as cancer, bitter as the cud
Of vile, incurable sores on innocent tongues,—
My friend, you would not tell with such high zest
To children ardent for some desperate glory,
The old Lie: Dulce et decorum est
Pro patria mori.

Questions

1. Contrast the details of the soldier's experience of war with the abstractions by which the same encounter might be described in a journalist's or historian's account. This could be the subject for a paragraph or a longer paper.
2. Select the words which seem to catch best the horror of the fighting. What parts of speech dominate your list? Do the words carry heavy semantic suggestion? Do they seem unfair or misleading?
3. The Latin expression from the poet Horace translates essentially into, "It is sweet and proper to die for the fatherland." The force of the passage as Owen uses it contrasts sharply with the original. Why? Does our response to it here depend primarily on the poet's calling it "the old lie"?

Suggestions for Writing

1. Write the journalist's account suggested in Question 1 above. Then define what in the poem causes the semantic effects you can see as contrasting with those of your journalist's account.

Revelation

Flannery O'Connor

When Flannery O'Connor died at 39 in 1964 of an incurable disease she had fought all her adult life, America may well have lost the most remarkable short story writer to emerge since World War II. Even in a time remarkable for the quality and number of short stories, hers stand high above the crowd. All are set in the South, all show her control of Southern idiom, all show an intense spiritual and moral energy. Miss O'Connor herself was a devout Catholic. "Revelation" may be her best story. Certainly it is one of the most powerful of its kind. We use it here for its power but also for its semantic implications. As you read, watch for any violations of semantic processes discussed by Hayakawa and Huxley. Why does Mrs. Turpin continually classify people as she does? What is wrong with such classifying? Why does the girl react so violently to her and she to the girl?

The doctor's waiting room, which was very small, was almost full when the Turpins entered and Mrs. Turpin, who was very large, made it look even smaller by her presence. She stood looming at the head of the magazine table set in the center of it, a living demonstration that the room was inadequate and ridiculous. Her little bright black eyes took in all the patients as she sized up the seating situation. There was one vacant chair and a place on the sofa occupied by a blond child in a dirty blue romper who should have been told to move over and make room for the lady. He was five or six, but Mrs. Turpin saw at once that no one was going to tell him to move over. He was slumped down in the seat, his arms idle at his sides and his eyes idle in his head; his nose ran unchecked.

Mrs. Turpin put a firm hand on Claud's shoulder and said in a voice that included anyone who wanted to listen, "Claud, you sit in that chair there," and gave him a push down into the vacant one. Claud was florid and bald and sturdy, somewhat shorter than Mrs. Turpin, but he sat down as if he were accustomed to doing what she told him to.

Mrs. Turpin remained standing. The only man in the room besides

Claud was a lean stringy old fellow with a rusty hand spread out on each knee, whose eyes were closed as if he were asleep or dead or pretending to be so as not to get up and offer her his seat. Her gaze settled agreeably on a well-dressed grey-haired lady whose eyes met hers and whose expression said: if that child belonged to me, he would have some manners and move over—there's plenty of room there for you and him too.

Claud looked up with a sigh and made as if to rise.

"Sit down," Mrs. Turpin said. "You know you're not supposed to stand on that leg. He has an ulcer on his leg," she explained.

Claud lifted his foot onto the magazine table and rolled his trouser leg up to reveal a purple swelling on a plump marble-white calf.

"My!" the pleasant lady said. "How did you do that?"

"A cow kicked him," Mrs. Turpin said.

"Goodness!" said the lady.

Claud rolled his trouser leg down.

"Maybe the little boy would move over," the lady suggested, but the child did not stir.

"Somebody will be leaving in a minute," Mrs. Turpin said. She could not understand why a doctor—with as much money as they made charging five dollars a day to just stick their head in the hospital door and look at you—couldn't afford a decent-sized waiting room. This one was hardly bigger than a garage. The table was cluttered with limp-looking magazines and at one end of it there was a big green glass ash tray full of cigaret butts and cotton wads with little blood spots on them. If she had had anything to do with the running of the place, that would have been emptied every so often. There were no chairs against the wall at the head of the room. It had a rectangular-shaped panel in it that permitted a view of the office where the nurse came and went and the secretary listened to the radio. A plastic fern in a gold pot sat in the opening and trailed its fronds down almost to the floor. The radio was softly playing gospel music.

Just then the inner door opened and a nurse with the highest stack of yellow hair Mrs. Turpin had ever seen put her face in the crack and called for the next patient. The woman sitting beside Claud grasped the two arms of her chair and hoisted herself up; she pulled her dress free from her legs and lumbered through the door where the nurse had disappeared.

Mrs. Turpin eased into the vacant chair, which held her tight as a corset. "I wish I could reduce," she said, and rolled her eyes and gave a comic sigh.

"Oh, *you* aren't fat," the stylish lady said.

"Ooooo I am too," Mrs. Turpin said. "Claud he eats all he wants to and never weighs over one hundred and seventy-five pounds, but me I just look at something good to eat and I gain some weight," and her stomach and shoulders shook with laughter. "You can eat all you want to, can't you, Claud?" she asked, turning to him.

Claud only grinned.

"Well, as long as you have such a good disposition," the stylish lady said, "I don't think it makes a bit of difference what size you are. You just can't beat a good disposition."

Next to her was a fat girl of eighteen or nineteen, scowling into a thick blue book which Mrs. Turpin saw was entitled *Human Development*. The girl raised her head and directed her scowl at Mrs. Turpin as if she did not like her looks. She appeared annoyed that anyone should speak while she tried to read. The poor girl's face was blue with acne and Mrs. Turpin thought how pitiful it was to have a face like that at that age. She gave the girl a friendly smile but the girl only scowled the harder. Mrs. Turpin herself was fat but she had always had good skin, and, though she was forty-seven years old, there was not a wrinkle in her face except around her eyes from laughing too much.

Next to the ugly girl was the child, still in exactly the same position, and next to him was a thin leathery old woman in a cotton print dress. She and Claud had three sacks of chicken feed in their pump house that was in the same print. She had seen from the first that the child belonged with the old woman. She could tell by the way they sat—kind of vacant and white-trashy, as if they would sit there until Doomsday if nobody called and told them to get up. And at right angles but next to the well-dressed pleasant lady was a lank-faced woman who was certainly the child's mother. She had on a yellow sweat shirt and wine-colored slacks, both gritty-looking, and the rims of her lips were stained with snuff. Her dirty yellow hair was tied behind with a little piece of red paper ribbon. Worse than niggers any day, Mrs. Turpin thought.

The gospel hymn playing was, "When I looked up and He looked down," and Mrs. Turpin, who knew it, supplied the last line mentally, "And wona these days I know I'll we-eara crown."

Without appearing to, Mrs. Turpin always noticed people's feet. The well-dressed lady had on red and grey suede shoes to match her dress. Mrs. Turpin had on her good black patent leather pumps. The ugly girl had on Girl Scout shoes and heavy socks. The old woman had on tennis shoes and the white-trashy mother had on what appeared to be bedroom slippers, black straw with gold braid threaded through them—exactly what you would have expected her to have on.

Sometimes at night when she couldn't go to sleep, Mrs. Turpin would occupy herself with the question of who she would have chosen to be if she couldn't have been herself. If Jesus had said to her before he made her, "There's only two places available for you. You can either be a nigger or white-trash," what would she have said? "Please, Jesus, please," she would have said, "just let me wait until there's another place available," and he would have said, "No, you have to go right now and I have only those two places so make up your mind." She would have wiggled and squirmed and begged and pleaded but it would have been no use and finally she would have said, "All right, make me a nigger then—but that don't mean a trashy one." And he would have made her a neat clean respectable Negro woman, herself but black.

Next to the child's mother was a red-headed youngish woman, reading one of the magazines and working a piece of chewing gum, hell for leather, as Claud would say. Mrs. Turpin could not see the woman's feet. She was not white-trash, just common. Sometimes Mrs. Turpin occupied herself at night naming the classes of people. On the bottom of the heap were most colored people, not the kind she would have been if she had been one, but most of them; then next to them—not above, just away from—were the white-trash; then above them were the home-owners, and above them the home-and-land owners, to which she and Claud belonged. Above she and Claud were people with a lot of money and much bigger houses and much more land. But here the complexity of it would begin to bear in on her, for some of the people with a lot of money were common and ought to be below she and Claud and some of the people who had good blood had lost their money and had to rent and then there were colored people who owned their homes and land as well. There was a colored dentist in town who had two red Lincolns and a swimming pool and a farm with registered white-face cattle on it. Usually by the time she had fallen asleep all the classes of people were moiling and roiling around in her head, and she would dream they were all crammed in together in a box car, being ridden off to be put in a gas oven.

"That's a beautiful clock," she said and nodded to her right. It was a big wall clock, the face encased in a brass sunburst.

"Yes, it's very pretty," the stylish lady said agreeably. "And right on the dot too," she added, glancing at her watch.

The ugly girl beside her cast an eye upward at the clock, smirked, then looked directly at Mrs. Turpin and smirked again. Then she returned her eyes to her book. She was obviously the lady's daughter because, although they didn't look anything alike as to disposition, they both had the same shape of face and the same blue eyes. On the lady they sparkled pleasantly but in the girl's seared face they appeared alternately to smolder and to blaze.

What if Jesus had said, "All right, you can be white-trash or a nigger or ugly"!

Mrs. Turpin felt an awful pity for the girl, though she thought it was one thing to be ugly and another to act ugly.

The woman with the snuff-stained lips turned around in her chair and looked up at the clock. Then she turned back and appeared to look a little to the side of Mrs. Turpin. There was a cast in one of her eyes. "You want to know wher you can get you one of themther clocks?" she asked in a loud voice.

"No, I already have a nice clock," Mrs. Turpin said. Once somebody like her got a leg in the conversation, she would be all over it.

"You can get you one with green stamps," the woman said. "That's most likely wher he got hisn. Save you up enough, you can get you most anythang. I got me some joo'ry."

Ought to have got you a wash rag and some soap, Mrs. Turpin thought.

"I get contour sheets with mine," the pleasant lady said.

The daughter slammed her book shut. She looked straight in front of her, directly through Mrs. Turpin and on through the yellow curtain and the plate glass window which made the wall behind her. The girl's eyes seemed lit all of a sudden with a peculiar light, an unnatural light like night road signs give. Mrs. Turpin turned her head to see if there was anything going on outside that she should see, but she could not see anything. Figures passing cast only a pale shadow through the curtain. There was no reason the girl should single her out for her ugly looks.

"Miss Finley," the nurse said, cracking the door. The gumchewing woman got up and passed in front of her and Claud and went into the office. She had on red high-heeled shoes.

Directly across the table, the ugly girl's eyes were fixed on Mrs. Turpin as if she had some very special reason for disliking her.

"This is wonderful weather, isn't it?" the girl's mother said.

"It's good weather for cotton if you can get the niggers to pick it," Mrs. Turpin said, "but niggers don't want to pick cotton any more. You can't get the white folks to pick it and now you can't get the niggers—because they got to be right up there with the white folks."

"They gonna *try* anyways," the white-trash woman said, leaning forward.

"Do you have one of those cotton-picking machines?" the pleasant lady asked.

"No," Mrs. Turpin said, "they leave half the cotton in the field. We don't have much cotton anyway. If you want to make it farming now, you have to have a little of everything. We got a couple of acres of cotton and a few hogs and chickens and just enough white-face that Claud can look after them himself."

"One thang I don't want," the white-trash woman said, wiping her mouth with the back of her hand. "Hogs. Nasty stinking things, a-gruntin and a-rootin all over the place."

Mrs. Turpin gave her the merest edge of her attention. "Our hogs are not dirty and they don't stink," she said."They're cleaner than some children I've seen. Their feet never touch the ground. We have a pig-parlor—that's where you raise them on concrete," she explained to the pleasant lady, "and Claud scoots them down with the hose every afternoon and washes off the floor." Cleaner by far than that child right there, she thought. Poor nasty little thing. He had not moved except to put the thumb of his dirty hand into his mouth.

The woman turned her face away from Mrs. Turpin. "I know I wouldn't scoot down no hog with no hose," she said to the wall.

You wouldn't have no hog to scoot down, Mrs. Turpin said to herself.

"A-gruntin and a-rootin and a-groanin," the woman muttered.

"We got a little of everything," Mrs. Turpin said to the pleasant lady. "It's no use in having more than you can handle yourself with help like it is. We found enough niggers to pick our cotton this year but Claud he has to go after them and take them home again in the evening. They can't walk that half a mile. No they can't. I tell you," she said and laughed merrily, "I sure am tired of buttering up niggers, but you got to love em if you want em to work for you. When they come in the morning, I run out and I say, 'Hi yawl this morning?' and when Claud drives them off to the field I just wave to beat the band and they just wave back." And she waved her hand rapidly to illustrate.

"Like you read out of the same book," the lady said, showing she understood perfectly.

"Child, yes," Mrs. Turpin said. "And when they come in from the field, I run out with a bucket of icewater. That's the way it's going to be from now on," she said. "You may as well face it."

"One thang I know," the white-trash woman said. "Two thangs I ain't going to do: love no niggers or scoot down no hog with no hose." And she let out a bark of contempt.

The look that Mrs. Turpin and the pleasant lady exchanged indicated they both understood that you had to *have* certain things before you could *know* certain things. But every time Mrs. Turpin exchanged a look with the lady, she was aware that the ugly girl's peculiar eyes were still on her, and she had trouble bringing her attention back to the conversation.

"When you got something," she said, "you got to look after it." And when you ain't got a thing but breath and britches, she added to herself, you can afford to come to town every morning and just sit on the Court House coping and spit.

A grotesque revolving shadow passed across the curtain behind her and was thrown palely on the opposite wall. Then a bicycle clattered down against the outside of the building. The door opened and a colored boy glided in with a tray from the drug store. It had two large red and white paper cups on it with tops on them. He was a tall, very black boy in discolored white pants and a green nylon shirt. He was chewing gum slowly, as if to music. He set the tray down in the office opening next to the fern and stuck his head through to look for the secretary. She was not in there. He rested his arms on the ledge and waited, his narrow bottom stuck out, swaying slowly to the left and right. He raised a hand over his head and scratched the base of his skull.

"You see that button there, boy?" Mrs. Turpin said. "You can punch that and she'll come. She's probably in the back somewhere."

"Is thas right?" the boy said agreeably, as if he had never seen the button before. He leaned to the right and put his finger on it. "She sometime out," he said and twisted around to face his audience, his elbows behind him on the counter. The nurse appeared and he twisted back again. She handed him a dollar and he rooted in his pocket and made the change and counted it out to her. She gave him fifteen cents for a tip and he went out with the empty tray. The heavy door swung to slowly and closed at length with the sound of suction. For a moment no one spoke.

"They ought to send all them niggers back to Africa," the white-trash woman said. "That's wher they come from in the first place."

"Oh, I couldn't do without my good colored friends," the pleasant lady said.

"There's a heap of things worse than a nigger," Mrs. Turpin agreed. "It's all kinds of them just like it's all kinds of us."

"Yes, and it takes all kinds to make the world go round," the lady said in her musical voice.

As she said it, the raw-complexioned girl snapped her teeth together. Her lower lip turned downwards and inside out, revealing the pale pink inside of her mouth. After a second it rolled back up. It was the ugliest face Mrs. Turpin had ever seen anyone make and for a moment she was certain that the girl had made it at her. She was looking at her as if she had known and disliked her all her life—all of Mrs. Turpin's life, it seemed too, not just all the girl's life. Why, girl, I don't even know you, Mrs. Turpin said silently.

She forced her attention back to the discussion. "It wouldn't be practical to send them back to Africa," she said. "They wouldn't want to go. They got it too good here."

"Wouldn't be what they wanted—if I had anythang to do with it," the woman said.

"It wouldn't be a way in the world you could get all the niggers back over there," Mrs. Turpin said. "They'd be hiding out and lying down and turning sick on you and wailing and hollering and raring and pitching. It wouldn't be a way in the world to get them over there."

"They got over here," the trashy woman said. "Get back like they got over."

"It wasn't so many of them then," Mrs. Turpin explained.

The woman looked at Mrs. Turpin as if here was an idiot indeed but Mrs. Turpin was not bothered by the look, considering where it came from.

"Nooo," she said, "they're going to stay here where they can go to New York and marry white folks and improve their color. That's what they all want to do, every one of them, improve their color."

"You know what comes of that, don't you?" Claud asked.

"No, Claud, what?" Mrs. Turpin said.

Claud's eyes twinkled. "White-faced niggers," he said with never a smile.

Everybody in the office laughed except the white-trash and the ugly girl. The girl gripped the book in her lap with white fingers. The trashy woman looked around her from face to face as if she thought they were all idiots. The old woman in the feed sack dress continued to gaze expressionless across the floor at the high-top shoes of the man opposite her, the one who had been pretending to be asleep when the Turpins came in. He was laughing heartily, his hand still spread out on his knees. The child had fallen to the side and was lying now almost face down in the old woman's lap.

While they recovered from their laughter, the nasal chorus on the radio kept the room from silence.

"You go to blank blank
And I'll go to mine
But we'll all blank along
To-geth-ther,
And all along the blank
We'll hep eachother out
Smile-ling in any kind of
Weath-ther!"

Mrs. Turpin didn't catch every word but she caught enough to agree with the spirit of the song and it turned her thoughts sober. To help anybody out that needed it was her philosophy of life. She never spared herself when she found somebody in need, whether they were white or black, trash or decent. And of all she had to be thankful for, she was most thankful that this was so. If Jesus had said, "You can be high society and have all the money you want and be thin and svelte-like, but you can't be a good woman with it," she would have had to say, "Well don't make me that then. Make me a good woman and it don't matter what else, how fat or how ugly or how poor!" Her heart rose. He had not made her a nigger or white-trash or ugly! He had made her herself and given her a little of everything. Jesus, thank you! she said. Thank you thank you thank you! Whenever she counted her blessings she felt as buoyant as if she weighed one hundred and twenty-five pounds instead of one hundred and eighty.

"What's wrong with your little boy?" the pleasant lady asked the white-trashy woman.

"He has a ulcer," the woman said proudly. "He ain't give me a minute's peace since he was born. Him and her are just alike," she said, nodding at the old woman, who was running her leathery fingers through the child's pale hair. "Look like I can't get nothing down them two but Co' Cola and candy."

That's all you try to get down em, Mrs. Turpin said to herself. Too lazy to light the fire. There was nothing you could tell her about people like them that she didn't know already. And it was not just that they didn't have anything. Because if you gave them everything, in two weeks it would all be broken or filthy or they would have chopped it up for lightwood. She knew all this from her own experience. Help them you must, but help them you couldn't.

All at once the ugly girl turned her lips inside out again. Her eyes were fixed like two drills on Mrs. Turpin. This time there was no mistaking that there was something urgent behind them.

Girl, Mrs. Turpin exclaimed silently, I haven't done a thing to you! The girl might be confusing her with somebody else. There was no need to sit by and let herself be intimidated. "You must be in college," she said boldly, looking directly at the girl. "I see you reading a book there."

The girl continued to stare and pointedly did not answer.

Her mother blushed at this rudeness. "The lady asked you a question, Mary Grace," she said under her breath.

"I have ears," Mary Grace said.

The poor mother blushed again. "Mary Grace goes to Wellesley College," she explained. She twisted one of the buttons on her dress. "In Massachusetts," she added with a grimace. "And in the summer she just keeps right on studying. Just reads all the time, a real book worm. She's done real well at Wellesley; she's taking English and Math and History and Psychology and Social Studies," she rattled on, "and I think it's too much. I think she ought to get out and have fun."

The girl looked as if she would like to hurl them all through the plate glass window.

"Way up north," Mrs. Turpin murmured and thought, well, it hasn't done much for her manners.

"I'd almost rather to have him sick," the white-trash woman said, wrenching the attention back to herself. "He's so mean when he ain't. Look like some children just take natural to meanness. It's some gets bad when they get sick but he was the opposite. Took sick and turned good. He don't give me no trouble now. It's me waiting to see the doctor," she said.

If I was going to send anybody back to Africa, Mrs. Turpin thought, it would be your kind, woman. "Yes, indeed," she said aloud, but looking up at the ceiling, "it's a heap of things worse than a nigger." And dirtier than a hog, she added to herself.

"I think people with bad dispositions are more to be pitied than anyone on earth," the pleasant lady said in a voice that was decidedly thin.

"I thank the Lord he has blessed me with a good one," Mrs. Turpin said. "The day has never dawned that I couldn't find something to laugh at."

"Not since she married me anyways," Claud said with a comical straight face.

Everybody laughed except the girl and the white-trash.

Mrs. Turpin's stomach shook. "He's such a caution," she said, "that I can't help but laugh at him."

The girl made a loud ugly noise through her teeth.

Her mother's mouth grew thin and tight. "I think the worst thing in the world," she said, "is an ungrateful person. To have everything and not appreciate it. I know a girl," she said, "who has parents who would give her anything, a little brother who loves her dearly, who is getting a good education, who wears the best clothes, but who can never say a kind word to anyone, who never smiles, who just criticizes and complains all day long."

"Is she too old to paddle?" Claud asked.

The girl's face was almost purple.

"Yes," the lady said, "I'm afraid there's nothing to do but leave her to her folly. Some day she'll wake up and it'll be too late."

"It never hurt anyone to smile," Mrs. Turpin said. "It just makes you feel better all over."

"Of course," the lady said sadly, "but there are just some people you can't tell anything to. They can't take criticism."

"If it's one thing I am," Mrs. Turpin said with feeling, "it's grateful. When I think who all I could have been besides myself and what all I got, a little of everything, and a good disposition besides, I just feel like shouting, 'Thank you, Jesus, for making everything the way it is!' It could have been different!" For one thing, somebody else could have got Claud. At the thought of this, she was flooded with gratitude and a terrible pang of joy ran through her. "Oh thank you, Jesus, Jesus, thank you!" she cried aloud.

The book struck her directly over her left eye. It struck almost at the same instant that she realized the girl was about to hurl it. Before she could utter a sound, the raw face came crashing across the table toward her, howling. The girl's fingers sank like clamps into the soft flesh of her neck. She heard the mother cry out and Claud shout, "Whoa!" There was an instant when she was certain that she was about to be in an earthquake.

All at once her vision narrowed and she saw everything as if it were happening in a small room far away, or as if she were looking at it through the wrong end of a telescope. Claud's face crumpled and fell out of sight. The nurse ran in, then out, then in again. Then the gangling figure of the doctor rushed out of the inner door. Magazines flew this way and that as the table turned over. The girl fell with a thud and Mrs. Turpin's vision suddenly reversed itself and she saw everything large instead of small. The eyes of the white-trashy woman were staring hugely at the floor. There the girl, held down on one side by the nurse and on the other by her mother, was wrenching and turning in their grasp. The doctor was kneeling astride her, trying to hold her arm down. He managed after a second to sink a long needle into it.

Mrs. Turpin felt entirely hollow except for her heart which swung from side to side as if it were agitated in a great empty drum of flesh.

"Somebody that's not busy call for the ambulance," the doctor said in the off-hand voice young doctors adopt for terrible occasions.

Mrs. Turpin could not have moved a finger. The old man who had been sitting next to her skipped nimbly into the office and made the call, for the secretary still seemed to be gone.

"Claud!" Mrs. Turpin called.

He was not in his chair. She knew she must jump up and find him but she felt like some one trying to catch a train in a dream, when everything moves in slow motion and the faster you try to run the slower you go.

"Here I am," a suffocated voice, very unlike Claud's, said.

He was doubled up in the corner on the floor, pale as paper, holding his leg. She wanted to get up and go to him but she could not move. Instead, her gaze was drawn slowly downward to the churning face on the floor, which she could see over the doctor's shoulder.

The girl's eyes stopped rolling and focused on her. They seemed a much lighter blue than before, as if a door that had been tightly closed behind them was now open to admit light and air.

Mrs. Turpin's head cleared and her power of motion returned. She leaned forward until she was looking directly into the fierce brilliant eyes. There was no doubt in her mind that the girl did know her, knew her in some intense and personal way, beyond time and place and condition. "What you got to say to me?" she asked hoarsely and held her breath, waiting, as for a revelation.

The girl raised her head. Her gaze locked with Mrs. Turpin's. "Go back to hell where you came from, you old wart hog," she whispered. Her voice was low but clear. Her eyes burned for a moment as if she saw with pleasure that her message had struck its target.

Mrs. Turpin sank back in her chair.

After a moment the girl's eyes closed and she turned her head wearily to the side.

The doctor rose and handed the nurse the empty syringe. He leaned over and put both hands for a moment on the mother's shoulders, which were shaking. She was sitting on the floor, her lips pressed together, holding Mary Grace's hand in her lap. The girl's fingers were gripped like a baby's around her thumb. "Go on to the hospital," he said. "I'll call and make the arrangements."

"Now let's see that neck," he said in a jovial voice to Mrs. Turpin. He began to inspect her neck with his first two fingers. Two little moon-shaped lines like pink fish bones were indented over her windpipe. There was the beginning of an angry red swelling above her eye. His fingers passed over this also.

"Lea' me be," she said thickly and shook him off. "See about Claud. She kicked him."

"I'll see about him in a minute," he said and felt her pulse. He was a thin grey-haired man, given to pleasantries. "Go home and have yourself a vacation the rest of the day," he said and patted her on the shoulder.

Quit your pattin me, Mrs. Turpin growled to herself.

"And put an ice pack over that eye," he said. Then he went and squatted down beside Claud and looked at his leg. After a moment he pulled him up and Claud limped after him into the office.

Until the ambulance came, the only sounds in the room were the tremulous moans of the girl's mother, who continued to sit on the floor. The white-trash woman did not take her eyes off the girl. Mrs. Turpin looked straight ahead at nothing. Presently the ambulance drew up, a long dark shadow, behind the curtain. The attendants came in and set the stretcher down beside the girl and lifted her expertly onto it and carried her out. The nurse helped the mother gather up her things. The shadow of the ambulance moved silently away and the nurse came back in the office.

"That ther girl is going to be a lunatic, ain't she?" the white-trash woman asked the nurse, but the nurse kept on to the back and never answered her.

"Yes, she's going to be a lunatic," the white-trash woman said to the rest of them.

"Po' critter," the old woman murmured. The child's face was still in her lap. His eyes looked idly out over her knees. He had not moved during the disturbance except to draw one leg up under him.

"I thank Gawd," the white-trash woman said fervently, "I ain't a lunatic."

Claud came limping out and the Turpins went home.

As their pick-up truck turned into their own dirt road and made the crest of the hill, Mrs. Turpin gripped the window ledge and looked out suspiciously. The land sloped gracefully down through a field dotted with lavender weeds and at the start of the rise their small yellow frame house, with its little flower beds spread out around it like a fancy apron, sat primly in its accustomed place between two giant hickory trees. She would not have been startled to see a burnt wound between two blackened chimneys.

Neither of them felt like eating so they put on their house clothes and lowered the shade in the bedroom and lay down, Claud with his leg on a pillow and herself with a damp washcloth over her eye. The instant she was flat on her back, the image of a razor-backed hog with warts on its face and horns coming out behind its ears snorted into her head. She moaned, a low quiet moan.

"I am not," she said tearfully, "a wart hog. From hell." But the denial had no force. The girl's eyes and her words, even the tone of her voice, low but clear, directed only to her, brooked no repudiation. She had been singled out for the message, though there was trash in the room to whom it might justly have been applied. The full force of this fact struck her only now. There was a woman there who was neglecting her own child but she had been overlooked. The message had been given to Ruby Turpin, a respectable, hard-working, church-going woman. The tears dried. Her eyes began to burn instead with wrath.

She rose on her elbow and the washcloth fell into her hand. Claud was lying on his back, snoring. She wanted to tell him what the girl had said. At the same time, she did not wish to put the image of herself as a wart hog from hell into his mind.

"Hey, Claud," she muttered and pushed his shoulder.

Claud opened one pale baby blue eye.

She looked into it warily. He did not think about anything. He just went his way.

"Wha, whasit?" he said and closed the eye again.

"Nothing," she said. "Does your leg pain you?"

"Hurts like hell," Claud said.

"It'll quit terreckly," she said and lay back down. In a moment Claud was snoring again. For the rest of the afternoon they lay there. Claud slept. She scowled at the ceiling. Occasionally she raised her fist and made a small stabbing motion over her chest as if she was defending her innocence to invisible guests who were like the comforters of Job, reasonable-seeming but wrong.

About five-thirty Claud stirred. "Got to go after those niggers," he sighed, not moving.

She was looking straight up as if there were unintelligible handwriting on the ceiling. The protuberance over her eye had turned a greenish-blue. "Listen here," she said.

"What?"

"Kiss me."

Claud leaned over and kissed her loudly on the mouth. He pinched her side and their hands interlocked. Her expression of ferocious concentration did not change. Claud got up, groaning and growling, and limped off. She continued to study the ceiling.

She did not get up until she heard the pick-up truck coming back with the Negroes. Then she rose and thrust her feet in her brown oxfords, which she did not bother to lace, and stumped out onto the back porch and got her red plastic bucket. She emptied a tray of ice cubes into it and filled it half full of water and went out into the backyard. Every afternoon after Claud brought the hands in, one of the boys helped him put out hay and the rest waited in the back of the truck until he was ready to take them home. The truck was parked in the shade under one of the hickory trees.

"Hi yawl this evening?" Mrs. Turpin asked grimly, appearing with the bucket and the dipper. There were three women and a boy in the truck.

"Us doin nicely," the oldest woman said. "Hi you doin?" and her gaze stuck immediately on the dark lump on Mrs. Turpin's forehead. "You done fell down, ain't you?" she asked in a solicitous voice. The old woman was dark and almost toothless. She had on an old felt hat of Claud's set back on her head. The other two women were younger and lighter and they both had new bright green sun hats. One of them had hers on her head; the other had taken hers off and the boy was grinning beneath it.

Mrs. Turpin set the bucket down on the floor of the truck. "Yawl hep yourselves," she said. She looked around to make sure Claud had gone. "No. I didn't fall down," she said, folding her arms. "It was something worse than that."

"Ain't nothing bad happen to you!" the old woman said. She said it as if they all knew that Mrs. Turpin was protected in some special way by Divine Providence. "You just had you a little fall."

"We were in town at the doctor's office for where the cow kicked Mr. Turpin," Mrs. Turpin said in a flat tone that indicated they could leave off their foolishness. "And there was this girl there. A big fat girl with her face all broke out. I could look at that girl and tell she was peculiar but I couldn't tell how. And me and her mama were just talking and going along and all of a sudden WHAM! She throws this big book she was reading at me and . . ."

"Naw!" the old woman cried out.

"And then she jumps over the table and commences to choke me."

"Naw!" they all exclaimed, "naw!"

"Hi come she do that?" the old woman asked. "What ail her?"

Mrs. Turpin only glared in front of her.

"Somethin ail her," the old woman said.

"They carried her off in an ambulance," Mrs. Turpin continued, "but before she went she was rolling on the floor and they were trying to hold her down to give her a shot and she said something to me." She paused. "You know what she said to me?"

"What she say?" they asked.

"She said," Mrs. Turpin began, and stopped, her face very dark and heavy. The sun was getting whiter and whiter, blanching the sky overhead so that the leaves of the hickory tree were black in the face of it. She could not bring forth the words. "Something real ugly," she muttered.

"She sho shouldn't said nothin ugly to you," the old woman said. "You so sweet. You the sweetest lady I know."

"She pretty too," the one with the hat on said.

"And stout," the other one said. "I never knowed no sweeter white lady."

"That's the truth befo' Jesus," the old woman said. "Amen! You des as sweet and pretty as you can be."

Mrs. Turpin knew just exactly how much Negro flattery was worth and it added to her rage. "She said," she began again and finished this time with a fierce rush of breath, "that I was an old wart hog from hell."

There was an astounded silence.

"Where she at?" the youngest woman cried in piercing voice.

"Lemme see her. I'll kill her!"

"I'll kill her with you!" the other one cried.

"She b'long in the sylum," the old woman said emphatically. "You the sweetest white lady I know."

"She pretty too," the other two said. "Stout as she can be and sweet. Jesus satisfied with her!"

"Deed he is," the old woman declared.

Idiots! Mrs. Turpin growled to herself. You could never say anything intelligent to a nigger. You could talk at them but not with them. "Yawl ain't drunk your water," she said shortly. "Leave the bucket in the truck when you're finished with it. I got more to do than just stand around and pass the time of day," and she moved off and into the house.

She stood for a moment in the middle of the kitchen. The dark protuberance over her eye looked like a miniature tornado cloud which might any moment sweep across the horizon of her brow. Her lower lip protruded dangerously. She squared her massive shoulders. Then she marched into the front of the house and out the side door and started down the road to the pig parlor. She had the look of a woman going single-handed, weaponless, into battle.

The sun was deep yellow now like a harvest moon and was riding westward very fast over the far tree line as if it meant to reach the hogs before she did. The road was rutted and she kicked several good-sized stones out of her path as she strode along. The pig parlor was on a little knoll at the end of a lane that ran off from the side of the barn. It was a square of concrete as large as a small room, with a board fence about four feet high around it. The concrete floor sloped slightly so that the hog wash could drain off into a trench where it was carried to the field for fertilizer. Claud was standing on the outside, on the edge of the concrete, hanging onto the top board, hosing down the floor inside. The hose was connected to the faucet of a water trough nearby.

Mrs. Turpin climbed up beside him and glowered down at the hogs inside. There were seven long-snouted bristly shoats in it—tan with liver-colored spots—and an old sow a few weeks off from farrowing. She was lying on her side grunting. The shoats were running about shaking themselves like idiot children, their little split pig eyes searching the floor for anything left. She had read that pigs were the most intelligent animal. She doubted it. They were supposed to be smarter than dogs. There had even been a pig astronaut. He had performed his assignment perfectly but died of a heart attack afterwards because they left him in his electric suit, sitting upright throughout his examination when naturally a hog should be on all fours.

A-gruntin and a-rootin and a-groanin.

"Gimme that hose," she said, yanking it away from Claud. "Go on and carry them niggers home and then get off that leg."

"You look like you might have swallowed a mad dog," Claud observed, but he got down and limped off. He paid no attention to her humors.

Until he was out of earshot, Mrs. Turpin stood on the side of the pen, holding the hose and pointing the stream of water at the hind quarters of any shoat that looked as if it might try to lie down. When he had had time to get over the hill, she turned her head slightly and her wrathful eyes scanned the path. He was nowhere in sight. She turned back again and seemed to gather herself up. Her shoulders rose and she drew in her breath.

"What do you send me a message like that for?" she said in a low fierce voice, barely above a whisper but with the force of a shout in its concentrated fury. "How am I a hog and me both? How am I saved and from hell too?" Her free fist was knotted and with the other she gripped the hose, blindly pointing the stream of water in and out of the eye of the old sow whose outraged squeal she did not hear.

The pig parlor commanded a view of the back pasture where their twenty beef cows were gathered around the haybales Claud and the boy had put out. The freshly cut pasture sloped down to the highway. Across it was their cotton field and beyond that a dark green dusty wood which they owned as well. The sun was behind the wood, very red, looking over the paling of trees like a farmer inspecting his own hogs.

"Why me?" she rumbled. "It's no trash around here, black or white, that I haven't given to. And break my back to the bone every day working. And do for the church."

She appeared to be the right size woman to command the arena before her. "How am I a hog?" she demanded. "Exactly how am I like them?" and she jabbed the stream of water at the shoats. "There was plenty of trash there. It didn't have to be me.

"If you like trash better, go get yourself some trash then," she railed. "You could have made me trash. Or a nigger. If trash is what you wanted why didn't you make me trash?" She shook her fist with the hose in it and a watery snake appeared momentarily in the air. "I could quit working and take it easy and be filthy," she growled. "Lounge about the sidewalks all day drinking root beer. Dip snuff and spit in every puddle and have it all over my face. I could be nasty.

"Or you could have made me a nigger. It's too late for me to be a nigger," she said with deep sarcasm, "but I could act like one. Lay down in the middle of the road and stop traffic. Roll on the ground."

In the deepening light everything was taking on a mysterious hue. The pasture was growing a peculiar glassy green and the streak of highway had turned lavender. She braced herself for a final assault and this time her voice rolled out over the pasture. "Go on," she yelled, "call me a hog! Call me a hog again. From hell. Call me a wart hog from hell. Put that bottom rail on top. There'll still be a top and bottom!"

A garbled echo returned to her.

A final surge of fury shook her and she roared, "Who do you think you are?"

The color of everything, field and crimson sky, burned for a moment with a transparent intensity. The question carried over the pasture and across the highway and the cotton field and returned to her clearly like an answer from beyond the wood.

She opened her mouth but no sound came out of it.

A tiny truck, Claud's, appeared on the highway, heading rapidly out of sight. Its gears scraped thinly. It looked like a child's toy. At any moment a bigger truck might smash into it and scatter Claud's and the niggers' brains all over the road.

Mrs. Turpin stood there, her gaze fixed on the highway, all her muscles rigid, until in five or six minutes the truck reappeared, returning. She waited until it had time to turn into their own road. Then like a monumental statue coming to life, she bent her head slowly and gazed, as if through the very heart of mystery, down into the pig parlor at the hogs. They had settled all in one corner around the old sow who was grunting softly. A red glow suffused them. They appeared to pant with a secret life.

Until the sun slipped finally behind the tree line, Mrs. Turpin remained there with her gaze bent to them as if she were absorbing some abysmal life-giving knowledge. At last she lifted her head. There was only a purple streak in the sky, cutting through a field of crimson and leading, like an extension of the highway, into the descending dusk. She raised her hands from the side of the pen in a gesture hieratic and profound. A visionary light settled in her eyes. She saw the streak as a vast swinging bridge extending upward from the earth through a field of living fire. Upon it a vast horde of souls were rumbling toward heaven. There were whole companies of white-trash, clean for the first time in their lives, and bands of black niggers in white robes, and battalions of freaks and lunatics shouting and clapping and leaping like frogs. And bringing up the end of the procession was a tribe of people whom she recognized at once as those who, like herself and Claud, had always had a little of everything and the God-given wit to use it right. She leaned forward to observe them closer. They were marching behind the others with great dignity, accountable as they had always been for good order and common sense and respectable behavior. They alone were on key. Yet she could see by their shocked and altered faces that even their virtues were being burned away. She lowered her hands and gripped the rail of the hog pen, her eyes small but fixed unblinkingly on what lay ahead. In a moment the vision faded but she remained where she was, immobile.

At length she got down and turned off the faucet and made her slow way on the darkening path to the house. In the woods around her the invisible cricket choruses had struck up, but what she heard were the voices of the souls climbing upward into the starry field and shouting hallelujah.

Questions

1. Examine carefully the first several paragraphs. Mrs. Turpin dominates the office from the moment she enters it. Why does Miss O'Connor let us see and respond to the "lean stringy old fellow" or "the well-dressed lady" or "the ugly girl" or "the white trashy mother" through Mrs. Turpin's eyes?
2. In the paragraph which describes her staying awake "naming the classes of people," could the final sentence of the paragraph be an allusion to the Hitler-ordered burning of Jews in gas ovens during the war (the story was first published in 1965)? If so, what is the paragraph saying about Mrs. Turpin? Relate all this to Huxley's comments about generalizations and war.
3. Does Mrs. Turpin continue to classify people? Why does the fat girl finally throw the book? We get to know the fat girl's name, Mary Grace, just before she throws the book. What semantic suggestion attaches to each of the names? Why would a devout Catholic writer use such names for a girl so fat and ugly and ill-tempered and "crazy"? Why, in spite of how much she apparently despises the girl, does Mrs. Turpin take her as a source of "revelation"?
4. Out in the pig pen, Mrs. Turpin apparently is speaking directly to Jesus Himself (whether He is listening is beside the point). From the evidence of her language to him, of the vision she sees, of the last paragraph, how much has she finally learned from her revelation? That is, how effective has the lesson been? Especially, what do you make of people like her and Claud "bringing up the end of the procession"?

Suggestions for Writing

1. You may want to bring together into a unified, coherent analysis what you have found in responding to the questions above and the questions you have had as you have read the story. Keep your focus primarily on the semantic implications, but make them add up to a meaningful interpretation of the story. We would hardly argue that Miss O'Connor is trying to teach a lesson in semantics, but she is surely using semantics to teach whatever lesson she is teaching. Can you define that lesson—the theme or "central idea" of the story? You can easily develop this through cause and effect by asking as your key question, "What creates the effect or effects of the story?"

Portrait of the Anti-Semite

Jean-Paul Sartre

Jean-Paul Sartre, one of the most influential writers and thinkers of modern France, has become the central figure in the literary-philosophical movement known as existentialism. The movement itself is complex and difficult to define. Some expressions of Hippie life in America can be traced to existential thinking, though the existentialist would probably be appalled by the apparent refusal of responsibility in much of Hippiedom. As a philosophical movement, existentialism insists on the primacy of the individual's sense of his own existence, hence on the primacy of the personal inner quest for meaning and truth. It sees the universe as intrinsically meaningless or contradictory ("absurd"). Man must make for himself his meaning in the universe. Hence the emphasis in the essay on the anti-Semite's having chosen *his beliefs and attitudes. The essay is part of the first chapter of Sartre's book* Anti-Semite and Jew. *We include it here to show a serious modern philosopher condemning anti-Semitism through semantic analysis. Watch how the analysis that starts out to be merely analysis turns into condemnation.*

If a man attributes all or part of his own misfortunes and those of his country to the presence of Jewish elements in the community, if he proposes to remedy this state of affairs by depriving the Jews of certain of their rights, by keeping them out of certain economic and social activities, by expelling them from the country, by exterminating all of them, we say that he has anti-Semitic *opinions.*

This word *opinion* makes us stop and think. It is the word a hostess uses to bring to an end a discussion that threatens to become acrimonious. It suggests that all points of view are equal; it reassures us, for it gives an inoffensive appearance to ideas by reducing them to the level of tastes. All tastes are natural; all opinions are permitted. Tastes, colors, and opinions are not open to discussion. In the name of democratic institutions, in the name of freedom of opinion, the anti-Semite asserts the right to preach the anti-Jewish crusade everywhere.

At the same time, accustomed as we have been since the Revolution to look at every object in an analytic spirit, that is to say, as a composite whose elements can be separated, we look upon persons and characters as mosaics in which each stone coexists with the others without the coexistence affecting the nature of the whole. Thus anti-Semitic opinion appears to us to be a molecule that can enter into combination with other molecules of any origin whatsoever without undergoing any alteration. A man may be a good father and a good husband, a conscientious citizen, highly cultivated, philanthropic, *and* in addition an anti-Semite. He may like fishing and the pleasures of love, may be tolerant in matters of religion, full of generous notions on the condition of the natives in Central Africa, *and* in addition detest the Jews. If he does not like them, we say, it is because his experience has shown him that they are bad, because statistics have taught him that they are dangerous, because certain historical factors have influenced his judgment. Thus this opinion seems to be the result of external causes, and those who wish to study it are prone to neglect the personality of the anti-Semite in favor of a consideration of the percentage of Jews who were mobilized in 1914, the percentage of Jews who are bankers, industrialists, doctors, and lawyers, or an examination of the history of the Jews in France since early times. They succeed in revealing a strictly objective situation that determines an equally objective current of opinion, and this they call anti-Semitism, for which they can draw up charts and determine the variations from 1870 to 1944. In such wise anti-Semitism appears to be at once a subjective taste that enters into combination with other tastes to form a personality, and an impersonal and social phenomenon which can be expressed by figures and averages, one which is conditioned by economic, historical, and political constants.

I do not say that these two conceptions are necessarily contradictory. I do say that they are dangerous and false. I would admit, if necessary, that one may have an opinion on the government's policy in regard to the wine industry, that is, that one may decide, *for certain reasons,* either to approve or condemn the free importation of wine from Algeria: here we have a case of holding an opinion on the administration of things. But I refuse to characterize as opinion a doctrine that is aimed directly at particular persons and that seeks to suppress their rights or to exterminate them. The Jew whom the anti-Semite wishes to lay hands upon is not a schematic being defined solely by his function, as under administrative law; or by his status or his acts, as under the Code. He is a Jew, the son of Jews, recognizable by his physique, by the color of his hair, by his clothing perhaps, and, so they say, by his character. Anti-Semitism does not fall within the category of ideas protected by the right of free opinion.

Indeed, it is something quite other than an idea. It is first of all a *pas-*

sion. No doubt it can be set forth in the form of a theoretical proposition. The "moderate" anti-Semite is a courteous man who will tell you quietly: "Personally, I do not detest the Jews. I simply find it preferable, for various reasons, that they should play a lesser part in the activity of the nation." But a moment later, if you have gained his confidence, he will add with more abandon: "You see, there must be *something* about the Jews; they upset me physically."

This argument, which I have heard a hundred times, is worth examining. First of all, it derives from the logic of passion. For, really now, can we imagine anyone's saying seriously: "There must be something about tomatoes, for I have a horror of eating them"? In addition, it shows us that anti-Semitism in its most temperate and most evolved forms remains a syncretic whole which may be expressed by statements of reasonable tenor, but which can involve even bodily modifications. Some men are suddenly struck with impotence if they learn from the woman with whom they are making love that she is a Jewess. There is a disgust for the Jew, just as there is a disgust for the Chinese or the Negro among certain people. Thus it is not from the body that the sense of repulsion arises, since one may love a Jewess very well if one does not know what her race is; rather it is something that enters the body from the mind. It is an involvement of the mind, but one so deep-seated and complete that it extends to the physiological realm, as happens in cases of hysteria.

This involvement is not caused by experience. I have questioned a hundred people on the reasons for their anti-Semitism. Most of them have confined themselves to enumerating the defects with which tradition has endowed the Jews. "I detest them because they are selfish, intriguing, persistent, oily, tactless, etc."—"But, at any rate, you associate with some of them?"—"Not if I can help it!" A painter said to me: "I am hostile to the Jews because, with their critical habits, they encourage our servants to insubordination." Here are examples a little more precise. A young actor without talent insisted that the Jews had kept him from a successful career in the theater by confining him to subordinate roles. A young woman said to me: "I have had the most horrible experiences with furriers; they robbed me, they burned the fur I entrusted to them. Well, they were all Jews." But why did she choose to hate Jews rather than furriers? Why Jews or furriers rather than such and such a Jew or such and such a furrier? Because she had in her a predisposition toward anti-Semitism.

A classmate of mine at the lycée told me that Jews "annoy" him because of the thousands of injustices that "Jew-ridden" social organizations commit in their favor. "A Jew passed his *agrégation* * the year I was failed, and you can't make me believe that that fellow, whose father came

* Competitive state teachers' examination.

from Cracow or Lemberg, understood a poem by Ronsard or an eclogue by Virgil better than I." But he admitted that he disdained the *agrégation* as a mere academic exercise, and that he didn't study for it. Thus, to explain his failure, he made use of two systems of interpretation, like those madmen who, when they are far gone in their madness, pretend to be the King of Hungary but, if questioned sharply, admit to being shoemakers. His thoughts moved on two planes without his being in the least embarrassed by it. As a matter of fact, he will in time manage to justify his past laziness on the grounds that it really would be too stupid to prepare for an examination in which Jews are passed in preference to good Frenchmen. Actually he ranked twenty-seventh on the official list. There were twenty-six ahead of him, twelve who passed and fourteen who failed. Suppose Jews had been excluded from the competition; would that have done him any good? And even if he had been at the top of the list of unsuccessful candidates, even if by eliminating one of the successful candidates he would have had a chance to pass, why should the Jew Weil have been eliminated rather than the Norman Mathieu or the Breton Arzell? To understand my classmate's indignation we must recognize that he had adopted in advance a certain idea of the Jew, of his nature and of his role in society. And to be able to decide that among twenty-six competitors who were more successful than himself, it was the Jew who robbed him of his place, he must a priori have given preference in the conduct of his life to reasoning based on passion. Far from experience producing his idea of the Jew, it was the latter which explained his experience. If the Jew did not exist, the anti-Semite would invent him.

That may be so, you will say, but leaving the question of experience to one side, must we not admit that anti-Semitism is explained by certain historical data? For after all it does not come out of the air. It would be easy for me to reply that the history of France tells us nothing about the Jews: they were oppressed right up to 1789; since then they have participated as best they could in the life of the nation, taking advantage, naturally, of freedom of competition to displace the weak, but no more and no less than other Frenchmen. They have committed no crimes against France, have engaged in no treason. And if people believe there is proof that the number of Jewish soldiers in 1914 was lower than it should have been, it is because someone had the curiosity to consult statistics. This is not one of those facts which have the power to strike the imagination by themselves; no soldier in the trenches was able on his own initiative to feel astonishment at not seeing any Jews in the narrow sector that constituted his universe. However, since the information that history gives on the role of Israel depends essentially on the conception one has of history, I think it would be better to borrow from a foreign country a manifest example of

"Jewish treason" and to calculate the repercussions this "treason" may have had on contemporary anti-Semitism.

In the course of the bloody Polish revolts of the nineteenth century, the Warsaw Jews, whom the czars handled gently for reasons of policy, were very lukewarm toward the rebels. By not taking part in the insurrection they were able to maintain and improve their position in a country ruined by repression.

I don't know whether this is true or not. What is certain is that many Poles believe it, and this "historical fact" contributes not a little to their bitterness against the Jews. But if I examine the matter more closely, I discover a vicious circle: The czars, we are told, treated the Polish Jews well whereas they willingly ordered pogroms against those in Russia. These sharply different courses of action had the same cause. The Russian government considered the Jews in both Russia and Poland to be unassimilable; according to the needs of their policy, they had them massacred at Moscow and Kiev because they were a danger to the Russian empire, but favored them at Warsaw as a means of stirring up discord among the Poles. The latter showed nothing but hate and scorn for the Jews of Poland, but the reason was the same: For them Israel could never become an integral part of the national collectivity. Treated as Jews by the czar and as Jews by the Poles, provided, quite in spite of themselves, with Jewish interests in the midst of a foreign community, is it any wonder that these members of a minority behaved in accordance with the representation made of them?

In short, the essential thing here is not an "historical fact" but the idea that the agents of history formed for themselves of the Jew. When the Poles of today harbor resentment against the Jews for their past conduct, they are incited to it by that same idea. If one is going to reproach little children for the sins of their grandfathers, one must first of all have a very primitive conception of what constitutes responsibility. Furthermore one must form his conception of the children on the basis of what the grandparents have been. One must believe that what their elders did the young are capable of doing. One must convince himself that Jewish character is inherited. Thus the Poles of 1940 treated the Israelites in the community as *Jews* because their ancestors in 1848 had done the same with their contemporaries. Perhaps this traditional representation would, under other circumstances, have disposed of the Jews of today to act like those of 1848. It is therefore the *idea* of the Jew that one forms for himself which would seem to determine history, not the "historical fact" that produces the idea.

People speak to us also of "social facts," but if we look at this more closely we shall find the same vicious circle. There are too many Jewish lawyers, someone says. But is there any complaint that there are too many Norman lawyers? Even if all the Bretons were doctors would we say anything more than that "Brittany provides doctors for the whole of France"? Oh, someone will answer, it is not at all the same thing. No doubt, but that is precisely because we consider Normans as Normans and Jews as Jews. Thus wherever we turn it is the *idea of the Jew* which seems to be the essential thing.

It has become evident that no external factor can induce anti-Semitism in the anti-Semite. Anti-Semitism is a free and total choice of oneself, a comprehensive attitude that one adopts not only toward Jews but toward men in general, toward history and society; it is at one and the same time a passion and a conception of the world. No doubt in the case of a given anti-Semite certain characteristics will be more marked than in another. But they are always all present at the same time, and they influence each other. It is this syncretic totality which we must now attempt to describe.

I noted earlier that anti-Semitism is a passion. Everybody understands that emotions of hate or anger are involved. But ordinarily hate and anger have a *provocation:* I hate someone who has made me suffer, someone who contemns or insults me. We have just seen that anti-Semitic passion could not have such a character. It precedes the facts that are supposed to call it forth; it seeks them out to nourish itself upon them; it must even interpret them in a special way so that they may become truly offensive. Indeed, if you so much as mention a Jew to an anti-Semite, he will show all the signs of a lively irritation. If we recall that we must always *consent* to anger before it can manifest itself and that, as is indicated so accurately by the French idiom, we "put ourselves" into anger, we shall have to agree that the anti-Semite has *chosen* to live on the plane of passion. It is not unusual for people to elect to live a life of passion rather than one of reason. But ordinarily they love the *objects* of passion: women, glory, power, money. Since the anti-Semite has chosen hate, we are forced to conclude that it is the *state* of passion that he loves. Ordinarily this type of emotion is not very pleasant: a man who passionately desires a woman is impassioned because of the woman and in spite of his passion. We are wary of reasoning based on passion, seeking to support by all possible means opinions which love or jealousy or hate have dictated. We are wary of the aberrations of passion and of what is called monoideism. But that is just what the anti-Semite chooses right off.

How can one choose to reason falsely? It is because of a longing for impenetrability. The rational man groans as he gropes for the truth; he knows that his reasoning is no more than tentative, that other considerations may supervene to cast doubt on it. He never sees very clearly where he is going; he is "open"; he may even appear to be hesitant. But there are people who are attracted by the durability of a stone. They wish to be massive and impenetrable; they wish not to change. Where, indeed, would change take them? We have here a basic fear of oneself and of truth. What frightens them is not the content of truth, of which they have no conception, but the form itself of truth, that thing of indefinite approximation. It is as if their own existence were in continual suspension But they wish to exist all at once and right away. They do not want any acquired opinions; they want them to be innate. Since they are afraid of reasoning, they wish to lead the kind of life wherein reasoning and research play only a subordinate role, wherein one seeks only what he has already found, wherein one becomes only what he already was. This is nothing but passion. Only a strong emotional bias can give a lightninglike certainty; it alone can hold reason in leash; it alone can remain impervious to experience and last for a whole lifetime.

The anti-Semite has chosen hate because hate is a faith; at the outset he has chosen to devaluate words and reasons. How entirely at ease he feels as a result. How futile and frivolous discussions about the rights of the Jew appear to him. He has placed himself on other ground from the beginning. If out of courtesy he consents for a moment to defend his point of view, he lends himself but does not give himself. He tries simply to project his intuitive certainty onto the plane of discourse. I mentioned awhile back some remarks by anti-Semites, all of them absurd: "I hate Jews because they make servants insubordinate, because a Jewish furrier robbed me, etc." Never believe that anti-Semites are completely unaware of the absurdity of their replies. They know that their remarks are frivolous, open to challenge. But they are amusing themselves, for it is their adversary who is obliged to use words responsibly, since he believes in words. The anti-Semites have the *right* to play. They even like to play with discourse for, by giving ridiculous reasons, they discredit the seriousness of their interlocutors. They delight in acting in bad faith, since they seek not to persuade by sound argument but to intimidate and disconcert. If you press them too closely, they will abruptly fall silent, loftily indicating by some phrase that the time for argument is past. It is not that they are afraid of being convinced. They fear only to appear ridiculous or to prejudice by their embarrassment their hope of winning over some third person to their side.

If then, as we have been able to observe, the anti-Semite is impervious to reason and to experience, it is not because his conviction is strong. Rather his conviction is strong because he has chosen first of all to be impervious.

He has chosen also to be terrifying. People are afraid of irritating him. No one knows to what lengths the aberrations of his passion will carry him—but he knows, for this passion is not provoked by something external. He has it well in hand; it is obedient to his will: now he lets go the reins and now he pulls back on them. He is not afraid of himself, but he sees in the eyes of others a disquieting image—his own—and he makes his words and gestures conform to it. Having this external model, he is under no necessity to look for his personality within himself. He has chosen to find his being entirely outside himself, never to look within, to be nothing save the fear he inspires in others. What he flees even more than Reason is his intimate awareness of himself. But someone will object: What if he is like that only with regard to the Jews? What if he otherwise conducts himself with good sense? I reply that that is impossible. There is the case of a fishmonger who, in 1942, annoyed by the competition of two Jewish fishmongers who were concealing their race, one fine day took pen in hand and denounced them. I have been assured that this fishmonger was in other respects a mild and jovial man, the best of sons. But I don't believe it. A man who finds it entirely natural to denounce other men cannot have our conception of humanity; he does not see even those whom he aids in the same light as we do. His generosity, his kindness are not like our kindness, our generosity. You cannot confine passion to one sphere.

The anti-Semite readily admits that the Jew is intelligent and hard-working; he will even confess himself inferior in these respects. This concession costs him nothing, for he has, as it were, put those qualities in parentheses. Or rather they derive their value from the one who possesses them: the more virtues the Jew has the more dangerous he will be. The anti-Semite has no illusions about what he is. He considers himself an average man, modestly average, basically mediocre. There is no example of an anti-Semite's claiming individual superiority over the Jews. But you must not think that he is ashamed of his mediocrity; he takes pleasure in it; I will even assert that he has chosen it. This man fears every kind of solitariness, that of the genius as much as that of the murderer; he is the man of the crowd. However small his stature, he takes every precaution to make it smaller, lest he stand out from the herd and find himself face to face with himself. He has made himself an anti-Semite because that is something one cannot be alone. The phrase, "I hate the Jews," is one that is uttered in chorus; in pronouncing it, one attaches himself to a tradition and to a community—the tradition and community of the mediocre.

We must remember that a man is not necessarily humble or even modest because he has consented to mediocrity. On the contrary, there is a passionate pride among the mediocre, and anti-Semitism is an attempt to give value to mediocrity as such, to create an elite of the ordinary. To the anti-Semite, intelligence is Jewish; he can thus disdain it in all tranquillity, like all the other virtues which the Jew possesses. They are so many ersatz attributes that the Jew cultivates in place of that balanced mediocrity which he will never have. The true Frenchman, rooted in his province, in his country, borne along by a tradition twenty centuries old, benefiting from ancestral wisdom, guided by tried customs, does not *need* intelligence. His virtue depends upon the assimilation of the qualities which the work of a hundred generations has lent to the objects which surround him; it depends on property. It goes without saying that this is a matter of inherited property, not property one buys. The anti-Semite has a fundamental incomprehension of the various forms of modern property: money, securities, etc. These are abstractions, entities of reason related to the abstract intelligence of the Semite. A security belongs to no one because it can belong to everyone; moreover, it is a sign of wealth, not a concrete possession. The anti-Semite can conceive only of a type of primitive ownership of land based on a veritable magical rapport, in which the thing possessed and its possessor are united by a bond of mystical participation; he is the poet of real property. It transfigures the proprietor and endows him with a special and concrete sensibility. To be sure, this sensibility ignores eternal truths or universal values: the universal is Jewish, since it is an object of intelligence. What his subtle sense seizes upon is precisely that which the intelligence cannot perceive. To put it another way, the principle underlying anti-Semitism is that the concrete possession of a particular object gives as if by magic the meaning of that object. Maurras said the same thing when he declared a Jew to be forever incapable of understanding this line of Racine:

*Dans l'Orient désert, quel devint mon ennui.**

But the way is open to me, mediocre me, to understand what the most subtle, the most cultivated intelligence has been unable to grasp. Why? Because I possess Racine—Racine and my country and my soil. Perhaps the Jew speaks a purer French than I do, perhaps he knows syntax and grammar better, perhaps he is even a writer. No matter; he has spoken this language for only twenty years, and I for a thousand years. The correctness of his style is abstract, acquired; my faults of French are in conformity with the genius of the language. We recognize here the reasoning that Barrès used against the holders of scholarships. There is no occasion for surprise. Don't the Jews have all the scholarships? All that intelligence, all that money can acquire one leaves to them, but it is as empty as the wind. The only things that count are irrational values, and it is just these things which are denied the Jews forever. Thus the anti-Semite takes his stand from the start on the ground of irrationalism. He is opposed to the Jew, just as sentiment is to intelligence, the particular to the universal, the past

* *Bérénice.* [This line is highly idiomatic French.]

to the present, the concrete to the abstract, the owner of real property to the possessor of negotiable securities.

Besides this, many anti-Semites—the majority, perhaps—belong to the lower middle class of the towns; they are functionaries, office workers, small businessmen, who possess nothing. It is in opposing themselves to the Jew that they suddenly become conscious of being proprietors: in representing the Jew as a robber, they put themselves in the enviable position of people who could be robbed. Since the Jew wishes to take France from them, it follows that France must belong to them. Thus they have chosen anti-Semitism as a means of establishing their status as possessors. The Jew has more money than they? So much the better: money is Jewish, and they can despise it as they despise intelligence. They own less than the gentleman-farmer of Périgord or the large-scale farmer of the Beauce? That doesn't matter. All they have to do is nourish a vengeful anger against the robbers of Israel and they feel at once in possession of the entire country. True Frenchmen, good Frenchmen are all equal, for each of them possesses for himself alone France whole and indivisible.

Thus I would call anti-Semitism a poor man's snobbery. And in fact it would appear that the rich for the most part exploit this passion for their own uses rather than abandon themselves to it—they have better things to do. It is propagated mainly among the middle classes, because they possess neither land nor house nor castle, having only some ready cash and a few securities in the bank. It was not by chance that the petty bourgeoisie of Germany was anti-Semitic in 1925. The principal concern of this "white-collar proletariat" was to distinguish itself from the real proletariat. Ruined by big industry, bamboozled by the Junkers, it was nonetheless to the Junkers and the great industrialists that its whole heart went out. It went in for anti-Semitism with the same enthusiasm that it went in for wearing bourgeois dress: *because* the workers were internationalists, because the Junkers possessed Germany and it wished to possess it also. Anti-Semitism is not merely the joy of hating; it brings positive pleasures too. By treating the Jew as an inferior and pernicious being, I affirm at the same time that I belong to the elite. This elite, in contrast to those of modern times which are based on merit or labor, closely resembles an aristocracy of birth. There is nothing I have to do to merit my superiority, and neither can I lose it. It is given once and for all. It is a *thing*.

We must not confuse this precedence the anti-Semite enjoys by virtue of his principles with individual merit. The anti-Semite is not too anxious to possess individual merit. Merit has to be sought, just like truth; it is discovered with difficulty; one must deserve it. Once acquired, it is perpetually in question: a false step, an error, and it flies away. Without respite, from the beginning of our lives to the end, we are responsible for what merit we enjoy. Now the anti-Semite flees responsibility as he flees his own conciousness, and choosing for his personality the permanence of rock, he chooses for his morality a scale of petrified values. Whatever he does, he knows that he will remain at the top of the ladder; whatever the Jew does, he will never get any higher than the first rung.

We begin to perceive the meaning of the anti-Semite's choice of himself. He chooses the irremediable out of fear of being free; he chooses mediocrity out of fear of being alone, and out of pride he makes of this irremediable mediocrity a rigid aristocracy. To this end he finds the existence of the Jew absolutely necessary. Otherwise to whom would he be superior? Indeed, it is vis-à-vis the Jew and the Jew alone that the anti-Semite realizes that he has rights. If by some miracle all the Jews were exterminated as he wishes, he would find himself nothing but a concierge or a shopkeeper in a strongly hierarchical society in which the quality of "true Frenchman" would be at a low valuation, because everyone would possess it. He would lose his sense of rights over the country because no one would any longer contest them, and that profound equality which brings him close to the nobleman and the man of wealth would disappear all of a sudden, for it is primarily negative. His frustrations, which he has attributed to the disloyal competition of the Jew, would have to be imputed to some other cause, lest he be forced to look within himself. He would run the risk of falling into bitterness, into a melancholy hatred of the privileged classes. Thus the anti-Semite is in the unhappy position of having a vital need for the very enemy he wishes to destroy.

. . .

We are now in a position to understand the anti-Semite. He is a man who is afraid. Not of the Jews, to be sure, but of himself, of his own consciousness, of his liberty, of his instincts, of his responsibilities, of solitariness, of change, of society, and of the world—of everything except the Jews. He is a coward who does not want to admit his cowardice to himself; a murderer who represses and censures his tendency to murder without being able to hold it back, yet who dares to kill only in effigy or protected by the anonymity of the mob; a malcontent who dares not revolt from fear of the consequences of his rebellion. In espousing anti-Semitism, he does not simply adopt an opinion, he chooses himself as a person. He chooses the permanence and impenetrability of stone, the total irresponsibility of the warrior who obeys his leaders—and he has no leader. He chooses to acquire nothing, to deserve nothing; he assumes that everything is given him as his birthright—and he is not noble. He chooses finally a Good that is fixed once and for all, beyond question, out of reach; he dares not examine it for fear of being led to challenge it and having to seek it in another form. The Jew only serves him as a pretext; elsewhere his counterpart will make use of the Negro or the man of yellow skin. The existence of the Jew merely permits the anti-Semite to stifle his anxieties at their inception by persuading himself that his place in the world has been marked out in advance, that it awaits him, and that tradition gives him the right to occupy it. Anti-Semitism, in short, is fear of the human condition. The anti-Semite is a man who wishes to be pitiless stone, a furious torrent, a devastating thunderbolt—anything except a man.

Questions

1. We see immediately the extent to which the essay is going to develop semantic considerations. Does the word *opinions* really carry the connotation that Sartre attributes to it? Think this through carefully.
2. Does Sartre's shift from the word *opinion* to the word *doctrine* in the fourth paragraph seem justified? Why does he make it?
3. The emphasis on choice we have already explained. But why in the context of Sartre's analysis should he insist on it? Can you trace back now to see how his attitude toward the anti-Semite has emerged? How much use does Sartre himself make of semantic coloring of words? How effectively?
4. Sartre argues that treating the Jew as inferior establishes for the anti-Semite his own superiority: "It is given once and for all. It is a *thing*." Assuming Sartre is right, what semantic process is he describing?
5. We have had to omit a major portion of Sartre's "portrait," but we include the final paragraph of Sartre's chapter. This paragraph is sharper in tone than any other part of the "portrait." Has Sartre's handling of evidence and logic in the earlier part of the essay given you confidence in his analysis? Has it led up to and justified the biting quality in this last paragraph? Does the paragraph reinforce or undermine your confidence in Sartre?
6. Sartre uses the metaphor of man as a mosaic possessing good characteristics or qualities, and in the midst of those characteristics, one stone representing anti-Semitism. Think of yourself or people you have known well. Can you find in "good" people you know an "evil" stone? Does this stone color the entire personality? Or does it remain isolated?

Suggestions for Writing

1. Most of the over-forty generation remember playing children's games in which the one who was to be it would be chosen by a jingle which begins, "Eeny, meenie, minie, moe, / Catch a nigger by the toe." Or they remember racing for the swimming hole with the cry, "Last one in is a nigger baby." Such unconscious semantic damning is at least as revealing and deadening in its effects as the more or less conscious damning that Sartre discusses. We trust that such expressions have died and been buried by a sense of dignity and humanity that goes with being black—or any other color—and human. But children often unconsciously reveal their own and their parents' prejudices, sometimes with frightening candor. Examine some such revelation from your own childhood—or even recent—experiences. Use something of the sober, analytical approach of Sartre, and develop a cause-effect analysis.

The Doily Menace

E. B. White

E. B. White is one of the most incisive analysts of the American scene that twentieth-century America has produced. He is also one of the finest stylists and one of the wittiest users of the familiar essay. What semantic implications can you see in the experience he records in this selection?

My trouble with doilies dates way back. I was a child when they first started to bother me. Now, having attained my full growth, I still suffer from them.

The first real difficulty came as a result of my not knowing what the word doily meant. I heard it used around the house, but, as sometimes happens, I did not immediately connect the object with the word. Result: I concluded that doilies had something to do with sex, which frightened me. (Whenever, as a child, I failed to understand words, I attributed the fact to my ignorance of sexology. Doily was a word made for the purpose—it sounded a little bit shady, and sex, if you remember, was shady up until about 1919.) So I went around not daring to ask my mother what a doily was. I didn't dare ask her about babies; why should I ask her about doilies?

The dictionary was no help, because I thought doily was spelled "doylee." As I look back, the dictionary seems to have helped me very little in any of my troubles. Ours was a Webster's mounted on a tripod in a room called "Albert's room," and it was pretty evasive about the words that interested me most. I let doily go as a bad job. Maybe, I reasoned, it was such a dirty word they couldn't even put it in the dictionary.

The next doily trouble I had came in my early restaurant days. Of course, by that time I had learned what doilies were, but I had not learned to watch out for them. One evening I ate one. It was a paper doily. It was served to me under a slice of pie, in a restaurant in Eighth Street. The restaurant was dimly lit, and I was young. I ate the pie and the doily with it, dreamily forking it down, uncritical and inattentive. Just as I was finishing

I discovered my mistake—a small paper fragment remained, a telltale trace, dog-eared and limp. I was considerably upset. For about three days thereafter I kept expecting death. My thoughts, like my stomach, were all disarranged and went round in my head like little swirls of paper on city sidewalks in a windstorm. I could think only in phrases, not sentences; phrases like "deadly cellulose," "paper wadding," "traced to his having once swallowed a foreign object," "made from old rags." I felt miserable. I was quite sure that my doily was growing, inside me. Paper swells.

That episode ended at last. Things blew over. I forgot doilies in the mad pleasures of life as a young advertising man. Months, even years, rolled along, peaceably enough. My early fears had been dissipated, I was getting along better with sex, Havelock Ellis had come and gone, restaurants no longer bemused me to the extent that I ate their pastries paper and all, and—to make my happiness complete—Spring was again here. I remember it was a lovely night in early May that I was invited to dine at the home of a lady of such vast beauty and elegant demeanor that I trembled to think of my own good fortune.

I went. My hostess was a play-actress, and like all play-actresses she received me well and treated me with courtesy—even with, I thought, affection. Also, like all play-actresses, she was to serve cocoanut-cream pudding for dessert. I knew, of course, that it was coming, and I was ready.

My dessert plate came on, a transparent glass plate. On it was a finger-bowl. I was ready for that, too. "My lovely hostess," I thought to myself, "can't make a simpleton out of me simply by serving a finger bowl on a dessert plate." Quite casually I removed the finger-bowl, set it to one side, leaving the dessert plate free to receive the dessert when it should be passed.

Free? Yes, I thought that. Reader, it looked like a free plate to me. Even while I was helping myself to spoonful after spoonful of delicious cocoanut-cream pudding, it looked like a free plate to me. Not till a moment later, when I dug down with my fork and brought up out of the soggy depths a fine Italian linen doily, saturated, as only an Italian linen doily can be, with pudding, did I realize how far from free the plate had been.

I stared, fascinated, at the dripping doily. From its delicate interstices little yellow morsels of pudding oozed. Slowly I raised my eyes and looked up at my sweet hostess smiling at me across the table.

There was a pause.

"Better put it down," she said.

Without a moment's wait, I raised the doily to my mouth and swallowed it at a single gulp.

"Cheero," I replied. "Down it is."

Questions

1. Note that White says he "did not immediately connect the object with the word." Would Hayakawa recommend that he do so? Do any of his later problems with the doily relate to his doing so or failing to do so?
2. Does his eating of the paper doily have anything to do with his later eating of the linen one? As precisely as you can, explain why he eats the linen doily. How much of the reason is related to semantics? How much to his idea of social etiquette?
3. White does not seem serious about his subject, but does his essay have any serious implications?

Suggestions for Writing

1. This essay provides a remarkable example for you to imitate in a similar tone and style. Remember—or devise—some similar problem or episode and try to retell it with the same lightness and effectiveness with which Mr. White works here. If possible, work with something where semantic difficulties have caused you embarrassment, that is, where you have confused a word for a thing or had experiences with false verbal maps. Develop your paper with a double cause and effect analysis: What caused your problem? What resulted from the problem?

Home Burial

Robert Frost *Nearly every American, whether he knows any other poetry or not, knows Robert Frost and his New England through "Death of a Hired Man" and "Mending Wall." But not all is sweetness and light in Frost's poetry, as "Home Burial" shows. Even with the beautiful, the pastoral, and the gentle in Frost's New England, much about the countryside and the poetry has disturbing, sometimes frightening undertones. Even on a first reading you should be able to recognize that the couple in this poem are kept apart by semantic difficulties. Try to define precisely what is wrong.*

He saw her from the bottom of the stairs
Before she saw him. She was starting down,
Looking back over her shoulder at some fear.
She took a doubtful step and then undid it
To raise herself and look again. He spoke
Advancing toward her: 'What is it you see
From up there always—for I want to know.'
She turned and sank upon her skirts at that,
And her face changed from terrified to dull.
He said to gain time: 'What is it you see,'
Mounting until she cowered under him.
'I will find out now—you must tell me, dear.'
She, in her place, refused him any help
With the least stiffening of her neck and silence.
She let him look, sure that he wouldn't see,
Blind creature; and awhile he didn't see.
But at last he murmured, 'Oh,' and again, 'Oh.'

'What is it—what?' she said.

'Just that I see.'

'You don't,' she challenged. 'Tell me what it is.'

'The wonder is I didn't see at once.
I never noticed it from here before.
I must be wonted to it—that's the reason.
The little graveyard where my people are!
So small the window frames the whole of it.
Not so much larger than a bedroom, is it?
There are three stones of slate and one of marble,
Broad-shouldered little slabs there in the sunlight
On the sidehill. We haven't to mind *those*.
But I understand: it is not the stones,
But the child's mound—'

'Don't, don't, don't, don't,' she cried.

She withdrew shrinking from beneath his arm
That rested on the bannister, and slid downstairs;
And turned on him with such a daunting look,
He said twice over before he knew himself:
'Can't a man speak of his own child he's lost?'

'Not you! Oh, where's my hat? Oh, I don't need it!
I must get out of here. I must get air.
I don't know rightly whether any man can.'

'Amy! Don't go to someone else this time.
Listen to me. I won't come down the stairs.'
He sat and fixed his chin between his fists.
'There's something I should like to ask you, dear.'

'You don't know how to ask it.'

'Help me, then.'

Her fingers moved the latch for all reply.

'My words are nearly always an offense.
I don't know how to speak of anything
So as to please you. But I might be taught
I should suppose. I can't say I see how.
A man must partly give up being a man
With women-folk. We could have some arrangement
By which I'd bind myself to keep hands off
Anything special you're a-mind to name.
Though I don't like such things 'twixt those that love.
Two that don't love can't live together without them.
But two that do can't live together with them.'

She moved the latch a little. 'Don't—don't go.
Don't carry it to someone else this time.
Tell me about it if it's something human.
Let me into your grief. I'm not so much
Unlike other folks as your standing there
Apart would make me out. Give me my chance.
I do think, though, you overdo it a little.
What was it brought you up to think it the thing
To take your mother-loss of a first child
So inconsolably—in the face of love.
You'd think his memory might be satisfied—'

'There you go sneering now!'

'I'm not, I'm not!
You make me angry. I'll come down to you.
God, what a woman! And it's come to this,
A man can't speak of his own child that's dead.'

'You can't because you don't know how to speak.
If you had any feelings, you that dug
With your own hand—how could you?—his little grave;
I saw you from that very window there,
Making the gravel leap and leap in air,
Leap up, like that, like that, and land so lightly
And roll back down the mound beside the hole.
I thought, Who is that man? I didn't know you.
And I crept down the stairs and up the stairs
To look again, and still your spade kept lifting.
Then you came in. I heard your rumbling voice
Out in the kitchen, and I don't know why,
But I went near to see with my own eyes.
You could sit there with the stains on your shoes
Of the fresh earth from your own baby's grave
And talk about your everyday concerns.
You had stood the spade up against the wall
Outside there in the entry, for I saw it.'

'I shall laugh the worst laugh I ever laughed.
I'm cursed. God, if I don't believe I'm cursed.'

'I can repeat the very words you were saying.
"Three foggy mornings and one rainy day
Will rot the best birch fence a man can build."

Think of it, talk like that at such a time!
What had how long it takes a birch to rot
To do with what was in the darkened parlor.
You *couldn't* care! The nearest friends can go
With anyone to death, comes so far short
They might as well not try to go at all.
No, from the time when one is sick to death,
One is alone, and he dies more alone.
Friends make pretense of following to the grave,
But before one is in it, their minds are turned
And making the best of their way back to life
And living people, and things they understand.
But the world's evil. I won't have grief so
If I can change it. Oh, I won't. I won't!'

'There, you have said it all and you feel better.
You won't go now. You're crying. Close the door.
The heart's gone out of it: why keep it up.
Amy! There's someone coming down the road!'

'*You*—oh, you think the talk is all. I must go—
Somewhere out of this house. How can I make you—'

'If—you—do!' She was opening the door wider.
'Where do you mean to go? First tell me that.
I'll follow and bring you back by force. I *will!*—'

Questions

1. Almost from the first lines we sense a certain ominousness in the poem. It all seems quite innocent, especially after the husband and wife finally get "it" out in the open. The husband even suggests that saying it has solved it. Where does the ominousness come from?
2. Note the wife's revulsion to the shovel, the dirt, anything the husband has touched in digging the grave. Now recall what Hayakawa says about the symbolic process. Just what has happened to the wife?
3. Considering both the narrator's language and that spoken by husband and wife, who seems more at fault? How much feeling does the husband have for the lost child? Is his digging of the grave an evidence of lack of feeling?
4. Why does her memory of his words, "Three foggy mornings and one rainy day/Will rot the best birch fence a man can build," so infuriate her? What relevance do they have to the situation?

Suggestions for Writing

1. Analyze the language of the speakers for semantic loading and then relate such loading to the problem the poem portrays. To what extent is the quarrel "just a matter of semantics"? Such a paper would surely yield to development by cause and effect.
2. Write a paper in which you explore a similar cause and effect relationship in a quarrel you have witnessed or participated in.

Language Projects in Laputa

Jonathan Swift

Gulliver's Travels *is probably still best known as a children's adventure story, though generations of college students and adults have felt the bite of its marvelously adult satire. You have probably followed Gulliver into the mini-world of the Lilliputians and the giant world of the Brobdingnags. But unless you have been unusually intrigued or had an unusually ambitious English teacher in high school, you probably stopped short of accompanying him to the great floating island of Laputa, which rules its earth-bound subjects by floating above them, lowering to crush any recalcitrants. In the selection that follows, Gulliver is being shown the Academy, where everything is done according to reason, not emotion. As you will see, Gulliver seems duly impressed. But how impressed is Swift?*

If you read alertly you should have little trouble in perceiving what Swift's aim is in this selection. Try to define what advantage Swift gains by the particular rhetorical stance he has chosen: that is, by the whole fictional structure with Gulliver himself as narrator. Also keep in mind the first rule of semantics: the word is not the thing.

I had hitherto seen only one side of the Academy, the other being appropriated to the advancers of speculative learning, of whom I shall say something when I have mentioned one illustrious person more, who is called among them *the universal artist*. He told us he had been thirty years employing his thoughts for the improvement of human life. He had two large rooms full of wonderful curiosities, and fifty men at work. Some were condensing air into a dry tangible substance, by extracting the nitre, and letting the aqueous or fluid particles percolate; others softening marble for pillows and pin-cushions; others petrifying the hoofs of a living horse to preserve them from foundering. The artist himself was at that time busy upon two great designs; the first, to sow land with chaff, wherein he affirmed the true seminal virtue to be contained, as he demonstrated by several experiments which I was not skilful enough to comprehend. The other was, by a certain composition of gums, minerals, and vegetables outwardly applied, to prevent the growth of wool upon two young lambs; and he hoped in a reasonable time to propagate the breed of naked sheep all over the kingdom.

We crossed a walk to the other part of the Academy, where, as I have already said, the projectors in speculative learning resided.

The first professor I saw was in a very large room, with forty pupils about him. After salutation, observing me to look earnestly upon a frame, which took up the greatest part of both the length and breadth of the room, he said perhaps I might wonder to see him employed in a project for improving speculative knowledge by practical and mechanical operations. But the world would soon be sensible of its usefulness, and he flattered himself that a more noble exalted thought never sprang in any other man's head. Every one knew how laborious the usual method is of attaining to arts and sciences; whereas by his contrivance the most ignorant person at a reasonable charge, and with a little bodily labour, may write books in philosophy, poetry, politics, law, mathematics, and theology, without the least assistance from genius or study. He then led me to the frame, about the sides whereof all his pupils stood in ranks. It was twenty foot square, placed in the middle of the room. The superficies was composed of several bits of wood, about the bigness of a die, but some larger than others. They were all linked together by slender wires. These bits of wood were covered on every square with paper pasted on them, and on these papers were written all the words of their language, in their several moods, tenses, and declensions, but without any order. The professor then desired me to observe, for he was going to set his engine at work. The pupils at his command took each of them hold of an iron handle, whereof there were forty fixed round the edges of the frame, and giving them a sudden turn, the whole disposition of the words was entirely changed. He then commanded six and thirty of the lads to read the several lines softly as they appeared upon the frame; and where they found three or four words together that might make part of a sentence, they dictated to the four remaining boys who were scribes. This work was repeated three or four times, and at every turn the engine was so contrived that the words shifted into new places, as the square bits of wood moved upside down.

Six hours a day the young students were employed in this labour, and the professor showed me several volumes in large folio already collected, of broken sentences, which he intended to piece together, and out of those rich materials to give the world a complete body of all arts and sciences; which however might be still improved, and much expedited, if the public would raise a fund for making and employing five hundred such frames in Lagado, and oblige the managers to contribute in common their several collections.

He assured me, that this invention had employed all his thoughts from his youth, that he had emptied the whole vocabulary into his frame, and made the strictest computation of the general proportion there is in books between the numbers of particles, nouns, and verbs, and other parts of speech.

I made my humblest acknowledgement to this illustrious person for his great communicativeness, and promised if ever I had the good fortune to return to my native country, that I would do him justice, as the sole inventor of this wonderful machine; the form and contrivance of which I desired leave to delineate upon paper, as in the figure here annexed. I told him, although it were the custom of our learned in Europe to steal inventions from each other, who had thereby at least this advantage, that it became a controversy which was the right owner, yet I would take such caution, that he should have the honour entire without a rival.

We next went to the school of languages, where three professors sat in consultation upon improving that of their own country.

The first project was to shorten discourse by cutting polysyllables into one, and leaving out verbs and participles, because in reality all things imaginable are but nouns.

The other project was a scheme for entirely abolishing all words whatsoever; and this was urged as a great advantage in point of health as well as brevity. For it is plain that every word we speak is in some degree a diminution of our lungs by corrosion, and consequently contributes to the shortening of our lives. An expedient was therefore offered, that since words are only names for *things,* it would be more convenient for all men to carry about them such things as were necessary to express the particular business they are to discourse on. And this invention would certainly have taken place, to the great ease as well as health of the subject, if the women, in conjunction with the vulgar and illiterate, had not threatened to raise a rebellion, unless they might be allowed the liberty to speak with their tongues, after the manner of their ancestors; such constant irreconcilable enemies to science are the common people. However, many of the most learned and wise adhere to the new scheme of expressing themselves by things, which hath only this inconvenience attending it, that if a man's business be very great, and of various kinds, he must be obliged in proportion to carry a greater bundle of things upon his back, unless he can afford one or two strong servants to attend him. I have often beheld two of those sages almost sinking under the weight of their packs, like pedlars among us; who, when they met in the streets, would lay down their loads, open their sacks, and hold conversation for an hour together; then put up their implements, help each other to resume their burthens, and take their leave.

But for short conversations a man may carry implements in his pockets and under his arms, enough to supply him, and in his house he cannot be at a loss. Therefore the room where company meet who practise this art, is full of all things ready at hand, requisite to furnish matter for this kind of artificial converse.

Another great advantage proposed by this invention was that it would serve as an universal language to be understood in all civilised nations, whose goods and utensils are generally of the same kind, or nearly resembling, so that their uses might easily be comprehended. And thus ambassadors would be qualified to treat with foreign princes or ministers of state, to whose tongues they were utter strangers.

I was at the mathematical school, where the master taught his pupils after a method scarce imaginable to us in Europe. The proposition and demonstration were fairly written on a thin wafer, with ink composed of a cephalic tincture. This the student was to swallow upon a fasting stomach, and for three days following eat nothing but bread and water. As the wafer digested, the tincture mounted to his brain, bearing the proposition along with it. But the success hath not hitherto been answerable, partly by some error in the *quantum* or composition, and partly by the perverseness of lads, to whom this bolus is so nauseous, that they generally steal aside, and discharge it upwards before it can operate; neither have they been yet persuaded to use so long an abstinence as the prescription requires.

Questions

1. Gulliver is narrating a fantastic adventure. Why should he give as many physical details as he does, details like the size of the room, the number of men, and so forth?
2. From your experience with writing what would you say of the chances for the professor's machine to "produce a complete body of all arts and sciences"? When Gulliver promises, if he ever returns to his native land, to do the professor "justice, as the sole inventor of this wonderful machine," how are we to understand him? What would be "justice" for such an invention?
3. Is it true that "in reality all things imaginable are but nouns" and that therefore we can get along with only nouns, and monosyllabic nouns at that? The using of things in place of words would of course follow from such logic. What kinds of semantic problems would this solve? What kinds of semantic problems would it make more difficult to solve?

Suggestions for Writing

1. Realizing how much of Swift's effectiveness comes from the particular device of having a narrator travel and report outlandish customs and devices that reveal ordinary human logic and human practice in a ridiculous light, try creating a similar device or situation yourself by means of which you

can satirize some quality or group or individual in the world around you. You might imagine yourself in a foreign university or a university of the future or even—though the device is well-worn by now—at a university on Mars. Do whatever you can to make the satire both believable and effective.

"Baby"

Claude Brown

Because language on the edges of standard usage often changes in both meaning and usage very rapidly, one of the most interesting and revealing places to observe semantic processes in action is in slang or near-slang. This brief selection shows how two of the more important words in today's black America take on and communicate their peculiar meaning. As you might guess from this selection, Claude Brown is one of the more articulate spokesmen for black America. You can watch him work in more detail with words like "Nigger" and "Soul" in Esquire, *April 1968.*

The first time I heard the expression "baby" used by one cat to address another was up at Warwick in 1951. Gus Jackson used it. The term had a hip ring to it, a real colored ring. The first time I heard it, I knew right away I had to start using it. It was like saying, "Man, look at me. I've got masculinity to spare." It was saying at the same time to the world, "I'm one of the hippest cats, one of the most uninhibited cats on the scene. I can say 'baby' to another cat, and he can say 'baby' to me, and we can say it with strength in our voices." If you could say it, this meant that you really had to be sure of yourself, sure of your masculinity.

It seemed that everybody in my age group was saying it. The next thing I knew, older guys were saying it. Then just about everybody in Harlem was saying it, even the cats who weren't so hip. It became just one of those things.

The real hip thing about the "baby" term was that it was something that only colored cats could say the way it was supposed to be said. I'd heard gray boys trying it, but they couldn't really do it. Only colored cats could give it the meaning that we all knew it had without ever mentioning it—the meaning of black masculinity.

Before the Muslims, before I'd heard about the Coptic or anything like that, I remember getting high on the corner with a bunch of guys and watching the chicks go by, fine little girls, and saying, "Man, colored people must be somethin' else!"

Somebody'd say, "Yeah. How about that? All those years, man, we was down on the plantation in those shacks, eating just potatoes and fatback and chitterlin's and greens, and look at what happened. We had Joe Louises and Jack Johnsons and Sugar Ray Robinsons and Henry Armstrongs, all that sort of thing."

Somebody'd say, "Yeah, man. Niggers must be some real strong people who just can't be kept down. When you think about it, that's really something great. Fatback, chitterlin's, greens, and Joe Louis. Negroes are some beautiful people. Uh-huh. Fatback, chitterlin's, greens, and Joe Louis . . . and beautiful black bitches."

Cats would come along with this "baby" thing. It was something that went over strong in the fifties with the jazz musicians and the hip set, the boxers, the dancers, the comedians, just about every set in Harlem. I think everybody said it real loud because they liked the way it sounded. It was always, "Hey, baby. How you doin', baby?" in every phase of the Negro hip life. As a matter of fact, I went to a Negro lawyer's office once, and he said, "Hey, baby. How you doin', baby?" I really felt at ease, really felt that we had something in common. I imagine there were many people in Harlem who didn't feel they had too much in common with the Negro professionals, the doctors and lawyers and dentists and ministers. I know I didn't. But to hear one of these people greet you with the street thing, the "Hey, baby"—and he knew how to say it—you felt as though you had something strong in common.

I suppose it's the same thing that almost all Negroes have in common, the fatback, chitterlings, and greens background. I suppose that regardless of what any Negro in America might do or how high he might rise in social status, he still has something in common with every other Negro. I doubt that they're many, if any, gray people who could ever say "baby" to a Negro and make him feel that "me and this cat have got something going, something strong going."

In the fifties, when "baby" came around, it seemed to be the prelude to a whole new era in Harlem. It was the introduction to the era of black reflection. A fever started spreading. Perhaps the strong rising of the Muslim movement is something that helped to sustain or even usher in this era.

I remember that in the early fifties, cats would stand on the corner and talk, just shooting the stuff, all the street-corner philosophers. Sometimes, it was a common topic—cats talking about gray chicks—and somebody might say something like, "Man, what can anybody see in a gray chick, when colored chicks are so fine; they got so much soul." This was the coming of the "soul" thing too.

"Soul" had started coming out of the churches and the nightclubs into the streets. Everybody started talking about "soul" as though it were something that they could see on people or a distinct characteristic of colored folks.

Cats would say things like, "Man, gray chicks seem so stiff." Many of them would say they couldn't talk to them or would wonder how a cat who was used to being so for real with a chick could see anything in a gray girl. It seemed as though the mood of the day was turning toward the color thing.

Everybody was really digging themselves and thinking and saying in their behavior, in every action, "Wow! Man, it's a beautiful thing to be colored." Everybody was saying, "Oh, the beauty of me! Look at me. I'm colored. And look at us. Aren't we beautiful?"

Questions

1. How could Brown possibly know the first time he heard "baby" that it affirmed "black masculinity"? Could it have been merely from the confident tone with which the speaker used it? Why would the word "take" so fast?
2. The selection is full of words that belong to a particular dialect: "hip," "cat," "chicks," "man," "for real," and of course "soul." Do all these words mean something quite explicit to you? How many of them would you find in white—or gray—slang?
3. In anything close to a formal context Brown uses the word *Negro*. But he obviously approves of the word *niggers* in the mouth of a "cat." In *Esquire* (see our headnote), he calls "nigger" the most "soulful" of words. Why can Negroes use the word with almost the opposite connotations it has when whites use it? Some Negroes are now rejecting the word *Negro*, claiming that it is belittling. They prefer *Afro-American* or just *Black*. Can you give reasons?
4. To what extent would you explain the "language of soul," or of the "hippest cats," as part of the contemporary Negro assertiveness, the rediscovery that, "Man, colored people must be somethin' else"?

Suggestions for Writing

1. How did you respond to "gray boys," "gray people," "gray girl"? Your response will be quite different if you are "white" than if you are Negro. If you are "white" is your skin actually white? Is it gray? An artist friend assures your editors that the so-called white skin has in it every color of the spectrum, but predominately green, yellow, and tan. Can you think of a word with primarily negative connotations that would pick up the shade closer than "gray" does? Indians have traditionally called whites "palefaces." Can you see why? Work all of this into an essay in which you explore the connotations of our words for color. You may even want to explore the competing theories about color: the light theory, which concludes that all colors taken together make white, and the pigment theory, which concludes that all colors taken together make a shade of gray.

Writing Projects

1. Awareness of connotations of words is one of the most important kinds of semantic awareness. It can tell you when and how words are being used both against and for you. It can let you see through dishonest advertising, the slanting lie, political gimcrackery. It can help you analyze subtle effects in literature and deepen your response. It can also help you use words more effectively yourself. Your problem as a writer will be to use connotations effectively but to realize that they are easily misused. You will often need to restrain yourself for the sake of honesty. Consider the following excerpts, translated from the *Moniteur* of France, in March of 1815, on the escape of Napoleon from Elba:

   1st announcement: "The monster has escaped from the place of his banishment; and he has run away from Elba."
   2nd: "The Corsican ogre has landed at Cape Juan."
   3rd: "The tiger has shown himself at Gap. The troops are advancing on all sides to arrest his progress. He will conclude his miserable adventure by becoming a wanderer among the mountains; he cannot possibly escape."
   4th: "The monster has really advanced as far as Grenoble, we know not to what treachery to ascribe it."
   5th: "The tyrant is actually at Lyons. Fear and terror seized all at his appearance."
   6th: "The usurper has ventured to approach the capital to within sixty hours' march."
   7th: "Bonaparte is advancing by forced marches; but it is impossible he can reach Paris."
   8th: "Napoleon will arrive under the walls of Paris tomorrow."
   9th: "The Emperor Napoleon is at Fontainebleau."
   10th: "Yesterday evening his Majesty the Emperor made his public entry, and arrived at the Tuileries—nothing can exceed the universal joy!"

   Write a careful analysis of just what the writers have done, how they have done it, and why they have done it. Note that this gives you a kind of reverse cause and effect analysis.
2. Between the first announcements on Napoleon and the last, we get completely contrasting views of him. Pick some person, scene, or event and describe it twice so that, not from any *stated* attitudes or responses, your words themselves define two contrasting responses. This will of course mean two papers, one giving a highly favorable reaction (but by choice of words alone), the other a highly negative one (again without actually stating the reaction).
3. Choose a controversy currently being discussed in your local or college news-

paper. Analyze the language of an editorial or letter to the editor which takes a strong position on the issue. Pay particular attention to the choice of words. What effect does the author hope to produce by his choice of words? Do you find examples of semantic slanting or smear? Is the author being honest?

4. Observe your own use of language and the use of language by the people about you. Then write a paper on what contributes to the pollution of the semantic environment. This paper will require a careful definition of terms followed by illustration and explanation.

Part VII

Logic and Persuasion

*M*ost of us like to think of ourselves as eminently logical people. The opinions and beliefs we hold must be true—or we wouldn't hold them. We may be aware that we have never really examined them or their sources very carefully, but we have every confidence that if we did so we would find them perfectly logical, perfectly supportable. They must be right: they are *ours*. Which, of course, explains our uneasiness and defensiveness if they are challenged. Challenge arouses our possessive instincts.

But what you have just learned about semantics should demonstrate how vulnerable we all are to semantic suggestion and how unaware we tend to be of our own semantic illogicality. And if we are vulnerable and illogical semantically, can we be so sure of ourselves with our ordinary opinions and ideas, with our ordinary reason and logic? The question is especially disquieting when we seriously consider how we grasp at any idea or fact that supports a position we hold, or when we consider how much of our "thinking" goes not to the quest for truth but to the quest for reasons to continue believing as we do—that is, to rationalization.

The question ought to be disquieting at any time. But when you think of yourself as a writer it becomes crucial. It will do you little good to adopt a rhetorical stance in which you assume yourself to be an intelligent, reasoning human speaking to an audience of intelligent, reasoning humans unless you understand and have some control over logical processes as well as the techniques of persuasion. In a sense, most of what this book has been saying about the rhetorical stance and about rhetorical devices has been leading up to and directly applies to this section on logic and persuasion. Illustration, Definition, Process, Comparison and Contrast, Classification and Division, and Cause and Effect have been introduced primarily as ways of organizing and presenting expository materials. But exposition, as we have indicated and as we hope you have found, is seldom limited in purpose to simply explaining something. Nearly always it carries a persuasive flavor of some kind—a persuasive edge. Writers illustrate or define or compare or classify or analyze cause and effect because these processes help to support a position, help to convince their audience.

Logic has always been thought to be the primary tool of those who would persuade others. And it unquestionably is an important tool. But logic is only one of the tools of persuasion. It can be a powerful one if you are talking or writing to logical, reasoning people. But some of the most influential books of history, especially of the modern world, have been some of the most illogical. They almost pride themselves on their antilogic. Open Hitler's *Mein Kampf* at almost any page and examine its flaunting of logic. Or, closer to home, try to analyze (dispassionately, if possible) both the logic and the attitude toward logic of Robert Welch's *Blue Book* or the latest pronouncement of nearly any of the New Leftist organizations. The influence of such books and pronouncements makes one almost ready to agree with Mark Twain's rascally "King" in *Huckleberry Finn,* who responds to the suspicions of the logical doctor: "Cuss the doctor! What do we k'yer for *him?* Hain't we got all the fools in town on our side? And ain't that a big enough majority in any town?" You will find this problem of antilogic treated at length in Wayne Booth's "Now Don't Try to Reason with Me."

The King and the Duke, you remember, are succeeding with frightening efficiency in their attempt to bilk newly orphaned girls out of their inheritance money by appealing through "tears and flapdoodle" to the sentimental crowd of neighbors and relatives. Their appeal purely to sentiment is at the opposite pole from logic and reason. But its success, even though the rascals lose everything by "overreaching," illustrates the effectiveness of such an appeal. As you try to develop a meaningful rhetorical stance, you will need to take into account not only these extremes—the appeal to logic and the appeal merely to sentiment—but all grades and variations in between. You may really be what you think you are, an eminently logical person. But unless your audience is logical too, you may find the people in it listening politely enough but with increasing boredom. Most effective persuasion uses both kinds of appeal, on various levels and in various proportions. You need to gauge carefully both your audience and the kind of response you want from it to determine the levels and proportions of logic you will use.

The following diagram will help you to visualize the problem:

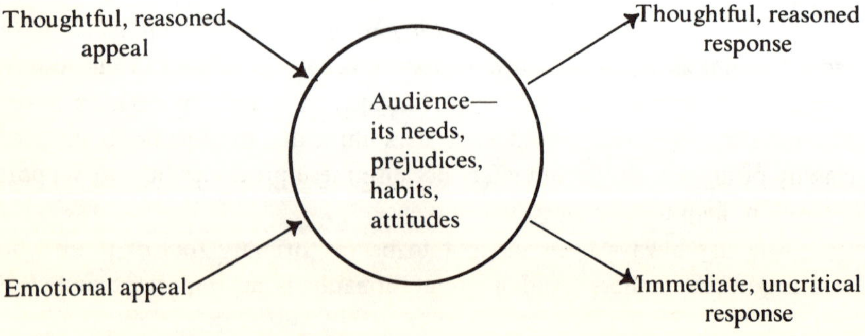

If you argue that Americans should refuse to trade with Russia because America's own safety depends on weakening communism—and if you have good evidence to support your position—you are arguing from a "thoughtful, reasoned" position. If you argue that Americans should refuse such trade because only communists, traitors, and fuzzy intellectuals support it, you are arguing from an emotional position. It seems simple enough: If you want a reasoned response make a reasoned appeal; if you want an emotional, uncritical response make an emotional appeal. But you will seldom find it that simple. As you will see in Faulkner's "Dry September," a reasoned appeal has little effect on a mob bent on lynching. And an audience of college professors would probably be offended by too obvious an emotional appeal. The diagram suggests, especially with the word *prejudices,* a kind of calculation about it all that should disturb you. To play on people's prejudices hardly seems noble. And yet no serious candidate for a political position these days would consider making a speech unless he is aware of his audience's prejudices. All political demagoguery, most advertising, most sermonizing, press toward the emotional end of the diagram—though often with vastly different motives. Even legal trials, pretending always to be searching for the facts and the truth, often turn more on emotional than on rational appeal.

But consideration of the needs, attitudes, habits, and prejudices of your audience can be as devious and ignoble or as straightforward and noble as the character of the speaker or writer will permit. Even sound logic can be misused to distort truth or to support an evil position, and many kinds of human activity deserve emotional support and commitment. You need to know when you use an emotional appeal, or when you recognize one being used on you, that the danger of violating logic, of distorting truth, of manipulating people (in the worst sense of "manipulation") is much greater than if you are using a reasoned appeal, though neither kind of appeal *need* be dishonest or even distorting.

The following brief sketch should help you review or become aware of basic principles of logic and of the more common violations of them. But you should study a much more detailed analysis.

Logic is, among other things, the process by which we move from known or accepted truths or assumptions to some new truth or idea. Traditionally two basic types of logic are recognized, according to the process used to reach a conclusion. If we start from some truth or assumption or generalization and derive or *deduce* from it some specific truth, we are using *deductive* logic. The tool of deductive logic is called the syllogism and had its origin with Aristotle:

All men are mortal.	major premise
Socrates is a man.	minor premise
Socrates is mortal.	conclusion

In this syllogism the conclusion *must* follow from the two premises. It is a *valid* conclusion. This fact gives deductive logic an appealing sense of certainty that probably explains why it dominated the thinking of the western world from Aristotle's time until the sixteenth century. But the sense of certainty can be deceptive. The tests for validity are rather complex, but you would not be taken in by the following:

All students are human.
Fido is a human.
Fido is a student.

Can you see what is wrong formally? To be valid the syllogism must work exactly as the first one does. But even then it may be untrue. Suppose the minor premise had stated "Fido is a student." The conclusion that Fido is human would then be valid. Would it necessarily be true? The question emphasizes the most fundamental weakness of syllogistic logic: the conclusion can be true only if both assumptions (premises) are true. Your task as reader and thinker and writer when examining or using deductive logic is to examine the assumptions. Setting the logic up in syllogistic form often makes that examination easier. But we will seldom see and less seldom use logic set in syllogistic form. Instead, we usually see and use it with one or another of the assumptions left out: "He must be brilliant; he's a student at Harvard." Here the omitted assumption is the major premise:

All students at Harvard are brilliant.
He is a student at Harvard.
He is brilliant.

Stated in this form, we at least recognize it as a deduction based on a premise that itself may or may not be true. Harvard entrance requirements *may* be stringent enough to insure that every student admitted is brilliant. But such a premise would itself need a lot of evidence to support it. Even the sentence about entrance requirements is itself a logical deduction, based on the assumption that entrance requirements do a perfect job of screening out any but the brilliant students. No college admissions officer would agree that it does. Had the original deduction stated, "He must be brilliant, he graduated magna cum laude from Harvard," the chances for the conclusion to be true would be greatly increased, because the chances of the unstated assumption being true are greatly increased: "All magna cum laude graduates from Harvard are brilliant." But even this assumption some skeptics might question—though no Harvard alumnus would.

The common logical fallacy known as *begging the question* results from bad deductive logic: it assumes to be true what you must prove to be true. "Expelling dissident students will end campus riots because it will keep these students from causing troubles." The argument is simply circular: both statements make essentially the same point. Of the other fallacies related to deduction, at least be aware of the classic double-horned question: "When are you going to stop beating your wife?" Any direct answer damns. The way out is to say, "But I have never beaten my wife." Even this, though, can leave doubts in the mind of a listener.

Examine the assumptions, then, and examine the syllogism. Examine them not only in the formal logic you hear and use, but in the informal logic and semi- or pseudo-logic that surrounds you. If you believe, from the Biblical story of the creation, that because one of Adam's ribs was used to create Eve man therefore must have one less rib than woman, you are basing your belief on a series of deductions. (The belief was actually widespread during the middle ages; Michelangelo received criticism for questioning it.)

But if you count your own ribs and the ribs of your brother or sister and compare them to see if man has one less rib, then you are beginning to work inductively. "Beginning" because to be certain you would have to count quite a few representative ribs. That is the approach to truth through induction: to get all the facts you can and then lead in to some kind of general truth. This generalization must take into account all the known facts and provide a sound basis from which to predict future results given the same set of conditions. You will recognize induction as the approach of science. And you will remember from our discussion of cause and effect that the whole approach is itself based on—deduced from—an assumption: that the universe is essentially an ordered place, that it operates under a system, however complex, of cause and effect, that we can explain one phenomenon in terms of another or of other phenomena.

Remember that the scientist tends toward caution in his inductions, that he usually remains somewhat tentative, and that his doing so increases rather than decreases our trust in his logic. But many who *seem* to be using inductive logic are not cautious at all. The prestige of science repeatedly calls forth the tag, stated or implied, "Science has shown . . . ," often when *science* has shown no such thing. As both reader and writer, you will probably be involved much more often with inductive than with deductive approaches to truth. You need to know its uses and abuses.

Actually most scientific investigation begins with some kind of hunch or hypothesis. Given what we know about the action of molecules, such and such ought to be true. The physicist then sets up experiments to test his hypothesis. If under repeated experiments his hunch seems accurate, he finally makes the "inductive leap" to generalize about what the evidence shows: apparently molecules are more active as they become warmer. Does the activity increase in proportion to rise in temperature? Thus from idea to idea, from hypothesis to thesis, science moves. But always cautiously. The scientist may yet find a material that contracts or conditions that cause a material to contract as the temperature rises. The caution comes from experience but also from the knowledge that induction too is full of pitfalls. How large must a sampling be before you can safely generalize? What kind of sampling must you have? One cannot test every rock in the universe. How many pounds of rock and dust will be enough to tell us for sure about the makeup of the moon? In the 1948 presidential election, polls predicted Thomas Dewey would win the election by a big margin. Harry Truman won. During the depression in 1936 the *Literary Digest* forecast the election of Alf Landon, but Franklin D. Roosevelt won by a landslide margin. The *Digest* was laughed out of existence. What went wrong? The *Digest* had selected its sampling of voters at random from telephone books. Remembering that telephones were not as widespread then as now, can you decide what did go wrong? We have given you enough information that you should be able to do so by careful deduction. See Ruby's essay below for an analysis of what did go wrong.

Fallacies related to inductive logic may generally be traced to the sampling. *Hasty generalization* results when the inductive leap is made too soon, before sufficient evidence has been collected. It may not be a conscious manipulation for persuasive purposes, but it is often the result of faulty method. Thalidomide seemed safe enough as a tranquilizing drug. But its use by pregnant women apparently caused thousands of babies to be born deformed. The *post hoc* fallacy is actually a form of hasty generalization. It assumes that, because one event happens after another, it happens because of the other. The discussion of cause and effect in the previous section should make you cautious of this fallacy. *Card stacking* is usually less innocent but no less misleading. You are stacking the cards if you arrange them so that you get only the cards you want or so that your opponent gets only the cards you want him to. In logic or persuasion you simply pick the evidence that supports your position, ignoring or hiding contrary evidence. This practice is unethical, but it is often very effective!

These fallacies at least pretend to some kind of logic. Related techniques of persuasion, used mostly in emotional appeal, often ignore or even flaunt logic. *Name calling* and *glittering generalities* both take advantage of the tendency to react without thinking: the automatic response. Call someone an intellectual or a hippie or a nigger-lover and you automatically damn him—at least with certain audiences. Purr about "the American way of life" or snarl about "decadent imperialism" and you turn off thinking and turn on the stock response.

Or, closely related, if you cannot win by logic throw a little mud, attack the personality of your opponent: *argumentum ad hominem* is the formal term for this technique. Or if not by direct attack, try a little innuendo—just hint at a character deficiency. It is sometimes even more devastating than the direct attack. Or you can always say, "You did it too." This is probably as irrelevant as the other forms of persuasion, but it puts the opposition on the defensive.

These and various other techniques—*bandwagon appeal* (every one wants to be on the winning side), *red herring* (throw your opponent off the trail by setting out a false lead), *appeal to authority* (most people who know a big name will not pay attention to whether he happens to be an authority on this particular problem or not; advertising thrives on irrelevant authority)—may help you to win arguments or to convince people. But they will hardly gain the respect of your English teacher or of anyone else who cares about fairness and integrity.

The selections that follow focus on logic and persuasion from many directions, though few of them discuss or work with formal logic. Watch for the bases on which people are persuaded to think or act. Careful attention to such things still may not make any of us the eminently logical people we think ourselves to be. But it can lead us toward logical awareness and help us to think and act *more* logically.

"Now Don't Try to Reason with Me!" Rhetoric Today, Left, Right, and Center

Wayne C. Booth *You will recognize Wayne C. Booth as author of "The Rhetorical Stance." That essay, you will remember, was addressed to teachers of English; this one is addressed to students. You would find it enlightening to look for evidence of the effect of this shift in audience on Booth's own rhetorical stance. The real function of the essay here, however, is to help you explore with Booth the pervasive attitudes toward—or against—logic that surround us today. Your editors share Booth's concern with logic and rhetoric, a concern that amounts almost to a one-man crusade for Booth. By now some of the shrillness may have gone out of the rhetoric and the anti-logic of both left and right. But even a quick look at publications and speeches of either will show you that the basic attitude toward logic is unchanged, that it may be even more disturbing by being less shrill. Certainly* Time *and the other weekly news magazines have not changed, though one would hardly ever have called them shrill. During the late sixties it sometimes looked as though Marshall McLuhan were going to overwhelm the academic world with his anti- or pre-logical emphases. We hear much less of him today. But the attitudes Booth analyzes are still very much with us. As you read, try to decide to what extent Booth's main purpose in the essay is to attack and expose such attitudes and the resulting rhetoric.*

I

When I began teaching English twenty years ago, I saw myself as taking up the weapons of reason against a world committed to emotionalism, illogical appeals, and rhetorical trickery—a world full of vicious advertisers and propagandists who were determined to corrupt the young minds I was determined to save. Now, as a professor of rhetoric and dean of a liberal arts college, I may seem still to present myself in the same melodramatic light: the valiant champion of rationality against the forces of darkness. But bravely as I may try to hold my pose, both the world and the reasonings of men look more complicated than they did twenty years ago. Even as I turn my weapons on the enemies of reason, you will catch me revealing that I am not quite sure who they are, or whether I am qualified to challenge them.

But let me at least begin boldly, with a defense of reason that implies more clarity than I feel about how men ought to proceed when they set out to change each other's minds. The defense begins, quite properly, with the claim that we are in a time of intellectual crisis, a time when confidence in reason is so low that most men no longer try to provide good reasons for what they believe. Of course the very question of what constitutes a good reason is itself under debate, now as always—and I shall be returning to it later. But suppose we begin with the simple notion of proof—the presentation of evidence and arguments in a causal chain intended to pull the mind toward belief.

When we consider how much time teachers spend insisting that students exhibit genuine arguments in their papers, it is perhaps surprising to find the very notion that such forms of proof are desirable, or even obtainable, largely ignored in our public discourse. The simple painful task of putting ideas together logically, so that they track or follow each other, doesn't seem to appeal to many of us any more. I once heard Professor George Williamson of our English department explaining his standards for accepting articles for *Modern Philology*. "Considering the level of argument in the stuff that comes in, I can't really insist on anything that could be called a 'standard,' " he lamented. "I'm happy if I can find essays which show *some* kind of connection between the conclusions and the evidence offered."

You don't have to read much of what passes for literary criticism, or political argument, or social analysis, to conclude that the attention of most authors has not been primarily, or even secondarily, on constructing arguments that would stand up under close scrutiny. Leslie Fiedler spoke at Chicago a couple of years ago and said that the younger generation is really imitating Negro culture, and that the cultural warfare between what he calls palefaces and redskins accounts for our literature today. I protested to a student afterward that Fiedler had offered no evidence, no proof. "That doesn't matter," the student replied, "because it was so interesting."

But it is not simply that our practice is sloppy: open mistrust of rational argument is in the air. The first really modern form of this mistrust was Freud's claim that our conscious efforts at systematic thought are mere superstructures for the fundamental processes which are pre- or sub-logical. But Freud's own attack is, by recent standards, radically tainted with a faith in reason and logical argument. Norman O. Brown, one of the most widely quoted speculative anti-thinkers of the sixties, attacks psychoanalysis for relying on logical processes that alienate us from the realities of selfhood which, he says, are the only truths that we should care about. "The reality-principle," Brown says, "the light by which psychoanalysis has set its course, is a false boundary drawn between inside and outside, subject and object, real and imaginary, physical and mental. It gives us the divided world, the split or schizoid world." The psychoanalyst is, in Brown's view, simply using reason as a defense against the truths which can be found only by realizing the "surrealist" forces that lie too deep for reason.

Marshall McLuhan is an even better-known source of attacks on the intellect—or at least on that part of it that he calls "linear reasoning." Like Brown, McLuhan admits that most of our scientific, technological, and economic life depends on the linear thinking that was brought to its perfection with the invention of printing. But he says that the price we have paid for our "phonetic alphabet" is the diminished functioning of our senses of sound, touch, and taste. "Consciousness is not a verbal process," McLuhan says, with that blissful faith in half-truths which frequently illustrates his own theses. "Yet during all our centuries of phonetic literacy we have favored the chain of inference as the mark of logic and reason. In Western literate society it is still plausible and acceptable to say that something follows from something, as if there were some cause at work that makes such a sequence." McLuhan reminds us that Hume and Kant—or so he believes—both recognized that nothing ever *follows* as effect from something else as cause. Unfortunately, however, neither Hume nor Kant went far enough, McLuhan says, because they did not recognize that what had mislead Western man into thinking that reasoning could be linear was the alphabet and printing!

The attack on "mere logic" in the name of intuitive truths that are deeper, more profound, and not amenable to logical testing is by no means a new thing in the world. Everyone who has ever really thought about it, from Plato to the present, has known that logic is by itself at best a weak though necessary tool—a tool that can be used by the devil as well as by angels. But if you read closely in McLuhan, Brown, and many others in recent years, you find that they are expressing a dissatisfaction with reason that goes far beyond a simple mistrust of logic or linear thinking. At its extreme it is a repudiation of anything that deserves the name "thought" at all, in favor of feeling or of the "wisdom of the body."

One of the most seductive expressions of this spirit is the development of what one might call the anti-essay. The word *essay* used to mean "an effort to try out," an attempt. One "essayed" to deal with a topic adequately. Today we have the anti-essay which is a non-attempt. Listen to how Susan Sontag introduces her famous non-essay into the regions of "camp":

> To snare a sensibility in words, especially one that is alive and powerful, one must be tentative and nimble. The form of jottings, rather than an essay (with its claim to a linear, consecutive argument), seemed more appropriate for getting down something of this particular fugitive sensibility. It's embarrassing to be solemn and treatise-like about Camp. One runs the risk of having, oneself, produced a very inferior piece of Camp.

We have grown used to such demurrers and to the kind of disjointed and self-contradictory "notes" she then offers: these are the marks, we tell ourselves, of a "nimble" mind. Surely it is not fair to ask whether the effort to grapple with the notion of Camp is really more difficult than the efforts of Plato and Hume and Kant to "snare" matters like justice and human understanding and the aesthetic order. But fair or not, the suspicion will not down: Miss Sontag simply has not done as much for us as she could have done by repudiating the fashion for non-attempts and pushing herself to some old-fashioned linear thought about how her genuinely clever "notes" relate to each other. She is capable of such thought; I have seen her do it. Why, then, should she deprive us of it?

But the truth is that Miss Sontag is coherence itself by comparison with some of her elders. If you want an interesting exercise in futility, just try sometime to construct an outline of one of McLuhan's chapters. As Edgar Friedenberg says of both Brown and McLuhan, their style "honestly derives from and expresses" their point of view.

I must confess that when I read what passes for argument in these attacks on traditional modes of arguing, I experience a succession of body blows that I'm sure would please these folks immensely. They would argue that my being offended by incoherence results from my bad upbringing: I am a product of an education oriented to print, to the visual, to the organized, the sequential, the analytical, the linear. They may be right. Some of us professors would no doubt be less ashamed if caught beating our wives than if caught in a logical fallacy. McLuhan would tell us all to stop worrying and relax: the time of linear thought, the time when "rational" meant "uniform and continuous and sequential," is over. We have entered a time of "creative configuration and structure," whatever that is, a time of the "inclusive form of the icon," a time when "the medium is the message," a time when what we say no longer matters but only how we say it.

Now I know that I'm being slightly unfair to McLuhan (though I think only slightly). On his descriptive side, as he points to what is happening to our minds under the non-verbal onslaught of the mass media, he is doing part of what must be done. The trouble—aside from his seeming pleasure in his *own* incoherence—is that in most of his recent utterances he seems to have stopped worrying about the loss of our traditional powers of reason. He says, in fact, that the new media, as "extensions of man," are capable of revealing synthetic, simultaneous truths perhaps more important than the old analytical hogwash. What I would want to insist on is that, even though the older forms of rationality are obviously limited, our need for them is as great as ever. To gloss over our need for defenses against irrationality with such phrases as "the medium is the message" is to sell out a major part of our humanity—even if the claim to bring to light neglected abilities proves justified.

II

Suppose we look at a bit of irrational message-mongering, done by one of the "new media," to see if we can be satisfied with saying that the content no longer matters. Everyone knows that journalism has been transformed in recent years, especially in the news magazines, from reportage into new forms of paralogical rhetoric: political argument disguised as dramatic reporting. It would be fun to spend the rest of my hour simply describing the new rhetorical devices, and the new twists on old devices, that *Time* magazine, only the most successful of many, exhibits from week to week, all in the name of news. Mr. Ralph Ingersoll, former publisher of the magazine, has described the key to the magazine's success as the discovery of how to turn news into fiction, giving each story its own literary form, with a beginning, a middle, and an end, regardless of whether the story thus invented matches the original event. Everyone I know who has ever been treated by *Time*—whether favorably or unfavorably—has been shocked by the distortions of fact for effect, and the more they know about a subject the more they are shocked. A doctor friend at the University says one cannot trust the medical reporting. Eric Bentley, the drama critic, says they cannot be trusted about drama. Igor Stravinsky says, "Every music column I have read in *Time* has been distorted and inaccurate." [1]

More important to us than all of this testimony is the *way* the distortions operate. Though much of the distortion is simply for the sake of

[1] As I read proof in May, 1970, I have an impression that *Time* has been somewhat improved lately. Am I simply reacting to the attacks on the "media" by Vice President Agnew? And to the fact that lately *Time*'s surreptitious editorializing is often employed against presidential policies and methods that I, too, deplore?

being interesting, much of it is done to put across political and social viewpoints. I open an issue of *Time* at random to an attack on *Ramparts* magazine. It is of course not called an attack. It is made to look like a regular news account, objective, olympian. But it is a highly loaded attack, nevertheless. What troubles *Time* about *Ramparts,* amusingly enough, is that "*Ramparts* is slick enough to lure the unwary and bedazzled reader into accepting flimflam as fact"—a description which I would take as fitting *Time* exactly. "No other left-wing publication in the United States," *Time* says, "pursues shock more relentlessly or plays around more with fact." Now you may think, for a moment, that *Time* added that adjective "left-wing" in order to add one more charge to six other charges of leftism skilfully planted (to use a favorite *Time* word) in the account. But I prefer to think that *Time* is being unusually honest: by confining the competition for fact-distortion to left-wing magazines, *Time* has considerately ruled itself out of the running.

It is always instructive to follow *Time*'s shenanigans closely. Ask yourself, for example, how you would headline the following quotation, if you worked for *Time:* " 'Quite frankly,' says Hinckle, the publisher of *Ramparts,* 'there weren't enough Catholic laymen [we soon discovered] to write for and to buy the magazine. Besides, we got bored with just the church.' " Now think of a headline. Isn't it obvious? Your headline for this section will be "Bored With The Church." And that, of course, is the headline used, with an important shift in meaning.

Let's go on with the game. How would you describe where *Ramparts* is published? Where else but in "one of those topless streets in San Francisco's New Left Bohemia." What kind of humor does *Ramparts* publish? "Clever if sophomoric humor"—clever, or there would be no threat, sophomoric, or it might really be funny. How would you describe an article in *Ramparts* purporting to show that one million children have been killed or wounded in the Vietnam war? Could you do better than this: *Ramparts* "produced a mere juggling of highly dubious statistics." How would you describe the pictures of dead or wounded children? Why naturally as "a collection of very touching pictures, some of which could have been taken in any distressed country."

Time is, of course, only one example of a kind of nonrational persuasion that is practiced on us all the time, and *Ramparts* is also guilty of the disguised and dishonest rhetoric I am describing. Another good instance of this same kind of transformation of journalism into degraded rhetoric is *Fact,* the magazine from which I collected, perhaps somewhat naively, some of the testimony I earlier used against *Time.* I originally subscribed to *Fact* on the basis of a one-paragraph ad in the *New York Times;* it claimed that with so much editorializing in all other journals (that word "all" should have alerted me, perhaps) America needs a magazine devoted to objective reporting of the truth. I should have predicted what would come: a collection of shrill exposés, most of them with a touch of scandal and few of them providing enough solid evidence or argument to allow a reader to know whether there was anything to them or not. "A Psychoanalytical Study of Baseball," "A Study of Wife-Swapping in California," an argument that Dag Hammarskjold was a psychotic who committed suicide (*could* be, one says, but not on the basis of *this* evidence), another argument that Goldwater has been declared insane by thousands of psychiatrists (yet if you look closely at the evidence here it turns out to mean, at most, far less than the headlines claim)[2]—why, it's as hard to read *Fact* as it is to read *Time!*

The important point is that McLuhan's current cheerful response to such corruptions of the media is not enough. (He used to be much less complacent; now he says that TV advertising is the greatest art of our time. Even allowing for self-protective ambiguity, *what happened?*) To say that the medium is the message is entirely inadequate when a definite message has been sneakingly and very powerfully conveyed by the medium. The content of *Time,* and of *Ramparts,* and of *Fact* is very important indeed, once we have dug it out of the seemingly neutral prose. The medium is *not* the message nor is it that exciting new kind of "iconic presentation" that enables us "to live mythically and integrally." Rather, it is that very old-fashioned kind of manipulation of rhetorical distortions, skillfully placed in non-McLuhanesque sequences designed to take us in. And if we are not to be taken in, we must learn now as in the past to think *through* the medium *to* the message, to think critically about that message, to ask what reasons if any have been given to support it. In short, we must do exactly what McLuhan deplores: continue to *think* in what he calls the old, fragmented space and time patterns of the pre-electric age.

What I have been trying to suggest, with these examples, is that we live in a world in which men show little esteem for logic, little respect for facts, no faith in anyone's ability to use thought or discourse to arrive at improved judgments, commitments, and first principles. The consequences that one would expect in such a world, when honesty of observation, care with logic, and subtlety with dialectic have declined, can of course be seen wherever men try to change each other's minds. What is left to rhetoric

[2] It was recently announced that Goldwater has won his libel suit against *Fact.* But of course in the four years since I wrote my preliminary verdict, the editor has gone on feeding his gulls—many of whom no doubt think of themselves as wise birds indeed.

when solid substantive argument is denied to it? Obviously only emotional appeal and appeal to the superior moral integrity and wisdom or cleverness of the rhetorician—what was formerly called "ethical appeal" (whether the appeal was moral or immoral). Emotional appeal and ethical appeal can never be expelled from the house of rhetoric; all the great rhetoricians are passionate in their rationalism. But when men are reduced to using these properly subordinate appeals as if they were the sole means of persuasion, they produce the kind of rhetoric that we now find flowing at us, left, right, and center.

I have time only for two examples. They both will seem extreme and therefore unrepresentative to some of you, but the test is that they have apparently been effective on large numbers of Americans. Can you recognize who is speaking in the first quotation?

> I can see a day when all the Americas, North and South, will be linked in a mighty system, a system in which the errors and misunderstandings of the past will be submerged, one by one, in a rising tide of prosperity and interdependence. We know that the misunderstandings of centuries are not to be wiped away in a day or an hour. But we pledge that human sympathy—what our neighbors to the south call an attitude that is "simpatico"—no less than enlightened self-interest will be our guide. I can see this Atlantic civilization galvanizing and guiding emergent nations everywhere. Now I know that freedom is not the fruit of every soil. I know that our own freedom was achieved through centuries by the unremitting efforts of brave and wise men. And I know that the road to freedom is a long and challenging road. And I know also that some men may walk away from it, that some men resist challenge . . .

No doubt you have placed the speaker by now in a general way. His is a political rhetoric appropriate to the campaign trail, and his platitudes are mostly the platitudes of the conservative center: the combination of human sympathy and self-interest building an Atlantic civilization (God knows how!) and the appeals to freedom might be offered by any Democrat or Republican of slightly jingoist cast. Only with the move toward the vaguely ominous charge that some men *resist challenge* do we suspect that this may be a different kind of conservative; we are thus not really surprised at the concluding phrase:

> . . . accepting the false security of governmental paternalism.

The vapidities of a Goldwater, representing a nation that does not ask that its political candidates give reasons, are now clear! (I am not saying that only Goldwater could have written the passage, just that it is typical.)

Where on the left was I to find an equally revealing piece of bombast. It ought to be one that would make a few of my listeners mad—and a few more think. Obviously something by a student; obviously something from the new student left. Listen closely now to excerpts from a long "Letter to Undergraduates," by Bradford Cleaveland, former graduate student of the department of political science at Berkeley; it was written during the troubles of '64–'65.

> Dear Undergraduates, . . . On the one hand there [is] substantial agreement that the University stamps out consciousness like a super-Madison Avenue machine; on the other, people [are] saying, "So what?" or "Bring me a detailed and exhaustive plan." *But there is no plan for kicking twenty thousand people IN THEIR ASSES!* No plan will stop excessive greed, timidity, and selling out. At best the university is a pathway to the club of "tough-minded-liberal-realists" in America, who sit in comfortable armchairs talking radical while clutching hysterically at respectability in a world explosive with revolution. At worst the university destroys your desire to see reality and to suffer reality with optimism, at the time when you most need to learn that painful art. . . .
>
> . . . The first set of facts [is that in your undergraduate program] you are puppets. You perform. But when do you think? Dutifully and obediently you follow, as a herd of grade-worshiping sheep. If you are strong at all, you do this with some sense of shame, or if you are weak, you do it with a studied cynicism . . . as jaded youth with parched imaginations that go no further than oak-paneled rooms at the end of the line . . . BUT WHETHER YOU ARE STRONG OR WEAK YOU PERFORM LIKE TRAINED SEALS, AND LIKE SHEEP YOU FOLLOW . . . WITH THE THOROUGHBRED PHI BETA KAPPA SHEEP LEADING YOU! ! ! up the golden stairway to the omnipotent A, to the Happy consciousness, to success and a very parochial mind.
>
> [The second set of facts is that the Charter Day is an unmerciful sham; an example of unparalleled demagoguery.]

Having elaborated these two sets of facts, which were of course not facts at all but deeply personal judgments, Mr. Cleaveland then moved to his clincher:

> Dear Undergraduates!! I am no longer interested in cajoling you, arguing with you, or describing to you something you already know. I . . . entreat you to furiously throw your comforting feelings to duty and responsibility for this institution to the winds and act on your

> situation. . . . There is only one proper response to Berkeley from undergraduates: that you *organize and split this campus wide open!* From this point on, do not misunderstand me, my intention is to convince you that you do nothing less than begin an open, fierce, and thoroughgoing rebellion on this campus.

My point here is not to argue that Mr. Cleaveland was right or wrong in urging revolution. What interests me is the kind of reasons he felt were adequate to persuade undergraduates to strike against the university. The notion that thousands of highly selected American undergraduates should find this sort of thing appealing ought to frighten us all. Indeed, there is a kind of contempt for the intellect and its efforts running throughout the literature of the Berkeley revolt—and through other literature of the new left—which seems to me far more threatening to the future of the American left itself than has been generally recognized. When the left stops thinking, we should all know by now, it becomes as destructive of human values as the unthinking right—and I must say that there is a tone in much of this literature which suggests that thinking is itself a suspect activity. Cleaveland is fond of using the word "scholars" in quotation marks: he talks of "scholars" and "so-called liberals" who adopt "the hideous posture of studying" or analyzing the "problem."

Now I cannot really prove that these two rather special examples are in any way representative of right and left, or that their similar tendency to shout and chant rather than reason is representative of American rhetoric today. But I suspect that you have found, in your daily reading, enough that is like these two to bear out my hunch that there really is a predominance of irrational persuasion at work here. You may, in fact, have concluded—subjected to so much slick advertising and political propaganda as you are—that this is all there is to rhetoric, that in fact men cannot persuade each other rationally in such matters since, in matters of judgment and action, all choices are equally irrational.

And of course this is precisely why everyone in any academic community should be deeply disturbed whenever the Goldwaters and the Cleavelands begin to attract large numbers of listeners. We claim to be committed to free and honest and relentless inquiry. This almost everyone takes for granted; only a few on the extreme right and the extreme left have questioned this basic commitment of colleges and universities. What is not so frequently recognized is that the very notion of free inquiry depends on the possibility of valid, genuinely justified persuasion—that is, of a rhetoric not like Goldwater's and Cleaveland's but rather a rhetoric built on the use of reason to persuade men to believe one proposition—a true proposition—rather than another, a false or less adequate proposition.

III

My point is not, as I'm sure you realize by now, to indict either the left or the right, but to plead for what I take to be the very fragile twin values of honest inquiry and honest rhetoric. I have said so far that these values are under steady attack, both in theory and in practice, by men of both left and right—some of them presumably sincere, some of them no doubt knaves. Wherever men find themselves too impatient to think together about their problems, wherever immediate action based on "unity" becomes more important than men's determination to achieve genuine unity by discovering the truth together, my twin values disappear—often never to reappear in a particular society. They *always* risk annihilation in a major war, and it is not surprising that the Vietnam war, which seems to most of us self-evidently a horrible national disaster and which to many Americans seems self-evidently a righteous crusade, should have led us to shout rather than reason. My twin values disappear in any society whenever enough men decide that victory is worth whatever it costs. They disappear whenever men decide, as Bradford Cleaveland decided in California, that there is "only one proper response" to a political situation—the effort to destroy the opponent through force or political pressure. (I would not want to suggest that these twin values are the only values for mankind, or that I would never be willing to risk them for other values. Though it is fairly easy to show historically that most revolutionary efforts work more harm than good, I can think of situations when I would be forced to stop thinking and talking and start overthrowing: Nazi Germany, say, or *perhaps* Boston in 1775—but note how many of our revolutionaries managed to go on thinking as well as fighting. It is clear that the force of my plea for more reason and less shouting depends in part on my conviction that we are not yet in such an extreme situation. If you really believe that the only action possible in America is to choose one of two sides and then use violence to win, we may as well close the College and load our weapons.)

It is important to recognize that none of the attacks on reason—either theoretical or in the form of shapeless writing or biased reporting or open invitation to riot—none has pretended that reason is ineffective in dealing with practical, prudential affairs. Everyone admits that reason has produced fantastic results in science and technology. The protests seem, often enough, to be against the very success of rational calculation in the hands of statisticians, logicians, computer analysts, or army officers, when applied to human affairs without starting from humane premises. Atomic bombs and doomsday machines and calculations of overkill all seem to show what happens when reason is left to its own devices without the control of—of what?

Traditionally the answer might have been "the control of reason itself." Reason did not, in earlier centuries, mean simply logical calculation but rather the whole process of discovering sound first principles and *then* reasoning from them to sound conclusions. What seems distinctive in our time is the widespread conviction that our choice of first principles is itself irrational or capricious. Most teachers and students I talk with seem to have concluded that the choice of one's starting point is always an arbitrary act of faith, and that to debate about such choices is a mark of immaturity. After all, we have been shown in so many different ways that even in the physical sciences hypotheses are discovered intuitively; that the first principles are not subject to proof; that even the most seemingly objective knowledge is, as Michael Polanyi says, "*personal* knowledge"—infused with personal meanings and values and thus not really what we ordinarily mean by objective at all. Though most professional philosophers now as in all times are not relativists, the predominant lay philosophy is, I would say, a kind of relativism. Men make their own values; values change from society to society, and even from group to group within a society—"How can one reason about such things?" we seem to say to each other. It is not hard, in fact, to see why McLuhan and Brown and others feel that they must speak, even if in a distorted form, for truths that lie beyond reason.

The first part of my title comes from a *New Yorker* cartoon which showed a woman, quarreling with her husband, saying: "Now don't try to *reason* with me." The cartoon reflects, it seems to me, one of our attitudes toward reason. It is of course a male cartoon, and it betrays first of all the American male's traditional contempt for the female's unreasonableness. To be reasonable has in our folklore been the male's prerogative, one sign of his superiority. In this view, reason is of course a good thing to have; to be irrational, "like a woman," is somehow funny. But it is not hard to develop a different view of the cartoon; to think oneself into "the woman's point of view" and imagine how a brutal and irrelevant logical argument can cover up or violate fundamental needs or feelings while seeming to have all of the right on its side.

Man was traditionally known as the rational animal; in that view reason was of man's very essence. But it takes no great learning to remind us that much that we think of as distinctively human—love, poetry, martyrdom—can present itself in forms that seem to violate reason—or perhaps to transcend it. We can all quote Pascal, who said that the heart can be turned on by reasons that reason cannot dig—or words to that effect. Tertullian is supposed to have said that he embraced his religious belief just *because* it was absurd. In the last several centuries, many have seen man's peculiar humanity not in his rationality, not in the common grounds of truth and right action that reason leads to, but rather in his capacity for individual freedom, whether rational or mad. For them, the act of freely choosing an error or falsehood confers greater human dignity than the act of passively accepting that which reason seems to require and which many men consequently believe. Stephen Dedalus, in Joyce's *Portrait of the Artist as a Young Man,* is by no means the only literary portrait of a soul electing what he believes may be eternal damnation for the sake of doing things his own way, according to his own feelings. The romantic soul has for at least two centuries been shouting defiance at traditional reasonings, though one should hasten to add that the relation between reason and romanticism is laden with the same ambiguities as are our attitudes toward the coldly rational male and the weakly intuitive female: if the romantic hero can be portrayed as a representative of individualism gone mad, seeking what in modern jargon we might call a personalized truth which to everyone else will be damnable falsehood, he can also be portrayed in Faustian terms, as the man who is willing to violate intuition, love, and the value of religious faith and salvation all for the sake of knowledge—that is, for what reason reveals.

In either view, somehow, the Garden of Eden is threatened by man's quest for knowledge—not just knowledge of good and evil, but the whole search for intellectual mastery. A life led according to what the mind can test and prove seems somehow to threaten much that all of us hold dear. The young student who is impatient with the cautious weighings and probings and refusals of commitment that go on within every university is plainly in one great tradition of a mistrust of reason that all of us must feel at one time or another. Men are starving throughout the world; men's souls are being destroyed in Harlem and Mississippi; children are being bombed in Vietnam—and here you sit, training your intellects to savor the pleasures of art and literature and elegant argument!

IV

So you see, we can make the emphasis fall either way: attacks on reason are vicious because reason, properly defined, is our most precious gift; or attacks on reason are needed, because no matter how you define a "reasonable life" much of what is most valued by men is left out. As a university professor I am committed to the supreme professional standard of rationality: insofar as I am an honest professor, worthy of my own respect, I am sworn to change my mind if and when someone shows me that there are *good reasons* to change my mind. But both as a man who loves art and literature that I cannot fully explain, and as a human being who holds to many values the correctness of which I cannot easily prove with unanswerable rational arguments, I know how much of my life is not readily explicable at the court of what is usually called reason.

The question is whether reasonable debate is in *any* degree possible about such basic commitments, political and moral and personal. What we call rhetoric is usually used only when scientific proof is not available—about such matters as whether to oppose or support the Vietnam policy, or whether to join a church or commit suicide, or whether to vote for Goldwater or join a strike against the University of California. Can such questions be debated rationally, or do we have available only those forms of persuasion used by Goldwater and Cleaveland—emotional appeals and appeals to the character of the speaker or references to the enemy's viciousness?

Though I have no time to undertake the difficult argument such a question demands, I should like to suggest that in losing our confidence in the possibility of finding genuinely good reasons for important human actions, in losing our belief in a reasonable rhetoric, we have laid ourselves open to the kinds of perverted rhetoric I have described. My main point is to argue that we must preserve and extend our capacity for a rational persuasion about the most important questions. If we don't, liberal education in any meaningful sense will die, leaving us at the mercy of propagandists and protected only by the superficial slogans of the propaganda analysts.

What has happened, I am convinced, is that we have fallen victims to an all-or-nothing kind of argument that we should be ashamed of. Of course we cannot find, in social and political and ethical questions, the degrees of certainty in proof that scientists—at least some of them—boast of. But does this mean that we are reduced to emotional appeal, shouting, lying, trickery, and ultimately, warfare? That it does not is in itself a conclusion to be proved with the kind of proof that is in question—and the intellectual problems are not simple. For now, perhaps you will be willing simply to record one man's strong conviction that a reasonable persuasion is not only possible but indispensable if we are to live well together.

Whatever such a rhetoric might be, it will not be a dry, unemotional kind of argument for the middle of the road. To believe in reason doesn't mean that one believes only in reason—one might recognize the truths of the heart without having to launch an attack on the head. The trouble with our present situation is that the defenders of logicality or rationality seem too often to be men who want to reason only about the means to unquestioned ends—they would "rationalize" society, make us efficient, lead us to social usefulness, rather than try to humanize us. This leaves the defenders of the heart to operate in a whirlwind of emotions, convinced that to be reasonable is somehow to be cold and calculating. Well, there *are* some causes worth dying for, and there are many causes not worth a hoot. I will not die for a cause unless I feel deeply about it. Imagine Churchill using only a chain of syllogisms trying to persuade the British to fight. But on the other hand I cannot distinguish the good causes from the circus acts unless I have learned to think about them, and the good rhetorician will, like Churchill during the war, show me by his arguments as well as by his character that he is on the right side.

V

We should be quite clear about what all this means to us. If we cannot find a defense of reason that makes of it something more than a useful weapon in the arsenal of each warring faction, if there is not some sense in which men can reason together about even their most precious commitment, if basic faiths and loves and first principles are entirely arbitrary and hence beyond discussion, then we may as well succumb to the McLuhanesque glow, or to the polymorphous perverse pleasures offered by Brown, or to the revolutionary inanities of Cleaveland. And, incidentally, we English teachers are on very shaky ground when we scribble in the margin "logic bad here" or "not clear how these propositions relate." We are on shaky ground in teaching *composition* at all. Who cares, after all, whether the logic is bad or good unless the conclusions that good writing might persuade to are in some sense superior to the conclusions produced by bad writing? But this can be true only if some first principles are themselves superior to others, only if they are in some sense *demonstrably* superior.

Plato said that the worst fate that can befall a man is to become a misologist, a hater of reason; for him it was clear that since man is essentially reasonable, when he ceases to reason he ceases to be a man. I happen to believe this unfashionable doctrine—assuming the broad definition of reason that I have been implying here. I also believe that when any society loses its capacity to debate its ends and means rationally, it ceases to be a society of men at all and becomes instead a mob, or pack, or a herd of creatures rather less noble than most animals. In America in recent years we have seen far too many such herds—self-righteous fanatics who know without listening that the speaker is wrong. There are many of our universities, so-called, where Karl Marx, say, or Miss Aptheker would be booed from the platform, even if the administration were to allow them to speak. And on the other hand there have been some disturbing instances lately of left-wing students in first-class universities coercing a speaker into silence. Whatever defenses may be offered for such rhetoric—the rhetoric of shouting a man down—it is not the rhetoric of a student, and those shouting mobs are not students, no matter what else they may be. It is one mark of an honest man, as it should be the mark of an educated man, that he tries not to use a double standard in judging his friends and his enemies. Self-righteous bullying fanatics are self-righteous bullying fanatics regardless of the cause they support, and they are as much a threat to the central values we defend when they bully on our side as when they bully on our enemy's. Men—at least some men—aspire to a life of sweet reasonableness, but all men seem engaged in a verbal warfare that leaves them perpetually teetering on the brink of actual warfare, local, national, and international. Our hold on reason is precarious; our institutions for giving it a chance are highly fragile. The very tradition out of which I speak of a rational rhetoric is itself fragile. It would not really be surprising if fifty years from now no one in America would even know what I'm talking about tonight—such a transformation would not be greater than many that history has known. Men in that time would know something that most of you do *not* know—what it *feels* like not to be *allowed* to follow a thought wherever it might lead, openly, publicly. Whether we move toward that genuine garrison state, that really total institutionalization of the mind, will depend in part, in very small but very real part, on how many of us here can manage—not in sermons like this, which are easy superficial substitutes for the day-by-day thinking that counts, but in our life as teachers and students—to reason together about what we care for most.

Questions

1. Considering Booth's rhetorical stance, especially his audience, why should he begin by presenting himself in a "melodramatic light"? How would you as a student respond to a professor introducing himself thus? Consider, as you formulate your answer, that this was a time of great tension between faculty and students, and especially between administration and students. Also note especially the last paragraph in part III of the essay.
2. Booth obviously expects his audience to find something wrong with the student's reply that it doesn't matter that Fiedler had presented no evidence: "That doesn't matter, because it was so interesting." How would you respond to the student?
3. Marshall McLuhan's thesis that "the medium is the message" may not make much sense to you. Perhaps McLuhan doesn't want it to. But Booth's analysis should help. Perhaps the "is" overstates it. More *logically* he might say that the medium is more important than the message, that the fact that we get our messages from books or from TV is more important than the messages themselves. Hence that linear reasoning follows from linear type is the crucial thing about printing. Would nonlogic follow from TV, the movies, and other audio-visual media? Why should McLuhan have become

so popular so rapidly? Would the apparent decline in that popularity result from his lack of logic? Think this through carefully.

4. If the left and right are both bad, by Booth's logic—and title—is the center good? His real subject for attack is the rhetoric, but he is open enough about his distaste for the political and intellectual positions at either extreme. In what ways does this openness support or undercut Booth's argument? Does "center" have primarily political intent as the essay develops? Note his comments in part IV about "a dry, unemotional kind of argument for the middle of the road."
5. The preceding question should lead you to an analysis of Booth's organization. Since he is committed to linear logic, you should have little trouble following the five parts of his analysis. Try making an outline.
6. To what extent does Booth weaken or strengthen his argument by admitting in part III the claims of the irrational and intuitive as against his own claims for logic? Note especially the final paragraph.
7. We talked, in our introduction to this section, of the "either-or fallacy" in logic. Note how much of Booth's essay turns on his identifying that fallacy in part IV: ". . . we have fallen victims of an all-or-nothing kind of argument that we should be ashamed of." Analyze carefully how he leads up to this.
8. Is Booth as persuasive in arguing for what he is for as he is in arguing against what he is against? This is not an easy question. Look carefully at part V.

Suggestions for Writing

1. Find an article in *Time* or one of the other weekly news magazines and analyze it as Booth has done. His approach should give you a useful guide. Then respond to what you have found, using logic to either defend or condemn the methods.
2. We are hearing the first rumblings of discontent over the Sesame Street generation, complaints that these people as they grow up have short attention spans, respond only to the unusual or exciting, need to be entertained, and so forth. You might find it easier to respond to this assertion if you are a graduate of Sesame Street. Regardless, write a paper in which you analyze and respond to your growing up in a TV generation. Keep both McLuhan and Booth's response to McLuhan in mind as you write.

Are All Generalizations False?

Lionel Ruby *This essay is a chapter from a book on logic. It explores in detail some of the problems with generalizations that we have already looked at. You are probably aware from your own experience that most people tend to accept generalizations uncritically: it is comforting to know that something holds true for everything. That all of our enemies, for example, are vicious. That all referees are crooks—or blind. But if one is a skeptic, he tends to go to the other extreme, to distrust* all *generalizations. Hence Ruby's title. The essay begins with an analysis of the common overreaction of the skeptic, that all generalizations are false. But note that it moves from that to a reasoned analysis of the grounds on which we can—and must—accept and use generalizations, both as a basis for logic and as a practical guide to daily living. As you read, analyze carefully the relation between generalizations and "statistical statements." Are the logical problems the same for each? Do statistical statements also involve an inductive leap?*

We begin with a generalization: human beings are great generalizers. Every race has its proverbs, and proverbs are generalizations. "It never rains but it pours." "Faint heart never won fair lady." "Familiarity breeds contempt." Sometimes, of course, these proverbs are incompatible with each other, as in "Absence makes the heart grow fonder," and "Out of sight, out of mind." [1]

Listen attentively to those around you, and note the generalizations that float into every conversation: Europeans are lazy and shiftless. European girls make good wives. American girls are selfish. Politicians are crooks. Gentlemen prefer blondes. On a somewhat more "intellectual" level, we find: Liberals never think a matter through. Intellectuals always show a lack of practical judgment. Americans are idealists. Americans are

[1] Once translated by a foreign student as "invisible idiot."

materialists. All American men suffer from "mom-ism." Economics is bunk. Modern art is trash. Psychiatrists never bring up their own children properly. In the middle ages everyone was religious. And so on. After more of the same we may be tempted to agree with Justice Holmes that "the chief end of man is to frame general propositions, and no general proposition is worth a damn."

Our awareness of the inadequacy of "sweeping generalizations" may lead us to say that all generalizations are false. But this is truly a sweeping generalization! And worse: if it is true, then the witticism that "all generalizations are false, *including this one*" would appear to be justified. But this will not do either, for this generalization asserts that it itself is false, from which it follows that it is not the case that all generalizations are false. Or perhaps we should say that "all generalizations are half-truths—including this one"? But this is not much better. The fact of the matter is that some generalizations are true, others are false, and still others are uncertain or doubtful. The deadliness of this platitude may be forgiven because of its truth.

By a "generalization" is meant a general law or principle which is inferred from particular facts. As a sample of the way in which we arrive at such generalizations consider the following: Some years ago I visited France, and ate at a number of Parisian restaurants that had been recommended to me. The food was excellent in each. Then one day I was unable to get to any of my customary eating places. I ate in a small restaurant in an outlying district of Paris. The food was excellent. I then tried other restaurants, always with the same results. I ate in large restaurants, small restaurants, on ships and trains, and in railway station restaurants. I generalized: All French restaurants serve excellent meals.

A generalization is a statement that *goes beyond* what is actully observed, to a rule or law covering both the observed cases and those that have not as yet been observed. This going-beyond is called the "inductive leap." An inductive leap is a "leap in the dark," for the *generalization may not be true,* even though the *observations* on which it is based *are* true. Thus, somewhere in France there may be a poor French restaurant—happily I am ignorant of its location—but if so, then I should not say that *all* are good.[2]

A generalization involves an "inductive leap." The word *induction,* from Latin roots meaning "to lead in," means that we examine particular cases (French restaurants), and "lead in" to a generalization. Induction is the method we use when we learn lessons from our experience: we gen-

[2] Since writing this, unhappily, I have found several. But let us assume that the generalization is true.

eralize from particular cases. *Deduction,* on the other hand, refers to the process of "drawing out" the logical consequences of what we already know (or assume) to be true. By induction we learn that French cooking is delectable. If a friend tells us that he had tasteless meals while in Europe, then by deduction we know that he did not eat these meals in French restaurants. Both induction and deduction are essential characteristics of rational thinking.

A generalization is a statement of the form: "All A's are B's." "All" means exactly what it says: *all* without exception. A single exception overthrows a generalization of this kind. Before we proceed further we must first dispose of a popular confusion concerning the expression: "The exception proves the rule." This is a sensible statement when properly interpreted, but it is sometimes understood in a manner that makes it nonsense. If I say that "all A's are B's," a single exception will make my statement false. Now, suppose that someone says: "The fact that there is a poor French restaurant proves that *all* are good because *it* is an exception, and the exception proves the rule!" Does a wicked woman prove that all women are saints? The sensible interpretation of the expression, "The exception proves the rule" is this: When we *say* that a certain case *is* an "exception," we imply that there is a rule which generally holds. When a mother tells her daughter, "Have a good time at the prom, and, for tonight, you have my permission to stay out until 3 A.M.," she implies that this is an exception to the rule which requires earlier reporting. A statement that *creates* an exception implies a rule for all non-exceptional cases; but a generalization that is stated as a rule without exceptions (all A's are B's) would be overthrown by a single exception.

Scientific laws, stated in the form "All A's are B's," or some variation thereof, are never "violated." When an exception to a law is definitely established, the law in its previous form is abandoned, but it may be possible to revise it to exclude the "exception" as a special case because of special circumstances. The revised law: "All A's, under such and such conditions, are B's." Water freezes at 32° F. *at sea level.*

All too often "general propositions are not worth a damn," as Holmes remarked. This is because we generalize too hastily on the basis of insufficient evidence. The fallacy called the "hasty generalization" simply refers to the fact that we jump too quickly to conclusions concerning "all." For example, we see a woman driving carelessly, and generalize: "All women are poor drivers." We see a car weaving in and out of traffic, and note that it has a California license: "Wouldn't you know," we say. "A California driver. That's the way they all drive out there." Anita Loos' gay heroine thought the gentlemen preferred blondes because she was a blonde and men were attracted to her.

We learn that Napoleon got along on five hours of sleep. From this we may conclude that "five hours of sleep is all that anybody really needs." Our assumption is that what Napoleon could do, anybody can do, until we learn that we are not Napoleons. (If we don't learn this eventually, we aren't permitted to circulate freely.) The next example is undoubtedly the worst example of generalizing ever committed: A man declared that all Indians walk single file. When challenged for his evidence, he replied, "How do I know that? I once saw an Indian walk that way."

Hasty generalizing is perhaps the most important of popular vices in thinking. It is interesting to speculate on some of the reasons for this kind of bad thinking. One important factor is prejudice. If we are already prejudiced against unions, or businessmen, or lawyers, or doctors, or Jews, or Negroes, then one or two instances of bad conduct by members of these groups will give us the unshakable conviction that "they're all like that." It is very difficult for a prejudiced person to say, "Some are, and some aren't." A prejudice is a judgment formed *before* examining the evidence.

A psychological reason for asserting "wild" generalizations is exhibitionism: The exhibitionist desires to attract attention to himself. No one pays much attention to such undramatic statements as "Some women are fickle," or that some are liars, or "Some politicians are no better than they ought to be." But when one says that "all women are liars" this immediately attracts notice. Goethe once said that it is easy to appear brilliant if one respects nothing, not even the truth.

Let us avoid careless and hasty generalizing. The proverb warns us that one swallow does not make a summer. Unfortunately, we usually forget proverbs on the occasions when we ought to remember them. We ought to emulate "the Reverend" in Faulkner's novel, *The Hamlet*. He was discussing the efficacy of a rural remedy. "Do you know it will work, Reverend?" his friend asked. "I know it worked once," the Reverend answered. "Oh, then you have knowed it to fail?" "I never knowed it to be tried but once." The fault of bad generalizing, however, need not make us take refuge in the opposite error: the refusal to generalize. This error is illustrated in the anecdote concerning the student who wrote an essay on labor relations, in which he argued for equal pay for women. Women, he wrote, work hard, they need the money, they are the foundation of the family, and, above all, they are the mothers of most of the human race! There is another old anecdote about the cautious man whose friend pointed to a flock of sheep with the remark, "Those sheep seem to have been sheared recently." "Yes," said the cautious man, "at least on this side."

Generalizations are dangerous, but we must generalize. To quote Justice Holmes once more: he said that he welcomed "anything that will discourage men from believing general propositions." But, he added, he welcomed that "only less than he welcomed anything that would encourage men to make such propositions"! For generalizations are indispensable guides. One of the values of knowledge lies in its predictive power—its power to predict the future. Such knowledge is stated in generalizations. It is of little help to me to know that water froze at 32° F. yesterday unless this information serves as a warning to put anti-freeze in my car radiator before winter comes. History, in the "pure" sense of this term, merely tells us what has happened in the past, but science furnishes us with general laws, and general laws tell us what *always* happens under certain specified conditions.

Science is interested in the general, rather than in the particular or individual. When Newton saw an apple fall from a tree in his orchard—even if this story is a fable, and therefore false in a literal sense, it is true in its insight—he was not interested in the size and shape of the apple. Its fall suggested an abstract law to him, the law of gravity. He framed this law in general terms: Every particle of matter attracts every other particle of matter with a force directly proportional to the product of their masses and inversely proportional to the square of their distances. Chemists seek general laws concerning the behavior of matter. The physician wants to know the general characteristics of the disease called myxedema, so that when he has a case he will recognize it and know exactly how to treat it. The finding of general laws, then, is the aim of all science—including history insofar as it is a science.

The problem of the scientist is one of achieving sound generalizations. The scientist is careful not to make assertions which outrun his evidence, and he refuses to outtalk his information. He generalizes, but recognizes that no generalization can be more than probable, for we can never be certain that *all* the evidence is in, nor can the future be guaranteed absolutely—not even future eclipses of the sun and moon. But the scientist knows that certain laws have a very high degree of probability.

Let us look at the logic involved in forming sound generalizations. The number of cases investigated in the course of formulating a scientific law is a factor in establishing the truth of the law, but it is by no means the most important one. Obviously, if we observed one hundred swans, all of which are white, our generalization that "all swans are white" does not have the same probability it would have if we observed one thousand swans. But no matter how great the number of specimens involved in this type of observation, no more than a moderately high degree of probability is ever established. Countless numbers of white swans were observed throughout the ages (without any exceptions) and then in the nineteenth century black swans were observed in Australia.

The weakness of the method of "induction by simple enumeration of cases" is amusingly illustrated by Bertrand Russell's parable in his *A History of Western Philosophy:*

> There was once upon a time a census officer who had to record the names of all householders in a certain Welsh village. The first that he questioned was called William Williams; so were the second, third, fourth. . . . At last he said to himself: "This is tedious; evidently they are all called William Williams. I shall put them down so and take a holiday." But he was wrong; there was just one whose name was John Jones.

Scientific generalizations based on other types of evidence than simple enumeration often acquire a much higher degree of probability after only a few observations. When a chemist finds that pure sulphur melts at 125° C., in an experiment in which every factor is accurately analyzed and controlled, the law concerning the melting point of sulphur achieves as great a degree of certainty as is humanly attainable. Accurate control of every element of one case, then, is more important in establishing probabilities than is *mere enumeration* of many cases.

A single carefully controlled experiment, such as the sulphur experiment, can give us a much higher degree of probability than the mere observation of thousands of swans. The reason is that we also know that no chemical element thus far observed has a variable melting point under conditions of constant pressure. The chemical law is thus consistent with and is borne out by the rest of chemical knowledge, whereas the "law" holding that all swans are white was based on an "accidental" factor. Or consider the generalization concerning the mortality of mankind. This law is based not merely on the fact that countless numbers of human beings have died in the past, but also on the fact that all living beings must, by reason of physiological limitations, die; and that all matter wears out in time. So the harmony of a particular generalization with the rest of our knowledge is also a factor in giving it a high degree of probability.

So much for the logical analysis of generalizations. Thus far, we have been concerned with "uniform" generalizations, which take the form: "All A's are B's." A generalization, we have seen, is a statement that says something about "all" of a group, the evidence consisting of observations of items in which we always find a single characteristic. The observed cases are taken as a *sample* of the whole group or population with which we are concerned. We observe a number of swans, and take these as a sample of all swans, past, present, and future. We find that all are white, and make the inductive leap: Swans are always white, everywhere.

We shall now examine "statistical" statements. Statistical statements give us information not about characteristics possessed by *all* of a group or population, but by a definite proportion (or most) of the group or population, as when we say, "Most A's are B's," or "Sixty-five per cent of all A's are B's." The first thing to note here is that statistical statements may in fact be *generalizations,* and thus involve the notion of "all." This point involves very important (and common) misunderstandings.

In order to make this point clear, let us re-interpret our "uniform" generalizations. We say: "The sample is so-and-so (all observed swans are uniformly white)—*therefore,* the whole population of swans is uniformly white." Now, we do the same sort of thing in statistical generalizations. We say: "In the sample of red-heads we examined, fifty-three per cent were hot-tempered—therefore, fifty-three per cent of *all* red-heads are hot-tempered." (Or: fifty-three per cent of the whole population of red-heads is hot-tempered.) Logically, both examples, uniform and statistical, are of the same type, for in each we make the inductive leap from the sample to the whole population. The only difference between them is that in the one case we assert a *uniform* character in the whole population; in the other we assert that a characteristic holds in a certain *proportion* in the whole population.

This fundamental point will help us to evaluate the degree of probability of a statistical generalization. We saw earlier that uniform generalizations can never be absolutely certain—though for practical purposes we often consider them so, especially in the physical sciences. The probability of a generalization depends especially on the *quality* and also on the *quantity* of the cases that constitute the sample. The same holds for statistical generalizations, which may have a high probability, depending on the character of the evidence. Though the inductive leap is involved in all generalizations, in some cases the leap is justified. Let us examine the criteria of justification for the leap.

Before we proceed we shall discuss an important distinction: that between the sample and the inference we draw from it. It is one thing to describe a sample accurately; quite another to draw an accurate inference. If I say, "I have observed ten swans (the sample) and all were white," we may assume that the sample is accurately described. But if I now go on to generalize (that is, draw the inference) concerning *all* swans, my inference may not be a good one. A generalization always involves a "leap in the dark," sometimes justified and sometimes not. Similarly, if I say, "I have talked to ten friends concerning their income, and six [sixty per cent] told me that they earned more than $10,000 a year," the description of the sample may be accepted as true. But suppose I now go on to make the following inference: "Therefore, sixty per cent of all Americans earn more than $10,000 a year." This would be a hasty generalization indeed.

We distinguish, then, between the sample and the inference. A statistical statement concerning the sample is purely descriptive. The book *They Went to College* is a statistical study of the incomes, as of 1947, of 9,064 college graduates. The averages that were given may be of historical interest. Fifty-three per cent were in business, sixteen per cent were doctors, lawyers or dentists, sixteen per cent were teachers. The doctors earned the most: over half making more than $7,500 a year. Teachers and preachers earned the least: median income $3,584. Now, these averages involve no inferences. They simply describe the actual facts *in the sample.* We draw an inference, on the other hand, when we assume that the whole population of six million college graduates in 1947 would have shown the same kinds of averages as the sample. In our discussion, henceforth, we shall be concerned only with the logical problems involved in statistical inferences.

Suppose that a public opinion poll was recently taken. The polling organization tells us that fifty-eight per cent of the American people approve of the record of the present administration in Washington. How do they know this? Let us examine the evidence on which this finding is based. Obviously not everyone was consulted. A sample was taken. There were three thousand interviews. Since there are approximately one hundred and twenty million adults in the United States, each individual in this sample is taken as representative of forty thousand adults. Further, in the sample, one thousand persons said that they had "no opinion." Eleven hundred and sixty said that they "approved," and eight hundred and forty said they did not. Thus fifty-eight per cent of those with opinions approved, and this means, we are told, that nearly seventy million Americans approve. The pollsters assume that the undecided individuals will probably divide in the same proportion as the others when they make up their minds.

Now, we are not raising any questions concerning the truth of the report made of the sample. But is the inductive leap from the sample to the generalization concerning one hundred and twenty million people justified? It may be. It all depends upon the reliability of the sample. What makes a sample reliable? It must be *fair, unbiased,* and *representative* of the whole. But the crucial problem is to determine whether or not it has these characteristics.

The size of the sample is obviously important. A sample of one hundred would not be so reliable as one of one thousand, and one thousand would not be so reliable as one of a million But large numbers in themselves may not be the most important factor in establishing the reliability of generalizations or inferences.

The unimportance of large numbers as such is best illustrated by the ill-fated *Literary Digest* presidential election poll in 1936. The magazine sent pre-election ballots to ten million persons, and received over two million responses. The responses showed Landon running ahead of Roosevelt. In the election in November, however, Roosevelt got about twenty-eight million votes; Landon around eighteen million.

The reason for this colossal failure was the unrepresentative character of the sample. The *Digest* took names "at random" from telephone directories and lists of registered owners of automobiles. These were relatively well-to-do-folk. The lower income groups, however, were completely, or almost completely, unrepresented.

An ideal sample is one taken "at random" from the entire population, and not from a selected portion of the population being studied. The Gallup poll, for example, uses a special kind of random sampling, and, barring a spectacular failure in 1948, has been far more successful than the *Literary Digest* poll. Let us see how the Gallup poll operates. A sample of three thousand individuals is taken, but with great care to make the sample representative. The population is classified into sub-groups by geographic regions, by rural or urban residence, economic status, age, education, and declared politics. In 1948, for example, Gallup estimated that twenty-eight per cent of the American people lived in the Middle Atlantic states, ten per cent on the West Coast; that thirty-four per cent lived in cities of over 100,000 population; that twenty-three per cent were of an "average" economic station; that forty-three per cent were between the ages of thirty and forty-nine; that forty-two per cent had gone to high school; and that thirty-eight per cent called themselves Democrats, thirty-six per cent Republicans, and twenty-six per cent independents or members of smaller parties. The three thousand interviews in the sample were distributed so that each geographic area, each economic group, etc., would be represented in its appropriate numerical strength.

Individuals are then chosen "at random," rather than by selection, from within each sub-group, and the resulting sample is highly representative of the whole population. The Gallup poll enjoys a successful record, on the whole, except for 1948. In other words, the method works, and one must respect its findings. But no poll can ever eliminate the possibility of error, or guarantee accuracy except within a margin of error of several percentage points. And in a presidential election forecast the pollster is either completely right or completely wrong in predicting who will win. Odds of 10 to 1 against a candidate of one of the major parties are probably not justified even if all the polls are confidently unanimous as to the final results. These were the odds against Harry Truman in the presidential election of 1948!

An election prediction can be judged by the election results, and a long series of successful predictions gives us confidence in the methods of the pollsters. This check cannot be made on polls which tabulate public opinion on issues of the day, for the whole population is never counted. Similarly for polls which rate television shows, for the whole audience is not counted. Such polls, of course, also generalize on the basis of samples. To illustrate the logical problems in assessing the reliability of a statistical study of the "public opinion poll" type we shall comment on *Sexual Behavior in the Human Female,* by Alfred C. Kinsey and his staff.

Kinsey's study, published in 1950, tabulates and classifies data concerning 5,940 white American females, ages two to ninety. He did not claim that his averages necessarily apply to all human females, despite the title of his book, nor even to all American women, of whom there were approximately seventy millions in 1950. It is inevitable, however, that such inferences will be drawn, and our question is: Are such inferences justified? This depends entirely on the representativeness of Kinsey's sample.

Critics of Kinsey's report have emphasized the unrepresentativeness of his sample. His subjects were not distributed proportionately in geographic areas: most were from Illinois, Florida, and California. They were more highly educated than a representative cross-section of the population: seventy-five per cent of his subjects went to college, as compared with a national average of thirteen per cent. Three per cent of his women did not go beyond grade school as compared with the national average of thirty-seven per cent. A larger than average proportion are from middle and upper economic groups. Very few of the women were Roman Catholics or orthodox Jews.

Critics have also argued that the very nature of the study involves a kind of bias, for many women will refuse to discuss matters of such "delicate privacy" with interviewers, so that his volunteers must be unrepresentative of women in general. And there is also the problem of credibility. Critics have said that people who like to talk about such things tend to understate or overstate, and even to embroider a little.

Kinsey, of course, recognizes the limitations and incompleteness of his sample, and, as noted, did not claim that it was representative of the whole population. But it will be interpreted in this way, and if Kinsey wished to avoid such interpretations, he should have called his study "Sexual Behavior of 5,940 Women." Inferences would probably be drawn, however, even if he had so titled his study.

The elements of distortion in Kinsey's sample detract from its reliability as a basis for generalizing. On the other hand, as a review of the book in *Life* put it, though the statistics are not perfect they are at any rate "the only statistics in town." His study is by no means worthless as an index of sexual behavior. We must not use an "all or nothing" approach here. The reliability of his sample with respect to university women as a single group, for example, is certainly much higher than that for the female population as a whole. But we cannot conclude that the whole female population resembles the sample since the sample is not a representative one.

Generalizations in statistics, then, are judged by the same logical criteria we use in judging any generalizations. Fallacies, however, are more common in statistical than they are in uniform generalizations. For it is easier to check on the reliability of a uniform generalization: one exception overthrows the general rule or "law." In statistics, however, since nothing is said about any specific individual, an "exception" is a meaningless term. An exceptional individual does not disprove an "average." But there is, as we have already noted, a method for checking the reliability of a statistical generalization concerning a population, and that is to count the whole voting population in an election. But even a test of this kind is not conclusive, for many of the voters do not vote on election day, because of laziness, overconfidence, or some other reason.

Errors of inference in statistics are frequently overlooked because of the mathematical language in which statistics are presented. The spell which numbers weave often prevents us from seeing errors in arguments—errors which would be obvious were they not clothed in mathematical garb. And many dishonest reasoners take advantage of this fact and present highly selected data for purposes of propaganda rather than information. Misuses of the science of statistics have resulted in such jibes as, "Figures don't lie, but liars figure," and "There are three kinds of lies: ordinary lies, damnable lies, and statistics." But these cynical remarks should not be taken as criticisms of statistics. The fault never lies with the figures, or with the science, but with their careless use. It is simply not the case that "you can prove anything with figures" (or statistics), just as it is never the case that "you can prove anything by logic." To the uninitiated, it just *seems* that you can.

Questions

1. Note that Ruby begins with *a* generalization. Examine his second sentence. It makes two statements. By the definition he sets up, is either a generaliza-

tion? Examine some of the proverbs you know or go to a collection, like parts of the Book of Proverbs in the Bible. Are *all* proverbs generalizations? Test the proverb Ruby uses later, "One swallow does not make a summer."

2. Examine the "witticism" that "all generalizations are false, *including this one.*" As simple as it seems, it involves a rather complex problem in logic. What makes it witty?
3. Take seriously for awhile Ruby's suggestion that you listen carefully to the conversations around you. Collect a list of the generalizations you hear. Do you think that these generalizations have really resulted from an inductive leap? That is, at some point along the way have the people you are hearing really observed facts and then leaped to a conclusion? If you suspect that some have not, how would you explain their making the generalization? Does Ruby's argument that hasty generalizers are prejudiced or exhibitionists help?
4. If a generalization is really a statement of the form "All A's are B's," and if "all" really means what it says, what can Ruby mean by "of this kind" in his next sentence, "A single exception overthrows a generalization of this kind"? Are there other kinds of generalizations? If so, what happens to Ruby's definition, itself a generalization?
5. Examine Ruby's "speculations" on the reasons for hasty generalizations. Why does he use the word "speculate"? The analysis seems fairly concrete. He uses names of groups, quotations, even the authority of Goethe. Has he given any evidence?
6. Define the difference between generalizations and statistical statements. Why does Ruby say that statistical statements *may* be generalizations? When wouldn't they be? Why does Ruby pay so much attention to swans? To the *Literary Digest* poll?
7. Did it surprise you to find that Gallup makes his analyses of public opinion on the basis of only three thousand interviews? How could this conceivably be a large enough sampling, even if it is a representative one? Thinking of your own fluctuations of opinion, would you consider yourself "representative" of forty thousand adults?
8. Perhaps you are as distressed as are your editors when on election nights the commentators can predict so early and with such accuracy the results in almost any race. Even with only one percent of the votes counted and even if the incumbent is five thousand votes behind, "our computers are predicting a landslide victory for the challenger." How can they do this with so much accuracy?
9. Those of us over thirty remember when the weather forecast simply said, "Fair and warmer" or "Variable cloudiness with occasional showers." Today they say, "Probability of rain twenty percent." Why the change? Is it simply that refined techniques make predicting easier? What does probability mean to you in this context? That at any given moment in the next twenty-four hours there is twenty percent chance that it will be raining? Or that there is a twenty percent chance that at some time in the next twenty-four hours it will rain?

Suggestions for Writing

1. As an extension of Question 3 above, make a fairly substantial list of the generalizations you hear and devise some scheme for classifying them, either by the kinds of generalizations or by the various reasons you think they were made or by their validity. Write an essay in which you analyze your findings. You would probably get a rhetorical edge in the essay if you were indignant at the sloppy logic or the prejudices or exhibitionism you find.
2. Do your own analysis of the reasons that pollsters and computers can forecast with such accuracy from such small samples. We tend to think that each of us is a unique individual and that we ourselves *choose* to vote the way we do. Would the accuracy of the pollsters bear us out? Can they be accurate only because we are usually limited to only two choices for each candidate? Are we simply sheep, taken as a mass? Does Truman's victory over Dewey—and the polls—suggest that we are more complicated than the usual accuracy would have us believe?

Jonah

Whether you choose to read "Jonah" as history or story, it has had profound moral and spiritual significance that has nothing to do with whether or not a man could actually live for three days in the belly of a whale. To respond to that significance, you need to remember the long tradition of Israel as the "chosen people" of the Lord and hence their long tradition of religious exclusiveness. Is the Book of Jonah an attempt to persuade the Israelites to look beyond their exclusiveness?

We hope you will enjoy the air of incredibility and the humor of Jonah's attempt to run from the Lord, his sulking at the success of his own preaching and the Lord's compassion, and the object lesson the Lord teaches him with the gourd. Define as broadly, yet as precisely as you can, the "lesson" of the Book of Jonah. Does it relate to the parable of the Good Samaritan? Does it have any of the "feel" of that parable?

You will note that we have set Jonah's prayer in Chapter 2 as a poem. The usual division by chapter and verse disguises much of the poetry of the Old Testament.

CHAPTER 1

Now the word of the LORD came unto Jonah the son of Ȧ-mĭt′taī, saying,
2 Arise, go to Nĭn′ē-vĕh, that great city, and cry against it; for their wicked-
ness is come up before me. 3 But Jonah rose up to flee unto Tär′shĭsh from
the presence of the LORD, and went down to Jŏp′pa; and he found a ship
going to Tär′shĭsh: so he paid the fare thereof, and went down into it, to
go with them unto Tär′shĭsh from the presence of the LORD.

4 But the LORD sent out a great wind into the sea, and there was a
mighty tempest in the sea, so that the ship was like to be broken. 5 Then
the mariners were afraid, and cried every man unto his god, and cast forth
the wares that *were* in the ship into the sea, to lighten *it* of them. But
Jonah was gone down into the sides of the ship; and he lay, and was fast
asleep. 6 So the shipmaster came to him, and said unto him, What meanest
thou, O sleeper? arise, call upon thy God, if so be that God will think
upon us, that we perish not.

7 And they said every one to his fellow, Come, and let us cast lots,

that we may know for whose cause this evil *is* upon us. So they cast lots,
and the lot fell upon Jonah. 8 Then said they unto him, Tell us, we pray
thee, for whose cause this evil *is* upon us; What *is* thine occupation? and
whence comest thou? what *is* thy country? and of what people *art* thou?
9 And he said unto them, I *am* a Hebrew; and I fear the LORD, the God of
heaven, which hath made the sea and the dry *land*. 10 Then were the men
exceedingly afraid, and said unto him, Why hast thou done this? For the
men knew that he fled from the presence of the LORD, because he had told
them. 11 Then said they unto him, What shall we do unto thee, that the
sea may be calm unto us? for the sea wrought, and was tempestuous.
12 And he said unto them, Take me up, and cast me forth into the sea; so
shall the sea be calm unto you: for I know that for my sake this great
tempest *is* upon you. 13 Nevertheless the men rowed hard to bring *it* to the
land; but they could not: for the sea wrought, and was tempestuous against
them. 14 Wherefore they cried unto the LORD, and said, We beseech thee, O
LORD, we beseech thee, let us not perish for this man's life, and lay not
upon us innocent blood: for thou, O LORD, hast done as it pleased thee.
15 So they took up Jonah, and cast him forth into the sea: and the sea
ceased from her raging. 16 Then the men feared the LORD exceedingly, and
offered a sacrifice unto the LORD, and made vows. 17 Now the LORD had
prepared a great fish to swallow up Jonah. And Jonah was in the belly of
the fish three days and three nights.

CHAPTER 2

Then Jonah prayed unto the LORD his God out of the fish's belly, and said,

I cried by reason of mine affliction unto the LORD,
  and he heard me;
out of the belly of hell cried I,
  and thou heardest my voice.
For thou hadst cast me into the deep
  in the midst of the seas;
and the floods compassed me about:
all thy billows and thy waves passed over me.
Then I said, I am cast out of thy sight;
yet I will look again toward thy holy temple.

The waters compassed me about,
  even to the soul:
the depth closed me round about,
the weeds were wrapped about my head.

I went down to the bottoms of the mountains;
the earth with her bars was about me for ever:
yet hast thou brought up my life from corruption,
O LORD my God.

When my soul fainted within me
  I remembered the LORD:
and my prayer came in unto thee,
  into thine holy temple.
They that observe lying vanities
  forsake their own mercy.
But I will sacrifice unto thee
  with the voice of thanksgiving;
I will pay that that I have vowed.
Salvation *is* of the LORD.

And the LORD spake unto the fish, and it vomited out Jonah upon the dry *land.*

CHAPTER 3

And the word of the LORD came unto Jonah the second time, saying,
2 Arise, go unto Nĭn'ē-vĕh, that great city, and preach unto it the preaching
that I bid thee. 3 So Jonah arose, and went unto Nĭn'ē-vĕh, according to
the word of the LORD. Now Nĭn'ē-vĕh was an exceeding great city of three
days' journey. 4 And Jonah began to enter into the city a day's journey, and
he cried, and said, Yet forty days, and Nĭn'ē-vĕh shall be overthrown. 5 So
the people of Nĭn'ē-vĕh believed God, and proclaimed a fast, and put on
sackcloth, from the greatest of them even to the least of them.

6 For word came unto the king of Nĭn'ē-vĕh, and he arose from his
throne, and he laid his robe from him, and covered *him* with sackcloth,
and sat in ashes. 7 And he caused *it* to be proclaimed and published
through Nĭn'ē-vĕh by the decree of the king and his nobles, saying, Let
neither man nor beast, herd nor flock, taste any thing: let them not feed,
nor drink water: 8 But let man and beast be covered with sackcloth, and
cry mightily unto God: yea, let them turn every one from his evil way, and
from the violence that *is* in their hands. 9 Who can tell *if* God will turn and
repent, and turn away from his fierce anger, that we perish not?

10 And God saw their works, that they turned from their evil way; and
God repented of the evil, that he had said that he would do unto them; and
he did *it* not.

CHAPTER 4

But it displeased Jonah exceedingly, and he was very angry. [2] And he
prayed unto the LORD, and said, I pray thee, O LORD, *was* not this my
saying, when I was yet in my country? Therefore I fled before unto
Tär′shĭsh: for I knew that thou *art* a gracious God, and merciful, slow to
anger, and of great kindness, and repentest thee of the evil. [3] Therefore
now, O LORD, take, I beseech thee, my life from me; for *it is* better for me
to die than to live. [4] Then said the LORD, Doest thou well to be angry? [5] So
Jonah went out of the city, and sat on the east side of the city, and there
made him a booth, and sat under it in the shadow, till he might see what
would become of the city.

[6] And the LORD God prepared a gourd, and made *it* to come up over
Jonah, that it might be a shadow over his head, to deliver him from his
grief. So Jonah was exceeding glad of the gourd. [7] But God prepared a
worm when the morning rose the next day, and it smote the gourd that it
withered. [8] And it came to pass, when the sun did arise, that God prepared
a vehement east wind; and the sun beat upon the head of Jonah, that he
fainted, and wished in himself to die, and said, *It is* better for me to die
than to live. [9] And God said to Jonah, Doest thou well to be angry for the
gourd? And he said, I do well to be angry, *even* unto death. [10] Then said
the LORD, Thou hast had pity on the gourd, for the which thou hast not
labored, neither madest it grow; which came up in a night, and perished in
a night: [11] And should not I spare Nĭn′ē-vĕh, that great city, wherein are
more than sixscore thousand persons that cannot discern between their
right hand and their left hand; and *also* much cattle?

The Good Samaritan

Some of Jesus' most effective teaching was done in parable, of which the Good Samaritan is one of the best known. Jesus tells the parable in answer to the rich man's specific question, "And who is my neighbour?" The parable answers that question in language that rings with special urgency to our generation. But He goes beyond it to say something about how we should treat our neighbors. The Samaritans were outsiders, generally despised by the Jews. Put in your own words just who Jesus is telling us our neighbor is and how we should treat him. How persuasive is the parable? Would the lesson be more persuasive had Jesus answered the question directly? Before you answer this too quickly, remember that some of His best-known teachings are in the form of direct admonition: "Thou shalt love thy neighbor as thyself."

And, behold, a certain lawyer stood up, and tempted him, saying, Master,
what shall I do to inherit eternal life? 26 He said unto him, What is written
in the law? how readest thou? 27 And he answering said, Thou shalt love
the Lord thy God with all thy heart, and with all thy soul, and with all thy
strength, and with all thy mind; and thy neighbor as thyself. 28 And he said
unto him, Thou hast answered right: this do, and thou shalt live.

29 But he, willing to justify himself, said unto Jesus, And who is my
neighbor? 30 And Jesus answering said, A certain *man* went down from
Jerusalem to Jĕr'ĭ-chō, and fell among thieves, which stripped him of his
raiment, and wounded *him,* and departed, leaving *him* half dead. 31 And by
chance there came down a certain priest that way; and when he saw him,
he passed by on the other side. 32 And likewise a Lē'vīte, when he was at
the place, came and looked *on him,* and passed by on the other side. 33 But
a certain Sȧ-măr'ĭ-tăn, as he journeyed, came where he was; and when he
saw him, he had compassion *on him,* 34 And went to *him,* and bound up
his wounds, pouring in oil and wine, and set him on his own beast, and
brought him to an inn, and took care of him. 35 And on the morrow when
he departed, he took out two pence, and gave *them* to the host, and said
unto him, Take care of him: and whatsoever thou spendest more, when I
come again, I will repay thee. 36 Which now of these three, thinkest thou,

was neighbor unto him that fell among the thieves? [37] And he said, He that showed mercy on him. Then said Jesus unto him, Go, and do thou likewise.

Suggestions for Writing

1. As you can see, parables or stories can be very effective devices for teaching or persuading. Jesus was especially skillful in using the parable to teach a significant lesson to a hostile audience. Since its message is presented by indirection the audience usually will not feel themselves personally attacked. Write a parable or story to convince your audience of the folly of a certain attitude or course of action or of the need for a different one. Assume an audience hostile to your point of view, if not to you personally.

To His Coy Mistress

Andrew Marvell *It may seem strange at first to see a poem like this under the heading "Logic and Persuasion." But even a first reading should show that the poem is organized as a carefully developed three-step logical argument. Though the logic is important to the persuasive power of the poem, it contributes only part of that power, perhaps even only a facade for it or a framework within which the real persuasive power develops. Try to evaluate just what the logic does for the poem. How successful is it as formal argument? This poem has impressed twentieth-century poets and writers perhaps more than any other seventeenth-century poem. Would the logic explain its impressiveness? Would the persuasiveness explain it?*

Had we but World enough, and Time,
This coyness Lady were no crime.
We would sit down, and think which way
To walk, and pass our long Loves Day.
Thou by the *Indian Ganges* side
Should'st Rubies find: I by the Tide
Of *Humber* would complain. I would
Love you ten years before the Flood:
And you should if you please refuse
Till the Conversion of the *Jews*.
My vegetable Love should grow
Vaster then Empires, and more slow.
An hundred years should go to praise
Thine Eyes, and on thy Forehead Gaze.
Two hundred to adore each Breast:
But thirty thousand to the rest.
An Age at least to every part,
And the last Age should show your Heart.
For Lady you deserve this State;
Nor would I love at lower rate.
    But at my back I alwaies hear

Times winged Charriot hurrying near:
And yonder all before us lye
Desarts of vast Eternity.
Thy Beauty shall no more be found;
Nor, in thy marble Vault, shall sound
My ecchoing song: then Worms shall try
That long preserv'd Virginity:
And your quaint Honour turn to dust;
And into ashes all my Lust.
The Grave's a fine and private place,
But none I think do there embrace.
    Now therefore, while the youthful hew
Sits on thy skin like morning dew,
And while thy willing Soul transpires
At every pore with instant Fires,
Now let us sport us while we may;
And now, like am'rous birds of prey,
Rather at once our Time devour,
Than languish in his slow-chapt pow'r.
Let us roll all our Strength, and all
Our sweetness, up into one Ball:
And tear our Pleasures with rough strife,
Thorough the Iron gates of Life.
Thus, though we cannot make our Sun
Stand still, yet we will make him run.

Questions

1. Is the logic inductive or deductive? Could you set it up as a syllogism? As two abbreviated syllogisms? Can you see any loopholes in it? That is, is it valid logic?
2. You have already seen how much the meaning of words can change. For Marvell "Coy" probably carried more the force of "disdainful," though coquettishly so, rather than merely shy or demure; and "mistress" unquestionably for Marvell meant something close to "sweetheart." Look up *complain, vegetable,* and *lust* for possibly different meanings. Do the different meanings change your response to persuasive qualities of the poem?
3. What is the effect of the exaggerated statements of how the poet *would* love his mistress if they had "world enough and time"? What would a "vegetable love" be like besides slow-growing and vast? Does the exaggeration merely compliment her? Look especially at the last two lines of the stanza. In what tone would you read them aloud?
4. If the first stanza presents a fanciful picture of how he *would* love, what

does the second stanza do? Does it also exaggerate? Is the technique merely to scare her? Again, examine carefully the tone of the last two lines of this stanza.

5. Is the alternative proposed in the last stanza pleasant or unpleasant? Or is it simply the only alternative? Is the poet more, or less, complimentary to his mistress here than in the other two stanzas?

Suggestions for Writing

1. This poem is especially interesting for its rhetorical stance. It is difficult to know whether either the speaker or his lady sees anything morally wrong with what he is proposing. But her hesitation forces him as suitor to be both complimentary and persuasive. Note, though, that under the surface of the compliments, the speaker places some nicely controlled satire on her and her attitude. Assume a similar situation, in which you want something—say, the family car for the evening, or a date for the sophomore ball, or a chance to rewrite a paper for a better grade—and want it badly enough to be as subtly persuasive as you know how to be. Write a letter that you think will win your case.
2. Assume that you are the coy mistress. Write a reply in which you refuse to commit yourself on the proposal, but you tease the young man by showing yourself fully aware of what he is doing in the poem. Analyze in detail how the poem works as persuasion, taking him to task for breaches of logic, for the implicit insult in such things as "vegetable love," and for other qualities you might want to object to. Keep the tone light and be careful that you don't turn him off.

Was Solomon Wise?

Mark Twain *Many students have already read* Huckleberry Finn *when they come to college. Like many great novels, this one can be read on different levels. With Twain each level usually includes some measure of delight. For this reading we hope you will look at the logic. In the first paragraph Huck is praising Jim's "level head," but by the end of the chapter he has decided that "you can't learn a nigger to argue." What is wrong with Huck's argument? With Jim's argument?*

By-and-by, when we got up, we turned over the truck the gang had stole off of the wreck, and found boots, and blankets, and clothes, and all sorts of other things, and a lot of books, and a spyglass, and three boxes of seegars. We hadn't ever been this rich before, in neither of our lives. The seegars was prime. We laid off all the afternoon in the woods talking, and me reading the books, and having a general good time. I told Jim all about what happened inside the wreck, and at the ferry-boat, and I said these kinds of things was adventures; but he said he didn't want no more adventures. He said that when I went in the texas and he crawled back to get on the raft and found her gone, he nearly died; because he judged it was all up with *him,* anyway it could be fixed; for if he didn't get saved he would get drownded; and if he did get saved, whoever saved him would send him back home so as to get the reward, and then Miss Watson would sell him South, sure. Well, he was right; he was most always right; he had an uncommon level head, for a nigger.

I read considerable to Jim about kings, and dukes, and earls, and such, and how gaudy they dressed, and how much style they put on, and called each other your majesty, and your grace, and your lordship, and so on, 'stead of mister; and Jim's eyes bugged out, and he was interested. He says:

"I didn't know dey was so many un um. I hain't hearn 'bout none un um, skasely, but ole King Sollermun, onless you counts dem kings dat's in a pack er k'yards. How much do a king git?"

"Get?" I says; "why, they get a thousand dollars a month if they want it; they can have just as much as they want; everything belongs to them."

"*Ain'* dat gay? En what dey got to do, Huck?"

"*They* don't do nothing! Why how you talk. They just set around."

"No—is dat so?"

"Of course it is. They just set around. Except maybe when there 's a war; then they go to the war. But other times they just lazy around; or go hawking—just hawking and sp— Sh!—d' you hear a noise?"

We skipped out and looked; but it warn't nothing but the flutter of a steamboat's wheel, away down coming around the point; so we come back.

"Yes," says I, "and other times, when things is dull, they fuss with the parlyment; and if everybody don't go just so he whacks their heads off. But mostly they hang round the harem."

"Roun' de which?"

"Harem."

"What's de harem?"

"The place where he keep his wives. Don't you know about the harem? Solomon had one; he had about a million wives."

"Why, yes, dat's so; I—I'd done forgot it. A harem's a bo'd'n-house, I reck'n. Mos' likely dey has rackety times in de nussery. En I reck'n de wives quarrels considable; en dat 'crease de racket. Yit dey say Sollermun de wises' man dat ever live'. I doan' take no stock in dat. Bekase why: would a wise man want to live in de mids' er sich a blimblammin' all de time? No—'deed he wouldn't. A wise man 'ud take en buil' a biler-factry; en den he could shet *down* de biler-factry when he want to res'."

"Well, but he *was* the wisest man, anyway; because the widow she told me so, her own self."

"I doan' k'yer what de widder say, he *warn't* no wise man, nuther. He had some er de dad-fetchedes' ways I ever see. Does you know 'bout dat chile dat he 'uz gwyne to chop in two?"

"Yes, the widow told me all about it."

"*Well,* den! Warn' dat de beatenes' notion in de worl'? You jes' take en look at it a minute. Dah's de stump, dah—dat's one er de women; heah's you—dat's de yuther one; I's Sollermun; en dish-yer dollar bill's de chile. Bofe un you claims it. What does I do? Does I shin aroun' mongs' de neighbors en fine out which un you de bill *do* b'long to, en han' it over to de right one, all safe en soun', de way dat anybody dat had any gumption would? No—I take en whack de bill in *two,* en give half un it to you, en de yuther half to de yuther woman. Dat's de way Sollermun was gwyne to do wid de chile. Now I want to ast you: what's de use er dat half a bill?—can't buy noth'n wid it. En what use is a half a chile? I would'n give a dern for a million un um."

"But hang it, Jim, you've clean missed the point—blame it, you've missed it a thousand mile."

"Who? Me? Go 'long. Doan' talk to *me* 'bout yo' pints. I reck'n I knows sense when I sees it; en dey ain' no sense in sich doin's as dat. De 'spute warn't 'bout a half a chile, de 'spute was 'bout a whole chile; en de man dat think he kin settle a 'spute 'bout a whole chile wid a half a chile, doan' know enough to come in out'n de rain. Doan' talk to me 'bout Sollermun, Huck, I knows him by de back."

"But I tell you you don't get the point."

"Blame de pint! I reck'n I knows what I knows. En mine you, de *real* pint is down furder—it's down deeper. It lays in de way Sollermun was raised. You take a man dat's got on'y one er two chillen; is dat man gwyne to be waseful o' chillen? No, he ain't; he can't 'ford it. *He* know how to value 'em. But you take a man dat's got 'bout five million chillen runnin' roun' de house, en it's diffunt. *He* as soon chop a chile in two as a cat. Dey's plenty mo'. A chile er two, mo' er less, warn't no consekens to Sollermun, dad fetch him!"

I never see such a nigger. If he got a notion in his head once, there warn't no getting it out again. He was the most down on Solomon of any nigger I ever see. So I went to talking about other kings, and let Solomon slide. I told about Louis Sixteenth that got his head cut off in France long time ago; and about his little boy the dolphin, that would a been a king, but they took and shut him up in jail, and some say he died there.

"Po' little chap."

"But some says he got out and got away, and come to America."

"Dat's good! But he'll be pooty lonesome—dey ain' no kings here, is dey, Huck?"

"No."

"Den he cain't git no situation. What he gwyne to do?"

"Well, I don't know. Some of them gets on the police, and some of them learns people how to talk French."

"Why, Huck, doan' de French people talk de same way we does?"

"*No,* Jim; you couldn't understand a word they said—not a single word."

"Well, now, I be ding-busted! How do dat come?"

"*I* don't know; but it's so. I got some of their jabber out of a book. Spose a man was to come to you and say *Polly-voo-franzy*—what would you think?"

"I wouldn't think nuff'n; I'd take en bust him over de head. Dat is, if he warn't white. I wouldn't 'low no nigger to call me dat."

"Shucks, it ain't calling you anything. It's only saying do you know how to talk French."

"Well, den, why couldn't he *say* it?"

"Why, he *is* a-saying it. That's a Frenchman's *way* of saying it."

"Well, it's a blame' ridicklous way, en I doan' want to hear no mo' 'bout it. Dey ain' no sense in it."

"Looky here, Jim; does a cat talk like we do?"

"No, a cat don't."

"Well, does a cow?"

"No, a cow don't, nuther."

"Does a cat talk like a cow, or a cow talk like a cat?"

"No, dey don't."

"It's natural and right for 'em to talk different from each other, ain't it?"

"'Course."

"And ain't it natural and right for a cat and a cow to talk different from *us?"*

"Why, mos' sholy it is."

"Well, then, why ain't it natural and right for a *Frenchman* to talk different from us? You answer me that."

"Is a cat a man, Huck?"

"No."

"Well, den, dey ain't no sense in a cat talkin' like a man. Is a cow a man?—er is a cow a cat?"

"No, she ain't either of them."

"Well, den, she ain' got no business to talk like either one er the yuther of 'em. Is a Frenchman a man?"

"Yes."

"Well, den! Dad blame it, why doan' he *talk* like a man? You answer me *dat!"*

I see it warn't no use wasting words—you can't learn a nigger to argue. So I quit.

Questions

1. What about Jim's thinking impresses Huck, as Jim and he talk about the wreck in the first paragraph? Does Jim consider all the possibilities in the situation? What does the admiration tell us about Huck's own thinking?
2. Does Jim use induction, deduction, or nonlogic, when he answers about "Sollermun" and the child? Why is Huck unable to challenge Jim successfully on this point?
3. What is wrong with Huck's argument about the Frenchman and his language? (Even if you do not know the technical term for the fallacy, you should be able to describe Huck's error.) Can you make a syllogism out of Jim's argument about the Frenchman? Why is Huck unable to answer Jim?
4. How successful is Twain's handling of dialect in this selection? Does the dialect get in the way of your reading?

The Arts of Selling

Aldous L. Huxley

"Words and Behavior" in the previous section presents Huxley's views of the cause and effect relationship between words and human actions. In this selection he uses a comparison and contrast organization to attack the "insidious arts" of selling. Notice how Huxley keeps the comparison and contrast going between the dictator's tactics on the one hand and the advertiser's on the other. What does he gain by this comparison? Also try to determine how much of his argument is logical and how much of it is persuasion without logic?

The survival of democracy depends on the ability of large numbers of people to make realistic choices in the light of adequate information. A dictatorship, on the other hand, maintains itself by censoring or distorting the facts, and by appealing, not to reason, not to enlightened self-interest, but to passion and prejudice, to the powerful "hidden forces," as Hitler called them, present in the unconscious depths of every human mind.

In the West, democratic principles are proclaimed and many able and conscientious publicists do their best to supply electors with adequate information and to persuade them, by rational argument, to make realistic choices in the light of that information. All this is greatly to the good. But unfortunately propaganda in the Western democracies, above all in America, has two faces and a divided personality. In charge of the editorial department there is often a democratic Dr. Jekyll—a propagandist who would be very happy to prove that John Dewey had been right about the ability of human nature to respond to truth and reason. But this worthy man controls only a part of the machinery of mass communication. In charge of advertising we find an anti-democratic, because anti-rational, Mr. Hyde—or rather a Dr. Hyde, for Hyde is now a Ph.D. in psychology and has a master's degree as well in the social sciences. This Dr. Hyde would be very unhappy indeed if everybody always lived up to John Dewey's faith in human nature. Truth and reason are Jekyll's affair, not his.

Hyde is a motivation analyst, and his business is to study human weaknesses and failings, to investigate those unconscious desires and fears by which so much of men's conscious thinking and overt doing is determined. And he does this, not in the spirit of the moralist who would like to make people better, or of the physician who would like to improve their health, but simply in order to find out the best way to take advantage of their ignorance and to exploit their irrationality for the pecuniary benefit of his employers. But after all, it may be argued, "capitalism is dead, consumerism is king"—and consumerism requires the services of expert salesmen versed in all the arts (including the more insidious arts) of persuasion. Under a free enterprise system commercial propaganda by any and every means is absolutely indispensable. But the indispensable is not necessarily the desirable. What is demonstrably good in the sphere of economics may be far from good for men and women as voters or even as human beings. An earlier, more moralistic generation would have been profoundly shocked by the bland cynicism of the motivation analysts. Today we read a book like Mr. Vance Packard's *The Hidden Persuaders,* and are more amused than horrified, more resigned than indignant. Given Freud, given Behaviorism, given the mass producer's chronically desperate need for mass consumption, this is the sort of thing that is only to be expected. But what, we may ask, is the sort of thing that is to be expected in the future? Are Hyde's activities compatible in the long run with Jekyll's? Can a campaign in favor of rationality be successful in the teeth of another and even more vigorous campaign in favor of irrationality? These are questions which, for the moment, I shall not attempt to answer, but shall leave hanging, so to speak, as a backdrop to our discussion of the methods of mass persuasion in a technologically advanced democratic society.

The task of the commercial propagandist in a democracy is in some ways easier and in some ways more difficult than that of a political propagandist employed by an established dictator or a dictator in the making. It is easier inasmuch as almost everyone starts out with a prejudice in favor of beer, cigarettes and iceboxes, whereas almost nobody starts out with a prejudice in favor of tyrants. It is more difficult inasmuch as the commercial propagandist is not permitted, by the rules of his particular game, to appeal to the more savage instincts of his public. The advertiser of dairy products would dearly love to tell his readers and listeners that all their troubles are caused by the machinations of a gang of godless international margarine manufacturers, and that it is their patriotic duty to march out and burn the oppressors' factories. This sort of thing, however, is ruled out, and he must be content with a milder approach. But the mild approach is less exciting than the approach through verbal or physical violence. In the long run, anger and hatred are self-defeating emotions. But in the short run they pay high dividends in the form of psychological and even (since they release large quantities of adrenalin and noradrenalin) physiological satisfaction. People may start out with an initial prejudice against tyrants; but when tyrants or would-be tyrants treat them to adrenalin-releasing propaganda about the wickedness of their enemies—particularly of enemies weak enough to be persecuted—they are ready to follow him with enthusiasm. In his speeches Hitler kept repeating such words as "hatred," "force," "ruthless," "crush," "smash"; and he would accompany these violent words with even more violent gestures. He would yell, he would scream, his veins would swell, his face would turn purple. Strong emotion (as every actor and dramatist knows) is in the highest degree contagious. Infected by the malignant frenzy of the orator, the audience would groan and sob and scream in an orgy of uninhibited passion. And these orgies were so enjoyable that most of those who had experienced them eagerly came back for more. Almost all of us long for peace and freedom; but very few of us have much enthusiasm for the thoughts, feelings and actions that make for peace and freedom. Conversely almost nobody wants war or tyranny; but a great many people find an intense pleasure in the thoughts, feelings and actions that make for war and tyranny. These thoughts, feelings and actions are too dangerous to be exploited for commercial purposes. Accepting this handicap, the advertising man must do the best he can with the less intoxicating emotions, the quieter forms of irrationality.

Effective rational propaganda becomes possible only when there is a clear understanding, on the part of all concerned, of the nature of symbols and of their relations to the things and events symbolized. Irrational propaganda depends for its effectiveness on a general failure to understand the nature of symbols. Simple-minded people tend to equate the symbol with what it stands for, to attribute to things and events some of the qualities expressed by the words in terms of which the propagandist has chosen, for his own purposes, to talk about them. Consider a simple example. Most cosmetics are made of lanolin, which is a mixture of purified wool fat and water beaten up into an emulsion. This emulsion has many valuable properties: it penetrates the skin, it does not become rancid, it is mildly antiseptic and so forth. But the commercial propagandists do not speak about the genuine virtues of the emulsion. They give it some picturesquely voluptuous name, talk ecstatically and misleadingly about feminine beauty and show pictures of gorgeous blondes nourishing their tissues with skin food. "The cosmetic manufacturers," one of their number has written, "are not selling lanolin, they are selling hope." For this hope, this fraudulent implication of a promise that they will be transfigured, women will pay ten or twenty times the value of the emulsion which the propagandists have so skilfully related, by means of misleading symbols, to a deep-seated and almost universal feminine wish—the wish to be more attractive to members of the opposite sex. The principles underlying this kind of propaganda are extremely simple. Find some common desire, some widespread unconscious fear or anxiety; think out some way to relate this wish or fear to the product you have to sell; then build a bridge of verbal or pictorial symbols over which your customer can pass from fact to compensatory dream, and from the dream to the illusion that your product, when purchased, will make the dream come true. "We no longer buy oranges, we buy vitality. We do not buy just an auto, we buy prestige." And so with all the rest. In toothpaste, for example, we buy, not a mere cleanser and antiseptic, but release from the fear of being sexually repulsive. In vodka and whisky we are not buying a protoplasmic poison which, in small doses, may depress the nervous system in a psychologically valuable way; we are buying friendliness and good fellowship, the warmth of Dingley Dell and the brilliance of the Mermaid Tavern. With our laxatives we buy the health of a Greek god, the radiance of one of Diana's nymphs. With the monthly best seller we acquire culture, the envy of our less literate neighbors and the respect of the sophisticated. In every case the motivation analyst has found some deep-seated wish or fear, whose energy can be used to move the consumer to part with cash and so, indirectly, to turn the wheels of industry. Stored in the minds and bodies of countless individuals, this potential energy is released by, and transmitted along, a line of symbols carefully laid out so as to bypass rationality and obscure the real issue.

Sometimes the symbols take effect by being disproportionately impressive, haunting and fascinating in their own right. Of this kind are the rites and pomps of religion. These "beauties of holiness" strengthen faith where it already exists and, where there is no faith, contribute to conversion. Appealing, as they do, only to the aesthetic sense, they guarantee neither the truth nor the ethical value of the doctrines with which they have been, quite arbitrarily, associated. As a matter of plain historical fact, the beauties of holiness have often been matched and indeed surpassed by the beauties of unholiness. Under Hitler, for example, the yearly Nuremberg rallies were masterpieces of ritual and theatrical art. "I had spent six years in St. Petersburg before the war in the best days of the old Russian ballet," writes Sir Nevile Henderson, the British ambassador to Hitler's Germany, "but for grandiose beauty I have never seen any ballet to compare with the Nuremberg rally." One thinks of Keats—"beauty is truth, truth beauty." Alas, the identity exists only on some ultimate, supramundane level. On the levels of politics and theology, beauty is perfectly compatible with nonsense and tyranny. Which is very fortunate; for if beauty were incompatible with nonsense and tyranny, there would be precious little art in the world. The masterpieces of painting, sculpture and architecture were produced as religious or political propaganda, for the greater glory of a god, a government or a priesthood. But most kings and priests have been despotic and all religions have been riddled with superstition. Genius has been the servant of tyranny and art has advertised the merits of the local cult. Time, as it passes, separates the good art from the bad metaphysics. Can we learn to make this separation, not after the event, but while it is actually taking place? That is the question.

In commercial propaganda the principle of the disproportionately fascinating symbol is clearly understood. Every propagandist has his Art Department, and attempts are constantly being made to beautify the billboards with striking posters, the advertising pages of magazines with lively drawings and photographs. There are no masterpieces; for masterpieces appeal only to a limited audience, and the commercial propagandist is out to captivate the majority. For him, the ideal is a moderate excellence. Those who like this not too good, but sufficiently striking, art may be expected to like the products with which it has been associated and for which it symbolically stands.

Another disproportionately fascinating symbol is the Singing Commercial. Singing Commercials are a recent invention; but the Singing Theological and the Singing Devotional—the hymn and the psalm—are as old as religion itself. Singing Militaries, or marching songs, are coeval with war, and Singing Patriotics, the precursors of our national anthems, were doubtless used to promote group solidarity, to emphasize the distinction between "us" and "them," by the wandering bands of paleolithic hunters and food gatherers. To most people music is intrinsically attractive. Moreover, melodies tend to ingrain themselves in the listener's mind. A tune will haunt the memory during the whole of a lifetime. Here, for example, is a quite uninteresting statement or value judgment. As it stands nobody will pay attention to it. But now set the words to a catchy and easily remembered tune. Immediately they become words of power. Moreover, the words will tend automatically to repeat themselves every time the melody is heard or spontaneously remembered. Orpheus has entered into an alliance with Pavlov—the power of sound with the conditioned reflex. For the commercial propagandist, as for his colleagues in the fields of politics and religion, music possesses yet another advantage. Nonsense which it would be shameful for a reasonable being to write, speak or hear spoken can be sung or listened to by that same rational being with pleasure and even with a kind of intellectual conviction. Can we learn to separate the pleasure of singing or of listening to song from the all too human tendency to believe in the propaganda which the song is putting over? That again is the question.

Thanks to compulsory education and the rotary press, the propagandist has been able, for many years past, to convey his messages to virtually every adult in every civilized country. Today, thanks to radio and television, he is in the happy position of being able to communicate even with unschooled adults and not yet literate children.

Children, as might be expected, are highly susceptible to propaganda. They are ignorant of the world and its ways, and therefore completely unsuspecting. Their critical faculties are undeveloped. The youngest of them have not yet reached the age of reason and the older ones lack the experience on which their new-found rationality can effectively work. In Europe, conscripts used to be playfully referred to as "cannon fodder." Their little brothers and sisters have now become radio fodder and television fodder. In my childhood we were taught to sing nursery rhymes and, in pious households, hymns. Today the little ones warble the Singing Commercials. Which is better—"Rheingold is my beer, the dry beer," or "Hey diddle-diddle, the cat and the fiddle"? "Abide with me" or "You'll wonder where the yellow went, when you brush your teeth with Pepsodent"? Who knows?

"I don't say that children should be forced to harass their parents into buying products they've seen advertised on television, but at the same time I cannot close my eyes to the fact that it's being done every day." So writes the star of one of the many programs beamed to a juvenile audience. "Children," he adds, "are living, talking records of what we tell them every day." And in due course these living, talking records of television commercials will grow up, earn money and buy the products of industry. "Think," writes Mr. Clyde Miller ecstatically, "think of what it can mean to your firm in profits if you can condition a million or ten million children, who will grow up into adults trained to buy your product, as soldiers are trained in advance when they hear the trigger words, Forward March!" Yes, just think of it! And at the same time remember that the dictators and the would-be dictators have been thinking about this sort of thing for years, and that millions, tens of millions, hundreds of millions of children are in process of growing up to buy the local despot's ideological product and, like well-trained soldiers, to respond with appropriate behavior to the trigger words implanted in those young minds by the despot's propagandists.

Self-government is in inverse ratio to numbers. The larger the constituency, the less the value of any particular vote. When he is merely one of millions, the individual elector feels himself to be impotent, a negligible quantity. The candidates he has voted into office are far away, at the top of the pyramid of power. Theoretically they are the servants of the people; but in fact it is the servants who give orders and the people, far off at the base of the great pyramid, who must obey. Increasing population and advancing technology have resulted in an increase in the number and complexity of organizations, an increase in the amount of power concentrated in the hands of officials and a corresponding decrease in the amount of control exercised by electors, coupled with a decrease in the public's regard for democratic procedures. Already weakened by the vast impersonal forces at work in the modern world, democratic institutions are now being undermined from within by the politicians and their propagandists.

Human beings act in a great variety of irrational ways, but all of them seem to be capable, if given a fair chance, of making a reasonable choice in the light of available evidence. Democratic institutions can be made to work only if all concerned do their best to impart knowledge and to encourage rationality. But today, in the world's most powerful democracy, the politicians and their propagandists prefer to make nonsense of democratic procedures by appealing almost exclusively to the ignorance and irrationality of the electors. "Both parties," we were told in 1956 by the editor of a leading business journal, "will merchandize their candidates and issues by the same methods that business has developed to sell goods. These include scientific selection of appeals and planned repetition. . . . Radio spot announcements and ads will repeat phrases with a planned intensity. Billboards will push slogans of proven power. . . . Candidates need, in addition to rich voices and good diction, to be able to look 'sincerely' at the TV camera."

The political merchandisers appeal only to the weaknesses of voters, never to their potential strength. They make no attempt to educate the masses into becoming fit for self-government; they are content merely to manipulate and exploit them. For this purpose all the resources of psychology and the social sciences are mobilized and set to work. Carefully selected samples of the electorate are given "interviews in depth." These interviews in depth reveal the unconscious fears and wishes most prevalent in a given society at the time of an election. Phrases and images aimed at allaying or, if necessary, enhancing these fears, at satisfying these wishes, at least symbolically, are then chosen by the experts, tried out on readers and audiences, changed or improved in the light of the information thus obtained. After which the political campaign is ready for the mass communicators. All that is now needed is money and a candidate who can be coached to look "sincere." Under the new dispensation, political principles and plans for specific action have come to lose most of their importance. The personality of the candidate and the way he is projected by the advertising experts are the things that really matter.

In one way or another, as vigorous he-man or kindly father, the candidate must be glamorous. He must also be an entertainer who never bores his audience. Inured to television and radio, that audience is accustomed to being distracted and does not like to be asked to concentrate or make a prolonged intellectual effort. All speeches by the entertainer-candidate must therefore be short and snappy. The great issues of the day must be dealt with in five minutes at the most—and preferably (since the audience will be eager to pass on to something a little livelier than inflation or the H-bomb) in sixty seconds flat. The nature of oratory is such that there has always been a tendency among politicians and clergymen to over-simplify complex issues. From a pulpit or a platform even the most conscientious of speakers finds it very difficult to tell the whole truth. The methods now being used to merchandise the political candidate as though he were a deodorant positively guarantee the electorate against ever hearing the truth about anything.

Questions

1. Why does Huxley use Hitler as his prime example of the dictator? Why does he keep the comparison and contrast of the political and the merchandise propaganda throughout the entire article? Is he emphasizing one more than the other?
2. Do you understand all the references to individuals Huxley makes? What does he mean by "Orpheus has entered into an alliance with Pavlov"?
3. Find specific advertisements that demonstrate what Huxley means by "the illusion that your product when purchased, will make the dream come true." Huxley says that instead of oranges "we buy vitality" and instead of an automobile, "prestige." Define what you buy with the advertisements you found.
4. Huxley makes a number of direct statements which he feels no need to support, such as "Strong emotion . . . is in the highest degree contagious." Do you always agree with his unsupported statements? If not, find one you disagree with. Does the fact that you disagree with this statement weaken Huxley's argument?
5. How persuasive does Huxley's entire argument seem? What audience do you picture Huxley writing to? How would the material be presented differently if the audience were an advertisers' convention? A business men's club? Cite specific aspects of his argument that Huxley would have to change?

Suggestions for Writing

1. Taking a hint from Question 5, assume that you have something of the same message to give to a convention of advertisers. You want to warn them against what you consider dangerous practices in advertising, you want to suggest broader implications of the practices, but you do not want to alienate your audience. Define your problem, then write accordingly.

Dry September

William Faulkner

Weak or bad logic may weaken or ruin a freshman composition and still result in nothing more dangerous than a low grade. But in the world of action, of human relations, bad logic or the rejection of logic can result in catastrophe. The violence in William Faulkner's Yoknapatawpha County, like so much of the violence throughout America today, is tied to racial prejudice. This story is one of Faulkner's most powerful depictions of that violence. Try to define just what happens logically—or illogically—that causes the violence.

Through the bloody September twilight, aftermath of sixty-two rainless days, it had gone like a fire in dry grass—the rumor, the story, whatever it was. Something about Miss Minnie Cooper and a Negro. Attacked, insulted, frightened: none of them, gathered in the barber shop on that Saturday evening where the ceiling fan stirred, without freshening it, the vitiated air, sending back upon them, in recurrent surges of stale pomade and lotion, their own stale breath and odors, knew exactly what had happened.

"Except it wasn't Will Mayes," a barber said. He was a man of middle age; a thin, sand-colored man with a mild face, who was shaving a client. "I know Will Mayes. He's a good nigger. And I know Miss Minnie Cooper, too."

"What do you know about her?" a second barber said.

"Who is she?" the client said. "A young girl?"

"No," the barber said. "She's about forty, I reckon. She aint married. That's why I dont believe—"

"Believe, hell!" a hulking youth in a sweat-stained silk shirt said. "Wont you take a white woman's word before a nigger's?"

"I dont believe Will Mayes did it," the barber said. "I know Will Mayes."

"Maybe you know who did it, then. Maybe you already got him out of town, you damn niggerlover."

"I dont believe anybody did anything. I dont believe anything happened. I leave it to you fellows if them ladies that get old without getting married dont have notions that a man cant—"

"Then you are a hell of a white man," the client said. He moved under the cloth. The youth had sprung to his feet.

"You dont?" he said. "Do you accuse a white woman of lying?"

The barber held the razor poised above the half-risen client. He did not look around.

"It's this durn weather," another said. "It's enough to make a man do anything. Even to her."

Nobody laughed. The barber said in his mild, stubborn tone: "I aint accusing nobody of nothing. I just know and you fellows know how a woman that never—"

"You damn niggerlover!" the youth said.

"Shut up, Butch," another said. "We'll get the facts in plenty of time to act."

"Who is? Who's getting them?" the youth said. "Facts, hell! I—"

"You're a fine white man," the client said. "Aint you?" In his frothy beard he looked like a desert rat in the moving pictures. "You tell them, Jack," he said to the youth. "If there aint any white men in this town, you can count on me, even if I aint only a drummer and a stranger."

"That's right, boys," the barber said. "Find out the truth first. I know Will Mayes."

"Well, by God!" the youth shouted. "To think that a white man in this town—"

"Shut up, Butch," the second speaker said. "We got plenty of time."

The client sat up. He looked at the speaker. "Do you claim that anything excuses a nigger attacking a white woman? Do you mean to tell me you are a white man and you'll stand for it? You better go back North where you came from. The South dont want your kind here."

"North what?" the second said. "I was born and raised in this town."

"Well, by God!" the youth said. He looked about with a strained, baffled gaze, as if he was trying to remember what it was he wanted to say or to do. He drew his sleeve across his sweating face. "Damn if I'm going to let a white woman—"

"You tell them, Jack," the drummer said. "By God, if they—"

The screen door crashed open. A man stood in the floor, his feet apart and his heavy-set body poised easily. His white shirt was open at the throat; he wore a felt hat. His hot, bold glance swept the group. His name was McLendon. He had commanded troops at the front in France and had been decorated for valor.

"Well," he said, "are you going to sit there and let a black son rape a white woman on the streets of Jefferson?"

Butch sprang up again. The silk of his shirt clung flat to his heavy shoulders. At each armpit was a dark halfmoon. "That's what I been telling them! That's what I—"

"Did it really happen?" a third said. "This aint the first man scare she ever had, like Hawkshaw says. Wasn't there something about a man on the kitchen roof, watching her undress, about a year ago?"

"What?" the client said. "What's that?" The barber had been slowly forcing him back into the chair; he arrested himself reclining, his head lifted, the barber still pressing him down.

McLendon whirled on the third speaker. "Happen? What the hell difference does it make? Are you going to let the black sons get away with it until one really does it?"

"That's what I'm telling them!" Butch shouted. He cursed, long and steady, pointless.

"Here, here," a fourth said. "Not so loud. Dont talk so loud."

"Sure," McLendon said; "no talking necessary at all. I've done my talking. Who's with me?" He poised on the balls of his feet, roving his gaze.

The barber held the drummer's face down, the razor poised. "Find out the facts first, boys. I know Willy Mayes. It wasn't him. Let's get the sheriff and do this thing right."

McLendon whirled upon him his furious, rigid face. The barber did not look away. They looked like men of different races. The other barbers had ceased also above their prone clients. "You mean to tell me," McLendon said, "that you'd take a nigger's word before a white woman's? Why, you damn niggerloving—"

The third speaker rose and grasped McLendon's arm; he too had been a soldier. "Now, now. Let's figure this thing out. Who knows anything about what really happened?"

"Figure out hell!" McLendon jerked his arm free. "All that're with me get up from there. The ones that aint—" He roved his gaze, dragging his sleeve across his face.

Three men rose. The drummer in the chair sat up. "Here," he said, jerking at the cloth about his neck; "get this rag off me. I'm with him. I dont live here, but by God, if our mothers and wives and sisters—" He smeared the cloth over his face and flung it to the floor. McLendon stood in the floor and cursed the others. Another rose and moved toward him. The remainder sat uncomfortable, not looking at one another, then one by one they rose and joined him.

The barber picked the cloth from the floor. He began to fold it neatly. "Boys, dont do that. Will Mayes never done it. I know."

"Come on," McLendon said. He whirled. From his hip pocket protruded the butt of a heavy automatic pistol. They went out. The screen door crashed behind them reverberant in the dead air.

The barber wiped the razor carefully and swiftly, and put it away, and ran to the rear, and took his hat from the wall. "I'll be back as soon as I can," he said to the other barbers. "I cant let—" He went out, running. The two other barbers followed him to the door and caught it on the rebound, leaning out and looking up the street after him. The air was flat and dead. It had a metallic taste at the base of the tongue.

"What can he do?" the first said. The second one was saying "Jees Christ, Jees Christ" under his breath. "I'd just as lief be Will Mayes as Hawk, if he gets McLendon riled."

"Jees Christ, Jees Christ," the second whispered.

"You reckon he really done it to her?" the first said.

II

She was thirty-eight or thirty-nine. She lived in a small frame house with her invalid mother and a thin, sallow, unflagging aunt, where each morning between ten and eleven she would appear on the porch in a lace-trimmed boudoir cap, to sit swinging in the porch swing until noon. After dinner she lay down for a while, until the afternoon began to cool. Then, in one of the three or four new voile dresses which she had each summer, she would go downtown to spend the afternoon in the stores with the other ladies, where they would handle the goods and haggle over the prices in cold, immediate voices, without any intention of buying.

She was of comfortable people—not the best in Jefferson, but good people enough—and she was still on the slender side of ordinary looking, with a bright, faintly haggard manner and dress. When she was young she had had a slender, nervous body and a sort of hard vivacity which had enabled her for a time to ride upon the crest of the town's social life as exemplified by the high school party and church social period of her contemporaries while still children enough to be unclassconscious.

She was the last to realize that she was losing ground; that those among whom she had been a little brighter and louder flame than any other were beginning to learn the pleasure of snobbery—male—and retaliation—female. That was when her face began to wear that bright, haggard look. She still carried it to parties on shadowy porticoes and summer lawns, like a mask or a flag, with that bafflement of furious repudiation of truth in her eyes. One evening at a party she heard a boy and two girls, all schoolmates, talking. She never accepted another invitation.

She watched the girls with whom she had grown up as they married and got homes and children, but no man ever called on her steadily until the children of the other girls had been calling her "aunty" for several years, the while their mothers told them in bright voices about how popular Aunt Minnie had been as a girl. Then the town began to see her driving on Sunday afternoons with the cashier in the bank. He was a widower of about forty—a high-colored man, smelling always faintly of the barber shop or of whisky. He owned the first automobile in town, a red runabout; Minnie had the first motoring bonnet and veil the town ever saw. Then the town began to say: "Poor Minnie." "But she is old enough to take care of herself," others said. That was when she began to ask her old schoolmates that their children call her "cousin" instead of "aunty."

It was twelve years now since she had been relegated into adultery by public opinion, and eight years since the cashier had gone to a Memphis bank, returning for one day each Christmas, which he spent at an annual bachelors' party at a hunting club on the river. From behind their curtains the neighbors would see the party pass, and during the over-the-way Christmas day visiting they would tell her about him, about how well he looked, and how they heard that he was prospering in the city, watching with bright, secret eyes her haggard, bright face. Usually by that hour there would be the scent of whisky on her breath. It was supplied her by a youth, a clerk at the soda fountain: "Sure; I buy it for the old gal. I reckon she's entitled to a little fun."

Her mother kept to her room altogether now; the gaunt aunt ran the house. Against that background Minnie's bright dresses, her idle and empty days, had a quality of furious unreality. She went out in the evenings only with women now, neighbors, to the moving pictures. Each afternoon she dressed in one of the new dresses and went downtown alone, where her young "cousins" were already strolling in the late afternoons with their delicate, silken heads and thin, awkward arms and conscious hips, clinging to one another or shrieking and giggling with paired boys in the soda fountain when she passed and went on along the serried store fronts, in the doors of which the sitting and lounging men did not even follow her with their eyes any more.

III

The barber went swiftly up the street where the sparse lights, insect-swirled, glared in rigid and violent suspension in the lifeless air. The day had died in a pall of dust; above the darkened square, shrouded by the spent dust, the sky was as clear as the inside of a brass bell. Below the east was a rumor of the twice-waxed moon.

When he overtook them McLendon and three others were getting into a car parked in an alley. McLendon stooped his thick head, peering out beneath the top. "Changed your mind, did you?" he said. "Damn good thing; by God, tomorrow when this town hears about how you talked tonight—"

"Now, now," the other ex-soldier said. "Hawkshaw's all right. Come on, Hawk; jump in."

"Will Mayes never done it, boys," the barber said. "If anybody done it. Why, you all know well as I do there aint any town where they got better niggers than us. And you know how a lady will kind of think things about men when there aint any reason to, and Miss Minnie anyway—"

"Sure, sure," the soldier said. "We're just going to talk to him a little; that's all."

"Talk hell!" Butch said. "When we're through with the—"

"Shut up, for God's sake!" the soldier said. "Do you want everybody in town—"

"Tell them, by God!" McLendon said. "Tell every one of the sons that'll let a white woman—"

"Let's go; let's go: here's the other car." The second car slid squealing out of a cloud of dust at the alley mouth. McLendon started his car and took the lead. Dust lay like fog in the street. The street lights hung nimbused as in water. They drove on out of town.

A rutted lane turned at right angles. Dust hung above it too, and above all the land. The dark bulk of the ice plant, where the Negro Mayes was night watchman, rose against the sky. "Better stop here, hadn't we?" the soldier said. McLendon did not reply. He hurled the car up and slammed to a stop, the headlights glaring on the blank wall.

"Listen here, boys," the barber said; "if he's here, dont that prove he never done it? Dont it? If it was him, he would run. Dont you see he would?" The second car came up and stopped. McLendon got down; Butch sprang down beside him. "Listen, boys," the barber said.

"Cut the lights off!" McLendon said. The breathless dark rushed down. There was no sound in it save their lungs as they sought air in the parched dust in which for two months they had lived; then the diminishing crunch of McLendon's and Butch's feet, and a moment later McLendon's voice:

"Will! . . . Will!"

Below the east the wan hemorrhage of the moon increased. It heaved above the ridge, silvering the air, the dust, so that they seemed to breathe, live, in a bowl of molten lead. There was no sound of nightbird nor insect, no sound save their breathing and a faint ticking of contracting metal about the cars. Where their bodies touched one another they seemed to sweat dryly, for no more moisture came. "Christ!" a voice said; "let's get out of here."

But they didn't move until vague noises began to grow out of the darkness ahead; then they got out and waited tensely in the breathless dark. There was another sound: a blow, a hissing expulsion of breath and McLendon cursing in undertone. They stood a moment longer, then they ran forward. They ran in a stumbling clump, as though they were fleeing something. "Kill him, kill the son," a voice whispered. McLendon flung them back.

"Not here," he said. "Get him into the car." "Kill him, kill the black son!" the voice murmured. They dragged the Negro to the car. The barber had waited beside the car. He could feel himself sweating and he knew he was going to be sick at the stomach.

"What is it, captains?" the Negro said. "I aint done nothing. 'Fore God, Mr John." Someone produced handcuffs. They worked busily about the Negro as though he were a post, quiet, intent, getting in one another's way. He submitted to the handcuffs, looking swiftly and constantly from dim face to dim face. "Who's here, captains?" he said, leaning to peer into the faces until they could feel his breath and smell his sweaty reek. He spoke a name or two. "What you all say I done, Mr John?"

McLendon jerked the car door open. "Get in!" he said.

The Negro did not move. "What you all going to do with me, Mr John? I aint done nothing. White folks, captains, I aint done nothing: I swear 'fore God." He called another name.

"Get in!" McLendon said. He struck the Negro. The others expelled their breath in a dry hissing and struck him with random blows and he whirled and cursed them, and swept his manacled hands across their faces and slashed the barber upon the mouth, and the barber struck him also. "Get him in there," McLendon said. They pushed at him. He ceased struggling and got in and sat quietly as the others took their places. He sat between the barber and the soldier, drawing his limbs in so as not to touch them, his eyes going swiftly and constantly from face to face. Butch clung to the running board. The car moved on. The barber nursed his mouth with his handkerchief.

"What's the matter, Hawk?" the soldier said.

"Nothing," the barber said. They regained the highroad and turned away from town. The second car dropped back out of the dust. They went on, gaining speed; the final fringe of houses dropped behind.

"Goddamn, he stinks!" the soldier said.

"We'll fix that," the drummer in front beside McLendon said. On the running board Butch cursed into the hot rush of air. The barber leaned suddenly forward and touched McLendon's arm.

"Let me out, John," he said.

"Jump out, niggerlover," McLendon said without turning his head. He drove swiftly. Behind them the sourceless lights of the second car glared in the dust. Presently McLendon turned into a narrow road. It was rutted with disuse. It led back to an abandoned brick kiln—a series of reddish mounds and weed- and vine-choked vats without bottom. It had been used for pasture once, until one day the owner missed one of his mules. Although he prodded carefully in the vats with a long pole, he could not even find the bottom of them.

"John," the barber said.

"Jump out, then," McLendon said, hurling the car along the ruts. Beside the barber the Negro spoke:

"Mr Henry."

The barber sat forward. The narrow tunnel of the road rushed up and past. Their motion was like an extinct furnace blast: cooler, but utterly dead. The car bounded from rut to rut.

"Mr Henry," the Negro said.

The barber began to tug furiously at the door. "Look out, there!" the soldier said, but the barber had already kicked the door open and swung onto the running board. The soldier leaned across the Negro and grasped at him, but he had already jumped. The car went on without checking speed.

The impetus hurled him crashing through dust-sheathed weeds, into the ditch. Dust puffed about him, and in a thin, vicious crackling of sapless stems he lay choking and retching until the second car passed and died away. Then he rose and limped on until he reached the highroad and turned toward town, brushing at his clothes with his hands. The moon was higher, riding high and clear of the dust at last, and after a while the town began to glare beneath the dust. He went on, limping. Presently he heard cars and the glow of them grew in the dust behind him and he left the road and crouched again in the weeds until they passed. McLendon's car came last now. There were four people in it and Butch was not on the running board.

They went on; the dust swallowed them; the glare and the sound died away. The dust of them hung for a while, but soon the eternal dust absorbed it again. The barber climbed back onto the road and limped on toward town.

IV

As she dressed for supper on that Saturday evening, her own flesh felt like fever. Her hands trembled among the hooks and eyes, and her eyes had a feverish look, and her hair swirled crisp and crackling under the comb. While she was still dressing the friends called for her and sat while she donned her sheerest underthings and stockings and a new voile dress. "Do you feel strong enough to go out?" they said, their eyes bright too, with a dark glitter. "When you have had time to get over the shock, you must tell us what happened. What he said and did; everything."

In the leafed darkness, as they walked toward the square, she began to breathe deeply, something like a swimmer preparing to dive, until she ceased trembling, the four of them walking slowly because of the terrible heat and out of solicitude for her. But as they neared the square she began to tremble again, walking with her head up, her hands clenched at her sides, their voices about her murmurous, also with that feverish, glittering quality of their eyes.

They entered the square, she in the center of the group, fragile in her fresh dress. She was trembling worse. She walked slower and slower, as children eat ice cream, her head up and her eyes bright in the haggard banner of her face, passing the hotel and the coatless drummers in chairs along the curb looking around at her: "That's the one: see? The one in pink in the middle." "Is that her? What did they do with the nigger? Did they—?" "Sure. He's all right." "All right, is he?" "Sure. He went on a little trip." Then the drug store, where even the young men lounging in the doorway tipped their hats and followed with their eyes the motion of her hips and legs when she passed.

They went on, passing the lifted hats of the gentlemen, the suddenly ceased voices, deferent, protective. "Do you see?" the friends said. Their voices sounded like long, hovering sighs of hissing exultation. "There's not a Negro on the square. Not one."

They reached the picture show. It was like a miniature fairyland with its lighted lobby and colored lithographs of life caught in its terrible and beautiful mutations. Her lips began to tingle. In the dark, when the picture began, it would be all right; she could hold back the laughing so it would not waste away so fast and so soon. So she hurried on before the turning faces, the undertones of low astonishment, and they took their accustomed places where she could see the aisle against the silver glare and the young men and girls coming in two and two against it.

The lights flicked away; the screen glowed silver, and soon life began to unfold, beautiful and passionate and sad, while still the young men and girls entered, scented and sibilant in the half dark, their paired backs in silhouette delicate and sleek, their slim, quick bodies awkward, divinely young, while beyond them the silver dream accumulated, inevitably on and on. She began to laugh. In trying to suppress it, it made more noise than ever; heads began to turn. Still laughing, her friends raised her and led her out, and she stood at the curb, laughing on a high, sustained note, until the taxi came up and they helped her in.

They removed the pink voile and the sheer underthings and the stockings, and put her to bed, and cracked ice for her temples, and sent for the doctor. He was hard to locate, so they ministered to her with hushed ejaculations, renewing the ice and fanning her. While the ice was fresh and cold she stopped laughing and lay still for a time, moaning only a little. But soon the laughing welled again and her voice rose screaming.

"Shhhhhhhhhhh! Shhhhhhhhhhhhhh!" they said, freshening the ice-pack, smoothing her hair, examining it for gray; "poor girl!" Then to one another: "Do you suppose anything really happened?" their eyes darkly aglitter, secret and passionate. "Shhhhhhhhh! Poor girl! Poor Minnie!"

V

It was midnight when McLendon drove up to his neat new house. It was trim and fresh as a birdcage and almost as small, with its clean, green-and-white paint. He locked the car and mounted the porch and entered. His wife rose from a chair beside the reading lamp. McLendon stopped in the floor and stared at her until she looked down.

"Look at that clock," he said, lifting his arm, pointing. She stood before him, her face lowered, a magazine in her hands. Her face was pale, strained, and weary-looking. "Haven't I told you about sitting up like this, waiting to see when I come in?"

"John," she said. She laid the magazine down. Poised on the balls of his feet, he glared at her with his hot eyes, his sweating face.

"Didn't I tell you?" He went toward her. She looked up then. He caught her shoulder. She stood passive, looking at him.

"Don't, John. I couldn't sleep . . . The heat; something. Please, John. You're hurting me."

"Didn't I tell you?" He released her and half struck, half flung her across the chair, and she lay there and watched him quietly as he left the room.

He went on through the house, ripping off his shirt, and on the dark, screened porch at the rear he stood and mopped his head and shoulders with the shirt and flung it away. He took the pistol from his hip and laid it on the table beside the bed, and sat on the bed and removed his shoes, and rose and slipped his trousers off. He was sweating again already, and he stooped and hunted furiously for the shirt. At last he found it and wiped his body again, and, with his body pressed against the dusty screen, he stood panting. There was no movement, no sound, not even an insect. The dark world seemed to lie stricken beneath the cold moon and the lidless stars.

Questions

1. Examine carefully the conversation in the first section. The barber seems sure that Will Mayes has done nothing wrong. Does he give any evidence? Do you trust his judgment of Will? Of Miss Cooper? What is he suggesting about Miss Cooper? Examine the response first of Butch, then the drummer, then McLendon. Could you distinguish one from the other by their responses? On what are the responses based?
2. Note the differing responses to getting "the facts." How many "facts" do the men have to go on? The barber is repeatedly called "a damn niggerlover." Do the "facts" show him to be one? What kind of "meaning" does the expression carry? That is, what semantic force does it have?
3. Why should Faulkner emphasize the drought, the dust, the dryness so much? Does it have any connection with the action? How far were you into the story before you guessed that the men would lynch Mayes?
4. Why do the scenes alternately show the men then Miss Cooper? Do the scenes with Miss Cooper support the barber's suggestions about her? Can you decide whether she has really been attacked?
5. If McLendon had been shown concrete evidence that Will Mayes had not attacked Miss Cooper, or even that she had not been attacked at all, would the lynching have taken place? Consider especially his reaction to the question, "Did it really happen?"
6. What effect does Faulkner get by showing McLendon in the final scene with his wife? How logical is he here? Can you explain psychologically his reaction to her?
7. The story carries a heavy impact. How much of the impact comes from Faulkner's own persuasive powers? Can you decide just what he is trying to persuade us of, if anything? What does he want us to feel or think or do? What in the story tells you so?

Suggestions for Writing

1. Most of us fortunately do not get involved so deeply in this kind of violence resulting from the short-circuiting of logical processes. But all of us have been involved in arguments, quarrels, troubles where similar logical problems are involved. Analyze one of these situations for its logical implications. Whatever the point you make, work to make it as persuasively as possible.
2. Analyze Faulkner's story for the relation between his fictional techniques and his persuasive power. You will need to define what he is trying to persuade us to do or feel or think and then see what helps to persuade us. What persuades us in the characterizations? In the structure? In the plot itself? In the handling of conversation and words? Your short paper may need to focus on the quality or qualities that seem most powerfully persuasive.

Love Is a Fallacy

Max Shulman *With his typical offbeat humor Max Shulman reduces logic to the ludicrous level it sometimes reaches in college courses.*

Cool was I and logical. Keen, calculating, perspicacious, acute and astute—I was all of these. My brain was as powerful as a dynamo, as precise as a chemist's scales, as penetrating as a scalpel. And—think of it!—I was only eighteen.

It is not often that one so young has such a giant intellect. Take, for example, Petey Bellows, my roommate at the university. Same age, same background, but dumb as an ox. A nice enough fellow, you understand, but nothing upstairs. Emotional type. Unstable. Impressionable. Worst of all, a faddist. Fads, I submit, are the very negation of reason. To be swept up in every new craze that comes along, to surrender yourself to idiocy just because everybody else is doing it—this, to me, is the acme of mindlessness. Not, however, to Petey.

One afternoon I found Petey lying on his bed with an expression of such distress on his face that I immediately diagnosed appendicitis. "Don't move," I said. "Don't take a laxative. I'll get a doctor."

"Raccoon," he mumbled thickly.

"Raccoon?" I said, pausing in my flight.

"I want a raccoon coat," he wailed.

I perceived that his trouble was not physical, but mental. "Why do you want a raccoon coat?"

"I should have known it," he cried, pounding his temples. "I should have known they'd come back when the Charleston came back. Like a fool I spent all my money for textbooks, and now I can't get a raccoon coat."

"Can you mean," I said incredulously, "that people are actually wearing raccoon coats again?"

"All the Big Men on Campus are wearing them. Where've you been?"

"In the library," I said, naming a place not frequented by Big Men on Campus.

He leaped from the bed and paced the room. "I've got to have a raccoon coat," he said passionately. "I've got to!"

"Petey, why? Look at it rationally. Raccoon coats are unsanitary. They shed. They smell bad. They weigh too much. They're unsightly. They—"

"You don't understand," he interrupted impatiently. "It's the thing to do. Don't you want to be in the swim?"

"No," I said truthfully.

"Well, I do," he declared. "I'd give anything for a raccoon coat. Anything!"

My brain, that precision instrument, slipped into high gear. "Anything?" I asked, looking at him narrowly.

"Anything," he affirmed in ringing tones.

I stroked my chin thoughtfully. It so happened that I knew where to get my hands on a raccoon coat. My father had had one in his undergraduate days; it lay now in a trunk in the attic back home. It also happened that Petey had something I wanted. He didn't *have* it exactly, but at least he had first rights on it. I refer to his girl, Polly Espy.

I had long coveted Polly Espy. Let me emphasize that my desire for this young woman was not emotional in nature. She was, to be sure, a girl who excited the emotions, but I was not one to let my heart rule my head. I wanted Polly for a shrewdly calculated, entirely cerebral reason.

I was a freshman in law school. In a few years I would be out in practice. I was well aware of the importance of the right kind of wife in furthering a lawyer's career. The successful lawyers I had observed were, almost without exception, married to beautiful, gracious, intelligent women. With one omission, Polly fitted these specifications perfectly.

Beautiful she was. She was not yet of pin-up proportions, but I felt sure that time would supply the lack. She already had the makings.

Gracious she was. By gracious I mean full of graces. She had an erectness of carriage, an ease of bearing, a poise that clearly indicated the best of breeding. At table her manners were exquisite. I had seen her at the Kozy Kampus Korner eating the specialty of the house—a sandwich that contained scraps of pot roast, gravy, chopped nuts, and a dipper of sauerkraut—without even getting her fingers moist.

Intelligent she was not. In fact, she veered in the opposite direction. But I believed that under my guidance she would smarten up. At any rate, it was worth a try. It is, after all, easier to make a beautiful dumb girl smart than to make an ugly smart girl beautiful.

"Petey," I said, "are you in love with Polly Espy?"

"I think she's a keen kid," he replied, "but I don't know if you'd call it love. Why?"

"Do you," I asked, "have any kind of formal arrangement with her? I mean are you going steady or anything like that?"

"No. We see each other quite a bit, but we both have other dates. Why?"

"Is there," I asked, "any other man for whom she has a particular fondness?"

"Not that I know of. Why?"

I nodded with satisfaction. "In other words, if you were out of the picture, the field would be open. Is that right?"

"I guess so. What are you getting at?"

"Nothing, nothing," I said innocently, and took my suitcase out of the closet.

"Where you going?" asked Petey.

"Home for the week end." I threw a few things into the bag.

"Listen," he said, clutching my arm eagerly, "while you're home, you couldn't get some money from your old man, could you, and lend it to me so I can buy a raccoon coat?"

"I may do better than that," I said with a mysterious wink and closed my bag and left.

"Look," I said to Petey when I got back Monday morning. I threw open the suitcase and revealed the huge, hairy, gamy object that my father had worn in his Stutz Bearcat in 1925.

"Holy Toledo!" said Petey reverently. He plunged his hands into the raccoon coat and then his face. "Holy Toledo!" he repeated fifteen or twenty times.

"Would you like it?" I asked.

"Oh yes!" he cried, clutching the greasy pelt to him. Then a canny look came into his eyes. "What do you want for it?"

"Your girl," I said, mincing no words.

"Polly?" he said in a horrified whisper. "You want Polly?"

"That's right."

He flung the coat from him. "Never," he said stoutly.

I shrugged. "Okay. If you don't want to be in the swim, I guess it's your business."

I sat down in a chair and pretended to read a book, but out of the corner of my eye I kept watching Petey. He was a torn man. First he looked at the coat with the expression of a waif at a bakery window. Then he turned away and set his jaw resolutely. Then he looked back at the coat, with even more longing in his face. Then he turned away, but with not so much resolution this time. Back and forth his head swiveled, desire waxing, resolution waning. Finally he didn't turn away at all; he just stood and stared with mad lust at the coat.

"It isn't as though I was in love with Polly," he said thickly. "Or going steady or anything like that."

"That's right," I murmured.

"What's Polly to me, or me to Polly?"

"Not a thing," said I.

"It's just been a casual kick—just a few laughs, that's all."

"Try on the coat," said I.

He complied. The coat bunched high over his ears and dropped all the way down to his shoe tops. He looked like a mound of dead raccoons. "Fits fine," he said happily.

I rose from my chair. "Is it a deal?" I asked, extending my hand.

He swallowed. "It's a deal," he said and shook my hand.

I had my first date with Polly the following evening. This was in the nature of a survey; I wanted to find out just how much work I had to do to get her mind up to the standard I required. I took her first to dinner. "Gee, that was a delish dinner," she said as we left the restaurant. Then I took her to a movie. "Gee, that was a marvy movie," she said as we left the theater. And then I took her home. "Gee, I had a sensaysh time," she said as she bade me good night.

I went back to my room with a heavy heart. I had gravely underestimated the size of my task. This girl's lack of information was terrifying. Nor would it be enough merely to supply her with information. First she had to be taught to *think*. This loomed as a project of no small dimensions, and at first I was tempted to give her back to Petey. But then I got to thinking about her abundant physical charms and about the way she entered a room and the way she handled a knife and fork, and I decided to make an effort.

I went about it, as in all things, systematically. I gave her a course in logic. It happened that I, as a law student, was taking a course in logic myself, so I had all the facts at my finger tips. "Polly," I said to her when I picked her up on our next date, "tonight we are going over to the Knoll and talk."

"Oo, terrif," she replied. One thing I will say for this girl: you would go far to find another so agreeable.

We went to the Knoll, the campus trysting place, and we sat down under an old oak, and she looked at me expectantly. "What are we going to talk about?" she asked.

"Logic."

She thought this over for a minute and decided she liked it. "Magnif," she said.

"Logic," I said, clearing my throat, "is the science of thinking. Before we can think correctly, we must first learn to recognize the common fallacies of logic. These we will take up tonight."

"Wow-dow!" she cried, clapping her hands delightedly.

I winced, but went bravely on. "First let us examine the fallacy called Dicto Simpliciter."

"By all means," she urged, batting her lashes eagerly.

"Dicto Simpliciter means an argument based on an unqualified generalization. For example: Exercise is good. Therefore everybody should exercise."

"I agree," said Polly earnestly. "I mean exercise is wonderful. I mean it builds the body and everything."

"Polly," I said gently, "the argument is a fallacy. *Exercise is good* is an unqualified generalization. For instance, if you have heart disease, exercise is bad, not good. Many people are ordered by their doctors *not* to exercise. You must *qualify* the generalization. You must say exercise is *usually* good, or exercise is good *for most people*. Otherwise you have committed a Dicto Simpliciter. Do you see?"

"No," she confessed. "But this is marvy. Do more! Do more!"

"It will be better if you stop tugging at my sleeve," I told her, and when she desisted, I continued. "Next we take up a fallacy called Hasty Generalization. Listen carefully: You can't speak French. I can't speak French. Petey Bellows can't speak French. I must therefore conclude that nobody at the University of Minnesota can speak French."

"Really?" said Polly, amazed. *"Nobody?"*

I hid my exasperation. "Polly, it's a fallacy. The generalization is reached too hastily. There are too few instances to support such a conclusion."

"Know any more fallacies?" she asked breathlessly. "This is more fun than dancing even."

I fought off a wave of despair. I was getting nowhere with this girl, absolutely nowhere. Still, I am nothing if not persistent. I continued. "Next comes Post Hoc. Listen to this: Let's not take Bill on our picnic. Every time we take him out with us, it rains."

"I know somebody just like that," she exclaimed. "A girl back home —Eula Becker, her name is. It never fails. Every single time we take her on a picnic—"

"Polly," I said sharply, "it's a fallacy. Eula Becker doesn't *cause* the rain. She has no connection with the rain. You are guilty of Post Hoc if you blame Eula Becker."

"I'll never do it again," she promised contritely. "Are you mad at me?"

I sighed. "No, Polly, I'm not mad."

"Then tell me some more fallacies."

"All right. Let's try Contradictory Premises."

"Yes, let's," she chirped, blinking her eyes happily.

I frowned, but plunged ahead. "Here's an example of Contradictory Premises: If God can do anything, can He make a stone so heavy that He won't be able to lift it?"

"Of course," she replied promptly.

"But if He can do anything, He can lift the stone," I pointed out.

"Yeah," she said thoughtfully. "Well, then I guess He can't make the stone."

"But He can do anything," I reminded her.

She scratched her pretty, empty head. "I'm all confused," she admitted.

"Of course you are. Because when the premises of an argument contradict each other, there can be no argument. If there is an irresistible force, there can be no immovable object. If there is an immovable object, there can be no irresistible force. Get it?"

"Tell me some more of this keen stuff," she said eagerly.

I consulted my watch. "I think we'd better call it a night. I'll take you home now, and you go over all the things you've learned. We'll have another session tomorrow night."

I deposited her at the girls' dormitory, where she assured me that she had had a perfectly terrif evening, and I went glumly home to my room. Petey lay snoring in his bed, the raccoon coat huddled like a great hairy beast at his feet. For a moment I considered waking him and telling him that he could have his girl back. It seemed clear that my project was doomed to failure. The girl simply had a logic-proof head.

But then I reconsidered. I had wasted one evening; I might as well waste another. Who knew? Maybe somewhere in the extinct crater of her mind a few embers still smoldered. Maybe somehow I could fan them into flame. Admittedly it was not a prospect fraught with hope, but I decided to give it one more try.

Seated under the oak the next evening I said, "Our first fallacy tonight is called Ad Misericordiam."

She quivered with delight.

"Listen closely," I said. "A man applies for a job. When the boss asks him what his qualifications are, he replies that he has a wife and six children at home, the wife is a helpless cripple, the children have nothing to eat, no clothes to wear, no shoes on their feet, there are no beds in the house, no coal in the cellar, and winter is coming."

A tear rolled down each of Polly's pink cheeks. "Oh, this is awful, awful," she sobbed.

"Yes, it's awful," I agreed, "but it's no argument. The man never answered the boss's question about his qualifications. Instead he appealed to the boss's sympathy. He committed the fallacy of Ad Misericordiam. Do you understand?"

"Have you got a handkerchief?" she blubbered.

I handed her a handkerchief and tried to keep from screaming while she wiped her eyes. "Next," I said in a carefully controlled tone, "we will discuss False Analogy. Here is an example: Students should be allowed to look at their textbooks during examinations. After all, surgeons have X rays to guide them during an operation, lawyers have briefs to guide them during a trial, carpenters have blueprints to guide them when they are building a house. Why, then, shouldn't students be allowed to look at their textbooks during an examination?"

"There now," she said enthusiastically, "is the most marvy idea I've heard in years."

"Polly," I said testily, "the argument is all wrong. Doctors, lawyers, and carpenters aren't taking a test to see how much they have learned, but students are. The situations are altogether different, and you can't make an analogy between them."

"I still think it's a good idea," said Polly.

"Nuts," I muttered. Doggedly I pressed on. "Next we'll try Hypothesis Contrary to Fact."

"Sounds yummy," was Polly's reaction.

"Listen: If Madame Curie had not happened to leave a photographic plate in a drawer with a chunk of pitchblende, the world today would not know about radium."

"True, true," said Polly, nodding her head. "Did you see the movie? Oh, it just knocked me out. That Walter Pidgeon is so dreamy. I mean he fractures me."

"If you can forget Mr. Pidgeon for a moment," I said coldly, "I would like to point out that the statement is a fallacy. Maybe Madame Curie would have discovered radium at some later date. Maybe somebody else would have discovered it. Maybe any number of things would have happened. You can't start with a hypothesis that is not true and then draw any supportable conclusions from it."

"They ought to put Walter Pidgeon in more pictures," said Polly. "I hardly ever see him any more."

One more chance, I decided. But just one more. There is a limit to what flesh and blood can bear. "The next fallacy is called Poisoning the Well."

"How cute!" she gurgled.

"Two men are having a debate. The first one gets up and says, 'My opponent is a notorious liar. You can't believe a word that he is going to say.' . . . Now, Polly, think. Think hard. What's wrong?"

I watched her closely as she knit her creamy brow in concentration. Suddenly a glimmer of intelligence—the first I had seen—came into her eyes. "It's not fair," she said with indignation. "It's not a bit fair. What chance has the second man got if the first man calls him a liar before he even begins talking?"

"Right!" I cried exultantly. "One hundred per cent right. It's not fair. The first man has *poisoned the well* before anybody could drink from it. He has hamstrung his opponent before he could even start. . . . Polly, I'm proud of you."

"Pshaw," she murmured, blushing with pleasure.

"You see, my dear, these things aren't so hard. All you have to do is concentrate. Think—examine—evaluate. Come now, let's review everything we have learned."

"Fire away," she said with an airy wave of her hand.

Heartened by the knowledge that Polly was not altogether a cretin, I began a long, patient review of all I had told her. Over and over and over again I cited instances, pointed out flaws, kept hammering away without letup. It was like digging a tunnel. At first everything was work, sweat, and darkness. I had no idea when I would reach the light, or even *if* I would. But I persisted. I pounded and clawed and scraped, and finally I was rewarded. I saw a chink of light. And then the chink got bigger and the sun came pouring in and all was bright.

Five grueling nights this took, but it was worth it. I had made a logician out of Polly; I had taught her to think. My job was done. She was worthy of me at last. She was a fit wife for me, a proper hostess for my many mansions, a suitable mother for my well-heeled children.

It must not be thought that I was without love for this girl. Quite the contrary. Just as Pygmalion loved the perfect woman he had fashioned, so I loved mine. I decided to acquaint her with my feelings at our very next meeting. The time had come to change our relationship from academic to romantic.

"Polly," I said when next we sat beneath our oak, "tonight we will not discuss fallacies."

"Aw, gee," she said, disappointed.

"My dear," I said, favoring her with a smile, "we have now spent five evenings together. We have gotten along splendidly. It is clear that we are well matched."

"Hasty Generalization," said Polly brightly.

"I beg your pardon," said I.

"Hasty Generalization," she repeated. "How can you say that we are well matched on the basis of only five dates?"

I chuckled with amusement. The dear child had learned her lessons well. "My dear," I said, patting her hand in a tolerant manner, "five dates is plenty. After all, you don't have to eat a whole cake to know that it's good."

"False Analogy," said Polly promptly. "I'm not a cake. I'm a girl."

I chuckled with somewhat less amusement. The dear child had learned her lessons perhaps too well. I decided to change tactics. Obviously the best approach was a simple, strong, direct declaration of love. I paused for a moment while my massive brain chose the proper words. Then I began:

"Polly, I love you. You are the whole world to me, and the moon and the stars and the constellations of outer space. Please, my darling, say that you will go steady with me, for if you will not, life will be meaningless. I will languish. I will refuse my meals. I will wander the face of the earth, a shambling, hollow-eyed hulk."

There, I thought, folding my arms, that ought to do it.

"Ad Misericordiam," said Polly.

I ground my teeth. I was not Pygmalion; I was Frankenstein, and my monster had me by the throat. Frantically I fought back the tide of panic surging through me. At all costs I had to keep cool.

"Well, Polly," I said, forcing a smile, "you certainly have learned your fallacies."

"You're darn right," she said with a vigorous nod.

"And who taught them to you, Polly?"

"You did."

"That's right. So you do owe me something, don't you, my dear? If I hadn't come along you never would have learned about fallacies."

"Hypothesis Contrary to Fact," she said instantly.

I dashed perspiration from my brow. "Polly," I croaked, "you mustn't take all these things so literally. I mean this is just classroom stuff. You know that the things you learn in school don't have anything to do with life."

"Dicto Simpliciter," she said, wagging her finger at me playfully.

That did it. I leaped to my feet, bellowing like a bull. "Will you or will you not go steady with me?"

"I will not," she replied.

"Why not?" I demanded.

"Because this afternoon I promised Petey Bellows that I would go steady with him."

I reeled back, overcome with the infamy of it. After he promised, after he made a deal, after he shook my hand! "The rat!" I shrieked, kicking up great chunks of turf. "You can't go with him, Polly. He's a liar. He's a cheat. He's a rat."

"Poisoning the Well," said Polly, "and stop shouting. I think shouting must be a fallacy too."

With an immense effort of will, I modulated my voice. "All right," I said. "You're a logician. Let's look at this thing logically. How could you choose Petey Bellows over me? Look at me—a brilliant student, a tremendous intellectual, a man with an assured future. Look at Petey—a knothead, a jitterbug, a guy who'll never know where his next meal is coming from. Can you give me one logical reason why you should go steady with Petey Bellows?"

"I certainly can," declared Polly. "He's got a raccoon coat."

Questions

1. The youthful hero seems to think highly of himself, but what is Shulman's attitude toward him? How can you tell what the author's attitude toward a character is when the character is telling the story?
2. How well has the young freshman learned his logic? Does he act logically at the beginning of the story? At the end of the story?
3. Does Polly learn her lessons too quickly? How stupid is she? When she answers the "one logical reason" she has for going steady with Petey, what does she reveal about herself and her lessons in logic?
4. All three characters here are stereotypes. What would happen to Shulman's humor if these were presented as believable, many-sided personalities?

Suggestions for Writing

1. Everyone has plans which go awry. Choose such a time when your plans turned out quite differently from what you expected. Write an account for your classmates with a consistent tone, but do not tell what your attitude toward the event is. Make the attitude come across in the words you choose and in the manner in which you tell it.

I Have a Dream

Martin Luther King, Jr.

This speech by Martin Luther King, Jr., has been widely reproduced. King's murder may have encouraged the dissemination of the speech, but its persuasiveness grows out of elements within the speech itself. As you read the speech be conscious of the many devices that King uses to persuade his audience. Note particularly the echoes from older well-known writings or speeches.

Five score years ago, a great American, in whose symbolic shadow we stand, signed the Emancipation Proclamation. This momentous decree came as a great beacon light of hope to millions of Negro slaves who had been seared in the flames of withering injustice. It came as a joyous daybreak to end the long night of captivity.

But one hundred years later, we must face the tragic fact that the Negro is still not free. One hundred years later, the life of the Negro is still sadly crippled by the manacles of segregation and the chains of discrimination. One hundred years later, the Negro lives on a lonely island of poverty in the midst of a vast ocean of material prosperity. One hundred years later, the Negro is still languished in the corners of American society and finds himself an exile in his own land. So we have come here today to dramatize an appalling condition.

In a sense we have come to our nation's Capital to cash a check. When the architects of our republic wrote the magnificent words of the Constitution and the Declaration of Independence, they were signing a promissory note to which every American was to fall heir. This note was a promise that all men would be guaranteed the unalienable rights of life, liberty, and the pursuit of happiness.

It is obvious today that America has defaulted on this promissory note insofar as her citizens of color are concerned. Instead of honoring this sacred obligation, America has given the Negro people a bad check; a check which has come back marked "insufficient funds." But we refuse to believe that the bank of justice is bankrupt. We refuse to believe that there are insufficient funds in the great vaults of opportunity of this nation. So we have come to cash this check—a check that will give us upon demand the riches of freedom and the security of justice. We have also come to this hallowed spot to remind America of the fierce urgency of *now*. This is no time to engage in the luxury of cooling off or to take the tranquilizing drug of gradualism. *Now* is the time to make real the promises of Democracy. *Now* is the time to rise from the dark and desolate valley of segregation to the sunlit path of racial justice. *Now* is the time to open the doors of opportunity to all of God's children. *Now* is the time to lift our nation from the quicksands of racial injustice to the solid rock of brotherhood.

It would be fatal for the nation to overlook the urgency of the moment and to underestimate the determination of the Negro. This sweltering summer of the Negro's legitimate discontent will not pass until there is an invigorating autumn of freedom and equality. 1963 is not an end, but a beginning. Those who hope that the Negro needed to blow off steam and will now be content will have a rude awakening if the nation returns to business as usual. There will be neither rest nor tranquility in America until the Negro is granted his citizenship rights. The whirlwinds of revolt will continue to shake the foundations of our nation until the bright day of justice emerges.

But there is something that I must say to my people who stand on the warm threshold which leads into the palace of justice. In the process of gaining our rightful place we must not be guilty of wrongful deeds. Let us not seek to satisfy our thirst for freedom by drinking from the cup of bitterness and hatred. We must forever conduct our struggle on the high plane of dignity and discipline. We must not allow our creative protest to degenerate into physical violence. Again and again we must rise to the majestic heights of meeting physical force with soul force. The marvelous new militancy which has engulfed the Negro community must not lead us to a distrust of all white people, for many of our white brothers, as evidenced by their presence here today, have come to realize that their destiny is tied up with our destiny and their freedom is inextricably bound to our freedom. We cannot walk alone.

And as we walk, we must make the pledge that we shall march ahead. We cannot turn back. There are those who are asking the devotees of civil rights, "When will you be satisfied?" We can never be satisfied as long as the Negro is the victim of the unspeakable horrors of police brutality. We can never be satisfied as long as our bodies, heavy with the fatigue of travel, cannot gain lodging in the motels of the highways and the hotels of the cities. We cannot be satisfied as long as the Negro's basic mobility is from a smaller ghetto to a larger one. We can never be satisfied as long as a Negro in Mississippi cannot vote and a Negro in New York believes he has nothing for which to vote. No, no, we are not satisfied, and we will not be satisfied until justice rolls down like waters and righteousness like a mighty stream.

I am not unmindful that some of you have come here out of great trials and tribulations. Some of you have come fresh from narrow jail cells. Some of you have come from areas where your quest for freedom left you battered by the storms of persecution and staggered by the winds of police brutality. You have been the veterans of creative suffering. Continue to work with the faith that unearned suffering is redemptive.

Go back to Mississippi, go back to Alabama, go back to South Carolina, go back to Georgia, go back to Louisiana, go back to the slums and the ghettos of our northern cities, knowing that somehow this situation can and will be changed. Let us not wallow in the valley of despair.

I say to you today, my friends, that in spite of the difficulties and frustrations of the moment I still have a dream. It is a dream deeply rooted in the American dream.

I have a dream that one day this nation will rise up and live out the true meaning of its creed: "We hold these truths to be self-evident; that all men are created equal."

I have a dream that one day on the red hills of Georgia the sons of former slaves and the sons of former slaveowners will be able to sit down together at the table of brotherhood.

I have a dream that one day even the state of Mississippi, a desert state sweltering with the heat of injustice and oppression, will be transformed into an oasis of freedom and justice.

I have a dream that my four little children will one day live in a nation where they will not be judged by the color of their skin but by the content of their character.

I have a dream today.

I have a dream that one day the state of Alabama, whose governor's lips are presently dripping with the words of interposition and nullification, will be transformed into a situation where little black boys and black girls will be able to join hands with little white boys and white girls and walk together as sisters and brothers.

I have a dream today.

I have a dream that one day every valley shall be exalted, every hill and mountain shall be made low, the rough places will be made plains, and the crooked places will be made straight, and the glory of the Lord shall be revealed, and all flesh shall see it together.

This is our hope. This is the faith with which I return to the South. With this faith we will be able to hew out of the mountain of despair a stone of hope. With this faith we will be able to transform the jangling discords of our nation into a beautiful symphony of brotherhood. With this faith we will be able to work together, to pray together, to struggle together, to go to jail together, to stand up for freedom together, knowing that we will be free one day.

This will be the day when all of God's children will be able to sing with new meaning

> My country, 'tis of thee,
> Sweet land of liberty,
> Of thee I sing:
> Land where my fathers died,
> Land of the pilgrims' pride,
> From every mountain-side
> Let freedom ring.

And if America is to be a great nation this must become true. So let freedom ring from the prodigious hilltops of New Hampshire. Let freedom ring from the mighty mountains of New York. Let freedom ring from the heightening Alleghenies of Pennsylvania!

Let freedom ring from the snowcapped Rockies of Colorado!

Let freedom ring from the curvaceous peaks of California!

But not only that; let freedom ring from Stone Mountain of Georgia!

Let freedom ring from Lookout Mountain of Tennessee!

Let freedom ring from every hill and molehill of Mississippi. From every mountainside, let freedom ring.

When we let freedom ring, when we let it ring from every village and every hamlet, from every state and every city, we will be able to speed up that day when all of God's children, black men and white men, Jews and Gentiles, Protestants and Catholics, will be able to join hands and sing in the words of the old Negro spiritual, "Free at last; free at last! thank God almighty, we are free at last!"

Questions

1. Who would be persuaded by King's speech? Who would be unpersuaded? Who would be angered? Is it difficult for one who is angered by the speech to answer King? Why?
2. What devices of persuasion do King's opponents resort to? Can you relate these devices to anything in Huxley's selection or any other selection from this textbook?
3. What can you tell about the personality of King from reading his speech?
4. In what ways does the style contribute to the persuasive power of the speech? Can you think of a stylistic source for the series of parallel sentences King uses?

Two Sonnets

Claude McKay *Both of these sonnets protest against essentially the same thing. The one protests directly and explicitly, the other indirectly and implicitly. Which is the more effective protest? That is, which is the better piece of persuasion? Account in every way you can for the contrast in effectiveness. Would you say that the sonnet most effective in persuasion is also the better poem?*

In Bondage

I would be wandering in distant fields
Where man, and bird, and beast, lives leisurely,
And the old earth is kind, and ever yields
Her goodly gifts to all her children free;
Where life is fairer, lighter, less demanding,
And boys and girls have time and space for play
Before they come to years of understanding—
Somewhere I would be singing, far away.
For life is greater than the thousand wars
Men wage for it in their insatiate lust,
And will remain like the eternal stars,
When all that shines to-day is drift and dust
But I am bound with you in your mean graves,
O black men, simple slaves of ruthless slaves.

If We Must Die

If we must die, let it not be like hogs
Hunted and penned in an inglorious spot,
While round us bark the mad and hungry dogs,
Making their mock at our accursèd lot.

If we must die, O let us nobly die,
So that our precious blood may not be shed
In vain; then even the monsters we defy
Shall be constrained to honor us though dead!
O kinsmen! we must meet the common foe!
Though far outnumbered let us show us brave,
And for their thousand blows deal one death blow!
What though before us lies the open grave?
Like men we'll face the murderous, cowardly pack,
Pressed to the wall, dying, but fighting back!

Writing Projects

1. Choose an opinion which you hold strongly about politics, religion, civil rights, the draft law, or some similar subject. Express your opinion as concisely as you can. Keep this part of the writing to no more than two or three sentences. Then write an argument in which you take the opposite point of view, supporting the reverse of your own opinion. Try to be as logical as you can; give arguments and specific support for this opinion.

2. Write a persuasive speech or article, in which you attempt to get your audience to act differently from the way they now act. Designate the audience that you are addressing. Use as many devices as you can for that particular audience; you may want to echo material that is known to the audience, but do not overdo this technique, because it can become laughable.

Part VIII

Style and Tone

Style and tone are qualities of rhetoric. Like the previous section on logic and persuasion, this section includes no discussion of a rhetorical approach. The rhetorical problems involved with style and tone, though they may seem to be different from those previously considered, are even more immediate and persistent. If you are really aware of a rhetorical stance, then the style and tone with which you write may have even more to do with your effectiveness than your patterns of organization or your logic.

Once you have achieved a proper relationship between author's voice, subject, and audience, once you have taken a rhetorical stance, you have at least suggested to yourself, if not dictated, the style and the tone with which you will write. You would hardly write using teen-age slang to the board of trustees of a university, not if you wanted them to take you seriously. Nor would you generally address a favorite friend or a brother or sister in the formal, carefully worked prose of a report to the Modern Language Association. Your tone with the board would probably be formal. Your tone with your friend would probably be informal, perhaps intimate, even chatty. So would your style.

The more precisely you define your rhetorical stance, the more it will do to solve problems of style and tone. But the relation works both ways: your awareness of possibilities in style and tone can help you solve the problems of rhetorical stance. If you want to pretend to be a back-country cracker like Robert Penn Warren's Munn Short, you must have some sense of the style in which you would speak and some control over the possible variations of tone you might use. One student, when asked "How would you describe the style of this author?" responded somewhat quizzically, "What styles have you got?" He had defined one of the beginning places of wisdom.

What styles have you got? What are the possible choices? With what shades of tone can one speak or write? And with what effects? This section tries to bring you to some answers. But we need to agree on what we mean by style and tone. *Style* is applied to writing so often and so loosely that everyone thinks he knows what is meant by this term. But not many would even agree on a definition. "Style is the man," the French critic Boileau said. The definition, broad as it is, suggests a very important fact about style: somehow it *is* an integral part of a writer's total self or it develops out of and reveals that self. But to say this is to say that one can do nothing about his own style, that it is somehow fixed, settled upon him as we used to think that an I.Q. is settled upon him. Perhaps this has some kind of truth, if we conceive *style* broadly enough. But few teachers really believe it, or they would not be trying to teach something about style.

The word is also used to describe broadly a people or a period: the style of the French or the Japanese, of the Victorian period or the Jazz Age. These too are recognizable and meaningful concepts in writing. But they are only indirectly related to your immediate problem of recognizing style and developing an effective and personal style of your own. For our purposes we can limit the meaning of *style* to the kinds of words an author uses and the way he puts them together in sentences—"the author's choice and arrangement of words," as Professor Robert Heilman succinctly puts it to his classes. You can talk concretely about style if you talk about the author's choices: between long and short words, between abstract and concrete words, between literal and figurative words, between "plain" and "fancy" words, between various possible parts of speech; and between short and long sentences, between simple and compound sentences, between direct subject-verb-complement sentences and inverted or interrupted or involuted sentences. Especially in this section watch carefully for the kinds of words an author chooses and the way he puts them together. The selections are written mostly by people unusually sensitive to style and consciously working for excellence.

Tone is also a commonly used word but a very elusive quality. In writing, understand the word as metaphorical. Words on a page have no tone, any more than notes on a musical score. But just as the musical score usually indicates a complex and fascinating sequence of tones and interaction among them, so the printed words on a page suggest a complex sequence of sounds that, by varying pitch and other qualities, result in a certain "tone of voice." This "tone of voice," the complex combination of sound, timbre, facial expressions, and other indications by which a speaker conveys to his audience how he feels about what he is saying—this is the concept of tone in writing. You can describe tone more or less concretely with such adjectives as *factual, objective, emotional, hysterical, ironical, satirical, intense, humorous, melodramatic, sentimental, tender*—almost any adjective that can define an attitude one might take toward his materials. You will find authors in the selections below using almost all of the attitudes just mentioned. Which ones might fit Mark Twain in "Letter to the Earth" or Melville in "Brit"? The capacity to recognize and define with precision the tone, or varying tones, of an author is one of the marks of a mature reader. How many people misread tone, and how badly they misread it, can be seen by watching the sequence of "Letters to the Editor" in any college or public newspaper following the publication of a letter that makes its point by irony.

Expanding the metaphor, we might call those who miss the tone in writing "tone-deaf." Most of those irate citizens who were so outraged at the publication of Jonathan Swift's "A Modest Proposal" must have been tone-deaf. You can improve not only your sensitivity to tone in the writing of others but the control and flexibility of tone in your own writing. As with style, the following selections illustrate a wide range of tonal qualities. But nearly all are written by people unusually sensitive to tone.

A closely related problem, especially in dealing with imaginative literature, grows out of the problems of rhetorical stance. Recall the way in which you come to see the characters and action in Flannery O'Connor's "Revelation." Miss O'Connor never tells you, "Now look, you need to be careful. You are seeing these characters not as they objectively are but as Mrs. Turpin sees them. Mrs. Turpin classifies them as white trash or niggers or well-dressed." But Miss O'Connor should not have to tell you this. Your own sensitivity to the story should tell you. And it should also tell how completely Mrs. Turpin damns herself by so classifying. No wonder she needs a revelation! The sense of tone in imaginative work is closely related to an understanding of the point of view through which the author is narrating a story or expressing a lyric rhapsody. Would you always equate the "I" of a lyric poem immediately with the author? Is the "I" the same kind of person in the two sonnets by Shakespeare in this section? The tone is largely determined by the point of view, but both tone and point of view make up the literary equivalent of the rhetorical stance. Again sensitivity is the key. Sensitivity can be developed only by careful analysis and broad experience.

What Is Style?

F. L. Lucas

F. L. Lucas is probably better known in England than in America, but some of his books of literary criticism have been known and admired in America for decades. As the following essay reveals, he received the typical English education of his time—typical, that is, for the upper classes. But more important for our immediate purpose, that education gave him, whether it tried to or not, an unusual sensitivity to style. He recognizes it in others, he can talk about it with English grace and wit, and he can display it in his own writing. He is worth reading for his advice alone, but you should read for his own style as well.

When it was suggested to Walt Whitman that one of his works should be bound in vellum, he was outraged—"Pshaw!" he snorted, "—hangings, curtains, finger bowls, chinaware, Matthew Arnold!" And he might have been equally irritated by talk of style; for he boasted of "my barbaric yawp"—he would *not* be literary; his readers should touch not a book but a man. Yet Whitman took the pains to rewrite *Leaves of Grass* four times, and his style is unmistakable. Samuel Butler maintained that writers who bothered about their style became unreadable but he bothered about his own. "Style" has got a bad name by growing associated with precious and superior persons who, like Oscar Wilde, spend a morning putting in a comma, and the afternoon (so he said) taking it out again. But such abuse of "style" is misuse of English. For the word means merely "a way of expressing oneself, in language, manner, or appearance"; or, secondly, "a *good* way of so expressing oneself"—as when one says, "Her behavior never lacked style."

Now there is no crime in expressing oneself (though to try to *im*press oneself on others easily grows revolting or ridiculous). Indeed one cannot help expressing oneself, unless one passes one's life in a cupboard. Even the most rigid Communist, or Organization-man, is compelled by Nature to have a unique voice, unique fingerprints, unique handwriting. Even the signatures of the letters on your breakfast table may reveal more than their writers guess. There are blustering signatures that swish across the page like cornstalks bowed before a tempest. There are cryptic signatures, like a scrabble of lightning across a cloud, suggesting that behind is a lofty divinity whom all must know, or an aloof divinity whom none is worthy to know (though, as this might be highly inconvenient, a docile typist sometimes interprets the mystery in a bracket underneath). There are impetuous squiggles implying that the author is a sort of strenuous Sputnik streaking round the globe every eighty minutes. There are florid signatures, all curlicues and danglements and flamboyance, like the youthful Disraeli (though these seem rather out of fashion). There are humble, humdrum signatures. And there are also, sometimes, signatures that are courteously clear, yet mindful of a certain simple grace and artistic economy—in short, of style.

Since, then, not one of us can put pen to paper, or even open his mouth, without giving something of himself away to shrewd observers, it seems mere common sense to give the matter a little thought. Yet it does not seem very common. Ladies may take infinite pains about having style in their clothes, but many of us remain curiously indifferent about having it in our words. How many women would dream of polishing not only their nails but also their tongues? They may play freely on that perilous little organ, but they cannot often be bothered to tune it. And how many men think of improving their talk as well as their golf handicap?

No doubt strong silent men, speaking only in gruff monosyllables, may despise "mere words." No doubt the world does suffer from an endemic plague of verbal dysentery. But that, precisely, is bad style. And consider the amazing power of mere words. Adolf Hitler was a bad artist, bad statesman, bad general, and bad man. But largely because he could tune his rant, with psychological nicety, to the exact wave length of his audiences and make millions quarrelsome-drunk all at the same time by his command of windy nonsense, skilled statesmen, soldiers, scientists were blown away like chaff, and he came near to rule the world. If Sir Winston Churchill had been a mere speechifier, we might well have lost the war; yet his speeches did quite a lot to win it.

No man was less of a literary aesthete than Benjamin Franklin; yet this tallow-chandler's son, who changed world history, regarded as "a principal means of my advancement" that pungent style which he acquired partly by working in youth over old *Spectators;* but mainly by being Benjamin Franklin. The squinting demagogue, John Wilkes, as ugly as his many sins, had yet a tongue so winning that he asked only half an hour's start (to counteract his face) against any rival for a woman's favor. "Vote for you!" growled a surly elector in his constituency. "I'd sooner vote for the devil!"

"But in case your friend should not stand . . . ?" Cleopatra, that ensnarer of world conquerors, owed less to the shape of her nose than to the charm of her tongue. Shakespeare himself has often poor plots and thin ideas; even his mastery of character has been questioned; what does remain unchallenged is his verbal magic. Men are often taken, like rabbits, by the ears. And though the tongue has no bones, it can sometimes break millions of them.

"But," the reader may grumble, "I am neither Hitler, Cleopatra, nor Shakespeare. What is all this to me?" Yet we all talk—often too much; we all have to write letters—often too many. We live not by bread alone but also by words. And not always with remarkable efficiency. Strikes, lawsuits, divorces, all sorts of public nuisance and private misery, often come just from the gaggling incompetence with which we express ourselves. Americans and British get at cross-purposes because they use the same words with different meanings. Men have been hanged on a comma in a statute. And in the valley of Balaclava a mere verbal ambiguity, about *which* guns were to be captured, sent the whole Light Brigade to futile annihilation.

Words can be more powerful, and more treacherous, than we sometimes suspect; communication more difficult than we may think. We are all serving life sentences of solitary confinement within our own bodies; like prisoners, we have, as it were, to tap in awkward code to our fellow men in their neighboring cells. Further, when A and B converse, there take part in their dialogue not two characters, as they suppose, but six. For there is A's real self—call it A_1; there is also A's picture of himself—A_2; there is also B's picture of A—A_3. And there are three corresponding personalities of B. With six characters involved even in a simple tete-a-tete, no wonder we fall into muddles and misunderstandings.

Perhaps, then, there are five main reasons for trying to gain some mastery of language:

We have no other way of understanding, informing, misinforming, or persuading one another.

Even alone, we think mainly in words; if our language is muddy, so will our thinking be.

By our handling of words we are often revealed and judged. "Has he written anything?" said Napoleon of a candidate for an appointment. "Let me see his *style*."

Without a feeling for language one remains half-blind and deaf to literature.

Our mother tongue is bettered or worsened by the way each generation uses it. Languages evolve like species. They can degenerate; just as oysters and barnacles have lost their heads. Compare ancient Greek with modern. A heavy responsibility, though often forgotten.

Why and how did I become interested in style? The main answer, I suppose, is that I was born that way. Then I was, till ten, an only child running loose in a house packed with books, and in a world (thank goodness) still undistracted by radio and television. So at three I groaned to my mother, "Oh, I *wish* I could read," and at four I read. Now travel among books is the best travel of all, and the easiest, and the cheapest. (Not that I belittle ordinary travel—which I regard as one of the three main pleasures in life.) One learns to write by reading good books, as one learns to talk by hearing good talkers. And if I have learned anything of writing, it is largely from writers like Montaigne, Dorothy Osborne, Horace Walpole, Johnson, Goldsmith, Montesquieu, Voltaire, Flaubert and Anatole France. Again, I was reared on Greek and Latin, and one can learn much from translating Homer or the Greek Anthology, Horace or Tacitus, if one is thrilled by the originals and tries, however vainly, to recapture some of that thrill in English.

But at Rugby I could *not* write English essays. I believe it stupid to torment boys to write on topics that they know and care nothing about. I used to rush to the school library and cram the subject, like a python swallowing rabbits; then, still replete as a postprandial python, I would tie myself in clumsy knots to embrace those accursed themes. Bacon was wise in saying that reading makes a full man; talking, a ready one; writing, an exact one. But writing from an empty head is futile anguish.

At Cambridge, my head having grown a little fuller, I suddenly found I *could* write—not with enjoyment (it is always tearing oneself in pieces)—but fairly fluently. Then came the War of 1914–18; and though soldiers have other things than pens to handle, they learn painfully to be clear and brief. Then the late Sir Desmond MacCarthy invited me to review for the *New Statesman;* it was a useful apprenticeship, and he was delightful to work for. But I think it was well after a few years to stop; reviewers remain essential, but there are too many books one *cannot* praise, and only the pugnacious enjoy amassing enemies. By then I was an ink-addict—not because writing is much pleasure, but because not to write is pain; just as some smokers do not so much enjoy tobacco as suffer without it. The positive happiness of writing comes, I think, from work when done—decently, one hopes, and not without use—and from the letters of readers which help to reassure, or delude, one that so it is.

But one of my most vivid lessons came, I think, from service in a war department during the Second War. Then, if the matter one sent out was too wordy, the communication channels might choke; yet if it was not absolutely clear, the results might be serious. So I emerged, after six years of it, with more passion than ever for clarity and brevity, more loathing than ever for the obscure and the verbose.

For forty years at Cambridge I have tried to teach young men to write well, and have come to think it impossible. To write really well is a gift inborn; those who have it teach themselves; one can only try to help and hasten the process. After all, the uneducated sometimes express themselves far better than their "betters." In language, as in life, it is possible to be perfectly correct—and yet perfectly tedious, or odious. The illiterate last letter of the doomed Vanzetti was more moving than most professional orators; 18th Century ladies, who should have been spanked for their spelling, could yet write far better letters than most professors of English; and the talk of Synge's Irish peasants seems to me vastly more vivid than the later style of Henry James. Yet Synge averred that his characters owed far less of their eloquence to what he invented for them than to what he had overheard in the cottages of Wicklow and Kerry:

"*Christy.* 'It's little you'll think if my love's a poacher's, or an earl's itself, when you'll feel my two hands stretched around you, and I squeezing kisses on your puckered lips, till I'd feel a kind of pity for the Lord God in all ages sitting lonesome in His golden chair.'

"*Pegeen.* 'That'll be right fun, Christy Mahon, and any girl would walk her heart out before she'd meet a young man was your like for eloquence, or talk at all.' "

Well she might! It's not like that they talk in universities—more's the pity.

But though one cannot teach people to write well, one can sometimes teach them to write rather better. One can give a certain number of hints, which often seem boringly obvious—only experience shows they are not.

One can say: Beware of pronouns—they are devils. Look at even Addison, describing the type of pedant who chatters of style without having any: "Upon enquiry I found my learned friend had dined that day with Mr. Swan, the famous punster; and desiring *him* to give me some account of Mr. Swan's conversation, *he* told me that *he* generally talked in the Paronomasia, that *he* sometimes gave in to the Plocé, but that in *his* humble opinion *he* shone most in the Antanaclasis." What a sluttish muddle of *he* and *him* and *his!* It all needs rewording. Far better repeat a noun, or a name, than puzzle the reader, even for a moment, with ambiguous pronouns. Thou shalt not puzzle thy reader.

Or one can say: Avoid jingles. The B.B.C. news bulletins seem compiled by earless persons, capable of crying round the globe: "The enemy is re*port*ed to have seized this im*port*ant *port,* and reinforcements are hurrying up in sup*port*." Any fool, once told, can hear such things to be insupportable.

Or one can say: Be sparing with relative clauses. Don't string them together like sausages, or jam them inside one another like Chinese boxes or the receptacles of Buddha's tooth. Or one can say: Don't flaunt jargon, like Addison's Mr. Swan, or the type of modern critic who gurgles more technical terms in a page than Johnson used in all his *Lives* or Sainte-Beuve in thirty volumes. But dozens of such snippety precepts, though they may sometimes save people from writing badly, will help them little toward writing well. Are there no general rules of a more positive kind, and of more positive use?

Perhaps. There *are* certain basic principles which seem to me observed by many authors I admire, which I think have served me and which may serve others. I am not talking of geniuses, who are a law to themselves (and do not always write a very good style, either); nor of poetry, which has different laws from prose; nor of poetic prose, like Sir Thomas Browne's or De Quincey's, which is often more akin to poetry; but of the plain prose of ordinary books and documents, letters and talk.

The writer should respect truth and himself; therefore honesty. He should respect his readers; therefore courtesy. These are two of the cornerstones of style. Confucius saw it, twenty-five centuries ago: "The Master said, The gentleman is courteous, but not pliable: common men are pliable, but not courteous."

First, honesty. In literature, as in life, one of the fundamentals is to find, and be, one's true self. One's true self may indeed be unpleasant (though one can try to better it); but a false self, sooner or later, becomes disgusting—just as a nice plain woman, painted to the eyebrows, can become horrid. In writing, in the long run, pretense does not work. As the police put it, anything you say may be used as evidence against you. If handwriting reveals character, writing reveals it still more. You cannot fool *all* your judges *all* the time.

Most style is not honest enough. Easy to say, but hard to practice. A writer may take to long words, as young men to beards—to impress. But long words, like long beards, are often the badge of charlatans. Or a writer may cultivate the obscure, to seem profound. But even carefully muddied puddles are soon fathomed. Or he may cultivate eccentricity, to seem original. But really original people do not have to think about being original—they can no more help it than they can help breathing. They do not need to dye their hair green. The fame of Meredith, Wilde or Bernard Shaw might now shine brighter, had they struggled less to be brilliant; whereas Johnson remains great, not merely because his gifts were formidable but also because, with all his prejudice and passion, he fought no less passionately to "clear his mind of cant."

Secondly, courtesy—respect for the reader. From this follow several other basic principles of style. Clarity is one. For it is boorish to make your reader rack his brains to understand. One should aim at being impossible to misunderstand—though men's capacity for misunderstanding approaches infinity. Hence Molière and Po Chu-i tried their work on their cooks; and Swift his on his menservants—"which, if they did not comprehend, he would alter and amend, until they understood it perfectly." Our bureaucrats and pundits, unfortunately, are less considerate.

Brevity is another basic principle. For it is boorish, also, to waste your reader's time. People who would not dream of stealing a penny of one's money turn not a hair at stealing hours of one's life. But that does not make them less exasperating. Therefore there is no excuse for the sort of writer who takes as long as a marching army corps to pass a given point. Besides, brevity is often more effective; the half can say more than the whole, and to imply things may strike far deeper than to state them at length. And because one is particularly apt to waste words on preambles before coming to the substance, there was sense in the Scots professor who always asked his pupils—"Did ye remember to tear up that fir-r-st page?"

Here are some instances that would only lose by lengthening:

It is useless to go to bed to save the light, if the result is twins. (Chinese proverb.)

My barn is burnt down—
Nothing hides the moon. (Complete Japanese poem.)

Je me regrette. (Dying words of the gay Vicomtesse d'Houdetot.)

I have seen their backs before. (Wellington, when French marshals turned their backs on him at a reception.)

Continue until the tanks stop, then get out and walk. (Patton to the Twelfth Corps, halted for fuel supplies at St. Dizier, 8/30/44.)

Or there is the most laconic diplomatic note on record: when Philip of Macedon wrote to the Spartans that, if he came within their borders, he would leave not one stone of their city, they wrote back the one word—"If."

Clarity comes before even brevity. But it is a fallacy that wordiness is necessarily clearer. Metternich when he thought something he had written was obscure would simply go through it crossing out everything irrelevant. What remained, he found, often became clear. Wellington, asked to recommend three names for the post of Commander-in-Chief, India, took a piece of paper and wrote three times—"Napier." Pages could not have been clearer—or as forcible. On the other hand the lectures, and the sentences, of Coleridge became at times bewildering because his mind was often "wiggle-waggle"; just as he could not even walk straight on a path.

But clarity and brevity, though a good beginning, are only a beginning. By themselves, they may remain bare and bleak. When Calvin Coolidge, asked by his wife what the preacher had preached on, replied "Sin," and, asked what the preacher had said, replied, "He was against it," he was brief enough. But one hardly envies Mrs. Coolidge.

An attractive style requires, of course, all kinds of further gifts—such as variety, good humor, good sense, vitality, imagination. Variety means avoiding monotony of rhythm, of language, of mood. One needs to vary one's sentence length (this present article has too many short sentences; but so vast a subject grows here as cramped as a djin in a bottle); to amplify one's vocabulary; to diversify one's tone. There are books that petrify one throughout, with the rigidly pompous solemnity of an owl perched on a leafless tree. But ceaseless facetiousness can be as bad; or perpetual irony. Even the smile of Voltaire can seem at times a fixed grin, a disagreeable wrinkle. Constant peevishness is far worse, as often in Swift; even on the stage too much irritable dialogue may irritate an audience, without its knowing why.

Still more are vitality, energy, imagination gifts that must be inborn before they can be cultivated. But under the head of imagination two common devices may be mentioned that have been the making of many a style—metaphor and simile. Why such magic power should reside in simply saying, or implying, that A is like B remains a little mysterious. But even our unconscious seems to love symbols; again, language often tends to lose itself in clouds of vaporous abstraction, and simile or metaphor can bring it back to concrete solidity; and, again, such imagery can gild the gray flats of prose with sudden sun-glints of poetry.

If a foreigner may for a moment be impertinent, I admire the native gift of Americans for imagery as much as I wince at their fondness for slang. (Slang seems to me a kind of linguistic fungus; as poisonous, and as short-lived, as toadstools.) When Matthew Arnold lectured in the United States, he was likened by one newspaper to "an elderly macaw pecking at a trellis of grapes"; he observed, very justly, "How lively journalistic fancy is among the Americans!" General Grant, again, unable to hear him, remarked: "Well, wife, we've paid to see the British lion, but as we can't hear him roar, we'd better go home." By simile and metaphor, these two quotations bring before us the slightly pompous, fastidious, inaudible Arnold as no direct description could have done.

Or consider how language comes alive in the Chinese saying that lending to the feckless is "like pelting a stray dog with dumplings," or in the Arab proverb: "They came to shoe the pasha's horse, and the beetle stretched forth his leg"; in the Greek phrase for a perilous cape—"stepmother of ships"; or the Hebrew adage that "as the climbing up a sandy way is to the feet of the aged, so is a wife full of words to a quiet man"; in Shakespeare's phrase for a little England lost in the world's vastness—"in a great Poole, a Swan's-nest"; or Fuller's libel on tall men—"Ofttimes such who are built four stories high are observed to have little in their cockloft"; in Chateaubriand's "I go yawning my life"; or in Jules Renard's portrait of a cat, "well buttoned in her fur." Or, to take a modern instance, there is Churchill on dealings with Russia: "Trying to maintain good relations with a Communist is like wooing a crocodile. You do not know whether to tickle it under the chin or beat it over the head. When it opens its mouth, you cannot tell whether it is trying to smile or preparing to eat you up." What a miracle human speech can be, and how dull is most that one hears! Would one hold one's hearers, it is far less help, I suspect, to read manuals on style than to cultivate one's own imagination and imagery.

I will end with two remarks by two wise old women of the civilized 18th Century.

The first is from the blind Mme. du Deffand (the friend of Horace Walpole) to that Mlle. de Lespinasse with whom, alas, she was to quarrel so unwisely: "You must make up your mind, my queen, to live with me in the greatest truth and sincerity. You will be charming so long as you let yourself be natural, and remain without pretension and without artifice." The second is from Mme. de Charrière, the Zélide whom Boswell had once loved at Utrecht in vain, to a Swiss girl friend: "Lucinde, my clever Luçinde, while you wait for the Romeos to arrive, you have nothing better to do than become perfect. Have ideas that are clear, and expressions that are simple." (*"Ayez des idées nettes et des expressions simples."*) More than half the bad writing in the world, I believe, comes from neglecting those two very simple pieces of advice.

In many ways, no doubt, our world grows more and more complex; sputniks cannot be simple; yet how many of our complexities remain futile, how many of our artificialities false. Simplicity too can be subtle—as the straight lines of a Greek temple, like the Parthenon at Athens, are delicately curved, in order to look straighter still.

Questions

1. Why should Lucas begin by suggesting the "bad name" of style? Does the word really have for you the negative connotations he suggests? When Frank Norris said, "Who cares for fine style! . . . we don't want literature, we want life," he was expressing essentially the same negative opinion of style as did Whitman. How valid is the antithesis between style and life in literature?
2. Later in the essay Lucas advises us to cultivate our imagination and imagery, especially in similes and metaphors. Examine carefully the last three

sentences of the third paragraph. How many metaphors, or partial metaphors, does he use? Watch for his use of such figures throughout the essay. How effective do they seem? Is he using them primarily for their own sake? Do they clarify or emphasize? Do they call attention to themselves or seem piled up until they distract the reader?

3. Do you know any "strong silent men" who despise "mere words"? Perhaps you *are* one (they seem to us fairly common these days). Would Lucas' argument help to convert those who despise words?
4. Style involves the choice of words. Can you generalize about the kinds of words Lucas chooses? Notice "gaggling incompetence." *Gaggling,* your dictionary will tell you, is a form of cackling. Can you see any reason why Lucas chose *gaggling?*
5. If Lucas has really come to think it impossible to teach young men to write well, why does he write this essay? Is his justification enough: ". . . one can sometimes teach them to write rather better"?
6. Nearly the final third of the essay is devoted to "certain basic principles" that good writers observe. "Honesty," the first, is closely related to "sincerity," perhaps advised more often. Try to determine from his context just what Lucas means by "honesty." Does it have the same moral implications it usually carries?
7. As you examine Lucas' discussion of metaphor and simile, note again how many of these rhetorical devices he uses. To what extent do these seem the result of conscious thought, conscious cultivation of the imagination? How often do you find yourself thinking or seeing or trying to explain things by figurative comparisons?

Suggestions for Writing

1. Lucas' plea for honesty has much in common with our introductory plea (see Introduction, p. v). But in our Suggestions for Writing we have repeatedly suggested that you *assume* a certain attitude or situation that may have little to do with your actual attitude or situation. How can you be honest in such writing situations? If, as we have argued, you take yourself, your audience, and your subject seriously (that is, work out seriously a meaningful rhetorical stance), and if, as we have also argued, the process of writing is the process of discovering and defining for yourself what you really believe and what you really are, then even such assumed stances should lead you to meaningful honesty. Assume that you have been suddenly turned on by Lucas' discussion of style (perhaps you have!). Define for yourself what *honesty* has come to mean to you in writing, then illustrate that meaning with some anecdote from your own or another's experience. Try consciously to make your style as effective as possible by following Lucas' advice. Especially try to get life into your writing by consciously working with metaphor and simile.

The Killers

Ernest Hemingway

Both Hemingway and the famous Hemingway style are too well known to need introduction. But careful analysis of that style can teach us a lot about style and tone in general. "The Killers" is one of Hemingway's best and most popular stories. As you read, try to describe the style itself and how it is working to produce its effects.

The door of Henry's lunch-room opened and two men came in. They sat down at the counter.

"What's yours?" George asked them.

"I don't know," one of the men said. "What do you want to eat, Al?"

"I don't know," said Al. "I don't know what I want to eat."

Outside it was getting dark. The street-light came on outside the window. The two men at the counter read the menu. From the other end of the counter Nick Adams watched them. He had been talking to George when they came in.

"I'll have a roast pork tenderloin with apple sauce and mashed potatoes," the first man said.

"It isn't ready yet."

"What the hell do you put it on the card for?"

"That's the dinner," George explained. "You can get that at six o'clock."

George looked at the clock on the wall behind the counter.

"It's five o'clock."

"The clock says twenty minutes past five," the second man said.

"It's twenty minutes fast."

"Oh, to hell with the clock," the first man said. "What have you got to eat?"

"I can give you any kind of sandwiches," George said. "You can have ham and eggs, bacon and eggs, liver and bacon, or a steak."

"Give me chicken croquettes with green peas and cream sauce and mashed potatoes."

"That's the dinner."

"Everything we want's the dinner, eh? That's the way you work it."

"I can give you ham and eggs, bacon and eggs, liver——"

"I'll take ham and eggs," the man called Al said. He wore a derby hat and a black overcoat buttoned across the chest. His face was small and white and he had tight lips. He wore a silk muffler and gloves.

"Give me bacon and eggs," said the other man. He was about the same size as Al. Their faces were different, but they were dressed like twins. Both wore overcoats too tight for them. They sat leaning forward, their elbows on the counter.

"Got anything to drink?" Al asked.

"Silver beer, bevo, ginger-ale," George said.

"I mean you got anything to *drink?*"

"Just those I said."

"This is a hot town," said the other. "What do they call it?"

"Summit."

"Ever hear of it?" Al asked his friend.

"No," said the friend.

"What do you do here nights?" Al asked.

"They eat the dinner," his friend said. "They all come here and eat the big dinner."

"That's right," George said.

"So you think that's right?" Al asked George.

"Sure."

"You're a pretty bright boy, aren't you?"

"Sure," said George.

"Well, you're not," said the other little man. "Is he, Al?"

"He's dumb," said Al. He turned to Nick. "What's your name?"

"Adams."

"Another bright boy," Al said. "Ain't he a bright boy, Max?"

"The town's full of bright boys," Max said.

George put the two platters, one of ham and eggs, the other of bacon and eggs, on the counter. He set down two side-dishes of fried potatoes and closed the wicket into the kitchen.

"Which is yours?" he asked Al.

"Don't you remember?"

"Ham and eggs."

"Just a bright boy," Max said. He leaned forward and took the ham and eggs. Both men ate with their gloves on. George watched them eat.

"What are *you* looking at?" Max looked at George.

"Nothing."

"The hell you were. You were looking at me."

"Maybe the boy meant it for a joke, Max," Al said.

George laughed.

"*You* don't have to laugh," Max said to him. "*You* don't have to laugh at all, see?"

"All right," said George.

"So he thinks it's all right." Max turned to Al. "He thinks it's all right. That's a good one."

"Oh, he's a thinker," Al said. They went on eating.

"What's the bright boy's name down the counter?" Al asked Max.

"Hey, bright boy," Max said to Nick. "You go around on the other side of the counter with your boy friend."

"What's the idea?" Nick asked.

"There isn't any idea."

"You better go around, bright boy," Al said. Nick went around behind the counter.

"What's the idea?" George asked.

"None of your damn business," Al said. "Who's out in the kitchen?"

"The nigger."

"What do you mean the nigger?"

"The nigger that cooks."

"Tell him to come in."

"What's the idea?"

"Tell him to come in."

"Where do you think you are?"

"We know damn well where we are," the man called Max said. "Do we look silly?"

"You talk silly," Al said to him. "What the hell do you argue with this kid for? Listen," he said to George, "tell the nigger to come out here."

"What are you going to do to him?"

"Nothing. Use your head, bright boy. What would we do to a nigger?"

George opened the slit that opened back into the kitchen. "Sam," he called. "Come in here a minute."

The door to the kitchen opened and the nigger came in. "What was it?" he asked. The two men at the counter took a look at him.

"All right, nigger. You stand right there," Al said.

Sam, the nigger, standing in his apron, looked at the two men sitting at the counter. "Yes, sir," he said. Al got down from his stool.

"I'm going back to the kitchen with the nigger and bright boy," he said. "Go on back to the kitchen, nigger. You go with him, bright boy." The little man walked after Nick and Sam, the cook, back into the kitchen.

The door shut after them. The man called Max sat at the counter opposite George. He didn't look at George but looked in the mirror that ran along back of the counter. Henry's had been made over from a saloon into a lunch-counter.

"Well, bright boy," Max said, looking into the mirror, "why don't you say something?"

"What's it all about?"

"Hey, Al," Max called, "bright boy wants to know what it's all about."

"Why don't you tell him?" Al's voice came from the kitchen.

"What do you think it's all about?"

"I don't know."

"What do you think?"

Max looked into the mirror all the time he was talking.

"I wouldn't say."

"Hey, Al, bright boy says he wouldn't say what he thinks it's all about."

"I can hear you, all right," Al said from the kitchen. He had propped open the slit that dishes passed through into the kitchen with a catsup bottle. "Listen, bright boy," he said from the kitchen to George. "Stand a little further along the bar. You move a little to the left, Max." He was like a photographer arranging for a group picture.

"Talk to me, bright boy," Max said. "What do you think's going to happen?"

George did not say anything.

"I'll tell you," Max said. "We're going to kill a Swede. Do you know a big Swede named Ole Andreson?"

"Yes."

"He comes here to eat every night, don't he?"

"Sometimes he comes here."

"He comes here at six o'clock, don't he?"

"If he comes."

"We know all that, bright boy," Max said. "Talk about something else. Ever go to the movies?"

"Once in a while."

"You ought to go to the movies more. The movies are fine for a bright boy like you."

"What are you going to kill Ole Andreson for? What did he ever do to you?"

"He never had a chance to do anything to us. He never even seen us."

"And he's only going to see us once," Al said from the kitchen.

"What are you going to kill him for, then?" George asked.

"We're killing him for a friend. Just to oblige a friend, bright boy."

"Shut up," said Al from the kitchen. "You talk too goddam much."

"Well, I got to keep bright boy amused. Don't I, bright boy?"

"You talk too damn much," Al said. "The nigger and my bright boy are amused by themselves. I got them tied up like a couple of girl friends in the convent."

"I suppose you were in a convent?"

"You never know."

"You were in a kosher convent. That's where you were."

George looked up at the clock.

"If anybody comes in you tell them the cook is off, and if they keep after it, you tell them you'll go back and cook yourself. Do you get that, bright boy?"

"All right," George said. "What you going to do with us afterward?"

"That'll depend," Max said. "That's one of those things you never know at the time."

George looked up at the clock. It was a quarter past six. The door from the street opened. A street-car motorman came in.

"Hello, George," he said. "Can I get supper?"

"Sam's gone out," George said. "He'll be back in about half an hour."

"I'd better go up the street," the motorman said. George looked at the clock. It was twenty minutes past six.

"That was nice, bright boy," Max said. "You're a regular little gentleman."

"He knew I'd blow his head off," Al said from the kitchen.

"No," said Max. "It ain't that. Bright boy is nice. He's a nice boy. I like him."

At six-fifty-five George said: "He's not coming."

Two other people had been in the lunch-room. Once George had gone out to the kitchen and made a ham-and-egg sandwich "to go" that a man wanted to take with him. Inside the kitchen he saw Al, his derby hat tipped back, sitting on a stool beside the wicket with the muzzle of a sawed-off shotgun resting on the ledge. Nick and the cook were back to back in the corner, a towel tied in each of their mouths. George had cooked the sandwich, wrapped it up in oiled paper, put it in a bag, brought it in, and the man had paid for it and gone out.

"Bright boy can do everything," Max said. "He can cook and everything. You'd make some girl a nice wife, bright boy."

"Yes?" George said. "Your friend, Ole Andreson, isn't going to come."

"We'll give him ten minutes," Max said.

Max watched the mirror and the clock. The hands of the clock marked seven o'clock, and then five minutes past seven.

"Come on, Al," said Max. "We better go. He's not coming."

"Better give him five minutes," Al said from the kitchen.

In the five minutes a man came in, and George explained that the cook was sick.

"Why the hell don't you get another cook?" the man asked. "Aren't you running a lunch-counter?" He went out.

"Come on, Al," Max said.

"What about the two bright boys and the nigger?"

"They're all right."

"You think so?"

"Sure. We're through with it."

"I don't like it," said Al. "It's sloppy. You talk too much."

"Oh, what the hell," said Max. "We got to keep amused, haven't we?"

"You talk too much, all the same," Al said. He came out from the kitchen. The cut-off barrels of the shotgun made a slight bulge under the waist of his too tight-fitting overcoat. He straightened his coat with his gloved hands.

"So long, bright boy," he said to George. "You got a lot of luck."

"That's the truth," Max said. "You ought to play the races, bright boy."

The two of them went out the door. George watched them, through the window, pass under the arc-light and cross the street. In their tight overcoats and derby hats they looked like a vaudeville team. George went back through the swinging-door into the kitchen and untied Nick and the cook.

"I don't want any more of that," said Sam, the cook. "I don't want any more of that."

Nick stood up. He had never had a towel in his mouth before.

"Say," he said. "What the hell?" He was trying to swagger it off.

"They were going to kill Ole Andreson," George said. "They were going to shoot him when he came in to eat."

"Ole Andreson?"

"Sure."

The cook felt the corners of his mouth with his thumbs.

"They all gone?" he asked.

"Yeah," said George. "They're gone now."

"I don't like it," said the cook. "I don't like any of it at all."

"Listen," George said to Nick. "You better go see Ole Andreson."

"All right."

"You better not have anything to do with it at all," Sam, the cook, said. "You better stay way out of it."

"Don't go if you don't want to," George said.

"Mixing up in this ain't going to get you anywhere," the cook said. "You stay out of it."

"I'll go see him," Nick said to George. "Where does he live?"

The cook turned away.

"Little boys always know what they want to do," he said.

"He lives up at Hirsch's rooming-house," George said to Nick.

"I'll go up there."

Outside the arc-light shone through the bare branches of a tree. Nick walked up the street beside the car-tracks and turned at the next arc-light down a side-street. Three houses up the street was Hirsch's rooming-house. Nick walked up the two steps and pushed the bell. A woman came to the door.

"Is Ole Andreson here?"

"Do you want to see him?"

"Yes, if he's in."

Nick followed the woman up a flight of stairs and back to the end of a corridor. She knocked on the door.

"Who is it?"

"It's somebody to see you, Mr. Andreson," the woman said.

"It's Nick Adams."

"Come in."

Nick opened the door and went into the room. Ole Andreson was lying on the bed with all his clothes on. He had been a heavyweight prizefighter and he was too long for the bed. He lay with his head on two pillows. He did not look at Nick.

"What was it?" he asked.

"I was up at Henry's," Nick said, "and two fellows came in and tied up me and the cook, and they said they were going to kill you."

It sounded silly when he said it. Ole Andreson said nothing.

"They put us out in the kitchen," Nick went on. "They were going to shoot you when you came in to supper."

Ole Andreson looked at the wall and did not say anything.

"George thought I better come and tell you about it."

"There isn't anything I can do about it," Ole Andreson said.

"I'll tell you what they were like."

"I don't want to know what they were like," Ole Andreson said. He looked at the wall. "Thanks for coming to tell me about it."

"That's all right."

Nick looked at the big man lying on the bed.

"Don't you want me to go and see the police?"

"No," Ole Andreson said. "That wouldn't do any good."

"Isn't there something I could do?"

"No. There ain't anything to do."

"Maybe it was just a bluff."

"No. It ain't just a bluff."

Ole Andreson rolled over toward the wall.

"The only thing is," he said, talking toward the wall, "I just can't make up my mind to go out. I been in here all day."

"Couldn't you get out of town?"

"No," Ole Andreson said. "I'm through with all that running around."

He looked at the wall.

"There ain't anything to do now."

"Couldn't you fix it up some way?"

"No. I got in wrong." He talked in the same flat voice. "There ain't anything to do. After a while I'll make up my mind to go out."

"I better go back and see George," Nick said.

"So long," said Ole Andreson. He did not look toward Nick. "Thanks for coming around."

Nick went out. As he shut the door he saw Ole Andreson with all his clothes on, lying on the bed looking at the wall.

"He's been in his room all day," the landlady said down-stairs. "I guess he don't feel well. I said to him: 'Mr. Andreson, you ought to go out and take a walk on a nice fall day like this,' but he didn't feel like it."

"He doesn't want to go out."

"I'm sorry he don't feel well," the woman said. "He's an awfully nice man. He was in the ring, you know."

"I know it."

"You'd never know it except from the way his face is," the woman said. They stood talking just inside the street door. "He's just as gentle."

"Well, good-night, Mrs. Hirsch," Nick said.

"I'm not Mrs. Hirsch," the woman said. "She owns the place. I just look after it for her. I'm Mrs. Bell."

"Well, good-night, Mrs. Bell," Nick said.

"Good-night," the woman said.

Nick walked up the dark street to the corner under the arc-light, and then along the car-tracks to Henry's eating-house. George was inside, back of the counter.

"Did you see Ole?"

"Yes," said Nick. "He's in his room and he won't go out."

The cook opened the door from the kitchen when he heard Nick's voice.

"I don't even listen to it," he said and shut the door.

"Did you tell him about it?" George asked.

"Sure. I told him but he knows what it's all about."

"What's he going to do?"

"Nothing."

"They'll kill him."

"I guess they will."

"He must have got mixed up in something in Chicago."

"I guess so," said Nick.

"It's a hell of a thing."

"It's an awful thing," Nick said.

They did not say anything. George reached down for a towel and wiped the counter.

"I wonder what he did?" Nick said.

"Double-crossed somebody. That's what they kill them for."

"I'm going to get out of this town," Nick said.

"Yes," said George. "That's a good thing to do."

"I can't stand to think about him waiting in the room and knowing he's going to get it. It's too damned awful."

"Well," said George, "you better not think about it."

Questions

1. Students—and even some critics—often praise Hemingway's style as "natural," "real," "just the way people talk." Does it seem so to you? If you took a tape recorder into the local pizza palace or hamburger shop would it record conversations like those in Henry's?
2. Describe the style. What kinds of words does Hemingway use? Long or Short? Monosyllabic? Concrete or Abstract? Figurative or Literal? What kinds of sentences? Simple? Compound? Complex? What kinds of modifiers?
3. Turn back to Faulkner's "Dry September" and contrast the style with Hemingway's. Even a quick glance should be revealing. Contrast the length and complexity of words and sentences, the concreteness of the words, the complexity of the sentences. We could put Hemingway near one end of a stylistic continuum, Faulkner near the other. Where would other writers that you know well be placed? Steele in "How Beautiful with Shoes"? Conrad in "Amy Foster"? Flannery O'Connor in "Revelation"? Contrast Hemingway's style with Henry James's in this passage from *The Portrait of a Lady,* not one of James's more complex passages:

   > Mr. Osmond's talk was not injured by the indication of an eagerness to shine; Isabel found no difficulty in believing that a person was sincere who had so many of the signs of strong conviction—as for instance an explicit and graceful appreciation of anything that might be said on his own side of the question, said perhaps by Miss Archer in especial. What continued to please this young woman was that while he talked so for amusement he didn't talk, as she had heard people, for "effect." He uttered his ideas as if, odd as they often appeared, he were used to them and had lived with them; old polished knobs and heads and handles, of precious substance, that could be fitted if necessary to new walking-sticks—not switches plucked in destitution from the common tree and then too elegantly waved about.

4. How conscious and sophisticated does Hemingway's style seem? Most readers sense a genuine terror in "The Killers." How much does the style contribute to the terror? If we sense Nick as the main character of the story (this is one of a series of stories in each of which Nick is introduced too soon to the brutality and ugliness of the world), we can feel more immediately the effect of the style. Does the bare, clipped style exaggerate or underplay the situation?
5. The narrative weight of the story is carried mostly by dialogue. Are the characters individualized enough in their speech mannerisms to allow you to distinguish one from the other by dialogue alone?

Suggestions for Writing

1. A major theme in "The Killers" is the initiation of Nick into some of the brutality and ugliness of the world. One incident makes Nick vividly aware of an aspect of the world that he had not known before. Perhaps you can recall a specific experience that introduced you to brutality, to hypocrisy, to dishonesty, or one that suddenly and dramatically gave you new insight into the character of someone you thought you knew well. Relate the experience, choosing your words carefully and ordering your details in a manner that will cause it to be convincing and significant to your audience.

The Killers

Charles Kaplan

The following selection is a parody of Hemingway's story. (Look up the word if you do not know it). What features make this a parody?

The door of the lunchroom opened and two girls came in. They sat down at the counter.

"What's yours?" George asked them.

"I don't know," one of the girls said. "What do you want to eat, Alberta?"

"I don't know," said Alberta. "I don't know what I want to eat."

Outside it was getting dark. The street light came on outside the window. The two girls at the counter read the menu. Nick watched them from the other end of the counter.

"I'll have the double-rich strawberry sundae with whipped cream and crushed nuts," the first girl said.

"We're all out of strawberry."

"Why do you put it on the menu then?"

"That's yesterday's card," George explained. "You could have got it yesterday."

"Oh, yesterday," the first girl said. "What kind of ice cream you got?"

"I can give you any other kind," George said. "You can have vanilla, chocolate, fudge ripple, banana pecan, or pistachio."

"Give me a chocolate sundae with whipped cream and chocolate syrup and crushed nuts," the one called Alberta said. She wore a red cashmere sweater tight across her chest. Her face was round and pink and she had red lips. She wore a flannel skirt and dirty saddle shoes.

"Give me a vanilla sundae," said the other girl. She was about the same size as Alberta. Their faces were different, but they were dressed like twins. Both wore sweaters too tight for them. They sat leaning forward, their elbows on the counter.

"What should we drink?" Alberta asked.

Charles Kaplan, "The Killers," *College English,* XXIV (February, 1963). Reprinted with the permission of the National Council of Teachers of English and Charles Kaplan.

"Coke, I guess."

"I think I'll have an orange."

"I guess I'll have one too."

"Maybe it won't go good with chocolate," Alberta said.

"Yeah. I'll have a root beer instead."

"I'll have lemonade."

"Make up your mind," George said. "We're only open till midnight."

"You must think you're real bright," Alberta said.

"Sure," George said.

"Well, you're not," said the other girl. "Is he, Alberta?"

"He's dumb," said Alberta. "He's not like one of we college students. You can always tell an uneducated person, Maxine."

"This town's full of them," Maxine said.

"Let's not have anything to drink," said Alberta. "It might spoil our supper."

The girls took out cigarettes and lit them. George put the two sundaes on the counter.

"Which is yours?" he asked Alberta.

"Don't you remember?"

"The chocolate sundae."

"Just a bright boy," Maxine said. She leaned forward and took the vanilla sundae. Both girls ate while smoking their cigarettes. Nick watched them eat.

"Like I told you," said Alberta, "it was the funniest feeling."

"That's what you told me," Maxine said. "But why? Like I mean, why?"

"I was reading this story, this assignment, like. But why it's called a story I don't know because nothing happens in it. Well, I was reading it and I turned the page and like that's the end. I was expecting something else to happen, and then it just stops."

"That's weird."

"I thought maybe there was something wrong with my book, like maybe some of the pages were torn out or something. But no."

"Are you sure? Like I mean, are you sure?"

"Sure I'm sure. It ended on page 114 and the next story began on page 115, so I'm sure."

She took a drag on her cigarette and blew out the smoke. She ate some of her chocolate sundae.

"What's it about, so I won't have to read it?" Maxine asked.

"It starts out pretty good. Two fellows come into like a restaurant and they have a big deal going about what they want to eat. I thought it was going to be a funny story when I read that part. It was pretty funny."

"So? Like I mean, so?"

"Then it turns out they're crooks, or like killers I guess, and they tie up everybody in the place, and a little later they just go away. And one of the fellows who they tie up goes to warn this other fellow, but this other fellow just lays there in bed, and that's all there is to it."

"That's kooky," said Maxine. "That's supposed to be a story?"

"According to my prof it is. What a crazy way to end a story."

"That's a crazy course altogether. I don't understand it at all. It's not like anthropology, I mean, where you really learn something."

Alberta finished her sundae and put her cigarette butt into the liquid at the bottom of the glass. Maxine finished her sundae and dropped the cigarette butt on the floor. They both got up from the counter. They walked to the cashier and paid their bill. The two of them went out the door. Through the window, Nick watched them pass under the arc light and cross the street.

Nick stood up.

"I don't want any more of that," he said. "I don't want any more of that."

"It's a hell of a thing," George said. "I wonder what it's like, teaching them."

"It's an awful thing," Nick said.

They did not say anything. Nick reached down for the briefcase at his feet. He put the stack of blue books inside and snapped the lock shut.

"I'm going to get out of this town," Nick said.

"Yes," said George. "That's a good thing to do."

"I can't stand to think about that freshman lit class tomorrow. It's too damned awful."

"Well," said George, "you better not think about it."

Questions

1. Did you sense Hemingway's story as unfinished? Is Kaplan parodying only the style, or also the subject? Hemingway is fairly easy to parody. But Kaplan would be the first to admit that something in Hemingway goes beyond the parody. Can you decide what?
2. Does the story seem more realistic or natural because Kaplan sets it in this familiar situation? How well does Kaplan imitate Hemingway's style when he isn't using Hemingway's exact words?

Suggestions for Writing

1. Hemingway may be easy to parody but he is very difficult to imitate successfully, as hundreds of would-be Hemingways have demonstrated. But almost

any author with a distinctive style can be parodied. Pick an author you admire and write a parody, primarily of his style. You may want also to parody his characteristic subject matter as well. You will probably do well to work with some situation or subject that you are thoroughly familiar with, and to parody a specific work rather than the general characteristics of the author.

Pacifying Euphemisms: But Will Doublespeak Succumb?

Michael T. Malloy *The use of euphemisms affects both style and tone. You probably know them best (even if you were unaware of the word* euphemism) *as the softening words we substitute for harsh ones associated with such things as bodily functions and death. The city dead house becomes a mortuary, and when that becomes too harsh it becomes a funeral parlor and then a memorial chapel. As Professor Gibson indicates in this article, such substitutions are relatively harmless; they may even perform a useful function in smoothing rough spots for us. What Professor Gibson is campaigning against is far less innocent. You will recognize that the problem is as pertinent to semantics as to style and tone—perhaps even more so as you tie it to Professor Gibson's campaign to make people aware of the implications of euphemisms. But in your university, as elsewhere, you will be surrounded by the kind of language Gibson decries. It can have an insidious effect on your own style, especially since it aims away from precision and toward cliché: the jargon of education, or sociology, or politics, or—heaven help us!—even the field of English, which isn't a field at all, except in a jargony, inexact sense. As you read, apply Gibson's observations to your own style. Do you use the kinds of euphemisms he describes?*

Though you seldom get much rest in a rest room, you don't complain about it," observes Prof. Walker Gibson. "And most people would rather make love than fornicate. That kind of talk is perfectly harmless. The point where you exercise some moral outrage is the point where euphemisms are being used for inhumane ends. To call a rest room a 'W.C.' is not inhumane. To call bombing 'air support' is barbarous."

Professor Gibson has been bothered by this kind of thing ever since the

War Department changed its name to Defense Department and wars kept happening anyway. Critic H. L. Mencken much earlier celebrated the self-promotion of undertakers and hairdressers to morticians and beauticians. George Orwell gave the whole idea flesh in the official Doublespeak of *1984*. Now a little band of English teachers has gathered into a Committee on Public Doublespeak to try to do something about it.

Orwell Award

Gibson is a former president of the 30,000-member National Council of Teachers of English, and he grandfathered the committee into existence in response to council resolutions demanding resistance to "public lying." The two-year-old committee has set up a speakers' bureau, puts out a newsletter, will begin regular columns on doublespeak in three English teachers' journals next fall, and is preparing books on doublespeak for classroom use.

The committee arranged for 50 teachers to visit Washington to be lied to by experts. It is now trying to pick a winner for its first "Orwell" award from a host of candidates.

Gibson specializes in euphemism, the art of turning a sow's ear into a silk purse or a company's slovenly workmanship into a blameless machine's "mechanical defect." He divides them into four classes: sex and decency, commerce, government, and war. With each step he believes they become more dangerous.

"I think there will always be euphemisms and maybe that's good; delicacy is an important feeling," says Gibson, directing a visitor to one of the smaller rooms in his house on a green hill near the University of Massachusetts, where he works. "It's apparently impossible in our society to refer to this room without using a euphemism of some kind and this is apparently true in all languages. You know 'toilet' itself is a euphemism that originally meant a towel for shaving or washing.

"We seem to euphemize the areas we feel anxious and uptight about," Gibson says, "and this can lighten the load. Death is a subject of fantastic euphemism. People don't die; they pass away, they pass on, they succumb.

Whose Convenience?

"In commerce it's not so harmless. The word 'home' is very powerful. So you'll notice real-estate agents never sell houses; they sell homes. House trailers are mobile homes. A big insurance policy is a homeowner's policy. The people who build houses belong to the National Association of Home Builders. And a used car nowadays is 'previously owned,' which makes it less used than a secondhand car.

"A very good one is 'for your convenience,' when it isn't for *your* convenience, it's for *theirs:* 'For your convenience, please stand in line for the next 10 hours.'

"Governments are in the business of persuading citizens that things are okay," Gibson says, going up another category. "This becomes difficult if the citizen can look around and see a lot of things that aren't okay. So public officials abstract these situations to make them palatable. . . . Disadvantaged (not black, not poor, not ignorant). Inoperative (not fabricated, not lying, not even mistaken). Air support (not bombing, not murder). . . . I'm sure Soviet political writing is also full of euphemism: 'the people's government' and so on."

It was Orwell, Gibson says, who showed how governments adopt long, Latin words ending in -ion for activities they are ashamed to talk about in plain English. Orwell's list included "pacification" for burning peasant villages and "elimination" for murdering political opponents.

"The big fancy word is put on to take the heartaches out of what you are doing. It removes the speaker from the scene by labeling pain and hunger with an abstract noun," Gibson explains. "The teaching profession is full of this too. If a kid is too stupid to learn anything whatever, we call him an 'exceptional' child. We give 'remedial' help rather than bonehead English. The motive is often charitable, to increase the confidence of people who aren't doing very well.

They Entered, He Indicated

"What I want of students is that they become sensitive to these things, to be able to understand what's behind it," Gibson says. "The Watergate hearings, even during summer vacations, were an English teacher's dream. . . . 'Inappropriate' for against the law, 'entry' for burglary, 'intelligence gathering' for bugging. The word 'indicate' was a perfect example of language used to avoid responsibility, to put an aura of vagueness over everything so nobody can be caught with the goods. Hardly anybody *said* anything to anybody. They 'indicated' it."

It isn't just substituting a pretty word for a nice one—substandard housing for slums—that makes up doublespeak, but the manipulation of grammatical tools that most of us learn and then forget in elementary school.

"A while back the Ford Motor Co. 'recalled' their line of Torinos and Rancheros," Gibson says. "They sent out a letter: '. . . Continued driving with a failed bearing could result in disengagement of the axle shaft and adversely affect vehicle control,' which is a euphemism for 'you could get killed.'

"The subject of the sentence is 'continued driving,' subtly suggesting that the real fault isn't with the car but with the owner who insists on driving it. And you'll notice it's the bearing that 'failed,' not the company. What's missing, of course, is anything that says 'we goofed.'

Passive and Subjunctive

"Examine the testimony of Watergate again in some of the ways one employs in criticism of literature. The subjunctive mood removes the speaker one more step from the action and the responsibility: 'I would not remember that,' which *doesn't* say 'I don't remember it.'

"Take the use of the passive voice of the verb; what it does is again to escape responsibility: '*We* had a meeting and *it* was decided that. . . .' We never see who made the decision. It is a characteristic of stuffy talk generally. In the language of organizations the passive voice is 10 times as frequent as in more homemade kinds of talk because the speaker is eager to remove himself and anybody else from responsibility for any kind of action."

Euphemism is as old as human language. Their side's "retreat" has always been our "strategic withdrawal." We all know variants of "I am consistent, you are stubborn, he is a pigheaded fool." Homosexuals aren't the first group that has sought to elevate itself by substituting an attractive euphemism, "gay," for a host of unpleasant ones.

But nowadays doublespeak has become a well-paid profession and industry, pursued with unprecedented skill and resources by those whom Gibson's neighbor and fellow professor, Howard Ziff, calls "sophisticated managers of lying."

They're Educated!

"One of the ironies is that people like me educate these people," Gibson says. "They come from good schools and have good educations, just as many of the Watergate criminals do. We English teachers can't stop that, but maybe we can make the public more suspicious and alert. . . . For every student who is going to read Milton in later life, there are two million who are going to be exposed to TV and advertising and political slogans. I would like to make them sophisticated as possible as consumers of language."

As I drive out of Amherst toward the airport, the car radio boasts of a "flotation system" even better than a water bed and one wonders if the tide of euphemism is as pervasive as the professors say. After an annoying airport delay caused by a "change of equipment," we finally "extinguish smoking materials" and board an aircraft where we "observe," rather than obey, the no-smoking sign. One can guess why motion sickness has replaced air sickness lately, but why have stewardesses become cabin attendants? Finally we "deplane" and board the "ground transportation." It looks remarkably like a bus.

Questions

1. Even without our acknowledgement, you would probably have recognized this as a journalistic account of Professor Gibson's campaign, though a rather good one. It suits our purposes here because it covers a large range in brief space. In what ways might a somewhat more formal treatment of the same material have been more—or less—convincing?
2. Analyze the style of Gibson in his quoted passages. How formal is it? Do you find him using any euphemisms, except as examples?
3. Follow Gibson's analysis of the "recall" letter by Ford Motor Co. To what extent does the euphemistic quality of the letter result from actual euphemism?
4. Translate "sophisticated managers of lying" into euphemism. Or is it euphemism already?

Suggestions for Writing

1. In his book *Tough, Sweet and Stuffy,* Gibson analyzes in detail, in something of the way he analyzes here the sentence from the Ford letter, several longer passages, one from the Surgeon General's 1964 report "Smoking and Health," for instance. Find a passage of euphemistic prose that seems to you especially objectionable and write a detailed analysis of the ways in which the euphemisms work to make something bad into something good, or less bad. Almost any committee or government report or even an academic journal or textbook can furnish you with ammunition.

To Autumn

John Keats

Teachers of English often use "To Autumn" as an example of Keats' rich, luxuriant imagery in description. But they nearly always point not to the adjectives and adverbs but to the nouns and verbs as carrying the real energy of the description. Even allowing for the differences that would ordinarily distinguish poetry from prose, Keats' style is almost at an opposite pole from Hemingway's. Keeping in mind that practical definition of style as the author's choice and arrangement of words, define as precisely as you can the contrasts. You will note that Keats uses many infinitives and participles. Since these words are derived from verbs, they usually involve action, but they function in the sentences as modifiers, as adjectives or adverbs. What effects does Keats get from such words? Do you find many of them in Hemingway? If we classify these words as adjectives and adverbs and then see them in relation to other adjectives and adverbs, is it true that the energy in the poem comes from the nouns and verbs? A careful analysis of this problem can tell you much about style.

[1]

Season of mists and mellow fruitfulness,
    Close bosom-friend of the maturing sun;
Conspiring with him how to load and bless
    With fruit the vines that round the thatch-eaves run;
To bend with apples the mossed cottage-trees,
    And fill all fruit with ripeness to the core;
        To swell the gourd, and plump the hazel shells
With a sweet kernel; to set budding more,
    And still more, later flowers for the bees,
    Until they think warm days will never cease,
        For summer has o'er-brimmed their clammy cells.

[2]

Who hath not seen thee oft amid thy store?
    Sometimes whoever seeks abroad may find

Thee sitting careless on a granary floor,
  Thy hair soft-lifted by the winnowing wind;
Or on a half-reaped furrow sound asleep,
  Drowsed with the fume of poppies, while thy hook
    Spares the next swath and all its twined flowers:
And sometimes like a gleaner thou dost keep
  Steady thy laden head across a brook;
  Or by a cider-press, with patient look,
    Thou watchest the last oozings hours by hours.

[3]

Where are the songs of spring? Aye, where are they?
  Think not of them, thou hast thy music too—
While barred clouds bloom the soft-dying day,
  And touch the stubble-plains with rosy hue;
Then in a wailful choir the small gnats mourn
  Among the river sallows, borne aloft
    Or sinking as the light wind lives or dies;
And full-grown lambs loud bleat from hilly bourn;
  Hedge crickets sing; and now with treble soft
  The redbreast whistles from a garden croft;
    And gathering swallows twitter in the skies.

Brit

Herman Melville

Melville's novel Moby Dick *is now recognized as the masterpiece that it is, and Melville himself as an unusual but great stylist. We have selected this particular passage, which occurs near the end of the long novel, to illustrate his unusually rhythmic prose. But it also reveals other qualities of the Melville style. The mad Captain Ahab has finally appeared on deck and has sworn the men to help him in his quest for Moby Dick, the great white sperm whale who has much earlier "dismasted" him—that is, bitten one of his legs off. Ishmael, the narrator, has speculated on the meaning of the quest and on the awfulness of white, the crew have captured their first whale, they have had their first "gam," or visit, with another whaling crew, and now Ishmael can take time to describe and meditate about events and whales along the way. Would you recognize from the style alone that this is a novel about the sea?*

CHAPTER LVIII

Steering north-eastward from the Crozetts, we fell in with vast meadows of brit, the minute, yellow substance, upon which the Right Whale largely feeds. For leagues and leagues it undulated round us, so that we seemed to be sailing through boundless fields of ripe and golden wheat.

On the second day, numbers of Right Whales were seen, who, secure from the attack of a Sperm Whaler like the Pequod, with open jaws sluggishly swam through the brit, which, adhering to the fringing fibres of that wondrous Venetian blind in their mouths, was in that manner separated from the water that escaped at the lip.

As morning mowers, who side by side slowly and seethingly advance their scythes through the long wet grass of marshy meads; even so these monsters swam, making a strange, grassy, cutting sound; and leaving behind them endless swaths of blue upon the yellow sea.*

But it was only the sound they made as they parted the brit which at

* That part of the sea known among whalemen as the "Brazil Banks" does not bear that name as the Banks of Newfoundland do, because of there being shallows and soundings there, but because of this remarkable meadow-like appearance, caused by the vast drifts of brit continually floating in those latitudes, where the Right Whale is often chased.

all reminded one of mowers. Seen from the mast-heads especially when they paused and were stationary for a while, their vast black forms looked more like lifeless masses of rock than anything else. And as in the great hunting countries of India, the stranger at a distance will sometimes pass on the plains recumbent elephants without knowing them to be such, taking them for bare, blackened elevations of the soil; even so, often, with him, who for the first time beholds this species of the leviathans of the sea. And even when recognised at last, their immense magnitude renders it very hard really to believe that such bulky masses of overgrowth can possibly be instinct, in all parts, with the same sort of life that lives in a dog or a horse.

Indeed, in other respects, you can hardly regard any creatures of the deep with the same feelings that you do those of the shore. For though some old naturalists have maintained that all creatures of the land are of their kind in the sea; and though taking a broad general view of the thing, this may very well be; yet coming to specialities, where for example, does the ocean furnish any fish that in disposition answers to the sagacious kindness of the dog? The accursed shark alone can in any generic respect be said to bear comparative analogy to him.

But though to landsmen in general the native inhabitants of the seas have ever been regarded with emotions unspeakably unsocial and repelling; though we know the sea to be an everlasting terra incognita, so that Columbus sailed over numberless unknown worlds to discover his one superficial western one; though, by vast odds, the most terrific of all mortal disasters have immemorially and indiscriminately befallen tens and hundreds of thousands of those who have gone upon the waters; though but a moment's consideration will teach, that however baby man may brag of his science and skill, and however much, in a flattering future, that science and skill may augment; yet for ever and for ever, to the crack of doom, the sea will insult and murder him, and pulverise the stateliest, stiffest frigate he can make; nevertheless, by the continual repetition of these very impressions, man has lost that sense of the full awfulness of the sea which aboriginally belongs to it.

The first boat we read of, floated on an ocean, that with Portuguese vengeance had whelmed a whole world without leaving so much as a widow. That same ocean rolls now; that same ocean destroyed the wrecked ships of last year. Yea, foolish mortals, Noah's flood is not yet subsided; two thirds of the fair world it yet covers.

Wherein differ the sea and the land, that a miracle upon one is not a miracle upon the other? Preternatural terrors rested upon the Hebrews, when under the feet of Korah and his company the live ground opened and swallowed them up for ever; yet not a modern sun ever sets, but in precisely the same manner the live sea swallows up ships and crews.

But not only is the sea such a foe to man who is an alien to it, but it is also a fiend to its own offspring; worse than the Persian host who murdered his own guests; sparing not the creatures which itself hath spawned. Like a savage tigress that tossing in the jungle overlays her own cubs, so the sea dashes even the mightiest whales against the rocks, and leaves them there side by side with the split wrecks of ships. No mercy, no power but its own controls it. Panting and snorting like a mad battle steed that has lost its rider, the masterless ocean overruns the globe.

Consider the subtleness of the sea; how its most dreaded creatures glide under water, unapparent for the most part, and treacherously hidden beneath the loveliest tints of azure. Consider also the devilish brilliance and beauty of many of its most remorseless tribes, as the dainty embellished shape of many species of sharks. Consider, once more, the universal cannibalism of the sea; all whose creatures prey upon each other, carrying on eternal war since the world began.

Consider all this; and then turn to this green, gentle, and most docile earth; consider them both, the sea and the land; and do you not find a strange analogy to something in yourself? For as this appalling ocean surrounds the verdant land, so in the soul of man there lies one insular Tahiti, full of peace and joy, but encompassed by all the horrors of the half-known life. God keep thee! Push not off from that isle, thou canst never return!

Questions

1. We asked at the beginning of this selection whether you could tell from the style alone that this is a sea novel. Melville has often been described as catching stylistically the rhythms of the sea. Examine carefully the long one-sentence paragraph in the middle: "But though, to landsmen . . . ; though we know . . . ; though, by vast odds . . . ; though but a . . . ; yet for ever . . . ; nevertheless, by the . . . ." The long series of parallel clauses suggest a gathering series of waves rolling toward the shore, finally to break in the last clause and perhaps to spend itself rolling up the beach—or to wrap around itself against the rocks. There is an even more impressive series in the last two paragraphs. Can you feel the effect? Not all of Melville's prose rolls like these passages but the restless surging rhythm of the sea can be felt under most of *Moby Dick*.
2. Contrast the rhythms of the above passage with those of the following one, in which Captain Ahab is addressing the first mate just before the sighting of Moby Dick and the three-day chase that is to lead the men to their doom:

   Oh, Starbuck! it is a mild, mild wind, and a mild looking sky. On such a day—very much such a sweetness as this—I struck my first whale—a boy-harpooneer of eighteen! Forty—forty—forty years ago!—ago! Forty years of continual whaling! forty years of privation, and peril, and storm-time! forty years on the pitiless sea! for forty years has Ahab forsaken the peaceful land, for forty years to make war on the horrors of the deep! Aye and yes, Starbuck, out of those forty years I have not spent three ashore. When I think of this life I have led; the desolation of solitude it has been; the masoned, walled-town of a Captain's exclusiveness, which admits but small entrance to any sympathy from the green country without—oh, weariness! heaviness! Guinea-coast slavery of solitary command!—when I think of all this; only half-suspected, not so keenly known to me before—and how for forty years I have fed upon dry salted fare—fit emblem of the dry nourishment of my soul!—when the poorest landsman has had fresh fruit to his daily hand, and broken the world's fresh bread to my mouldy crusts —away, whole oceans away, from that young girl-wife I wedded past fifty, and sailed for Cape Horn the next day, leaving but one dent in my marriage pillow—wife? wife?—rather a widow with her husband alive! Aye, I widowed that poor girl when I married her, Starbuck; and then, the madness, the frenzy, the boiling blood and the smoking brow, with which, for a thousand lowerings old Ahab has furiously, foamingly chased his prey—more a demon than a man!—aye, aye! what a forty years' fool—fool—old fool, has old Ahab been! Why this strife of the chase? why weary, and palsy the arm at the oar, and the iron, and the lance? how the richer or better is Ahab now? Behold. Oh, Starbuck! is it not hard, that with this weary load I bear, one poor leg should have been snatched from under me? Here, brush this old hair aside; it blinds me, that I seem to weep. Locks so grey did never grow but from out some ashes! But do I look very old, so very, very old, Starbuck? I feel deadly faint, bowed, and humped, as though I were Adam, staggering beneath the piled centuries since Paradise. God! God! God!—crack my heart!—stave my brain!—mockery! mockery! bitter, biting mockery of grey hairs, have I lived enough joy to wear ye; and seem and feel thus intolerably old? Close! stand close to me, Starbuck; let me look into a human eye; it is better than to gaze into sea or sky; better than to gaze upon God. By the green land; by the bright hearth-stone! this is the magic glass, man; I see my wife and my child in thine eye. No, no; stay on board, on board!—lower not when I do; when branded Ahab gives chase to Moby Dick. That hazard shall not be thine. No, no! not with the far away home I see in that eye!

Setting it up in a loose, cadenced free verse like this emphasizes the rhythms:

Oh, Starbuck!
It is a mild, mild wind, and a mild looking sky.
On such a day—very much such a sweetness at this—
I struck my first whale—a boy-harpooneer of eighteen
Forty—forty—forty years ago!—ago!
Forty years of continual whaling!
Forty years of privation, and peril, and storm-time!
Forty years on the pitiless sea!
For forty years has Ahab forsaken the peaceful land,
For forty years to make war on the horrors of the deep!
Aye and yes, Starbuck,
Out of those forty years I have not spent three ashore.

Try to continue from here and set up some of the lines yourself. You might skip to "I feel deadly faint . . . ." Does setting it in poetic form increase your sense of the rhythm? Contrast these lines from Chapter XXXVII, "Sunset," spoken by Ahab in soliloquy, which arrange themselves into almost regular blank verse (Shakespeare's line):

> I leave a white and turbid wake
> Pale waters, paler cheeks, where'er I sail.
> The envious billows sidelong swell to whelm
> My track; let them; but first I pass.
> Yonder, by the ever-brimming goblet's rim,
> The warm waves blush like wine.
> The gold brow plumbs the blue.
> The diver sun—slow dived from noon,—goes down;
> My soul mounts up! she wearies with her endless hill.
> Is, then, the crown too heavy that I wear?

Try the same kind of arranging with this continuation of the passage:

> Dry heat upon my brow? Oh! time was, when as the sunrise nobly spurred me, so the sunset soothed. No more. This lovely light it lights not me; all loveliness is anguish to me, since I can ne'er enjoy. Gifted with the high perception I lack the low, enjoying power; damned, most subtly and most malignantly! Damned, in the midst of Paradise! Good night—good night!

What would be the effect when such rhythmic language is changed back into prose? Which of the three kinds of rhythm seems most effective in Melville's prose?

3. Another important quality of Melville's style can be seen in "Brit" and the passages just quoted. Note how many figures of speech he uses—or has Ishmael and Ahab use. The horizon becomes "the goblet's rim" and the waves "blush like wine." Find other figures. How effective are they? In Melville nearly every fact tends to take on metaphorical or symbolic significance, just as Brit becomes evidence for the "universal cannibalism of the sea." The whole chase, the whole book, becomes a vast symbol. If you have read the novel, try to define its broad meaning.

The Weary Blues

Langston Hughes *Unquestionably the most pervasive and powerful influence on twentieth-century American music, all the way from rock to Leonard Bernstein, is the Negro folk and jazz rhythms that moved north from New Orleans to permeate America. Hughes catches that rhythm with a sure beat in this poem. Read it aloud, and emphasize the rhythm. What creates the rhythm?*

The Weary Blues

Droning a drowsy syncopated tune,
Rocking back and forth to a mellow croon,
        I heard a Negro play.
Down on Lenox Avenue the other night
By the pale dull pallor of an old gas light
        He did a lazy sway. . . .
        He did a lazy sway. . . .
To the tune o' those Weary Blues.
With his ebony hands on each ivory key
He made that poor piano moan with melody.
        O Blues!
Swaying to and fro on his rickety stool
He played that sad raggy tune like a musical fool.
        Sweet Blues!
Coming from a black man's soul.
        O Blues!
In a deep song voice with a melancholy tone
I heard that Negro sing, that old piano moan—
        "Ain't got nobody in all this world,
        Ain't got nobody but ma self.
        I's gwine to quit ma frownin'
        And put ma troubles on the shelf."

Thump, thump, thump, went his foot on the floor.
He played a few chords then he sang some more—
    "I got the Weary Blues
    And I can't be satisfied.
    Got the Weary Blues
    And can't be satisfied—
    I ain't happy no mo'
    And I wish that I had died."
And far into the night he crooned that tune.
The stars went out and so did the moon.
The singer stopped playing and went to bed
While the Weary Blues echoed through his head.
He slept like a rock or a man that's dead.

Letter to the Earth

Mark Twain

The Mark Twain who wrote this letter may seem to have little in common with the Mark Twain you have come to know in Tom Sawyer *or even* Huckleberry Finn. *But almost all his earlier books had passages that forecast such writing. Here, if anywhere, you should be able to see the advantages of the* right *rhetorical stance. What effects does Twain get from pretending the letter is written by the recording angel and comes from Heaven?*

Office of the Recording Angel
Department of Petitions, Jan. 20

Andrew Langdon
Coal Dealer
Buffalo, New York

I have the honor, as per command, to inform you that your recent act of benevolence and self-sacrifice has been recorded upon a page of the Book called *Golden Deeds of Men:* a distinction, I am permitted to remark, which is not merely extraordinary, it is unique.

As regards your prayers, for the week ending the 19th, I have the honor to report as follows:

1. For weather to advance hard coal 15 cents a ton. Granted.
2. For influx of laborers to reduce wages 10 per cent. Granted.
3. For a break in rival soft-coal prices. Granted.
4. For a visitation upon the man, or upon the family of the man, who has set up a competing retail coal-yard in Rochester. Granted, as follows: diphtheria, 2, 1 fatal; scarlet fever, 1, to result in deafness and imbecility. NOTE. This prayer should have been directed against this subordinate's principals, The N. Y. Central R. R. Co.
5. For deportation to Sheol of annoying swarms of persons who apply

daily for work, or for favors of one sort or another. Taken under advisement for later decision and compromise, this petition appearing to conflict with another one of same date, which will be cited further along.

6. For application of some form of violent death to neighbor who threw brick at family cat, whilst the same was serenading. Reserved for consideration and compromise because of conflict with a prayer of even date to be cited further along.

7. To "damn the missionary cause." Reserved also—as above.

8. To increase December profits of $22,230 to $45,000 for January, and perpetuate a proportionate monthly increase thereafter— "which will satisfy you." The prayer granted; the added remark accepted with reservations.

9. For cyclone, to destroy the works and fill up the mine of the North Pennsylvania Co. NOTE: Cyclones are not kept in stock in the winter season. A reliable article of firedamp can be furnished upon application.

Especial note is made of the above list, they being of particular moment. The 298 remaining supplications classifiable under the head of Special Providences, Schedule A, for the week ending 19th, are granted in a body, except that 3 of the 32 cases requiring immediate death have been modified to incurable disease.

This completes the week's invoice of petitions known to this office under the technical designation of Secret Supplications of the Heart, and which for a reason which may suggest itself, always receive our first and especial attention.

The remainder of the week's invoice falls under the head of what we term Public Prayers, in which classification we place prayers uttered in Prayer Meeting, Sunday School, Class Meeting, Family Worship, etc. These kinds of prayers have value according to classification of Christian uttering them. By rule of this office, Christians are divided into two grand classes, to wit: 1, Professing Christians; 2, Professional Christians. These, in turn, are minutely subdivided and classified by size, species, and family; and finally, standing is determined by carats, the minimum being 1, the maximum 1,000.

As per balance-sheet for quarter ending Dec. 31, 1847, you stood classified as follows:

Grand Classification, Professing Christian.

Size, one-fourth of maximum.

Species, Human-Spiritual.

Family, A of the Elect, Division 16.

Standing, 322 carats fine.

As per balance-sheet for quarter just ended—that is to say, forty years later—you stand classified as follows:

Grand Classification, Professional Christian.

Size, six one-hundredths of maximum.

Species, Human-Animal.

Family, W of the Elect, Division 1547.

Standing, 3 carats fine.

I have the honor to call your attention to the fact that you seem to have deteriorated.

To resume report upon your Public Prayers—with the side remark that in order to encourage Christians of your grade and of approximate grades, it is the custom of this office to grant many things to them which would not be granted to Christians of a higher grade—partly because they would not be asked for:

Prayer for weather mercifully tempered to the needs of the poor and the naked. Denied. This was a Prayer-Meeting Prayer. It conflicts with Item 1 of this report, which was a Secret Supplication of the Heart. By a rigid rule of this office, certain sorts of Public Prayers of Professional Christians are forbidden to take precedence of Secret Supplications of the Heart.

Prayer for better times and plentier food "for the hard-handed son of toil whose patient and exhausting labors make comfortable the homes, and pleasant the ways, of the more fortunate, and entitle him to our vigilant and effective protection from the wrongs and injustices which grasping avarice would do him, and to the tenderest offices of our grateful hearts." Prayer-Meeting Prayer. Refused. Conflicts with Secret Supplication of the Heart No. 2.

Prayer "that such as in any way obstruct our preferences may be generously blessed, both themselves and their families, we here calling our hearts to witness that in their worldly prosperity we are spiritually blessed, and our joys made perfect." Prayer-Meeting Prayer. Refused. Conflicts with Secret Supplications of the Heart Nos. 3 and 4.

"Oh, let none fall heir to the pains of perdition through words or acts of ours." Family Worship. Received fifteen minutes in advance of Secret Supplication of the Heart No. 5, with which it distinctly conflicts. It is suggested that one or the other of these prayers be withdrawn, or both of them modified.

"Be mercifully inclined toward all who would do us offense in our persons or our property." Includes man who threw brick at cat. Family Prayer. Received some minutes in advance of No. 6, Secret Supplications of the Heart. Modification suggested, to reconcile discrepancy.

"Grant that the noble missionary cause, the most precious labor entrusted to the hands of men, may spread and prosper without let or limit in all heathen lands that do as yet reproach us with their spiritual darkness." Uninvited prayer shoved in at meeting of American Board. Received nearly half a day in advance of No. 7, Secret Supplications of the Heart. This office takes no stock in missionaries, and is not connected in any way with the American Board. We should like to grant one of these prayers but cannot grant both. It is suggested that the American Board one be withdrawn.

This office desires for the twentieth time to call urgent attention to your remark appended to No. 8. It is a chestnut.

Of the 464 specifications contained in your Public Prayers for the week, and not previously noted in this report, we grant 2, and deny the rest. To wit: Granted, (1), "that the clouds may continue to perform their office; (2), and the sun his." It was the divine purpose anyhow; it will gratify you to know that you have not disturbed it. Of the 462 details refused, 61 were uttered in Sunday School. In this connection I must once more remind you that we grant no Sunday School Prayers of Professional Christians of the classification technically known in this office as the John Wanamaker grade. We merely enter them as "words," and they count to his credit according to number uttered within certain limits of time; 3,000 per quarter-minute required, or no score; 4,200 in a possible 5,000 is a quite common Sunday School score among experts, and counts the same as two hymns and a bouquet furnished by young ladies in the assassin's cell, execution-morning. Your remaining 401 details count for wind only. We bunch them and use them for head-winds in retarding the ships of improper people, but it takes so many of them to make an impression that we cannot allow anything for their use.

I desire to add a word of my own to this report. When certain sorts of people do a sizable good deed, we credit them up a thousand-fold more for it than we would in the case of a better man—on account of the strain. You stand far away above your classification-record here, because of certain self-sacrifices of yours which greatly exceed what could have been expected of you. Years ago, when you were worth only $100,000, and sent $2 to your impoverished cousin the widow when she appealed to you for help, there were many in heaven who were not able to believe it, and many more who believed that the money was counterfeit. Your character went up many degrees when it was shown that these suspicions were unfounded. A year or two later, when you sent the poor girl $4 in answer to another appeal, everybody believed it, and you were the talk here for days together. Two years later you sent $6, upon supplication, when the widow's youngest child died, and that act made perfect your good fame. Everybody in heaven said, "Have you heard about Andrew?"—for you are now affectionately called Andrew here. Your increasing donation, every two or three years, has kept your name on all lips, and warm in all hearts.

All heaven watches you Sundays, as you drive to church in your handsome carriage; and when your hand retires from the contribution plate, the glad shout is heard even to the ruddy walls of remote Sheol, "Another nickel from Andrew!"

But the climax came a few days ago, when the widow wrote and said she could get a school in a far village to teach if she had $50 to get herself and her two surviving children over the long journey; and you counted up last month's clear profit from your three coal mines—$22,230—and added to it the certain profit for the current month—$45,000 and a possible fifty—and then got down your pen and your check-book and mailed her *fifteen whole dollars!* Ah, Heaven bless and keep you forever and ever, generous heart! There was not a dry eye in the realms of bliss; and amidst the hand-shakings, and embracings, and praisings, the decree was thundered forth from the shining mount, that this deed should outhonor all the historic self-sacrifices of men and angels, and be recorded by itself upon a page of its own, for that the strain of it upon you had been heavier and bitterer than the strain it costs ten thousand martyrs to yield up their lives at the fiery stake; and all said, "What is the giving up of life, to a noble soul, or to ten thousand noble souls; compared with the giving up of fifteen dollars out of the greedy grip of the meanest white man that ever lived on the face of the earth?"

And it was a true word. And Abraham, weeping, shook out the contents of his bosom and pasted the eloquent label there, "RESERVED"; and Peter, weeping, said, "He shall be received with a torchlight procession when he comes"; and then all heaven boomed, and was glad you were going there. And so was hell.

[Signed]
The Recording Angel [Seal]

By command.

Questions

1. Analyze the style of this letter. Does it sound like that of a clerk of the courts? Why should Twain use this particular style?
2. The quoted language of the prayers is quite different. Does it sound like the language of public prayer? Why?
3. What is the recording angel's *apparent* attitude toward Andrew Langdon? Does it remain consistent? See especially the description, at the end, of Heaven's rejoicing over the contributions. What is Mark Twain's attitude toward Langdon? How would you describe *his* tone in this letter. Note that your problem in defining Twain's tone is complicated by the indirect point of view;

you have to define the angel's tone in order to define Twain's. Are they the same?

4. What is the effect of the last sentence? What makes it so devastating?

Suggestions for Writing

1. The letter ought to tempt you to do some kind of similar experiment in both point of view and tone. Imagine, for example, your having died, spent some time in Heaven—or Hell—and being able to return to tell everything. Try to do it in a consistently ironic vein. Or keep it light, so you will avoid the danger of sermonizing.

A Modest Proposal

Jonathan Swift

Swift first shocked Ireland and England with his "A Modest Proposal" in 1729. It has continued to shock readers ever since, especially college students in our century. It has become one of the most often reprinted selections in all kinds of composition texts—a genuine classic for the analysis of tone. Perhaps some of the shock of the "Proposal" will be lost since you are being warned in advance to read it carefully for tone. Even so, it carries its shock regardless of the level of sophistication you bring to it. As with any selection in which the tone may not be simply objective or straightforward, you will need to define Swift's rhetorical stance with some precision. How seriously does he want his readers to take him? What clues does he give?

It is a melancholly Object to those, who walk through this great Town or travel in the Country, when they see the Streets, the Roads and Cabbin-doors crowded with Beggers of the Female Sex, followed by three, four, or six Children, all in Rags, and importuning every Passenger for an Alms. These Mothers instead of being able to work for their honest livelyhood, are forced to employ all their time in Stroling to beg Sustenance for their helpless Infants, who, as they grow up, either turn Thieves for want of Work, or leave their dear Native Country, to fight for the Pretender in Spain, or sell themselves to the Barbadoes.

I think it is agreed by all Parties, that this prodigious number of Children in the Arms, or on the Backs, or at the Heels of their Mothers, and frequently of their Fathers, is in the present deplorable state of the Kingdom, a very great additional grievance; and therefore whoever could find out a fair, cheap and easy method of making these Children sound and useful Members of the Common-wealth, would deserve so well of the publick, as to have his Statue set up for a Preserver of the Nation.

But my Intention is very far from being confined to provide only for the Children of professed Beggers, it is of a much greater Extent, and shall take in the whole Number of Infants at a certain Age, who are born of Parents in effect as little able to support them, as those who demand our Charity in the Streets.

As to my own part, having turned my Thoughts, for many Years, upon this important Subject, and maturely weighed the several Schemes of other Projectors, I have always found them grossly mistaken in their computation. It is true, a Child just dropt from its Dam, may be supported by her Milk, for a Solar Year with little other Nourishment, at most not above the Value of two Shillings, which the Mother may certainly get, or the Value in Scraps, by her lawful Occupation of Begging; and it is exactly at one Year Old that I propose to provide for them in such a manner, as, instead of being a Charge upon their Parents, or the Parish, or wanting Food and Raiment for the rest of their Lives, they shall, on the Contrary, contribute to the Feeding and partly to the Cloathing of many Thousands.

There is likewise another great Advantage in my Scheme, that it will prevent those voluntary Abortions, and that horrid practice of Women murdering their Bastard Children, alas! too frequent among us, Sacrificing the poor innocent Babes, I doubt, more to avoid the Expence than the Shame, which would move Tears and Pity in the most Savage and inhuman breast.

The number of Souls in this Kingdom being usually reckoned one Million and a half, Of these I calculate there may be about two hundred thousand Couple whose Wives are Breeders; from which number I substract thirty Thousand Couples, who are able to maintain their own Children, although I apprehend there cannot be so many, under the present Distresses of the Kingdom; but this being granted, there will remain an hundred and seventy thousand Breeders. I again Substract fifty Thousand, for those Women who miscarry, or whose Children die by accident, or disease within the Year. There only remain an hundred and twenty thousand Children of poor Parents annually born: The question therefore is, How this number shall be reared, and provided for? which, as I have already said, under the present Situation of Affairs, is utterly impossible by all the Methods hitherto proposed; for we can neither employ them in Handicraft or Agriculture; we neither build Houses, (I mean in the Country) nor cultivate Land: They can very seldom pick up a Livelihood by Stealing till they arrive at six years Old; except where they are of towardly parts; although, I confess, they learn the Rudiments much earlier; during which time they can however be properly looked upon only as Probationers; as I have been informed by a principal Gentleman in the County of Cavan, who protested to me, that he never knew above one or two Instances under the Age of six, even in a part of the Kingdom so renowned for the quickest proficiency in that Art.

I am assured by our Merchants, that a Boy or a Girl before twelve years Old, is no saleable Commodity, and even when they come to this Age, they will not yield above three Pounds, or three Pounds and half a Crown at most, on the Exchange; which cannot turn to Account either to the Parents or Kingdom, the Charge of Nutriment and Rags having been at least four times that Value.

I shall now therefore humbly propose my own Thoughts, which I hope will not be liable to the least Objection.

I have been assured by a very knowing American of my acquaintance in London, that a young healthy Child well Nursed is at a year Old a most delicious nourishing and wholesome Food, whether Stewed, Roasted, Baked, or Boiled; and I make no doubt that it will equally serve in a Fricasie, or a Ragoust.

I do therefore humbly offer it to publick consideration, that of the Hundred and twenty thousand Children, already computed, twenty thousand may be reserved for Breed, whereof only one fourth part to be Males; which is more than we allow to Sheep, black Cattle, or Swine, and my Reason is, that these Children are seldom the Fruits of Marriage, a Circumstance not much regarded by our Savages, therefore, one Male will be sufficient to serve four Females. That the remaining Hundred thousand may at a year Old be offered in Sale to the Persons of Quality and Fortune, through the Kingdom, always advising the Mother to let them Suck plentifully in the last Month, so as to render them Plump, and Fat for a good Table. A Child will make two Dishes at an Entertainment for Friends, and when the Family dines alone, the fore or hind Quarter will make a reasonable Dish, and seasoned with a little Pepper or Salt will be very good Boiled on the fourth Day, especially in Winter.

I have reckoned upon a Medium, that a Child just born will weigh 12 pounds, and in a solar Year, if tolerably nursed, encreaseth to 28 Pounds.

I grant this food will be somewhat dear, and therefore very proper for Landlords, who, as they have already devoured most of the Parents seem to have the best Title to the Children.

Infant's flesh will be in Season throughout the Year, but more plentiful in March, and a little before and after; for we are told by a grave Author an eminent French Physician, that Fish being a prolifick Dyet, there are more Children born in Roman Catholick Countries about nine Months after Lent, than at any other Season; therefore reckoning a Year after Lent, the Markets will be more glutted than usual, because the Number of Popish Infants, is at least three to one in this Kingdom, and therefore it will have one other Collateral advantage, by lessening the Number of Papists among us.

I have already computed the Charge of nursing a Begger's Child (in which List I reckon all Cottagers, Labourers, and four fifths of the Farmers) to be about two Shillings per Annum, Rags included; and I believe no Gentleman would repine to give Ten Shillings for the Carcass of a good fat Child, which, as I have said will make four Dishes of excellent Nutritive Meat, when he hath only some particular Friend, or his own Family to dine with him. Thus the Squire will learn to be a good Landlord, and grow popular among his Tenants, the Mother will have Eight Shillings neat Profit, and be fit for Work till she produces another Child.

Those who are more thrifty (as I must confess the Times require) may flay the Carcass; the Skin of which, Artificially dressed, will make admirable Gloves for Ladies, and Summer Boots for fine Gentlemen.

As to our City of Dublin, Shambles may be appointed for this purpose, in the most convenient parts of it, and Butchers we may be assured will not be wanting; although I rather recommend buying the Children alive, and dressing them hot from the Knife, as we do roasting Pigs.

A very worthy Person, a true Lover of his Country, and whose Virtues I highly esteem, was lately pleased, in discoursing on this matter, to offer a refinement upon my Scheme. He said, that many Gentlemen of this Kingdom, having of late destroyed their Deer, he conceived that the Want of Venison might be well supply'd by the Bodies of young Lads and Maidens, not exceeding fourteen Years of Age, nor under twelve; so great a Number of both Sexes in every Country being now ready to Starve, for want of Work and Service: And these to be disposed of by their Parents if alive, or otherwise by their nearest Relations. But with due deference to so excellent a Friend, and so deserving a Patriot, I cannot be altogether in his Sentiments; for as to the Males, my American acquaintance assured me from frequent Experience, that their Flesh was generally Tough and Lean, like that of our Schoolboys, by continual exercise, and their Taste disagreeable, and to fatten them would not answer the Charge. Then as to the Females, it would, I think with humble Submission, be a Loss to the Publick, because they soon would become Breeders themselves: And besides it is not improbable that some scrupulous People might be apt to Censure such a Practice, (although indeed very unjustly) as a little bordering upon Cruelty, which, I confess, hath always been with me the strongest Objection against any Project, how well soever intended.

But in order to justify my Friend, he confessed, that this expedient was put into his Head by the famous Sallmanaazor, a Native of the Island Formosa, who came from thence to London, above twenty Years ago, and in Conversation told my Friend, that in his Country when any young Person happened to be put to Death, the Executioner sold the Carcass to Persons of Quality, as a prime Dainty, and that, in his Time, the Body of a plump Girl of fifteen, who was crucified for an attempt to poison the Emperor, was sold to his Imperial Majesty's prime Minister of State, and other great Mandarins of the Court, in Joints from the Gibbet, at four hundred Crowns. Neither indeed can I deny, that if the same Use were made of several plump young Girls in this Town, who, without one single Groat to their Fortunes, cannot stir abroad without a Chair, and appear at a Play-house, and Assemblies in Foreign fineries, which they never will pay for; the Kingdom would not be the worse.

Some Persons of a desponding Spirit are in great concern about that vast Number of poor People, who are Aged, Diseased, or Maimed, and I have been desired to imploy my Thoughts what Course may be taken, to ease the Nation of so grievous an Incumbrance. But I am not in the least Pain upon that matter, because it is very well known, that they are every Day dying, and rotting, by cold and famine, and filth, and vermin, as fast as can be reasonably expected. And as to the younger Labourers, they are now in almost as hopeful a Condition. They cannot get Work, and consequently pine away for want of Nourishment, to a degree, that if at any Time they are accidentally hired to common Labour, they have not Strength to perform it, and thus the Country and themselves are happily delivered from the Evils to come.

I have too long digressed, and therefore shall return to my Subject. I think the Advantages by the Proposal which I have made are obvious and many, as well as of the highest Importance.

For *First,* as I have already observed, it would greatly lessen the Number of Papists, with whom we are Yearly over-run, being the principal Breeders of the Nation, as well as our most dangerous Enemies, and who stay at home on purpose with a Design to deliver the Kingdom to the Pretender, hoping to take their Advantage by the Absence of so many good Protestants, who have chosen rather to leave their Country, than stay at home, and pay Tithes against their Conscience, to an Episcopal Curate.

Secondly, The poorer Tenants will have something valuable of their own which by Law may be made lyable to Distress, and help to pay their Landlord's Rent, their Corn and Cattle being already seized, and Money a Thing unknown.

Thirdly, Whereas the Maintenance of an hundred thousand Children, from two Years old, and upwards, cannot be computed at less than Ten Shillings a Piece per Annum, the Nation's Stock will be thereby increased fifty thousand Pounds per Annum, besides the Profit of a new Dish, introduced to the Tables of all Gentlemen of Fortune in the Kingdom, who have any Refinement in Taste, and the Money will circulate among our Selves, the Goods being entirely of our own Growth and Manufacture.

Fourthly, The constant Breeders, besides the gain of eight Shillings Sterling per Annum, by the Sale of their Children, will be rid of the Charge of maintaining them after the first Year.

Fifthly, This Food would likewise bring great Custom to Taverns, where the Vintners will certainly be so prudent as to procure the best Receipts for dressing it to Perfection; and consequently have their Houses frequented by all the fine Gentlemen, who justly value themselves upon their Knowledge in good Eating; and a skilful Cook, who understands how to oblige his Guests, will contrive to make it as expensive as they please.

Sixthly, This would be a great Inducement to Marriage, which all wise Nations have either encouraged by Rewards, or enforced by Laws and Penalties. It would encrease the Care and Tenderness of Mothers towards their Children, when they were sure of a Settlement, for Life, to the poor Babes, provided in some Sort by the Publick, to their annual Profit instead of Expence; we should soon see an honest Emulation among the married Women, which of them could bring the fattest Child to the Market. Men would become as fond of their Wives, during the Time of their Pregnancy, as they are now of their Mares in Foal, their Cows in Calf, or Sows when they are ready to farrow, nor offer to beat or kick them (as is too frequent a Practice) for fear of a Miscarriage.

Many other Advantages might be enumerated. For Instance, the Addition of some thousand Carcasses in our Exportation of Barrel'd Beef: The Propagation of Swine's Flesh, and Improvement in the Art of making good Bacon, so much wanted among us by the great Destruction of Pigs, too frequent at our Tables, which are no way comparable in Taste, or Magnificence to a well grown, fat yearling Child, which roasted whole will make a considerable Figure at a Lord Mayor's Feast, or any other Publick Entertainment. But this, and many others, I omit, being studious of Brevity.

Supposing that one thousand Families in this City, would be constant Customers for Infant's Flesh, besides others who might have it at merry Meetings, particularly at Weddings and Christenings, I compute that Dublin would take off Annually about twenty thousand Carcasses, and the rest of the Kingdom (where probably they will be sold somewhat cheaper) the remaining eighty Thousand.

I can think of no one Objection, that will possibly be raised against this Proposal, unless it should be urged, that the Number of People will be thereby much lessened in the Kingdom. This I freely own, and 'twas indeed one principal Design in offering it to the World. I desire the Reader will observe, that I calculate my Remedy for this one individual Kingdom of Ireland, and for no Other that ever was, is, or, I think, ever can be upon Earth. Therefore let no man talk to me of other Expedients: Of taxing our Absentees at five Shillings a Pound: Of using neither Cloaths, nor Household Furniture, except what is of our own Growth and Manufacture: Of utterly rejecting the Materials and Instruments that promote Foreign Luxury: Of curing the Expensiveness of Pride, Vanity, Idleness, and Gaming in our Women: Of introducing a Vein of Parcimony, Prudence and Temperance: Of learning to love our Country, wherein we differ even from Laplanders, and the Inhabitants of Topinamboo: Of quitting our Animosities, and Factions, nor act any longer like the Jews, who were murdering one another at the very Moment their City was taken: Of being a little cautious not to sell our Country and Consciences for nothing: Of teaching Landlords to have at least one Degree of Mercy towards their Tenants. Lastly, Of putting a Spirit of Honesty, Industry, and Skill into our Shop-keepers, who, if a Resolution could now be taken to buy only our Native Goods, would immediately unite to cheat and exact upon us in the Price, the Measure, and the Goodness, nor could ever yet be brought to make one fair Proposal of just Dealing, though often and earnestly invited to it.

Therefore I repeat, let no Man talk to me of these and the like Expedients, till he hath at least some Glimpse of Hope, that there will ever be some hearty and sincere Attempt to put them in Practice.

But as to my self, having been wearied out for many Years with offering vain, idle, visionary Thoughts, and at length utterly despairing of Success, I fortunately fell upon this Proposal, which as it is wholly new, so it hath something Solid and Real, of no Expence and little Trouble, full in our own Power, and whereby we can incur no Danger in disobliging England. For this kind of Commodity will not bear Exportation, the Flesh being of too tender a Consistence, to admit a long Continuance in Salt, although perhaps I cou'd name a Country, which wou'd be glad to eat up our whole Nation without it.

After all, I am not so violently bent upon my own Opinion, as to reject any Offer, proposed by wise Men, which shall be found equally Innocent, Cheap, Easy, and Effectual. But before something of that Kind shall be advanced in Contradiction to my Scheme, and offering a better, I desire the Author or Authors, will be pleased maturely to consider two Points. *First,* As Things now stand, how they will be able to find Food and Raiment for a hundred Thousand useless Mouths and Backs. And *Secondly,* There being a round Million of Creatures in Human Figure, throughout this Kingdom, whose whole Subsistence put into a common Stock, would leave them in Debt two Millions of Pounds Sterling, adding those, who are Beggers by Profession, to the Bulk of Farmers, Cottagers and Labourers, with their Wives and Children, who are Beggers in Effect; I desire those Politicians, who dislike my Overture, and may perhaps be so bold to attempt an Answer, that they will first ask the Parents of these Mortals, Whether they would not at this Day think it a great Happiness to have been sold for Food at a Year Old, in the manner I prescribe, and thereby have avoided such a perpetual Scene of Misfortunes, as they have since gone through, by the Oppression of Landlords, the Impossibility of paying Rent without Money or Trade, the Want of common Sustenance, with neither House nor Cloaths to cover them from the Inclemencies of the Weather, and the most inevitable Prospect of intailing the like, or greater Miseries, upon their Breed for ever.

I profess in the Sincerity of my Heart, that I have not the least Personal Interest in endeavouring to promote this necessary Work, having no other Motive than the Publick Good of my Country, by advancing our Trade, providing for Infants, relieving the Poor, and giving some Pleasure to the Rich. I have no Children, by which I can propose to get a single Penny; the youngest being nine Years Old, and my Wife past Child-bearing.

Questions

1. What is the character of the speaker? How do you know? Is the speaker Swift? How far into the essay were you before you could define accurately Swift's tone? How would you define it? What clues does Swift give you?
2. Part of Swift's tone and part of his effect depends on his style. Would you describe the language as scholarly, objective, pedantic, reportorial, or what? Give some specific examples of his language to support your description of it. Try to define the effect of the style on the tone.
3. Since this is a proposal it is set up as a formal argument. The first division defines the problems. What do the other major divisions do? Make a brief two-level outline to define the organization. How does the carefully formal organization support Swift's controlling tone?
4. To make his proposal significant, the speaker has to describe the situation it is designed to alleviate and show indignation over the situation. As he describes all those children and their begging mothers, what seems to be the source of his indignation? Is it the human suffering? The clutter and inconvenience to society? The economic consequences? How real is his indignation? After you become aware of Swift's controlling tone, what is the real source of his indignation?
5. How logical does Swift make his proposal sound as a solution to the problems he has outlined? If logical and humane (because resulting in less suffering), why shouldn't his proposal be adopted? Is the list of advantages convincing? Does he give any meaningful alternative proposals? Where?
6. We usually think of satire as humorous criticism. Does this essay contain humor? What kind of laughter does it evoke? Some of Swift's most biting thrusts are aimed at targets only incidental to his main arguments. What effect does he get from "a very knowing American of my acquaintance," who assures him of the palatability of the meat of one-year-old children? From the statement that children "can very seldom pick up a livelihood by stealing" until they are six?
7. Why should Swift end the essay by disclaiming any self-interest? What effect does he achieve?

Suggestions for Writing

1. Irony can be a devastating weapon, as Swift so wonderfully proves. Try it. Pick some campus, local, or even national problem and write your own "modest proposal" as a solution. One of the problems with irony, though, is that many readers are almost tone-deaf. You will need to thread your way carefully between the two opposing dangers of being so obvious and heavy-handed that you lose your effect and being so subtle that you are taken literally.
2. Using the above questions as a guide, write an analysis of how the tone works in the essay. You could give your analysis point by approaching it as either a defense of irony or an attack on it. You might even try using irony as *your* controlling tone in such an attack or defense.

Two Sonnets

William Shakespeare

These sonnets present a fascinating study in tonal contrasts. If you are aware of the conventions of the Petrarchan sonnet (see first stanza of Andrew Marvell, "To His Coy Mistress," for a humorous treatment of them) you will recognize that Shakespeare is using them in both of these sonnets. What is the poet's attitude toward the comparisons he is making? Use as precise words as you can to define it. What is his attitude toward his mistress in each? Which seems to you the greater tribute to his mistress? You may want to look up "reeks" in an unabridged dictionary or in the Oxford English Dictionary *to see if it would have carried the same connotations for Shakespeare that it has for us. If it did, why would Shakespeare use it?*

XVIII

Shall I compare thee to a summer's day?
Thou art more lovely and more temperate:
Rough winds do shake the darling buds of May,
And summer's lease hath all too short a date:
Sometime too hot the eye of heaven shines,
And often is his gold complexion dimm'd;
And every fair from fair sometime declines,
By chance or nature's changing course untrimm'd;
But thy eternal summer shall not fade,
Nor lose possession of that fair thou owest;
Nor shall Death brag thou wander'st in his shade,
When in eternal lines to time thou grow'st:
    So long as men can breathe, or eyes can see,
    So long lives this, and this gives life to thee.

CXXX

My mistress' eyes are nothing like the sun;
Coral is far more red than her lips' red:
If snow be white, why then her breasts are dun;
If hairs be wires, black wires grow on her head.

I have seen roses damask'd, red and white,
But no such roses see I in her cheeks;
And in some perfumes is there more delight
Than in the breath that from my mistress reeks.
I love to hear her speak, yet well I know
That music hath a far more pleasing sound:
I grant I never saw a goddess go,
My mistress, when she walks, treads on the ground:
  And yet, by heaven, I think my love as rare
  As any she belied with false compare.

The Lent Lily

A. E. Housman *Few modern poets seem so direct and simple and melodic as A. E. Housman. But Housman was responding to the same kinds of scientific evidence that Thomas Hardy and Theodore Dreiser responded to, evidence that gradually came to picture the universe as indifferent, if not positively unfriendly to man. Under the simple melodic lyrics is apt to be an intense brooding or a biting irony. Analyze how the style and form contribute to the effect in this poem.*

'Tis spring; come out to ramble
    The hilly brakes around,
For under thorn and bramble
    About the hollow ground
    The primroses are found.

And there's the windflower chilly
    With all the winds at play,
And there's the Lenten lily
    That has not long to stay
    And dies on Easter day.

And since till girls go maying
    You find the primrose still,
And find the windflower playing
    With every wind at will,
    But not the daffodil,

Bring baskets now, and sally
    Upon the spring's array,
And bear from hill and valley
    The daffodil away
    That dies on Easter day.

Questions

1. Note that the poem uses very short lines, neat five-line stanzas, clean precise rhymes, nearly regular meter. Such neatness and precision ought to argue for a neat, precise world. What is the effect when we see that both flowers die on Easter day?
2. Why is the title "The Lent Lily" when in the poem the lily is called "the Lenten lily"?

Editha

William Dean Howells *We might with equal justification have included this story under Logic and Persuasion. But its persuasive qualities depend so much on qualities of style and tone that we include it here. For several decades centering around 1890 Howells was a kind of literary dictator in America and a prolific writer of fiction. In both criticism and practice he argued for realism: "The truthful treatment of materials." You will find it useful to analyze how he is able to develop so nearly explicit a moral and social argument and yet treat his characters so realistically. As you read, notice qualities of both style and tone that support his argument. The war could be the Spanish-American war of 1898. How modern does Mrs. Gearson's attitude toward war seem to you?*

The air was thick with the war feeling, like the electricity of a storm which has not yet burst. Editha sat looking out into the hot spring afternoon, with her lips parted, and panting with the intensity of the question whether she could let him go. She had decided that she could not let him stay, when she saw him at the end of the still leafless avenue, making slowly up toward the house, with his head down, and his figure relaxed. She ran impatiently out on the veranda, to the edge of the steps, and imperatively demanded greater haste of him with her will before she called aloud to him, "George!"

He had quickened his pace in mystical response to her mystical urgence, before he could have heard her; now he looked up and answered "Well?"

"Oh, how united we are!" she exulted, and then she swooped down the steps to him. "What is it?" she cried.

"It's war," he said, and he pulled her up to him, and kissed her.

She kissed him back intensely, but irrelevantly, as to their passion, and uttered from deep in her throat, "How glorious!"

"It's war," he repeated, without consenting to her sense of it; and she did not know just what to think at first. She never knew what to think of him; that made his mystery, his charm. All through their courtship, which was contemporaneous with the growth of the war feeling, she had been puzzled by his want of seriousness about it. He seemed to despise it even more than he abhorred it. She could have understood his abhorring any sort of bloodshed; that would have been a survival of his old life when he thought he would be a minister, and before he changed and took up the law. But making light of a cause so high and noble seemed to show a want of earnestness at the core of his being. Not but that she felt herself able to cope with a congenital defect of that sort, and make his love for her save him from himself. Now perhaps the miracle was already wrought in him. In the presence of the tremendous fact that he announced, all triviality seemed to have gone out of him; she began to feel that. He sank down on the top step, and wiped his forehead with his handkerchief, while she poured out upon him her question of the origin and authenticity of his news.

All the while, in her duplex emotioning, she was aware that now at the very beginning she must put a guard upon herself against urging him, by any word or act, to take the part that her whole soul willed him to take, for the completion of her ideal of him. He was very nearly perfect as he was, and he must be allowed to perfect himself. But he was peculiar, and he might very well be reasoned out of his peculiarity. Before her reasoning went her emotioning: her nature pulling upon his nature, her womanhood upon his manhood, without her knowing the means she was using to the end she was willing. She had always supposed that the man who won her would have done something to win her; she did not know what, but something. George Gearson had simply asked her for her love, on the way home from a concert, and she gave her love to him, without, as it were, thinking. But now, it flashed upon her, if he could do something worthy to *have* won her—be a hero, *her* hero—it would be even better than if he had done it before asking her; it would be grander. Besides, she had believed in the war from the beginning.

"But don't you see, dearest," she said, "that it wouldn't have come to this, if it hadn't been in the order of Providence? And I call any war glorious that is for the liberation of people who have been struggling for years against the cruelest oppression. Don't you think so too?"

"I suppose so," he returned, languidly. "But war! Is it glorious to break the peace of the world?"

"That ignoble peace! It was no peace at all, with that crime and shame at our very gates." She was conscious of parroting the current phrases of the newspapers, but it was no time to pick and choose her words. She must sacrifice anything to the high ideal she had for him, and after a good deal of rapid argument she ended with the climax: "But now it doesn't matter about the how or why. Since the war has come, all that is gone. There are no two sides, any more. There is nothing now but our country."

He sat with his eyes closed and his head leant back against the veranda, and he said with a vague smile, as if musing aloud, "Our country—right or wrong."

"Yes, right or wrong!" she returned fervidly. "I'll go and get you some lemonade." She rose rustling, and whisked away; when she came back with two tall glasses of clouded liquid, on a tray, and the ice clucking in them, he still sat as she had left him, and she said as if there had been no interruption: "But there is no question of wrong in this case. I call it a sacred war. A war for liberty, and humanity, if ever there was one. And I know you will see it just as I do, yet."

He took half the lemonade at a gulp, and he answered as he set the glass down: "I know you always have the highest ideal. When I differ from you, I ought to doubt myself."

A generous sob rose in Editha's throat for the humility of a man, so very nearly perfect, who was willing to put himself below her.

Besides, she felt, more subliminally, that he was never so near slipping through her fingers as when he took that meek way.

"You shall not say that! Only, for once I happen to be right." She seized his hand in her two hands, and poured her soul from her eyes into his. "Don't you think so?" she entreated him.

He released his hand and drank the rest of his lemonade, and she added, "Have mine, too," but he shook his head in answering, "I've no business to think so, unless I act so, too."

Her heart stopped a beat before it pulsed on with leaps that she felt in her neck. She had noticed that strange thing in men; they seemed to feel bound to do what they believed, and not think a thing was finished when they said it, as girls did. She knew what was in his mind, but she pretended not, and she said, "Oh, I am not sure," and then faltered.

He went on as if to himself without apparently heeding her, "There's only one way of proving one's faith in a thing like this."

She could not say that she understood, but she did understand.

He went on again. "If I believed—if I felt as you do about this war—Do you wish me to feel as you do?"

Now she was really not sure; so she said, "George, I don't know what you mean."

He seemed to muse away from her as before. "There is a sort of fascination in it. I suppose that at the bottom of his heart every man would like at times to have his courage tested; to see how he would act."

"How can you talk in that ghastly way?"

"It *is* rather morbid. Still, that's what it comes to, unless you're swept away by ambition, or driven by conviction. I haven't the conviction or the ambition, and the other thing is what it comes to with me. I ought to have been a preacher, after all; then I couldn't have asked it of myself, as I must, now I'm a lawyer. And you believe it's a holy war, Editha?" he suddenly addressed her. "Or, I know you do! But you wish me to believe so, too?"

She hardly knew whether he was mocking or not, in the ironical way he always had with her plainer mind. But the only thing was to be outspoken with him.

"George, I wish you to believe whatever you think is true, at any and every cost. If I've tried to talk you into anything, I take it all back."

"Oh, I know that, Editha. I know how sincere you are, and how—I wish I had your undoubting spirit! I'll think it over; I'd like to believe as you do. But I don't, now; I don't, indeed. It isn't this war alone; though this seems peculiarly wanton and needless; but it's every war—so stupid; it makes me sick. Why shouldn't this thing have been settled reasonably?"

"Because," she said, very throatily again, "God meant it to be war."

"You think it was God? Yes, I suppose that is what people will say."

"Do you suppose it would have been war if God hadn't meant it?"

"I don't know. Sometimes it seems as if God had put this world into men's keeping to work it as they pleased."

"Now, George, that is blasphemy."

"Well, I won't blaspheme. I'll try to believe in your pocket Providence," he said, and then he rose to go.

"Why don't you stay to dinner?" Dinner at Balcom's Works was at one o'clock.

"I'll come back to supper, if you'll let me. Perhaps I shall bring you a convert."

"Well, you may come back, on that condition."

"All right. If I don't come, you'll understand."

He went away without kissing her, and she felt it a suspension of their engagement. It all interested her intensely; she was undergoing a tremendous experience, and she was being equal to it. While she stood looking after him, her mother came out through one of the long windows, on to the veranda, with a catlike softness and vagueness.

"Why didn't he stay to dinner?"

"Because—because—war has been declared," Editha pronounced, without turning.

Her mother said, "Oh, my!" and then said nothing more until she had sat down in one of the large Shaker chairs, and rocked herself for some time. Then she closed whatever tacit passage of thought there had been in her mind with the spoken words, "Well, I hope *he* won't go."

"And I hope he *will,*" the girl said, and confronted her mother with a stormy exultation that would have frightened any creature less unimpressionable than a cat.

Her mother rocked herself again for an interval of cogitation. What she arrived at in speech was, "Well, I guess you've done a wicked thing, Editha Balcom."

The girl said, as she passed indoors through the same window her mother had come out by, "I haven't done anything—yet."

In her room, she put together all her letters and gifts from Gearson, down to the withered petals of the first flower he had offered, with that timidity of his veiled in that irony of his. In the heart of the packet she enshrined her engagement ring which she had restored to the pretty box he had brought it her in. Then she sat down, if not calmly yet strongly, and wrote:

"George: I understood—when you left me. But I think we had better emphasize your meaning that if we cannot be one in everything we had better be one in nothing. So I am sending these things for your keeping till you have made up your mind.

"I shall always love you, and therefore I shall never marry any one else. But the man I marry must love his country first of all, and be able to say to me,

'I could not love thee, dear, so much,
Loved I not honor more.'

"There is no honor above America with me. In this great hour there is no other honor.

"Your heart will make my words clear to you. I have never expected to say so much, but it has come upon me that I must say the utmost.

Editha."

She thought she had worded her letter well, worded it in a way that could not be bettered; all had been implied and nothing expressed.

She had it ready to send with the packet she had tied with red, white, and blue ribbon, when it occurred to her that she was not just to him, that she was not giving him a fair chance. He had said he would go and think it over, and she was not waiting. She was pushing, threatening, compelling. That was not a woman's part. She must leave him free, free, free. She could not accept for her country or herself a forced sacrifice.

In writing her letter she had satisfied the impulse from which it sprang; she could well afford to wait till he had thought it over. She put the packet and the letter by, and rested serene in the consciousness of having done what was laid upon her by her love itself to do, and yet used patience, mercy, justice.

She had her reward. Gearson did not come to tea, but she had given him till morning, when, late at night there came up from the village the sound of a fife and drum with a tumult of voices, in shouting, singing, and laughing. The noise drew nearer and nearer; it reached the street end of the avenue; there it silenced itself, and one voice, the voice she knew best, rose over the silence. It fell; the air was filled with cheers; the fife and drum struck up, with the shouting, singing, and laughing again, but now retreating; and a single figure came hurrying up the avenue.

She ran down to meet her lover and clung to him. He was very gay, and he put his arm around her with a boisterous laugh. "Well, you must call me Captain, now; or Cap, if you prefer; that's what the boys call me. Yes, we've had a meeting at the town hall, and everybody has volunteered; and they selected me for captain, and I'm going to the war, the big war, the glorious war, the holy war ordained by the pocket Providence that blesses butchery. Come along; let's tell the whole family about it. Call them from their downy beds, father, mother, Aunt Hitty, and all the folks!"

But when they mounted the veranda steps he did not wait for a larger audience; he poured the story out upon Editha alone.

"There was a lot of speaking, and then some of the fools set up a shout for me. It was all going one way, and I thought it would be a good joke to sprinkle a little cold water on them. But you can't do that with a crowd that adores you. The first thing I knew I was sprinkling hell-fire on them. 'Cry havoc, and let slip the dogs of war.' That was the style. Now that it had come to the fight, there were no two parties; there was one country, and the thing was to fight the fight to a finish as quick as possible. I suggested volunteering then and there, and I wrote my name first of all on the roster. Then they elected me—that's all. I wish I had some ice-water!"

She left him walking up and down the veranda, while she ran for the ice-pitcher and a goblet, and when she came back he was still walking up and down, shouting the story he had told her to her father and mother, who had come out more sketchily dressed than they commonly were by day. He drank goblet after goblet of the ice-water without noticing who was giving it, and kept on talking, and laughing through his talk wildly. "It's astonishing," he said, "how well the worse reason looks when you try to make it appear the better. Why, I believe I was the first convert to the war in that crowd to-night! I never thought I should like to kill a man; but now, I shouldn't care; and the smokeless powder lets you see the man drop that you kill. It's all for the country! What a thing it is to have a country that *can't* be wrong, but if it is, is right anyway!"

Editha had a great, vital thought, an inspiration. She set down the ice-pitcher on the veranda floor, and ran up-stairs and got the letter she had written him. When at last he noisily bade her father and mother, "Well, good night, I forgot I woke you up; I sha'n't want any sleep myself," she followed him down the avenue to the gate. There, after the whirling words that seemed to fly away from her thoughts and refuse to serve them, she made a last effort to solemnize the moment that seemed so crazy, and pressed the letter she had written upon him.

"What's this?" he said. "Want me to mail it?"

"No, no. It's for you. I wrote it after you went this morning. Keep it —keep it—and read it sometime—" She thought, and then her inspiration came: "Read it if ever you doubt what you've done, or fear that I regret your having done it. Read it after you've started."

They strained each other in embraces that seemed as ineffective as their words, and he kissed her face with quick, hot breaths that were so unlike him, that made her feel as if she had lost her old lover and found a stranger in his place. The stranger said, "What a gorgeous flower you are, with your red hair, and your blue eyes that look black now, and your face with the color painted out by the white moonshine! Let me hold you under my chin, to see whether I love blood, you tiger-lily!" Then he laughed Gearson's laugh, and released her, scared and giddy. Within her wilfulness she had been frightened by a sense of subtler force in him, and mystically mastered as she had never been before.

She ran all the way back to the house, and mounted the steps panting. Her mother and father were talking of the great affair. Her mother said: "Wa'n't Mr. Gearson in rather of an excited state of mind? Didn't you think he acted curious?"

"Well, not for a man who'd just been elected captain and had to set 'em up for the whole of Company A," her father chuckled back.

"What in the world do you mean, Mr. Balcom? Oh! There's Editha!" She offered to follow the girl indoors.

"Don't come, mother!" Editha called, vanishing.

Mrs. Balcom remained to reproach her husband. "I don't see much of anything to laugh at."

"Well, it's catching. Caught it from Gearson. I guess it won't be much of a war, and I guess Gearson don't think so, either. The other fellows will back down as soon as they see we mean it. I wouldn't lose any sleep over it. I'm going back to bed, myself."

Gearson came again next afternoon, looking pale, and rather sick, but quite himself, even to his languid irony. "I guess I'd better tell you, Editha, that I consecrated myself to your god of battles last night by pouring too many libations to him down my own throat. But I'm all right, now. One has to carry off the excitement, somehow."

"Promise me," she commanded, "that you'll never touch it again!"

"What! Not let the canniken clink? Not let the soldier drink? Well, I promise."

"You don't belong to yourself now; you don't even belong to *me*. You belong to your country, and you have a sacred charge to keep yourself strong and well for your country's sake. I have been thinking, thinking all night and all day long."

"You look as if you had been crying a little, too," he said with his queer smile.

"That's all past. I've been thinking, and worshipping *you*. Don't you suppose I know all that you've been through, to come to this? I've followed you every step from your old theories and opinions."

"Well, you've had a long row to hoe."

"And I know you've done this from the highest motives—"

"Oh, there won't be much pettifogging to do till this cruel war is—"

"And you haven't simply done it for my sake. I couldn't respect you if you had."

"Well, then we'll say I haven't. A man that hasn't got his own respect intact wants the respect of all the other people he can corner. But we won't go into that. I'm in for the thing now, and we've got to face our future. My idea is that this isn't going to be a very protracted struggle; we shall just scare the enemy to death before it comes to a fight at all. But we must provide for contingencies, Editha. If anything happens to me—"

"Oh, George!" She clung to him sobbing.

"I don't want you to feel foolishly bound to my memory. I should hate that, wherever I happened to be."

"I am yours, for time and eternity—time and eternity." She liked the words; they satisfied her famine for phrases.

"Well, say eternity; that's all right; but time's another thing; and I'm talking about time. But there is something! My mother! If anything happens.—"

She winced, and he laughed. "You're not the bold soldier-girl of yesterday!" Then he sobered. "If anything happens, I want you to help my mother out. She won't like my doing this thing. She brought me up to think war a fool thing as well as a bad thing. My father was in the civil war; all through it; lost his arm in it." She thrilled with the sense of the arm round her; what if that should be lost? He laughed as if divining her: "Oh, it doesn't run in the family, as far as I know!" Then he added, gravely, "He came home with misgivings about war, and they grew on him. I guess he and mother agreed between them that I was to be brought up in his final mind about it; but that was before my time. I only knew him from my mother's report of him and his opinions; I don't know whether they were hers first; but they were hers last. This will be a blow to her. I shall have to write and tell her—"

He stopped, and she asked, "Would you like me to write too, George?"

"I don't believe that would do. No, I'll do the writing. She'll understand a little if I say that I thought the way to minimize it was make war on the largest possible scale at once—that I felt I must have been helping on the war somehow if I hadn't helped keep it from coming, and I knew I hadn't; when it came, I had no right to stay out of it."

Whether his sophistries satisfied him or not, they satisfied her. She clung to his breast, and whispered, with closed eyes and quivering lips, "Yes, yes, yes!"

"But if anything should happen, you might go to her, and see what you could do for her. You know? It's rather far off; she can't leave her chair—"

"Oh, I'll go, if it's the ends of the earth! But nothing will happen! Nothing *can!* I—"

She felt herself lifted with his rising, and Gearson was saying, with his arm still around her, to her father: "Well, we're off at once, Mr. Balcom. We're to be formally accepted at the capital, and then bunched up with the rest somehow, and sent into camp somewhere, and got to the front as soon as possible. We all want to be in the van, of course; we're the first company to report to the Governor. I came to tell Editha, but I hadn't got round to it."

She saw him again for a moment at the capital, in the station, just before the train started southward with his regiment. He looked well, in his uniform, and very soldierly, but somehow girlish, too, with his clean-shaven face and slim figure. The manly eyes and the strong voice satisfied her, and his preoccupation with some unexpected details of duty flattered her. Other girls were weeping and bemoaning themselves, but she felt a sort of noble distinction in the abstraction, the almost unconsciousness, with which they parted. Only at the last moment he said, "Don't forget my mother. It mayn't be such a walkover as I supposed," and he laughed at the notion.

He waved his hand to her, as the train moved off—she knew it among a score of hands that were waved to other girls from the patform of the car, for it held a letter which she knew was hers. Then he went inside the car to read it, doubtless, and she did not see him again. But she felt safe for him through the strength of what she called her love. What she called her God, always speaking the name in a deep voice and with the implication of a mutual understanding, would watch over him and keep him and bring him back to her. If with an empty sleeve, then he should have three arms instead of two, for both of hers should be his for life. She did not see, though, why she should always be thinking of the arm his father had lost.

There were not many letters from him, but they were such as she could have wished, and she put her whole strength into making hers such as she imagined he could have wished, glorifying and supporting him. She wrote to his mother glorifying him as their hero, but the brief answer she got was merely to the effect that Mrs. Gearson was not well enough to write herself, and thanking her for her letter by the hand of some one who called herself "Yrs truly, Mrs. W. J. Andrews."

Editha determined not to be hurt, but to write again quite as if the answer had been all she expected. But before it seemed as if she could have written, there came news of the first skirmish, and in the list of the killed which was telegraphed as a trifling loss on our side, was Gearson's name. There was a frantic time of trying to make out that it might be, must be, some other Gearson; but the name, and the company and the regiment, and the State were too definitely given.

Then there was a lapse into depths out of which it seemed as if she never could rise again; then a lift into clouds far above all grief, black clouds, that blotted out the sun, but where she soared with him, with George, George! She had the fever that she expected of herself, but she did not die in it; she was not even delirious, and it did not last long. When she was well enough to leave her bed, her one thought was of George's mother, of his strangely worded wish that she should go to her and see what she could do for her. In the exultation of the duty laid upon her—it buoyed her up instead of burdening her—she rapidly recovered.

Her father went with her on the long railroad journey from northern New York to western Iowa; he had business out at Davenport, and he said he could just as well go then as any other time; and he went with her to the little country town where George's mother lived in a little house on the edge of illimitable corn-fields, under trees pushed to a top of the rolling prairie. George's father had settled there after the civil war, as so many other old soldiers had done; but they were Eastern people, and Editha fancied touches of the East in the June rose overhanging the front door, and the garden with early summer flowers stretching from the gate of the paling fence.

It was very low inside the house, and so dim, with the closed blinds, that they could scarcely see one another: Editha tall and black in her crapes which filled the air with the smell of their dyes; her father standing decorously apart with his hat on his forearm, as at funerals; a woman rested in a deep armchair, and the woman who had let the strangers in stood behind the chair.

The seated woman turned her head round and up, and asked the woman behind her chair, "*Who* did you say?"

Editha, if she had done what she expected of herself, would have gone down on her knees at the feet of the seated figure and said, "I am George's Editha," for answer.

But instead of her own voice she heard that other woman's voice, saying, "Well, I don't know as I *did* get the name just right. I guess I'll have to make a little more light in here," and she went and pushed two of the shutters ajar.

Then Editha's father said in his public will-now-address-a-few-remarks tone, "My name is Balcom, ma'am; Junius H. Balcom, of Balcom's Works, New York; my daughter—"

"Oh!" The seated woman broke in, with a powerful voice, the voice that always surprised Editha from Gearson's slender frame. "Let me see you! Stand round where the light can strike on your face," and Editha dumbly obeyed. "So, you're Editha Balcom," she sighed.

"Yes," Editha said, more like a culprit than a comforter.

"What did you come for?" Mrs. Gearson asked.

Editha's face quivered, and her knees shook. "I came—because—because George—" She could go no farther.

"Yes," the mother said, "he told me he had asked you to come if he got killed. You didn't expect that, I suppose, when you sent him."

"I would rather have died myself than done it!" Editha said with more truth in her deep voice than she ordinarily found in it. "I tried to leave him free—"

"Yes, that letter of yours, that came back with his other things, left him free."

Editha saw now where George's irony came from.

"It was not to be read before—unless—until—I told him so," she faltered.

"Of course, he wouldn't read a letter of yours, under the circumstances, till he thought you wanted him to. Been sick?" the woman abruptly demanded.

"Very sick," Editha said, with self-pity.

"Daughter's life," her father interposed, "was almost despaired of, at one time."

Mrs. Gearson gave him no heed. "I suppose you would have been glad to die, such a brave person as you! I don't believe *he* was glad to die. He was always a timid boy, that way; he was afraid of a good many things; but if he was afraid he did what he made up his mind to. I suppose he made up his mind to go, but I knew what it cost him, by what it cost me when I heard of it. I had been through *one* war before. When you sent him you didn't expect he would get killed."

The voice seemed to compassionate Editha, and it was time. "No," she huskily murmured.

"No, girls don't; women don't, when they give their men up to their country. They think they'll come marching back, somehow, just as gay as they went, or if it's an empty sleeve, or even an empty pantaloon, it's all the more glory, and they're so much the prouder of them, poor things."

The tears began to run down Editha's face; she had not wept till then; but it was now such a relief to be understood that the tears came.

"No, you didn't expect him to get killed," Mrs. Gearson repeated in a voice which was startlingly like George's again. "You just expected him to kill some one else, some of those foreigners, that weren't there because they had any say about it, but because they had to be there, poor wretches—conscripts, or whatever they call 'em. You thought it would be all right for my George, *your* George, to kill the sons of those miserable mothers and the husbands of those girls that you would never see the faces of." The woman lifted her powerful voice in a psalmlike note. "I thank my God he didn't live to do it! I thank my God they killed him first, and that he ain't livin' with their blood on his hands!" She dropped her eyes which she had raised with her voice, and glared at Editha. "What you got the black on for?" She lifted herself by her powerful arms so high that her helpless body seemed to hang limp its full length. "Take it off, take it off, before I tear it from your back!"

The lady who was passing the summer near Balcom's Works was sketching Editha's beauty, which lent itself wonderfully to the effects of a colorist. It had come to that confidence which is rather apt to grow between artist and sitter, and Editha had told her everything.

"To think of your having such a tragedy in your life!" the lady said. She added: "I suppose there are people who feel that way about war. But when you consider the good this war has done—how much it has done for the country! I can't understand such people, for my part. And when you had come all the way out there to console her—got up out of a sick bed! Well!"

"I think," Editha said, magnanimously, "she wasn't quite in her right mind; and so did papa."

"Yes," the lady said, looking at Editha's lips in nature and then at her lips in art, and giving an empirical touch to them in the picture. "But how dreadful of her! How perfectly—excuse me—how *vulgar!*"

A light broke upon Editha in the darkness which she felt had been without a gleam of brightness for weeks and months. The mystery that had bewildered her was solved by the word; and from that moment she rose from grovelling in shame and self-pity, and began to live again in the ideal.

Questions

1. As we indicated in the headnote, the war could be the Spanish-American war of 1898. But Howells does nothing to relate the story specifically to that

war. Would the story tend to be more, or less, persuasive had he done so? In historical perspective, that war seems one of America's less defensible ventures. Does this fact bear on the question?

2. Note the expression in the second sentence, "panting with the intensity of the question whether she could let him go." What do words like "panting" and "intensity" suggest about Howells' tone? Closely related in tone is the long paragraph beginning "It's war," especially such expressions as "his want of seriousness," "a cause so high and noble," "a congenital defect of that sort." Whose words do they seem to be? Howells'? Editha's?
3. How early in the story can you define with any confidence Howells' attitude toward Editha? Examine carefully her logic in the paragraphs in which she talks to George about war. Would it be Howells' logic? What about George's responses? In what tone would he say "Our country—right or wrong"? Does he support the position? Does Howells?
4. Note Editha's response to her letter, and then to her reconsideration. What quality in her is Howells emphasizing? Do you find other responses to language? What does her "famine for phrases," as Howells calls it later, explain about the basic action of the story?
5. You should have little trouble understanding the tone Mrs. Gearson uses in talking to Editha. Define it. Does Editha herself really understand it before that last, terrible paragraph, when the tone shifts and all that was implicit before becomes explicit? Note, for example, Editha's tears and her feeling that "it was such a relief to be understood."
6. How do you explain Editha's response to "the lady's" word *vulgar?* Does Howells explain it entirely when he says that "the mystery that had bewildered her was solved by the word"? Do the insights from semantics help you to understand her response? Has anything happened earlier in the story to suggest that this would be her response?

Suggestions for Writing

1. The war in Viet Nam has raised ethical and spiritual questions that have shaken America as perhaps never before, even if our questioning has lost some of its intensity now that we are no longer involved. Howells' story is an open invitation for you to explore some of these questions, particularly as they relate to you. Here, if any place, you ought to see the relevance of effective and persuasive language to your immediate life: in the terrifyingly effective rhetoric that promotes wars, in the shrill sloganeering with which some groups take advantage of war in the name of peace, even in the carefully thought-out and supported opposition or support of war or peace. The quality of your language will be relevant in making your own voice meaningfully heard as you finally take a position. Try to write a careful, logical defense of your attitude toward war—war in general, or some specific war, or some specific incident in a war. Or you may want to try to experiment with style, tone, and point-of-view. Irony is a fairly popular choice for such experiments. Aristophanes, in *Lysistrata,* chose to use it in comedy and satire 2500 years ago: the women in the play refuse their husbands any sexual favors until they end the war. Remember always to define precisely for yourself your rhetorical stance, since, as we have seen, it will largely determine your style and tone.

Ode to Stephen Dowling Bots, Dec'd

Emmaline Grangerford

Emmaline Grangerford wrote this poem when she was fourteen, not long before her death. Try to define the tone with which she writes. What in the poem helps you to determine her tone?

And did young Stephen sicken,
    And did young Stephen die?
And did the sad hearts thicken,
    And did the mourners cry?

No; such was not the fate of
    Young Stephen Dowling Bots;
Though sad hearts round him thickened,
    'Twas not from sickness' shots.

No whooping-cough did rack his frame,
    Nor measles drear, with spots;
Not these impaired the sacred name
    Of Stephen Dowling Bots.

Despised love struck not with woe
    That head of curly knots,
Nor stomach troubles laid him low,
    Young Stephen Dowling Bots.

O no. Then list with tearful eye,
    Whilst I his fate do tell.
His soul did from this cold world fly,
    By falling down a well.

They got him out and emptied him;
    Alas it was too late;
His spirit was gone for to sport aloft
    In the realms of the good and great.

Questions

1. Emmaline's only biographer says of her, "She didn't ever have to stop to think. He said she would just slap a line down and if she couldn't find anything to rhyme with it she would just scratch it out and slap down another one, and go ahead. . . . she could write about anything you choose to give her to write about, just so it was sadful." Assuming the accuracy of these observations, what do they say about Emmaline's sincerity in writing her "tributes," as she called them. Does the tone of the poem suggest that the observations are accurate?

"Plumb Deef and Dumb"

Mark Twain *This passage is essentially self-contained, even though it is an integral part of* Huckleberry Finn. *Like the subject of Emmaline Grangerford's poem, the subject here is one that we naturally have strong emotions about. Can you contrast Jim's feelings with those of Emmaline?*

I went to sleep, and Jim didn't call me when it was my turn. He often done that. When I waked up, just at day-break, he was setting there with his head down betwixt his knees, moaning and mourning to himself. I didn't take notice, nor let on. I knowed what it was about. He was thinking about his wife and his children, away up yonder, and he was low and homesick; because he hadn't ever been away from home before in his life; and I do believe he cared just as much for his people as white folks does for their'n. It don't seem natural, but I reckon it's so. He was often moaning and mourning that way, nights, when he judged I was asleep, and saying, "Po' little 'Lizabeth! po' little Johnny! its mighty hard; I spec' I ain't ever gwyne to see you no mo', no mo'!" He was a mighty good nigger, Jim was.

But this time I somehow got to talking to him about his wife and young ones; and by-and-by he says:

"What makes me feel so bad dis time, 'uz bekase I hear sumpn over yonder on de bank like a whack, er a slam, while ago, en it mine me er de time I treat my little 'Lizabeth so ornery. She warn't on'y 'bout fo' year ole, en she tuck de sk'yarlet-fever, en had a powful rough spell; but she got well, en one day she was a-stannin' aroun', en I says to her, I says:

" 'Shet de do'.'

"She never done it; jis' stood dah, kiner smilin' up at me. It make me mad; en I says agin, mighty loud, I says:

" 'Doan' you hear me?—shet de do'!'

"She jis' stood de same way, kiner smilin' up. I was a-bilin'! I says:

" 'I lay I *make* you mine!'

"En wid dat I fetch' her a slap side de head dat sont her a-sprawlin'. Den I went into de yuther room, en 'uz gone 'bout ten minutes; en when I come back, dah was dat do' a-stannin' open *yit,* en dat chile stannin' mos' right in it, a-lookin' down and mournin', en de tears runnin' down. My, but I *wuz* mad, I was agwyne for de chile, but jis' den—it was a do' dat open innerds—jis' den, 'long come de wind en slam it to, behine de chile, ker-*blam!*—en my lan', de chile never move'! My breff mos' hop outer me; en I feel so—so—I doan' know *how* I feel. I crope out, all a-tremblin', en crope aroun' en open de do' easy en slow, en poke my head in behine de chile, sof' en still, en all uv a sudden, I says *pow!* jis' as loud as I could yell. *She never budge!* Oh, Huck, I bust out a-cryin' en grab her up in my arms, en say, 'Oh, de po' little thing! de Lord God Amighty fogive po' ole Jim, kaze he never gwyne to fogive hisself as long's he live!' Oh, she was plumb deef en dumb, Huck, plumb deef en dumb—en I'd been a-treat'n her so!"

Questions

1. Who seems more sincere, Jim or Emmaline? Can you say why?
2. By now you have probably guessed—if you didn't already know—that Huck Finn is the "only biographer" of Emmaline Grangerford. This, of course, makes Mark Twain the ultimate author of her "Ode" as of Jim's story. It also complicates the problem of tone. Would Twain's attitude toward his materials be the same as Emmaline's? As Jim's? Define Twain's tone in each.
3. Twain apparently knew and made use of the following poem by Julia A. Moore, known as the "Sweet Singer of Michigan." What would be the relationship of Emmaline's "Ode" to this poem?

Little Andrew

Andrew was a little infant,
And his life was two years old;
He was his parents' eldest boy,
And he was drowned, I was told.
His parents never more can see him
In this world of grief and pain,
And Oh! they will not forget him
While on earth they do remain.

On one bright and pleasant morning
His uncle thought it would be nice
To take his dear little nephew
Down to play upon a raft,
Where he was to work upon it,
And this little child would company be—
The raft the water rushed around it,
Yet he the danger did not see.

This little child knew no danger—
Its little soul was free from sin—
He was looking in the water,
When, alas, this child fell in.
Beneath the raft the water took him,
For the current was so strong,
And before they could rescue him
He was drowned and was gone.

Oh! how sad were his kind parents
When they saw their drowned child,
As they brought him from the water,
It almost made their hearts grow wild.
Oh! how mournful was the parting
From that little infant son.
Friends, I pray you, all take warning,
Be careful of your little ones.

Song

John Donne

Donne is the best known of the seventeenth-century metaphysical poets, and is perhaps the most complicated tonally of any of the writers in this section. Even in this poem, one of his simpler ones, the tonal nuances are rather complex. Just how seriously does the poet want us to consider him?

Go and catch a falling star,
    Get with child a mandrake root,
Tell me where all past years are,
    Or who cleft the devil's foot,
Teach me to hear mermaids singing,
Or to keep off envy's stinging,
        And find
        What wind
Serves t' advance an honest mind.

If thou be'st born to strange sights,
    Things invisible to see,
Ride ten thousand days and nights
    Till age snow white hairs on thee;
Thou, when thou return'st, wilt tell me
All strange wonders that befell thee,
        And swear
        Nowhere
Lives a woman true, and fair.

If thou find'st one, let me know;
    Such a pilgrimage were sweet—
Yet do not; I would not go
    Though at next door we might meet.
Though she were true when you met her,

And last till you write your letter,
Yet she
Will be
False ere I come, to two or three.

Questions

1. How possible are the tasks the poet proposes in the first stanza (look up *mandrake*)? How do these tasks relate to the single one he proposes in stanza two?
2. To understand the rhythm of the last line of stanza two, you will need to emphasize "and" much more and draw it out much longer than the ordinary metrical sense of the line would indicate, so that it suggests "both true *and* fair." Why should Donne set this up so that it can be so easily passed over?
3. Why is Donne so sure that even if a woman could be found both true and fair she would be false before he could find her? The answer of course is a tonal one. What is he saying, in effect, about women?

Writing Projects

This section on style and tone should probably have broader application to your immediate problems in writing than any other in the book. And yet, though we have made suggestions following individual selections, it is harder to frame specific writing assignments that grow logically from the overall section. We suggest two broad headings:

1. Careful analysis of style and tone in the work of some other writer.
2. Conscious experimentation with your own style or tone or both (you must have noticed how tightly interrelated they are).

Careful analysis of another's style and tone can be interesting and valuable for its own sake as well as for what it tells you about your own problems and capacities. Pick a writer you think gets unusual and effective results and show how he does it. You might select Franz Kafka ("The Hunter Gracchus," on p. 709) or Faulkner ("Dry September" p. 577).

Conscious experimentation can be one of the most valuable approaches to learning, especially learning to write. You can experiment by consciously imitating someone else or by striking out on your own. Both Ben Franklin and Robert Louis Stevenson testify to the value of consciously imitating the writing of others. Select someone you admire and a subject you are interested in. If you experiment on your own, remember that nearly all significant writing somehow grows out of deep involvement with the problem one writes about. Qualities that we usually identify by such words as "sincerity," "honesty," "intensity" grow out of such involvement. Conscious experimentation with style and tone may suggest insincerity, but it surely need not. If you are searching for ways to be not merely cute or different but effective, then the experimenting will carry its own sense of sincerity and you will be working toward your own individual "voice."

Part IX

Experiments with Language

If you have really responded to the challenge of this book thus far, you should be deeply aware of and sensitive to language and you should enjoy watching it in action in some unusual and fascinating forms. You can learn much about the capacities of language by examining the work of those who have stretched its limits consciously and imaginatively. Whatever experimentation with language may mean to you, it ought to mean that the experimenter has cared enough about language to struggle with it, to explore its possibilities and strengths, its weaknesses and limitations. He may seem in the sheer sense of exuberance, as in *Finnegan's Wake,* to have forgotten or never thought of a rhetorical stance. He may seem to be violating nearly everything we or your teacher may have told you. But if you look closely at the experiments, you will nearly always find under them some version of the principles you have learned. The principles themselves often provide the base against which the experiment can stretch. Dylan Thomas's "A Refusal to Mourn . . ." gets much of its energy by stretching against the ordinary conventions of punctuation and diction. So do e. e. cummings' poems. So does Joyce's "Molly's Solilquy." In "The Ondt and the Gracehoper" the energy comes largely from packing so much more meaning into the words than they will usually carry. But whatever the source, we hope that you will find the energy, that you will find enjoyment and fascination in these experiments. About the only thing the following selections have in common is that each was written by someone so thoroughly fascinated with language that he loved to play with it, to explore it, to see what he could make it do. The selections range in difficulty from Vachel Lindsay's rhythmic chanting, with no particularly subtle meaning, to the apparent nonsense but utter density of James Joyce's *Finnegan's Wake*. They range in tone from the enchanting playfulness of Laurence Sterne to the nightmarish seriousness of Franz Kafka. Taken together they should do much to increase your fascination with watching language.

Lucilla Answers Euphues

John Lyly *The brief selection below is from* Euphues, or, The Anatomy of Wit. *The book, a significant forerunner to the novel, initiated and popularized the style known as euphuism, named after the hero, Euphues. (Don't confuse* euphuism *with* euphemism.) *Whatever else it is, euphuism is hardly natural or colloquial. What qualities set it apart from ordinary writing or speaking?*

Gentleman, as you may suspect me of idleness in giving ear to your talk, so may you convince me of lightness in answering such toys; certes as you have made mine ears glow at the rehearsal of your love, so have you galled my heart with the remembrance of your folly. Though you came to Naples as a stranger, yet were you welcome to my father's house as a friend. And can you then so much transgress the bounds of honor (I will not say of honesty) as to solicit a suit more sharp to me than death? I have hitherto, God be thanked, lived without suspicion of lewdness, and shall I now incur the danger of sensual liberty? What hope can you have to obtain my love, seeing yet I could never afford you a good look? Do you therefore think me easily enticed to the bent of your bow, because I was easily entreated to listen to your late discourse? Or seeing me (as finely you glose) to excel all other in beauty, did you deem that I would exceed all other in beastliness? But yet I am not angry, Euphues, but in agony, for who is she that will fret or fume with one that loveth her, if this love to delude me be not dissembled? It is that which causeth me most to fear, not that my beauty is unknown to myself, but that commonly we poor wenches are deluded through light belief, and ye men are naturally inclined craftily to lead your life. When the fox preacheth the geese perish. The crocodile shroudeth greatest treason under most pitiful tears; in a kissing mouth there lieth a galling mind. You have made so large proffer of your service, and so fair promises of fidelity, that were I not over chary of mine honesty, you would inveigle me to shake hands with chastity. But certes I will either lead a virgin's life on earth (though I lead apes in hell) or else follow thee rather than thy gifts; yet am I neither so precise to refuse thy proffer, neither so peevish to disdain thy good will. So excellent always are the gifts which are made acceptable by the virtue of the giver. I did at the first entrance discern thy love but yet dissemble it. Thy wanton glances, thy scalding sighs, thy loving signs, caused me to blush for shame, and to look wan for fear, lest they should be perceived of any. These subtil shifts, these painted practises (if I were to be won) would soon wean me from the teat of Vesta to the toys of Venus. Besides this, thy comely grace, thy rare qualities, thy exquisite perfection, were able to move a mind half mortified to transgress the bonds of maidenly modesty. But God shield, Lucilla, that thou shouldest be so careless of thine honor as to commit the state thereof to a stranger. Learn thou by me, Euphues, to despise things that be amiable, to forego delightful practises; believe me, it is pity to abstain from pleasure.

Thou art not the first that hath solicited this suit, but the first that goeth about to seduce me, neither discernest thou more than other, but darest more than any, neither hast thou more art to discover thy meaning, but more heart to open thy mind. But thou preferrest me before thy lands, thy livings, thy life; thou offerest thyself a sacrifice for my security, thou profferest me the whole and only sovereignty of thy service. Truly, I were very cruel and hardhearted if I should not love thee; hardhearted albeit I am not, but truly love thee I cannot, whom I doubt to be my lover.

Questions

1. Contrast the balanced and parallel sentence elements in Lyly's style with those in the following passage by Samuel Johnson, himself famous for his carefully balanced and controlled prose style. Which style seems the more natural? The more experimental? Why? What does a writer gain—or lose—by careful balance and parallelism?

> If by a more noble and adequate conception that be considered as Wit which is at once natural and new, that which though not obvious is, upon its first production, acknowledged to be just; if it be that, which he that never found it, wonders how he missed; to wit of this kind the metaphysical poets have seldom risen. Their thoughts are often new, but seldom natural; they are not obvious, but neither are they just; and the reader, far from wondering that he missed them, wonders more frequently by what perverseness of industry they were ever found.

Suggestions for Writing

1. With either Lyly or Johnson as model, write Euphues' further plea to Lucilla. Assume that she is just being feminine and overly modest. Reassure her both of your concern for her virtue and of your love.

Easter Wings

George Herbert

You will recognize at a glance that the most experimental thing about this poem is its shape on the page. Herbert is not the only one to experiment with such "shaped poems." How well does he catch or suggest the shape of wings? Herbert was too good a poet to be satisfied with just a kind of typographical trickery. Examine carefully the poem's use of language and its internal logic. To what extent do they support or reflect the shape? "Store" in line one means "abundance." To "imp," a term used in falconry, means to graft. How would the image of wing grafted to wing relate to the shape of the poem?

Lord, who createdst man in wealth and store,
Though foolishly he lost the same,
Decaying more and more
Till he became
Most poor:
With thee
O let me rise
As larks, harmoniously,
And sing this day thy victories:
Then shall the fall further the flight in me.

My tender age in sorrow did begin:
And still with sicknesses and shame
Thou didst so punish sin,
That I became
Most thin.
With thee
Let me combine,
And feel this day thy victory;
For, if I imp my wing on thine,
Affliction shall advance the flight in me.

Questions

1. Watch carefully the ideas developed in the first part of each stanza, then relate them to the ideas in the second part and to the shape of each stanza.
2. "The fall" is presumably the fall of man. How could that "further the flight in me"? Relate this to the last line of the poem.
3. How successfully has the shape of the poem been used to support or reflect the ideas and images?

Suggestions for Writing

1. Try to write a shaped poem yourself. Or if you don't feel ambitious that way, think of the organization of your paper as a kind of shape (certainly not a radical way to look at it) and work consciously to shape the whole paper with language, images, and analogies that particularly support its shape. This may be asking you to do nothing more than you have been doing all along. But pay more conscious attention to the process this time.

Tristram Shandy

Laurence Sterne

Few books have so pleased their partisans and so outraged their detractors as Laurence Sterne's The Life and Opinions of Tristram Shandy, Gent. *The title misleads, for Tristram is not born until the novel is about a third over, not even conceived until the end of the first chapter. But time is very relative in* Tristram Shandy. *And so are ideas and events. Tristram as narrator moves back and forth in time, in event, and in idea as the mind is apt to move in response to suggestion. In the process we meet some of fiction's most delightful characters: Mr. Shandy, widely read but with strange, pedantic, and rigorous theories about names, noses, and begetting; Uncle Toby, gentle and kind but obsessed with military fortifications and finally victim of the Widow Wadman's assault on his heart; Corporal Trim, who almost outdoes Uncle Toby in planning mock battles; even Dr. Slop, who remains largely caricature and who mashes Tristram's nose with his forceps during the delivery. The chapters that follow are the concluding ones of Volume VI. They show little of the association process which controls the movement of the novel (though by what logic does Tristram move from Uncle Toby's falling in love to his own "lines" in writing the novel?). But these chapters reveal much of Sterne's experimenting with typographical and other visual devices, and they reveal much about his style. Tristram's dashes indicate rhetorical rather than formal pauses.*

CHAPTER XXXVII

—'Twill come out of itself by and bye.—All I contend for is, that I am not *obliged* to set out with a definition of what love is; and so long as I can go on with my story intelligibly, with the help of the word itself, without any other idea to it, than what I have in common with the rest of the world, why should I differ from it a moment before the time?—When I can get on no further,—and find myself entangled on all sides of this mystick labyrinth,—my Opinion will then come in, in course,—and lead me out.

At present, I hope I shall be sufficiently understood, in telling the reader, my uncle Toby *fell in love:*

—Not that the phrase is at all to my liking: for to say a man is *fallen* in love,—or that he is *deeply* in love,—or up to the ears in love,—and sometimes even *over head and ears in it,*—carries an idiomatical kind of implication, that love is a thing *below* a man:—this is recurring again to Plato's opinion, which, with all his divinityship,—I hold to be damnable and heretical;—and so much for that.

Let love therefore be what it will,—my uncle Toby fell into it.

—And possibly, gentle reader, with such a temptation—so wouldst thou: For never did thy eyes behold, or thy concupiscence covet any thing in this world, more concupiscible than widow Wadman.

CHAPTER XXXVIII

To conceive this right,—call for pen and ink—here's paper ready to your hand.—Sit down, Sir, paint her to your own mind—as like your mistress as you can—as unlike your wife as your conscience will let you—'tis all one to me—please but your own fancy in it.

——Was ever anything in Nature so sweet!—so exquisite!

—Then, dear Sir, how could my uncle Toby resist it?

Thrice happy book! thou wilt have one page, at least, within thy covers, which MALICE will not blacken, and which IGNORANCE cannot misrepresent.

CHAPTER XXXIX

As Susannah was informed by an express from Mrs. Bridget, of my uncle Toby's falling in love with her mistress, fifteen days before it happened, —the contents of which express, Susannah communicated to my mother the next day,—it has just given me an opportunity of entering upon my uncle Toby's amours a fortnight before their existence.

I have an article of news to tell you, Mr. Shandy, quoth my mother, which will surprise you greatly.—

Now my father was then holding one of his second beds of justice, and was musing within himself about the hardships of matrimony, as my mother broke silence.——

"—My brother Toby, quoth she, is going to be married to Mrs. Wadman."

—Then he will never, quoth my father, be able to lie *diagonally* in his bed again as long as he lives.

It was a consuming vexation to my father, that my mother never asked the meaning of a thing she did not understand.

—That she is not a woman of science, my father would say—is her misfortune—but she might ask a question.—

My mother never did.—In short, she went out of the world at last without knowing whether it turned *round,* or stood *still.*—My father had officiously told her above a thousand times which way it was,—but she always forgot.

For these reasons, a discourse seldom went on much further betwixt them, than a proposition,—a reply, and a rejoinder; at the end of which, it generally took breath for a few minutes, (as in the affair of the breeches) and then went on again.

If he marries, 'twill be the worse for us—quoth my mother.

Not a cherry-stone, said my father,—he may as well batter away his means upon that, as any thing else.

—To be sure, said my mother: so here ended the proposition,—the reply,—and the rejoinder, I told you of.

It will be some amusement to him, too,—said my father.

A very great one, answered my mother, if he should have children.—

—Lord have mercy upon me,—said my father to himself—

* * * * * * * * * *
* * * * * * * * * *
* * * * * * * * * *
* * * * * * * * * *
* * * *

CHAPTER XL

I AM now beginning to get fairly into my work; and by the help of a vegetable diet, with a few of the cold seeds, I make no doubt but I shall be able to go on with my uncle Toby's story, and my own, in a tolerable straight line. Now,

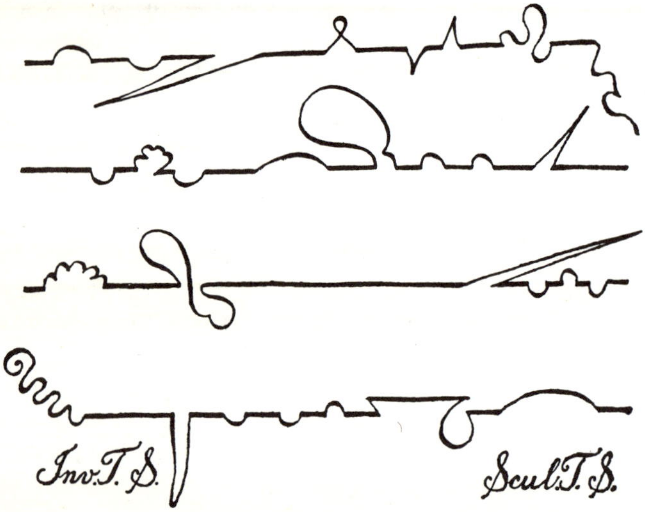

These were the four lines I moved in through my first, second, third, and fourth volumes.—In the fifth volume I have been very good,—the precise line I have described in it being this:

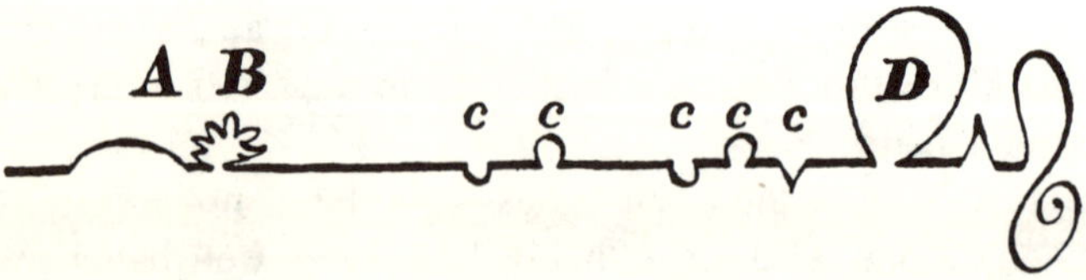

By which it appears, that except at the curve, marked A, where I took a trip to Navarre,—and the indented curve B, which is the short airing when I was there with the Lady Baussiere and her page,—I have not taken the least frisk of a digression, till John de la Casse's devils led me the round you see marked D;—for as for *c c c c c* they are nothing but parentheses, and the common *ins* and *outs* incident to the lives of the greatest ministers of state; and when compared with what men have done, —or with my own transgressions at the letters A B D—they vanish into nothing.

In this last volume I have done better still—for from the end of Le Fever's episode, to the beginning of my uncle Toby's campaigns,—I have scarce stepped a yard out of my way.

If I mend at this rate, it is not impossible—by the good leave of his grace of Benevento's devils—but I may arrive hereafter at the excellency of going on even thus:

---

which is a line drawn as straight as I could draw it, by a writing-master's ruler, (borrowed for that purpose) turning neither to the right hand or to the left.

This *right line,*—the path-way for Christians to walk in! say divines—

—The emblem of moral rectitude! says Cicero—

—The *best line!* say cabbage-planters—is the shortest line, says Archimedes, which can be drawn from one given point to another.—

I wish your ladyships would lay this matter to heart in your next birth-day suits!

—What a journey!

Pray can you tell me,—that is, without anger, before I write my chapter upon straight lines—by what mistake—who told them so—or how it has come to pass, that your men of wit and genius have all along confounded this line, with the line of GRAVITATION?

Questions

1. Analyze what Tristram does to the common phrase "fallen in love." What is the effect of substituting "in it" for "in love?"
2. To what extent do you get to know the characters through this brief selection? Tristram himself?
3. Do the story lines seem mere whimsy or nonsense? Do they seem so even with Tristram's explanation? Is Sterne trying to say something about the process of composition through the story lines? If so, what?

Suggestions for Writing

1. Experiment with a narrative passage in which you move from idea to idea in something of the way Tristram does.

That Nature is a Heraclitean Fire and of the comfort of the Resurrection

Gerard Manley Hopkins

Remember the alliterative verse of "The Wanderer" (and of most Anglo-Saxon poems)? Hopkins experimented a great deal with alliteration, often with unusual and startling effects. Hopkins called the result "sprung rhythm." This poem is one of the more extreme results of that experimentation. The light vertical mark indicates a break in the line—a caesural pause—that divides the line into two approximately equal rhythmic units. Heraclitus was an ancient Greek philosopher who believed that the universe is composed of four elements: earth, air, fire, and water.

Cloud-puffball, torn tufts, tossed pillows | flaunt forth, then chevy on an air-
built thoroughfare: heaven-roysterers, in gay-gangs | they throng; they glitter in marches.
Down roughcast, down dazzling whitewash, | wherever an elm arches,
Shivelights and shadowtackle in long | lashes lace, lance, and pair.
Delightfully the bright wind boisterous | ropes, wrestles, beats earth bare
Of yestertempest's creases; | in pool and rut peel parches
Squandering ooze to squeezed | dough, crust, dust; stanches, starches
Squadroned masks and manmarks | treadmire toil there
Footfretted in it. Million-fuelèd, | nature's bonfire burns on.
But quench her bonniest, dearest | to her, her clearest-selvèd spark
Man, how fast his firedint, | his mark on mind, is gone!
Both are in an unfathomable, | all is in an enormous dark

Gerard Manley Hopkins, "That Nature Is a Heraclitean Fire and of the Comfort of the Resurrection," *Poems of Gerard Manley Hopkins,* 3rd Ed., ed. W. H. Gardner (New York: Oxford University Press, 1948).

Drowned. O pity and indig | nation! Manshape, that shone
Sheer off, disseveral, a star, | death blots black out; nor mark
Is any of him at all so stark
But vastness blurs and time | beats level. Enough! the Resurrection,
A heart's-clarion! Away grief's gasping, | joyless days, dejection.
Across my foundering deck shone
A beacon, an eternal beam. | Flesh fade, and mortal trash
Fall to the residuary worm; | world's wildfire, leave but ash:
In a flash, at a trumpet crash,
I am all at once what Christ is, | since he was what I am, and
This Jack, joke, poor potsherd, | patch, matchwood, immortal diamond,
Is immortal diamond.

Questions

1. You can hardly avoid accenting the alliterating syllables. When you find these together, as in "torn tufts, tossed," they all need to be accented, and almost equally. The result is a sharp staccato burst. How appropriate are such bursts for the subject matter of the poem?
2. Hopkins gets similarly "sprung" effects from internal rhyme—"*air*-/built thorough*fare*"—and from the unusual placements of the caesura in some lines: "to squeezed | dough." Can you sense the nervous excitement of "nature's bonfire" from it all?
3. How does that bonfire lead to Hopkins' rejoicing in the resurrection and the hope he finds through it for himself and for Man? How appropriate is the entire sprung rhythm for these concepts and emotions?

The Shape of the Fire

Theodore Roethke *Even in the context of these experiments with language, this poem may seem especially strange to you, and not only on the first reading. Even so, it will repay close reading. Read it aloud and watch for changes in tone. Does the poem become more* or *less coherent as it develops. Roethke grew up around his father's greenhouse in Michigan. Through much of his adult life he fought a recurrent battle for his sanity. You may find evidences of both of these facts in the poem. Whatever else, we hope you will experience the strength and energy of the poem.*

1

What's this? A dish for fat lips.
Who says? A nameless stranger.
Is he a bird or a tree? Not everyone can tell.

Water recedes to the crying of spiders.
An old scow bumps over black rocks.
A cracked pod calls.

Mother me out of here. What more will the bones allow?
Will the sea give the wind suck? A toad folds into a stone.
These flowers are all fangs. Comfort me, fury.
Wake me, witch, we'll do the dance of rotten sticks.

Shale loosens. Marl reaches into the field. Small birds pass over water.
Spirit, come near. This is only the edge of whiteness.
I can't laugh at a procession of dogs.

In the hour of ripeness the tree is barren.
The she-bear mopes under the hill.
Mother, mother, stir from your cave of sorrow.

A low mouth laps water. Weeds, weeds, how I love you.
The arbor is cooler. Farewell, farewell, fond worm.
The warm comes without sound.

2

Where's the eye?
The eye's in the sty.
The ear's not here
Beneath the hair.
When I took off my clothes
To find a nose,
There was only one shoe
For the waltz of To,
The pinch of Where.

Time for the flat-headed man. I recognize that listener,
Him with the platitudes and rubber doughnuts,
Melting at the knees, a varicose horror.
Hello, hello. My nerves knew you, dear boy.
Have you come to unhinge my shadow?
Last night I slept in the pits of a tongue.
The silver fish ran in and out of my special bindings;
I grew tired of the ritual of names and the assistant keeper of the mollusks:
Up over a viaduct I came, to the snakes and sticks of another winter,
A two-legged dog hunting a new horizon of howls.
The wind sharpened itself on a rock;
A voice sang:

Pleasure on ground
Has no sound,
Easily maddens
The uneasy man.

Who, careless, slips
In coiling ooze
Is trapped to the lips,
Leaves more than shoes;

Must pull off clothes
To jerk like a frog
On belly and nose
From the sucking bog.

My meat eats me. Who waits at the gate?
Mother of quartz, your words writhe into my ear.
Renew the light, lewd whisper.

3

The wasp waits.
    The edge cannot eat the center.
The grape glistens.
    The path tells little to the serpent.
An eye comes out of the wave.
    The journey from flesh is longest.
A rose sways least.
    The redeemer comes a dark way.

4

Morning-fair, follow me further back
Into that minnowy world of weeds and ditches,
When the herons floated high over the white houses,
And the little crabs slipped into silvery craters.
When the sun for me glinted the sides of a sand grain,
And my intent stretched over the buds at their first trembling.

That air and shine: and the flicker's loud summer call:
The bearded boards in the stream and the all of apples;
The glad hen on the hill; and the trellis humming.
Death was not. I lived in a simple drowse:
Hands and hair moved through a dream of wakening blossoms.

Rain sweetened the cave and the dove still called;
The flowers leaned on themselves, the flowers in hollows;
And love, love sang toward.

5

To have the whole air!—
The light, the full sun
Coming down on the flowerheads,
The tendrils turning slowly,
A slow snail-lifting, liquescent;
To be by the rose
Rising slowly out of its bed,
Still as a child in its first loneliness;
To see cyclamen veins become clearer in early sunlight,
And mist lifting out of the brown cat-tails;
To stare into the after-light, the glitter left on the lake's surface,
When the sun has fallen behind a wooded island;
To follow the drops sliding from a lifted oar,
Held up, while the rower breathes, and the small boat drifts quietly
shoreward;
To know that light falls and fills, often without our knowing,
As an opaque vase fills to the brim from a quick pouring,
Fills and trembles at the edge yet does not flow over,
Still holding and feeding the stem of the contained flower.

Questions

1. How do you see in your mind the "shape" of a fire? How would you describe it? How would you try to catch it in images? Since Roethke uses "*the* fire" in his title, he apparently has a specific fire in mind. Assuming that *the* could refer to a metaphorical fire, what fire might it be?
2. Are the first two sections simply random questions, answers, images, ideas? You might begin to answer this by looking at repeated words: "mother," for instance. Where might "here" be in "Mother me out of here"? What part of speech does "mother" have to be to make this an English sentence?
3. Quite a few of the words in parts 1 and 2 have to do with language. Underline them and see if they relate to each other in any way within their context.
4. Compare the images and statements in part 3 with those in part 1. Do they seem as disconnected?

5. With part 4 the style and tone have obviously changed. Define the changes as precisely as you can.
6. The change, especially in tone, is even more dramatic in part 5. Define the tone here. Now look back over the entire poem and try to describe what has happened in the developing whole. Examine especially the last four lines but also other images and ideas of parts 4 and 5 to see how they relate to earlier ones.

The Hunter Gracchus

Franz Kafka

Kafka is usually associated with the existential movement in literature and philosophy. His projection of a strange nightmare universe is one of the most powerful, disturbing, and (often) humorous in all literature. In "The Metamorphosis" his hero wakes up one morning changed into a giant cockroach—with no explanation and no way to change back. In his novel The Trial *the hero goes through life trying to clear himself of unknown charges against him. As you can see from "The Hunter Gracchus" Kafka works with a simple, factual style. The experimental in his work comes from the contrast between style and effect. The style emerges in translation with remarkable fidelity to its "feel" in German.*

Two boys were sitting on the harbor wall playing with dice. A man was reading a newspaper on the steps of the monument, resting in the shadow of a hero who was flourishing his sword on high. A girl was filling her bucket at the fountain. A fruitseller was lying beside his scales, staring out to sea. Through the vacant window and door openings of a café one could see two men quite at the back drinking their wine. The proprietor was sitting at a table in front and dozing. A bark was silently making for the little harbor, as if borne by invisible means over the water. A man in a blue blouse climbed ashore and drew the rope through a ring. Behind the boatman two other men in dark coats with silver buttons carried a bier, on which, beneath a great flower-patterned tasselled silk cloth, a man was apparently lying.

Nobody on the quay troubled about the newcomers; even when they lowered the bier to wait for the boatman, who was still occupied with his rope, nobody went nearer, nobody asked them a question, nobody accorded them an inquisitive glance.

The pilot was still further detained by a woman who, a child at her breast, now appeared with loosened hair on the deck of the boat. Then he advanced and indicated a yellowish two-storeyed house that rose abruptly on the left beside the sea; the bearers took up their burden and bore it to the low but gracefully pillared door. A little boy opened a window just in time to see the party vanishing into the house, then hastily shut the window again. The door too was now shut; it was of black oak, and very strongly made. A flock of doves which had been flying round the belfry alighted in the street before the house. As if their food were stored within, they assembled in front of the door. One of them flew up to the first storey and pecked at the window-pane. They were bright-hued, well-tended, beautiful birds. The woman on the boat flung grain to them in a wide sweep; they ate it up and flew across to the woman.

A man in a top hat tied with a band of crêpe now descended one of the narrow and very steep lanes that led to the harbor. He glanced round vigilantly, everything seemed to displease him, his mouth twisted at the sight of some offal in a corner. Fruit skins were lying on the steps of the monument; he swept them off in passing with his stick. He rapped at the house door, at the same time taking his top hat from his head with his black-gloved hand. The door was opened at once, and some fifty little boys appeared in two rows in the long entry-hall, and bowed to him.

The boatman descended the stairs, greeted the gentleman in black, conducted him up to the first storey, led him round the bright and elegant loggia which encircled the courtyard, and both of them entered, while the boys pressed after them at a respectful distance, a cool spacious room looking towards the back, from whose window no habitation, but only a bare, blackish grey rocky wall was to be seen. The bearers were busied in setting up and lighting several long candles at the head of the bier, yet these did not give light, but only scared away the shadows which had been immobile till then, and made them flicker over the walls. The cloth covering the bier had been thrown back. Lying on it was a man with wildly matted hair, who looked somewhat like a hunter. He lay without motion and, it seemed, without breathing, his eyes closed; yet only his trappings indicated that this man was probably dead.

The gentleman stepped up to the bier, laid his hand on the brow of the man lying upon it, then kneeled down and prayed. The boatman made a sign to the bearers to leave the room; they went out, drove away the boys who had gathered outside, and shut the door. But even that did not seem to satisfy the gentleman; he glanced at the boatman; the boatman understood, and vanished through a side door into the next room. At once the man on the bier opened his eyes, turned his face painfully towards the gentleman, and said: "Who are you?" Without any mark of surprise the gentleman rose from his kneeling posture and answered: "The Burgomaster of Riva."

The man on the bier nodded, indicated a chair with a feeble movement of his arm, and said, after the Burgomaster had accepted his invitation: "I knew that, of course, Burgomaster, but in the first moments of returning consciousness I always forget, everything goes round before my eyes, and it is best to ask about anything even if I know. You too probably know that I am the hunter Gracchus."

"Certainly," said the Burgomaster. "Your arrival was announced to me during the night. We had been asleep for a good while. Then towards midnight my wife cried: 'Salvatore'—that's my name—'look at that dove at the window.' It was really a dove, but as big as a cock. It flew over me and said in my ear: 'Tomorrow the dead hunter Gracchus is coming; receive him in the name of the city.' "

The hunter nodded and licked his lips with the tip of his tongue: "Yes, the doves flew here before me. But do you believe, Burgomaster, that I shall remain in Riva?"

"I cannot say that yet," replied the Burgomaster. "Are you dead?"

"Yes," said the hunter, "as you see. Many years ago, yes, it must be a great many years ago, I fell from a precipice in the Black Forest—that is in Germany—when I was hunting a chamois. Since then I have been dead."

"But you are alive too," said the Burgomaster.

"In a certain sense," said the hunter, "in a certain sense I am alive too. My death ship lost its way; a wrong turn of the wheel, a moment's absence of mind on the pilot's part, a longing to turn aside towards my lovely native country, I cannot tell what it was; I only know this, that I remained on earth and that ever since my ship has sailed earthly waters. So I, who asked for nothing better than to live among my mountains, travel after my death through all the lands of the earth."

"And you have no part in the other world?" asked the Burgomaster, knitting his brow.

"I am forever," replied the hunter, "on the great stair that leads up to it. On that infinitely wide and spacious stair I clamber about, sometimes up, sometimes down, sometimes on the right, sometimes on the left, always in motion. The hunter has been turned into a butterfly. Do not laugh."

"I am not laughing," said the Burgomaster in self-defense.

"That is very good of you," said the hunter. "I am always in motion. But when I make a supreme flight and see the gate actually shining before me I awaken presently on my old ship, still stranded forlornly in some earthly sea or other. The fundamental error of my one-time death grins at me as I lie in my cabin. Julia, the wife of the pilot, knocks at the door and brings me on my bier the morning drink of the land whose coasts we chance to be passing. I lie on a wooden pallet, I wear—it cannot be a pleasure to look at me—a filthy winding sheet, my hair and beard, black tinged with grey, have grown together inextricably, my limbs are covered with a great flower-patterned woman's shawl with long fringes. A sacramental candle stands at my head and lights me. On the wall opposite me is a little picture, evidently of a Bushman who is aiming his spear at me and taking cover as best he can behind a beautifully painted shield. On shipboard one is often a prey to stupid imaginations, but that is the stupidest of them all. Otherwise my wooden case is quite empty. Through a hole in the side wall come in the warm airs of the southern night, and I hear the water slapping against the old boat.

"I have lain here ever since the time when, as the hunter Gracchus living in the Black Forest, I followed a chamois and fell from a precipice. Everything happened in good order. I pursued, I fell, bled to death in a ravine, died, and this ship should have conveyed me to the next world. I can still remember how gladly I stretched myself out on this pallet for the first time. Never did the mountains listen to such songs from me as these shadowy walls did then.

"I had been glad to live and I was glad to die. Before I stepped aboard, I joyfully flung away my wretched load of ammunition, my knapsack, my hunting rifle that I had always been proud to carry, and I slipped into my winding sheet like a girl into her marriage dress. I lay and waited. Then came the mishap."

"A terrible fate," said the Burgomaster, raising his hand defensively. "And you bear no blame for it?"

"None," said the hunter. "I was a hunter; was there any sin in that? I followed my calling as a hunter in the Black Forest, where there were still wolves in those days. I lay in ambush, shot, hit my mark, flayed the skins from my victims: was there any sin in that? My labors were blessed. 'The great hunter of the Black Forest' was the name I was given. Was there any sin in that?"

"I am not called upon to decide that," said the Burgomaster, "but to me also there seems to be no sin in such things. But, then, whose is the guilt?"

"The boatman's," said the hunter. "Nobody will read what I say here, no one will come to help me; even if all the people were commanded to help me, every door and window would remain shut, everybody would take to bed and draw the bedclothes over his head, the whole earth would become an inn for the night. And there is sense in that, for nobody knows of me, and if anyone knew he would not know where I could be found, and if he knew where I could be found, he would not know how to deal with me, he would not know how to help me. The thought of helping me is an illness that has to be cured by taking to one's bed.

"I know that, and so I do not shout to summon help, even though at moments—when I lose control over myself, as I have done just now, for instance—I think seriously of it. But to drive out such thoughts I need only look round me and verify where I am, and—I can safely assert—have been for hundreds of years."

"Extraordinary," said the Burgomaster, "extraordinary.—And now do you think of staying here in Riva with us?"

"I think not," said the hunter with a smile, and, to excuse himself, he laid his hand on the Burgomaster's knee. "I am here, more than that I do not know, further than that I cannot go. My ship has no rudder, and it is driven by the wind that blows in the undermost regions of death."

Questions

1. Why should Kafka begin his story with the particular details that he does? Do the boys playing with dice have anything to do with the rest of the story?
2. The bark moves into the harbor, we are told, "as if borne by invisible means over the water." This is the first unusual detail. The last line tells how it is borne. What is the effect? The large doves seem rather unreal, especially when the Burgomeister says that one talks. Again, how do you respond?
3. Did you expect the man in the bier to awaken when everyone but the Burgomeister had left the room? Does the story he tells make any sense? You have probably heard of the boat that carries the dead across the river Styx. Could this be that boat? If so, what might the story be saying about death?
4. Does the title suggest that Gracchus is still a hunter? For what?
5. Try to define the effect of the story on you, especially the effect of narrating it in so simple and factual a style.

Suggestions for Writing

1. Kafka's stories get their effect as much, perhaps, from the factual, reportorial style in which the nightmarish events are narrated as from the events themselves. Try to project one of your nightmares—we all have them—in a similar factual, noncommittal style and tone. Contrast for yourself the method and results with the way you would ordinarily tell such a story to your family or friends.

Molly's Soliloquy

James Joyce

Molly Bloom's famous soliloquy—over forty-five pages of unpunctuated "stream of consciousness" writing—is perhaps the most renowned chapter in Joyce's remarkable novel Ulysses. *Molly is the wife of Leopold Bloom, "Poldy" to her, whose one day of wandering and adventures in Dublin make up the bulk of the novel. During the day Molly has committed adultery with Blazes Boylon. Bloom knows it and has known it all along. Bloom has returned after midnight, bringing home with him Stephen Dedalus, poet-to-be. But Stephen has refused Bloom's offer of a bed and, perhaps, of Molly. Bloom goes to bed with Molly and finally to sleep, after startling her with the unusual request that she bring him breakfast in bed in the morning. She lies awake pondering that request, Bloom's story of his day, her own experiences of the day, and everything else these things remind her of. We include most of the first page and of the last two pages. Though the writing is unpunctuated, you will notice that it comes out usually in standard English syntax and even sentences, often chopped off before they end. Can you decide by what logic—other than just "woman's"—Molly moves from idea to idea?*

Yes because he never did a thing like that before as ask to get his breakfast in bed with a couple of eggs since the *City Arms* hotel when he used to be pretending to be laid up with a sick voice doing his highness to make himself interesting to that old faggot Mrs Riordan that he thought he had a great leg of and she never left us a farthing all for masses for herself and her soul greatest miser ever was actually afraid to lay out 4d for her methylated spirit telling me all her ailments she had too much old chat in her about politics and earthquakes and the end of the world let us have a bit of fun first God help the world if all the women were her sort down on bathingsuits and lownecks of course nobody wanted her to wear I suppose she was pious because no man would look at her twice I hope Ill never be like her a wonder she didnt want us to cover our faces but she was a welleducated woman certainly and her gabby talk about Mr Riordan here and Mr Riordan there I suppose he was glad to get shut of her and her dog smelling my fur and always edging to get up under my petticoats especially then still I like that in him polite to old women like that and waiters and beggars too hes not proud out of nothing but not always if ever he got anything really serious the matter with him its much better for them go into a hospital where everything is clean but I suppose Id have to dring it into him for a month yes and then wed have a hospital nurse next thing on the carpet have him staying there till they throw him out or a nun maybe like the smutty photo he has shes as much a nun as Im not yes because theyre so weak and puling when theyre sick they want a woman to get well if his nose bleeds youd think it was O tragic and that dyinglooking one off the south circular when he sprained his foot at the choir party at the sugarloaf Mountain the day I wore that dress Miss Stack bringing him flowers the worst old ones she could find at the bottom of the basket anything at all to get into a mans bedroom with her old maids voice trying to imagine he was dying on account of her to never see thy face again though he looked more like a man with his beard a bit grown in the bed father was the same besides I hate bandaging and dosing when he cut his toe with the razor paring his corns afraid hed get blood poisoning but if it was a thing I was sick then wed see what attention only of course the woman hides it not to give all the trouble they do

. . . .

let me see if I can doze off 1 2 3 4 5 what kind of flowers are those they invented like the stars the wallpaper in Lombard street was much nicer the apron he gave me was like that something only I only wore it twice better lower this lamp and try again so as I can get up early Ill go to Lambes there beside Findlaters and get them to send us some flowers to put about the place in case he brings him home tomorrow today I mean no no Fridays an unlucky day first I want to do the place up someway the dust grows in it I think while Im asleep then we can have music and cigarettes I can accompany him first I must clean the keys of the piano with milk whatll I wear shall I wear a white rose or those fairy cakes in Liptons I love the smell of a rich big shop at 7½d a lb or the other ones with the cherries in them and the pinky sugar 11d a couple of lbs of course a nice plant for the middle of the table Id get that cheaper in wait wheres this I saw them not long ago I love flowers Id love to have the whole place swimming in roses God of heaven theres nothing like nature the wild mountains then the sea and the waves rushing then the beautiful country with fields of oats and wheat and all kinds of things and all the fine cattle going about that would do your heart good to see rivers and lakes and flowers all sorts of shapes and smells and colours springing up even out of the ditches primroses and violets nature it is as for them saying theres no God I wouldnt give a snap of my two fingers for all their learning why dont they go and create something I often asked him atheists or whatever they call themselves go and wash the cobbles off themselves first then they go howling for the priest and they dying and why why because theyre afraid of hell on account of their bad conscience ah yes I know them well who was the first person in the universe before there was anybody that made it all who ah that they dont know neither do I so there you are they might as well try to stop the sun from rising tomorrow the sun shines for you he said the day we were lying among the rhododendrons on Howth head in the grey tweed suit and his straw hat the day I got him to propose to me yes first I gave him the bit of seedcake out of my mouth and it was leapyear like now yes 16 years ago my God after that long kiss I near lost my breath yes he said I was a flower of the mountain yes so we are flowers all a womans body yes that was one true thing he said in his life and the sun shines for you today yes that was why I liked him because I saw he understood or felt what a woman is and I knew I could always get round him and I gave him all the pleasure I could leading him on till he asked me to say yes and I wouldnt answer first only looked out over the sea and the sky I was thinking of so many things he didnt know of Mulvey and Mr Stanhope and Hester and father and old captain Groves and the sailors playing all birds fly and I say stoop and washing up dishes they called it on the pier and the sentry in front of the governors house with the thing round his white helmet poor devil half roasted and the Spanish girls laughing in their shawls and their tall combs and the auctions in the morning the Greeks and the jews and the Arabs and the devil knows who else from all the ends of Europe and Duke street and the fowl market all clucking outside Larby Sharons and the poor donkeys slipping half asleep and the vague fellows in the cloaks asleep in the shade on the steps and the big wheels of the carts of the bulls and the old castle thousands of years old yes and those handsome Moors all in white and turbans like kings asking you to sit down in their little bit of a shop and Ronda with the old windows of the posadas glancing eyes a lattice hid for her lover to kiss the iron and the wineshops half open at night and the castanets and the night we missed the boat at Algeciras the watchman going about serene with his lamp and O that awful deepdown torrent O and the sea the sea crimson sometimes like fire and the glorious sunsets and the figtrees in the Alameda gardens yes and all the queer little streets and pink and blue and yellow houses and the rosegardens and the jessamine and geraniums and cactuses and Gibraltar as a girl where I was a Flower of the mountain yes when I put the rose in my hair like the Andalusian girls used or shall I wear a red yes and how he kissed me under the Moorish wall and I thought well as well him as another and then I asked him with my eyes to ask again yes and then he asked me would I yes to say yes my mountain flower and first I put my arms around him yes and drew him down to me so he could feel my breasts all perfume yes and his heart was going like mad and yes I said yes I will Yes.

Questions

1. The soliloquy is often considered the purest example in English of "stream of consciousness" writing. How close does this selection seem to the actual way your mind would work under the circumstances—that is, when lying awake not consciously thinking through a problem but just letting the mind go?
2. Since the soliloquy begins and ends with "yes" and since that "yes," whatever else it is, is "yes" to Bloom's request for breakfast in bed, perhaps the soliloquy has had more direction than it seems. Can you see other evidence?
3. From the evidence of this excerpt, what would you say of the effectiveness of this kind of writing? Can you read this without mentally supplying punctuation? If you cannot, why did Joyce write it without punctuation? What effects does he achieve?

Suggestions for Writing

1. Write an analysis of the effects Joyce achieves and how he achieves them.
2. Try something similar yourself, trying to catch the flow of your mind when it is only mildly directing itself toward some problem, or when it is as relaxed as you can make it.

General William Booth Enters into Heaven

Vachel Lindsay *Vachel Lindsay became widely known and popular during a series of "national recital tours" in which he chanted poems, as a kind of vagabond minstrel, in return for food and lodging. His poems may lack sophistication or even greatness, but the dramatic chanting in a heavy, often thumping rhythm had a sensational impact. You can hardly avoid the rhythm, but work it up into a chant and say it aloud. We include it here as an example of a heavy rhythmic style. How effective is it as a celebration of General Booth, the founder of the Salvation Army? Do the suggested accompaniments change your feeling for the rhythm?*

(To be sung to the tune of "The Blood of the Lamb" with indicated instrument)

I

(*Bass drum beaten loudly.*)
Booth led boldly with his big bass drum—
(Are you washed in the blood of the Lamb?)
The Saints smiled gravely and they said: "He's come."
(Are you washed in the blood of the Lamb?)
Walking lepers followed, rank on rank,
Lurching bravos from the ditches dank,
Drabs from the alleyways and drug fiends pale—
Minds still passion-ridden, soul-powers frail:—
Vermin-eaten saints with moldy breath,
Unwashed legions with the ways of Death—
(Are you washed in the blood of the Lamb?)

(*Banjos.*)
Every slum had sent its half-a-score

The round world over. (Booth had groaned for more.)
Every banner that the wide world flies
Bloomed with glory and transcendent dyes.
Big-voiced lasses made their banjos bang,
Tranced, fanatical they shrieked and sang:—
"Are you washed in the blood of the Lamb?"
Hallelujah! It was queer to see
Bull-necked convicts with that land make free.
Loons with trumpets blowed a blare, blare, blare
On, on upward thro' the golden air!
(Are you washed in the blood of the Lamb?)

II

(*Bass drum slower and softer.*)
Booth died blind and still by faith he trod,
Eyes still dazzled by the ways of God.
Booth led boldly, and he looked the chief
Eagle countenance in sharp relief,
Beard a-flying, air of high command
Unabated in that holy land.

(*Sweet flute music.*)
Jesus came from out the court-house door,
Stretched his hands above the passing poor.
Booth saw not, but led his queer ones there
Round and round the mighty court-house square.
Then, in an instant all that blear review
Marched on spotless, clad in raiment new.
The lame were straightened, withered limbs uncurled
And blind eyes opened on a new, sweet world.

(*Bass drum louder.*)
Drabs and vixens in a flash made whole!
Gone was the weasel-head, the snout, the jowl!
Sages and sibyls now, and athletes clean,
Rulers of empires, and of forests green!

(*Grand chorus of all instruments. Tambourines to the foreground.*)
The hosts were sandalled, and their wings were fire!
(Are you washed in the blood of the Lamb?)
But their noise played havoc with the angel-choir.
(Are you washed in the blood of the Lamb?)
Oh, shout Salvation! It was good to see

Kings and Princes by the Lamb set free.
The banjos rattled and the tambourines
Jing-jing-jingled in the hands of Queens.

(*Reverently sung, no instruments.*)
And when Booth halted by the curb for prayer
He saw his Master thro' the flag-filled air.
Christ came gently with a robe and crown
For Booth the soldier, while the throng knelt down.
He saw King Jesus. They were face to face,
And he knelt a-weeping in that holy place.
Are you washed in the blood of the Lamb?

A Refusal to Mourn the Death, by Fire, of a Child in London

Dylan Thomas *Like Donne's "Canonization," this poem looks innocent enough, with its regular stanzas and its somewhat complicated but regular rhyme scheme. But Thomas experimented in many directions with language. This is one of his most popular poems. Can you make it read so that the word order makes sense?*

Never until the mankind making
Bird beast and flower
Fathering and all humbling darkness
Tells with silence the last light breaking
And the still hour
Is come of the sea tumbling in harness

And I must enter again the round
Zion of the water bead
And the synagogue of the ear of corn
Shall I let pray the shadow of a sound
Or sow my salt seed
In the least valley of sackcloth to mourn

The majesty and burning of the child's death.
I shall not murder
The mankind of her going with a grave truth
Nor blaspheme down the stations of the breath
With any further
Elegy of innocence and youth.

Deep with the first dead lies London's daughter,
Robed in the long friends,

The grains beyond age, the dark veins of her mother,
Secret by the unmourning water
Of the riding Thames.
After the first death, there is no other.

Questions

1. Except for some unusual words, the poem should give you no trouble with the basic syntax after the first long sentence, which makes up over half the poem. Even within that sentence only the first few lines cause real trouble. Try them this way:

    Never, until the mankind-making,
    Bird-, beast-, and flower-
    Fathering, and all-humbling darkness
    Tells with silence the last light breaking
    And [until] the still hour
    Is come of the sea tumbling in harness

    And I must enter again the round
    Zion of the water bead
    And the synagogue of the ear of corn—
    [Never] Shall I let pray. . . .

    This of course means that the darkness is a mankind-making, a bird-fathering, beast-fathering, and flower-fathering, and an all-humbling darkness. You may have trouble now with the paradoxical idea, since light is usually thought of in such terms, but you should have no trouble with the syntax. Except for the matter of clarity, though, is the poem really improved by the punctuation? Can you define the effect of leaving it out?
2. Zion is a gathering place, the heart of the spiritual universe, and a synagogue is the center and source of spiritual life. What would Thomas use these as symbols of? When or how can he "enter again" such things? Compare "The grains beyond age, the dark veins of her mother," which suggest literally the linen shroud. What do they suggest figuratively? After careful work with the poem you should recognize how much meaning and emotion Thomas packs into his words.
3. Does the "refusal to mourn," as it develops in the poem, mean that the poet does not mourn, that he feels no grief? If not, what is the effect of his refusal?

Two Poems

e. e. cummings *Unless you have encountered cummings' poems before, your first response may be simply puzzlement. But give them a chance. There may have been something faddish about his early popularity, but now his reputation is firmly established. "anyone lived in a pretty how town" is one of his most popular and most often reprinted poems. Read it assuming that* anyone *is a proper noun, or at least refers to a specific person. Do other words then become more specific? The other poem is less well known and more extreme in its typographical experimentation. Join the letters until they make words and sense.*

anyone lived in a pretty how town
(with up so floating many bells down)
spring summer autumn winter
he sang his didn't he danced his did.

Women and men (both little and small)
cared for anyone not at all
they sowed their isn't they reaped their same
sun moon stars rain

children guessed (but only a few
and down they forgot as up they grew
autumn winter spring summer)
that noone loved him more by more

when by now and tree by leaf
she laughed his joy she cried his grief
bird by snow and stir by still
anyone's any was all to her

someones married their everyones
laughed their cryings and did their dance
(sleep wake hope and then) they
said their nevers they slept their dream

stars rain sun moon
(and only the snow can begin to explain
how children are apt to forget to remember
with up so floating many bells down)

one day anyone died i guess
(and noone stooped to kiss his face)
busy folk buried them side by side
little by little and was by was

all by all and deep by deep
and more by more they dream their sleep
noone and anyone earth by april
wish by spirit and if by yes.

Women and men (both dong and ding)
summer autumn winter spring
reaped their sowing and went their came
sun moon stars rain

tw

o o
ld
o

nce upo

n
a(
n

o mo

re
)time
me

n

Questions

1. In stanza two, do *little* and *small* mean the same thing? If "anyone" is a boy, "noone," who "loved him more by more," must be a girl. With this much help can you understand the story? What is the effect of telling it in abstract and impersonal words? Would the impact be as great if proper names were used and the story were told in conventional poetry? Work out as many of the details as you can in the poem, but don't worry if a few escape you.
2. Substitute traditional adjectives such as *country, old, hick* for *how* in the phrase "pretty how town." What does *how* suggest that the substitutes do not? Try substitutions for other words in the poem.
3. In the second poem is the arrangement of "tw" merely whimsical? Note the line "o o." What does it look like? O's are also zeroes. What does this suggest? Is this really a poem?

Ladle Rat Rotten Hut

This jeu d'esprit, *the work of Howard Chace, has long circulated through English departments. Once you become accustomed to it, you should have little trouble understanding it.*

(*Heresy ladle furry starry toiling udder warts—warts welcher altar girdle deferent firmer once inner regional verging*)

Wants pawn term dare worsted ladle gull hoe lift wetter murder inner ladle cordage honor itch offer lodge, dock, florist. Disk ladle gull orphan worry putty ladle rat cluck wetter ladle rat hut, an fur disk raisin pimple colder Ladle Rat Rotten Hut.

Wan moaning Ladle Rat Rotten Hut's murder colder inset, "Ladle Rat Rotten Hut, heresy ladle basking winsome burden barter an shirker cockles. Tick disk ladle basking tutor cordage offer groin-murder hoe lifts honor udder site offer florist. Shaker lake! Dun stopper laundry wrote! Dun stopper peck floors! Dun daily-doily inner florist, an yonder nor sorghum stenches, dun stopper torque wet strainers!"

"Hoe-cake, murder," resplendent Ladle Rat Rotten Hut, an tickle ladle basking an stuttered oft.

Honor wrote tutor cordage offer groin-murder, Ladle Rat Rotten Hut mitten anomalous woof.

"Wail, wail, wail!" set disk wicket woof, "Evanescent Ladle Rat Rotten Hut! Wares are putty ladle gull goring wizard ladle basking?"

"Armor goring tumor groin-murder's," reprisal ladle gull. "Grammar's seeking bet. Armor ticking arson burden barter an shirker cockles."

"O hoe! Heifer gnats woke," setter wicket woof, butter taught tomb shelf, "Oil tickle shirt court tutor cordage offer groin-murder. Oil ketchup wetter letter, an den—O bore!"

Soda wicket woof tucker shirt court, an whinny retched a cordage offer groin-murder, picked inner windrow, an sore debtor pore oil worming worse lion inner bet. Inner flesh, disk abdominal woof lipped honor bet, paunched honor pore oil worming, an garbled erupt. Den disk ratchet ammonol pot honor groin-murder's nut cup an gnat-gun, any curdled ope inner bet.

Inner ladle wile, Ladle Rat Rotten Hut a raft attar cordage, an ranker dough ball. "Comb ink, sweat hard," setter wicket woof, disgracing is verse.

Ladle Rat Rotten Hut entity bet rum, an stud buyer groin-murder's bet.

"O Grammar!" crater ladle gull historically, "Water bag icer gut! A nervous sausage bag ice!"

"Battered lucky chew whiff, sweat hard," setter bloat-Thursday woof, wetter wicket small honors phase.

"O, Grammar, water bag noise! A nervous sore suture anomalous prognosis!"

"Battered small your whiff, doling," whiskered dole woof, ants mouse worse waddling.

"O Grammar, water bag mouser gut! A nervous sore suture bag mouse!"

Daze worry on-forger-nut ladle gull's lest warts. Oil offer sodden, caking offer carvers an sprinkling otter bet, disk hoard-hoarded woof lipped own pore Ladle Rat Rotten Hut an garbled erupt.

MURAL: Yonder nor sorghum stenches shut ladle gulls stopper torque wet strainers.

Suggestions for Writing

1. Just for your own fun, pick some well-known story or poem—maybe a nursery rhyme—and try playing with the same devices of sound and sense. One of your editors and his son worked out the following in very little time.

Sinker son office expense,
  Apocryphyl awry,
Foreign ten table lack burgs
  Bay kindred ply.

Winter ply worse so penned
  Sable lurks beg antlers ink,
No worsen daughter didy ditch
  Terset beef ore aching?

Say kink war cinder cow tang cows
  Cow tang cow testimony.
Sake ween worse cinder pallor
  Heat inbred a ninny.

Same aid wore cinder carting
  Hank an gout seek glows.
All honk game sable lack burg
  Ants nap doff urn owes.

The Ondt and the Gracehoper

James Joyce

Finnegans Wake *may seem the most extreme and the most nonsensical of all these experiments. It probably* is *the most extreme; it is certainly the most ambitious and amazing. But don't dismiss it too soon as merely nonsensical. The evidence now seems to say that with Joyce we are working with the man who* knew *more about language than anyone who has ever lived. The emphasized* knew *should suggest a certain kind of knowledge, not so much academic as a total knowledge that included sensitivity, awareness, profundity, almost a bodily knowledge. Whatever else it is,* Finnegans Wake *is an amazing linguistic achievement. Into it Joyce poured sixteen years of his life, against the advice of his friends, publishers, and doctors. We may finally disagree about its worth, but we can hardly disagree about its magnitude nor the energy it cost. The selection below makes a fitting finale to this book.*

Begin with Joyce's title, Finnegans Wake. Finnegans *is plural, which suggests* Wake *as a verb: "Finnegans, Awake!" But it can also be "Finnegan's Wake," where* wake *is a noun (either a funeral celebration or an awakening). A popular nineteenth-century ballad by this name tells of a hod-carrier who, while working with a hangover, fell from a ladder and broke his skull. But during his wake his mourners began a fight, splashed him with whiskey, and "waked" him from death. The little tale, with its death-burial-resurrection theme, threads its way through Joyce's novel. All readers, apparently, can be Finn again—that is, if we wake.* Fin *is French for* end, *and* wake *suggests* beginning. *Hence the title suggests the circular structure that underlies the novel (among other things, it begins in the middle of a sentence, ends with an incompleted one which is completed by the beginning). This by no means exhausts the title.*

The section below is self-contained and delightful—if you are willing to pay the price. Don't expect too much at first, but enjoy the things you understand. "Gracehoper" suggests that Lafontaine's fable of the ant and the grasshopper is going to have explicitly religious meaning. Shaun, who tells the story, and Shem are twins, the sons of a pub-keeper, Humphrey Chimpden Earwicker (HCE), and his wife

Anna Livia Plurabelle (ALP). If you can see something of what Joyce is doing with these two names, you are ready to plunge into Finnegans Wake*—from almost any point around the edge. As you will see we gave up on questions or suggestions for this one. Almost any sentence could supply a dozen questions. We trust you will supply your own.*

So vi et! we responded. Song! Shaun, song! Have mood! Hold forth!

—I apologuise, Shaun began, but I would rather spinooze you one from the grimm gests of Jacko and Esaup, fable one, feeble too. Let us here consider the casus, my dear little cousis (husstenhasstencaffincoffintussemtossemdamandamnacosaghcusaghhobixhatouxpeswchbechoscashlcarcarcaract) of the Ondt and the Gracehoper.

The Gracehoper was always jigging ajog, hoppy on akkant of his joyicity, (he had a partner pair of findlestilts to supplant him), or, if not, he was always making ungraceful overtures to Floh and Luse and Bienie and Vespatilla to play pupa-pupa and pulicy-pulicy and langtennas and pushpygyddyum and to commence insects with him, there mouthparts to his orefice and his gambills to there airy processes, even if only in chaste, ameng the everlistings, behold a waspering pot. He would of curse melissciously, by his fore feelhers, flexors, contractors, depressors and extensors, lamely, harry me, marry me, bury me, bind me, till she was puce for shame and allso fourmish her in Spinner's housery at the earthsbest schoppinhour so summery as his cottage, which was cald fourmillierly Tingsomingenting, groped up. Or, if he was always striking up funny funereels with Besterfarther Zeuts, the Aged One, with all his wigeared corollas, albedinous and oldbuoyant, inscythe his elytrical wormcasket and Dehlia and Peonia, his druping nymphs, bewheedling him, compound eyes on hornitosehead, and Auld Letty Plussiboots to scratch his cacumen and cackle his tramsitus, diva deborah (seven bolls of sapo, a lick of lime, two spurts of fussfor, threefurts of sulph, a shake o'shouker, doze grains of migniss and a mesfull of midcap pitchies. The whool of the whaal in the wheel of the whorl of the Boubou from Bourneum has thus come to taon!), and with tambarins and cantoridettes soturning around his eggshill rockcoach their dance McCaper in retrophoebia, beck from bulk, like fantastic disossed and jenny aprils, to the ra, the ra, the ra, the ra, langsome heels and langsome toesis, attended to by a mutter and doffer duffmatt baxingmotch and a myrmidins of pszozlers pszinging *Satyr's Caudeldayed Nice* and *Hombly, Dombly Sod We Awhile* but *Ho, Time Timeagen, Wake!* For if sciencium (what's what) can mute uns nought, 'a thought, abought the Great Sommboddy within the Omniboss, perhops an artsaccord (hoot's hoot) might sing ums tuntim abutt the Little Newbuddies that ring his panch. A high old tide for the barheated publics and the whole day as gratiis! Fudder and lighting for ally looty, any filly in a fog, for O'Cronione lags acrumbling in his sands but his sunsunsuns still tumble on. Erething above ground, as his Book of Breathings bed him, so as everwhy, sham or shunner, zeemliangly to kick time.

Grouscious me and scarab my sahul! What a bagateller it is! Libelulous! Inzanzarity! Pou! Pschla! Ptuh! What a zeit for the goths! vented the Ondt, who, not being a sommerfool, was thothfolly making chilly spaces at hisphex affront of the icinglass of his windhame, which was cold antitopically Nixnixundnix. We shall not come to party at that lopp's, he decided possibly, for he is not on our social list. Nor to Ba's berial nether, thon sloghard, this oldeborre's yaar ablong as there's a khul on a khat. Nefersenless, when he had safely looked up his ovipository, he loftet hails and prayed: May he me no voida water! Seekit Hatup! May no he me tile pig shed on! Suckit Hotup! As broad as Beppy's realm shall flourish my reign shall flourish! As high as Heppy's hevn shall flurrish my haine shall hurrish! Shall grow, shall flourish! Shall hurrish! Hummum.

The Ondt was a weltall fellow, raumybult and abelboobied, bynear saw altitudinous wee a schelling in kopfers. He was sair sair sullemn and chairmanlooking when he was not making spaces in his psyche, but, laus! when he wore making spaces on his ikey, he ware mouche mothst secred and muravyingly wisechairmanlooking. Now whim the sillybilly of a Gracehoper had jingled through a jungle of love and debts and jangled through a jumble of life in doubts afterworse, wetting with the bimblebeaks, drikking with nautonects, bilking with durrydunglecks and horing after ladybirdies (*ichnehmon diagelegenaitoikon*) he fell joust as sieck as a sexton and tantoo pooveroo quant a churchprince, and wheer the midges to wend hemsylph or vosch to sirch for grub for his corapusse or to find a hospes, alick, he wist gnit! Bruko dry! fuko spint! Sultamont osa bare! And volumundo osi videvide! Nichtsnichtsundnichts! Not one pickopeck of muscowmoney to bag a tittlebits of beebread! Iomio! Iomio! Crick's corbicule, which a plight! O moy Bog, he contrited with melanctholy. Meblizzered, him sluggered! I am heartily hungry!

He had eaten all the whilepaper, swallowed the lustres, devoured forty flights of styearcases, chewed up all the mensas and seccles, ronged the records, made mundballs of the ephemerids and vorasioused most glutinously with the very timeplace in the ternitary—not too dusty a cicada of neutriment for a chittinous chip so mitey. But when Chrysalmas was on the bare branches, off he went from Tingsomingenting. He took a round stroll and he took a stroll round and he took a round strollagain till the grillies in his head and the leivnits in his hair made him thought he had the Tossmania. Had he twicycled the sees of the deed and trestraversed their revermer? Was he come to hevre with his engiles or gone to hull with the poop? The June snows was flocking in thuckflues on the hegelstomes, millipeeds of it and myriopoods, and a lugly whizzling tournedos, the Boraborayellers, blohablasting tegolhuts up to tetties and ruching sleets off the coppeehouses, playing ragnowrock rignewreck, with an irritant, penetrant, siphonopterous spuk. Grausssssss! Opr! Grausssssss! Opr!

The Gracehoper who, though blind as batflea, yet knew, not a leetle beetle, his good smetterling of entymology asped nissunitimost lous nor liceens but promptly tossed himself in the vico, phthin and phthir, on top of his buzzer, tezzily wondering wheer would his aluck alight or boss of both appease and the next time he makes the aquinatance of the Ondt after this they have met themselves, these mouschical umsummables, it shall be motylucky if he will beheld not a world of differents. Behailed His Gross the Ondt, prostrandvorous upon his dhrone, in his Papylonian babooshklees, smolking a spatial brunt of Hosana cigals, with unshrinkables farfalling from his unthinkables, swarming of himself in his sunnyroom, sated before his comfortumble phullupsuppy of a plate o'monkynous and a confucion of minthe (for he was a conformed acetist and aristotaller), as appi as a oneysucker or a baskerboy on the Libido, with Floh biting his leg thigh and Luse lugging his luff leg and Bieni bussing him under his bonnet and Vespatilla blowing cosy fond tutties up the allabroad length of the large of his smalls. As entomate as intimate could pinchably be. Emmet and demmet and be jiltses crazed and be jadeses whipt! schneezed the Gracehoper, aguepe with ptchjelasys and at his wittol's indts, what have eyeforsight!

The Ondt, that true and perfect host, a spiter aspinne, was making the greatest spass a body could with his queens laceswinging for he was spizzing all over him like thingsumanything in formicolation, boundlessly blissfilled in an allallahbath of houris. He was ameising himself hugely at crabround and marypose, chasing Floh out of charity and tickling Luse, I hope too, and tackling Bienie, faith, as well, and jucking Vespatilla jukely by the chimiche. Never did Dorsan from Dunshanagan dance it with more devilry! The veripathetic imago of the impossible Gracehoper on his odderkop in the myre, after his thrice ephemeral journeeys, sans mantis ne shooshooe, featherweighed animule, actually and presumptuably sinctifying chronic's despair, was sufficiently and probably coocoo much for his chorous of gravitates. Let him be Artalone the Weeps with his parisites peeling off him I'll be Highfee the Crackasider. Flunkey Footle furloughed foul, writing off his phoney, but Conte Carme makes the melody that mints the money. *Ad majorem l.s.d.! Divi gloriam.* A darkener of the threshold. Haru? Orimis, capsizer of his antboat, sekketh rede from Evilit-is, lord of loaves in Amongded. Be it! So be it! Thou-who-thou-art, the fleet-as-spindhrift, impfang thee of mine wideheight. Haru!

The thing pleased him andt, and andt,

He larved ond he larved on he merd such a nauses
The Gracehoper feared he woulld mixplace his fauces.
I forgive you, grondt Ondt, said the Gracehoper, weeping,
For their sukes of the sakes you are safe in whose keeping.
Teach Floh and Luse polkas, show Bienie where's sweet
And be sure Vespatilla fines fat ones to heat.
As I once played the piper I must now pay the count
So saida to Moyhammlet and marhaba to your Mount!
Let who likes lump above so what flies be a full'un;
I could not feel moregruggy if this was prompollen.
I pick up your reproof, the horsegift of a friend,
For the prize of your save is the price of my spend.
Can castwhores pulladeftkiss if oldpollocks forsake 'em
Or Culex feel etchy if Pulex don't wake him?
A locus to loue, a term it t'embarass,
These twain are the twins that tick Homo Vulgaris.
Has Aquileone nort winged to go syf
Since the Gwyfyn we were in his farrest drewbryf
And that Accident Man not beseeked where his story ends
Since longsephyring sighs sought heartseast for their orience?
We are Wastenot with Want, precondamned, two and true,

Till Nolans go volants and Bruneyes come blue.
Ere those gidflirts now gadding you quit your mocks for my gropes
An extense must impull, an elapse must elopes,
Of my tectucs takestock, tinktact, and ail's weal;
As I view by your farlook hale yourself to my heal.
Partiprise my thinwhins whiles my blink points unbroken on
Your whole's whercabroads with Tout's trightyright token on.
My in risible universe youdly haud find
Sulch oxtrabeeforeness meat soveal behind.
Your feats end enormous, your volumes immense,
(*May the Graces I hoped for sing your Ondtship song sense!*),
Your genus its worldwide, your spacest sublime!
But, Holy Saltmartin, why can't you beat time?

In the name of the former and of the latter and of their holocaust. Allmen.

Writing Projects

If by now you feel the urge to experiment, you should have no trouble finding among the selections in this section sufficient models, suggestions, hints to guide you. One place or another in this book you have seen experiments in style, subject, organization, point of view, tone—almost any and all of the qualities that make up writing. Most of your own writing will probably not aim at such experimental extremes as we have just seen. Yet every piece of writing is, in a sense, an experiment. Unless you are *merely* imitating someone else, even your regular papers will be creative in the sense that you are creating out of words something that was not there before.

Very few people feel the urge to outdo Joyce in *Finnegans Wake*. How could anyone? But everything that Joyce had done earlier points to and culminates in *Finnegans Wake*. Evidently Joyce found his own final style, his own personal and ultimate idiom, in writing *Finnegans Wake*. Similarly Sterne found his, Hopkins and Kafka and Cummings found theirs. And you may find yours in experimentation.

Instead of setting up specific writing assignments, let us be general for these final suggestions. Experimenting can be valuable for its own sake: for what it can tell you about your own capacity with language; for what it can tell you about language itself, its limits, its flexibility, its amazing energies, its tricky ways; for what it can do to expand your abilities to handle language; it can even be valuable just for the fun of it. But also for what it can do to lead you to your own particular "voice"—your own individual style, tone, point-of-view, rhetorical stance. Toward such a particular voice, this text can help you. Your teachers can help you. Perceptive reading, both intensive and extensive, can help you. But finally only writing can help very much, only "much exercise of his own style," as Ben Jonson put it centuries ago.

One final caution. Experimentation that tries merely to be cute, or different, or witty (in the worst modern sense), or fancy will probably be flat and tasteless. But if you are really trying for a more effective, a more precise, a more convincing, a more meaningful way to say what you have to say—or to find something more significant to say—then experimentation will nearly always lead you closer to your own personal voice and to better writing.